GREEK MEMORIES

Greek Memories aims to identify and examine the central concepts underlying the theories and practices of memory in the Greek world, from the archaic period to late antiquity, across all the main literary genres, and to trace some fundamental changes in these theories and practices. It explores the interaction and development of different 'disciplinary' approaches to memory in ancient Greece, which will enable a fuller and deeper understanding of the whole phenomenon, and of its specific manifestations. This collection of papers contributes to enriching the current scholarly discussion by re-focusing it on the question of how various theories and practices of memory, recollection, and forgetting play themselves out in specific texts and authors from ancient Greece, within a wide chronological span (from the Homeric poems to Plotinus), and across a broad range of genres and disciplines (epic and lyric poetry, tragedy, comedy, historiography, philosophy and scientific prose treatises).

LUCA CASTAGNOLI is Stavros Niarchos Foundation Clarendon Associate Professor in Ancient Greek Philosophy at the University of Oxford and Stavros Niarchos Foundation Clarendon Fellow in Ancient Greek Philosophy at Oriel College. He is the author of *Ancient Self-Refutation: The Logic and History of the Self-Refutation Argument from Democritus to Augustine* (Cambridge, 2010) and the editor of *The Cambridge Companion to Ancient Logic* (forthcoming).

PAOLA CECCARELLI is Lecturer in Classical Greek History at University College London. She has published widely in the field of Greek cultural history and is the author of monographs on the ancient weapon dance, *La pirrica nell'antichità greco romana* (1998), and Greek epistolography, *Ancient Greek Letter Writing: A Cultural History (600 BC–150 BC)* (2013).

GREEK MEMORIES

Theories and Practices

EDITED BY

LUCA CASTAGNOLI

University of Oxford

PAOLA CECCARELLI

University College London

CAMBRIDGE
UNIVERSITY PRESS

CAMBRIDGE
UNIVERSITY PRESS

University Printing House, Cambridge CB2 8BS, United Kingdom

One Liberty Plaza, 20th Floor, New York, NY 10006, USA

477 Williamstown Road, Port Melbourne, VIC 3207, Australia

314–321, 3rd Floor, Plot 3, Splendor Forum, Jasola District Centre, New Delhi – 110025, India

79 Anson Road, #06-04/06, Singapore 079906

Cambridge University Press is part of the University of Cambridge.

It furthers the University's mission by disseminating knowledge in the pursuit of education, learning, and research at the highest international levels of excellence.

www.cambridge.org
Information on this title: www.cambridge.org/9781108471725
DOI: 10.1017/9781108559157

First published 2019

Printed and bound in Great Britain by Clays Ltd, Elcograf S.p.A.

A catalogue record for this publication is available from the British Library.

Library of Congress Cataloging-in-Publication Data
Names: Castagnoli, Luca, 1975– editor.
Title: Greek memories : theories and practices / edited by Luca Castagnoli,
University of Oxford, Paola Ceccarelli, University College London.
Description: New York : Cambridge University Press, 2018. |
Includes bibliographical references and index.
Identifiers: LCCN 2018038871 | ISBN 9781108471725 (hardback) |
ISBN 9781108458351 (paperback)
Subjects: LCSH: Philosophy, Ancient. | Classical literature. |
Memory (Philosophy)
Classification: LCC B177.G74 2018 | DDC 880.9–dc23
LC record available at https://lccn.loc.gov/2018038871

ISBN 978-1-108-47172-5 Hardback

Contents

v

Contributors

PETER AGÓCS is Lecturer in Classics in the Department of Greek and Latin of University College London.

CLAUDE CALAME is Directeur d'études at the École des Hautes Études en Sciences Sociales, and a member of the Centre AnHiMA (Anthropologie et histoire des mondes anciens) in Paris.

LILAH GRACE CANEVARO is Lecturer in Greek in the School of History, Classics and Archaeology of the University of Edinburgh.

MIRKO CANEVARO is Reader in Greek History in the School of History, Classics and Archaeology of the University of Edinburgh.

ANDREA CAPRA is Associate Professor (Reader) in Greek Literature in the Department of Classics and Ancient History of Durham University.

LUCA CASTAGNOLI is Associate Professor of Ancient Greek Philosophy at the University of Oxford and Stavros Niarchos Foundation Clarendon Fellow at Oriel College, Oxford.

PAOLA CECCARELLI is Lecturer in Classical Greek History in the Department of History of University College London.

RICCARDO CHIARADONNA is Professor of Ancient Philosophy at Roma Tre University.

STEPHEN R. L. CLARK is Emeritus Professor of Philosophy at the University of Liverpool.

CATHERINE DARBO-PESCHANSKI is Directeur de Recherches at the CNRS, and a member of the Centre Léon Robin de Recherche sur la Pensée Antique (CNRS/Université Paris-Sorbonne).

R. A. H. KING is Professor of History of Philosophy at the University of Bern.

SILVIA MILANEZI is Professor of Ancient History in the Department of History of the Université Paris-Est Créteil Val-de-Marne.

MARIA MICHELA SASSI is Professor of History of Ancient Philosophy at the University of Pisa.

STEVEN D. SMITH is Professor of Comparative Literature, Languages and Linguistics at Hofstra University.

EMIDIO SPINELLI is Professor of History of Ancient Philosophy at the Sapienza University of Rome.

YNON WYGODA is Fellow of the Martin Buber Society of Fellows in the Humanities and Social Sciences at the Hebrew University of Jerusalem.

Abbreviations

Greek authors' names and works are abbreviated according to the *Oxford Classical Dictionary*, 4th edn. In the case of less well-known authors/works, please refer to the *Index Locorum*, where we have indicated the abbreviation used in this volume.

ARV²	J. D. Beazley, *Attic Red-Figure Vase Painters*, 2nd edn. Oxford, 1963.
Bernabé	A. Bernabé, *Poetae Epici Graeci (PEG). Testimonia et fragmenta*, i–ii. Leipzig and Berlin, 1988–2007.
Campbell	D. A. Campbell (ed. and trans.), *Greek Lyric*, vols. 1–5 (Loeb Classical Library). Cambridge, MA, 1982–1993.
CEG	P. A. Hansen, *Carmina Epigraphica Graeca*, vols. I–II. Berlin, 1983–1989.
Decleva Caizzi	F. Decleva Caizzi, *Antisthenis Fragmenta*. Milano and Varese, 1966.
DK	H. Diels, *Die Fragmente der Vorsokratiker, griechisch und deutsch*, I-III, 6. verb. Auflage, hrsg. von W. Kranz. Berlin, 1952.
FGrHist	F. Jacoby, *Die Fragmente der griechischen Historiker*. Leiden, 1923–1958.
I. Iasos	W. Blumel, *Die Inschriften von Iasos*, vols. I–II. Bonn, 1985.
IC	M. Guarducci, *Inscriptiones Creticae*. Rome, 1935–1950.
IG I-XIV	*Inscriptiones Graecae*. Berlin, 1873–
IvP	M. Fränkel, *Altertümer von Pergamon (Band VIII, 2): Die Inschriften von Pergamon*. Berlin, 1895.
K.-A.	R. Kassel and C. Austin (eds.), *Poetae Comici Graeci (PCG)*, I-VIII. Berlin 1983–

Kannicht	R. Kannicht (ed.), *Tragicorum Graecorum Fragmenta (TrGF) 5. i–ii: Euripides*. Göttingen, 2004.
L.-P.	E. Lobel and D. L. Page, *Poetarum Lesbiorum Fragmenta*. Oxford, 1955.
LSJ	H. G. Liddell, R. Scott, and H. S. Jones, *A Greek–English Lexicon*. Oxford, 1996⁹.
Page, *FGE*	D. L. Page, *Further Greek Epigrams: Epigrams before A.D. 50 from the Greek Anthology and other sources, not included in 'Hellenistic Epigrams' or 'The Garland of Philip'*. Cambridge, 1981.
Pfeiffer	R. Pfeiffer, *Callimachus*, I-II. Oxford, 1949–1953.
PMG	D. L. Page (ed.), *Poetae Melici Graeci*. Oxford, 1962.
PMGF	*Poetarum Melicorum Graecorum Fragmenta, vol. I. Alcman Stesichorus Ibycus*, post D. L. Page ed. Malcolm Davies. Oxford, 1991.
Radt	S. Radt (ed.), *Tragicorum Graecorum Fragmenta (TrGF) 3: Aeschylus*. Göttingen, 1985; 2nd edn, 2008.
Radt	S. Radt (ed.), *Tragicorum Graecorum Fragmenta (TrGF) 4: Sophocles*. Göttingen, 1977; 2nd edn, 1999.
SEG	*Supplementum Epigraphicum Graecum*. 1923–
Usener	H. Usener, *Epicurea*. Leipzig, 1887.
V.	E. M. Voigt (ed.), *Sappho et Alcaeus*. Amsterdam, 1971.
Wehrli	F. Wehrli, *Die Schule des Aristoteles*. 2nd edn. Basel, 1967–1969.
W²	M. L. West (ed.), *Iambi et elegi Graeci*, 2nd edn, 2 vols. Oxford, 1992 [1971].
West	M. L. West (ed.), *Greek Epic Fragments from the Seventh to the Fifth Centuries BC*. Cambridge, MA, 2003.

Introduction

Luca Castagnoli and Paola Ceccarelli

μέγιστον δὲ καὶ κάλλιστον ἐξεύρημα εὕρηται ἐς τὸν βίον μνάμα καὶ ἐς πάντα χρήσιμον, ἐς φιλοσοφίαν τε καὶ σοφίαν.

The greatest and finest discovery to be found for life is memory; it is useful for all purposes, for inquiry and wisdom.

This celebration of memory, which opens the final section of the anonymous Greek treatise known as *Dissoi Logoi* (*Contrasting Arguments*),[1] finds an echo in numerous other texts, both ancient and modern. Nowadays it is widely agreed that memory not only is a cognitive faculty fundamental for the acquisition, retention, organisation and transmission of information, but is also essential to our self-definition as individuals, to direct our actions and shape our experiences and feelings in our everyday life, just as it is essential to the identity, functioning and decision-making of larger groups and communities. Indeed, memory, as a way to locate ourselves within the world, as individuals or communities, is central to our human existence: deprived of memory, as individuals we lose not only a fundamental share of our knowledge of the world, but also our sense of self; and without shared memories a society loses its unity and coherence in time. And yet, the term 'memory' is used in such a variety of ways and in such a wide range of contexts that defining what it refers to is not easy: 'memory eludes our attempts at understanding it'.[2]

Because of the significance, breadth and elusiveness of the concept of memory, it is not surprising that since antiquity human beings have reflected upon, and debated, the sources, nature, functioning, uses, powers and limitations of memory. Close examination of different theories of memory, whether explicit or implicitly manifested in different usages of the

---

[1] *Dissoi logoi* 9.1. On the treatise, whose date is uncertain (see the cautious position of Burnyeat 1998), see Becker and Scholz 2004, who favour a late fifth century BC date, and the discussion (with further references) in Sassi's chapter in this volume, pp. 346–8.
[2] Nikulin 2015: 4.

vocabulary of memory and in different 'memory practices', can reveal fundamentally diverse conceptions of human psychology, the relation between human nature and the divine, and the way in which human beings, as individuals and societies, construct and preserve their knowledge, identities and interactions through time. The picture is complicated by the fact that, with the increasing specialisation of distinct and ever-narrowing areas of research, memory has featured more and more as a separate object of study in a number of different disciplines: literature and literary criticism, rhetoric, history and historiography, philosophy, pedagogy, cognitive and clinical psychology, neuroscience, anthropology, sociology, political theory, to mention only the most important. This vast multi-disciplinary attention towards memory has expanded and enriched our understanding of the breadth and complexity of the phenomenon; it has not consistently led, however, to sustained inter-disciplinary approaches to the study of memory.[3]

The present collection of studies exploring ancient Greek theories and practices of memory spans a variety of literary genres, and a number of what were recognised in antiquity, or would later be recognised, as distinct disciplines. We hope that the analysis of how different approaches to memory co-existed, developed and cross-fertilised across the centuries within the same broad cultural tradition can exemplify the fruitfulness of an approach to the study of memory that crosses disciplinary boundaries.

Over the last few decades the surge of new research and publications on memory across all the disciplines mentioned above has been accompanied by an effort to distinguish and catalogue the variety of ways in which we talk of memory in different contexts, and the many different 'types' or 'kinds' of memory corresponding to them.[4] In fact, the taxonomy of *memories*, rather than the inquiry into memory as a monolithic phenomenon, is often the focus in recent studies. Without trying to approximate the exhaustiveness of the list presented in the appendix of Tulving's playful article 'Are There 256 Different Kinds of Memory?',[5] it will be useful to introduce some key distinctions made in these taxonomies.[6] The first of

---

[3] For an ambitious manifesto of 'memory studies' as a properly inter-disciplinary field, see Roediger and Wertsch 2008.

[4] This systematising effort is reflected, for example, in the recent publication of a number of handbooks and companions on memory and 'memory studies' (e.g. Tulving and Craik 2000, which looks at memory from a psychological, cognitive, neuronal point of view, and Erll and Nünning 2008), as well as on 'metamemory', understood as the way in which humans control their memories (e.g. Dunsloky and Tauber 2016).

[5] Tulving 2007: 50–2.

[6] The following discussion is based on Fentress and Wickham 1992; Assmann 2008; Nikulin 2015; Sutton 2010 and Michaelian and Sutton 2017, as well as the above-mentioned handbooks.

such distinctions is one that has already been presented above, between *individual* and *collective* memory. It is on individual memory that most of the psychological and philosophical inquiry has traditionally tended to focus. The distinction between *declarative* and *non-declarative* memory is a standard one within individual memory. Declarative memory, the kind of memory that can be linguistically expressed in a declarative sentence, can in turn be *episodic* or *recollective*, if it concerns a past experience of the individual (I remember visiting Rome last year), or *semantic* or *propositional* (I remember that Rome is the capital city of Italy). Non-declarative memory includes *habit* or *procedural* memory, the kind of memory involved in our ability to do something, which cannot be codified as a set of declarative sentences, and need not even be entertained consciously (I remember how to ride a bike).[7] A different taxonomy, which only partially overlaps with the one just introduced, focuses on the kinds of items we can remember (corresponding to different possible grammatical objects of the verb 'to remember'): *things or people* (I remember my schoolteacher), *properties* (I remember the smell of jasmine), *actions* (I remember to turn off the heating), *experiences* (I remember eating ice cream yesterday), *events* (I remember that Socrates died in 399 BC), *facts* (I remember that the atomic number of uranium is 92). At least some of our action memories are 'prospective', as they concern the future performance of previously planned actions. As for collective or 'social' memory, the complex ways in which shared memories are negotiated, constructed, preserved and transmitted within large communities, societies and cultures (e.g. the German collective memory of the Holocaust) have been at the centre of a real scholarly boom over the last few decades, especially in history and the social sciences. Finally, more and more attention has been placed in recent years on *external memory*, as something distinct from, and supplementing (but also, possibly, endangering), individual or collective memory: for example, the external memory of an archive, a book, or the internet.

It is an important question of philosophy of memory whether all these different kinds of memories really have the same nature and ontological status, or the variety of uses of the term 'memory' risks obscuring essential differences in the phenomena described. Those who take episodic memory, with its connection to the past experience of individuals, as our 'core' notion of memory, will look with suspicion at kinds of memory which appear

---

[7] The distinction between short- and long-term memory, important in cognitive psychology and neuroscience, is less relevant to our discussion; all the examples of declarative and non-declarative memories given above would count as long-term memories.

radically different in their workings and functions (e.g. semantic memory, or collective memory). But the breadth and apparent dishomogeneity of the kinds of memories classified in modern taxonomies need not be discounted as the merely contingent result of the fact that the term 'memory' and its cognates have come to be used so broadly (*too* broadly, according to some) in English (the same, *mutatis mutandis*, for many other modern languages). Many elements of the modern taxonomies appear equally applicable to ancient Greek language and culture, including those elements that appear more deviant to some modern theorists. For instance, the Homeric verse 'Be men, my friends, and remember fierce strength' (ἀνέρες ἔστε, φίλοι, μνήσασθε δὲ θούριδος ἀλκῆς, *Il.* 15.487) is usually interpreted, like a number of similar expressions (e.g. 'let us remember sleep', 'let us remember food and drink'), as an appeal to 'action', 'prospective memory'.[8] And yet, equating the two would be too simplistic: as Bakker has pointed out, there is a link in ancient Greek between the verb μιμνήσκομαι, 'I remember', seemingly designating a cognitive ability, and forms deriving from its root μεν-, such as μένος ('vigour', 'strength') or μαίνομαι ('to be in a rage'), which refer to physical and emotionally charged impulses; the link is provided by the notion of embodiment.[9] Similarly, when the poet says, at the beginning of the Homeric Hymn to Apollo, 'I shall remember and not forget Apollo who shoots from afar' (μνήσομαι οὐδὲ λάθωμαι Ἀπόλλωνος ἑκάτοιο, *Hom. Hy. Ap.* 1), mentioning Apollo is meant to make him present to the ritual action.[10] Remembering Apollo has a performative function and force that are not captured by the 'memory of people' of our taxonomy of memory.[11]

[8] For a catalogue of these expressions, see Simondon 1982: 23–59, who considers them under the label 'mémoire d'action'; see also Bakker 2002a: 70 and nn. 11–12; Nikkanen 2012. For exhortations to remember battle, see e.g. *Il.* 6.112; 8.174; 11.287; for forgetting battle, *Il.* 13.721–2; 15.322; 16.356–7; 22.282; for remembering to stand guard: *Il.* 7.371; 10.99; 18.299; eating and drinking: *Il.* 19.231; 24.129, 601, 602, 613; *Od.* 10.177; 20.246; sleep: *Od.* 7.138; 16.481.

[9] Bakker 2008: 67–70. When Athena/Mentes 'reminds' (ὑπέμνησεν) Telemachus of his father in *Od.* 1.320–3, she is not activating the memory of his father (whom he has never known), but rather, in Bakker's words (2008: 70–1), she is giving him 'a shot of paternal *menos*'. It is however interesting to note that Telemachus 'in his phrenes understood, and was amazed in his thumos' (ὁ δὲ φρεσὶν ᾗσι νοήσας | θάμβησεν κατὰ θυμόν), recognizing the presence of a god: there is a cognitive aspect to this embodiment. On the etymology of μιμνήσκω see, besides Bakker 2008: 67–9, Benveniste 1954; Chantraine 1969: 702–3; Simondon 1982: 18–19; Beekes 2010: 953–4, and 929–31 for μένος, μέμονα; and Ustinova 2012 for the interconnection of memory and μανία, 'madness', 'inspiration'.

[10] Bakker 2002a; Bakker 2008: 67: 'the act of remembering will perform and make present the thing remembered'.

[11] For another example of the difficulty of matching ancient conceptions of memory with modern taxonomies, cf. Castagnoli's discussion, in this volume, of the difference between Aristotle's 'memory of the past' and 'our' episodic memory.

It is thus important to note that, despite the continuities and connections between the ancient and modern perspectives, the particular language, theories and practices of memory (both individual and collective) are always inextricably linked to their particular environment, to their society or culture, and to the different media in use in it. Each society has different ways of remembering, and of thinking and talking about memory. As Vernant pointed out in his path-breaking paper on 'Mythic Aspects of Memory', 'at different periods and in different cultures, there are close links between the techniques for mental recall, the inner organization of the function of memory, the place it occupies in the system of the ego, and the ways men picture memory to themselves'.[12] The aim of this volume is to examine the emergence and development of some central ideas and themes underlying the theories and practices of memory in the Greek world, from the archaic period to late antiquity, across a number of literary genres, through a selection of case studies highlighting both shared traits and specificities. The following ten sections provide a sample of some of these central ideas and themes explored in the sixteen chapters, and offer some essential background for their analyses.

1. Memory, Time and History

Although, as we have seen, memory is not necessarily 'of the past', memory is intimately connected to time more generally: it is a means by which individuals and communities situate themselves in history, either retrospectively or prospectively.[13] But the relationship of memory and time is not a simple one. A common trope within archaic and classical Greek poetry is that the relationship of memory and time is profoundly antagonistic: memory salvages matters of value for the identity of an individual or group against the relentless ravages of time, Chronos, the 'all-subduer' (πανδαμάτωρ) who threatens to pulverise any and all human achievements into oblivion.[14] Thus for instance Simonides affirms that 'Time is sharp of teeth, and wears away all things, even the most violent' (fr. 88 W²); a fragment from an unknown play of Sophocles states that 'time makes all things dark and brings them to oblivion' (χρόνος δ' ἀμαυροῖ πάντα κεἰς λήθην ἄγει, F 954). The same notion reappears in the words of the

---

[12] Vernant 1959 [2006: 115].

[13] Bakker 2002b: 11; Calame 2006b: 13–37. On Greek constructions of time, see the essays in Darbo-Peschanski 2000.

[14] Time the 'all-subduer': Simonides 531 *PMG*; Bacchylides *Ep.* 13.205; παντελὴς χρόνος, 'time that accomplishes all', Aesch. *Cho.* 965. Chronos does not play a role in Hesiod's *Theogony*, and there are no traces of a connection of Chronos with Mnemosyne (Memory) and the Muses; but for

eponymous protagonist of Sophocles' *Oedipus at Colonus*: 'to the gods alone old age and death never come, but all-powerful time sinks everything else into chaos' (τὰ δ' ἄλλα συγχεῖ πάνθ' ὁ παγκρατὴς χρόνος, Soph. *OC* 607–9).[15]

Yet, even as time is hailed as all-destroyer, the possibility that a memory of deeds survives through time, and because of time, is affirmed: time is not only a powerful destroyer, but also provides the matrix for productive creation; its destructive action can be resisted, and in time things are born and grow.[16] Time can also serve to bring out the truth, whittling away the inessential or outright false. Thus Bacchylides argues that 'truth loves to prevail, and all-conquering time always fosters the deed that is well done; but the foolish speech of enemies dwindles out of sight ...' (ἁ δ' ἀλαθεία φιλεῖ | νικᾶν, ὅ τε πανδ[α]μάτωρ | χρόνος τὸ καλῶς | ἐ]ργμένον αἰὲν ἀ[έξει· | δυσμενέων δὲ μα[ταία | γλῶσσ' ἀϊδ]ὴς μιν[ύθει, *Ep.* 13, 204–9). A similarly striking, slightly paradoxical proclamation of the resilience of human deeds is made by Pindar: 'Once deeds are done, whether in justice or contrary to it, not even Time, the father of all, could undo their outcome. But with a fortunate destiny forgetfulness may result.'[17] This is not a topic limited to lyric and elegiac poetry: tragedy too abounds in such statements. The double power of Chronos is best exemplified in the opening of Ajax's great speech: 'All

---

Pherecydes of Syros, in the sixth century, Chronos is one of three divinities who were not born, but always existed, and who open his *Theogony*: 'Zas and Chronos always were and Chthonie' (fr. 14 Schibli = DK 7 B1 = D.L. 1. 119), cf. fr. 60 Schibli = DK 7 A 8 = Damascius *De Principiis* 124b. Pherecydes here plays on the (paretymological) closeness of Kronos and Chronos: see Schibli 1990: 135–9; Kirk and Raven 1957: 54–7. Chronos also appears in the Derveni papyrus, rather surprisingly as the equivalent of Olympos ('Olympos and time are the same', Ὀλυμπ[ος καὶ χ]ρόνος τὸ αὐτόν, col. 12.3, with Betegh 2004: 249–52); for a discussion of the role of Chronos in the Orphic cosmogonies, see Betegh 2004: 140–52. Plutarch (*Is. Os.* 32) states that there are some 'Greeks who say that Kronos is but a figurative name for Chronos'; Cic. *ND* 2.25 (64) had called this idea an 'ancient belief'. For the influence of Kronos on the Western notion of Chronos/Time, Panofsky 1939: 69–91 ('Father Time') is still essential. But the Muse (*Moisa*), Truth (*alatheia*), Kronos and Chronos (Time) are inextricably interlinked also in Pindar's *Olympian* 10 (discussed in detail by Agócs in this volume, pp. 79–81, esp. at vv. 3–7 and 49–55; the association is early.

15 Cf. also Soph. *Aj.* 714–15: 'The long time makes all fade (πάνθ' ὁ μέγας χρόνος μαραίνει), and so I would not say that anything was beyond belief.' For discussion of statements underlining the destructivity of time, see Bakker 2002b.

16 See Bakker 2002b, who refers to passages such as Hdt. 5.9.3: 'In the long time everything can happen', contrasting it with the destructive *chronos* Herodotus confronts at the opening of the *Histories*.

17 Pind. *Ol.* 2. 15–18: τῶν δὲ πεπραγμένων | ἐν δίκᾳ τε καὶ παρὰ δίκαν ἀποίητον οὐδ' ἂν | Χρόνος ὁ πάντων πατὴρ δύναιτο θέμεν ἔργων τέλος· | λάθα δὲ πότμῳ σὺν εὐδαίμονι γένοιτ' ἂν (transl. Race).

things long and countless time brings to birth in darkness and covers after they have been revealed.'[18]

One poet who persistently explored the complex relationship between time and memory in his oeuvre is Simonides, who in his epigram for the fallen at Thermopylae famously stated that their glory, remembered in his poem, would defeat time: 'Of the dead at Thermopylae glorious is the fortune, fair the fate, an altar the tomb, in place of laments remembrance (μνᾶστις), of pity praise. Such a shroud as this neither dank decay nor time that subdues all will render faint' (531, 1–5 *PMG*). Glory and remembrance survive here detached from, and indeed beyond, the physical monument; yet next to such 'optimistic' statements, pessimistic views about the possibility of both stone monuments and poetry to survive abound.[19] Simonides' attention to remembrance and time is attested also in some other of his surviving fragments; noteworthy in particular is the 'Plataea' elegy, 11.24–5 W², because of its fascinating twist in the request for help addressed to the Muse 'so that someone later recall the men who for Sparta ...', (ἵνα τις [μνή]σεται ὑ[∪∪– | ἀνδρῶ]ν, οἳ Σπάρτηι ...).[20] This attention attracted the interest of later authors: Theocritus, Callimachus, and possibly already Aristotle feature Simonides in stories that have to do with remembrance, or allude to his poems on memorialisation.[21]

---

[18] Soph. *Ai.* 646–7: ἅπανθ' ὁ μακρὸς κἀναρίθμητος χρόνος | φύει τ' ἄδηλα καὶ φανέντα κρύπτεται (transl. Lloyd-Jones).

[19] For the divorce between physical marker and poem in 531 *PMG*, see Steiner 1999, but also Fearn 2013, who emphasises Simonides' ability to engage with the written support of his epigrams. Pessimistic statements: e.g. the song composed as an answer to Cleobulos of Lindos, 581 *PMG*, affirming the foolishness of trusting in the staying power of a statue, and more generally Austin 1967; Brillante 2015.

[20] See also 89 W² 'and I say that no one equals Simonides in memory'; 521 *PMG*; frr. 19 and 20 W²; and particularly interesting, the probably Simonidean 947 *PMG* (= 254 Poltera): 'The Muse does not, deprived of resources, taste the present only (οὐκ ἀπόρως γεύει τὸ παρὸν μόνον) but goes forward, harvesting all things.'

[21] Callimachus: *Aetia* fr. 64 Pf. ('the Tomb of Simonides', a poem appropriately defined by Bing 1988: 69 as 'a commemoration of a commemoration of a commemoration'; ll. 9–10: ὃς τὰ περισσά | .. καὶ] μνήμην πρῶτος ὃς ἐφρασάμην, 'who first invented the extra ... and memory' are particularly intriguing), with Morrison 2013. Theocritus: *Idyll* 16. 36–47, the Scopadae 'would have lain forgotten, leaving behind those many and prosperous things, among the wretched dead for long ages, if a divine singer, the Ceian, had not sounded his varied songs to the many-stringed lyre and made them famous among men of future generations' (42–6). Aristotle, *Physics* iv.13, 222b16–19 (= 645 *PMG*): 'in time all things come into being and are destroyed. That is why some consider time the wisest of things; but the Pythagorean Paron considered it the most incapable of learning, since people forget in time.' Commenting on Aristotle on the basis of a passage from Eudemus (fr. 90 Wehrli), Simplicius (*On Aristotle's Physics* ix 754, 5–17) identifies the first position with that of Simonides, who at Olympia would have praised time as very wise, because in it both learning and recollection occur; as for the Pythagorean Paron, Simplicius advances the hypothesis that Paron may not have been a personal name, but simply the participle 'being present'. Whatever the truth of this,

The Simonidean attention to memory, remembrance or commemoration, and their ability to resist the destructive power of time is shared by early Greek historiography: it appears for instance prominently in the proem of Herodotus' *Histories*, 'so that what has come to be through men may not become extinct with time' (ὡς μήτε τὰ γενόμενα ἐξ ἀνθρώπων τῷ χρόνῳ ἐξίτηλα γένηται, 1.1). Those engaged in historiographical endeavours continue the tradition of trying to render their recorded memories 'timeless', immune from oblivion, or, in Thucydides' phrase, 'a possession for all posterity' (1.22.4). The Muse of history, Klio, is after all a daughter of Memory, whether she works within an intentionalist framework or not.[22] And yet, the emergence of historiography also offered different means of thinking about time and recording events. In archaic Greece the high value placed on memory (to the point of its deification: see Section 2 below) had not led, in Vernant's words, 'to any attempts to explore the past or to the construction of an architecture of time. Memory is revered as the instrument of knowledge, omniscience, or as the instrument for escape from time … Memory [also in Plato's theory of anamnesis] is not the "thought of time" but an escape from it.'[23] Historiography, in contrast, develops a distinctive discursive configuration, which among other things emphasises writing; it also, importantly, 'colonises' time by developing various temporal frameworks, from those grounded in specific *polis*-communities to abstract conceptions of universal history.[24] Nowadays we know better than to oppose 'history' and 'memory' and have begun to understand (written) historiography as one of the forms in which historical memory manifests itself;[25] and one of its important contributions is its ability to articulate significantly more differentiated conceptions of time than those to be found in oral traditions.

it is striking that it is someone 'present' who argues that time does not bring any wisdom. Good discussion of this passage in Brillante 2015: 211–3, with further references.

[22] On the relationship between memory and history, see most recently Grethlein 2010: 1–11; Price 2012; Smith 2012. For the concept of 'intentional history', see n. 25 below and M. Canevaro's chapter in this volume.

[23] Vernant 1959 [2006]: 134–5. Indeed, the phenomenon of the floating gap, and the attending hourglass effect typical of oral tradition, applies to Greece as well: see Thomas 2001.

[24] For the development of chronological frameworks negotiating and articulating time, see Clarke 2008. For the distinction between non-historical *polis*-oriented genres, such as elegy, and the works of the first historians, who work with a larger scope and context, and are thus encouraged to use the past in a different way and for new purposes, see e.g. Grethlein 2010. Calame 2006b offers four case studies illustrating the way in which spatio-temporal frameworks are discursively constructed in Hesiod, in Bacchylides, in the inscription concerning the foundation of Cyrene and in the (Dionysiac? Orphic?) gold lamellae.

[25] See for instance Gehrke 2001, who puts forward the notion of 'intentional history'; Luraghi 2010, who makes the case for an 'intentional history' directed by the people, which becomes a foundation for identity, exactly as collective memory is assumed to do; Shrimpton 1997: 28–9 and 2014, who argues that 'ancient history was predominantly memory'; and Darbo-Peschanski's chapter, below.

2. The Divine Nature and Transtemporal Power of Memory

The ability of memory to 'see' (and give access to) events and figures, irrespective of whether they belong to the past, the present or the future, is reflected in the genealogy and power of the Muses, daughters of Mnemosyne, the Memory goddess, and Zeus (Hesiod, *Theogony* 52–63; 915–17). Mnemosyne herself appears as a primeval, pre-Olympian deity, born of the union of Gaia (Earth) and Ouranos (Heaven), and sister of Themis (Order), among others (Hes. *Theog.* 132–5).[26] When, in the Homeric *Hymn to Hermes*, the young Hermes picks up his lyre and begins to sing the story of how gods and earth came to be, 'first among the gods he honoured Mnemosyne, mother of the Muses, in his song; for she had obtained the son of Maia as her lot' (Μνημοσύνην μὲν πρῶτα θεῶν ἐγέραιρεν ἀοιδῇ, |μητέρα Μουσάων· ἣ γὰρ λάχε Μαιάδος υἱόν, *Hy. Herm.* 429–30). The young god then continues with the other divinities, describing how they came to be: the power of Mnemosyne and her daughters, the Muses, here enables the very possibility of talking and singing of the distant past.[27] It is clearly by virtue of their kinship with memory that the Muses represented for the Greeks omniscient sources of super-human knowledge that mortals might access through the medium of inspired poetry; hence the poet's typical address and request for help, famously exemplified in Homer *Iliad* 2.484–93, or Hesiod *Theogony* 22–33.[28] At the same time, this is a knowledge impossible for human beings to control: to Hesiod's invocation the Muses reply that 'we know how to speak many false things as though

[26] For Mnemosyne as the mother of the Muses, see also Eumel. 16 Bernabé (= 34 West) and the very similar Solon fr. 13.1–2 W²; Pind. *Paean* 6.54–6; Pind. *Isthm.* 6.74–5; Terpander fr. 4 Campbell ('Let us pour a libation to the Muses daughters of Memory', σπένδωμεν ταῖς Μνάμας παισὶν Μούσαις). Alcman frr. 3.1, 8, 9, 27 and 28 Campbell also has the usual genealogy (or simply addresses the Muses as Olympian); but an alternative tradition, attested in Alcman fr. 67 Campbell, made the Muses the daughters of Gaia and Ouranos, just like Mnemosyne herself in the Hesiodic tradition (cf. Diod. Sic. 4.7.1). Mimnermus fr. 13 W² and Musaeus fr. 82/86 Bernabé mention two generations of Muses, a first born of Ouranos (or Kronos in Musaeus), a second of Zeus and Mnemosyne.

[27] There are other traces of a connection between Hermes and Mnemosyne/memory, possibly because a messenger needs to be able to remember and repeat precisely a message. Thus, a metrical inscription of ca. 500 BC on a herm from the Athenian Acropolis proclaims that 'To Hermes this brilliant gift the herald Oin[obios? Oiniades?] giving thanks dedicated here as a memorial' (because of his memory?) (ηερμεί[αι ⋮ τόδε] | ἄγαλμα [⋮ διδὸς] | χάριν ⋮ ἐν[θάδε ⋮ ἔ]- | θεκεν ⋮ | Οἰν[...]- |ς ς ⋮ κ̄ερυχς ⋮ μ[νεμ]- | οσύνες ⋮ ηέ[νεκα], *IG* I³ 776 = *CEG* I 234, with Furley 2011: 166); Apollonius of Rhodes 1. 640–5 narrates of the herald Aethalides, to whom Hermes, his father, had granted a memory of all things, that never grew dim (οἱ μνῆστιν πόρε πάντων | ἄφθιτον), to the point that even after he died, in Hades, forgetfulness (λήθη) did not sweep over his soul. For the connection between Aethalides' memory, Pythagoras and immortality, see note 107 below.

[28] For the relation between memory, the Muses, poetic inspiration and knowledge, see e.g. Notopoulos 1938; Murray 1981, who points out how *Iliad* 2.484–93 (the invocation to the Muses before the

they were real; but we know, when we will, to utter true things' (ἴδμεν ψεύδεα πολλὰ λέγειν ἐτύμοισιν ὁμοῖα, | ἴδμεν δ᾽, εὖτ᾽ ἐθέλωμεν, ἀληθέα γηρύσασθαι, Hes. *Theog.* 27–8).[29] Although the Muses can be deceitful, they can, if they so desire, proclaim *alēthea*, things that are, literally, 'not hidden' or 'not forgotten', and thus true.[30]

In the *Iliad*, this special knowledge is linked to the Muses' ability to be always present: 'for you are goddesses and are in all places and know all things, while we hear only report and know nothing' (ὑμεῖς γὰρ θεαί ἐστε πάρεστέ τε ἴστέ τε πάντα, / ἡμεῖς δὲ κλέος οἶον ἀκούομεν οὐδέ τι ἴδμεν, *Il.* 2.485–6); the Muses know by virtue of having witnessed (presumably seen) what they know.[31] Their knowledge concerns not only the past, cosmogonic (e.g. Hesiod) and heroic (e.g. Homer), but also the present and the future: the Muses sing 'what is, what shall be and what was' (τά τ᾽ ἐόντα τά τ᾽ ἐσσόμενα πρό τ᾽ ἐόντα, *Theog.* 38).[32] The same nexus connecting Mnemosyne and the Muses to wisdom and sight (or its opposite, blindness) is present in one of Pindar's *Paeans*: 'And I pray to Ouranos' well-robed daughter, Mnemosyne, and to her children [i.e. the Muses], to provide facility, for blind are the minds of men, if anyone without the Heliconians seeks the deep path of wisdom.'[33] This is then a special type of knowledge, dependent on a special type of remembering: not so much recollection or retrieval of past experience from a memory storage as constant 'mindfulness' or 'presence'. This type of knowledge the Muses

---

Catalogue of Ships) is a request not just for inspiration, but also for facts; Collins 1999; Yamagata 2005; Ustinova 2012, who links this inspiration to μανία; for Plato's take on this, see Capra's chapter in this volume, pp. 182–3.

[29] For the history of the interpretations offered of these verses (mainly, criticism of heroic poetry as opposed to the Hesiodic brand of hexameter poetry; or acknowledgement that language imitates reality, but may at times *be* reality, and that humans cannot discern the difference), see Pucci 2007: 60–70.

[30] For the etymology and meaning of ἀλήθεια, see Chantraine 1969: 618–9, s.v. λανθάνω; Beekes 2010, s.v. ἀληθής: composed of privative α and λήθη, 'forgetfulness', or perhaps, more generally, privative α and the root λαθ- 'to be hidden, unknown'; Cole 1983; for further references, see Capra's and Wygoda's chapters in the volume, pp. 183 and nn. 15–16, and 207 n. 33.

[31] The Muses have a 'protocartographic' view (so Purves 2010: 2 and passim) of the *eusynoptos* ('easily taken in at a glance') plot of the *Iliad*, and ultimately of the world: maybe a hint of what will later develop into the technique of the *loci*, and at any rate a clear pointer to the importance of representation. See also Alcman fr. 133 Campbell, discussed below.

[32] A similar formulation appears slightly earlier in the text: the Muses have given Hesiod a 'divine voice, so that I could sing the glory of things past and things to happen' (αὐδὴν | θέσπιν, ἵνα κλείοιμι τά τ᾽ ἐσσόμενα πρό τ᾽ ἐόντα, Hes. *Theog.* 31–2). See West 1966: 166 for discussion and further passages; Pucci 2007: 74.

[33] Pind. *Paea.* 7b, 15–20: ἐ]πεύχο[μαι] δ᾽ Οὐρανοῦ τ᾽ εὐπέπλῳ θυγατρὶ | Μναμ[ο]σύ[ν]ᾳ κόραισί τ᾽ εὐ-| μαχανίαν διδόμεν. | τ]υφλα[ὶ γὰ]ρ ἀνδρῶν φρένες, | ὅ]στις ἄνευθ᾽ Ἑλικωνιάδων | βαθεῖαν ε . . [. .]. ων ἐρευνᾷ σοφίας ὁδόν (Race's text and translation).

share with diviners: Calchas is introduced in the *Iliad* as 'he who knew the things that were, that were to be, and that had been' (ὃς ἤδη τά τ' ἐόντα τά τ' ἐσσόμενα πρό τ' ἐόντα, *Iliad* 1.70).[34] The late (Byzantine) *Etymologicum Gudianum* preserves, under the entry μνήμη, 'Memory', a tantalizing piece of information: 'Alcman calls her "big-eyed" (or: "she that looks with the mind"); for we view the past through the intellect' (Ἀλκμὰν δέ, φασί, δόρκον αὐτὴν καλεῖ· βλέπομεν γὰρ τῇ διανοίᾳ τὰ ἀρχαῖα, fr. 133 Campbell). It is impossible to know whether Alcman himself had restricted memory to the past, or whether this is an inference or elaboration of the redactor of the *Etymologicum Gudianum*; what certainly goes back to Alcman, after Homer and before Pindar, is the connection between sight and memory.[35]

A different, but possibly just as ancient, tradition made of Memory herself one of three Muses: 'the sons of Aloeus held that the Muses were three in number, and gave them the names of Practice (*Meletē*), Memory (*Mnēmē*) and Song (*Aoidē*)',[36] names which clearly reflect the three essential aspects of the poetic work, and thus emphasise the connection between memory and poetic activity. According to another variant, preserved by Plutarch, 'all the Muses were in some places called "Remembrances" (*mneiai*), as in Chios'.[37] And Pindar is explicit as to the connection between the Muses and memory: 'the Muse loves to remember' (Μοῖσα μεμνᾶσθαι φιλεῖ, *Nem.* 1.12). What all this makes clear is the strong connection between early Greek song-culture, with its authoritative status, and the goddess of Memory. The existence of such a connection is easy to understand in a culture in which writing played a very limited role; but the connection remained very much alive also after the rise of the written word to prominence, as illustrated by the later reference to the Muses as 'Remembrances' in Plutarch, or by the group of

---

[34] Fundamental discussion of the power of the Muses and seers (and of the *aoidoi*) in Vernant 1959; Detienne 1996: 40–52. On 'Epic remembering' and the peculiarly performative importance of memory to the audience of the Homeric poems, see Bakker 2008.

[35] Elsner and Squire 2016 discuss the connection between sight and memory, focusing in particular on the Roman world; see also Agocs's chapter in this volume, p. 73.

[36] Pausanias 9.26.2. In the same context, Pausanias names Eupheme (Praise) as the nurse of the Muses, highlighting the link of the Muses with praise poetry (Paus. 9.29.5). Detailed discussion of the Muses and the traditions concerning them in Otto 1956. Vernant 1960 proposes a fascinating interpretation of these names, which he connects to a Pythagorean perspective, in which *meletē* and *ameleia* were closely connected to memory and oblivion; Plato would later rework this tradition (see below, pp. 19–20, and Sassi's chapter, pp. 344–7, 360–1).

[37] Plut. *Quaest. Conv.* 9.14.1, 743D. On the nature of the Muses' activity and its change in time, see Spentzou 2002; Murray 2004; Skarsouli 2006.

Zeus, Mnemosyne and the Muses in the 'Apotheosis of Homer' relief of Archelaos of Priene.[38]

3. The Impact of the Introduction of Writing on Greek Conceptions of Memory and Memorial Practices

This theme has been studied extensively;[39] but much is still open to discussion, and a number of chapters in this volume engage with this issue from different perspectives. No one disputes that the introduction and diffusion of writing had momentous cultural consequences in the Greek world; but it was the society which accepted writing that ultimately determined the use to be made of the new technology,[40] and the way in which this use was conceptualised and assessed, also in light of earlier ideas on the power and function of memory. Thus, earlier forms of conceptualisation not only remained alive alongside new developments, but contributed to shaping those developments. To mention here only one example: Plato not only adopted the writing metaphors of the wax tablet (*Theaetetus* 191b–195c) and the book of the mind (*Philebus* 38c–39c)[41] to explore psychological models of human memory, but also reflected on the epistemological shortcomings of both metaphors, or at least of the types of memory they illustrate. More generally, he famously questioned the adoption of writing itself, and its products, as tools for the acquisition and transmission of knowledge, denouncing, in a written text, the *Phaedrus*, the dangers posed by the technology of writing to human memory (*Phaedrus* 274b–278a).[42] On the other hand, with his 'theory of recollection' (*anamnēsis*) he also appropriated, and transformed, the traditional idea of divinely grounded, orally transmitted mnemonic wisdom, and turned it into a human, creative, *recollective* process of learning to be pursued through dialogical inquiry (see especially *Meno, Phaedo* and *Phaedrus*).[43] This process ultimately amounted for Plato also to a rediscovery of the true (and quasi-divine)

---

[38] The Archelaos relief, dated to the mid-second century BC, was found in Italy but came most probably from Alexandria; it is now in the British Museum (BM 2191). Photo and detailed discussion of the relief, and of the memory politics of the second sophistic, in Zeitlin 2001.

[39] Starting with Havelock 1963, 1982; more recent studies include e.g. Thomas 1992; Small 1997; Derderian 2001. See also Agócs' chapter in this volume.

[40] Thomas 2009.

[41] On the *Philebus*, see King's chapter in this volume.

[42] Cf. e.g. Ferrari 1987, Morgan 2000, Werner 2012, Capra 2014a; and Sassi's chapter in this volume, pp. 345–6, for a comparison with Alcidamas' misgivings about writing.

[43] For Plato's 'theory of recollection', see Section 7 below.

nature and powers of our immortal soul.[44] He thus opposed, in the name of genuine recollection, a particular form of philosophical inquiry to the passive memorising practices and techniques central to the activity of poets and sophists;[45] practices and activities that had been encouraged and expanded, rather than replaced, by the diffusion of writing.

It is beyond doubt, then, that the language and imagery of writing imposed itself in Greece as the prevalent way to describe memory and its processes, as can be seen through recurrent metaphors that appear pervasively in all genres, from lyric poetry to tragedy, from comedy to philosophical texts.[46] But did writing also change the way in which memory was used, and the past (mythical and non-mythical) was re-presented, recreated, recomposed? The complex answer which emerges from several chapters in this volume is: not always, not necessarily.[47]

4. Memory and Archives

The presence of long 'catalogues' is a distinctive feature of the early epic poems: the best-known example is the *Catalogue of Ships* in *Iliad* 2.494–760, preceded by an invocation to the Muses, and followed by a catalogue of the best Greek warriors and horses (*Il.* 2.761–79), and then by yet another catalogue of the Trojans (*Il.* 2.815–77). These catalogues can be seen – again in Vernant's words – as 'the archive of a society that has no writing'; 'through them, the repertoire of knowledge and familiar references enabling a social group to piece its past together is established and transmitted'.[48] Once writing became available, repertoires of knowledge originally transmitted through memory continued to be performed and transmitted orally, but also began to be externally stored: on stone, and, when written on parchment or papyrus, in archives. Diogenes

---

[44] For the role of memory in Orphism, another clear influence upon Plato's theory of recollection, see Section 5 below.

[45] On Plato's criticism of sophistic teaching and its attitude towards memory, see Wygoda's chapter in this volume.

[46] For a comprehensive list and discussion of these metaphors, see Agócs' chapter in this volume.

[47] See especially the chapters of Darbo-Peschanski, who follows Assmann in thinking that writing brought a marked change to conceptions of memory, and shows what these changes were in the field of ancient historiography; of Calame, who shows with his discussion of Theocritus 18 that cultural memory, even after the introduction of writing, was still also ritual, connective memory; and of Agócs, who argues that, at least from an ideological point of view, writing in poetry reinforced mnemonic performance.

[48] Vernant 1959 [2006: 119]. Similarly, the Hesiodic *Ēhoiai* ('catalogue of women') offered a system of genealogies that covered the whole heroic age, offering a picture of the *oikoumenē* (inhabited world) and its organisation.

Laertius preserves a tradition according to which Heraclitus dedicated his book *On Nature* in the temple of Artemis at Ephesus, thus putting his work under the protection of a force beyond human control – just as the earliest group of Cretan laws was inscribed on the steps and walls of the temple of Apollo Pythios.[49] But although decrees, laws and other official documents continued to be inscribed on stone, in the agora, on the acropolis, or in Panhellenic sanctuaries, very soon civic archives became reference points.[50] And from the fourth century BC onwards, private citizens also deposited documents in these archives.[51] Just as the language and practice of writing deeply informed the conceptualisation of memory (see Section 3), the vocabulary of (oral) memory was adapted to the new archival practice for written texts, or rather used alongside terms for writing, and it is possible to trace its evolution. Thus, when a Cretan city, ca. 500 BC, decides to appoint someone who will keep track of its 'memories', they appoint a certain Spensithios (and his descendants) 'so that he be for the city in public affairs both sacred and human scribe and recorder' (πόλι τὰ δαμόσια τά τε θιήια καὶ τἀνθρώπινα ποινικάζεν τε καὶ μναμονεύφην, ll. 3–5); and they decree that 'no one else is to be scribe for the *polis* or recorder in public affairs, neither sacred nor secular, except Spensithios himself and his descendants' (ποινικάζεν δὲ | [π]όλι καὶ μναμονεῦφεν τὰ δαμόσια μήτε τὰ θιήι-| α μήτε τἀνθρώπινα μηδέν' ἄλον αἰ μὴ Σπενσίθ[ι]-| [ο]ν αὐτόν τε καὶ γενιὰν τονυ, ll. 5–8).[52] On what materials Spensithios would write is not said, nor are indications given as to what exactly he would have to remember; the decision itself to appoint Spensithios was recorded on both sides of a bronze mitra, that is on an object not originally meant for writing. Writing and remembering are presented here in parallel, and numerous interpreters take the two terms 'scribe' and 'recorder' as a hendiadys; and yet presumably they cover different, if related, functions. Similarly, a decree from Halicarnassus, ca. 450 BC, mentions functionaries called *mnēmones*, who are not really (or not simply) archivists, since

---

[49] D. L. 9.1.6. Laws on the walls of the Pythion: *I. Cret.* IV 1–40, ca. 600 BC to ca. 525 BC. The curses of the inscriptions known as *Teiorum dirae* (see below) are meant to offer the same type of protection.

[50] At Athens, in the Metroon. The orators appeal to inscriptions that everyone can see, but also bring out archival documents that are then read by a clerk. For the debate on which carried authority, the stone or the archival document, see e.g. Sickinger 1999: chs. 3–5.

[51] On the basis of the statement in Epicurus' will, preserved in D. L. 10.16–17, that the philosopher's bequest had been deposited in the Athenian Metroon, and of the presence of archontal dates on his writings, Clay (1982) has suggested that Epicurus deposited his writings in the Athenian archive; this is uncertain, but the importance attributed by Epicurus to memory and to a specific form of writing for memory, the epitome, cannot be disputed (see below, and Spinelli's chapter in this volume).

[52] Jeffery and Morpurgo-Davies 1970 (*SEG* 28.631).

there is no mention of a physical archive or of written documents to be archived anywhere in the text.[53] But by Aristotle's time *mnēmones* becomes the name for magistrates in charge of the archives (*Pol.* 6.1321b34–40), which are thus conceptualised as 'external memories', to adopt the jargon of the modern taxonomies introduced above; and it is as guardians of the 'mnemonic writings' (τῶν μνημονικῶν γραμμάτων) that they are attested in a Hellenistic inscription from Paros.[54]

Besides physical archives, the late classical period sees the birth of literary archives: collections of epigrams circulate, composed of copies of inscribed epigrams, of texts imitating 'real' epigrams written on stone, or of purely literary epigrams.[55] In the Athens of Lycurgus, official texts of the works of the three great tragedians are established, in what is clearly a memorialising gesture;[56] similarly, in Ptolemaic Alexandria (and elsewhere), books are collected, and an attempt is made at recovering a text (and creating a canon) of earlier authors. In the Hellenistic age, the project of the Callimachean *Aitia* is a way of defining the relationship of the past to the present, and to catalogue it. Through the stories he recounts, Callimachus creates a collective cultural memory, and repositions the archaic and classical Greek past in relation to the new realities of Ptolemaic Alexandria. Callimachus plays with these old memory traditions, adopting and adjusting them to his needs: thus for instance when he invokes the goddesses (evidently the Muses), asking them to tell him why in Anaphe and Lindos those who make sacrifices do so pronouncing shameful words and blasphemies respectively, the Muse Calliope opens her speech as follows: 'First, commit to your memory Aegletes (i.e., Apollo) and Anaphe, the neighbour to

---

[53] Meiggs and Lewis 1988: 69–72, no. 32 = Osborne and Rhodes 2017: 180–7, no. 132, on which see in particular Carawan 2008. On the *mnēmones*, see also Darbo-Peschanski's chapter in this volume. For a brief survey of the development of written law alongside memory and a 'mnemonic' vocabulary, see Hawke 2011: 122–6.

[54] Cf. Lambrinoudakis and Wörrle 1983 = *SEG* 33.679. Mnemonic writings (contracts, deeds of sale and similar documents, it would seem, kept in the temple of Apollo Artemis and Leto, and in an official copy in the temple of Hestia) are mentioned at ll. 4, 9, 14, 21, 25, 36 and, in conclusion, at l. 84. *Mnēmones* are also attested in other cities, as e.g. at Iasos ca. 367–354 BC (*I.Iasos* 1). As Carawan 2008 points out, there is here no mention at all of paperwork or archival material: what the *mnēmones* do at Iasos at this moment in time is 'to sell with' someone else, that is, they provide themselves as official witnesses to a transaction. Aristotle mentions together *hieromnēmones, epistatai* and *mnēmones* as magistrates in charge of written private contracts, verdicts of legal proceedings and registration of legal proceedings.

[55] On epigrammatic collections, see Petrovic 2013, with further bibliography. On why it matters whether epigrams are inscribed or quasi-inscriptional, see Bing 2009: 210, who points to the different contexts (and memories of contexts) activated in each case. See further Bing 2009: 168 on the Aristotelian 'recognition through memory' (ἀναγνώρισις διὰ μνήμης, *Poet.* 16.1455a), and how it applies to reading.

[56] See [Plut.] *Vit. Dec. or.* 841f, with Hanink 2014: 60–89.

Laconian Thera, and the Minyans, beginning when the heroes sailed ...'.[57] Callimachus uses here traditional formulations and metaphors (π]ρῶτ[ον ἐνὶ μ]νήμῃ κάτθεο, 7c.6, or ἄρχμενος ὡς, 7c7), adjusting them to a very different context, in which it is the poet who takes the initiative: the dialogue between Callimachus and the Muses, which structures the first two books of the *Aitia*, was framed within the (diegematic and autobiographical) narrative report of a dream by a younger 'Callimachus', who at times intervenes independently in the narrative.[58]

Another way in which post-classical Greece reacted to the enormous growth of literature and knowledge preserved by writing and the difficulty of accessing and 'remembering' it all was the use of the epitome as a way of summarising and abridging written texts.[59] At the beginning of the Hellenistic age Epicurus provides an early and especially interesting example of the practice, since in some letters to his friends he epitomises parts of his own massive 37-book treatise *On Nature*, and explicitly comments on the function of these letters as memory aids. For example, in the opening of his *Letter to Herodotus*, he explains its nature and function as follows: 'For those who are unable to study carefully all my physical writings or to go into the longer treatises at all, I have myself prepared an epitome of the whole system, Herodotus, to preserve in the memory enough of the principal doctrines' (ἐπιτομὴν τῆς ὅλης πραγματείας εἰς τὸ κατασχεῖν τῶν ὁλοσχερωτάτων δοξῶν τὴν μνήμην ἱκανῶς, Epic. *Herod.* 35).[60] The length of the treatise is not the only reason why memorising and retaining its teachings might be difficult, even for those who have full access to them and the leisure to study them. The clarity and synoptic view afforded by the epitomisation will be themselves an invaluable aid for memory, as Epicurus also comments in his *Letter to Pythocles*: 'To aid your memory you ask me for a clear and concise statement concerning celestial phenomena; for what we have written on this subject elsewhere is, you tell me, hard to remember, although you have my books constantly with you' (Epic. *Pyth.* 84).[61]

[57] Fr. 7c.1–7 Harder = fr 7.19–25 Pfeiffer = 9.19–25 Massimilla; see also Stephens 2015.
[58] Cf. Harder 2012: 152–3; Morrison 2011. For the metaphor of 'committing something to the mind' in early classical authors, see Agócs' chapter in this volume.
[59] On the development of the epitome as a genre, from the fourth century BC onwards, see e.g. Dubischar 2016.
[60] For Galen's strikingly similar account of the function of an epitome in the Imperial age, cf. his *Synopsis librorum suorum de pulsibus* 431.1–432.17.
[61] For a similar point, cf. also *Herod.* 37. For in-depth study of these texts, and the complex ways in which Epicurus' theory of memory informed his writing practices, see Spinelli's chapter in this volume.

A very different Greek way of epitomising, canonising and memorialising the past is the collection of fragments; a particularly fascinating example is offered by Athenaeus' *Deipnosophistae* (*Sophists at Dinner*). This is not simply a work that preserves fragments of the past; it also plays with memory feats. Athenaeus claims to be repeating the conversation of the participants at a banquet held by a certain Larensis; the banqueters themselves remember, in the course of their conversation, long catalogues, starting from types of foods, and continuing with vessels, or famous courtesans. They cite from little-known authors, and then challenge each other as to the accuracy of their references; and thus challenge also the reader's memory. As Too has commented, 'at Larensis' dinner, the privileged textual performance is the feat of memory, and literary (dis)course is most often the catalogue. Banqueters announce that they will "recite" (καταλέξω, 573B), or that they will "call to memory" (cf. μνησθήσομαι, 585B) passages … In gesturing at the limits of human memory, Athenaeus raises the issue of exclusion and inclusion of the library.'[62]

5. The Persistence of Memory as a Powerful Divinity

While the introduction and diffusion of writing brought changes to Greek memorial practices and ideas, the goddess Mnemosyne continued to enjoy a conspicuous presence in the Greek cultural imaginary – and was the object of worship at both the civic and the individual level. Pausanias mentions the presence of images of Mnemosyne and the Muses, together with those of Athena, Zeus and Apollo, in Athens (Paus. 1.2.5), in a place dedicated in his time to the worship of Dionysus. Images of Mnemosyne and the Muses were on the altar of Athena at Tegea in Arcadia (Paus. 8.46.3), and, unsurprisingly, there was a cult of Mnemosyne and the Muses on the Helicon (Paus. 9.29.1). But Mnemosyne is also present in at least three sanctuaries of Asklepios: in the Asklepieia of the Piraeus and at Pergamon, the goddess receives ritual offerings during the night preceding the incubation, evidently to ensure that the incubant will remember the healing dream from Asklepios, and possibly to help the incubant give some logical coherence to the vague images of dreams; at Epidauros her presence is also attested by two bases inscribed with her name.[63] Yet another cult of Mnemosyne

---

[62] Too 2010: 111–12.

[63] Cf. respectively the fourth-century BC *lex sacra* from the Piraeus, *IG* II² 4962.19–25; the *lex sacra* from Pergamon *IvP* III 161A; and two bases from Epidauros simply inscribed Μναμοσύνα,

existed in Lebadeia, in connection with the oracle of Trophonius: the
person who wanted to consult the oracle had to drink first from the waters
of Lethe ('Oblivion') and then from the waters of Mnemosyne, before
descending into the hole of Trophonius, so as to be able to later remember
what he would learn. Once he had returned to the surface, the consultant
was 'again taken in hand by the priests, who set him upon a chair called the
chair of Mnemosyne (ἐπὶ θρόνον Μνημοσύνης μὲν καλούμενον), which
stands not far from the shrine'; the priests then asked the consultant to
report all that he had learned (Paus. 9.39.5–13). It is worth noting that
drinking from the waters of Mnemosyne is meant to help the consultant
to learn about the future, by preparing him to retain a memory of what
he would see: here, again, Mnemosyne ultimately helps human beings to
access what is to happen, rather than the past (cf. Section 2). Pausanias' testimony also brings out a specifically religious and ritual aspect of memory,
linked to the otherworld and Hades.[64]

This aspect also emerges prominently in some 'Orphic' (or 'Orphic-
Dionysiac') gold 'tablets' or 'leaves' (*lamellae*) dating from the sixth century
BC to the third century AD. Orphism was a complex and heterogeneous set
of theological and anthropological beliefs, mystery cults and purification
rites; the Orphics claimed the mythical lyre-player and singer Orpheus,
son of the Muse Calliope (and thus grandson of Mnemosyne), as their
prophet. One of the Orphic beliefs is that human souls are condemned
to live a bodily existence, as in a prison, through a cycle of reincarnations,
as the result of some kind of original sin, and consequent fall from their
divine status. The Orphic ritual practices and adoption of a pure lifestyle
were meant to help the initiates to prepare to regain their higher status
and place, and instructions were given as to how the soul should behave
after death to make this re-ascension possible. Some of the extant *lamellae*,
in retracing the path of the soul in the underworld, mention a lake of
Memory, from whose waters the thirsty soul desires to drink, while it must
avoid another spring (unnamed in the *lamellae*, but evidently a spring of
Forgetfulness);[65] furthermore, one *lamella* from Rome, dated to the second

---

IG IV² 1.303 and Peek, *Asklepieion* 128. For ample discussion of the presence and role of Mnemosyne
    at the healing sanctuaries of Asklepios, see Ahearne-Kroll 2014.
[64] For more on the problem of the memory (or non-memory) of the dead, see Ogden 2001: 231–50.
[65] Four tablets mention the spring and the lake of Memory: nos 1, from a female grave in Hipponion,
    ca. 400 BC; 2, from Petelia, fourth century BC; 8, from Entella (Sicily), ca. third century BC; 25,
    from Pharsalos in Thessaly, ca. 350 BC, in Graf and Johnston's 2007 numbering, corresponding to
    Bernabé–Jiménez San Cristóbal 2008: L1, L3, L2 and L4; eight tablets with a shorter form can be
    grouped with these, L5a–f, L6 and L6a (corresponding to Graf and Johnston 2007 nos 10, 11, 12, 16,
    13, 14, 29 and 18), which all mention water from the fountain of eternal flow. For detailed discussion

century AD, invites the underworld gods to accept the *lamella* itself as 'a gift of memory, sung of among mortals' (Μνημοσύνης τόδε δῶρον ἀοίδιμον ἀνθρώποισι), while two of the *lamellae* describing the lake of Memory also claim to be themselves a 'work of Memory' (no. 1.1: Μναμοσύνας τόδε ἔργον and no. 2.12: Μνημοσύνης τόδε ἔργον). The tablets are called a 'work of Mnemosyne' because the initiate needs to remember them in order to take the right course after death: they are an aid to memory. Indeed, an Orphic hymn calls on Mnemosyne to 'awaken the memory of the pious ritual in the initiates and send forgetfulness far from them' (*Orph. Hy.* 77.9–10). Here Mnemosyne is not called upon to keep alive great deeds, or an oral tradition through successive generations; rather, she is asked to allow an individual soul to remember, and thus find its way back to its own divine origin.[66] Indeed, the formula that the initiate has to pronounce in numerous tablets in answer to the inquiries made of him, 'I am a child of Earth (Gaia) and of Starry Heaven (Ouranos)', affirms man's affinity with the gods, his Titanian origin, and in particular the brotherhood of the initiate to Mnemosyne herself, daughter of Gaia and Ouranos.[67]

The otherworldly geography of the tablets finds an echo in numerous Platonic dialogues: in the myth of Er in the *Republic*, for example, the souls of the dead who are about to return to the world of the living for their next reincarnation come together in the 'Plain of Oblivion' (Λήθης πεδίον), and drink the water of the river Ἀμελής ('Carelessness'). This water brings oblivion and 'cannot be contained in a vase' (621a):[68] it is clearly a dangerous water, similar to that flowing from the spring first encountered

---

of the (non-cyclical) spatio-temporal framework of the tablets, see Calame 2006b: 229–88, who interprets the tablets as Dionysiac rather than Orphic.

[66] Memory here has a soteriological role (on the place of this hymn within the collection and on its meaning, see Graf 2009: 172); for comparison with Plato, see Bernabé 2011 and 2013. Similarly, Bernabé–Jiménez San Cristóbal 2008: 16–17 state that 'it is possible … that the predominance of Mnemosyne in the tablets is related to the role that some philosophers attribute to memory as an instrument of salvation', with specific reference to Pythagoras and Pythagorean doctrines. The exact origin and function of the celebration and practice of memory in the later Pythagorean tradition (cf. e.g. Iamblichus' *Life of Pythagoras* 29.164–6) is difficult to reconstruct. For the idea that Pythagoras understood memory as a source of survival and identity through time, see n. 107 below.

[67] This phrase appears in all of the above-mentioned tablets. See discussion in Bernabé–Jiménez San Cristóbal 2008: 39–44.

[68] This might resonate with the idea that being forced to carry water in leaky jars is a punishment for the uninitiated in Pl. *Gorg.* 493b (see Vernant 1960, who further links this to Pythagorean traditions) and [Pl.] *Axioch.* 371e, where the 'thirst of Tantalus' is another punishment for the wicked. At *Axioch.* 371b the judgement of the souls after death happens in the 'Plain of Truth' (Ἀληθείας πεδίον). Ἀληθείας πεδίον appears first in Ar. *Ran.* 186, again when talking of the underworld and the initiates; it is mentioned also in Pl. *Phdr.* 248b, in a different context (for discussion of the context of this occurrence, see Capra's chapter in this volume), and this is yet another example of the permeability of these accounts. See also Bernabé 2011 and 2013.

by the initiates in the narrative of the golden *lamellae*. Although the souls cannot avoid drinking the water of forgetfulness, because of the terrible heat of the Plain of Oblivion (thus forgetting their previous lives and their experiences in the underworld), some of them drink more than the right amount, if their thirst is not restrained by philosophical understanding (621a). With this detail, which does not receive any further comment or explanation in the dialogue, Plato is appropriating and transforming the Orphic tradition of thinking about the dangers of forgetfulness: presumably the souls who have drunk too much of the water of oblivion will be unable, in their next incarnation, to recollect their immortal, quasi-divine nature, distinct from their bodily prison, and the eternal truths akin to them. And this is the result of their complete forgetfulness of the sights and experiences of their after-death journey, including their vision of the cosmic order of the 'spindle of Necessity', and of the three Moirai (Fates) who, to the music of the Sirens, sing the past, the present and the future, exactly like the Muses of the epic tradition (616b–617c).[69]

6.   The Dynamic Tension between Memory and Forgetting

As we have seen in the previous section, the Orphic tablets and the tradition to which they belong draw a distinction between the waters of Oblivion, which the initiates must avoid, and those of Memory, which offer to the initiates the possibility of preserving, and perhaps rediscovering, their true divine selves. This is one of the many forms that the constant tension between remembering and forgetting took in ancient Greek culture. But this tension cuts across all conceptualisations and practices of memory through time and genres, and involves individuals as well as society at large: 'any recalling of the past involves selection, both deliberate and unintended. Choosing what to remember must entail also the choice of what to forget, what to pass over in silence, and what to obscure.'[70] Importantly, in this dialectic remembering and forgetting can carry very different values in different contexts. And while both remembrance and oblivion may simply 'happen' accidentally, there is often an ethical or political side to decisions about what to forget or remember.[71]

---

[69] For critical analysis of the myth of Er and other Platonic eschatological myths, see e.g. Halliwell 2007 and Annas 1982. On the relationship between the Muses and the Sirens, see p. 22 below.

[70] Flower 2006: 2. Hindsight plays a crucial role in the selection.

[71] See Michaelian and Sutton 2017 for some fascinating thoughts about the ethical issues raised by notions such as the right to be forgotten, the right to forget, or conversely the duty to remember. On 'active forgetting', see Wygoda's chapter in this volume.

But let us start from the beginning! Remembrance of the great deeds of past men, and their survival through poetry, through a(n inscribed) monument or a descendant (a σῆμα, 'sign', that is also a μνῆμα, a 'memory monument'), were viewed positively in Greek culture from very early on.[72] The Homeric heroes want to leave behind κλέος ἄφθιτον, an 'imperishable renown'; Herodotus presents the display of his inquiry 'so that things done by man not be forgotten in time (τῷ χρόνῳ ἐξίτηλα γένηται), and that great and marvelous deeds, some displayed by the Hellenes, some by the barbarians, not lose their glory'.[73] Men desire to gain for themselves an 'immortal memory' (ἀθάνατον μνήμην), or an 'immortal reputation' (ἀθάνατον δόξαν), a 'memory forever' (μνήμην ἀίδιον), a 'memory for all time' (μνήμην εἰς τὸν ἄπαντα χρόνον), in literary texts as well as in inscriptions dated from the classical to the imperial period.[74] The obvious enemy is oblivion, which menaces and corrodes everything through the passage of time.

Remembrance (being remembered, not being forgotten) is thus positively marked; conversely, the erasure of a person, a family, or an action from the collective memory, because of some actual or alleged misdeed, is the ultimate punishment. In her poems Sappho promises remembrance: 'Someone, I say, will remember us in the future'.[75] But she may also choose to condemn a rival to oblivion, in what Segal appropriately defined as a curse-like poem: 'But when you die you will lie there, and afterwards there will never be any recollection of you or any longing for you (οὐδέ ποτα μναμοσύνα σέθεν ἔσσετ᾽ οὐδὲ πόθα εἰς ὕστερον) since you have no share in the roses of Pieria; unseen (ἀφάνης) in the house of Hades also, flown from our midst, you will go to and fro among the shadowy corpses.'[76]

---

[72] For the semantics of *sēma* and *mnēma*, see e.g. Svenbro 1993: 31–8, as well as 68: 'the *sēma* indicates, the *mnēma* recalls'. For the change in memorial practices from the eighth to the fourth century BC, see Sourvinou-Inwood 1995.

[73] On the semantics of *kleos aphthiton*, see e.g. Nagy 1979; Finkelberg 2007 (with further references). On the opening of Herodotus' work, see also Darbo-Peschanski's chapter in this volume.

[74] See Habicht 1998 for full discussion and examples, both epigraphical and literary; it is worth adding to the latter at least Thuc. 2.41.4 (μνημεῖα κακῶν τε κἀγαθῶν ἀίδια).

[75] μνάσεσθαί τινά φαιμι † καὶ ἕτερον † ἀμμέων, fr. 147 L.-P. = 147 Campbell. The passage is quoted by Dio Chrysostom 37.47; what follows might also refer to the poem, implying a continued and intense reflection on remembrance and oblivion: 'For before now forgetfulness has tripped and cheated others, but good judgement has not cheated any man of worth' (λάθα μὲν γὰρ ἤδη τινὰς καὶ ἑτέρους ἔσφηλε καὶ ἐψεύσατο, γνώμη δ᾽ ἀνδρῶν ἀγαθῶν οὐδένα).

[76] Fr. 55 L.-P. = 55 Campbell, whose translation we follow, with Segal 1989: 331–2. For further discussion of Sappho on memory, and her influence on Plato, cf. Capra's chapter in this volume.

At the same time, some forms of memory can be extraordinarily dangerous. For example, listening to the song of the Sirens, who are at times represented in ways which are reminiscent of the Muses, can bring utter destruction.[77] Aeschylean tragedy is full of situations in which the memory of some earlier event (or this memory personified as the ἀλάστωρ, 'the Avenger') drives the action, pushing the hero towards his ultimate destiny, catastrophe, while this same memory paralyses the chorus with dread. The gods of course remember: they are μνήστορες, 'remembering' (Aesch. *Sept.* 180), and Zeus is πολυμνήστωρ, 'much-remembering' (Aesch. *Suppl.* 535). Divine remembrance can be implacable, as in the song of the Erinyes (Furies): 'We are skilled in plotting, powerful in execution, and we remember evil deeds'; or in the image of Hades surveying everything with his recording mind, and calling mortals to account.[78] This divine remembrance is strongly linked to retribution and justice. And yet, remembering can be characterised as a symptom of a bad or foolish character, when what the memory focuses upon is past quarrels: in Euripides' *Andromache*, for example, the messenger concludes his narrative of the death of Neoptolemus, stating that Apollo 'like a base mortal, remembered old quarrels. How then can he be wise?' (ἐμνημόνευσε δ᾽, ὥσπερ ἄνθρωπος κακός, | παλαιὰ νείκη. πῶς ἂν οὖν εἴη σοφός; Eur. *Andr.* 1164–5). The implication clearly is that at times even the gods should forget.

Indeed, if excessive or inappropriate remembering is negatively marked,[79] some forms of forgetting acquire positive connotations. Already in Hesiod's *Theogony* the poetic activity of the daughters of Mnemosyne, the Muses, is described as 'a forgetting of evils and a relief from sorrow' (λησμοσύνην τε κακῶν ἄμπαυμά τε μερμηράων, *Theog.* 55).[80] This is evidently a positive form of oblivion, of which numerous examples exist in lyric and tragic poetry: a character in Sophocles' *Thyestes* affirms that 'there

---

[77] In a nicely balanced phrase, the Sirens claim to know the past (like the Muses), as well as everything that happens on earth (ἴδμεν γάρ τοι πάνθ᾽ ὅσ᾽ ἐνὶ Τροίῃ εὐρείῃ | Ἀργεῖοι Τρῶές τε θεῶν ἰότητι μόγησαν, | ἴδμεν δ᾽, ὅσσα γένηται ἐπὶ χθονὶ πουλυβοτείρῃ, Hom. *Od.* 12. 189–91). On the emptiness of this claim and on its meaning for the Odyssean and the Iliadic tradition, see Pucci 1979; Schur 2014 (with further references).

[78] Aesch. *Eum.* 381–3: εὐμήχανοί τε καὶ τέλειοι, κακῶν τε μνήμονες (the Erinyes); and Aesch. *Eum.* 273–5 (Hades), on which see Agócs' chapter in this volume.

[79] For discussion of whether excessive displays of memory were avoided as inappropriate and rhetorically counterproductive in the Greek orators of the fourth century BC, see M. Canevaro's chapter in this volume.

[80] Cf. Hes. *Theog.* 93–103: the gift of the Muses to the humans is such, that 'even if someone who has unhappiness in his newly anguished spirit is parched in his heart with grieving, yet when a poet, servant of the Muses, sings of the glorious deeds of people of old (κλεῖα προτέρων ἀνθρώπων) and the blessed gods who possess Olympus, he forgets his sorrows at once and does not remember his anguish at all (αἶψ᾽ ὅ γε δυσφροσυνέων ἐπιλήθεται οὐδέ τι κηδέων | μέμνηται); for quickly the gifts

is a certain pleasure in words, if they cause one to forget the troubles one has' (ἔνεστι γάρ τις καὶ λόγοισιν ἡδονή, | λήθην ὅταν ποιῶσι τῶν ὄντων κακῶν, fr. 259.1–2). Oblivion is often associated with the state brought about by sleep: thus, for instance, when Orestes, persecuted by the Erinyes of his mother, wakes up after eventually falling asleep, he exclaims: 'Sweet magic of sleep (φίλον ὕπνου θέλγητρον), healer of pain, how sweetly you came to me, how needed! O revered Forgetfulness of troubles (ὦ πότνια Λήθη τῶν κακῶν), how wise a goddess (θεός) you are, and invoked by every suffering soul!' (Eur. *Or.* 211–15).

Oblivion can thus be a positive force in human life, when it offers temporary respite from evils. But oblivion can have a positive and more enduring value in itself, if it frees the human souls of unnecessary, dangerous ideas and attachments: a long line of philosophers, from Plato to Plotinus, argues for a positive value of forgetting some things in order to be able to recollect what is really important – in fact they argue for the essential function of this type of forgetting towards philosophical enlightenment. We have mentioned in Section 3 that Plato described the process of learning as a form of recollection of knowledge once possessed by the soul in its pre-natal disembodied state; the process, which involves the philosophical activity of dialectical examination of ourselves and others, requires, as a necessary precondition, a conscious endeavour to 'forget' (not be mindful of) our bodily experiences, desires and attachments, and to disregard the false teachings of traditional *paideia*, which overall amount to a form of self-forgetfulness, oblivion of our true natures.[81]

We should not forget, however, that when Oblivion first appears as a divinity in Greek literature it is as part of a group of rather unpleasant figures. According to Hesiod, Night gave birth to Eris (Strife); 'and loathsome Strife bore painful Toil and Oblivion (Lethe) and Hunger and tearful Pains, and Combats and Battles and Murders and Slaughters, and Quarrels and Lies and Tales and Disputes, and Lawlessness and Recklessness, much like one another, and Oath, who indeed brings most woe upon human beings on the earth, whenever someone willfully swears a false oath' (Hes. *Theog.* 227–32).[82] It might be surprising to see Oblivion so solidly included in the dysfunctional family of Strife, until one realises that memory is strongly

---

of the goddesses have turned it aside' (Most's translation). On this passage, see Ford 1992: 52–4, who points out that what is at stake here is not aesthetic pleasure, but rather 'being taken elsewhere'.

[81] For the emphasis on the importance of forgetfulness in the exercise of philosophical inquiry, see Wygoda's and Capra's chapters in this volume; for the legacy of this idea in the later Platonic tradition, see Clark's chapter.

[82] Transl. Most, slightly modified. Things are not so grim in the Orphic hymns, where Lethe is sister of Sleep (who brings the oblivion of cares) and death: *Orph. Hy.* 85.8. On Memory and Oblivion in the Orphic hymns, see Morand 2001: 58, 91–2, 221–3.

tied with reciprocity (see Section 8 below), and thus is an essential element in keeping communities together. Lethe may owe its negative connotation here to this fact, as well as to its connection with death (Hades is sometimes described as the house – or the plain – of Lethe).[83] At any rate, the notion that oblivion is 'hateful' is certainly not limited to Hesiod.[84]

This tension between remembering and forgetting, and between their positive and negative connotations is also, importantly, at the centre of the political contract that organises the *polis*.[85] According to Plutarch, there was an altar dedicated to Lethe in Athens;[86] furthermore, the day on which the conflict between Athena and Poseidon for the possession of the land of Attica had supposedly occurred, Boedromion 2, was omitted by Athenians in their calendar, and thus officially condemned to oblivion.[87] Plutarch's report of the existence of an altar to Lethe in Athens may seem in itself dubious; but it is not surprising if we read it against the broader context of the politics of forgetting (and remembering: see Section 8 below for official sacrifices to Memory and the Charites in Teos). A number of early Greek laws include among the sanctions against murderers or traitors, that is against people who committed the highest offences against the community, the complete destruction of their *genos* and the demolition of their house, and in some cases the refusal of an individual burial.[88] In the case of Athens, however, we see something different: from early on, Athens developed the practice of inscribing the names of traitors on stelai and displaying them prominently, thus ensuring the perpetuation of a negative memory. This practice was consistent with the emphasis on display through writing and public, 'democratic' education, as conveyed by the recurrent epigraphical formula σκοπεῖν τῶι βουλομένωι ('for whoever wants to see') and its variants.[89]

---

[83] Plain of Lethe: Ar. *Ran.* 186; halls of Lethe: Simon. 67 Page *FGE* (*Anth. Pal.* 7.25).

[84] Cf. eg Sophocles F. 568: λάθα Πιερίσιν στυγερὰ | κἀνήρατος· ὦ δύνασις | θνατοῖς εὐποτμότάιυ μελέων,| ἀνέχουσα βίου βραχὺν ἰσθμόν ('Oblivion is hateful to the Pierians and unlovely! Oh power of song, thing happiest for mortals, you who maintain the narrow channel of their life! [transl. Lloyd-Jones]). The abstract *dynasis* in connection with song and, conversely, oblivion is reminiscent of the links between *dynamis, mnēmē* and powerful reading in the fifth-century inscription from Teos discussed below (n. 105).

[85] The foundational discussion is Loraux 1997 [2002]; see also Loraux' remarkable essay 'On Amnesty and its Opposite', in Loraux 1988, as well as Ma 2009, with further bibliography.

[86] *Quaest. Conv.* 9.6, 741AB. The conflict between the two gods was represented on the West pediment of the Parthenon; it was thus central for fifth-century Athens (cf. Paus. 1.24.5).

[87] Plut. *De frat. amor.* 18, 489b, cf. *Quaest. Conv.* 9.6, 741B, with Parker 2005: 476–7.

[88] See Connor 1985; Flower 2006: 18–21. One may compare Herodotus' choice of explicitly ignoring names he knows: cf. Wygoda's chapter, p. 210 n. 44. For such sanctions as applied at Teos and Abdera in the first part of the fifth century BC, see below.

[89] For a detailed study of these formulae in Attic inscriptions, see Hedrick 1999; Sickinger 2009. Particularly significant for our purposes are ὅπως ἂν φαίνηται, φανηρὸν ἦ, 'so that it may be clear'

The most striking practice in terms of memory politics is a particular type of memory sanction: the amnesty. This was required to achieve a reconciliation after a period of *stasis*, civic discord. In the case of Athens, one of the events that marked the history of the *polis* was the oligarchic revolution of 404/3 BC, with its democratic resolution. The *Athēnaiōn Politeia* (*Constitution of Athens*) preserves the terms on which the reconciliation was effected. Among the various clauses, fundamental was the decision of implementing a universal amnesty, covering everybody except the oligarchic leadership, the Thirty, the Ten, the Eleven, and those who had been governors of Peiraeus; even these could be covered by the amnesty if they accepted to give public account of their activity.[90] The key phrase here is μηδενὶ πρὸς μηδένα μνησικακεῖν ἐξεῖναι, 'that it be not allowed for anyone to remember past injuries against anyone'. The amnesty did not imply forced personal oblivion – oblivion cannot be enforced – but it prohibited the public recalling of the past events covered by the amnesty. That this was not easy to achieve is shown by the fact that, as again recorded in the *Athēnaiōn Politeia*, it was necessary to put to death, without trial, someone who had begun stirring up grudges;[91] this was applauded as a good decision, since 'never since he was put to death has anybody broken the amnesty, but the Athenians appear both in private and public to have behaved towards the past disasters in the most completely honourable and statesmanlike manner of any people in history'.[92] Similar decisions were taken more than once, in other cities and contexts, in the years that followed; the use of the same vocabulary shows the thin line between remembering and forgetting as one of the ways Greek communities dealt with events which were difficult to accept.[93]

(157 instances including variants) and ὅπως ἂν ὑπάρχῃ ὑπόμνημα, 'so that a memory may remain' (36 instances).

[90] [Arist.] *Ath. Pol.* 39.6; see also Xen. *Hell.* 2.4.43: 'by sending to the others their friends and kinsmen, they persuaded them to become reconciled. And, pledged as they were under oath, that in very truth they would not remember past grievances (καὶ ὀμόσαντες ὅρκους ἦ μὴν μὴ μνησικακήσειν), the two parties even to this day live together as fellow-citizens and the commons abide by their oaths' (transl. Bronson).

[91] [Arist.] *Ath. Pol.* 40.2; the term is again *mnēsikakein*.

[92] For a thorough discussion of the complexities of remembering and forgetting in this particular historical situation, see Wolpert 2002; Shear 2011.

[93] Cf. for Cyrene Diod. Sic. 14.34.6, ca. 401 BC: 'After the battle the Cyrenaeans negotiated with each other and agreed to be reconciled, and they immediately swore oaths not to remember past injuries and lived together as one body in the city.' Decree of Dikaia, ca. 364 BC (*SEG* 57.576; text and translation in Gray 2015: 42–8): 'I will not bear grudges (*ou mnēsikakēsō oudeni oute logōi oute ergōi*) towards anyone in word or deed' (fifth decree, with the Oath, ll 72–3). For the interplay between public monuments and private memory and the dynamics of remembering and forgetting in Athens after the revolution against Demetrius Poliorcetes in 286 BC, see Shear 2012; for a detailed study of instances of amnesty in the Hellenistic period, see Rubinstein 2013.

7. Memory, Cognition and Knowledge

As we have seen, the extraordinary powers of the Muses, daughters of Mnemosyne, sprang from a unique capacity for cognition, a sort of omnitemporal and direct access to reality, guaranteeing superhuman knowledge. An early connection between memory itself and cognition, human or divine, also appears, at least implicitly, in the Homeric and Hesiodic poems. Several passages seem to draw an indirect link between *nous* (a form of reliable recognition or understanding) and memory, when they associate *nous* with mindfulness or attention, and express the latter concept negatively, via a litotes which adopts the vocabulary of hiddenness and forgetfulness (the root of *lanthanō/lēthē*; cf. Section 2). Think, for example, of Homer, *Iliad* 23.414–5: 'And I myself [Antilochos] will devise these things and recognise how to pass him at a narrow pan of the road, and it will not escape my mind' (ταῦτα δ' ἐγὼν αὐτὸς τεχνήσομαι ἠδὲ νοήσω | στεινωπῷ ἐν ὁδῷ παραδύμεναι, οὐδέ με λήσει); or Hesiod, *Works and Days* 267–9: 'The eye of Zeus sees everything and recognises everything. If it so pleases him, he casts his glance downward upon these things as well, and it does not escape his mind what kind of justice is this that the city keeps within it' (πάντα ἰδὼν Διὸς ὀφθαλμὸς καὶ πάντα νοήσας | καί νυ τάδ', αἴ κ' ἐθέλησ', ἐπιδέρκεται, οὐδέ ἑ λήθει, | οἵην δὴ καὶ τήνδε δίκην πόλις ἐντὸς ἐέργει.).[94]

One of the questions that remained at the centre of the Greeks' speculation throughout is whether memory itself should be identified with knowledge, or rather seen as a necessary but not sufficient condition for it, a stepping stone or component in the process of human cognitive development that leads to knowledge. In his poem, which aims to offer a new, correct description of *physis*, including a theology which debunks traditional conceptions of the gods, Empedocles still invokes a Muse, whom he describes as πολυμνήστη, 'much-remembering' (DK 31B3).[95] We have already seen how Plato rejected the epistemological value of certain forms of memory, and especially of certain passive *uses* of memory, which can in fact become dangerous stumbling blocks for our cognitive development (Section 6 above); but in several dialogues he also identified the highest achievements of philosophical dialectic, learning and the acquisition of

---

[94] Cf. Nagy 1990: ch. 8. Hesychius μ 1488 s.v. μναμονόοι (Pind. fr. 341 Sn.?) states that the Muses were also called μναμονόοι and μνηστῆρες.

[95] Cf. Hardie 2013, with discussion of the meaning of πολυμνήστη, 'much-remembering' and/or 'much-courted'.

knowledge, as a form of 'recollection' (*anamnēsis*) of eternal, intelligible and divine objects (the 'Forms') to which the best part of our soul, reason, can (re-)gain access from within itself, in virtue of its originary metaphysical affinity with them (see especially *Meno* 81a–86c; *Phaedo* 72e–78b; *Phaedrus* 246a–256b).[96]

Several developments of the later Greek philosophical tradition can be seen as a reflection upon Plato's nuanced discourse on memory.[97] Many, within the Platonic tradition, endorsed and systematised Plato's insights.[98] On the other hand, many others, from Aristotle onwards, explicitly engaged with, and rejected, Platonic innatism, and re-focused on memory as a fully human experience, which we share with lower forms of life (most animals), and on its role in the preservation and collection of our past experiences within a broadly empiricist epistemology. But even these critics adopted some of the vocabulary and imagery for conceptualising memory which Plato had explored, but ultimately either discarded or considered epistemologically inferior (vocabulary and imagery that, as we have seen in Section 3, Plato himself had borrowed and adapted from the Greek cultural tradition of the early and classical periods). For example, in the theory of memory he developed in the first chapter of *On Memory and Recollection* Aristotle fused Plato's imagery of imprints on wax (*Theaetetus*) with Plato's language of pictures or representations (*Philebus*): 'For it is clear that one must think of what is so generated by means of perception in the soul and in the part of the body which contains it as a sort of picture (οἷον ζωγράφημά τι), the having of which we say is memory; for the change that occurs marks in a sort of imprint (οἷον τύπον), as it were, of the percept, as people do who seal things with signet rings (καθάπερ οἱ σφραγιζόμενοι τοῖς δακτυλίοις)' (*Mem.* 1, 450a27–32).[99] In their rejection of innatism, the Stoics adopted the idea of the human mind as a *tabula rasa*: 'When a man is born, the Stoics say, he has the commanding-part of his soul as a sheet of papyrus ready for writing upon (χάρτην εὔεργον εἰς ἀπογραφήν) ... The first method of inscription is through the senses. For by perceiving something, e.g. white, they have a memory of it when it has departed. And when many memories of a similar kind have occurred, we

---

[96] The literature on Plato's theory of recollection is vast: for some good introductions, see Vlastos 1994, Scott 1995, Dancy 2004, Kahn 2006. For the connection between mundane forgetting and recollection of the forms in the *Phaedrus*, see Capra's chapter in this volume.

[97] Cf. Tarrant 2005, Helmig 2012.

[98] Cf. Chiaradonna's and Clark's chapters in this volume for the most important representative of the later part of this tradition, Plotinus.

[99] For discussion of Aristotle's theory, and further references, see Castagnoli's chapter in this volume.

then say we have experience... Reason, for which we are called rational, is said to be completed from our "preconceptions" [concepts which arise naturally as the result of repeated experiences][100] during our first seven years' (Aetius 4.11.1–4).[101] Even more strikingly, the epistemological process which from sense perception, through the accumulation and preservation of memories and the emergence of a unified 'experience' (*empeiria*), finally leads to knowledge and scientific understanding[102] had been sketched in passing, and rejected as an unsatisfactory way of approaching philosophical inquiry, by Socrates in Plato's *Phaedo*: 'When I was a young man I was wonderfully keen on that wisdom which they call inquiry into nature ... are living creatures nurtured when heat and cold produce a kind of putrefaction, as some say? Do we think with our blood, or air, or fire, or none of these, and does the brain provide our sense of hearing and sight and smell, from which come memory and opinion, and from memory and opinion which has become stable comes knowledge?' (*Phaedo* 96a–b).

The investigation into the physiology of memory, envisaged in this passage as an interest of the early *physiologoi*, and the study of the phenomenology, pathologies and therapeutics of memory were of course pursued in ancient Greek medicine, and are attested from the Hippocratic writings to late antiquity.[103] But ancient medicine also debated the role of memory, as a source of experience, in medicine itself. A branch of medical empiricism, espoused by the so-called 'memorist' (*mnēmoneutikoi*) doctors, emphasised the central cognitive and performative role of memory in medical theory and practice, in opposition to various forms of medical 'rationalism'.[104] A skilled doctor's ample and structured memory of past observations of symptoms and therapeutic effects, both personal (*autopsia*) and collected from others (*historia*), was considered cognitively rich enough to guide his medical practice, and to amount to medical knowledge.

Although memory scepticism was not a prominent issue in the ancient Greek reflection on memory,[105] unlike in modern discussions, the ancient sceptics not only targeted some of the theories of memory proposed by their

---

[100] For the Epicurean description of a preconception as a 'memory (*mnēmē*) of what has frequently become externally evident', cf. D.L. 10.33.

[101] For the Stoic theory of memory, and the debate within the Stoic school on whether memories should be understood as imprints in the soul, see Ierodiakonou 2007.

[102] For Aristotle's own influential description of this process, cf. *Metaph.* 1.1.980a27–981a7; *APo.* 2.19.

[103] See Julião-Lo Presti-Perler-van der Eijk 2016.

[104] See Frede 1990.

[105] For two interesting but elusively short ancient texts, cf. Pl. *Tht.* 166b1–4 (Protagoras) and Eus. *PE* 14.7.9 (the Academic sceptic Lacydes).

rival 'dogmatic' schools,[106] but also, in the case of the Pyrrhonists, adopted memory as a practical 'standard' (*kritērion*) of action. A Pyrrhonian sceptic will be able to live his everyday life in the absence of any knowledge, or indeed belief, about the world, by relying, non-dogmatically, on his present perceptions and feelings and what they remind him of, on the basis of his past experiences, i.e. by relying on 'commemorative' signs (ὑπομνηστικὰ σημεῖα, S.E. *PH* 2.197–202). For example, his present hunger will remind the sceptic that, in the past, a similar feeling was satisfactorily satisfied by food, without any need to discover the hidden essences or causes of things (such as the nature of food and its properties, or the physiological mechanism of hunger, or the way in which the processes of digestion and nutrition work). For the Pyrrhonists, memory and past experience have a fundamental survival function, not dissimilarly than in animals; but they should not be adopted as a body of knowledge or as instruments for scientific and philosophical discovery.

There is another hot topic in modern discussions of memory that was surprisingly undertheorised in ancient Greek thought: the role of memory in securing the *personal* identity of individuals over time,[107] and in constructing their self-knowledge and self-understanding. At the end of antiquity, Augustine, a Latin thinker and writer deeply influenced by Greek culture, although mostly via its appropriation and transformations in the Roman world of the late Republic and Empire, once again adopted epistemological and pedagogical models deeply rooted in the Platonic tradition of thinking about the powers of memory, and tailored them to the framework of his Christian theology.[108] In particular, at certain times he espoused a form of innatism strongly reminiscent of Plato's theory of recollection (cf. especially *Confessions* X),[109] and the idea that proper learning can only come from the 'teacher within' (*On the Teacher*), and not from the reception and memorisation of information from external

---

[106] See Ierodiakonou 2007.

[107] For some interesting exceptions, cf. e.g. Euripides' *Heracles*, in which the shifting memories of Heracles' biography recorded by various characters, including Heracles himself, and the chorus are the ever-changing and 'slippery site on which the identity of the hero is erected' (Dunn 2007: 85) – but the language of memory is not explicitly used; Heraclides' anecdote about Pythagoras' extraordinary ability to remember his past lives, which he had chosen as a proxy for immortality (D. L. 8.4–5: 'Heraclides Ponticus says that [Pythagoras] says about himself that he was once Aethalides, and was deemed a son of Hermes; and that Hermes told him to choose whatever he wanted except immortality, and so he asked that both alive and dead he should remember what happened'); and Lucretius *DRN* 3.843–64, which suggests that the continuity of our memories is a necessary condition for our persistence as individuals (discussion in Warren 2001 and Sorabji 2006: ch. 5).

[108] Cf. Hochschild 2012.

[109] Cf. Teske 2001, Castagnoli 2006a.

secular sources.[110] But he also went beyond that tradition, and ultimately identified memory as the core of our self, not just as human beings, generically, but as *individuals*: 'Great is the power of memory. It is a true marvel, O my God, a profound and infinite multiplicity! And this is the mind, and this I myself am' (*Conf.* 10.17. 26). He thus recognised memory as an essential source of self-understanding and self-transformation, while using a work of memory, the *Confessions*, to re-construct and make sense of his own spiritual journey towards those goals, and to inspire his audience to undertake a similar journey.[111] From this point of view, with his philosophy of memory Augustine was at one and the same time the last of the Greeks and the first of the moderns.

8.   Memory, Reciprocity, Justice and Retribution

The principle of reciprocity was of paramount importance in the ancient Greek world, from Homer onwards, and memory played an important role in its enactment. Indeed, the earliest such example in Greek literature, the exchange of gifts between Diomedes and Glaucus on the battlefield of Troy, is sparked by Diomedes' request to know the lineage of his adversary, Glaucus' narrative and Diomedes' acknowledgement of the earlier link of guest-friendship of their families (*Il.* 6.119–36). Although the role of remembrance is not foregrounded as such here, numerous other texts link explicitly memory with reciprocity or retribution. Thus, for instance, Solon's elegy to the Muses – a text that is very much about justice and retribution – foregrounds the Muses' mother Mnemosyne from the very first verse.[112]

The Muses, Mnemosyne and Mneme are often mentioned together with the Charites or 'Graces', 'pleasure-bestowing divinities' who represent the seductive power of beauty. The Charites enhance all sort of things with their grace, from artworks to persuasive oratory, but they particularly favour poetry: they are close to the Muses, with whom they live on the Olympus. Poets are inspired by the Muses, and the Charites enhance their song endowing it with *charis* ('grace').[113] But a strong link also exists

---

[110] Cf. Burnyeat 1987.

[111] For a useful introduction to the *Confessions*, cf. Clark 2004.

[112] Solon fr. 13.1–2 W²: 'Resplendent daughters of Mnemosyne and Olympian Zeus, Pierian Muses, hearken to my prayer' (Μνημοσύνης καὶ Ζηνὸς Ὀλυμπίου ἀγλαὰ τέκνα, | Μοῦσαι Πιερίδες, κλῦτέ μοι εὐχομένῳ). On reciprocity in ancient Greece, see the essays in Gill, Postlethwaite and Seaford 1998; on memory and justice in Solon, see Skarsouli 2006.

[113] Hes. *Theog.* 64: 'Next to them (the Muses, on the Olympus) have their dwellings the Charites and Desire' (πὰρ δ' αὐτῇς Χάριτές τε καὶ Ἵμερος οἰκί' ἔχουσιν). Bacchylides mentions Muses and

between memory and the *charis* of reciprocity, for in any situation in which a *charis*-giving gift is offered, a *charis*-giving return is also expected. In the case of dedications, the gift offered by the dedicant to the god functions, through its permanence, as a memorial of the exchange.[114] In other pragmatic situations, the necessity of remembering the gift and reciprocating it is explicitly proclaimed. Thus, Theognis says that 'the *charis* returned to a benefactor of the worthless ones is of the most trifling sort; this is equal to sowing seeds in a sea of grey brine … But the good sort are aware to the highest degree of what they have experienced, and retain the memory of the good deeds done, and *charis* thereafter (μνῆμα δ' ἔχουσ' ἀγαθῶν καὶ χάριν ἐξοπίσω)' (Theogn. 105–12). The close (and reciprocal) connection between lack of memory and lack of *charis* is explicit in Pindar: 'But the *charis* of long ago is asleep, and mortals are unremembering' (ἀλλὰ παλαιὰ γὰρ | εὕδει χάρις, ἀμνάμονες δὲ βροτοί, *Isthm.* 7.16–19).[115]

This connection of memory with reciprocity, and thus with justice, applies not only to the notion of *charis*, but also to the Charites as goddesses. Aristotle is quite clear on the fact that justice is a form of reciprocity, and that reciprocal giving is essential to the *polis*; it is for this reason, he adds, that 'we set up a shrine of the Graces in a public place, to remind men to return a kindness; for that is a special characteristic of grace, since it is a duty not only to repay a service done once, but another time to take the initiative in doing a service oneself'.[116]

We find one such shrine, or at any rate cult, in Hellenistic Teos. In ca. 203 BC, the Ionian city of Teos decided, after the king Antiochos III had conquered it and then rendered it inviolable, to thank the king by reorganising its religious calendar and its civic space, the *agora*, by erecting

---

Charites together at the beginning of his *Dithyramb* 5 (for the Athenians): 'There are countless paths of divine song for one who has received gifts from the Pierian Muses, and upon whose songs the violet-eyed maidens, the garland-bearing Charites, cast honour.' Cf. the chorus of Eur. *Her.* 673–5: 'Never will I cease to link in one the Charites and the Muses, sweetest union' (οὐ παύσομαι τὰς Χάριτας | Μούσαις συγκαταμειγνύς, | ἁδίσταν συζυγίαν). Further examples in MacLachlan 1993; Fisher 2010.

[114] E.g in the statuette dedicated by Mantiklos, which bears the inscription: 'Mantiklos dedicated me as a tithe to Apollo of the silver bow; do you, Phoibos, give some pleasing favour in return (*chariettan amoiban*)' *CEG* 326, dated ca. 700–675 BC, with Furley 2011: 154–5. On *charis* and reciprocity, see Parker 1998.

[115] On memory and forgetting in this ode, see Agócs 2009. For the connection between memory and reciprocity in tragedy, see Ceccarelli's chapter in this volume; for its continuation in the Second Sophistic, see Smith's chapter in this volume.

[116] Arist. *NE* 5.1133a (Rackham's translation). Ample discussion of the various forms taken by *charis*, with numerous references, in Azoulay 2004: 52–8; see also MacLachlan 1993: 73–86. For a list of cults and sanctuaries of the Charites in the Greek world, see Fisher 2010: 77–84, who however omits Teos.

a statue of the king, and by performing 'a sacrifice upon the common hearth of the city to the king, the Charites and Memory (τῶι τε βασιλεῖ καὶ Χάρισιν καὶ Μνήμη), as entrance-ritual (*eisitētēria*) each year' when the new city colleges entered office.[117] The Charites are here associated with Memory and with the king as recipients of a civic sacrifice, which is meant to remember and perpetuate the reciprocal link between the deeds of the king and the Teans' gratitude.

There was a precedent at Teos for this very explicit and central role of memory: two inscriptions dated to the first half of the fifth century, between 480 and 450 BC, one long known, the second published only in 1981, detail a list of sanctions to be enforced on offenders, in a situation of crisis caused by the return to Teos of a number of citizens from its colony, Abdera. These sanctions are to be enforced also through a curse: each year, both at Teos (the mother-city) and at Abdera, at specific moments, the *timouchoi* (the main magistrates) must pronounce the curse.[118] There is one interesting difference between the two texts. The older one prescribes that the magistrates pronounce the curse ΕΠΙ ΔΥΝΑΜΕΙ: a strange expression, that has been understood as either 'forcefully, so that it be effective', or 'next to the altar (or statue) of Dynamis'. It also adds a very detailed provision that whoever destroys the stele on which the curse is written, disfigures the letters, or renders them illegible shall fall under the same curse. The newer text has a slightly different provision: whoever is *timouchos* or *tamias* ('treasurer') is to *read* what is *written* on the stele ΕΠΙ ΜΝΗΜΗ ΚΑΙ ΔΥΝΑΜΕΙ: again, either 'so that it remains in memory and power' or 'next to the altar/statue of Memory and Dynamis'. The sacrifice to Antiochos III, Memory and the Charites in the document we saw above suggests that the presence of an altar to Memory in Teos is not impossible; however, most scholars tend towards the first interpretation ('for the purpose of memory and reinforcement').[119] Either way, it is interesting that a text that

---

[117] See Ma 1999: 311–7, Epigraphic dossier no. 18, ll. 33–7 (= *SEG* 41.1003, II) for text and translation; Ma 1999: 221–2 for discussion.

[118] Respectively, Meiggs and Lewis 1988 no. 30 ll. 29–35: οἵτινες τιμοχέοντες : |30 τὴν ἐπαρὴν : μὴ ποιήσεα-| ν : ἐπὶ Δυνάμει : καθημέν-| ο τὠγῶνος : Ἀνθεστηρίο-| ισιν : καὶ Ἡρακλέοισιν : | καὶ Δίοισιν : ἐν τῆιπαρῆ-| 35 ι : ἔχεσθαι (= Osborne and Rhodes 2017 no. 102 B ll. 29–35, who print δυνάμει minuscule); and Herrmann 1981 (a stele inscribed on four sides) d ll. 1–23 = Osborne and Rhodes 2017 no. 102 C (d) 1–23: [beginning lost] Ἀνθ[εστη]ρ[ί]-| οισιν : καὶ Ἡ-| ρακλέοισι-| ν : καὶ {ι} Δίοι-|5 σιν : ἐν Ἀβδ[ή]-| ρο[ι]σιν : Ἀνθ[ε]-| εστηρίοι[σ]-| ιν : καὶ Ἡρα[κ]-| λέοισιν : κ[α]-|10 ι Ζηνὸς : εορ-| τῆι : ὅστις δ-| ε τιμοχέων | ἢ ταμιεύων | μὴ 'ναλέξεε-|15 ν : τὰ γεγραθ-| μένα : ἐν τῆι | [σ]τήληι : ἐπὶ | μνήμηι : καὶ | δυνάμει : ἢ [φ]-|20 οινικογρα-| φέων : κελευ-| [ό]ντων τιμό-| χων : κεῖνον [continuation is lost].

[119] Discussion in Herrmann 1981: 11–12.

foregrounds reading should put emphasis on memory, presumably because the act of reading ensures that a written record will stay alive in the shared social memory of the community. As for the punishment: the curse calls for the complete extinction of the traitor and his family (ἀπόλλυσθαι : καὶ αὐτὸν : καὶ γένος : τὸ κένο, 'that he and his genos may perish', is regularly repeated throughout these texts), that is, for their complete erasure from memory.

9. Memory and Gender

Can we recognise traces of 'gendered remembering' (or forgetting) in ancient Greece, whether at the level of language and conceptualisation or at the level of memorial practices? There is an evident contrast between myth, in which the divinities having to do with memory, remembering and forgetting are all female (for example, Mnemosyne or Mneme, the Muses, and Lethe in Hesiod; the Mother of the Gods protecting the archive of the Metroon at Athens), and everyday life, where memory and memory matters appear to be for the most part in the hands of men, who have official control over them.[120] Both epic poetry and the *polis* exercise a normative control over official practices of remembrance and assign specific forms of memory according to gender; but a number of texts subvert these expectations. For example, Helen comes close to the ability of controlling and manipulating memories in the *Iliad* when she weaves images of the war, but especially in the *Odyssey*, where her use of the drug *nēpenthēs* allows her to control the emotional impact of her own and her guests' memories.[121] But the things on which men and women tend to focus, and their reactions to remembering, are often different. In epic poetry, war and the glory that ensues from it are the domain of men; lament belongs (mostly) to women. Hector eventually decides to withstand Achilles, and to die 'not ingloriously (ἀκλειῶς), but having accomplished some great

---

[120] See Bouvier 2011: 11–13; Loraux 1990: 106, who among other adduces Dinarchus, *Against Demosthenes* 86, affirming that the Mother of the Gods 'is the city's guardian of all written contracts', and goes on to suggest that 'for civic archives the Metröon is like the Mother's body standing ready for the father's writing' (70 and 77). Cf. the similar, and similarly authoritative, rewriting of individuals' (and especially women's) memories at the end of the Thucydidean Pericles' *Funeral oration* (Thuc. 2.43–5). Wagner-Hasel 2011 tries to find a role in the ancient world for women in the transmission of memories, which would explain the femininity of the goddesses of remembrance and song; weaving (patterning) is a possibility.

[121] Hom. *Il.* 3.124–7; *Od.* 4.219–22: 'Then Helen, daughter of Zeus, took other counsel. Straightway she cast into the wine of which they were drinking a drug to quiet all pain and strife, and bring forgetfulness of every ill (κακῶν ἐπίληθον ἁπάντων).' On Helen and memory, see L.-G. Canevaro's chapter in this volume, as well as the chapters of Capra and Calame.

deed for the hearing of men that are yet to be' (Hom. *Il.* 22.305): he wants
to be remembered in the future for his actions. Andromache instead regrets
that Hector did not give her a last word while dying, a 'dense word' that
she could have called back to her mind day and night while crying; she
knows (and Hector knows) that she herself will be a living memory of
Hector (and of his defeat and death) in some Greek's dwelling.[122]

Memory is also often the function of women in Greek tragedy (regularly
so in funerary tasks); unsurprisingly, these are often emotional memories,
and strongly marked as such. Thus, when in Aeschylus' *Libation-bearers*
Orestes, disguised as a stranger, brings news of his own (supposed) death,
the nurse sent to fetch Aegisthus remembers both the old troubles that fell
on the house, and, even more unendurable to her, the small tasks she used
to accomplish in bringing up the baby, the nursing, the washing of the
laundry (Aesch. *Cho.* 740–65). These personal memories mark a striking
contrast with Clytemnestra's own recollection of the curse upon her house
(Aesch. *Cho.* 691–718), although both sets of memories are triggered by
the same event. But possibly the best example of gendered remembering
in tragedy is Hecuba's long lament at the end of Euripides' *Trojan Women*.
The herald has just brought the body of her grandson Astyanax and the
shield of her son Hector: Andromache is being carried away, but she has
asked that the shield remain in Troy, and that Astyanax be buried in it
(Eur. *Tro.* 1127–46). Responsibility for the burial of Astyanax rests thus
with Hecuba; and she begins by addressing the boy, remembering the time
spent together, his words as a child, his kisses – to move abruptly to the
impossibility of the normal form of commemoration, an epigram.[123] For
'what could a poet (μουσοποιός) write upon your tomb? "This child the
Argives killed upon a time – in terror"? The epitaph brings disgrace upon
Greece.'[124] The presence of the shield, in which the child is going to be
buried, reminds us of epic death (the death of Hector) – but also of the
incongruity of epic death when it concerns a child. Already earlier, when
she could still hope that Astyanax would be taken away with Andromache,
Hecuba had lamented over her other sons – but had also added: 'But the
dead forget their grief' (ὁ θανὼν δ' ἐπιλάθεται ἀλγέων, Eur. *Tro.* 606).

---

[122] Hom. *Il.* 24.274–5: οὐδέ τί μοι εἶπες πυκινὸν ἔπος, οὗ τέ κεν αἰεὶ | μεμνῄμην νύκτάς τε καὶ ἤματα
δάκρυ χέουσα; and Hom. *Il.* 6.454–65, with L.-G. Canevaro's chapter in this volume.

[123] Writing an epigram on the tomb is of course an anachronism: normally, writing is not at its
place in the heroic world of tragedy. On the significance and power of such anachronisms, see
Easterling 1985.

[124] Eur. *Tro.* 1188–91: τί καί ποτε | γράψειεν ἄν σε μουσοποιὸς ἐν τάφῳ; | Τὸν παῖδα τόνδ' ἔκτειναν
Ἀργεῖοί ποτε| δείσαντες; αἰσχρὸν τοὐπίγραμμά γ' Ἑλλάδι.

She now turns to the shield, noticing how it preserves upon the strap the mark (τύπος) of the body of Hector, and on the rim its sweat. The shield is what remains of Hector: 'everything in this ritual is a figure of absence and embodies the paradox of embodied absence'.[125] As the lament advances, the very value of commemorative song is questioned, as Hecuba stresses the price to pay: 'If the god did not overturn our mortal world and enclose it beneath the earth, we would not, having vanished, be the subject of hymns, giving song to the Muses of mortals after us' (ἀφανεῖς ἂν ὄντες οὐκ ἂν ὑμνήθημεν ἂν | μούσαις ἀοιδὰς δόντες ὑστέρων βροτῶν, 1242–50). As Pucci has pointed out, 'we have here an indicting statement, a discourse of protest'.[126] While the official commemorative discourse of the *polis* gives a place to female mourning and memorialising (even if a very limited place), trying to tie everyone into the solidarity of community mourning, tragedy allows a glimpse into the difficulties of such a commemoration.[127]

10. Objects – Monuments or Relics – and Places as Sites of Memory

The role of monuments and objects in structuring and organising memory, or in preserving and supporting it, has most often been studied in the context of relics, and with a particular focus on the Hellenistic and imperial period (e.g. the so-called Lindian chronicle, or the extraordinary collection of relics kept in the temple of Sikyon, mentioned in Ampelius' *Liber Memorialis* 8.5).[128] But epic poetry and tragedy already offer examples of situations in which monuments, physical props, or objects mentioned but

---

[125] Segal 1993: 30; overall discussion of the end of the play at 29–32 (an expanded version of Segal 1989: 352–4). See Rodighiero 2016 for a splendid discussion of the collapse of cultural collective memory, and of communicative memory as well, in *Trojan Women*: the Trojans' memories will move over to the Greeks.

[126] Pucci 1977: 182.

[127] See Shear 2013 for a detailed study of the memory politics of the Athenian funeral oration (for women, esp. pp. 524–5): Shear suggests that these orations provided women and children, who had not participated in the action, with memories they could cherish, memories whose power would be reinforced by the ritual context. It is true that at least on that day the *polis* would come together, and that out of the individual memory a collective memory would be created; tragedy illustrates the power of this discourse, but also its limits (so does also Socrates' admission that the majestic feeling created by the words of the orators remains with him for three days, and that 'it is scarcely on the fourth or fifth day that I recover myself (ἀναμιμνῄσκομαι ἐμαυτοῦ) and remember that I really am here on earth', Pl. *Menex.* 235c). Arrington 2015 has recently emphasised the importance of private commemoration of the war-dead even in fifth century BC Athens. On commemoration of war, see the studies in Low, Oliver and Rhodes 2012, and in Giangiulio, Franchi and Proietti, forthcoming.

[128] On the Lindian chronicle, see Higbie 2003; on Ampelius and Sikyon, see Scheer 1996.

absent from the scene, are used as focalisers of memories and to trigger action. For example, in Sophocles' *Electra*, the chorus encourages the eponymous heroine by stating that 'the lord of the Greeks [Agamemnon], who gave you birth, will never be unmindful (οὐ γάρ ποτ' ἀμναστεῖ), nor will the double-edged bronze-covered axe of long ago, which in most shameless disgrace annihilated him' (484–6). The axe is here humanised: the instrument of the king's death remembers, exactly as the king himself will forever remember. These memories are, in turn, what must sustain Electra's desire for revenge. Later in the play, the urn carried by Orestes, supposedly containing Orestes' ashes but actually empty, will trigger the flood of Electra's memories. As Mueller remarks, '*Electra*'s characters dialogue with and through objects'.[129]

As for places, it has been remarked that landscape in ancient Greece is truly a landscape of memory.[130] A place, a specific view, may trigger a memory: thus, in Euripides' *Ion*, Creusa explains to Ion that 'when I saw Apollo's temple, I retraced an ancient memory. My mind was there, even though I was here' (ἐγὼ δ' ἰδοῦσα τούσδ' Ἀπόλλωνος δόμους / μνήμην παλαιὰν ἀνεμετρησάμην τινά. / ἐκεῖσε τὸν νοῦν ἔσχον ἐνθάδ' οὖσά περ, Eur. *Ion* 249–51).[131] It is not rare that in the course of a play a character or the chorus recall something that had happened before in the landscape that forms the scene of the actual plot. At the beginning of Aeschylus' *Eumenides*, for instance, the Pythia lists in her prayer all the previous owners of the sanctuary, mentioning Gaia, Themis, Phoibe and Apollo, other divinities, Athena, the nymphs of the Corycian cave, and continues: 'Bromios possesses this place, nor do I forget him (οὐδ᾽ ἀμνημονῶ), ever since the god led the army of the bacchants, having stitched a death

---

[129] Mueller 2016: 126, cf. Simondon 1982: 219: 'pas plus que la mémoire du mort, la mémoire de la hache n'est pas une mémoire consciente et subjective: elle est, au sens propre, une mémoire objective se confondant avec la trace matérielle, μαρτύριον du forfait'; and Soph. *El.* v. 1126 ff: ὦ φιλτάτου μνημεῖον ἀνθρώπων ἐμοὶ / ψυχῆς Ὀρέστου λοιπόν ..., 'Oh remaining memorial of the life of Orestes, dearest of men to me ...'. Important treatment of objects and memory in the epos in Ford 1992: 137–71; cf. also Grethlein 2008, Garcia 2013, and L.-G. Canevaro's chapter below. For tragedy, see Mueller 2016.

[130] The concept of 'lieux de mémoire', put forward by Pierre Nora (see e.g. Nora 1989), has become enormously influential; it has been taken in rather different directions than initially envisaged by Nora, who opposed 'lieux de mémoire' to 'milieux de mémoire', arguing that the very existence of sites of memory, seen as 'sites of residual continuity', was the consequence of the disappearance of real ('organic') environments of memory. For the ancient world, see Alcock 1996; Cole 2004; Ma 2009; Stein-Hölkeskamp and Hölkeskamp 2010, with further literature.

[131] Zeitlin 1995 analyses tragic ecphraseis such as those in Euripides' *Ion* as part of a shift towards imagery as a mode of knowing and reconfiguring the *kleos*: ecphraseis signal that what is happening is memorable; but this is part and parcel of a fifth-century development of modes of memorisation.

for Pentheus like that of a hare. I call on the streams of Pleistus and the strength of Poseidon, and highest Zeus, the Fulfiller; and then I take my seat as prophetess upon my throne.' We have here in a few deft strokes the whole history of the sacred place of Delphi, narrated with precise references to visible landmarks.[132] Indeed, numerous tragic plays end with aetiologies that make sense of a specific cultural and memorial landscape.[133] Myths or events – and so the past relevant to a community's or an individual's identity – are inscribed into the landscape, through the names the landscape bears, through the trees and rivers and monuments that inhabit it. This is visible in literary texts, from Homer down to late antiquity, but also – for instance – in the archaeologically attested offerings presented to Mycenean tombs in the context of hero cults.[134] But the text that best illustrates the significance of landscape as memory landscape, as something of a special cultural significance, is Pausanias' *Periegesis*. His description of Greece (be it Delphi, Athens, or the rugged landscape of Arcadia) results from the interplay between perception of the actual place and reactivation of the mental memory connected to it; it is as much a travel description as a memory pilgrimage.[135]

The observation that objects and places often act as seats and prompts for memory, and can be deliberately used in this way, may have led to the introduction and development of the most famous ancient mnemonic technique: the technique of memory 'places' (*loci*). The poet Simonides was credited since late antiquity as its inventor. According to Cicero's testimony, the invention was prompted by the unfortunate set of events which occurred at a symposium which Simonides attended to declaim an ode in praise of the host, Scopas. While Simonides was called outside, shortly after his performance, the roof of the hall collapsed, killing Scopas and all the

---

[132] Aesch. *Eum.* 1–29, with Schlesier 2010.

[133] On tragic (and particularly Euripidean) aetiologies, see e.g. Scullion 1999–2000 and Dunn 2000; Seaford 2009. However we may view the degree of innovation in Euripides, these aetiologies are interventions into the collective cultural memory.

[134] Names and landscape: see e.g. Calame 1988 for Laconia, and now the essays, covering all of the ancient world, in Hawes 2017. Homer: see for instance *Il.* 7.84–91, the imagined epigram on the tomb of a warrior slain by Hector, conveying forever the latter's *kleos*, with Petrovic 2016 who compares other archaic funerary epigrams on stone, or *Od.* 11.66–78, the tomb of Elpenor, also initially imagined, with Dimock 1989: 140–4; on both passages, Derderian 2001: 50–1. Grethlein 2008 discusses 'landmarks' as 'timemarks', further showing the implicit awareness, already in the *epos*, of the fact that the 'mark' may in time undergo a shift in both reference and meaning. Hero cults and tombs: for a recent treatment, see the studies in Henry and Kelp 2016. Landscape and tumuli of the Troad: Minchin 2016.

[135] See e.g. Galli 2005: 260–3, linking travel and pilgrimage; Alcock 1996 (a seminal study); Alcock, Cherry and Elsner 2001.

other diners, and mangling their corpses beyond recognition. Simonides was able to identify the bodies by consulting his mental memory image of the order in which the guests were sitting at the banquet. As a result of this, Simonides 'inferred that persons desiring to train this faculty of the mind [memory] must select places and form mental images of the things they wish to remember and store those images in the places, so that the order of the places will preserve the order of the things, and the images of the things will denote the things themselves, and we shall employ the places and images respectively as a wax writing-tablet and the letters written on it' (*Itaque iis, qui hanc partem ingenii exercerent, locos esse capiendos et ea, quae memoria tenere uellent, effingenda animo atque in iis locis collocanda; sic fore ut ordinem rerum locorum ordo conseruaret, res autem ipsas rerum effigies notaret atque ut locis pro cera simulacris pro litteris uteremur*, Cicero, *De oratore* 2.86.354).[136] Even if this attribution of the invention of the *loci* technique to Simonides, and the connected anecdote, are late and disputed, they are not surprising given the well-attested Simonidean emphasis on the powers of memory (discussed in Section 1 above).[137] A version of the anecdote already appears in the third century BC in Callimachus' *Aitia*, fragment 64; in the same fragment Simonides is referred to as 'the holy man from Ceos, who first invented the extra [lacuna] memory' (Κήϊον ἄνδρα τὸν ἱερόν, ὃς τὰ περισσά [lacuna] μνήμην πρῶτος ὃς ἐφρασάμην).[138] Similarly, it is not surprising that Cicero describes the technique of imposing mental images over memory places in terms of writing letters on the wax tablet of our memory, adopting the imagery so pervasive in Greek culture and philosophy (see Section 3 above).

Even if the full 'architectural' version of the technique based on the setting of images in buildings were a Roman invention, or at least a Roman development, the association between words to memorise and objects already appears as a mnemonic technique in the Greek *Dissoi Logoi*, in the same section celebrating the 'discovery' of memory with which we have opened this introduction: 'you must associate what you hear with what you know, like in the following. Does one need to remember "Chrysippus" (*Chrysippon*)? One must associate it with "gold" (*chryson*) and "horse" (*hippon*). Another case is that of "Pyrilampes" (*Pyrilampē*); one must associate it with "fire" (*pyr*) and "to shine" (*lampein*)' (*Dissoi Logoi* 9.4–5). Here

---

[136] Translation Sutton and Rackham. For an analogous testimony, see Quintilian 11.2.11–16, who discusses several variants of the anecdote.

[137] On the technique, and the question of its Simonidean origin, see Yates 1966: 27–9; Blum 1969: 41–6; Small 1997: 82–6; Baroin 2007.

[138] See Stephens 2015.

the semantic association between memories and objects is deliberate and artificial, and clearly lacks the experiential and affective dimension which characterises the examples of 'objects of memory' discussed at the beginning of the chapter.

This was an all too brief, and necessarily selective, survey of some of the central ideas and themes underlying the theories and practices of memory (and forgetting) in the ancient Greek world. We hope, however, that such a survey will be sufficient to convey some sense of why these ideas and themes cannot be fully understood in isolation, and why a synchronic and diachronic contextualisation of different ancient approaches to memory, across generic and disciplinary boundaries, can enrich the results of individual inquiries. The sixteen chapters of this volume, presented in rough chronological order, identify and examine a selection of instructive examples of:

(1) explicit discursive reflections or 'theories' on memory, recollecting and forgetting as divine and human experiences or powers, both individual and collective, and

(2) the role of these reflections in shaping certain 'practices' of remembrance, thought, communication and writing.

In Chapter 1 ('Women and Memory: the *Iliad* and the *Kosovo Cycle*'), Lilah Grace Canevaro explores the role of women as vessels of memory in archaic Greek epic and in the South Slavic epic cycle. Having introduced the way in which Homeric epics are inextricably linked with early reflections on, and practices of, remembering and memorialising, she examines the narrative strategies adopted by Homer to conceptualise the relationship between memory itself and women. Canevaro argues that women, who are characters with limited agency in Homeric epic, not only memorialise their men through words (e.g. lamentations), actions (e.g. weaving) and objects, but also *as* objects. It is primarily because they individually remember and articulate their losses that the women become vessels for the preservation of the collective memory of those who have died; but they also become living memorials through their own bodily survival, which is however much more ephemeral than the *kleos* afforded by poetry itself. In a further step, the chapter shows that this characterisation of women is not unique to Homer, or indeed the Greek tradition, by exploring the similar relationship between women and memory in South Slavic epic songs.

The theme of the 'materiality' of memory is also discussed by Peter Agócs in Chapter 2 ('Speaking in the Wax Tablets of Memory'). The chapter focuses on the way in which early fifth-century BC poetry, which is especially concerned with social memory and commemoration (both the 'praise-poetry' of Pindar and Bacchylides and relevant passages in the tragic poets), reflects upon and represents its own 'writtenness'. In particular, the chapter examines some of the implications of the pervasive metaphor of the 'wax tablets of the mind': the act of fixing something in memory is conceived as internal inscription. By its choice of sources and its focus on the way in which the materiality of written texts interacted in the social *imaginaire* with more traditional habits and ideologies of 'oral' memory, the chapter provides a link between Chapters 1 (Canevaro on epics) and 3 (Ceccarelli on tragedy), and discusses the archaic and early classical antecedents for themes explored in later chapters (particularly those of Capra, King, Castagnoli and Sassi). The chapter also breaks new ground by defining what, precisely, the poetic text, as the *written voice* of a society's past and future memory, meant to its early fifth-century audiences.

A group of eight chapters on memory in the classical period forms the largest section of the volume. The first three chapters of this group all concern memory in the classical *polis*, and more specifically Athens, for reasons which have to do with the amount of available evidence. At the same time, they cover a variety of genres, in which memory is a significant concern – from tragedy to comedy to oratory. A chapter on Greek historiography follows, offering an overview on changing conceptions of memory from the fifth to the third century BC. Together, these chapters form the cultural and generic backdrop for the four chapters that look into some specific aspects of philosophical conceptualisations of memory and forgetting formulated by Plato and Aristotle during this period.

Chapter 3 ('Economies of Memory in Greek Tragedy') by Paola Ceccarelli explores the interaction between immaterial memory, the materiality of writing and forms of reciprocity. It begins by surveying the various ways in which tragic playwrights bring memory into play, both within the world of their dramas and in terms of compositional practice, before focusing on remembrance as an essential element in the dynamics of reciprocity. Ceccarelli's first case study is Sophocles' *Ajax*, in which social ties and economies of gratitude break down since some of the main protagonists refuse to remember: the Atreidae resolutely consign to oblivion Ajax's Homeric services to the common Greek cause, opting to focus entirely on his present betrayal; and Ajax himself is haughtily indifferent to Tecmessa's appeal to remember his social obligations to his next of kin. The behaviour of all these heroes contrasts with the investment in memory as a prerequisite for reciprocity (and justice) shown by Tecmessa, Teucer and the chorus. In Euripides' *Suppliants*, the problem of how to ensure gratitude across time resurfaces. Whereas Theseus appears willing to trust the Argives' oral commitment to remember and repay his help in future, Athena feels called upon to intervene: the goddess insists on a written contract sanctioned by an oath put on record in a Panhellenic sanctuary as the only guarantee of memory and reciprocity, very much in line with the broader developments of writing and the externalisation of memory in the wider socio-political context.

In Chapter 4 ('Aristophanes and his Muses, or Memory in a Comic Key') Silvia Milanezi examines the distinctive and sophisticated discourse on memory of comic poets, especially Aristophanes. She focuses on three interrelated aspects: (1) the role of the Muses, daughters of Mnemosyne, as comic characters; (2) the uses to which the poetics of comedy puts memory, in particular through the dramatisation of the importance and risks of the right or wrong training of memory; (3) the relationship between comic memory and the memorialising practices of the city. Overall, the chapter aims to illuminate the ways in which structures of remembrance and memorialisation present in other genres (especially philosophy and tragedy) are commented upon and made fun of in comedy, as well as the ways in which playwrights, through intertextual dialogue with predecessors and rival dramatists, paved the way for the construction of a 'Dionysiac' record, a written external memory of the dramatic competitions. The analysis of the emphasis on the language of memory in the depiction of the interaction between Socrates and Strepsiades in the *Clouds* introduces a key theme which is explored further in a Platonic context by Capra and Wygoda in Chapters 7 and 8.

The idea that appeals to memory can be exploited as powerful instruments of persuasion, and the corresponding rhetorical practices are investigated by Mirko Canevaro in Chapter 5 ('Memory, the Orators, and the Public in Fourth-Century BC Athens'). Through close analysis of the fourth-century BC Greek orators' frequent allusions to shared memories, especially of poetical texts, but also of laws, recent events and debates, Canevaro draws a nuanced picture of what was considered appropriate for an Athenian citizen to remember. He argues, against extensive scholarly consensus, that our evidence does not attest to the idea that there might be an inappropriate, excessive, elitist and 'undemocratic' memory, but only that inappropriate *uses* of memory can be made. In fact, the orators' claims that their audience surely remember a certain fact, or law, are at times used to manipulate and misdirect the audience's expectations, lending authority to the orators' own questionable, and sometimes false, statements. In such a way, they rely at one and the same time on the presumptions of the audience and on the deficiencies of their memory. These rhetorical manipulations of the memory of individuals could also achieve the goal of constructing new shared collective memories within the memory communities addressed by orators. This complex dynamic in the use (and abuse) of memory claims and ascriptions attests to the enduring authority of memory, collective and individual, in the public discourse, a theme also explored, from a different viewpoint, by Calame in Chapter 11.

In Chapter 6 ('Place and Nature of Memory in Greek Historiography') Catherine Darbo-Peschanski identifies some milestones in the ever-shifting conceptualisation of memory, and its relationship to time, the past and the inquiry into the past, in the development of Greek historiography. The chapter begins by arguing that epic and lyric *kleos*, as memorialisation of past men and deeds, plays a limited role in Greek historiography: even if *kleos* may result from *historia*, it does not motivate its making. Mnemosyne, as divine memory, is absent; but individual memory as a psychological faculty is also conspicuously absent from Herodotus' work, whose *historia* resembles more the pattern of judicial inquiry supported by the institutional memory of the *mnēmones*. In Thucydides, psychological memory appears, but as a weak and unreliable faculty, one of the instruments of rhetorical persuasion, deprived of the cognitive power required for genuine historical inquiry. As for Xenophon, memory is neither an important psychological faculty nor a tool of *historia*, nor one of the aims or products of the historical narrative. Polybius will allow the language of memory back into the map of history, but only in the sense that historical narratives produce memories, and not that memory is a useful historiographical tool. By problematising the unstable conceptualisation and surprisingly limited appreciation of the role of memory in Greek historiography, the chapter reveals models of memory which are at the crossroad of epic and poetic modes of remembrance, on the one hand, and philosophico-scientific ways of envisaging the cognitive role of memory, on the other.

Starting with Chapter 7, philosophical approaches to memory come to the fore. While the subtle influence of Sappho's 'proto-philosophical' poetics of beauty and memory upon Socrates' 'palinode' praise of Eros in Plato's *Phaedrus* has already been identified in the scholarly literature, in Chapter 7 ('Lyric Oblivion: When Sappho Taught Socrates How to Forget') Andrea Capra identifies a new crucial, and neglected, poetic echo. Socrates appropriates and radically reshapes Sappho's poem 16 (Voigt) so as to argue that a true lover must be able to *forget* (the perceptible world and its values) in order to be able to *recollect* (the intelligible Forms). Even if he redirects the focus of erotic contemplation towards what he takes to be a higher form of beauty, Plato fully endorses Sappho's lesson on how to forget: Plato's Sappho becomes a 'master of oblivion'. While references to forgetting, whether collective or individual, and to its risks and rewards are frequent in the previous chapters, Capra's analysis places the concept at centre stage. In this way the chapter is closely linked to Wygoda's (Chapter 8) and Clark's (Chapter 15), who both stress the (oft-neglected) role of forgetting as the counterpart of recollecting in the Platonic tradition. It also introduces the theme of how Plato's philosophy of memory originally appropriates and rethinks key parts of the Greek cultural tradition.

Despite the extensive attention given to Plato's theories of memory and recollection, little has been made of the leitmotif of Socrates' frequent avowals of *forgetfulness* in Plato's corpus. In Chapter 8 ('Socratic Forgetfulness and Platonic Irony') Ynon Wygoda fills the gap, showing systematically how Socrates' confessions of forgetfulness represent a particularly interesting case of Socratic irony: Socrates' own insistence on a strong faculty of memory as an essential prerequisite for a life of inquiry such as his own (on which cf. also Sassi's Chapter 16) and the frequent testimonies in the dramatic fiction to his capacity to remember accurately previous arguments seem to undercut the frankness of Socrates' confessions. Through a close reading of key passages in the *Meno* and the *Protagoras*, Wygoda reveals the essential pedagogical message underlying Socrates' irony: it is only thanks to forgetfulness (understood as an active and deliberate process of disregard and rejection of traditional, external authorities) that dialectical inquiry and learning (understood as genuine, philosophical recollection from within) can take place (the Plotinian reception of this Platonic idea features prominently in Clark's Chapter 15).

Another key Platonic text on memory, recollection and forgetting, the *Philebus*, is the focus of Richard King's discussion in Chapter 9 ('Memory and Recollection in Plato's *Philebus*: Use and Definitions'). King aims to clarify the different functions and mechanics of memory (*mnēmē*) and two distinct forms of recollection (*anamnēsis*), showing how the definitions of memory, recollection and forgetting are advanced by Socrates in the dialogue within the broader context of an elaborate methodology of enquiry, learning and teaching. The main objectives of the chapter are: (1) to clarify the domain of the objects of memory and recollection (a question explored in the context of Aristotle's theory by Castagnoli in Chapter 10); (2) to illuminate the relation of memory and recollection to the soul and some of its other more primitive faculties (including, crucially, sense perception); (3) to explain Plato's use of the 'book of the mind' simile, according to which in memory an inner scribe and painter cooperate within our soul. The Platonic simile clearly appropriates the tradition examined by Agócs in Chapter 2, but also transforms and problematises it in the context of a theory which makes the soul incorporeal. King also argues for a deflationary reading of the role of mental images or pictures in the workings of memory, as side effects of the discursive written reports of the scribe, rather than structural factors in the production of memory, opinion and expectation.

The questions of the domain of the objects of memory and of the role of mental images in the workings of memory are taken up by Luca Castagnoli in his analysis of Aristotle's theory of memory in Chapter 10 ('Is Memory of the Past? Aristotle on the Objects of Memory'). He argues that Aristotle's claim that 'memory is of the past' constitutes an original break with the cultural tradition which associated Mnemosyne, and her daughters the Muses, with knowledge of the present and the future as well as of the past, a tradition which had been appropriated and transformed by Plato's adoption of *anamnēsis* as the route to knowledge of a-temporal truths in dialogues such as the *Phaedo* and the *Phaedrus* (cf. Capra and Wygoda in Chapters 8 and 9). Castagnoli concludes that for Aristotle memory is of the past in the narrow sense that, strictly speaking, we can remember only what we have experienced in the past as an object of our *sense-perception*, and only through the medium of mental images (Aristotle's adoption of the wax tablet metaphor for memory, mediated via Plato's *Theaetetus*, ultimately belongs to the cultural tradition investigated by Agócs in Chapter 2). Therefore, intelligible objects can be said to be remembered only 'accidentally', since they are the domain of a higher intellectual faculty which as human beings we do not share, unlike memory, with animals. Despite the fact that memory is essential to the process of learning (cf. Sassi in Chapter 16), memory and knowledge never coincide.

The next two chapters look at two case studies of Hellenistic developments, literary and philosophical. The role of memory in Callimachus and the interaction of text and performance in his work have recently received much attention.[139] In Chapter 11 ('Hellenistic Cultural Memory: Helen and Menelaus Between Heroic Fiction, Ritual Practice and Poetic Praise of the Royal Power (Theocritus 18)'), Claude Calame offers a close analysis of a text less studied from this point of view, Theocritus' *Idyll* 18. His purpose is to challenge what he takes to be two persistent misconceptions on the subject of historical collective memory. First, the use of writing in composition, communication and tradition does not imply any loss of pragmatic dimension, nor a transition to literature in the modern sense of the term

---

[139] E.g. Acosta-Hughes and Stephens 2012; Morrison 2011.

(the issue of what changes in memory practices and conceptualisations were wrought by the introduction of writing is also discussed by Agócs and Darbo-Peschanski in Chapters 2 and 6). Second, regardless of the presence or absence of writing, the ancient 'myths' concerned with the heroic past and the ancient history of a community remain an integral part of that community's historical collective memory. Not only is the memory of a central episode of the Trojan war's heroic past resurrected by Theocritus in Ptolemaic Alexandria through narrative means that recall those of earlier epic and lyric poetry; this Greek cultural memory is also connected to present circumstances which it is called upon to legitimate.

For his part, in Chapter 12 ('*Physiologia medicans*: The Epicurean Road to Happiness') Emidio Spinelli investigates the close relationship between the Epicureans' materialistic theory of memory and their practices of writing, communicating and 'living' their philosophy. Spinelli illustrates how memory was not only a central faculty in the Epicurean empiricist epistemology and an object of study in its own right for Epicurean physics and psychology (memory was understood as a sort of 'imprint' or material change in the atomic structure of the mind). Memorisation of the key tenets of the school was fundamental to the Epicurean therapy and way of life, and therefore ultimately as a source of happiness, and rote learning through repetition was encouraged by Epicurus and assisted through devices such as the epitomes provided by his own philosophical letters. By showing the complex interrelations between Epicurean theories and practices of memory, the chapter enters into a fruitful dialectical exchange with the very different Platonic approach depicted by Capra and Wygoda in Chapters 7 and 8.

Three chapters on the imperial period follow. In Chapter 13 ('Claudius Aelianus: Memory, Mnemonics, and Literature in the Age of Caracalla') Steven Smith investigates Claudius Aelianus' complex and reflective approach, both conservative and creative, to the memorialisation of Greek culture in the context of the third-century CE Roman empire: Aelianus is keenly aware that his act of re-membering the fragmentary remains of Greek culture is itself a matter of art. The prominent role of memory in Claudius Aelianus' *Historia animalium* is identified and analysed from three interconnected perspectives: (1) narratives in which Aelianus eulogises the natural memory of animals, and conceptualises human *moral* failures as failures of memory, which destroy the fabric of reciprocity and justice in human communities (cf. Ceccarelli's Chapter 3), but also involve the crucial forgetting of our special relationship with the Muses; (2) reflections on the degree to which memory is a product of nature (*phusis*) or art (*technē*), and criticisms of artificial mnemonic tools (a theme closely connected to Sassi's inquiry in Chapter 16; here, Smith extends his discussion to include Philostratus and other representatives of the Second Sophistics); (3) the political dimension of memory, alluding to Caracalla's manipulation of public memory (through *damnatio memoriae*) after the murder of Geta in 211 AD. As Spinelli does for the Epicureans in Chapter 12, Smith also stresses the complex way in which Aelianus' theoretical reflections on memory informed his own writing practices.

The next two chapters offer complementary reconstructions of two distinct but related aspects of the reception of Platonic and Aristotelian insights on memory in Plotinus. In Chapter 14 ('Plotinus on Memory, Recollection and Discursive Thought') Riccardo Chiaradonna focuses closely on a key Plotinian text on memory and recollection, *Enneads* 4.3.25–31. The two forms of memory discussed in that text are shown to stand in a complex dialectical relation with Aristotle's theory of memory and perception (on which, cf. Castagnoli in Chapter 10), on the one hand, and with Plato's theory of recollection (cf. especially Capra in Chapter 7), on the other. Chiaradonna clarifies how Plotinus' creative appropriation and transformation of the philosophy of memory of his two great predecessors (including, crucially, the rejection of the wax tablet model for memory discussed by Agócs in Chapter 2, and by several other contributors) is central to his own philosophical system, and is strictly related to fundamental tenets of his psychology and epistemology. In this way, for Plotinus the study of memory has the crucial role of revealing the soul's internal structure, with its different and hierarchically ordered metaphysical and cognitive levels.

Stephen Clark offers a wide-ranging exploration of different aspects of Plotinus' extensive interest in memory, and forgetfulness, in Chapter 15 ('Plotinus: Remembering and Forgetting'). Having briefly introduced Plotinus' rejection of the wax tablet model for memory, on the grounds that memory is an active power and not a passive physical mechanism (for more details, cf. Chiaradonna's chapter), Clark investigates Plotinus' familiarity with the ancient mnemonic techniques of *topoi*, 'places' (cf. Sassi in Chapter 16). He then originally connects this theme with the Platonic insight (investigated by Capra and Wygoda in Chapters 7 and 8) of the necessity of *forgetting* the sensible world and ourselves, that is our embodied life and experiences, in order to be able to re-ascend to the true realities of our divine origins (beauty and love play an important role in the ascent, together with astronomical observations). What is distinctive of Plotinus' position is that forgetting, like recollecting, requires effort and exercise, and the practice of certain techniques.

The volume closes with a chapter that offers a retrospect on philosophical approaches to memory and their broader cultural influences and context. In Chapter 16 ('Greek Philosophers on How to Memorise – and Learn'), Maria Michela Sassi provides a comprehensive study of how Greek philosophers, from the Sophists to Plotinus, not only constantly stressed the importance of memory and memorising, but also offered reasons for choosing what and how to memorise. Sassi identifies and examines, in particular, an important thread of Greek thought that insisted on memorisation as a *natural* process. This thread not only focused on memory as an individual human phenomenon, in opposition to the tradition making of Mnemosyne a divine source of inspiration and super-human knowledge; it also rejected the artificial devices adopted by the practitioners of various kinds of mnemotechnics (cf. Smith's discussion in Chapter 13). Sassi also stresses the importance of memory, and not only recollection, for Plato's philosophical method – an approach which is particularly interesting in light of predominant trends in Platonic scholarship, and which usefully complements Capra's and Wygoda's analyses in Chapters 7 and 8 – and argues that the importance of mnemotechniques in Aristotle's theory (see Castagnoli's Chapter 10) has been overplayed by scholars. Sassi's discussion highlights changes in attitudes to memory through time, and shows once more how much the development of the philosophical discourse on memory was deeply indebted to the broader cultural context.

Collectively, these sixteen studies in the history of Greek memories aspire to enrich the current vibrant scholarly discussion; in particular, they aim to re-focus it on the question of how various theories and practices of memory, recollection and forgetting play themselves out in a selection of Greek texts and authors, within a wide chronological span (from the Homeric poems to Plotinus), and across a broad range of literary genres (epic and lyric poetry, tragedy, comedy, historiography, philosophy and scientific prose treatises). Our main interest is in how the Greeks thought about their memories and memory practices, how they described them, what they took them to mean, how they conceptualised their power – hence the prevalent focus on texts rather than rituals, monuments, or social memories. In the wake of Halbwachs (1925), and more recently of Assmann (1992), much work has been devoted to the relationship between cultural memory, intentional history (the 'invention' of shared traditions) and identity, in ancient Greece and elsewhere; the approach has been mainly sociological, and the primary goal has been that of disclosing the 'constructed' nature of the past, and of the shared memories of such a past.[140] But less extensive attention has been given to the specific and different ways in which the relationship between these elements was explicitly *conceptualised* in Greek thought, and to how this conceptualisation shaped, in subtle and complex fashion, individual and collective *practices* of memory, remembrance and forgetfulness.[141] There are also of course a number of important studies on theories of memory and recollection in Greek philosophy from Plato to Plotinus;[142] but these studies often do not undertake the task to place ancient philosophical reflections on memory within the broader cultural and literary framework in which they originated, or to show how philosophical theories of memory shaped philosophical practices of inquiry, teaching and communication.[143]

Our rationale for the approach pursued here is thus not mere desire for chronological and thematic breadth; we believe that through exploration of the interaction and development of different generic and 'disciplinary' approaches to memory in ancient Greece – and more specifically through the juxtaposition of contributions addressing on the one hand the larger cultural context, and on the other specific theoretical reflections – a fuller and deeper understanding of the whole phenomenon, and of its specific manifestations, will be favoured. This approach also aims to open up further discussion on the way in which certain fundamental Greek approaches to memory bridge generic and chronological boundaries, or fail to do so.

* * *

We would like to thank a number of individuals and institutions who have helped us in bringing this project to fruition. Our contributors joined this enterprise with infectious enthusiasm, and then showed remarkable

---

[140] A brief introduction to this approach in Darbo-Peschanski's and Calame's chapters in this volume. We can mention here only some landmarks: Connerton 1989; Fentress and Wickham 1992; and, on the ancient Greek world in particular, Gehrke 2001 (intentional history); Giangiulio (2010). Grethlein 2010 touches upon some of the questions we have raised, but focuses exclusively on the fifth century BC, on the three genres of poetry, oratory and history, and on the past – and there is much more to memory than its relationship with the past. The discussion of memory by Calame 2006b, structured around four case studies, and proposing a shift in the way we should look at space, time and the process of identity creation, articulates a challenge that needs to be taken up and further explored.

[141] The only study that offers a precise, semantic analysis across a number of literary genres and over a relatively long span of time is Simondon 1982, which, while still very useful as a collection of data, does not venture beyond the archaic and classical ages and is methodologically rather outdated.

[142] See especially Sorabji 1972; Coleman 1992; Scott 1995; Sassi 2007; King 2009.

[143] See Carruthers 1990 for this kind of approach to medieval memory.

patience when we encountered unexpected delays in the development of this edited volume. We owe much to the anonymous readers for the Press, both for endorsing the project and for offering constructive criticisms that enabled us to improve the final product. Finally, we are profoundly grateful to the Department of Classics at Durham University, where we both worked when we began this project, for funding a seminar series on memory as well as the conference from which the idea of this volume arose – as well as our current institutions, Oriel College, Oxford, and University College London, which have supported us throughout the editorial process.

PART I

Archaic and Early Classical Configurations of Memory

CHAPTER I

Women and Memory: *The* Iliad *and the* Kosovo Cycle

Lilah Grace Canevaro

The Homeric epics are inextricably linked with ideas of remembering and memorialising. Originating as oral poems, their transmission at least at an early stage was dependent on the memory of the bard; studies such as those of Minchin, Bakker and Clay have drawn on cognitive psychology to explore the mnemonic methods used by the bards to recall the poems and to keep them consistent in re-performance.[1] That the epics create a shared memory of the past has been the focus of studies in cultural memory and intentional history such as those of Assmann and more recently Gehrke and Grethlein.[2] Homeric memory simultaneously separates the heroes of the past from the 'men who are now' (οἶοι νῦν βροτοί εἰσ᾿, *Il.* 5.304, 12.383, 449, 20.287) and bridges this gap by *enacting* the past to bring it into the present.[3] The very theme of the *Iliad,* the 'glorious deeds of men and gods' (κλέα ἀνδρῶν τε θεῶν τε), is a product of memory; glorious deeds are memorialised and perpetuated through the medium of poetry itself – and all of this stems from the Muses, daughters of Memory.[4]

This chapter focuses on one particular aspect of Homeric memory, more specifically memorialisation: the way in which women in the *Iliad* act as vessels for the preservation of memory. It examines the narrative strategies the poet adopts to treat the relationship between memory and women, and argues that women, who are nominally characters with limited agency in Homeric epic, memorialise their men through words, through objects,

---

[1] Minchin 2001, Bakker 2005 and Clay 2011. We may note, with Clay 2011: 118, an early link between mnemonics and memorialisation: the 'discovery' of mnemonics has been traditionally attributed to Simonides, who used the mnemonic technique of *loci* to remember a set of dinner guests and in the process preserved their memory. For discussion of some ancient reflections on the role and limitations of mnemonic techniques, cf. Sassi's chapter in this volume.

[2] E.g. Assmann 1992 (2011); Gehrke 2001; Grethlein 2010.

[3] Bakker 2002a.

[4] For the relationship between Memory and the Muses, see the Introduction to this volume.

and *as* objects.[5] In a further step, this chapter shows that this characterisation of women as vessels of memory is not unique to Homer, or indeed the Greek tradition, by exploring the relationship between women and memory in South Slavic songs. It concludes with a consideration of the type of memory preserved by these women, in contrast with that preserved by epic itself.

The *Iliad*'s wartime setting naturally foregrounds loss and memorialisation, and poses specific challenges to the depiction of women. The differentiated gender roles inherent in warfare highlight the restricted agency of women, in contrast to their men who repeatedly choose to fight.[6] This restriction means that the narrative approach has to change to accommodate women when they become the focus of attention. Rather than relating glorious deeds, when the poet turns to women he offers more static moments of reflection on memory and loss. It is because they remember and articulate loss that the women act as vessels for the preservation of the memory of those who have died; but they also become memorials through their bodily survival. Such distinct gender roles are evident also in South Slavic epic, which is a useful comparandum, not only in terms of context and techniques of performance, but also from a thematic point of view:[7] the *Kosovo Cycle* too is set in wartime and shares with the *Iliad* the challenges to the narrative posed by women.[8]

As a number of scholars have emphasised, inasmuch as they are agents Iliadic women often appear occupied with weaving, which in itself can become a means of memorialisation.[9] Weaving epitomises the Homeric ideal of domestic stability and conversely can come to symbolise the disruption of the household brought about by war. At *Iliad* 6.490–2 Hector

---

[5] For further discussion of the commemorative function of women and their objects, and specifically the *limitations* of both, see Canevaro forthcoming, a study which forms part of my wider work on 'Women and Objects in Greek Epic' (project funded by the Leverhulme Trust).

[6] It is well noted that Odyssean women, because of the poem's peacetime setting, have more agency than their Iliadic counterparts. Penelope, for example, controls events at home in her husband's absence, and Odysseus is constantly at the mercy of one strong female character or another. Without war as the driving force, gender roles are not quite so starkly delineated, or at least are differentiated in different terms.

[7] South Slavic epic, like the Homeric poems, originated as an oral tradition. As recently as the 1930s Milman Parry was able to experience it as 'a still living oral poetry' (Lord 1954: 3) though the tradition has now declined. Most bards now perform in an artificial context, reciting songs learned from books rather than through oral transmission. For a recent study, see I. Petrovic 2016.

[8] The corpus of songs is comprised of a number of 'Cycles': the most prominent are the Kosovo cycle (with which this chapter is concerned), the heroic Marko cycle, fifteenth- to nineteenth-century songs about outlaws and border raiders, and a later surge of new material following the first Serbian uprising in 1804.

[9] See for instance Snyder 1981, Pantelia 1993, Scheid and Svenbro 1996, Clayton 2004 and Mueller 2010.

delineates gender roles and sets up the activity of weaving as a foil for warfare when he commands Andromache:[10]

> ἀλλ᾽ εἰς οἶκον ἰοῦσα τὰ σ᾽ αὐτῆς ἔργα κόμιζε,
> ἱστόν τ᾽ ἠλακάτην τε, καὶ ἀμφιπόλοισι κέλευε
> ἔργον ἐποίχεσθαι· πόλεμος δ᾽ ἄνδρεσσι μελήσει

> Go therefore back to our house, and take up your own work,
> the loom and the distaff, and see to it that your handmaidens
> ply their work also; but the men must see to the fighting.[11]

At *Iliad* 6.456 Hector fears that after the fall of Troy Andromache will be taken away to work at another loom:[12] that transferral of Andromache and, crucially, her weaving for another family will symbolise the end of Hector's household. She is treated both as an object herself, to be taken away as part of the spoils of war, and as a creator of objects, valuable and integral to the home.

In the hands of a small number of exceptional female characters weaving can do more than signify domestic continuity. In *Iliad* 3 Helen memorialises the story of the Trojan war by weaving it, assuming a role akin to that of the poet, whilst Penelope commemorates her husband by delaying the completion of her weaving.[13] In fact, it is fitting that Penelope's situation operates in reverse: she memorialises through *un*weaving because, unlike the Iliadic women whose men are fated to die in battle, she is intent on preserving the memory of her *living* husband. In her case, it is the *completion* of the weaving which threatens domestic upheaval and the oblivion of Odysseus in Ithaca.[14] This diversity of the memorialising potential of weaving is brought out most pointedly by comparing Helen in *Iliad* 3 with Andromache in *Iliad* 22. Both women are said to be in the inner palace, weaving patterns into double-folded purple garments.[15] However, the subject matter of their weaving is very different, and characteristic of their respective situations: Andromache weaves flowers, motifs appropriate to the domestic sphere and with connotations of life and hope which contrast

---

[10] On gender roles in *Iliad* 6 see esp. Arthur Katz 1981, Graziosi and Haubold 2010: 29–32.

[11] The *Iliad* text is that of West 1998 and 2000; all *Iliad* translations are from Lattimore 1951.

[12] καί κεν ἐν Ἄργει ἐοῦσα πρὸς ἄλλης ἱστὸν ὑφαίνοις.

[13] See Mueller 2007.

[14] This idea of an eternal present and a perpetual remaking is so dominant in the poem that, as Clayton 2004 notes, many later interpretations of the *Odyssey* and indeed much Homeric scholarship seem almost to forget that Penelope does eventually complete her weaving.

[15] Inner palace: *Il.* 3.125 ἐν μεγάρωι, clarified at *Il.* 3.142 ὡρμᾶτ᾽ ἐκ θαλάμοιο; 22.440 μυχῶι δόμου ὑψηλοῖο. Pantelia 1993: 494 notes the importance of privacy: 'weavers could isolate themselves and perform their art away from the public eye'. The garments: *Il.* 3.126 δίπλακα μαρμαρέην, 22.441 δίπλακα πορφυρέην.

with the events unfolding outside the walls and reflect her naïveté;[16] Helen weaves scenes from the Trojan war. She intrudes into the martial male sphere and her awareness of the events unfolding around her both marks a contrast with Andromache and indicates her unique status within the *Iliad*.[17] Within the wider framework of the *Iliad* these episodes have a structural importance: they connect the third and third-last books and parallel the first battle with the last one.[18] Both women have, at different levels, a similar purpose in the *Iliad*: Helen caused the war, and is the reason why the deeds of men will be remembered; Andromache is there to preserve the memory of her man. Helen in her weaving preserves memory of the Trojan war using her privileged knowledge in a way that at the same time is appropriate to and subverts the domestic female sphere. She also manages to establish some *kleos* for herself *en route*, as she is said to weave the conflicts suffered on account of her (3.128 οὕς ἕθεν εἵνεκ᾽ ἔπασχον).[19] In contrast, Andromache weaves in ignorance and so her creation stands as no memorial of war: it would be – but in the circumstances cannot become – a symbol of peaceful domesticity. Her act of memorialising, in the tragic situation in which she finds herself, is not in the form of her weaving, but in her decision to burn the robes she has made when she hears Hector is dead.[20] This act represents the end of Andromache's own life and activity in Troy – even if she carries on living.

Andromache's life without her husband is predicted by Hector himself at *Iliad* 6.454–65. He expresses his vision in epigrammatic mode (460–1):[21]

---

[16] De Jong 2012 *s.v.* notes that though the etymology of θρόνα is obscure, already in antiquity it was taken to mean either 'decorations' or 'flowers': cf. the scholia on this passage. The poet explicitly comments on this naïveté when he calls her νηπίη (Graziosi and Haubold 2010: 30 translate 'poor innocent') at *Il.* 22.445.

[17] See for example other points in *Iliad* 3: she is casually visited by Iris, she and her attendants are given epithets more appropriate to goddesses, and she assumes a bard-like position in the *teichoskopia* (3.178–244).

[18] The point about books may appear arbitrary, given that the very idea of book division is a later construct, but it is the clearest way in which to express proportion in the text as it became fixed and transmitted.

[19] Similarly, in *Odyssey* 15 she gives Telemachus a robe she has woven which will act as 'a monument (μνῆμα) to the hands of Helen' (15.126); as Helen herself says, this robe is meant for Telemachus' future wife, but will meanwhile be kept by his mother: it thus remains in female hands. Somewhat ironically, the object travels from one weaver, Helen, to a woman famed for her unweaving, Penelope, from an unfaithful woman to the most faithful one. For discussion of Helen's weaving for *kleos*, see Mueller 2010.

[20] *Il.* 22.512 ἀλλ᾽ ἤτοι τά γε πάντα καταφλέξω πυρὶ κηλέῳ. This observation is made in Easterling 1991: 149. See further below.

[21] The lines are called an epigram by [Plutarch] *On Homer* 11 ch. 215; see also ΣbT *ad* 6.460b Erbse, Elmer 2005. On tracing the first allusions to epigram back to Homer, see Baumbach-Petrovic-Petrovic 2010: 7. For detailed discussion of epigrams in Homer (and Homeric language in epigrams),

Ἕκτορος ἥδε γυνή, ὃς ἀριστεύεσκε μάχεσθαι
Τρώων ἱπποδάμων, ὅτε Ἴλιον ἀμφεμάχοντο.

This is the wife of Hector, who was ever the bravest fighter of
the Trojans, breakers of horses, in the days when they fought
about Ilion.

An epigram acts as 'a machine for producing *kleos*'.[22] This epigram
performs just such a role, memorialising Hector and his achievements.
However, the 'reading' of this epigram is not initiated by the stone on
which it is carved, but by the presence of Andromache herself – she
perpetuates her husband's memory by her very existence. She takes the
place of a monument, a tomb or a *sēma*: 'Like a monument, she provokes
a response in those who see her.'[23] That she must be seen is key;[24] for an
epigram to have its effect it must be 'read', as 'in a culture where *kléos*
has a fundamental part to play, what is written remains incomplete until
such time as it is provided with a voice'.[25] So for Andromache to preserve
her husband's memory her shame and fall from glory must be witnessed
and discussed. This is not easy to bear – neither for Andromache nor for
Hector himself, who breaks down when he contemplates Andromache's
future. Not only is a woman expected to stay behind, wait and, ultimately, grieve, but she also becomes the mechanism by which heroes preserve their heroic deeds: a constant physical reminder of her own loss.
Svenbro asks: 'Is it really possible for one individual to be the *mnêma* of
another?'[26] In the case of the widowed Andromache, the answer is yes. As
inscribed epigrams 'constitute a kind of literary "site of memory"',[27] so
Andromache herself, the uninscribed epigram's very context, becomes a
living *lieu de mémoire*.

As the women become living monuments, memorialising *as* objects, so
the objects surrounding them share their function and allow the women
to memorialise *through* objects. There has been a surge of recent scholarly interest in how objects shape memory: for example Grethlein has

focusing on the two epigrams imagined by Hector, see A. Petrovic 2016. Clay 2016 uses Hector's
sepulchral epigram in *Iliad* 7 to reflect on epic's awareness of writing.

[22] Svenbro 1993: 164.

[23] Scodel 1992: 59. Also Graziosi and Haubold 2010 *ad* 460–1: 'Andromache functions as a σῆμα,
a living memorial of Hector's past achievements in war.' The importance of *sēmata* is noted by
Grethlein 2008: 29 who describes them as 'spatially sanctified acts of memory'.

[24] That Andromache must be *seen* is significant, as for the Greeks to see, rather than to hear, is to
know: see esp. Snell 1924 for the visual nature of Greek epistemology.

[25] Svenbro 1993: 44.

[26] Svenbro 1993: 93.

[27] Baumbach-Petrovic-Petrovic 2010: 9–10; on *lieux de mémoire*, cf. Nora 1984–92.

provided a systematic overview of commemorative objects in the Homeric epics.[28] This chapter adds to such analyses by showing how objects linked to the women's world fit with the narrative tone adopted in response to the women's limited agency.[29] The abundance of objects suggests the absence of human agents;[30] the objects, and indeed the women, point to the absence of the men who are destined never to return. In *Iliad* 22 Andromache expresses her grief through objects, the only thing over which she, as a woman confined to the domestic sphere, has control. First, when she hears lamentation from the walls, 'the shuttle dropped from her hand to the ground' (22.448 χαμαὶ δέ οἱ ἔκπεσε κερκίς). Weaving in epic, as we have seen, symbolises domestic stability and continuity. The dropping of the shuttle, therefore, signifies impending domestic upheaval: Andromache fears not only for her husband's life but also for her domestic stability.[31]

Second, when Andromache sees that her husband is dead she faints (22.466–7), dropping her headdress (22.468). As the scholiast comments, this reminder of old happiness emphasises Andromache's pitiful predicament: the headdress symbolises marriage, its loss the marriage's end and ensuing grief.[32] The physical description of the headdress is elaborate, culminating in the veil which 'is in itself a symbol of marriage', and Homer adds to it by giving the story of its origin.[33] The episode is important structurally, as it reinforces the link between this scene and the scene of Hector's departure in *Iliad* 6.[34] There (6.413–40) we hear of Andromache's past, how her father Eetion was killed by Achilles, leaving her without a family and therefore totally dependent on her husband Hector; here, in a complex rearrangement of the same elements, while Hector is being killed by

---

[28] Grethlein 2008. See also Crielaard 2003, Bassi 2005, Hartmann 2010.

[29] Mueller 2010 offers another gendered analysis of Homeric objects, with a focus on the memorialising potential of women's objects in the *Odyssey.*

[30] Here I hint at a model of human–object entanglement, the result of which is that solitary objects evoke their human 'counterparts'. Furthermore, the term 'agent' is a complex and loaded one which would require unpacking. Both these issues can be clarified by use of New Materialist theory – but this is beyond the scope of the current chapter.

[31] Cf. Pantelia 1993: 496.

[32] Σ bT *ad* 22.468–72 Erbse.

[33] Richardson 1993: 157. Although the veil can be used in any everyday context (a woman would cover her head when leaving the house), here it is being used for particular poignant effect. Cf. Grethlein 2008: 40: 'The presence of the past in material goods is often used by the Homeric narrator to create additional meaning and to highlight the narrative.' Grethlein also usefully provides a list of so-called 'biographical objects' in the Homeric poems.

[34] Connections noted by e.g. Graziosi and Haubold 2010 *ad* 6.417–20, 417. For a sensitive reading of *Iliad* 22 alongside book 6, particularly in terms of formulaic and non-formulaic elements, see Segal 1971. Grethlein 2007 takes up this question of formulae, considering how much the scene in *Iliad* 22 owes to the bathing type scene.

Achilles, Andromache expresses her grief through an object given to her in Eetion's house, on the occasion of her marriage. In a further link, the removal of the headdress also echoes the poignant scene of Hector taking off his helmet and putting it on the floor at 6.472–3.[35] The object is of symbolic importance to Hector 'of the shining helmet', and takes on its resonance precisely when Hector is furthest from the male sphere (the battlefield) and closest to the female.[36] The episode also emphasises the bride-price paid for her, important here because of the change in fortune Andromache predicts after her husband's death. It serves as a reminder of Andromache's value as an object herself, a commodity: one which, after Hector's death, might very well re-enter the market. Furthermore, the fall of the headdress serves to link Andromache's grief with that of Hecabe earlier in the book, as when she hears of her son's death she 'threw the shining veil far from her' (22.406–7 ἀπὸ δὲ λιπαρὴν ἔρριψε καλύπτρην | τηλόσε). In both cases, the act of throwing away head-gear marks a turning point: Andromache's move from wife to widow, and Hecabe's from mother to mother-in-mourning.[37]

In a final expression of grief, Andromache vows to burn Hector's clothes. Taken in relation to her weaving, this act frames the whole scene of Andromache's realisation: her vow to destroy the clothes (22.510–14) stands in stark contrast with the domestic stability expressed by her weaving in blissful ignorance (22.440–1). Though by weaving a garment and preparing a bath Andromache is foreshadowing the impending funeral rites in which Hector's body will be washed, anointed and clothed, she does so unknowingly; that she intends the clothing solely for her *living* husband is made evident by her intention to burn the clothes once she hears he is dead. The clothing symbolises two ideals: one, domestic security in life; the other, a decent burial in death (the contrast not between alive and dead, but between γυμνόν in death and decently shrouded). At this point in the narrative, Hector is deprived of both. Andromache therefore vows to burn the garments: female objects (made by χερσὶ γυναικῶν) over which she has control. She believes this is the best way to bring Hector *kleos*. Here Andromache's grief and obligation drive her to act, to strive to play

---

[35] ἀπὸ κρατός 6.472 and 22.468.

[36] Arthur Katz 1981: 31.

[37] There is, however, an important difference: whilst Hecabe threw off her καλύπτρην, Andromache discards her κρήδεμνον. This latter word is used both of Andromache's headdress and of the towers of Troy (*Il.*16.100 Τροίης ἱερὰ κρήδεμνα), a lexical crossover which forges a strong connection between woman and city, and more specifically between the downfall of both. For a discussion of Homeric *krēdemna*, see Scully 1990.

some role following Hector's death. And this is a dramatic statement, as the destruction of woven objects born of a long, laborious creative process is no small thing. As Mueller (2016: 46) writes: 'In societies where human hands laboriously produce every thread of a garment, clothing does not merely symbolize wealth – it *is* wealth.'

The ultimate expression of the women's grief at the loss of their men is lamentation.[38] Such laments usually follow the epic convention of an 'ascending scale of affection' with a crescendo culminating in the wife's lament.[39] In family-focused *Iliad* 22 this is indeed the case: Andromache's lament is left until last, further emphasised by the dramatic delay while news reaches her. In 'universal and transcendent' *Iliad* 24, however, Andromache goes first and unexpectedly leaves the final and prime spot open for Helen.[40] This is less a reflection on Andromache's importance and more a characterisation of Helen and her role in the poem. Pantelia rightly claims that Helen's position in the order of laments is dictated 'by virtue of her particular understanding of the importance of heroic *kleos* and poetry as the means for conferring it'.[41] Indeed, throughout the *Iliad*, Helen is characterised by her elevated status and her appearances are linked with poetry and an awareness of its potential as a tool for the preservation of memory.[42] Helen's sustained interest in *kleos* throughout the *Iliad* makes her the ideal character to conclude the poem, even over Hector's own wife: we will see below that this prioritising of *kleos* over the usual form of lament is linked with the different types of memory preserved by each.

Andromache in both her laments speaks not just as a wife, but as a mother. She speaks little of Hector himself and, although she refers in each lament to her widowhood, the majority of her lament is given over to the fate of their son Astyanax. This could of course be a way of enhancing the pathos of the situation, focusing on the youngest and most vulnerable victim; but I suggest it also provides a further connection with the female

---

[38] I refer here only to the γόοι of the kinswomen, excluding from my analysis the θρῆνοι of the professional mourners: for more on this distinction see Alexiou 2000 [1974]: 102. See further Alexiou 2000 [1974]: 133 and 161 on the conventional nature of the laments in *Il.* 24; Easterling 1991. On male laments in the *Iliad*, see below.

[39] Arthur Katz 1981: 27 (following Kakrides 1949): 'Its outstanding feature is the elevation of conjugal love over the love of friends and relatives.' Richardson 1993: 350 disagrees: 'it is natural that [Andromache] should lead the laments'. Either way, one should note that although she is not given the climactic position in the speeches, her actions mark her out as the chief mourner who 'usually clasps the head of the dead man with both hands' (Alexiou 2000 [1974]: 6).

[40] Pantelia 2002: 25. Helen also appears in sequence with these women in the pleas to Hector in *Iliad* 6; there the order was Hecabe, Helen, Andromache.

[41] Pantelia 2002: 21.

[42] See 3.121–8 (weaving), 3.146–244 (*teichoskopia*), 6.318–68 (comforting Hector).

act of memorialising. Svenbro writes: 'the Greeks believed humans could achieve immortality in two ways: through "generation" (*génesis*) or through "renown" (*kléos*)'.[43] I have shown that Andromache shows less interest in *kleos* than does Helen; generation is the focus of her speech. Through procreation and the continuation of Hector's line she preserves his memory, and her concern for her son's future is inextricably linked to a concern for memorialising her husband.

It should be noted that lament is not an exclusively female expression in the *Iliad*; it is only predominantly so. There are some important male laments, such as Achilles for Patroclus and Priam for Hector, which in formulation have much in common with the female laments.[44] However, as Gagliardi has shown, they are very different in their effect, and in fact this difference highlights the distinct gender roles in the poem.[45] The female laments are an end in themselves, an expression of grief which does not translate into action. Women can express themselves only through words (and, as we have seen, objects). The male laments, by contrast, propel the men into action; they are a means to an end: vengeance and, ultimately, *kleos*. Furthermore, whilst the women use their lament to memorialise the dead, the men often use their lament as an impetus to seek glory not for the fallen but for themselves.[46] Thus, the difference in the way men and women lament maps onto a more general gendered difference in the male and female mechanisms of memorialisation.

A comparison with South Slavic epic demonstrates that the relationship between women and memory is configured in a similar way in that oral tradition – partly because women perform a similar social role.[47] Since Milman Parry's groundbreaking work, comparisons between Greek and South Slavic epic have been well established.[48] Most of Parry and Lord's

---

[43] Svenbro 1993: 65.

[44] Achilles' lament for Patroclus: *Il.* 18.324–42, 19.315–37; Priam's lament for Hector: *Il.* 22.415–28.

[45] For analyses, see Gagliardi 2007: 191–207. She argues that these male laments are probably not true to life, but are a poetic construct with female laments used as a model.

[46] Gagliardi 2007: 194.

[47] Of course, this is not the only tradition with which comparisons can be drawn. One might similarly use as a comparandum the women of Mani, for example, on which see Seremetakis 1991. For a comparison with this nexus as presented by Tennyson and the Pre-Raphaelites, see Canevaro 2014.

[48] See e.g. Lord 1954, Parry 1971. Note, however, that the focus of Parry and Lord's fieldwork was the Muslim subgenre, rather than the Christian songs with which I am primarily concerned here. The examples I use in this chapter come from the branch of the tradition alternatively known as Serbo-Croatian. I use the term 'South Slavic', however, following the logic of e.g. Foley 1996: 'Although "South Slavic" is employed by linguists to denote the language family that also includes Bulgarian, Slovenian and Macedonian, it seems best to err on the side of inclusiveness rather than of parochialism or segregation.' In the analysis that follows, I have used the translations of Rootham 1920.

work, and indeed much of the work they inspired, focused on compositional techniques. Thematic comparisons feature too, but they often emerge when discussing larger compositional building blocks such as type scenes and narrative patterns. Their analyses also focused primarily on the corpus of Muslim songs. What I propose to offer here is a comparison between Greek and South Slavic epic which adopts a thematic approach, focusing on the depiction of women and which, precisely because it is the lesser frequented by Classicists, concentrates on the Christian *corpus*.

The Kosovo cycle is based around a key event in Serbian history: the defeat of the Serbs and their allies by the Turks at Kosovo on 15 June 1389.[49] Women are central to some of these songs and give their names to their poems; however, even in these instances they are portrayed as powerless, left alone in the domestic sphere whilst the men go off to fight and, ultimately, to die. In the *Maiden of Kossovo* a girl wanders the battlefield in the bloody aftermath, seeking the hero who pledged to marry her upon his return. As she tends the wounds of a soldier, he reveals that her betrothed and his companions lie among the dead – she must return home alone. In the *Death of the Mother of the Jugovitch* God allows a woman to fly to the battlefield, where she sees her nine fallen sons and dead husband but manages to keep calm. She then faces her sons' widows and children, but still holds firm. The next day two bloodstained ravens drop into her bosom the severed hand of her son. She is finally overwhelmed with grief and her heart breaks. In *Tsar Lazar and Tsaritsa Militsa*, a song thematically related to the preceding one as Militsa is the sister of the Jugovitch, Militsa begs her brothers to keep away from the battle. Despite having Prince Lazar's blessing to stay behind, all choose instead an honourable death; even the servant refuses to stay at home. News of the battle's grim outcome is brought to Militsa first by two black ravens, then by a servant carrying his right hand in his left.

The fundamental difference between the male and female spheres in the songs of the Kosovo Cycle, as in the *Iliad*, lies in the element of choice. The men have 'a masculine epic idiom of action':[50] they can choose whether or not to fight, can choose between an earthly or heavenly kingdom, to die an honourable death or to live a shameful life. That the brothers in *Tsar Lazar and Tsaritsa Militsa* choose martyrs' deaths over inglorious lives as cowards closely resembles the choice made by Achilles and other Iliadic heroes.[51]

---

[49] There is some debate over the exact details of this battle, as historical information is limited; much is reconstructed from the songs themselves, and from accounts of contemporaneous battles. The Serbian empire may not have fallen until 1459 but this battle was seen, from soon after the event itself, as a crucial turning point.

[50] Koljević 1980: 168.

[51] *Iliad* 9.410–16 Achilles reveals the choice he made. See Graziosi and Haubold 2005: 104.

The speech Sarpedon delivers in *Iliad* 12 (310–28), for example, outlines why he and Glaukos should choose to face death in the first line of battle, and in *Iliad* 6 Hector insists: 'I would feel deep shame before the Trojans, and the Trojan women with trailing garments, if like a coward I were to shrink aside from the fighting' (6.441–3). The women are not confronted with such choices in the Greek and South Slavic traditions.

In the Kosovo Cycle and *Iliad* 6 the outcome of the battle is predetermined. Both the male and female characters are aware of this – Hector knows that 'there will come a day when sacred Ilion shall perish' (6.448 ἔσσεται ἦμαρ ὅτ' ἄν ποτ' ὀλώληι Ἴλιος ἱρή) and Andromache warns that 'presently the Achaeans, gathering together, will set upon you and kill you' (6.409–10 τάχα γάρ σε κατακτενέουσιν Ἀχαιοί |πάντες ἐφορμηθέντες). But whereas the men choose to go into battle as doomed heroes or martyrs, all the women can do is try in vain to avert disaster. Tsaritsa Militsa begs: 'Leave me one at least of these my brothers, That I have a brother left to swear by' (12–13) and Andromache pleads with Hector, begging him to 'stay here on the rampart' (6.431 αὐτοῦ μίμν' ἐπὶ πύργωι).

The values of the respective heroes are formulated slightly differently. Hector's main concern is with *kleos*:

> ἐπεὶ μάθον ἔμμεναι ἐσθλός
> αἰεὶ καὶ πρώτοισι μετὰ Τρώεσσι μάχεσθαι,
> ἀρνύμενος πατρός τε μέγα κλέος ἠδ' ἐμὸν αὐτοῦ.
>
> I have learned to be valiant
> and to fight always among the foremost ranks of the Trojans,
> winning for my own self great glory, and for my father. (*Il.* 6.444–6)

The heroes of Kosovo are intent upon the honourable cross and the heavenly kingdom; Tsaritsa Militsa's second brother, for example, intends 'to shed his blood for Christ his honour, for the Holy Cross to fight and perish' (66–7). This difference stems from the very nature of the two conflicts; whilst the Achaeans and the Trojans share the same pantheon, the Kosovo Cycle tells of a religious war in which Christians battle Muslims and the ultimate goal is to ensure the superiority of one faith over the other. There are similarities between the two traditions, however, as both involve an element of memorialisation. *Kleos* may be the achievement of 'acoustic renown' *par excellence*,[52] but martyrdom can have the same lasting impact: in *Tsar Lazar and Tsaritsa Militsa* Milosh 'left glory to the name of Serbia, while there

---

[52] To use the formulation of Svenbro 1993: 164.

lives a people and Kossovo' (190–1). Whatever the concern of their men, the predicament of the women is the same: with the possible exception of Helen, they have little option of self-memorialisation. The closest they can come to a martyr's death is by proxy – indeed the fate of their men on the battlefield does sometimes prove the death of them: the Mother of the Jugovitch dies of heartbreak when she sees the gory evidence of her family's demise, and Andromache considers this possibility when she says 'for me it would be far better to sink into the earth when I have lost you' (6.410–11 ἐμοὶ δέ κε κέρδιον εἴη | σεῦ' ἀφαμαρτούσηι χθόνα δύμεναι).

This gender divide is physically manifest in both the *Iliad* and the *Kosovo Cycle*. 'The Scaean gates separate two radically different worlds, and they are the dividing line between city and battlefield';[53] appropriately, this is where Hector and Andromache part. In *Iliad* 6 Hector commands her 'Go therefore back to our house, and take up your own work' (6.490), and in *Iliad* 22 she learns of her husband's death while she is on the battlements. Similarly, Militsa's brother bids her: 'Go Militsa, to thy fair white tower' (58), and she 'comes down from her white slender tower' (127) to hear the news from the ravens: she is as removed from the action as Andromache on the battlement. In the *Maiden of Kossovo* the wounded hero urges 'return thee to thy fair white castle' (130), after he asks the maiden in surprise 'What dost thou upon the field of battle?' (33) – her presence in the military sphere is hardly to be expected, and is only accepted because she forms part of the aftermath rather than the battle itself.

Broader parallels can be drawn between Andromache and Tsaritsa Militsa, two young wives: in Militsa's pleading she focuses on her own family as does Andromache in her pleas in *Iliad* 6; both try to keep their menfolk back from battle; both faint at a point of high emotion; and both receive their bad news when abandoned at home. Similarly Hector's mother Hecabe and the Mother of the Jugovitch bear some resemblance: both in their laments focus on one son out of many, and are concerned with the inversion of the natural order symbolised by the loss of their children.

Just as Andromache in *Iliad* 22, powerless to change the course of events on the battlefield, expresses her grief through objects, the sections of the Kosovo songs which focus on the female characters, after the men have left, are characterised more by symbolic language than by narrative. As Koljević comments, 'instead of telling a story these poems enact a tragic drama

---

[53] Arthur Katz 1981: 20. On Homer's use of spatial markers, see esp. Clay 2011 – she also makes the compelling observation that whereas on the battlefield (i.e. the male sphere) locations are spatial, in the female sphere they are emotional (41).

of the mind, and this gives rise to their epic idiom in which tokens and symbols work out their ominous forebodings'.[54] The *Death of the Mother of the Jugovitch* is deeply symbolic from the outset (perhaps because of the extremity of the tragedy about to unfold); the Mother is given a falcon's eyes and a swan's wings, and the outcome of the battle is represented by two ravens carrying a severed hand. This is a 'tale which unfolds in pure retrospect of tokens of death'.[55] In *Tsar Lazar and Tsaritsa Militsa*, when the men have gone to battle the narrative language gives way to a sequence of images: instead of the heroes returning, 'Flying, come two ravens, two black ravens' (118); the servant comes carrying his right hand in his left (144); the dead are represented by many broken battle-lances (170). In both poems it is through a severed hand that the news is brought home: this gruesome token represents a passing of action, an end to the men's ability to *do* anything, and it is now up to the women to act, though in a different, symbolic, way. In *The Maiden of Kossovo* the heroes give the maiden items by which to remember them (a mantle, a ring, a bracelet) and by the end of the song these men, and the narrative with them, are reduced to these tokens alone. The maiden is explicitly seen as a vessel for memory, as each hero says of his token: 'By it thou wilt keep me in remembrance' (63) and 'By this shall my name live with thee' (111).

Lamentation as a predominantly female act also spans both traditions. Just as the *Iliad* closes on the funeral of Hector, so also at the end of the *Maiden of Kossovo*: 'From her white throat pour her lamentations' (135), as the maiden contemplates her inability to save the lover she describes as a 'young and tender sapling' (137). In the *Mother of the Jugovitch* the widows are joined in their mourning by 'lions', horses and falcons which 'roar their grief' (20) and 'scream in sorrow' (22), and before her death the Mother whispers a lament to the hand of her son, her 'fair green apple' (78).

Although women in the Homeric and South Slavic epics preserve the memory of their men, this preservation lasts only for as long as the women themselves continue to live. The women can only offer short-term, imperfect memory. Lament has been shown by Derderian to be a 'synchronic oral genre', in contrast to epic which is diachronic, as the commemorative function of lament does not operate beyond a one-off extemporaneous performance.[56] Lament alone cannot constitute a memorial, but needs poetry to preserve it: as Pantelia notes, 'the laments themselves, as songs

[54] Koljević 1980: 168
[55] Koljević 1980: 172.
[56] Derderian 2001: 10.

embedded in the epic narrative, contribute to the primary function of epic poetry, which is to preserve the memory of the hero beyond the limitations of his society'.[57] In short, laments are themselves only synchronic (i.e. they happen soon after death), but can contribute to diachronic memory. It is for this reason that Helen's lament is so incongruously prioritised in *Iliad* 24: she is the most aware of *kleos* and its diachronic potential. It is for this reason too that when Iliadic men express their lament they do not stop there, but use it as an impetus to *kleos*-seeking action, and heroes in the Kosovo Cycle depend not on a single lament but on a story to be told again and again, 'while there lives a people and Kossovo'.

As Grethlein has shown, the commemorative function of objects does not stand the test of time: 'the fragility and ambiguity of material relics and the eternity of the poetic tradition highlight each other in their discrepancy'.[58] That Andromache remembers Hector by *destroying* his clothes epitomises this transience of objects. Epigram should properly be a 'diachronic supplement to lament';[59] but the epigrammatic role of women is enacted by a 'reading' of the *woman*, not of an inscription in stone. As in the case of the other Iliadic non-*sēma*, that which Hector imagines at *Il.* 7.73–93, *kleos* is perpetuated not by the *sēma* itself but by the poetry in which it is memorialised.[60] Though women in the *Iliad* memorialise through objects *and* as epigrams, the two are never put together and so neither can last. Not even Helen's woven memorial is as perfect as it seems: she weaves the struggles Τρώων θ' ἱπποδάμων καὶ Ἀχαιῶν χαλκοχιτώνων (*Il.* 3.127 'of Trojans, breakers of horses, and bronze-armored Achaians') *before* Iris comes to her and takes her to see the amazing deeds Τρώων θ' ἱπποδάμων καὶ Ἀχαιῶν χαλκοχιτώνων (*Il.* 3.131). The order and repetition might point to Helen's semi-divine status, her privileged knowledge that comes from something more than empirical experience; it may, however, suggest that when Helen weaves she does not yet see.[61] When Iris calls Helen to the walls to tell Priam about the warriors down below, Helen's knowledge is certainly marked as limited; she searches for her brothers (*Il.* 3.236–42), because she does not know what the poet tells us: that 'the

---

[57] Pantelia 2002: 23.

[58] Grethlein 2008: 35. For discussion of the limitations of women and objects as commemorators, see further Canevaro forthcoming.

[59] Derderian 2001: 12. On written epigrams extending a person's memory, see e.g. Day 2010: 7.

[60] Hector proposes a duel and boasts that the Achaeans will erect a *sēma* so that men of the future will hear about his victory; the duel, however, does not happen, and so the *sēma* will never materialise. See Clay 2011: 58 n. 41 and further 119, now with Clay 2016.

[61] The line is made up of formulaic elements, but it is not very common as it appears elsewhere only at *Il.* 3.251 and 8.71.

teeming earth lay already upon them' (3.243 τοὺς δ' ἤδη κάτεχεν φυσίζοος αἶα). She might have been summoned for her privileged knowledge, but it only gets her so far – she is missing something. It seems likely, then, that a similar suggestion of limitation is operating also in the weaving passage. Like Andromache weaving in *Iliad* 22 when she has not yet heard of Hector's death, Helen too in her weaving does not have all the information. Furthermore, Helen's weaving itself is limited in that she does not complete it.[62] Iris calls her away while she is weaving, interrupting the act itself and stalling the finished product. Ultimately Helen knows less than the poet does – and so the men continue to seek everlasting fame in poetry.[63]

We still remember Andromache's headdress, Hector's epigram, Helen's tapestry and Hecabe's lament, but only because they have been preserved in Homer's poem. Homeric women act as vessels for the preservation of memory in their own right for as long as they are alive, but for this memory to continue it must be immortalised through epic. To conclude with some examples from the *Odyssey*, when Penelope philosophises about *kleos* in *Odyssey* 19 she points out that men are short-lived (*Od.* 19.328 ἄνθρωποι δὲ μινυνθάδιοι τελέθουσιν). The adjective μινυνθάδιοι highlights the ephemerality of any mode of memorialisation that depends on mortals. What we really need is reputation, rumour, *kleos*: things which can be transmitted orally after our death. When Agamemnon praises Penelope in *Odyssey* 24.195–8, he formulates Penelope's achievement in terms of her remembering Odysseus. Throughout his long absence, memory of Odysseus is kept alive by the fidelity and constancy of his wife, and Penelope is explicitly praised for acting as a vessel for memory – she is even given *kleos* for it. However, for this *kleos* to last it must enter into song, and song fashioned by the immortals no less (197–8 τεύξουσι δ'ἐπιχθονίοισιν ἀοιδὴν | ἀθάνατοι). Even the most constant – or conniving – woman has her limitations.

---

[62] Unlike – lest we forget – Penelope.
[63] Graziosi and Haubold 2010: 6–7.

CHAPTER 2

Speaking in the Wax Tablets of Memory

Peter Agócs

The relationship between memory and writing is an important theme in classical Greek culture. Poets and thinkers imagined writing as a sort of externalised memory, and memory as a kind of writing on the 'wax' of the soul – a dominant metaphor drawn from poetic language which still seems to inform and shape Plato's and Aristotle's philosophical discussions of memory and recollection.[1] This chapter aims to tease out some of the implications of the pervasive metaphor of the 'wax tablets of the mind', focusing on the earliest occurrences of the metaphor in Pindar and the Attic tragedians. In particular, it argues that the 'wax tablets' metaphor is not only a way of imagining how living human memory works: rather, it also reciprocally helped to define the culture's attitude to the written text, whether poetry or prose, as a new kind of aesthetic object – a voice distinct from any particular performance or context of performance. It also helped people to grapple with the problems that the technology of writing posed for a culture which still defined its most powerful and authoritative forms of literary speech as living, performed voice. The argument that follows falls into three sections, each of which describes one element in this nexus of ideas: the idea, familiar already in Homer's songs, of the poem as a kind of memory; memory as a kind of writing on the soul; and the written text, conversely, as the fixed and objectified 'memory' of a living voice. Section 1 briefly examines how writing, as a theme, emerged in the early fifth-century song culture, at a time when the dominant poetics of song were still powerfully shaped by the idea of *kleos* and externalised memory. Section 2 examines the various occurrences of the 'wax tablets' ('memory as writing') metaphor in Attic tragedy, before studying how Pindar, in the

---

[1] Cf. King's, Castagnoli's and Sassi's chapters in this volume. On the tendency of philosophical discussions to treat Plato's use of the 'wax block' analogy in *Theaetetus* 191a5–196c9 (on which see pp. 77–8, 244–6, and 349) in isolation from its wider cultural context and place in the earlier poetic tradition, see Zuckerman 2015: 2–3 and Sansone 1975: 59.

proem of *Olympian* 10, uses it to define his own lyric utterance as an act of reminding, assimilating the technology of literacy to the older (but still present) discourse of *kleos*. Section 3 broadens the focus to examine how fifth-century authors of song and prose negotiated the tensions created by the introduction of writing: a new kind of inscribed '*logos*' or voice that, as Socrates' myth so memorably puts it in the *Phaedrus* (274d5–275e), cannot, in the absence of its 'father', talk back or defend itself when questioned.

1 Song as Memory

At the turn of the sixth century BC, writing gave Greek culture a new metaphor with which to imagine the act of remembering. It was also, however, integrated into existing traditions of oral performance. The poetic text, in particular, was still (at least at the level of its overt poetics) defined by its vocality and its role in a wider 'culture of memory' based primarily on notions of tradition and the spoken word. Pindar and the tragedians appropriate and continue the ancient ideology of song as commemoration and memorialisation – the most powerful single medium of oral memory in the culture. In this tradition, expressed most succinctly in the Hesiodic genealogy which makes the Muses the daughters of Mnemosyne and Zeus,[2] song is valued for its ability to preserve a true account of the past and to grant a kind of immortality, in cultural memory, to individuals and their deeds.[3] As 'praise' and 'memory', song challenges the omnipresent power of λήθη. It 'awakens Mnemosyne' by reviving the memory of old traditions or creating new *kleos*, strengthening the 'mindfulness' and care (χάρις) which binds society to its individual and collective histories, its heroes and its gods.[4] Pindar's epinicians, in particular, emphasise reciprocal exchange between victor, poet and community, and their gods and ancestors.[5]

But late archaic song modifies the picture of a continuous tradition of *kleos* guaranteed by the Muse in subtle ways. Most strikingly, perhaps, we find a tendency, evident in both Theognis and Pindar, as well as in the poetry of Simonides, to invest the memorialising properties of song in objects, or, alternatively, to dispute the value of such metaphorical

---

[2] Hes. *Th.* 53–5, 915–17 with Detienne 1967: 9–14 and Simondon 1982: 103–12. For the relationship between Memory and the Muses, cf. also the Introduction of this volume.

[3] On 'cultural memory' as a concept, see Assmann 1992.

[4] See e.g. Pind. *Ol.* 8.76; *Pyth.* 9.104; *Isthm.* 4.19–24; *Isthm.* 7.10–21. On charis, see Simondon 1982: 47 65; Goldhill 1991: 132; Maclachlan 1993; Day 2010: 232–80.

[5] On this idea of χάρις or reciprocal exchange (with bibliography), see Agócs 2009; for its connection with memory, see also Ceccarelli's chapter in this volume.

investment. Theognis (19–37) uses the analogy of a sealed tablet or amphora
to mark his songs (τοῖσδ' ἔπεσιν, 20) as an authorial possession immune
to tampering.[6] In *Nemean* 7, Pindar says (12–16) that 'great acts of courage,
lacking songs, are trapped in great darkness; we know of a mirror for fair
deeds in one way only: if by the grace of Mnemosyne of the radiant head-
band they find ransom for labours in famous songs of words'.[7] Simonides,
Pindar's older colleague and rival, is likewise supposed to have called
poetry 'speaking painting'.[8] Likewise, the proem to Pindar's *Nemean* 5 famously rejects the analogy between poetry and 'statue-making', extolling the
power of song, as a form of oral *kleos*, to travel the world untrammelled by
the monument's ties to a particular place.

This new emphasis on the song as an aesthetic object and a spatial form,
as something permanent and lasting beyond the frame of any single communicative or performative act, coincides with a tendency, in Pindar and
other poets, to emphasise the role of the poet's learned craft (τέχνη) alongside the divinely given knowledge, insight and vocality vouchsafed him by
Homeric and Hesiodic tradition. The τέχνη-language that comes to the
fore in their poetry (Pindar's song can be a portico with golden columns,
a Delphic treasury, a funeral stele of Parian marble, or a finely worked
fillet such as Grecian goldsmiths make)[9] expresses the power of song to
act as a 'sign' or 'reminder' (σῆμα/μνῆμα)[10] of something absent. Like the
monuments with which it now contrasts itself, song *externalises* memory: it
is an *Erinnerungsfigur* or *lieu de mémoire*.[11] Although this objectification of
the song has certain clear precedents in Homer (the warrior's tomb, the
Achaean Wall, Achilles' Shield), the pervasiveness and explicitness of these
poetological metaphors in early fifth-century song must be in some way
connected to the increasing prevalence of literacy in Greek culture. The
magic of performance was now underwritten by the permanence of fixed
written texts, which themselves became the 'sign' of an absent performance

---

[6] Ford 1985: 85 ('The seal is significant not because it names an author or a singer but because it identifies a "text"').

[7] Frontisi-Ducroux and Vernant 1997: 51–250 (on *Nem.* 7.14–16: 117–18). Here and in what follows,
   all translations, unless otherwise indicated, are my own.

[8] Plut. *De glor. ath.* 3. 346f (= T 101 Poltera) and M. Psellus 821BC (*Migne, PG* vol. 122), with
   Carson 1992.

[9] The mentioned passages are *Ol*.6. init., *Pyth*.6.5–14, *Nem*.4.79–82 (cf. *Nem*.8.46–7, *Isthm*. 8.61–
   2) and *Nem*.7.77–9 (cf. *Nem*.8.15). On these object-analogies: Goldhill 1991: 30–1; Steiner 1993,
   1994: 91–9 and 2001: 251–94; Ford 1992: 138–71 and especially 2002: 93–130; also Porter 2010: 453–523.

[10] In Homer, a σῆμα is a mark, sign or token, or (e.g. *Il*.7.419) a barrow; on μνῆμα, see LSJ s.v. Both
   words are common in funerary epigram; *mnēma* also occurs on dedications (*agalmata*). On 'signs'
   in early song, see Nagy 1983; Ford 1992: 137–45; Steiner 1994: 10–60 and Scodel 2002: esp. 99–105.

[11] *Erinnerungsfigur*: Assmann 1992: 37–8; cf. Nora 1984–1992. Halbwachs 1925 spoke, in the Platonic-
   Aristotelian tradition, of 'memory images'.

and a vocality that could, as it were, be re-animated through reference to the fixed sign. The 'memory for story' typical of *epos* is supplemented by a 'memory for words' based on the entextualised transcript, but the social function is identical.

The emphasis on songs as permanent objects coincides in the early fifth century with a new explicitness and boldness in the texts about the technology of writing itself. Although literacy was by no means 'new', it nevertheless constituted a new theme in the conservative repertory of song and poetry. The emergence of writing as a theme for song is paralleled by an unprecedented burst of images of writers and readers (usually but not exclusively boys or youths and their teachers) on Attic red-figure symposium vases of the 480s.[12] A little later, Aeschylus and Pindar make the earliest explicit literary references in the Greek tradition to writing and reading alphabetic script.[13] In the speech from *Prometheus Bound* where the Titan describes how the τέχναι he invented saved humanity from savagery, he defines writing (460–1) as 'the combination of letters, the memory of all things, a craft-skilled woman, mother of the Muse' (γραμμάτων τε συνθέσεις, μνήμην ἁπάντων, μουσομήτορ' ἐργάνην). Here then, in a play probably composed around the middle of the fifth century,[14] writing *is* Memory. She is also, in a nod to Hesiod and the traditional metonymy 'Muse' for 'song', the mother of verbal art itself.[15] In Euripides' *Palamedes* (fr. 578.1–2 Kannicht) the hero describes writing as 'a medicine (*pharmakon*) against forgetting (*lēthē*) | *voiceless and yet speaking*' encoded in syllables and letters.[16] When Socrates in the *Phaedrus* (274c5–275b2) dissects the myth of *grammata* as a '*pharmakon* of wisdom and memory', or when in the *Laws* (5.741c) the Athenian Stranger describes writing tablets as 'cypresswood memories covered in letters', Plato is thus responding to a nexus of associations established in earlier poetry. It is this nexus of associations that the next section will explore.

---

[12] Pfeiffer 1968: 25–8; Immerwahr 1964 and 1973; Lissarrague 1987: 119–33; Harris 1989: 97.

[13] The earliest allusion to writing (γράφειν) in Greek literature is the πίναξ of Proitos at *Il.*6.168–70 (σήματα λυγρά ... θυμοφθόρα πολλά). The earliest dateable and unambiguous use of γράφειν to mean 'alphabetic writing' are Pind. *Ol.*10.3 (p. 79 below) and *Ol.*3.3.

[14] Griffith 1977: 252–4.

[15] Note that most MSS (Griffith 1983: 169–70) have μνήμην θ' ἁπάντων, giving us 'number, writing, *and* memory'. 'Muse': Detienne 1967: 10–11 n. 7. ἐργάνη (Stobaeus: the codd. have meretricious ἐργάτιν for ἐργάτην) also evokes the Attic cult of Athena Ergane: Deubner 1932: 35–6, Parke 1977: 92–3; Simon 2002: 38–9; Parker 2005: 409, 464–5.

[16] Translation after Collard and Cropp 2008. ἄφωνα καὶ φωνοῦντα (Collard, Cropp and Gilbert 2004: 98–9) may refer to 'consonants and vowels': the correction τε θείς deserves consideration. cf. Gorgias 82 F11a, 30 (ii: 301, 25–6 DK).

2 The Mind as Writing-tablet

The notion of memory as a kind of writing that externalises its contents in
the inscribed sign appears first in Pindar and the tragedians. We will begin
with the latter. Later in *Prometheus Bound*, when asked to tell Io about
her future wanderings, the Titan frames his prophecy with two formulaic
speech-tags. Beginning the tale, he says (705–6):

> σύ τ' Ἰνάχειον σπέρμα, **τοὺς ἐμοὺς λόγους**
> **θυμῷ βάλ'**, ὡς ἂν τέρματ' ἐκμάθῃς ὁδοῦ.

> And you, seed of Inachus, **thrust my words into your *thumos*,**
> so that you may learn how your journey will end.

But when he begins the second half of the account (788–9), the injunction
takes a different form:

> σοὶ πρῶτον, Ἰοῖ, πολύδονον πλάνην φράσω,
> **ἣν ἐγγράφου σὺ μνήμοσιν δέλτοις φρενῶν.**

> First, Io, I shall tell you about the wanderings on which you will
> be driven: **inscribe them on the memorious tablets of your
> *phrenes*.**

The first phrase echoes a familiar Homeric formula:

> ἄλλο δέ τοι ἐρέω, **σὺ δ' ἐνὶ φρεσὶ βάλλεο σῇσιν**[17]

> I'll tell you something else: **thrust it into your *phrenes***

which is used to introduce a set of instructions, or to contradict an interlocutor. Recurring in Hesiod and parainetic elegy, where it underscores
the distance between 'teacher' and 'pupil',[18] it calls attention to the message
(ἔπος) the speaker is about to impart, suggesting his words are worth full
attention. The phraseology is that with which Homeric Greek describes
any emotion, mental impression, plan, thought or vital force arriving or
stoked from 'outside' the person, or indeed any act of giving something to
someone.[19] Remembering (like perceiving, knowing and feeling) is never
really a 'mental event' in Homer. What for Aristotle would become the
functions of the soul are distributed across a range of (often overlapping)

---

[17] *Il.* 1.297; 4.39; 5.259, etc. cf. *HAp.* 261 with Nieddu 1984: 214.
[18] See e.g. Theogn. 1049–54 and Hes. *Op.* 107, 274, 491, 688, 797.
[19] Sansone 1975: 54–8. Homer normally uses βάλλειν, ἐσβάλλειν (cf. LSJ s.v. I.6). In memory contexts,
the implied object is normally an *epos* (but cf. *Il.* 9.434–5; *Od.* 2. 79, 11.428 where the corresponding
phrase refers to emotion or intention).

'organs' or 'places' (φρήν/φρένες, πραπίδες, θυμός) that, like the active and passive work (thinking, feeling, remembering) which they perform, are basically somatic.[20] At least with respect to memory, *phrenes* and *thumos* function as an empty space where experience, thought and utterance are internalised for later use and rumination.[21] The sense of a definite place is clearer with the *phrenes* than with *thumos*; but the terms must refer to the same sense of inner experience.[22] The *phrenes*, at least, extend both sideways and down.[23] How consciousness' receptacle works is left unexplained; but since the language tends to equate memory and attention, 'knowing' (οἶδα) and 'seeing' (ἰδεῖν), *phrenes* and *thumos* may be a place where objects, once retained, present themselves to recognition by the inner sight (*noos*).[24] Post-Homeric texts are more explicit about recollection as visualisation. For Empedocles, it is the πράπιδες that, when trained as Pythagoras' were in wisdom and recollection, can reach beyond a man's lifetime by a span of ten or twenty generations, 'seeing' past and future lives.[25] In Pindar, if you've forgotten something, your *phrenes* have 'missed' it.[26]

Spatial metaphors are basic to how humans, as corporeal beings, imagine consciousness. But Prometheus' image of 'memorious' or 'mindful' tablets in the *phrenes* pushes the idea of the receptacle of consciousness in new directions. The act of fixing something in the mind is conceived as inscription. The language is strongly poeticised – μνήμων, transferred from the person to the passive surface of remembering, merges the subject of remembering with the vehicle and tenor (expressed in the defining genitive φρενῶν) of the metaphor – but also literal.[27] *Deltoi* are *tablets*:[28] thin boards

---

[20] One hesitates to speak of 'faculties' in connection with these concepts. Of the other Homeric 'organs' of life and consciousness, ψυχή, κραδίη/κῆρ/ἦτορ, and νόος, only the last seems to have no somatic existence. The literature on Homeric concepts of mind is vast: see Snell 1953: 8–22 and 1977; Fränkel 1975: 74–85; Ireland and Steel 1975; Jahn 1987; Darcus Sullivan 1989 and 1990 (on Pindar and Bacchylides) and 1994, 36–41 (esp. n. 48) and 54–60 (esp. n. 82), 1995; Padel 1992: 12–48; Clarke 1999 (esp. 61–126).

[21] This applies also to learning skills: e.g. *Od.* 22.347–8.

[22] Sansone 1975: 54–8 posits a difference. The *phrenes* are sometimes identified with the lungs (cf. esp. *Il.*16. 503–4 with Onians 1951: 13–83; Clarke 1999: 74–89); *thumos* seems less confined to a zone of the body. But they occur in hendiadys (cf. e.g. *Il.* 1.193; Theogn. 1050).

[23] In Homer (*Il.* 19.125) emotion 'strikes deep into the *phrēn*'. Pindar associates the 'deep *phrēn*' with emotion (e.g. the victor's μέριμνα or the poet's χρέος) and poetic inspiration (e.g. *Nem.* 4.6–8). 'Good counsel' and 'wise thought' are also traditionally 'deep': see Silk 1974: 121 n. 13.

[24] On *noos* as intentionality, see Clarke 1999: 120–6. Alcman probably (fr. 133 *PMGF* = 191 Calame) punned on 'seeing' memory: see above, Introduction, p. 11.

[25] fr. 129 DK.

[26] *Pyth.* 4.42: τῶν δ᾽ἐλάθοντο φρένες.

[27] LSJ s.v.; Steiner 1994: 25.

[28] A Semitic loan-word: Masson 1967: 61–5.

(πίνακες)[29] with a hollow centre filled with wax. When applied to the mind, the tablet metaphor involves a transference: even as the tablets are an image of the remembering mind, they have a memory of their own – the 'memory' of the wax.

The tablets are in fact the tragedians' only metaphor for memory, even as memory is the only context in tragedy where writing figures as the vehicle of a metaphor. The metaphor was certainly conventional and clichéd (if hardly dead)[30] by the time it is first attested in extant poetry. This is clear from the naturalness with which the *Prometheus* poet deploys it. Aeschylus uses it six times (first in *Supplices*); Sophocles thrice; it is missing in extant Euripides. It can hardly have been invented by Aeschylus:[31] indeed, it must have migrated to poetry from the metaphorical repertory of everyday discourse. Often, it appears (as in the *Prometheus Bound*) as a substitute for the older metaphor of 'fixing in the mind', with the same idea of memory motivating action. In a *kommos* of *Choephori*, Electra tells her brother to remember their father's sufferings. 'Such', she says, 'is the tale you hear: write it down in your mind'.[32] 'Yes, write it down', sings the chorus: 'let the words pierce right through your ears to the calm abyss of the mind' (δι' ὤτων δὲ συν-| τέτραινε μῦθον ἡσύχῳ φρενῶν βάθει).[33] The story and its memory, once internalised, must stir Orestes to revenge. In *Suppliants* (179) Danaos, preparing to meet the Argive host, tells his daughters:

αἰνῶ φυλάξαι τἄμ' ἔπη **δελτουμένας**

I advise you: guard my words, **writing them on the wax tablet**.[34]

The image recurs at 991–2.[35] Sophocles uses it in *Triptolemus*, one of his earliest plays, and in the *Philoctetes*, one of his last.[36] In *Trachiniae* (682–3), Deianeira, preparing the poison that will kill her husband, declares that she forgot none of the dying centaur's instructions, 'but held them safe like writing unwashable from a tablet (δέλτος) of bronze'.[37]

---

[29] *Pinax* in Homer means a 'board' or 'plank', but also a writing tablet (n. 13 above).

[30] For the distinction: Silk 1974: 27–8.

[31] Sansone 1975: 59–60.

[32] l. 450 (Garvie 1986: 166; Untersteiner 2002: 114 and 309 ad loc.) is insecure and certainly lacunose.

[33] Aesch. *Cho.* 451–2 (translation after Sommerstein). See Garvie 1986: 166–7 ad loc., reading βάθει with Sommerstein 2008 for cod. M's difficult βάσει ('step') of (Untersteiner 2002: ad loc.) the movement of the revenge plot.

[34] *Deltoumenas* is a *hapax*: Σ *ad loc* paraphrases with ἀπογραφομένας ('transcribing').

[35] See Sansone 1975: 61.

[36] fr. 597 Radt; *Phil.* 1325.

[37] Jebb ad loc. While we have examples of δέλτοι made from materials other than wood – the usual material was boxwood (hence πύξιον: Pollux IV.18) while Eur. *IA* 39 speaks of pine – it is not the material of the support that Sophocles is thinking of, but the writing surface itself. The metal's

Some instances of writing tablets in drama (two strictly *non*-metaphorical, the third a development of the metaphor) pertain to a discourse of *eschatological memory*. The notion that the gods 'watch' human actions appears already in Homer and Hesiod. There are the 'Prayers' of the *Iliad* (9.502–4), Hesiod's 'thrice countless immortal watchers, φύλακες, of mortal men' who wander over the earth cloaked in fog (*Op.* 252–4), and Dike herself (*Op.* 259–60), who sits by her father telling him of the evil *noos* of unjust men. An Aeschylean fragment (fr. 281a Radt = *P.Oxy.* 2256 fr. 9a) of uncertain genre takes up the Hesiodic image of Justice at the throne of Zeus (l.10), re-imagining her as a writer. Dike speaks: her τιμή as the god's emissary is to make the lives of just (*dikaios*) men easy and to change the lives of the bad not by charms or force, but by recording their sins 'on the tablet of Zeus' (21, γράφουσα τὰ⟨μ⟩πλακήματ' ἐν δέλτῳ Διός).[38] 'When', her interlocutor[39] asks, 'will you open the tablet?' 'When for them [the bad people] the day brings the appointed reckoning.'[40] The divine record is stored away until it is consulted: the inscrutable slowness of Zeus's justice,[41] subjected to the discipline of script, becomes an infallible and methodical archiving of sins. In *Eumenides* (273–5), the Erinyes, singing of the punishment which awaits Orestes in the Underworld, describe a 'great assessor of mortals, Hades, beneath the earth' who 'watches everything with tablet-writing mind' (δελτογράφῳ δὲ πάντ' ἐπωπᾷ φρενί). Every action is archived for future use when, as εὔθυνος he prepares the audit of our actions.

The underworld judge may attest Orphic/Pythagorean influence; but the fact he is a writer and an *euthynos* (a word which may allude to a legal procedure well-attested in the classical city)[42] foreshadows the world of Athenian legality which plays such a important part in the drama's denouement. In 458, their city, on the cusp of its radical democracy, had begun to deploy writing, particularly on stone, on a scale unparalleled in any earlier Greek state. It was increasingly identified with equality, the rule of law

---

hardness and monumentality, and the force needed to inscribe it, show Deianeira's ironic reverence for the monster's words.

[38] I follow the interpretation and supplements of Sommerstein 2008.

[39] Perhaps the chorus.

[40] εὖτ' ἂν τέλ]ῃ σφιν ἡμέρα τὸ κύριον, *vel sim.*

[41] See e.g. Solon fr. 13 W². Cf. also *com. adesp.* fr. 921 K.-A.; Hesych. s.v. σκυτάλαι (van Looy 1964: 229–30).

[42] While εὔθυνος (the inquisitor who examines the conduct of retiring officials) and εὔθυναι are not attested this early, the language implies such a procedure (Solmsen 1944: 28–9; Sommerstein 1989: 130 ad loc.; Steiner 1994: 109–10). As described by Arist. *Ath. Pol.* 48.4, *euthynai* involve written denunciations. εὐθύνειν of Zeus: *Pers.* 828 (with Garvie 2009: 316–17).

and democratic Athens herself.[43] While it is unlikely that Athenian legal procedure kept records of judgements as early as the 450s, or that forensic evidence (witness statements, for example) was presented in written form as it is in the fourth-century orators,[44] writing's real-world uses are less important than the conceptual leap that identifies the perfect memory with the archive.[45] Memory-writing assumes the implicit authority of real written text. Euripides pillories the conceit in one of his *Melanippe* plays (fr. 506 Kannicht, probably *the Wise*[46]) where the speaker, probably the heroine, voicing advanced sophistic ideas, says that Justice is not an anthropomorphic, spiritualised force, but something 'close by': manifested, perhaps, in everyday human relations. She denies that human crimes 'leap up' to the gods and that Zeus could have a tablet: were the whole sky a writing surface, it could never accommodate the tale of human crime.

There is another side to tablet memory, connected to the ephemeral nature of the medium. Wax tablets were used for jottings and 'notes to self',[47] for letters, and, as the Hellenistic poets show, for drafts of works that, when finished, might be copied to papyrus.[48] The metaphor thus describes not only recording and preservation, but also forgetting. Aeschylus speaks of a man's image 'drawn' (γεγραμμένος) in the mind: just so, the fading of memory is a wiping out, sudden or gradual, of the inscribed 'sketch' or 'text'.[49] The term for 'rubbing' out letters is ἐξαλείφω, the word used for scrubbing someone from a register or list, or of the cancellation of debts.[50] This gives rise to some striking metaphors. Eteokles, gearing up for war, can speak of the 'erasure' that threatens the city's shrines (*Sept.* 15);[51] the chorus of the *Prometheus* (534–5) wishes that their good intentions might 'abide ... and never *melt* away' (ἀλλά μοι τόδ' ἐμμένοι | καὶ μήποτ' ἐκτακείη). To scrape the old wax off a writing-tablet is ἐκκνίζω; new wax is

---

[43] Eur. *Suppl.* 433–6 is the classic fifth-century statement.

[44] On written documents' fourth-century use in law and business: Thomas 1992: 148–9; Gagarin 2008: 176–205. γραφή, a form of public indictment, is attested at Athens ca. 440–420 (Gagarin 2008: 111–14 traces it back to the sixth century).

[45] Solmsen 1944: 28.

[46] See van Looy 1964: 225–32, 322–6; Collard, Cropp and Lee 1995: 278.

[47] For an interesting reference to such 'notes' in the Hippocratic Corpus, see van der Eijk 1997: 97.

[48] For some instances, see n. 122 below. As a medium, *deltoi* arguably imply the relative impermanence of the poetic text.

[49] Cf. Aesch. *Ag.* 1327–9, referring either to the palimpsesting of papyrus by washing, a process attested later, or (Fraenkel 1950 iii: 621–2 ad loc.) to erasure of a wet ink sketch from a whitened board (λεύκωμα): cf. Soph. *Trach.* 685; Eur. fr. 618 Kannicht (both 'tablets').

[50] See *DGE* s.v. ἐξαλείφω, 1.1–2. The verb ἀλείφω is also attested in Cypriote texts as a term for inscribing with brush and ink: see Heubeck 1979: 157.

[51] Cf. Aesch. *Cho.* 503 (Garvie 1986: 182–3 ad loc.).

'melted on' (ἐπιτήκειν);[52] but the same wax, as in a joke in *Clouds* (771–2) that turns on the destruction of documents, can melt and take the writing with it. Critias (fr. 6 W², 10–12), describing the effects of drunkenness, says that 'forgetfulness melts away memory from the mind (λῆστις δ' ἐκτήκει μνημοσύνην πραπίδων)'.

In the 'wax tablets', it is not (as in Homer) the experience that is internalised or forgotten, but rather the 'writing' – a graphic *symbol* for the remembered word, experience or concept. Quite apart from the unique symbolism, often complex and pertaining for example to what is 'inscribed' and how, that animates particular poetic uses of the trope, they all share a simple semantics in which the content of memory is replaced with a written 'sign' (σῆμα), which itself refers us to whatever is no longer present to lived experience. Memories, as mental representations, are thus transformed into referential signs.[53] Writing and image-making (both senses of γράφειν) constitute the final link in a chain of Greek thought about signs (σήματα/μνήματα), that draws together Homeric poetics – the heard performance of the *aoidos* as a living 'sign' of an absent world; the tomb (also σῆμα) as a 'sign' of the absent man – with the language of seeing and interpreting 'signs' (σήματα, κληδόνες) expressed in chance words and occurrences, the organs of a sacrificial animal, or the flight of birds, all of which established an extensive hermeneutics in the Greek culture's earliest phases. To put it another way, the Greeks had a theory of 'reading' before they discovered *grammata*.[54]

This semantics presents the older language of internalised experience with a transparent explanatory mechanism. As noted in numerous studies by Geoffrey Lloyd, the distinction between image/analogy and literal description is not strictly realised in the fifth century, even in philosophical or scientific prose, appearing only with Aristotle's division of phrases into 'strict' (κυρίως) and 'transferred' (κατὰ μεταφοράν) usages.[55] The Hippocratic texts, for example, often invoke analogies from crafts or everyday life to explain changes in the body.[56] There is no easy leap from our own interpretative categories to these fifth-century descriptive metaphors

---

[52] See Hdt. 7. 239 and *Suda* ε 2094 s.v. ἐπέτηξε with ε 1608 s.v. ἐξέκνισεν.
[53] These passages belong to the period when it becomes possible for Greek poets to speak of mental 'images': e.g. Aesch. *Ag.* 799–804 (Fraenkel 1950 ii: 363).
[54] See e.g. Eur. *Suppl.* 212, with Svenbro 1993: 8–25; Padel 1992: 16–18 and Steiner 1994: 10–60.
[55] Lloyd 1990: 20–38 and Zuckerman 2015: 7.
[56] Padel 1992: 10 n. 19 and 33–40 (the quotation comes from 34); Lloyd 1966: 357–8; 1987: 172–214; 1990: 23–4. Although some fifth-century texts (e.g. Ar. *Thesm.* 55 ἀντονομάζει) refer to troped language, a theory of metaphor emerges only in Aristotle.

or even those of fourth-century philosophy. Mental contents as inscribed in a book (*Phlb.* 38c–39a),[57] or impressed like the image on a signet ring in the receiving 'wax' of the mind (*Tht.* 191d–196e), form the basis of famous descriptions of memory in Plato.[58] In one model for memory presented and rejected in *Theaetetus*, the ease with which we remember something, like the durability of the 'inscription', depends on the consistency of the wax.[59] The wax and signet ring recur in Aristotle's impression model of sense perception (*An.* 2.12 424a17–26) and in the *De memoria*'s analysis of memory (450a28–451a14).[60] His treatment of memories as belonging to a larger class of mental traces or representations (φαντάσματα; εἰκόνες), and his statement that cognition (νοεῖν) is 'impossible' without such 'pictures',[61] shows how natural recourse to graphic imagery became a way of imagining the invisible processes of mental representation and memory. Aristotle too sees the 'consistency' of memory in material terms (450a32–450b11). In Plato, and particularly in Aristotle, many difficult problems depend on how the 'wax block', an inheritance of the poets' folk psychology, is intended.[62] Is it a serious model of how embodied consciousness works, or a 'mere' analogy? The idea of memory as an image 'inscribed' in mental space receives its developed form in the late fifth century with the *ars memoriae*, ascribed in the tradition to the poet Simonides – a system that influenced Aristotle's theorising here.[63] Many scientific explanations develop from ordinary language, and no science, however much it mistrusts them, can do without metaphors.

Perhaps the most interesting use of the 'wax tablets' metaphor in early classical poetry occurs, however, in Pindar, where it shapes the poet's

---

[57] See King's chapter in this volume.

[58] Recollection is compared (*Tht.* 197c–199e) to finding and catching birds in an aviary. Carruthers 1990: 16–45; Coleman 1992: 1–38.

[59] Appeal to somatic properties to explain differences in mental functioning is a feature in Homeric (Clarke 1999: 88–9, 97–106) and Presocratic thought (e.g. Heraclitus: Padel 1992: 41).

[60] See Castagnoli's chapter in this volume; see also (on Plato) Lang 1980, Penner 2013 and Zuckerman 2015.

[61] *Mem.* 449b31–2 with Sorabji 1972. At 450a28–32 Aristotle compares the affection (πάθος) caused by perception in the soul – of which memory (μνήμη) is the lasting 'possession' (ἕξις) – to ζωγράφημά τι, 'a kind of painted picture' (another sense of γράφειν). The simile is repeated at 450b21–451a2, again *apropos* of mental error.

[62] See Sorabji 1972, and compare Nussbaum 1978; Schofield 1978; Annas 1992; Caston 1996 and 2005; Labarrière 2000.

[63] Simonides: fr. 510 *PMG* = T80 Poltera. Discussing how mental representations (φαντάσματα) can be called up on demand, *An.* 3.3 427b19–21 compares this to how practitioners of the *ars memoriae* create and call up mnemonic images (cf. Sorabji 1972: ix–x, 2–8, 22–34); Coleman 1992: 39–59 with Carruthers 1990 and Yates 1966. For some qualifications on Aristotle's interest in mnemotechnics, cf. Sassi's chapter in this volume.

representation of his song as text and commemorative object, and thus opens the way to our next theme: written song as a form of externalised memory. After the famous σήματα λυγρά with which Proitos deceives the hero Bellerophon in *Iliad* 6 (169), Pindar is the first poet in the tradition to use the verb γράφειν in the sense 'to write'.[64] A marginal scholion to *pae.* viib, 24 (fr. 52h Maehler = C2 Rutherford) tells us that he mentioned a wax tablet (δέλτου) immediately after a passage of great poetological interest; the context, however, is uncertain.[65] But the proem of his tenth *Olympian*, where we also find the earliest dated use of the verb 'to read' (ἀναγιγνώσκειν) in any Greek text, is a place where we can examine Pindar's use of the metaphor more closely:[66]

str. 1, 1 τὸν Ὀλυμπιονίκαν ἀνάγνωτέ μοι
Ἀρχεστράτου παῖδα, πόθι φρενός
ἐμᾶς γέγραπται· γλυκὺ γὰρ αὐτῷ μέλος ὀφείλων
ἐπιλέλαθ'· ὦ Μοῖσ, ἀλλὰ σὺ καὶ θυγάτηρ

Ἀλάθεια Διός, ὀρθᾷ χερί
ἐρύκετον ψευδέων   5
ἐνιπὰν ἀλιτόξενον.

ant. 1, 1 ἔκαθεν γὰρ ἐπελθὼν ὁ μέλλων χρόνος
ἐμὸν καταίσχυνε βαθὺ χρέος.
ὅμως δὲ λῦσαι δυνατὸς ὀξεῖαν ἐπιμομφὰν
τόκος †θνατῶν·[67] νῦν ψᾶφον ἑλισσομέναν
ὀπᾷ κῦμα κατακλύσσει ῥέον,   10

ὀπᾷ τε κοινὸν λόγον
φίλαν τείσομεν ἐς χάριν.

Read out for me the name of the Olympic victor, the son of Archestratos: where is it inscribed upon my *phrēn*? For I owe to him a sweet song, and have forgotten. O Muse, let you and the daughter of Zeus, Truth, ward off from me the charge of harming my guest friend with broken promises.

For what was then the future has approached from afar and brought shame in passing upon my deep debt. Still, the interest is able to free a man from sharp reproach. Let him see now: just as the flowing wave swamps the pebble rolled along, so shall we

---

[64] n. 13 above.

[65] Rutherford 2001: 250.

[66] I have learned much from Hubbard 1985: 67–9; see also Lomiento in Gentili, Catenacci, Giannini and Lomiento 2013: esp. 250–1 and 555–9 and now Budelmann 2017: 54–9.

[67] ὀνάτωρ Hermann; ὁρᾷτ' ὢν νυν Schneidewin; ὁράτω νῦν Fennell (the reading translated here *exempli gratia*).

pay back the debt of all [or 'a theme of general concern'] to the
satisfaction of reciprocity.[68]

The tone is hard to parse, but the preponderance of what for Pindar's own
standards are fairly earthy commercial metaphors suggests humour.[69] The
speaker asks someone (the 'you' he addresses is plural and undefined) to
'read out' the victor's name. πόθι introduces an indirect question: he is
rummaging in the archive.[70] 'Read out' in the first instance means 'remind'.
'Pindar' owed a song to Agesidamos, a child boxer from Western Locri, but
has forgotten the debt. He calls upon the Muse and 'Truth, daughter of
Zeus' (ll.3–6) to defend him from the reproach of having harmed a friend.
'Future time, coming from afar, has approached and shamed my deep
debt.'[71] The song is late:[72] Time, who remembers everything, has caught the
speaker out.[73] In calling the Muse and Truth as witnesses who will 'ward
off' the charges against him, he vaguely associates the 'wax tablets' image
with the idea of forensic *evidence* (nothing is forgotten: look! the name has
been there all along!).[74] Debt and repayment, a standard motivation for praise, through reciprocity, as a response to the event that it
commemorates,[75] are then enacted through the metaphor of 'repayment
with interest'[76] and the simile of the wave that overflows the pebble on
the shore.[77] The currency of repayment is the ode itself, which like the sea
will overwhelm any possible 'debt'.[78] The simile ends with the assurance

---

[68] Translation after Race 1997.
[69] Gildersleeve 1885: 214. 'Song for money' in Pindar is often accompanied by a lightening of tone: e.g.
    *Isthm.*2 init. and *Pyth.*11.38–45.
[70] In Gildersleeve 1885, but largely neglected by later commentators.
[71] Why is the debt 'deep'? Most likely because the *phrenes* are 'deep' (n. 23 above) and the poet's 'debt'
    is also his 'inspiration'.
[72] *Ol.*10 and 11 commemorate a victory won in 476 BC, the year of *Ol.*1 and *Ol.*2–3.
[73] Cf. with e.g. *Ol.*10, 55 and *Ol.*1, 33.
[74] We might compare Aristotle and Plato on error in recollection.
[75] On this 'χρέος motif': Bundy 1986: 10–11.
[76] Here there is uncertainty in the text: see n. 67 above. I will not discuss the scholiasts' influential
    theory (cf. Σ 1b i: 308 and Σ *Ol.*11 inscr. i: 342 Drachmann) that the 'interest' refers to a different
    poem (*Ol.*11): see Bundy 1986.
[77] Another mnemonic image, this time from the sphere of accuracy in counting (Verdenius 1988: 60
    ad loc., sees an allusion to Athenian dikastic voting and a metaphorical 'condemnation').
[78] Song as flowing water: Nünlist 1998: ch. 8; Verdenius 1988: ad loc. κοινὸν λόγον ... τείσομεν is a
    problem. The identity of *logos* and song was recognised by Aristarchus (Σ 15a [1: 313 Dr.]): other
    scholiasts (15b) explain it as something 'won by many' (ie. victors: *logos* would mean 'praise': a sense
    attested in Pindar), or 'performed by many voices' (ie. by a chorus). For the moderns, it is: 1) a debt
    'known to all' (Farnell 1930, Nassen 1975); 2) an account addressed to the community (Verdenius
    1988: 61 ad loc.); or 3) a narrative of Panhellenic importance (Eckerman 2008). The first translation is
    closest to the spirit of the surrounding metaphor. The ambiguity is intrinsic and hence intended: the
    song is at once 'debt', 'praise' (of individual and community) and 'myth' (a vehicle of 'praise').

of mutual satisfaction at the restoration of balanced reciprocity (χάρις), which is also friendship and love.[79]

This *quasi*-narrative of debt, recollection and repayment is assembled by the reader from clues Pindar lets drop. But let us return to the opening. The speaker asks his addressees to 'read' a name from the place where it is written in his own mind. ἀναγιγνώσκειν, which refers to the mental and vocal effort of 'recognising' words and sentences, translating them from graphic representation into syllabic sounds and combining those sounds into phrases, is of the Greek words for 'to read' the one most strongly associated in later times with public acts of 'reading out'.[80] The evidence concealed in the speaker's mind requires a voice to transpose it from the space of graphic representation into the space of sonority. Who is the 'reader'? The scholiasts think of the Muses or the chorus.[81] One might indeed read the imperative as directed toward performers and audience, or any potential singer, reciter, or reader.[82] Without wanting to force the issue (for Pindar here is definitely *not* directly addressing the performance of poetic texts), there is at least an *implication* of self-reference, for the voice whose utterance constitutes for us the text of the ode is inviting us (or the Muse and Truth) to 'read out'. Pindar alludes to another level of enactment on which the object of reading (and, implicitly, the acts of voicing and reminding) is the text itself – the verbal object that begins with this demand to 'read' and remind. It is the voice of someone absent, restored to presence with each act of 'reading out'. Writing literally 're-minds': the name of the boy from Locri will 'speak out' as long as the text survives. In this respect, the Pindaric text seems to have affinities with epigraphic inscription, especially funerary inscriptions and epigrams on stone. This passage thus forms a link between the two 'sides' of the tablets image – 'memory as text' and 'writing as memory'. It is to the latter theme that we will turn in the final section of the chapter.

---

[79] Note the mention following (l.13) of Atrekeia ('Exactness': Kromer 1976: 421), which accomplishes the transition from the opening theme of debt to the praise of the Locrians.

[80] Chantraine 1950; Svenbro 1993: 4–5; Gavrilov 1997: 73. Pindar's phrase resembles formulae in the fourth-century oratory: e.g. Andoc. 1.47; Dem. 18.118.

[81] Cf. Σ 1a, d (i: 308.13–14 Dr.) ὁ λόγος πρὸς τὰς Μούσας, ἢ πρὸς τοὺς τοῦ χοροῦ. with 1d (i: 308–9: Muses), 1h (i: 309: Muses). Note however that the scholiasts' paraphrase is not careful enough: it refers to plural Muses, while Pindar mentions only one.

[82] Verdenius 1988: 56.

3 The Written Text as a Form of Memory

Prometheus' confident assimilation of memory to writing is one side of a pervasive cultural theme. Pindar's ode represents the other. It attests the ease with which fifth-century thought assimilated literacy to a still-vibrant tradition of *kleos* theory. The semantics of memory as internalised writing are relevant to the cultural construction of text as an authoritative form of 'memory': a way of creating permanent 'memory objects'. Euripides associates texts with the transmission of mythological knowledge;[83] in the closing scene of *Supplices*, he makes Athena emphasise the role of script as monument and witness (μνημεῖα/μαρτύρημα, 1204).[84] In some cases, the persuasiveness of a text is entirely bound up with the idea of long transmission in writing. Collectors of oracles (χρησμόλογοι) appealed to such authority;[85] the practitioners of Orphic/Bacchic religion made similar claims about their sacred books.[86] On an Attic red-figure cup in the Fitzwilliam Museum in Cambridge, the severed head of Orpheus is shown dictating to an amanuensis with tablet and stylus (Figure 2.1).[87] In this image (the only one from antiquity, so far as I am aware, to show the making of an 'oral dictated text', a theoretical notion made famous by Lord's *Singer of Tales*) the painter articulates a claim of precedence: the evolving canon of 'Orphic' texts (poems by the greatest of singers, the mortal son of a Muse and grandson of Mnemosyne) surpasses other traditions in the purity of its descent from the source. Acusilaos of Argos, Pindar's close contemporary, also claimed that his three books of *Genealogies* (to judge from surviving fragments an Ionian-dialect prose paraphrase of the Hesiodic tradition) came from bronze tablets recovered by his father from the foundations of the family house.[88] But for 'Orphic' initiates, their texts were not only the authoritative truth but also protective talismans ('the work [or "gift"] of Memory') to be carried to the other side by the departed.[89] It is hardly by chance that writing, in these cases, reinforces claims of timeless sacred authority of a kind more familiar from Abrahamic religions, but largely absent in the 'official' religious practice of the *polis*. Writing's claims of

---

[83] Eur. *Hipp.* 451–2 (with Barrett 1964: 241–2 ad loc.); cf. *IA* 798.

[84] Steiner 1994: 63–71; Ceccarelli, this volume.

[85] For χρησμόλογοι as performers of written oracles, see Flower 2008. The most famous, Onomacritus (Hdt. 7.6), fell short of his employer's ideal of textual authority. These assumptions are parodied in the oracle scene of *Birds* (959–91).

[86] e.g. Eur. *Hipp.* 953–4.

[87] P. of Ruvo 1346 (Corpus Christi College) = *ARV²* 1401,1 (ill. Guthrie 1952: pl.7); cf. the hydria in Dunedin (Eur. 48.266 = *ARV²* 1174,1 (no scribe).

[88] *FGrHist* 2 T 1.

[89] Cf. the 'gold tablets' F474, F476, 12 and F491, 3 Bernabé (*PEG* ii.2).

Figure 2.1 Loan Ant.103.25. Stemless Cup. Head of Orpheus uttering oracles, 410 BC
© Fitzwilliam Museum, Cambridge. Lewis Collection.

authenticity fed back into the psychology of memory, creating demands of accuracy realisable only in the *ars memoriae*, where memory, through disciplined visualisation, makes itself more like a space of mental writing.

The semantics of writing can, however, be turned against textual authority. Written communication is fraught with uncertainties. In Aeschylus' *Supplices* (946–9), Pelasgus invokes the superiority of honest democratic speech over the written and sealed proclamations of Eastern kings, in a way that prefigures Plato's critique of the inscrutability of a written text in the *Phaedrus*,[90] and Lévi-Strauss' assimilation of writing to practices of state control in *Tristes Tropiques*. In Plato, writing deceives by its sheer interpretability. According to Socrates (275e1) texts, mere εἴδωλα (images) of living speech, 'roll about all over the place' (κυλινδεῖται ... πανταχοῦ): one cannot predict whose hands they will land in, or what they will become in the absence of an author to control their interpretation.[91] The authority invested in written *logos* can deceive, as Theseus learns at his own cost in *Hippolytus*. In tragedy, writing is often gendered female and associated with

[90] 274c–275e; see Friis Johansen and Whittle 1980 iii: 250–2 ad loc. and Steiner 1994: 168–9.
[91] For Plato's lack of faith in written communication as a means of transmitting knowledge and his association of it with 'play' see Yunis 2011: 225. For Plato's views on the risks posed by writing and memory for philosophical recollection, cf. also Capra's chapter in this volume.

forgery, concealment and intrigue;[92] for Herodotus, it is used primarily by tyrants and barbarian empires.[93] The proof of Palamedes' treason in Euripides' play was a *pinax* containing a forged letter written in 'Phrygian characters': the naive *protos heuretes* undone by his own 'invention'.[94] In the fourth century, Alcidamas and Isocrates, Gorgias' most famous pupils, grapple with the value of writing in composing speeches and training the orator.[95] Alcidamas (*On Sophists*, 29) writes that written speeches are not *logoi* at all, but εἴδωλα καὶ σχήματα καὶ μιμήματα λόγων ('images and forms and imitations of *logoi*') of no use in the cut-and-thrust of real oratory.[96]

This definition of text as a representation of living *logos* brings out what James Porter calls 'the paradox of the voice that lies buried in written language'.[97] The Greeks, as we do, would ask about a text 'what does it *say*?',[98] and the recipient of text is often positioned as a 'listener' (ὁ ἀκούων), a habit persistent in authors of the Imperial period, which points to long-institutionalised practices of voiced reading.[99] Fifth-century drama often invokes the vocality of text. In *Seven Against Thebes*, the mottoes on the Argive shields 'speak'. Theseus in *Hippolytus* 'hears' the screams of Phaedra's silent letter: βοᾷ βοᾷ δέλτος ἄλαστα.[100] When Iphigenia (*IT* 759–65) gives the δέλτος (tablet) containing her letter to Pylades for transportation to Argos, she adds: 'if you keep the tablet unharmed, all by herself she'll silently communicate her contents (τὰγγραμμένα); but if the *grammata* are lost at sea, saving yourself you'll save my *logoi* too'. A famous early fifth-century dedication from Halicarnassus enacts a dialogue between the reader's voice and the 'artful voice of the stone'.[101]

As Svenbro describes them, early dedications are 'machines' designed to ensure *kleos* (in his memorable phrase '*renom sonore*').[102] Especially before the mid-sixth century, the inscribed object often addresses the reader as 'I'. The Mantiklos kouros (326 *CEG*) 'says':

---

[92] Steiner 1994: 40 n. 97.

[93] Thomas 1992: 130; Ceccarelli 2013: 127–8.

[94] Collard, Cropp and Gilbert 2004: 92–7.

[95] Muir 2001: xiii–xv; cf. Porter 2010: 335–47. Van der Eijk 1997: 95–6 discusses Hippocratic suspicion of writing.

[96] The comparison of written speech, as an εἰκὼν λόγου, to a statue is made already in §28; at §32, he compares written text to a 'mirror' of the writer's thought.

[97] Porter 2010: 338.

[98] See e.g. Hdt.1.124.

[99] Svenbro 1993: 160–86; Schenkeveld 1992; Gavrilov 1997: 70–3; Johnson 2010: 17–31.

[100] l.877, cf. 858, 865, 879–80, 1056.

[101] 429 *CEG*, with Tueller 2010 (esp. 54–7); cf. Svenbro 1993: 56–63.

[102] Svenbro 1993: 26–63 ('machine': 62, 164); on inscriptional voice now, see Vestrheim 2010.

Μάντικλός μ' ἀνέθηκε ϝεκαβόλωι ἀργυροτόξσωι
τᾶς δεκάτας· τὺ δὲ, Φοῖβε, δίδοι χαρίϝετταν ἀμοιβ[ά]ν

Mantiklos dedicated me to the far-striking [god] of the silver bow
as a tenth: you, Phoebus, give pleasing reciprocation.

The epigram sets itself in the moment of its own reception when Mantiklos
(mentioned only in the third person) is absent. This is a fictional voice. The
part after the caesura in the second hexameter is the most interesting: the
reader, having heard herself assert Mantiklos' piety in a narrative statement,
is now committed to reproducing an efficacious prayer for χάρις.[103] These
so-called *oggetti parlanti* remain within the usual framework of oral
communication: they require the addressee to adopt the position of the
speaking subject – in this case, the voice of the dedication. This is arguably
true of later, less 'egocentric' inscriptions as well. Early letters – whether
Herodotus' invented literary versions or real ones on folded strips of lead –
embed the message in a third-person quotation formula, identifying the
absent speaker and mediating the shift from the voice of the reader to that
of the text.[104]

As utterances composed by one person for others to perform, choral odes
grapple with the same situation of deferred reception.[105] Theirs is an exciting
pragmatic situation that brings the problems of fictional voice to the fore with
unremitting clarity. In choral song, the authorial 'I' is often marked by its
absence or distance from the communicative present. This is part of its wider
tendency to distinguish time of composition from time of reception, using
either moment as the temporal *origo* from which to describe the unfolding
utterance.[106] In the poetic *sphragis*, the voice of the poem describes its author
in the third person. As Calame notes, this sets up an effect of double framing
(a '*dédoublement du je*') in which the singer ascribes her utterance to the absent
author.[107] Another trope frequent in the praise poetry of Bacchylides and
Pindar, but largely missing in other genres, is the *sending* of songs.[108] The lyric
speaker stands in the moment of composition looking forward to a future
instance of performance from which he will be absent.[109] Two odes of Pindar

---

[103] On the statuette and its inscription: Day 2010: 33–48.
[104] e.g. Hdt. 3.40.1: Ἄμασις Πολυκράτεϊ ὧδε λέγει· ἡδὺ μὲν πυνθάνεσθαι ἄνδρα φίλον καὶ ξεῖνον εὖ πρήσσοντα ... For real early letters: Harris 1989: 111; Ceccarelli 2013: 36–47, 335–56.
[105] On differences in how epigram and lyric monody 'address' a recipient: Schmitz 2010.
[106] D'Alessio 2004.
[107] Cf. Alcm. fr. 39 *PMGF* = 91 Calame, with Calame 1995: 20–4.
[108] See Tedeschi 1985. Examples: Pind. *Ol*.6; *Ol*.7.7–9; *Ol*.9.25ff; *Pyth*.2.67ff; *Pyth*.3; *Nem*.3.76ff; *Isthm*.2, 45–8; fr.14ab2.4; Bacch. 5.1–16; fr.20B, C.
[109] e.g. *Nem*.3.1–14, 63–84: 10–12 (ἐγὼ ... κείνων) the composing 'I' is clearly distinguished from the *komos* that will perform.

address the messenger responsible for conveying the song to the victor's city, referring obliquely to the existence of a text.[110] These allusions, like those of 'techne-language', remain subtle hints in a poetic discourse that is overwhelmingly occasional and performative. In general, references to writing on any medium are rare in early fifth-century 'high' poetry, and mention of papyrus rolls is unknown in 'high' lyric and tragedy. This is interesting, given that it was the book roll which assured the text's survival.[111]

By the late sixth century, Greek prose was emerging as a literary form with its own artistry and diction. Early prose writers – Hippocratic doctors, philosophers and historiographers alike – are conscious of the novelty of the enterprise. Prose defines itself first of all as λόγος ('speech'), but has a more comfortable relationship to writtenness.[112] Whatever the real mechanism of composition, and despite the occurrence of public 'readings',[113] prose unlike poetry was *written*, and its tradition was a competitive dialogue between 'writers'.[114] Apart from that of Herodotus, all early historiographical proems make reference to writing. In Thucydides and his Sicilian precursor Antiochus of Syracuse it comes in the aorist tense of the whole *opus*.[115]

Bearing this in mind, it is interesting to find even Thucydides responding to the problems of entextualised voice. In all fields, the explosive emergence of prose literature is driven by a spirit of competition in which traditions are questioned, predecessors rejected and new standards of truth proposed.[116] The authority invoked is that of the authorial voice. The 'egotism' of prose engenders a preponderance of 'I-statements' and self reference, asserting both the importance of the writer's topic and his superior discretion.[117] Proems are instructive. Philosophers sometimes begin *in*

---

[110] Cf. *Ol*.6.87–96 and *Isthm*.2.47–8. In the former, the proxy is a Laconian 'message stick'; while the latter tells him to ἀπόνειμον (a word which can, as Svenbro 1993: 19 n. 54 and Catenacci 1999 show, mean 'read') ταῦτα, 'what I have just said': in fact a set of instructions in the preceding lines on how to use and re-use the corpus of Pindaric odes composed for the family of Theron (τούσδ' ὕμνους, 45: on this passage see Athanassaki 2012: 155–6). As the lyric speaker says, 'I did not labour on [these] in order for them to stand around killing time' (ἐπεί τοι / οὐκ ἐλινύσοντας αὐτοὺς ἐργασάμαν, 45–6).

[111] On comic poets' books: Harvey 1966: 601–2; on their absence in tragedy: Easterling 1985: 5–6. Note that Aesch. *Pers*. 333 (Dumortier 1975: 208) uses a book-roll metaphor of narrating.

[112] In Attic, σύγγραμμα comes to mean 'prose treatise'; ὑπόμνημα, obviously interesting for its connection to 'reminding', emerges in fourth-century prose where it refers to 'jottings' or 'memoranda'.

[113] Lucian, *Herodotus*, 1–2; Thomas 1992: 4, 123–7 and 2000 on the performativity of prose.

[114] We must separate prose from oratory, where writtenness becomes an issue only after 400.

[115] Antiochus *FGrHist* 555 F 2. In Thucydides' case, the work is unfinished.

[116] Lloyd 1987: 56–78; 1990; 1999; Fowler 1996: 69; Goldhill 2002.

[117] Lloyd 1987: 56–70; Fowler 1996: 69 n. 61 for a list of fifth-century prose proems.

medias res;[118] this is also the rule in the Hippocratic Corpus.[119] But the historiographical proem from the beginning insists on a telling shift from third- to first-person enunciation:

Ἑκαταῖος Μιλήσιος ὧδε μυθεῖται· τάδε γράφω,
ὡς μοι δοκεῖ ἀληθέα εἶναι ... (Hecataeus, *FGrHist* 1 F 1)

Thus speaks Hecataeus of Miletus: I write these things here as they seem to me to be true ...

The embedding again bridges the gap between the text's impersonal physicality and the speaker who narrates and describes, argues and judges.[120] In Hecataeus the shift from third-person frame to first-person narration is instantaneous. In Thucydides, the egocentric narrator appears with little fanfare halfway through the proem (1.3). In Herodotus, it happens well inside the text (1.5.3), when the authorial voice emerges to mark the limits of history as he sees them, and to begin the authorial narrative.[121] So despite the real differences between the approaches to writtenness of historiographical prose and poetry, the prose author's voice is also entextualised.

It has long been clear that we need to move away from a view that stresses the *effects* of literacy on consciousness, to one that emphasises rhetorical contexts and modes of use. Styles of allusion to writing are deployed for specific aims within different regimes of textuality. The structured use of writing terms persists, for example in Hellenistic poetry, where different genres evince different protocols of allusion to the text *as* text. *Deltoi*, for example, are found in 'light' poetry where the text, treating itself ironically as a 'draft' and emphasising its own place in a tradition of written literature, underplays its own permanence. In epic and didactic, genres that aspire to the traditional elevation of hexameter song, such references are unknown.[122] Reference to writtenness and writing media has a rhetorical purpose. In classical Greece, the historiographer is a writer; the poet cannot be so direct; both, however, respond to conditions in which reading is a

---

[118] Philolaus of Croton: 44B1 DK (no trace of 'egocentrism') vs. Heraclitus of Ephesus 22B1; Diogenes of Apollonia 64B1; Ion of Chios fr. 114 Leurini (*FGrHist* 392 F24ab) and Critias 88B32 (all 'egocentric'). Alcmaeon of Croton (24B1) presents his book as a record of oral teaching.

[119] On Hippocratic anonymity, see van der Eijk 2007: 98–9; on proems: 113–15; on the egocentric voice: 115–19.

[120] Svenbro 1993: 148–50 ('transcript': p. 150). On the historian as judge, see Darbo-Peschanski's chapter in this volume.

[121] Asheri et al. 2007: 78 ad loc.; Evans 1991: 105–6; Fowler 1996: 83; Goldhill 2002: 11–15.

[122] For δέλτοι in Hellenistic 'light' verse: cf. Call. *Aet.* fr. 1, 21 Pf. with fr. 75. 66 Pf. = 174 Massimilla (the 'tablets' of a learned source); Strato *Anth. Pal.* 12.2; Asclepiades *Anth. Pal.* 12.162, 3 = 23 Gow-Page; *Batrachomyomachia*, 3. Epic is never 'written'; on its speciously 'oral' source citations, see Norden 1916: 123–4; Hunter 1989: 187–8; Hinds 1998: 1–2.

form of vocalisation. The 'tablets of memory' contain thought and conceal it:[123] their contents had to be re-activated and converted back into sound.

As we have seen, this is true *par excellence* of poetic texts. There is a vogue among red-figure vase-painters in the first quarter of the fifth century for writing snippets of text on represented book rolls: these, where legible, are always in 'poetic' diction. 'Homeric hymns', 'wisdom' themes and *melos* are represented.[124] From about 440 BC, book rolls in vase-painting become common props of the Muses, and Sappho is shown reading aloud.[125] For vase-painters, often illiterate, book rolls were associated particularly with the memorisation and re-performance of song. In the 'education' scenes of the fifth century's first quarter, they appear together with musical instruments. Their main mode of use seems to have been in recitation and memorisation. Performing rhapsodes memorised texts, but so did ordinary learners. In two early 'school' scenes the book roll is in the hands of an older man; the boy stands in front of him reciting; the text seems to be there as a means to control accuracy. Music teaching too was done face to face, with the teacher singing or demonstrating and the student repeating until the song was learned.[126] Late anecdotes suggest that Pindar and Euripides trained their choruses in this way.[127]

The need to internalise text before it can be restored to life is reflected in the ideology that drives Athenian education. In a song from Euripides' *Erechtheus* the chorus of old men, while listing the symposium as one of the blessings of peace (ἡσυχία), sings of 'opening the voice of wax tablets in which wise poets win fame' – a metaphorical description of performance from memory of learning acquired from tablets.[128] The earliest third-party description of epinician in performance is the frustrated singing of a Simonidean song at the symposium in *Clouds* (1355–7 = fr. 507 *PMG* and 16 Poltera). Schoolroom and symposium are linked: in the first, a man acquires a mind well stocked with morally improving thoughts and songs that he will use in the second, and which, as the century progresses,

---

[123] The word for 'opening' a tablet is ἀναπτύσσω: cf. e.g. Aesch. fr. 281a Radt, 22 and Eur. *Tro.* 663 (with Bagnall 2000 and van Minnen 2001).

[124] Beazley 1948; Immerwahr 1964 and 1973; Sider 2010.

[125] Athens NM 1260 = *ARV²* 1060, 145.

[126] E.g. Beck 1975 nos. 100, 105, 106, 109, 114.

[127] The term for memorisation by dictation seems to have been ὑπολέγειν (Plut. *De Audiend.* 46b). Ar. *Ran* 151–3 (Ford 2003: 27 n. 43) distinguishes lyrics learned 'by ear' from ῥήσεις copied for memorisation.

[128] Fr. 369, 6 Kannicht (Collard, Cropp and Lee 1995: 184–5; Ford 2003: 31–2). Lissarrague 1987: 130, 132 notes the presence of drinking cups on the Douris 'school cup'.

also contribute to the foundation of a sound literary style.[129] The ubiquitous mode of literary reception was still performance: reading, as a kind of reduced performance, facilitated the interaction of listeners with the entextualised poem. Most vase paintings showing 'private' reading incorporate a listener.[130] Although silent reading was common enough that scenes in tragedy and comedy turn on characters' ability to perform it,[131] the texts thus read are letters or oracles rather than poems. As Johnson (2000 and 2010) has shown, voiced reading was how poetic texts were consumed even down to the developed book culture of the Roman Empire. Hellenistic and Roman sources show the importance attached to impeccable vocal delivery (ὑπόκρισις) in reading.[132] The practice of silent reading did not, therefore, affect the underlying idea that written text is transcribed utterance enacted by the reader. Fifth-century poetry texts thus expect to be memorised, internalised and reperformed *as voice*.

This helps to explain how it was that in a society so saturated with verse texts (inscribed on stone or bronze, copied on papyrus, or kept in the more tenuous medium of wax tablets), the ideal shape of poetry remains vocal; it also explains the lack of references to book rolls in fifth-century non-comic poetry. Like a modern musical score, the aesthetic fullness of a Greek poem could only, in its indigenous context, be experienced in *interpretation*. In a culture where the poetic text was a machine that guaranteed re-performance, it was not autonomous, but rather locked into a system of use that subordinated text to voice.[133] Poetry's powers and dignity were bound up with its cultural role and proclaimed effects, all of which foreground its ability to leap off the page and attain real enactment in performance;[134] it grew out of and sunk back into a still vibrant oral tradition, and indeed sought to modify that tradition with new κλέος. At least in ideological terms, written poetry *reinforced* performance.[135] Returning for a moment to Pindar, the praise-singer's main aim is not the production of a physical text – although that may be one (for us, important) result of his activity – but rather a vocal act that preserves the *kleos* ('what is heard') of

---

[129] Pl. *Prot.*325e–6b and Ion of Chios *FGrHist* 392 F 6 with Ford 2003: 20–31, 34–5. For similar practices of internalising text in the Middle Ages: Carruthers 1990: 169–79.

[130] On ancient reading as a group practice: Johnson 2000: 615–25; use of *lectores*: Harris 1989: 30–6; Starr 1990–91; Schenkeveld 1992.

[131] Knox 1968 and Johnson 2000: 593–600.

[132] E.g. Dion. Thrac. §2 (i.1: 6 *GG*). The theme appears as early as Aristotle (Porter 2010: 315–19) and is treated by Quintilian (Johnson 2010: 27–30).

[133] Arist. *Poet.* 1450b18–19, 1460a11–18 is the first to claim the autonomy of the poetic text.

[134] Cf. (with respect to tragedy) Easterling 1985: 5–6.

[135] Cf. Thomas 1992: 62–3.

the man, and the occasion it enacts, in the living tradition of song and in the collective memory. This emphasis on oral fame may look like a feint, but the claims of immortality it grounds are a necessary part of song's mystique. If these texts are a kind of written memory, they bear the imprint of a voice 'set upon a golden bough to sing ... of what is past, or passing, or to come'.

Memory and Forgetting in the Classical Period

PART II

Memory and Forgetting in the
Classical Period

CHAPTER 3

Economies of Memory in Greek Tragedy

Paola Ceccarelli

In memory of Lucio Ceccarelli

1 Introduction

Memory is central to Greek tragedy. The earliest instance of audience reaction we are aware of, the story of the disastrous reception by the Athenians of Phrynichus' play *The Sack of Miletus*, foregrounds memory. Here is how Herodotus narrates the affair: 'The Athenians made clear their deep grief for the capture of Miletus in various ways, and in particular, when Phrynichus composed a play entitled "The Fall of Miletus" and produced it, the whole theater fell to weeping; they fined Phrynichus a thousand drachmas *for reminding them of their own evils* (ἀναμνήσαντα οἰκήια κακά), and forbade anybody ever to make use of that play again.'[1] In discussing this play, Herodotus emphasizes tragedy's power of 'recalling', in this case sufferings that were too close for comfort to the Athenians as a community. But the fine imposed on the playwright also focuses on memory, inasmuch as it corresponds to a *damnatio memoriae*: the play was not allowed to be re-staged and left no further trace in performance history.[2]

Tragic plays brought events of the past onto the stage. Whether these stories came from the epic past or the more recent one, they were important to the Athenian audience and their cultural identity as a civic community.[3]

---

[1] Hdt. 6.21. On the story, see e.g. Loraux 1998: 84–6; Rosenbloom 1993, esp. 163–5 on how tragedy moved from this recalling of 'one's own sufferings' to using the sufferings of others to comment on one's own condition, thus making the more general (and fundamental) point that tragedy involves the spectator's sense of identity; Munn 2000: 22–3, 30–3; Kottman 2003, who focuses on the collective tears of the Athenians over 'their own catastrophe': 'the polis emerges here as a kind of organized remembrance', 87; Uhlig and Hunter 2017: 5–7.

[2] For the paradox of a cancellation that ensures a 'negative' memory, see Flower 2006: 17–23, and the Introduction to this volume, p. 24.

[3] Re-performances will have functioned in different ways (see for instance the fascinating discussions by Nervegna 2014 and Hartwig 2014, the former focusing on tragedy, the latter on comedy; Uhlig and Hunter 2017, and specifically on theatre as a 'memory machine', Hanink 2017. It is worth noting that the known instances of fifth-century first performances outside Athens (*Aetnaian Women, Andromache, Archelaus*) focus on myths pertinent to the place of first performance.

These stories, repeated and represented in various contexts, from the tales told to children by their nurses to the tragic and dithyrambic performances that revolved around myths and legends, from the funeral orations over the war-dead to the monuments and paintings that adorned the city, formed part of the cultural memory shared by all Athenians; each play brought these shared memories afresh to the attention of the audience.[4] The comic poet Antiphanes could state, in comparing comedy and tragedy, that the life of tragic poets is easy, since they can rely on existing plots, of which they only need to 'remind' (ὑπομνῆσαι) the audience; by contrast, comic poets must each time invent everything anew.[5] Put differently, tragic playwrights could rely on the fact that the mention of a specific hero or place would inevitably conjure images and stories in the minds of the spectators – an important difference to comedy, which of course also operated according to a set of generic conventions but did not in the same way deliberately redeploy familiar material.

At the same time, it is crucial to emphasize that the common stock of stories on which tragedians drew in fashioning their plays formed the background against which they invented their own versions of the stories: each tragic play offered specific, subtle variations of the same set of well-known stories. Much of the interest for the spectator would have resided in remembering other versions, and wondering about the variations: meaning would arise out of the differences.[6] We are here looking at another kind of memory: not any longer cultural memory of a shared mythical past, but specific recollection by individual spectators of earlier particular narratives and performances referring to that common and culturally shared past. Even though variation was limited by the necessity of conforming to the main lines of the traditional plot, tragedy presented the spectators with potential variation in the narrative recall and dramatic interpretation of a distant past.[7] And some of the departures could be stark and shocking (and

[4] Nurses' stories: Buxton 1994: 18–23, and more generally 9–16 on the plurality of voices and narrators. Funeral oration: Thomas 1989: 196–237 (the 'official tradition'). On the interface between tragedy and funeral oration (and more largely orators' speeches), see the important discussion by Hanink 2013. For a survey of the different 'carriers' of Athenian social memory, see Steinbock 2013b: 48–98.

[5] Antiphanes F 189, 1–5 and 17–18, with Burian 1997 (and specifically 183 for the passage of Antiphanes); Taplin 2010.

[6] That specific versions, and not a generic plot only, were remembered is clear from Aristophanic paratragedy: the parodies of Euripides' plays *Telephus* or *Palamedes*, to take only two examples, in Aristophanes' *Acharnians* and *Thesmophoriazusae* respectively, make sense only if we assume that the public remembered these specific plays, and not just the overall story. See Milanezi's chapter in this volume.

[7] Aristotle *Poetics*, 1451b17–21. This does not apply to the few plays with a 'historical' subject: here, at least in the case of the first performance, the play is plotted directly against the personal, direct experience of a near past. I discuss the implications of this below.

then themselves become canonical): it makes a difference to the story of Medea whether the Corinthians or Medea herself murdered her children. Even more important to the Athenians would have been variations on myths that were part of the story of early Athens, such as the war against Eumolpos or the city's intervention in securing the burial of the Seven.[8]

Thus, while it is certainly true that tragedy relied on – and further reinforced – a common shared heritage of collective and cultural memory, tragic performances also must have conveyed a (potentially destabilizing) sense that this shared past could be presented and viewed in different ways, and that new versions, taking their place besides old ones, could potentially alter or even obliterate older variants.[9]

Furthermore, tragic plays were performed in a ritual festival context that spoke of the present, and to the present. Contemporary events, and the collective and individual memory of such events, formed the background for the understanding of what happened on stage – a process facilitated, in the specific case of Greek tragedy, by the festival context of its performance, with its multiple connections to contemporary events: the display of the tribute of the allies, the parade of the children of the Athenians who had died in war, the presence of the generals, the proclamation of honours for benefactors.[10] As a result, tragic performances in Athens had the potential to play simultaneously on multiple 'memorial' registers: on a shared memory central to the common identity of the community of spectators, whether cultural or collective, whether concerning the mythical or the recent past;[11] and on the specific remembrance of previous performances, which brought with itself an awareness of the fact that cultural memories (the memories of the mythical past) might be presented and shaped in different ways – an awareness that might further have led to questions as to whether also collective memory of recent events might be thus (re)shaped.

---

[8] Variations on the Medea story: see Dunn 2000: 15–16, who emphasizes the pointed way in which Euripides alludes to other versions; Mastronarde 2002: 44–53; war against Eumolpos and burial of the Seven: Hanink 2013; Steinbock 2013b: 155–210; and below.

[9] One might compare the development that led to Hecataeus' statement about the diversity, and consequently ridiculousness, of Greek myths, in the proem to his *Genealogies* (*FGrHist* 1 F 1): cf. Fowler 2001.

[10] Goldhill 1987 and 2000; Rhodes 2003; Steinbock 2013b: 59–60. List and discussion of the 'preplay' events in Pickard-Cambridge 1988: 58–63; for the proclamation of honours at the moment of the tragic contest, see Wilson 2009; Ceccarelli 2010.

[11] I here follow Chaniotis 2009: 255–9 in distinguishing between cultural and collective memory: the first refers to shared memories of a past time, mythical, or simply going back in time beyond the experience of the living community; the second, to shared memories of something that is still within the experience of the community.

The plays themselves are thus interventions in social memory, as Ruth Scodel has brilliantly shown for the *Eumenides*.[12] But this tension between memory and construction (or oblivion) of the past plays itself out also on stage: memory and remembrance, and their counterpart, oblivion, are often discussed and problematized within the plays themselves. Individuals, collectivities and divinities (forces beyond the control of man) remember or forget in various ways.[13]

2   Marked and Unmarked Remembering, by Individuals and Groups

Memories appear on stage most obviously and frequently in an unmarked way, when characters (as individuals, or as a chorus) relate past events, whether having heard about them from the elders of the community or having witnessed the events in person, as in messenger reports. Thus, the chorus of Theban women remember the story of the house of Laios, and the chorus of old men in Argos remember the departure of the Atreidai for Troy.[14] Similarly, the chorus of old Persians at the opening of Aeschylus' *Persians* remember those who left, listing them in a catalogue, and continue with a description of the passing of the Hellespont (something the Persian Elders may or may not have seen themselves), as the memory of the warriors who left merges with vague predictions and fears about the future.[15] In such reminiscences there is often a certain indeterminacy, which reflects the fact that these may be mediated, as well as collective, memories; in line with the indeterminacy of these memories, the text usually does not foreground memory itself as a mental faculty.

If the text of a choral ode explicitly reflects on memory, through the use of terms of remembering or oblivion for instance, it does so for a

---

[12] Scodel 2008: 119, 133–8.

[13] This manipulation of memory often takes place with reference to writing, whether metaphorical or real: besides Scodel 2008, see Agócs' chapter in this volume; Ceccarelli 2013: 66–87, 187–91, 257–63. For a discussion of memory in tragedy, organized according to the headings of 'human memory', 'divine memory' and 'conscience of destiny', see Simondon 1982: 193–256. Schlesier 2010 focuses on memories associated with Dionysos; Popescu 2014 offers a brief survey.

[14] Respectively, Aesch. *Sept.* 766–91; Aesch. *Ag.* 40–83 and 104–257. In the latter passage, the chorus points out that the source of their authority is their age (104–6), which inspires them with the power of singing persuasively; it is thus not 'autoptic' vision (which they could also have claimed) that gives them authority. Cf. Fraenkel 1950 II 59–65, who at 63–4 proposes a comparison with Eur. *Her.* 678 ἔτι τοι γέρων ἀοιδὸς κελαδῶ Μναμοσύναν, 'Old singer that I am, I sing the praise of Mnemosyne'.

[15] Aesch. *Pers.* 1–64 and 65–139. The repetition of πόθος, at 133 and 138, is worth noting: the Elders remember, and because they remember they miss the departed warriors.

particular reason, as in the chorus of the *Agamemnon*. In this play memory appears early on as one of the driving forces of the plot, but not in the words of the chorus. Rather, the chorus quotes someone else – the seer Calchas: 'for there awaits, to arise hereafter, a fearsome, guileful keeper of the house, a Wrath that remembers and will avenge a child' (μίμνει ... μνάμων Μῆνις τεκνόποινος).[16] Here, it is the very ability of the chorus to remember the words of Calchas (rather than simply summarize them) that gives the theme of the 'remembering wrath' such strength: not only does the chorus remember words about remembering (without focusing on this fact), in a 'box in the box' effect that is significant, not least from an illocutionary point of view; it is also the verbatim recall (as opposed to a vague recollection) of the seer's utterance that generates the desired atmosphere of preordained doom.[17]

When specific individuals (as opposed to the chorus) remember, such as messengers who report on events that happened offstage, the assumption seems to be that their memory is reliable;[18] and in most such cases, no vocabulary specific to memory and remembrance, or conversely forgetting, is used. When references to remembering appear, they are mostly self-reflections by the individual narrating, meant to explicate his personal relationship to the narrative. A good example of this pointed reference to remembering occurs in Aeschylus' *Persians*. The messenger opens his narrative of the events at Salamis by stressing that his account is based on what he saw, and not on the reports of others (266); he continues by emphasizing the pain that recalling the events causes him (285: φεῦ, τῶν Ἀθηνῶν ὡς στένω μεμνημένος). At this point the chorus intervenes, encouraging him (and, by extension, everyone) to remember Athens (μεμνῆσθαί τοι πάρα) and, more specifically, how many Persian women have lost their husbands.[19] Following these words and those of the queen,

---

[16] Aesch. *Ag.* 155, a very marked alliteration emphasizing the connection (possibly also etymological: cf. Muellner 1996: 177–95) between persistent memory and wrath/vengeance/retribution. On this prophecy, see Goldhill 2004: 74–8. Zeitlin and Goldhill both emphasize how the memory of the sacrifice of Iphigenia pervades the play, both as cause of its development, and as a model for the other murders.

[17] Precision here implies reliability. Like prophecy, curses and oaths derive much of their power from being performed with precision, in the appropriate performative context: see Fletcher 2012.

[18] On messenger speeches in tragedy, cf. Barrett 2002; for cases that go against the norm (emphasizing a self-reflexive element and attention to memory), see 194–8, and my discussion below. Scodel 2008 offers an insightful discussion of the herald's report in Aeschylus' *Agamemnon*, which reveals it as a self-conscious attempt at controlling memory.

[19] On 'memory' as one of the important themes of *Persians*, see Hall 1996: 1, who does however not elaborate. Herodotus narrates that after the destruction of Sardis, Darius asked Zeus to grant him vengeance over the Athenians, and charged a servant to repeat three times, whenever dinner was served, 'Master, remember the Athenians' (δέσποτα, μέμνεο τῶν Ἀθηναίων, Hdt. 5.105.2), a

the messenger indeed launches into an enumeration of the noble Persians who died, an enumeration which he closes again with a 'selective memory' statement: 'That much I mention about the commanders (τοσόνδε ταγῶν νῦν ὑπεμνήσθην πέρι, 329); but of our many evil losses I report but few.'[20] In his second, extended three-part narrative (353–432, 447–71, and 480–514), a narrative which answers direct requests for information by the queen, the messenger simply recounts events; he again concludes with a self-reflexive statement, stating that what has been told is true (ταῦτ' ἔστ' ἀληθῆ), but that he has omitted many of the evils inflicted by the god upon the Persians (513–14). The references to recollection made by the messenger emphasize the authority and correctness of the account given, highlight the effect of remembering on himself, and underscore the distance between his narrative (based on his memory of the events) and the events themselves. What the audiences (internal and external) hear is an explicitly selective account, which therefore leaves open to contemporaries and eyewitnesses (the external audience) the possibility to activate their own memories of the events to fill in the gaps.

This is how most messenger reports in tragedy function; but there are instances where a wedge presents itself, explicitly, between the events and their recalling and retelling by the messenger. This is what happens for instance at the end of Sophocles' *Oedipus Tyrannus*. The messenger who informs the chorus of Jocasta's death and Oedipus' own blinding begins by stating that the chorus (and the spectators) will be spared the worst of the suffering, because they do not see the events (literally, 'because the spectacle is absent', ἡ γὰρ ὄψις οὐ πάρα, 1238); 'but equally, so far as my memory serves (ὅσον γε κἀν ἐμοὶ μνήμης ἔνι, 1239), you will learn the sufferings of that unhappy woman'. Memory and the words of the messenger are what allows a knowledge of the events; but at the same time, the messenger's words make clear how much the events are mediated by his memory, and so how selective his report will, by necessity, be.[21]

---

story that is referred back to in the sixth book, as a prelude to Marathon: 'The Persian was going about his own business, for his servant was constantly reminding him to remember the Athenians' (ἀναμιμνήσκοντός τε αἰεὶ τοῦ θεράποντος μεμνῆσθαί μιν τῶν Ἀθηναίων, Hdt. 6. 94). We may have in this story an early instance of reception of the 'memory theme' of the *Persians*.

[20] Of course the ultimate model for any report in which the messenger, on the verge of starting on a catalogue, states that he will mention 'but a few' is the epic singer's invocation to the Muses, Hom. *Il.* 2.484–93.

[21] Barrett 2002: 196–7 points out that 'in emphasizing his own mediating function in the constitution of his narrative, the *exangelos* marks his report as selective, flawed, and unconventional'. See also Segal 1995: 156: 'The emphasis on memory is striking when one considers how much memory in the play has distorted the recollection of the past. Jocasta, Oedipus, and the Old Herdsman have all shown highly selective memories' (1057, 1131; cf. 870–1).

Most of the remaining explicit references to memory involve requests to remember some past events, thus setting up the space for a narrative development, or orders to bear in mind instructions in the future.[22] But designating something in the past as explicitly 'worthy of memory' may also have the pointed, specific purpose to remove it from the dynamics of memorial flux. This happens to be the case when some form of temporally deferred reciprocity is at stake. For if a debt for services rendered is not paid off instantly, the two parties inevitably rely on some kind of memory of the initially extended favour. A system of either interpersonal or generalized reciprocities relies for its proper functioning not just on trust, accountability and a commitment to a sense of distributive justice, but also on a remembrance of things past, which underwrites both the 'credit' of the benefactor, who (we may assume) is strongly invested in a precise and authentic recollection of his deeds, and the 'debt' of the bene-ficiary, who may (for obvious reasons) be less inclined to keep an accurate account of services received fresh and foremost in mind. The mainten-ance – or, conversely, unavailability – of a consensual memory of specific events thus has significant socio-political implications, and in what follows I want to explore with reference to a particularly striking example each from Sophocles and Euripides what can happen when the latent tension between the investment in reliable remembrance and the forces of flux or indeed oblivion explodes on stage. I will conclude by briefly mapping tragedy's negotiation of this issue (and the trajectory that can arguably be traced from Sophocles to Euripides) against more general developments in fifth-century Athenian culture.

3 Memory and Failed Reciprocities in Sophocles' *Ajax*

The play opens with a conversation between Odysseus and Athena, concerning very recent events: the identity of the person who has slaughtered the cattle of the Achaean army and the reason why this has been done. What has happened is worked out without any explicit references to memory. This turns out to be programmatic: throughout the play, there is a sharp division between Ajax and his circle on the one hand and the Argive commanders on the other, a division only marginally mediated by

---

[22] Remembrance as trigger for action: much of Sophocles' *Oedipus Tyrannus* functions in this way. Instructions: for instance Aesch. *Cho.* 680–2, the (invented) instructions of Strophios to Orestes, delivered by Orestes himself: 'Stranger, since in any case you are bound for Argos, keep my message in mind most faithfully (πανδίκως μεμνημένος) and tell his parents Orestes is dead.' Remembrance of a painful past: Soph. *Phil.* 1169. See Simondon 1982, passim.

Odysseus at the end; and, as it turns out, most references to the past (and
pointedly, all references to memory except one) are made by Ajax and his
circle. Thus, when Ajax comes to himself and realises what he has done,
he obsessively contrasts his recent actions with his earlier deeds during the
war and those of his father, also at Troy; Tecmessa similarly contrasts Ajax's
present situation with the past.[23] In contrast to this investment in the past,
their adversaries, the Atreidae, seem to live entirely in the present – a present in which, Ajax states, there is no place left for him.

The first to play the memory card is Tecmessa. In her attempt to convince
Ajax that death is not the only choice left to him, she retells her own story,
mentions Ajax's father, mother and young son, and eventually comes back
to herself and her utter dependence on Ajax (485–524).[24] At this point, at the
end of her speech, she explicitly foregrounds remembrance, linking it to reciprocity (*charis*) and nobility (*eugeneia*):

> ἀλλ' ἴσχε κἀμοῦ <u>μνῆστιν</u>· ἀνδρί τοι χρεὼν
> <u>μνήμην</u> προσεῖναι, τερπνὸν εἴ τί που πάθοι.
> <u>χάρις χάριν</u> γάρ ἐστιν ἡ τίκτουσ' ἀεί·
> ὅτου δ' ἀπορρεῖ <u>μνῆστις</u> εὖ πεπονθότος,
> οὐκ ἂν γένοιτ' ἔθ' οὗτος <u>εὐγενὴς</u> ἀνήρ.

> Think of me also; a man should keep it in his memory, should
> some pleasure come his way; for it is always a kindness that
> begets a kindness; and if a man allows the memory of a
> kindness to slip away, he can no longer be accounted a noble
> man. (vv. 520–4)

Tecmessa's speech here is highly wrought – and places memory (and
reciprocities dependent on memory) left, right and centre. The rare
term *mnēstis* appears twice, in the same position, yet with antithetical
force, at the beginning and at the end of Tecmessa's appeal:[25] in 520, she

---

[23] At vv. 364–6, 372–6, 405–7, 414–17, Ajax contrasts the past and present situation; in his first great
speech, vv. 430–80, he adds the comparison with his own father's deeds. Tecmessa emphasizes the
changed behaviour of Ajax (he cries, something he would not have done before: 317–22; he speaks
words that in time past he would never have spoken, 410–11). For the *Ajax*, I follow the text and
translation (with occasional modification) of Lloyd-Jones in the Loeb Classical Library.

[24] In a scene and with words that are closely modelled on the encounter and conversation between
Hector and Andromache in *Iliad* 6, and that thus set up Ajax as an anti-Hector (and eventually an
anti-Achilles): splendid discussion in Winnington-Ingram 1980: 15–19.

[25] μνῆστις appears in one of Odysseus' deceitful speeches, in a formulation typical of the Homeric
'behavioural memory', as the hero asserts that 'we did not have any thought of supper' (οὐδέ τις
ἡμῖν δόρπου μνῆστις ἔη, *Od.* 13.280); in Alcman, fr. 118 *PMGF*/175 Calame (a fragment deprived of
context: ἔστι παρέντων μνᾶστιν † ἐπιθέσθαι, 'we may (preserve?) the memory of those who were
present'); in Simonides' epigram for the Fallen at the Thermopylae (531 *PMG*); in Herodotus 7.158
(in Gelon's speech, in a context of disregarded reciprocity); note also Soph. *Trach.* 108: <u>εὔμναστον</u>

admonishes Ajax to keep his *mnēstis* of her intact; in 523, she reflects on the dire consequences that ensue for someone unwilling or unable to cultivate *mnēstis* – and specifically *mnēstis* of services received – properly. The repetition and emphatic positioning ensure that the audience will recall this particular passage when the noun recurs later on in the play. The two uses of *mnēstis* frame references to memory (521: μνήμην) and gratitude (522, in pointed polyptoton: χάρις χάριν), which, exactly like memory, creates links between people.[26] This is an appeal particularly appropriate to someone like Ajax, who is angry at what he perceives to be the ingratitude of the Greeks.[27]

Furthermore, the passage itself is closely linked to other parts of the play, by both content and terminological allusions. Tecmessa is here deftly reusing what had been Ajax's own conclusion: just a few verses earlier, after examining his options, Ajax had concluded that 'a noble man can only either live with honour or die a honourable death' (479–80: ἀλλ' ἢ καλῶς ζῆν ἢ καλῶς τεθνηκέναι | τὸν εὐγενῆ χρή). Tecmessa picks up on the notion of 'noble man' (εὐγενὴς ἀνήρ) but tries to redefine it: for her, a noble man is someone implicated in a network of reciprocities who does not allow the memory of a received kindness to slip away. The play itself enacts such a network of reciprocities through allusive echoes between this passage and other parts of the play. The chorus had introduced Tecmessa's speech by emphasizing the importance of listening to friends (δὸς ἀνδράσι φίλοις | γνώμης κρατῆσαι, 'allow your friends to rule your judgment', vv. 483–4). But the emphasis on the bonds of φιλία, friendship, between the members of Ajax's circle (the chorus, Tecmessa, Teucer and Eurysaces, Ajax himself, who does initially address the chorus as φίλοι, although in the course of the play Ajax retires more and more into himself) runs throughout the play;[28] it is highlighted *e contrario* by Ajax's liminal death in a secluded space, alone.

ἀνδρός δεῖμα. After the fifth century, it is found mostly in epic poetry (four times in Apollonius Rhodius, twice in Nicander, once in Quintus of Smyrna, seventeen times in Nonnius); once in Theocritus 28.23; and in some poems of the *Anthologia Graeca*.

[26] The fact that the *charis* alluded to by Tecmessa here has an 'erotic edge' (Finglass 2011: 289, with parallels) does not make her reflection less universal.

[27] The connection between *charis* and memory is traditional, and already attested in Hesiod, *Theog.* 503 (ἀπεμνήσαντο χάριν εὐεργεσιάων) and Theognis 101–12: see Finglass 2011: 288, with further references, and the Introduction to this volume, pp. 30–2. Within Sophocles' plays, one may compare *OC* 779; extensive discussion in Simondon 1982: 193–222, who notes how the verb ἀπορρεῖ, literally 'flows away', conveys the image of time passing.

[28] The contrast between friends and enemies (φίλος vs ἐχθρός) and the frequent reference to the relationship between father and sons are important themes of the play (see Finglass 2011: 55–6). They can both be subsumed in the larger topic of *charis*, reciprocity. The notion is mooted by the chorus

Tecmessa's words work only in part: they do not suffice to deter Ajax
from his chosen path, but they remind him of his closest kin: he calls for
his son, and while holding him he entrusts him to the protection of his
own brother Teucer and of the warriors that accompanied him to Troy
from Salamis. Even while he proposes to sever the bonds that connected
him to his family (χωρὶς ὄντ' ἐμοῦ, 'even though you are without me', 561),
Ajax ensures that the chorus will relay his command to Teucer, to bring the
boy home, to their father Telamon and Ajax's mother Eriboea, in what he
explicitly calls a 'charge of gratitude' that he lays on them (κοινὴν ... χάριν,
566).[29] This reflection on the bonds created by friendship informs also the
following words by the chorus: faced with Ajax's determination, the chorus
lament the hero's sufferings, but also the further sufferings that he will
cause, emphasizing first the grief that Ajax's madness is giving 'his friends'
(φίλοις, 615), and then the grief it will cause his mother and father (624–
35). Between the mention of their own grief and that of the parents, the
chorus manage to squeeze in a pointed remark on those who are mindless
of Ajax's services, the Atreidai:

> the deeds of greatest valour done earlier by his hands have been let drop,
> having won no friendship from men incapable of friendship (τὰ πρὶν δ'ἔργα
> χεροῖν | μεγίστας ἀρετᾶς | ἄφιλα παρ' ἀφίλοις ἔπεσ' ἔπεσε, 616–19).[30]

The second time memory features prominently and explicitly in the play
is in the chorus' song after Ajax's second speech, the deceitful speech in
which the hero pretends to reconsider. In this speech, Ajax pretends to
have changed his views, in light of the fact that nothing is beyond expectation in the long and countless time:

> I have lately (ἀρτίως) learned that our enemy (ἐχθρὸς) must be hated as one
> who will sometime become a friend (ὡς καὶ φιλήσων αὖθις), and in helping
> a friend (φίλον) I shall aim to assist him as one assists a man who will not
> remain a friend forever (ὡς αἰὲν οὐ μενοῦντα), since for most mortals the
> harbour of friendship cannot be trusted (ἄπιστός ἐσθ' ἑταιρείας λιμήν).
> (678–83).

---

early on, in their statement that 'little men are best supported by the great, and the great by smaller
men' (vv. 160–1). In-depth treatment of φιλία and enmity in the *Ajax* in Blundell 1989: 60–105.

[29] Indeed, when Teucer gives orders for the rescue of Eurysaces, at vv. 990–1, the chorus will remember
Ajax's request, just as it is being taken care of.

[30] Finglass 2011: 320 draws attention to the polyptoton ἄφιλα παρ'ἀφίλοις, which recalls (and might
have done so for the audience) an earlier one by Tecmessa, also emphasizing commonality and
reciprocity, at 265–7: 'would you prefer, if given a choice, to grieve your friends (φίλους)
but enjoy happiness yourself, or to join in sorrow with your companions (κοινὸς ἐν κοινοῖσι
λυπεῖσθαι)?'.

Ajax here presents traditional notions on the changeability of life; the chorus is overjoyed at this sudden change of attitude, a change that clashes with all they (and tradition) knew about the hero.[31] And so, the chorus sings,

> Now it is my wish to dance! … Ah, now once more, now, o Zeus, can the bright light of day shine upon the swift ships that glide over the sea, now that Ajax once more forgets his pain (ὅτ'Αἴας λαθίπονος πάλιν), and has fulfilled the ordinances of the gods with all their sacrifices, doing them reverence with all obedience. All things are withered by mighty time (πανθ'ὁ μέγας χρόνος μαραίνει); and I would say that nothing was unpredictable, now that Ajax, beyond our hopes, has repented (μετανεγνώσθη) of his anger against the son of Atreus and his great quarrel. (701–18)

The perceived change in Ajax's disposition is emphasized in multiple ways: by the use of the rare term λαθίπονος, joined with πάλιν (once again: but here, it means that Ajax is back to what he was before); by the declaration that Ajax has repented; and possibly by the fact that the chorus ends their song with a reference to all-consuming time, the very topic with which Ajax had opened his own speech (ἅπανθ' ὁ μακρὸς κἀναρίθμητος χρόνος | φύει τ'ἄδηλα καὶ φανέντα κρύπτεται, 645–6), reinforcing the message of fluidity and changeability that seems to pervade this part of the play.[32]

As it turns out, Ajax has not forgotten – the first inkling of the trouble to come emerges in the following scene, which involves the arrival of a messenger, announcing the arrival of Teucer, and the chorus. When he hears that Ajax has left, the messenger, answering to the chorus, reports the words exchanged between Teucer and Calchas. This is a case of normal, unmarked recalling, where the messenger derives his authority from the fact that he was present at the scene, as in numerous messenger speeches.[33] And yet, this normal recalling shifts very quickly

---

[31] In *Odyssey* 11. 543–6 Ajax is described as staying alone, full of wrath, even in Hades, for having lost the contest for the weapons of Hector. For parallels to the image of friendship as a harbour, see Finglass 2011: 339 (Theognis 113–14 is particularly relevant here).

[32] The mention of the grievous anger of the goddess (μῆνιν βαρεῖαν, 656), and even more Ajax's decision to bury Hector's sword in the ground so that no one may ever see it again (657–63) are however pointers in the other direction. Knox 1961: 3–4 and n. 11 highlights the similarities between Sophocles' *Ajax* and *Oedipus at Colonus* for what concerns the status of men, gods and the passing of time. Memory and remembrance indeed play a central role in that play as well. To the passages listed by Knox, one can add the striking way in which Theseus discusses Oedipus' request of being buried in Athens: 'You ask for life's last service; but for all between you have no memory, or no care' (τὰ δ' ἐν μέσῳ ἢ λῆστιν ἴσχεις ἢ δι' οὐδενὸς ποιῇ, Soph. *OC* 583–4); in his further reply, Theseus will point out that Oedipus asks for a *charis*.

[33] v. 748: τοσοῦτον οἶδα καὶ παρὼν ἐνέτυχον. Cf. Barrett (2002) 74–5, and discussion above.

into something else, when, through the words of Calchas, the messenger reports words pronounced by Ajax even before leaving for Troy, and then again when at Troy – arrogant words, the cause of his downfall, twice cited verbatim – but words that Calchas himself cannot have heard by being present. Indeed, the messenger quickly restates that the authority for this part rests with Calchas ('so much the prophet said', 780). The information that this is the critical day, and that if Ajax is kept indoors he may survive, comes, however, too late: the next part of the drama focuses on Ajax's suicide on a solitary beach, and on the search by Tecmessa and the chorus.

At this point the members of Ajax's circle – Tecmessa, the chorus, Teucer – cannot but realize that Ajax has voided his obligations towards them. Tecmessa says so explicitly, using the same term she had employed in her appeal, χάρις:

> ἔγνωκα γὰρ δὴ φωτὸς ἠπατημένη
> καὶ τῆς παλαιᾶς χάριτος ἐκβεβλημένη
>
> For I see that he has deceived me and cast me out from
> the favour (*charis*) I once enjoyed. (807–8)

As for the chorus, they feel that Ajax's death is their own: 'Alas my lord, you have killed me your fellow sailor!' (901–2);[34] and yet they can spare a thought for Tecmessa (903: 'O poor lady!'). Finally, although Teucer laments his own fate at length, now that Ajax is no more, he too feels that he failed to help his brother (992–1039). Yet interestingly, they all maintain alive their own obligations towards him: and this entails remembering, in various ways. Tecmessa remembers him almost 'inadvertently', when at 904, in dialogue with the chorus, she says:

> ὡς ὧδε τοῦδ' ἔχοντος αἰάζειν πάρα.
>
> it is so with him, and we can only lament.

She is in fact here quoting Ajax's own words: the hero had opened his first speech with a reflection on his name:

> αἰαῖ· τίς ἄν ποτ' ὤεθ' ὧδ' ἐπώνυμον
> τοὐμὸν ξυνοίσειν ὄνομα τοῖς ἐμοῖς κακοῖς;
> νῦν γὰρ πάρεστι καὶ δὶς αἰάζειν ἐμοὶ

---

[34] Finglass 2011: 401 on the particular bond shared by the chorus and Ajax as sailors, a bond mentioned already in 348–9.

> Alas! Who ever would have thought that my name would
> come to harmonise with my sorrows? For now I can say
> 'Alas' a second time ... (v. 430–2)

After the first *agon* between Menelaus and Teucer, the chorus worry over
the boy, and about the body of Ajax; they dwell on a physical – if bleak –
memorial,[35] with words recalling another memorial:

> Come as quickly as you can, Teucer, hasten to find a hollow trench for this
> man, where he shall occupy the dank tomb, a memorial forever for mortals
> (σπεῦσον κοίλην κάπετόν τιν' ἰδεῖν | τῷδ', ἔνθα βροτοῖς τὸν ἀείμνηστον |
> τάφον εὐρώεντα καθέξει, 1164–7).

The phrase 'hollow trench' used here for the tomb of Ajax recalls the depos-
ition of Hector's bones in a tomb in the *Iliad* (ἐς κοίλην κάπετον θέσαν,
Hom. *Il.* 24.797). This allusion would have been all the more easy to perceive, as a connection between the two heroes appears more than once in
the play: they are linked by Hector's sword, on which Ajax kills himself.
Thus, 'the Chorus' hope that Ajax's grave will be an "always-remembered
tomb" (ἀείμνηστος τάφος, 1166–7) is enacted by the play itself, just as the
Iliad had constructed an "always-remembered tomb" for Hector'.[36]

More poignantly, the idea of gratitude being either honoured in
memory or slipping away into oblivion reappears with force in the speech
that Teucer delivers to rebut Agamemnon's insults and his attempt to deny
Ajax a proper burial:

> Alas, how quickly gratitude to the dead flows away (χάρις διαρρεῖ) from
> men and is found to have turned to betrayal, if this man no longer, even for
> a brief mention, remembers you (ἔτ' ἴσχει μνῆστιν),[37] Ajax, even though it
> was for his sake you toiled so often in battle, offering your own life to the
> spear! No, your assistance is dead and gone, all flung aside (ἐρριμμένα)! Fool
> and foolish talker, do you no longer remember anything (οὐ μνημονεύεις
> οὐκέτ' οὐδέν) of the time when you were trapped inside your defences ...
> (Soph. *Ai.* 1269–73)

---

[35] Henrichs 1993: 170 comments: 'the tomb of Ajax is both ἀείμνηστος (1166) and εὐρώεις (1167), a
place where memory (μνήμη) coexists precariously with mold (εὐρώς)'. This is the turning point
towards the construction of a hero cult for Ajax.

[36] Easterling 1988: 96–7; Barker 2009: 314, who points out that starting from this moment (once
deprived of Ajax) the chorus begins to actively take charge. On the tomb of Ajax and the aetiology of cult, which looks into the future from the past perspective of the tragic choruses, see
Henrichs 1993.

[37] διαρρεῖ here corresponds to ἀπορρεῖ in Tecmessa's earlier speech (952–3); here as earlier in Tecmessa's
speech, μνῆστιν ἴσχειν implies a positive recollection.

Teucer proceeds to remind Agamemnon of the help Ajax gave the Achaeans, when the Trojans led by Hector were already at the ships, and of the time when Ajax met Hector in duel – but it is only the arrival of Odysseus that will resolve the conflict: Agamemnon seems to hold no memory of what (the Homeric) Ajax has done for him. Any notion of (deferred) reciprocity between Ajax and the sons of Atreus breaks down since the latter refuse to acknowledge – or have simply become oblivious to – the services previously rendered by the former. The Atreidae seem to possess only short-term memory, a pragmatic sort of memory, as the only explicit reference to memory they make in all of the play shows:

> O. παῦσαι: κρατεῖς τοι τῶν φίλων νικώμενος.
> A. μέμνησ' ὁποίῳ φωτὶ τὴν χάριν δίδως.

> Od. Enough! You win, when you give in to your friends.
> Ag. Remember to what sort of man you show this kindness!
> (Soph. Ai. 1353–54)

In Agamemnon's view, Ajax has failed to show the *charis* which would merit *charis* in return. But Odysseus, who does remember, and who realises the value of friendship, can juxtapose the past and the present: 'This man was an enemy, but he was once noble' (ὅδ' ἐχθρὸς ἀνήρ, ἀλλὰ γενναῖός ποτ' ἦν, 1356). Ultimately, Odysseus prevails, even if he does not convince Agamemnon; he also fails to persuade Teucer that it is appropriate to let him help bury Ajax: as Teucer points out, this might displease the dead.[38] The *philoi* of Ajax take up positions close to those that were Ajax's; and to counterbalance the failure of reciprocal fairness in the human sphere, Teucer invests in the superior memory of the gods, more specifically the divinities responsible for retributive justice (Soph. Ai. 1389–92, Teucer speaking):

> For that, may the father who is first on Olympus and the unforgetting Erinys (μνήμων τ' Ἐρινὺς) and Justice who accomplishes her ends (*telesphoros*) destroy them [the Atridae] cruelly, as they are cruel, they who wished to cast this man out outrageously in unworthy fashion.

Sophocles' meditation on the failure of memory in the *Ajax*, which entailed a failure of reciprocity grounded in gratitude (*charis*), and

---

[38] An evident pointer to the epic tradition, specifically to the encounter between Odysseus and Ajax in Hades, narrated in *Od.* 11. 543–64: Odysseus asks whether Ajax won't forgive him even in death (οὐκ ἄρ' ἔμελλες | οὐδὲ θανὼν λήσεσθαι ἐμοὶ χόλου εἵνεκα τευχέων); the hero does not answer and goes his way. Indeed, Teucer says, Ajax's 'black blood' (but the Greek has μένος, 1413, a term that is linked with the root μεν – of memory: see the Introduction, p. 4) continues to flow.

ultimately of justice, provides a useful foil for how the same cluster of ideas gets negotiated in Euripides' *Suppliants*.

4   Euripides on How to Ensure Proper Remembrance of Things Past

One of the most striking reflections on collective memory and its strengths and values appears in Euripides' *Suppliant Women*, a play probably performed in the 420s.[39] The scene is set at Eleusis: the mothers of the Argive warriors who died attacking Thebes have come to Athens, with their king Adrastos, to ask Theseus' help in retrieving the bodies of their sons, which the Thebans refuse to give back for burial.[40] Theseus eventually agrees to their request, even though this implies a battle against the Thebans, and recovers the bodies. With this, the main strand of the action is over, and the rest of the play focuses on the performance of the funeral rites: the burning of the bodies, the funeral speech of Adrastos (857–917), and the lamentations of the Argive wives, mothers and children. With the end of the lamentations (1164), the action appears to have come to an end and the play is seemingly over – but for a surprising, fascinating coda. Theseus reappears on stage and addresses Adrastos and the Argive women; his words make clear that what he is going to say concerns the two cities, Athens and Argos.[41] After stating that he and the city are giving

---

[39] Collard 2007. The play has been extensively discussed; the most important studies are listed in Steinbock 2013b: 155–6 n. 1, to which should be added at least Kavoulaki 2008, Storey 2008, Hanink 2013, Wohl 2015: 89–109. For *Suppliant Women* I follow the text and translation (with occasional modification) of D. Kovacs in the Loeb Classical Library.

[40] Whether or not the play alludes to the events that followed the Athenian defeat at Delion in 424 BC, as narrated by Thucydides, is disputed: see e.g. Bowie 1997 (for) and Zuntz 1955: 4 (against), with Collard 2007. In any case it was a burning contemporary issue for a play performed in wartime. Hanink 2013 and Steinbock 2013b: 155–210 compare the versions of the story in Aeschylus' *Eleusinians* (which featured a peaceful, diplomatic resolution of the issue), Euripides' *Suppliant Women* (in which the Athenians accepted to fight the Thebans to retrieve the bodies of the Argives), and the speeches of the orators (funeral orations, but also Isocrates), showing how each chose to draw on a version appropriate to the actual historical context. For an overall interpretation of the play not as an encomion of Athens, but rather as a play concerned with the forging of correct relations between Greek communities (also an issue of burning actuality in the Athenian empire), see Kavoulaki 2008. Athens, Argos and Thebes are the *poleis* primarily involved in the play, but the chance of a side dig at other communities is not passed over: Adrastus pointedly asks for Theseus' help, because 'Sparta is savage and devious in its ways, and the other states are small and weak'; only Athens can help (Eur. *Suppl.* 186–9).

[41] See Collard 1975: nn. 1165–8, as well as Morwood 2007: 234 and Wohl 2015: 106, for the importance at v. 1165 of the word 'race' (γυναῖκες Ἀργεῖαι γένος): this is no longer a personal, humanitarian affair, but a political one; the Argive orphans are reflected in the orphans sitting in the theatre, the Argive mothers in the Athenian citizens.

back to the Argives the bones of the Seven as a present (δωρούμεθα), he adds (1169–75):

ὑμᾶς δὲ τῶνδε χρὴ χάριν μεμνημένους
σώζειν, ὁρῶντας ὧν ἐκύρσατ' ἐξ ἐμοῦ,
παισίν θ' ὑπειπεῖν τούσδε τοὺς αὐτοὺς λόγους,
τιμᾶν πόλιν τήνδ', ἐκ τέκνων ἀεὶ τέκνοις
μνήμην παραγγέλλοντας ὧν ἐκύρσατε.
Ζεὺς δὲ ξυνίστωρ οἵ τ' ἐν οὐρανῷ θεοὶ
οἵων ὑφ' ἡμῶν στείχετ' ἠξιωμένοι.

You must remember these things and maintain your gratitude for them, as you look upon what you have won from me, and you must suggest to these boys here these very words, to honour this city, always handing down from one generation of children to another the memory of what you have won. And let Zeus and the gods in heaven be witnesses of what treatment you have been thought worthy by us as you go on your way.

Theseus here calls for the establishment of an oral tradition as a means of preserving the expected gratitude (and ensuing obligations) or, to use an economic idiom, the credit and debt that link benefactor and beneficiary: the mothers are to hand down the memory of the good deeds of Athens to their children, and the children in turn will take care to pass this memory on to the next generation. Theseus is extremely precise in his instructions: the mothers and children must repeat a set of specific words, the very words pronounced by Theseus, 'to honour this *polis*': the demonstrative τήνδε would have had its full effect on stage; if projected into the future, in the words of the mothers and children as they pass them on, it would have the effect of making the past present over and over again. Theseus closes his instruction by invoking the gods as witnesses (all-seeing, from their position in the sky, and συνίστωρες): they are to be his only guarantee.

Adrastos agrees, and in his answer echoes some of the very terms used by Theseus:[42]

Θησεῦ, ξύνισμεν πάνθ' ὅσ' Ἀργείαν χθόνα
δέδρακας ἐσθλὰ δεομένην εὐεργετῶν,
χάριν τ' ἀγήρων ἕξομεν· γενναῖα γὰρ
παθόντες ὑμᾶς ἀντιδρᾶν ὀφείλομεν.

---

[42] 1176: ξυνίσμεν, cf. 1174: ξυνίστωρ '(Zeus) witness'; 1178: χάριν τ' ἀγήρων ἕξομεν = 1169: χάριν.

> Theseus, we are conscious of all the good you have done to the
> land of Argos when it needed a benefactor, and our gratitude will
> never grow old. Since we have received such noble treatment, we
> must treat you nobly in turn. (1176–9)

Everything seems in order, and the Argives are already leaving when Athena
appears and stops the proceedings. She goes on to argue that Theseus
should not give away the bodies so lightly: he must first require a sworn
oath from the Argives that they will never attack Attica. The wording of
the oath is set out in extraordinary detail, 'the most detailed prescription
for an oath in Greek literature':[43]

> Do not give these bones to these children to carry away to the land of Argos,
> letting them go so lightly, but in return for your labours and those of your
> city first exact an oath. This man here, Adrastus, must swear: he has the
> authority to take an oath on behalf of the whole land of Danaus' sons since
> he is the king. This is the oath: that the Argives will never move a hostile
> army against this land, and that, if others do so, they will use their own
> might to stop them. They must pray that the land of Argos may perish mis-
> erably if they violate the oath and march against the city. (1185–95)

This is already quite specific – but it is not enough for Athena: the oath
must be accompanied by sacrifices, performed over a bronze tripod which
Heracles, coming back from having destroyed Troy, once ordered Theseus
to set up at the Pythian shrine, as he was leaving for another mission (1196–
200).[44] Over this tripod, Athena orders, the sacrifice must be accomplished:

> ἐν τῷδε λαιμοὺς τρεῖς τριῶν μήλων τεμὼν
> ἔγγραψον ὅρκους τρίποδος ἐν κοίλῳ κύτει,
> κἄπειτα σῴζειν θεῷ δὸς ᾧ Δελφῶν μέλει,
> μνημεῖά θ' ὅρκων μαρτύρημά θ' Ἑλλάδι. (1201–4)

> Having cut over this tripod the throats of three sheep inscribe the
> oaths on its curved hollow, and then give it for safekeeping to the
> god who rules Delphi, a memorial of the oath and a witness to it in
> the eyes of Hellas.

---

[43] Fletcher 2012: 18.

[44] On oath sacrifices, see Torrance 2014: 138–40; on the political meaning of this oath and on its
connection with the alliance with Argos in Aeschylus' *Eumenides*, Torrance 2014: 149–51. More generally on interstate relations and oaths, Bayliss in Sommerstein and Bayliss 2013: 147–304. On the
historical background in the 420s, see Storey 2008: 24–6; Bowie 1997: 45–7. A treaty with Argos was
ratified in July 420: cf. *IG* I³ 83 and Thuc. 5.47, 82.5 (discussed below, n. 52). The terms presented
here (a one-sided obligation) differ radically from those of the agreement of 420 BC; but as Bowie
1997: 55 n. 128 points out, tragic treaties emphasize benefits to Athens (he compares Aesch. *Eum.*
767–74; Soph. *OC* 1518–34; Eur. *Heracl.* 1030–44).

Furthermore, in a quasi-magical ritual, the sacrificial knife with which Theseus will cut the throats must be buried in the depths of the earth (ἐς γαίας μυχούς), right next to the pyre of the Seven dead: 'For if the Argives ever return to the city, this knife, when displayed, will make them afraid and cause them an evil journey home' (*Suppl.* 1208–9). Only then may Theseus escort the Argive bodies out of the country.

The oral memory of the great deed accomplished by the Athenians, an oral memory handed over to the Argives to preserve, and with which Theseus had been content, is here, under Athena's directions, modified into a ritual (oaths, sacrifice) of which the inscription on bronze forms an important part.[45] Moreover, the goddess orders that the inscribed vase, which at this point symbolizes that memory, be located in a Panhellenic centre, Delphi, following a procedure that was commonly practised by the Greek cities. This instruction serves the purpose of removing the memory of the deed from its initially exclusive Argive-Athenian context and entrusting it to the god (Apollo) of a Panhellenic sanctuary, placing it under the protection of a divinity honoured across the Greek world.[46] Here it is important to note that the main purpose of the writing does not seem to be publicity, for the oaths are incised inside the vase: the writing on the bronze of this very special, 'historical' tripod (once given to Theseus by Heracles, and thus reflecting the earlier connections between the two cities) has a fundamentally sacred, ritual value.

To say that a written memory here replaces oral memory would be going too far. But clearly, the elaborate finale of the *Suppliant Women* displays awareness of the power of ritual to 'embody' remembrance. Furthermore, public writing is now, and in a very positive sense, the guardian of common memory and oaths, in contradistinction to the practice of simply 'remembering'. This public writing receives a peculiar 'added value' from the support on which it is engraved, from the ritual that accompanies both the taking of the oath and its engraving, and from the status of the location where the tripod and the text it bears are finally located, Delphi.[47] But the

---

[45] Cf. Day 2010: 106: writing a treaty on a special tripod 'appears as one in a series of ritualized acts (besides oath taking etc.) and becomes an integral part of the monument that preserves the relationship between Argos and Athens'.

[46] Numerous treaties have survived from Olympia: cf. e.g. the alliance of Sybaris and its allies with the Serdaioi, ca. 550–525 BC, or the treaty between Eleans and Heraeans of the early fifth century BC, Meiggs and Lewis 1988 nos. 10 and 17, both inscribed on bronze tablets. This latter document includes an explicit warning that 'if anyone injures this writing, whether private man or magistrate or community, he shall be liable to the sacred fine herein written': this is powerful writing (compare the inscription from Teos discussed in the introduction to this volume, pp. 32–3); see Bayliss in Sommerstein and Bayliss 2013: 158–60.

[47] Bowie 1997: 55–6 follows Krummen in suggesting that the (presumed) continued existence of the tripod in Delphi stands as a reminder of the splendour of Athens' military and moral leadership (but

most fascinating aspect of this epilogue is not so much the endorsement of this complex way of preserving a memory: after all, writing and its public exposure are normal in the last quarter of the fifth century. Rather, it is the way in which Athena explicitly disowns alternative forms of remembering, and in particular (oral) transmission of gratitude from elders to future generations. Her striking dismissal of this practice as insufficient has telling parallels elsewhere in the tragic corpus as well as other contemporary sources, and clearly points to a deep worry about traditional procedures of remembrance and the reciprocity grounded in and by memory. A passage in Thucydides illustrates the point. Before the outbreak of the war, in 433 BC, the Corinthians try to convince the Athenians not to back Corcyra by calling on favours (*charis*) Athens owed, sufficient 'according to the laws of the Greeks': namely, the support that the Corinthians gave to Athens in the war against Aegina, which took place before the Persian invasions (an affair mentioned in Herodotus 6.89), and the fact that Corinth prevented the Spartans from aiding Samos against Athens. They close this part of their speech with the exhortation to 'bear these facts in mind, and let every young man learn of them by one who is older, and let them determine to render us like for like'.[48] *Charis* is one of the buzzwords in the speech of the Corinthians, but their speech fails to convince the Athenians. Part of the issue in Thucydides' passage is surely the contrast between young and old men, a contrast that appears more than once in his work; but there is also here an appeal to an oral tradition, which should have preserved the memory of a service, a *charis*, but fails. In this context, it is worth noting that there is a marked increase in inscribed honorific decrees in Athens around 430 BC, in particular proxeny decrees: the good deeds accomplished by foreigners for the Athenians tend to be now commemorated in stone.[49]

Furthermore, *Suppliant Women* is one of the few plays in which the positive side of written law is explicitly stressed, in Theseus' answer to the Theban herald, who affirms proudly to come from a city ruled by one man and not by the rabble, a city where no man can fool the others with slick, flattering words. In his reply, Theseus stresses that in a city held by a tyrant

---

see further below on the tripod). There is also possibly here an allusion to the (oral only) alliance concluded between Athens and Argos at the end of Aeschylus' *Oresteia* (*Eum.* 762–74): see e.g. Torrance 2013: 172; a specific intertextual memory could thus also have been activated.

[48] Thuc. 1. 41–2. The contrast between young and old is relatively frequent, but here it is developed in a very specific way, in connection with remembering past benefactions. For Thucydides' take on the (very scarce) reliability of human memory, see 2.54.3, and Darbo-Peschanski's chapter in this volume.

[49] See Meyer 2013, esp. 458 and 467 for honorific decrees, 471–2 for treaties and regulations; Ferrario 2006 emphasizes the increase in written (monumental) commemoration at Athens in the last quarter of the fifth century, whether through honorific decrees or individual funerary monuments.

there are no common laws (νόμοι/κοινοί, 430–1), for one person only has power, holding the law by himself – and this is unjust (καὶ τόδ'οὐκέτ' ἔστ' ἴσον, 432). By contrast, written laws in particular enable comprehensive protection against willful injustice (Eur. *Suppl.* 433–44):

γεγραμμένων δὲ τῶν νόμων ὅ τ' ἀσθενὴς/ὁ πλούσιός τε τὴν δίκην
ἴσην ἔχει

When the laws are written, both the weak and the rich have justice equally.

As pointed out by Stinton, this is the only passage in all of fifth-century Greek literature that states explicitly that written laws are a guarantee of equality, which is not in itself a self-evident notion: 'statutory laws in states where they were not written down, e.g. Sparta, were not thought any the less binding, or less *nomoi*, on that account'.[50] However, the decision to move the written laws from the acropolis to the agora, the appearance of formulae of disclosure (such as σκοπεῖν τῷ βουλομένῳ, 'so that anyone who desires may see', attested in five Athenian inscriptions all dated to the 430s/420s) and, more generally, the emphasis that inscriptions place on the importance of publication on stone, as well as other historical developments, show that the idea that written laws help enforce equality (and democracy) must have found increasingly broad circulation.[51] The idea that writing down the laws was a central element of the *polis'* identity may thus have been widely shared in Athens. In the context of international diplomacy, publication of written agreements was also commonplace in the fifth century: the alliances between Sybaris and her allies and the Serdaioi, for instance, or that between the Eleans and the Heraeans, written on bronze plates dedicated at Olympia, go back to the sixth century.[52] In 420,

---

[50] Stinton (in Collard 1975: 441–2). The distinction between *agraphoi nomoi* (divine, natural, universal, international laws) and man-made, positive laws of particular cities is different from the point at issue here. On written and unwritten laws, and their authority, see Harris 2006: 41–61 (unwritten esp. at 45; relationship between unwritten and written, 53–7).

[51] For the report that the decision to move the laws was taken by Ephialtes, cf. Anaximenes of Lampsacus, *FGrHist* 72 F 13 (although note Wilamowitz' sceptical position on this, with Jacoby's comments, ad loc.; see Loraux 2002: 72 or Sickinger 1999: 30, who accept the account, and Meyer 2013: 478 n. 114, who does not); for analysis of disclosure formulae, cf. Hedrick 1999: 410–11 (list in his appendix 2), with Meyer 2013. One does not have to believe that this notion is true (and for instance the issue of the authority ordering the writing down of the laws is not addressed; yet it is crucial), nor that it was shared over all of Greece (it emphatically was not). The law cited by Andoc. *Myst.* 83–6 (86: ἀγράφῳ νόμῳ τὰς ἀρχὰς μὴ χρῆσθαι) shows the centrality of written laws; later political theory connected the development of law with the beginnings of writing, cf. Plato *Leg.* 680a, and the detailed discussion in Harris 2006.

[52] Respectively, Meiggs and Lewis 1988 nos. 10 and 17; see also the agreement between Argos, Cnossus and Tylissus, Osborne and Rhodes 2017 no. 126, or the treaty between Sparta and the Erxadieis, Osborne and Rhodes 2017 no. 128, both dated to ca. 450 BC.

Athens made a treaty with Argos, Mantinea and Elis, whose text is quoted in its entirety by Thucydides; an inscribed, incomplete copy of the treaty has survived, corresponding to the first part of Thucydides' text (5.47.1–8), but sufficient to show that Thucydides' text is entirely reliable.[53] A clause of this treaty, preserved only in Thucydides, stated that copies of the treaty should be erected at Athens on the Acropolis, in Argos at the temple of Apollo in the agora, in Mantinea at the temple of Zeus in the agora, and at Olympia on a bronze stele. It further prescribed renewal of the oaths by all allies every two years, in Elis 30 days before the Olympic games, and in Athens 10 days before the Panathenaic games. The parallels with Athena's intervention on behalf of the Athenians in the *Suppliant Women*, to ensure that the future expectations of good, reciprocal behaviour on the part of the Argives be soundly and permanently enshrined in Panhellenic memory, are obvious, irrespective of whether the play post- or predates the treaty.

In light of all this, it is remarkable that the writing of laws and agreements should have surfaced, and so forcefully, in this tragedy only. It is probably not an accident that the play is *Suppliant Women*, a play in which persuasion and writing are presented in an optimistic perspective; and it is certainly not an accident that these words on the positive value of written laws are put in the mouth of the 'democratic' Theseus, even as those on the positive value of written treaties are in the mouth of Athena. In Sophocles' oeuvre, we can still detect resistance of the tragic genre to integrate writing (and its memorial powers) into the world of the plays, in a conscious avoidance of what would have been an anachronistic presence in the heroic age in which the plays are set; Euripides, by contrast, does not wish to bypass reflection on the power of the written word, not least as a guarantor of 'contractual memories'.[54] References to the complex interface of writing, memory and (sustained) reciprocity begin to register more insistently in at least some of his plays, overriding the generic conventions he inherited. And yet, the issues raised by the 'novel' way of enshrining memory suggested by Athena will not have been lost, on at least some members of the audience: the contrived, if not entirely 'fabricated', status

---

[53] Treaty: *IG* I³ 83 = Osborne and Rhodes 2017 no. 165, from Athens; cf. Thucydides 5.47 (5.47.10 for the renewal of the oaths; 5.47.11 for the clause on inscription), and Bolmarcich 2007; Hornblower 2008: 109–20.

[54] It is well known that while Aeschylus and Sophocles (just as Pindar) exploit the metaphor of writing as memory, Euripides does not. Detailed discussion of the appearances of writing (real and metaphorical) in tragedy in Torrance 2013, esp. 135–82; Ceccarelli 2013: 183–235 and 258–64; see also Agócs' chapter in this volume.

of tripod and knife (the first conveniently dedicated away from Athens, the second buried underground, so as to make examination impossible), and the change in the place of burial of the Seven (here sent back to Argos: the shrine will simply indicate the location of cremation) undermine the claim to a direct tradition.[55]

[55] Dunn 2000: 12–15.

CHAPTER 4

Aristophanes and his Muses, or Memory in a Comic Key

Silvia Milanezi

> Listen, good sir, and see if I speak the truth. Man is by nature a crea-
> ture born to suffer, and his life must endure many sorrows. And so, he
> has discovered these comforting distractions from his anxieties. For
> the mind, forgetting its own cares and entertained at someone else's
> suffering, ends up pleasured, and learning something to boot.
>
> Timocles, *Women at the Dionysia*, F 6

In a seminal article, Jean-Pierre Vernant has shown how poetics and history
are entangled in Ancient Greek thought. They come together in the figure
of Mnemosyne, who is not only a psychological category ('memory'), but
also a Goddess ('Memory').[1] Lying with Zeus for nine nights, Mnemosyne,
according to Hesiod, gave birth to the Muses, whose *geras* ('privilege', 'pre-
rogative') it is to delight gods and men with their songs.[2] Since they are
able to sing what is, what was and what will be, the Muses' songs are
grounded in comprehensive divine knowledge, which comprises a complete recall of the past as well as full awareness of future events. Even their
'new' performances are thus always re-enactments of a universal memory.
The gift of song that the Muses distribute among men is not supposed
to be a distinction that singles out a particular man for his own personal
advantage and glory. Those who receive the Muses' gift become the reposi-
tories of the goddesses' divine memory, which conveys both knowledge
and oblivion of pains.[3] Their performances, thanks to the Muses' gift, recreate a divine harmony as they share memory with their audience. This
archaic conception of Memory and the Muses certainly evolved, but
Greek poetics can hardly be detached from the authority of the Muses.
Whatever their poetic endeavour, their commissioners or the context of
their performances, singers and poets draw attention to their relationship

---

[1] Vernant 1959: 1–29.
[2] Hes. *Theog.* 36–42; 96–103.
[3] Hes. *Theog.* 55.

with the Muses, a relationship that grants them authority and competence in poetic matters as the legitimate keepers of their divine *geras*.[4]

The comic poets pay tribute to Mnemosyne and the Muses and use a wide range of vocabulary linked to them[5] and to different aspects of memory, such as the disposition to learn practical and spiritual matters, to remember and to act or perform accordingly.[6] Comic poets endeavour to instruct their audiences, preparing them to respond to their production. By doing so, they create a shared public ground that becomes a (comic) history, not only of their craft but also of the Dionysiac competition in Athens.

In what follows, I begin by stressing the importance of the comic Muses and their role in the dramatic competition; I then turn my attention to the training of memory and its results. In my conclusion, I emphasize the relationship between comic memory and civic memory.

1   Mnemosyne and the Comic Muses

Mnemosyne is directly invoked only once in the comic *corpus*, in the *Lysistrata*,[7] to send her Muse to the chorus for a song that involves memory of the past – the battles of Artemision and Thermopylae, in which, thanks to their harmonious relationship, Athenians and Spartans triumphed over the Persians.[8] Mnemosyne and the Muses, or the song they inspire, should guarantee, thanks also to Artemis and diplomacy, the return of the old friendship (*philia*) that has been lost during the Peloponnesian War. In a way, these lines encapsulate three central aspects of the poetics of comedy (or its rhetoric): the relationship between the comic poet and the Muses, which reveals the poet's allegiance to the Greek poetic tradition; the positive results of song; and the possibility to distribute praise or blame.

Strikingly, even when literacy becomes widespread in classical Athens, when musical and dramatic contests are offered to Dionysus,

---

4 See Biles 2011: 20–1.
5 e.g. μουσική: Ar. *Ach.* 851; *Eq.* 188; *Ran.* 729, 797, 1493; *Plut.*, 190; see also F 347 K.-A.: *trugōidopoiomousikē*; Cratin. F 308 K.-A.; Theophil. *Kitharoidos* F 5 K.-A.; Anaxil. *Hyakinthos* F 27 K.-A.; Antiph. *Tritagonistes* F 207 K.-A.; Men. *Thesauros* F 178 K.-A.; ἄμουσος: Ar. *Vesp.* 1074; Ar. *Thesm.* 159.
6 e.g. μιμνήσκω: Ar. *Eq.* 526, 1052, 1180; *Vesp.* 443; *Pax* 501, 1060, 1275; *Ran.* 593, 1469; *Eccl.* 286, 951, 1155; Hermipp. F. 81 K.-A.; Men. *Sam.* 8; μνημεῖον: Ar. *Eq.* 268; μνῆμα: Anaxipp. *Phrear.* F 8 K.-A.; Diph. *Enagizontes vel Enagismata* F 37 K.-A.; μνημόσυνον: Ar. *Vesp.* 538, 559; μνημονεύω: Ar. *Eccl.* 264; Men. *Pk.* 332; *Sam.* 170; 709; *Adespota*, F 821 K.-A.; μνήμων: Ar. *Nub.* 414, 484; *Pax* 761; μνημονικός: Ar. *Nub.* 483; Cratin. *Panoptai*, F 162 K.-A.; μνημόνευμα: Men. *Pk.* 796; ἀμνημονέω: Men. *Sam.* 73.
7 Μναμόνα, Ar. *Lys.* 1248, the Doric form for the Attic Μνημοσύνη (cf. Μῶά for Μοῦσα in *Lys.* 1249).
8 Ar. *Lys.* 1249–61.

poets/*didaskaloi* do not let Mnemosyne or the Muses go. On the contrary, they call onstage a multiplicity of Muses,[9] possibly one for every poetic genre,[10] one for every poet/singer or *didaskalos*,[11] one for every Greek region.[12] Invoked or evoked alone or together,[13] the Muses also appeared as characters in some comedies now lost.[14] Even when they quote, parody or mock their ancestors' Muses, or compete against those of their contemporaries, comic poets re-enact the relationship they had established with them.[15] Their allegiance to tradition is all the more impressive as comic poets also stress their bonds with Dionysus and even specifically with *Kōmōidia*: the latter becomes Cratinus' wife,[16] while Dionysus is 'nourisher' of the choreutai.[17] But the god can invite the chorus to join in the celebration of the Muses before the dramatic contests, emphasizing that without them there is no competition.[18] As for the Muses, they are summoned to preside over the chorus' dances and, as in Hesiod, to sing their songs 'from the beginning' (ἐξ ἀρχῆς),[19] displaying for humankind the wonders of the world.[20]

---

[9] Ar. *Eq.* 505–6 (the chorus of Knights refers to the musical contests in Athens). See also Ar. *Ra.* 356 and 873, in which these same contests are defined as ὄργια Μουσῶν or ἀγῶνα μουσικώτατα. Anaxil. F 27 K.-A. evokes the children of *Mousikē*, as numerous as the beasts born to Africa.

[10] Poets' Muses (in general): Ar. *Av.* 912–4; Comic Muses: Ar. *Vesp.* 1015–22; Tragic: Ar. *Thesm.* 41–3 (Agathon's thiasos of Muses) and 107–10; Euripides' Muse, Ar. *Ran.* 1305–8; see also 874–81; 1300; Muses of a lyric poet seeking patronage: Ar. *Av.* 904–57; lascivious or Ionian Muses, Ar. *Eccl.* 882–3; Bucolic Muse, Ar. *Av.* 737–9; Nightingale's friend, Ar. *Av.* 658–60; Birds' friend, Ar. *Av.* 783; Frogs' friends or lovers, Ar. *Ran.* 229–30.

[11] Aristophanes' Muse: *Vesp.* 1021–2; Phrynichus' Muse opposed to Euripides', *Ran.* 1301–3; Euripides' Muses, *Ran.* 1305–8.

[12] Laconian Muse: Ar. *Lys.* 1295–7; Muse of Acharnai: Ar. *Ach.* 665–6.

[13] *Adespota*, fr. 1051 (*CGFP*, fr. 293ª 7, P. Giss. 152).

[14] At least five plays taking their title from the Muses are known: Epicharmus' *Hebe's Wedding or Muses* (according to Athenaeus 3.110b, *Muses* was a revised version of *Hebe's Wedding*: cf. Olson 2007: 8 and 42); Phrynichus' *Muses* (on which see below, p. 118); the *Muses* of Euphro (*Suda* ε 3815; *PCG* V, 288, T 1; no surviving fragments) and Euphanes (F 1 K.-A. = Athenaeus, 8.343b); and Polyzelus' *Birth of the Muses* (*Suda* π 1961; F 8–11 K.-A.). Moreover, *Suda* ω 272 attributes a comedy *Muses* to the comic poet Ophelio; see, however, the doubts of Kassel and Austin, *PCG* VII, 97 T 1.

[15] On the archaic aspects of memory, see above n. 1, and in this volume, Introduction; see also Agócs' chapter. Comic poets pay their respects to Pindar, for example, by stressing the prophetic ability of the Muses, which become theirs: see Ar. *Av.* 724.

[16] Cratinus presented *Komodia* as his wife: Kassel-Austin, *PCG* IV. 219–32 and particularly T ii IV 219 = Schol. Ar. *Eq.* 400 = *Suda* κ 2216. See Rosen 2000: 23–39; Biles 2011: 146–54; Bakola 2010: 59–63.

[17] Ar. *Nub.* 519. See also Cratin. *Boukoloi*, F 17–22 K.-A., with Bakola 2010: 23 and 42–9, who observes that Cratinus constructs his agonistic rhetoric by stressing his relationship with Dionysus.

[18] Dionysus prepares a sacrifice and prays that he may be able to judge the poets 'most musically' (ἀγῶνα κρῖναι τόνδε μουσικώτατα, Ar. *Ran.* 873), and then asks the chorus to sing for the Muses, 874; this is followed by the invocation to the Muses, in which the chorus invites them to attend to the competition, 875–80.

[19] Ar. *Pax* 773–80; cf. Hes. *Theog.* 45 and 115, as well as Hes. *Theog.* 1.

[20] Hermipp. *Phormophoroi* F 63 K.-A.

Calling for the Muses' protection and alliance, comic poets enforce their right to sing, that is to say, their right to introduce their poetics, to compete, and, thanks to their poetic skills, to convey a new kind of knowledge.

In Athens, dramatic poets or musicians competing in the Dionysiac contest first underwent a selection by the city.[21] Comic poets recall the request presented to the city to grant them (or those acting in their name as *didaskaloi*) the right to compete: the competitors at the Dionysia were winners of a first contest, a contest that preceded the appointment of the *chorēgoi*, the actors and the musicians.[22] In that situation, too, the *didaskaloi*, or their coryphaeus, merged into the 'poetic comic I' thanks to the conventions of the genre, appealed to the Muses and their patronage: their victory would depend not only on their own musical skills, but also on those of everyone involved, including the *chorēgoi*, whose generosity and *philotimia* could give them the dramatic victory.[23] And, last but not least, the Muses, inspirers of the poets' art, and identified with their songs, could enlighten the minds of judges and audience. Excellence is thus the outcome of a sum of skills that only the Muses can provide. Under the power of the Muses, the city legitimated the comic Muse, the poet's Muse, making it part of the civic voice, of civic history.

It is thus not surprising to find the poet's Muse or a multiplicity of Muses in the comic productions, or to discover them among comic characters. Phrynichus' *Muses*, produced at the Lenaea of 405 BC, is probably the best-known play showcasing the goddesses.[24] Phrynichus seems to have brought on stage a chorus of Muses. We can only guess what the Muses' role was, what their appearance or their dances were, and what relationship they established with the poet *didaskalos* of this play and with the audience, since only a few lines of this comedy are still available to us.[25] Phrynichus' Muses surely could, as choruses do, distribute praise, honour and scorn; but, just like the poet they protected, they could also become the target of mockery and insult.[26]

It is actually in the context of the rivalry characteristic of competitions that the *didaskalos*, as the epinician singer, introduces his Muses; better, he makes the chorus introduce them, speak on their behalf and stir

---

[21] See [Arist.] *Ath. Pol.* 56; Wilson 2000: 61–5.

[22] Cf. Wilson 2000: 61; Milanezi 2011.

[23] Addresses to the Muses asking for their patronage often appear in *parabaseis* (Ar. *Ach.* 665–6; *Pax* 775–80; *Av.* 737; *Ran.* 674–5; F 348 K.-A.; Cratin. F 237 K.-A.). See Biles 2011: 53 and n. 159; 241.

[24] *PCG* VII, 409–11. On this topic, see Harvey 2000: 91–134 and, particularly, 103–8.

[25] From this play only eight lines are preserved (F 32–5 K.-A.), in which the Muses are not named.

[26] See in particular Ar. *Pax* 773–818.

up the rivalry between them and the other Muses.[27] Play after play the members of the chorus and their coryphaei construct the *persona comica* suited to their *didaskalos* and, thanks to their Muse, those of their rivals. Aristophanes' choruses thus present their rivals' Muses as procuresses given to debauchery,[28] while theirs take pride in honesty and courage.[29] Loyal allies to the poets and their choruses, the Muses are invited to react to frigid tragic *didaskaloi* such as Morsimus and Melanthius and to spit on them, as if they were comic rivals.[30] In other words, they are invited to play the blame (*psogos*) game that is an important part of the comic competition. Thanks to the Muses, there is no genre frontier for the choruses and the comic poet: the comic *didaskalos* is the sum total of musical memories; he introduces them in his plays; he can even recreate an entire Dionysiac contest on stage, as Aristophanes did in his *Frogs,* and perhaps in his *Gerytades.*[31] So it is unsurprising when the coryphaeus affirms in one of Aristophanes' lost comedies that it is unnecessary 'to summon the curly-tressed Muses or yell for the Olympian Graces to join the chorus, for our poet says they're already present':[32] the Muses are the poetry of the poet, the memory that he is spreading, thanks also to his contemporaries and ancestors in craft.

Bacchylides' saying, that 'the poet owes to the poet, in the past and still now' as 'it is not easy to find out the gates of words unspoken',[33] also applies to the comic poets. They knew the *poikilia* of the poetic craft and the peculiarity of the comic muse and understood that, as the Muses' protégés, they should pass on poetic memories and fix them in the public mind, play after play, training the musical memory of the citizen.

2 Memory, Learning, Acting and Performing

Comic poets deal with divine, but also human memory. One of the aspects of the latter is recollection. Characters and chorus often evoke recent or past deeds and events. These memories, whether glad or sad, whether

[27] *Ran.* 1300–3. *Vesp.* 1015–70. For the epinician poet and the Muse, see Agócs, this volume, pp. 69–71, 79–81; Darbo-Peschanski, this volume, pp. 163–4.
[28] *Vesp.* 1025–8. On the image, see Taillardat 1965: 427–30 and particularly 428 §735; Imperio 2004: 280–1.
[29] *Vesp.* 1015–70.
[30] *Pax* 815–7. The chorus invites the Muses to consider Carcinus' sons as quails in a poultry yard (*Pax* 781–95) and to refuse to admit them to their chorus.
[31] F 156 K.-A. On plots dealing with the dramatic contests, and particularly the *Thesmophoriazusae,* see Voelke 2004; Biles 2011: 173, 249.
[32] *Thesm.* II, F 348 (translation by Rusten et al., in Rusten 2011). See also Imperio 2004: 94.
[33] fr. 5 Sn.-Maehl. See also Gentili 2011: 91.

personal or civic, become song, drama. Lovers cry over their lost partners and love tokens;[34] men rejoice in their past deeds or cry over their lost youth or old age;[35] while citizens sing their exploits at war and the favours of the gods.[36] Even those memories that should be buried, such as the loss of a son or the painful memories of the civil war, become part of the comic craft.[37] Importantly, comic recollection appears also as a disposition to learn, as a training method, and, ultimately, as a performance. The relationship between master and disciple, often presented onstage, is a source of good laughter, as poets make the most of the master's experience and of the student's clumsiness.[38] In *Clouds*, as in *Wasps*, instead of introducing young men willing to learn, Aristophanes presents old men being taught. While in *Wasps* a father is instructed, against his own will, by his son, in *Clouds* an indebted peasant is eager to be admitted to Socrates' school.[39] By these comic reversals, the poet increases the ridicule of his characters' situation, revitalizing at the same time a traditional pattern.

In *Clouds*, the chorus promises Socrates' pupil-to-be, Strepsiades, absolute happiness among the Athenians and all the Greeks, if he is mindful (or possessed of a good memory: *mnēmōn*), is a deep-thinker and has got an enduring soul.[40] As for Socrates, he explicitly states that he

---

34 Ar. *Plut.* 991: 'so that wearing my cloak he would remember me' (ἵνα τοὐμὸν ἱμάτιον φορῶν μεμνῇτό μου).

35 *Vesp.* 1200–7 (the past events Philocleon should remember when in polite company); Ar. *Eq.* 1052–3: 'but cherish your good hawk, remembering in your soul that he brought you those Lacedaemonian fish in chains' (Ἀλλ' ἱέρακα φίλει μεμνημένος ἐν φρεσίν, ὅς σοι/ἤγαγε συνδήσας Λακεδαιμονίων κορακίνους); *Nub.* 998–9: 'not to talk back to your father, nor remind him maliciously, by calling him Iapetus, of the age when he brought you up as a chick' (μηδ' ἀντειπεῖν τῷ πατρὶ μηδὲν μηδ' Ἰαπετὸν καλέσαντα/μνησικακῆσαι τὴν ἡλικίαν ἐξ ἧς ἐνεοττοτροφήθης).

36 Cf. the exchange between Sausage-Seller and Demos, Ar. *Eq.* 1178–80: 'Athena sends you this meat cooked in its own gravy, along with this dish of tripe and some paunch.' [Demos]: 'She did well to remember the peplos I offered her' (Καλῶς γ' ἐπόησε τοῦ πέπλου μεμνημένη). See also the comic recollection of the battle of Naxos of 460 BC, Ar. *Vesp.* 354: 'Do you recall how (μέμνησαι δῆθ' ὅτ'), when you were with the army at the taking of Naxos, you descended so readily from the top of the wall by means of the spits you had stolen?'; and the fond recollection of the happy times when there was no war, *Pax* 571 (ἀλλ' ἀναμνησθέντες ὦνδρες τῆς διαίτης τῆς παλαιᾶς). In *Eq.* 268, μνημεῖον ἀνδρείας is at the core of a civic (demagogic) honorary proposition whose effect would be the building of a monument celebrating forever the memory of the Athenian warriors' deeds. For other examples of recollection, see e.g. *Vesp.* 449; *Eccl.* 22.

37 Loss of children in war: Ar. *Lys.* 588–90 (at Lysistrata's complaint that the women carry double the weight of the war, giving birth and then sending their children as hoplite, the magistrate answers 'Silence! let that memory sleep!', Σίγα, μὴ μνησικακήσῃς). For bad memories of wars, see also Ar. *Pax* 1275: οὐ παύσει μεμνημένος ἀσπίδος ἡμῖν; Ar. *Plut.* 1146 (civil war): Μὴ μνησικακήσῃς, εἰ σὺ Φυλὴν κατέλαβες.

38 Ar. *Vesp.* 1122–64; *Nub.* 223–803; Eup. *Taxiarchoi*, F 269 K.-A.; Alex. *Linos* F 140 K.-A.

39 Ar. *Vesp.* 1122–64; *Nub.* 223–803.

40 Ar. *Nub.* 414: εἰ μνήμων εἶ καὶ φροντιστὴς καὶ τὸ ταλαίπωρον ἔνεστιν ἐν τῇ ψυχῇ. See also 129 and Dover 1968 ad loc.

requires memory from those yearning to follow on his path (βραχέα σου πυθέσθαι βούλομαι,/εἰ μνημονικὸς εἶ).[41] In his eagerness to be admitted to the *Phrontistērion*, Strepsiades, assessed by his Master in a parody of *dokimasia*, reveals the selective aspects of his memory and the cunning nature of his character: he considers himself fit for the instruction he aims to acquire as he has a good memory – that is to say, a good memory when someone owes him something, but none otherwise.[42] This malicious affirmation also mirrors his conception – or misconception – of the *logoi* that the comic Socrates is supposed to teach:[43] Strepsiades desires to master the most enchanting and powerful discourse ever, the clever discourse able to bend and change reality, or rather the laws, written or unwritten.[44] Once competent in these matters Strepsiades will be able to sweep away the tantalizing memories of his debts, to wipe them out definitively not only from his consciousness and from its double, the *grammateion* in which they are inscribed,[45] but also from his creditors' – or so he thinks. As the comic plot evolves, it becomes clear that Strepsiades' mind is not fit for Socrates' teaching: his memory, just as a sieve, cannot retain anything.[46]

The entire scene depicting Strepsiades' education is central to our concerns with memory. Aristophanes makes the most of Socrates' comic pedagogical methods, confronting two ill-assorted characters speaking different languages. Strepsiades is unable to incorporate Socrates' twisted philological, materialistic or 'philosophical' teachings, meant to brush away his old mind and memories, and to prepare the ideal ground whence the discourse Strepsiades is eager to master will sprout. Being short-sighted, Strepsiades fails to understand the real or the technical meaning of the terms *mnēmōn* and *mnēmonikos*, respectively used by the Clouds and by Socrates. From the viewpoint of the comic Socrates, to be gifted with good memory, *mnēmonikos*, implies the capacity to acquire by training

---

[41] Ar. *Nub.* 483; compare Pl. *Resp.* 486c–d: the forgetful soul (ἐπιλήσμονα ψυχήν) cannot be considered among the competent lovers of wisdom, because it is steeped in oblivion (λήθης πλέως) and so cannot retain knowledge; the philosophical soul must be gifted with memory (μνημονικὴν αὐτὴν δεῖν εἶναι).

[42] Ar. *Nub.* 483–5: δύο τρόπω, νὴ τὸν Δία./ἢν μέν γ᾽ ὀφείληταί τι μοι, μνήμων πάνυ,/ἐὰν δ᾽ ὀφείλω σχέτλιος, ἐπιλήσμων πάνυ. See also *Nub.* 487, and, for another example of selective memory, Metag. *Aurai or Mamakuthos*, F 2 K.-A. It is no coincidence if Cratinus uses the same vocabulary in his *Panoptai*, F 162 (ἀλλοτριογνώμοις ἐπιλήσμοσι μνημονικοῖσιν): Aristophanes and Cratinus are using and mocking a technical vocabulary pertaining to the philosophical discourse.

[43] Ar. *Nub.* 112–15; 657.

[44] Ar. *Nub.* 98–9; 239–62. See also 1038–43 in which this personified Discourse presents himself and his craft onstage.

[45] Ar. *Nub.* 19–20.

[46] Ar. *Nub.* 492; 627–31; 646; 654; 785–90.

an immediate memory,[47] thanks to the constant examining of reality and the dialogic method.[48] This training gives access to new information that should be internalized, stored into memory. *Mnēmōn* is he who is able to remember what he has learned or has been taught, to summarize, to join in the abstract dialogue, to think freely, to create, to live by his own mind, and even dare to cross the traditional boundaries of knowledge, as the comic Socrates does.[49]

From the beginning Socrates understands that Strepsiades is clumsy and forgetful.[50] Nonetheless, he tries to instruct him, but eventually sends Strepsiades home when he observes that his forgetful disciple is also unable to meditate.[51] But even if Strepsiades shows his total inability to retain new ideas or theoretical concepts, to conceptualize, to internalize the rudimentary knowledge required to follow Socrates' steps, in short his inability to embrace a *mousikē* that goes further than elementary spelling, maths or memorization of trivia, he is not totally deprived of memories. In fact, his dreadful debts hang on his mind as his creditors before his door.

Nor are the Socratic lessons entirely lost on Strepsiades. Somehow varnished by the teaching methods and the ideas he has picked up from the comic Socrates, and mimicking his Master, Strepsiades persuades his son of the relevance of Socratic instruction and convinces him to enter the *phrontistērion*.[52] He also gets rid, at least temporarily, of his creditors,[53] encouraged by his son's skills. Strepsiades proves his point: he has a good memory, but not when asked to pay his debts. However when his son, thanks to his youth and memory, becomes Socrates' comic double, breathing subtle ideas and mastering perfectly the discourse that Strepsiades was so eager to possess, he cannot stand the extent of his

---

[47] On this topic, see Cerri 2012: 182–3. On techniques used for training memory, see Pl. *Hipp. Mai.* 285e; *Hipp. Min.* 368d–369a, and Sassi's chapter below, 346–8; on its dangers: *Phdr.* 274e–275a.

[48] On memory in the dialogic encounter, see Cerri 2012: 182–3. Aristophanes parodies Socrates' dialogic method, transforming it into a question-answer barren exercise, Strepsiades being impervious to the pursuit of knowledge.

[49] For an interesting analogy on this point with the Platonic Socrates, cf. Wygoda's chapter in this volume.

[50] Ar. *Nub.* 628–31 (οὐκ εἶδον οὕτως ἄνδρ' ἄγροικον οὐδαμοῦ/οὐδ' ἄπορον οὐδὲ σκαιὸν οὐδ' ἐπιλήσμονα,/ὅστις σκαλαθυρμάτι' ἄττα μικρὰ μανθάνων/ταῦτ' ἐπιλέλησται πρὶν μαθεῖν); 790 (ἐπιλησμότατον καὶ σκαιότατον γερόντιον); 785–6 (ἀλλ' εὐθὺς ἐπιλήθει σύ γ' ἄττ' ἂν καὶ μάθης./ἐπεὶ τί νυνὶ πρῶτον ἐδιδάχθης; λέγε.). See also 492 (ἄνθρωπος ἀμαθὴς οὑτοσὶ καὶ βάρβαρος); 655 (ἀγρεῖος εἶ καὶ σκαιός).

[51] Ar. *Nub.* 695–9; 723–90.

[52] See particularly Ar. *Nub.* 814–45.

[53] Ar. *Nub.* 1214–302.

misfortune. His unrestrained Socratic son not only disrupts his life and his musical memory,[54] but eventually also the city.

But the play on memory goes further. In fact, by having Socrates train Strepsiades onstage, the comic poet is also instructing the audience to appreciate, to judge and to get the measure of the accuracy of Strepsiades' instruction and memory, and its gaps. In other words, whether they want to or not, the audience are invited to take Socrates' part and respond with a boisterous laughter to Strepsiades' clumsiness, as clever men should do. In a way Aristophanes transforms the audience into an enclosed Socratic circle forbidden to the delusional Strepsiades. With Socrates and his disciples he only shares the shabby appearance, the lack of cloak and shoes.[55]

Strepsiades' training is a comic disaster. Till the end of *Clouds*, Aristophanes plays with his character's selective memory and his inability to think properly. Burning the *phrontistērion*, Strepsiades proves that he forgets or chooses to forget that Socrates cannot be accountable for Strepsiades' own choice and its consequences.

In *Clouds*, the poet plays with memory in order to make fun of philosophical ideas and enquiries, and particularly of Socratic maieutic. This is perhaps why, in this comedy, the Clouds, forming the chorus, replace the Muses, Memory's daughters, vouching for the comic Socratic *paideia* or *mousikē*. As the Muses, these goddesses first sing their father,[56] then Athens and the *Dionysia*,[57] becoming not only the patronesses of the philosophers but also of all poets and men whose crafts spring from their mind.[58] In other words, the Clouds are the new Muses, who hail Strepsiades as the 'hunter of speeches dear to the Muses'.[59] This is perhaps why they require memory from those seeking to follow their path.

2.1   *Musical Memory, Action and Reception*

Learning and training transform the acquired memories into action, that is to say, into performances. The fourth-century comic poet Dionysius (I) presents, in *The Men who Shared a Name*, a Master Chef instructing an apprentice: after a long monologue in which a Head Cook teaches him how

---

[54] Ar. *Nub.* 1353–78.
[55] Ar. *Nub.* 501–2; for Socrates' and his disciples' appearance, *Nub.* 102–4. On this topic, see Stone 1977: 441–2; Dover 1968: 501–2; Fisher 1984: 145; Cerri 2012: 186–7.
[56] Ar. *Nub.* 270–1; 275–8. See Hes. *Theog.* 42–52.
[57] Ar. *Nub.* 298–313.
[58] Ar. *Nub.* 316–18; 331–3.
[59] Ar. *Nub.* 358: θηρατὰ λόγων φιλομούσων.

to buy food, and how to prepare and serve a banquet, the apprentice is asked
to remember what he is being taught and to act accordingly.[60] Memory
here should equal action, that is to say, the transformation of a theoretical
learning into deeds: in this case, how to become in turn a reputed cook. But
the master's words also convey a command or a comic menace: the apprentice must stick to his own ground, never trespassing on the established
boundaries that characterize their relationship. Long before the production
of Dionysius' play, Aristophanes had, in his *Women at the Thesmophoria*,
dealt with the role of memory in a scene of dramatic instruction aimed at
preparing the student for a dramatic performance. At the same time, in
Women at the Thesmophoria, a play concerned with *mimēsis*, the poet offers
a comic reflection on why apprenticeship of musical memory is important.
By enhancing the audience's ability to appreciate a drama, the poet aims to
obtain the desired victory in the dramatic competition.

Having learnt that the women assembled in the *Thesmophorion* are
going to sentence to death the poet who insults and mistreats them in his
dramas,[61] Euripides persuades his Inlaw to disguise himself as a woman,
in order to attend their assembly and present the poet's defence.[62] Lacking
the ability to merge with the character he is supposed to play, and thus
unmasked, the Inlaw risks an outrageous punishment. As Euripides' double
in cunning, he chooses a *mēchanē* issued from Euripides' craft to save himself. Mimicking the cunning Palamedes, he sends a message to Euripides,
but this fails to bring the poet on stage. Eventually, as the Inlaw plays Helen's
lament from another of Euripides' plays, the poet appears as Menelaus. But
even together they cannot move the women, so another Euripidean trick is
needed, out of the myriads he has in stock.[63] Euripides had not instructed
his Inlaw to perform pieces from his *Palamedes* or *Helen*. But when the poet
appears in the *parodos* costumed as Perseus, the Inlaw recognizes his cue.
Accordingly, he responds playing Andromeda's part, all the more convincingly, since the Scythian archer to whose care the women have consigned
him has fastened him to a post, tightening his bonds, exactly as Andromeda
had been bound.[64] But Euripides' tragic plot fails to free his Inlaw from the
women's grip; as a tragic hero, the poet faces now an *aporia*:

---

[60] *Homonymoi* F 3 K.-A. See also Dionysius, *Thesmophorus*, F 2 K.-A.; and Rusten 2011: 566–8.
[61] Ar. *Thesm.* 82–5; 181–2; 372–9.
[62] Ar. *Thesm.* 71–86. See also 181–2; 372–9.
[63] Ar. *Thesm.* 927. On Euripides' *mēchanai*, see Beta 2004: 232–7.
[64] Ar. *Thesm.* 1004.

Αἰαῖ· τί δράσω; Πρὸς τίνας στρεφθῶ λόγους;
Ἀλλ' οὐκ ἂν ἐνδέξαιτο βάρβαρος φύσις.
Σκαιοῖσι γάρ τοι καινὰ προσφέρων σοφὰ
μάτην ἀναλίσκοις ἄν. Ἀλλ' ἄλλην τινὰ
τούτῳ πρέπουσαν μηχανὴν προσοιστέον.

Alas, what shall I do? To what speeches shall I turn?
But the barbarian nature couldn't grasp them.
To lavish strange ingenuities upon yokels
Would be in vain. Some other device,
Suitable for this man, must be brought out.[65]

In a fit of pique, Euripides attributes his failure to the Scythian archer's barbarian nature. Quoting a line of his own *Medea*, he underlines the uselessness of offering the hapless something wise.[66] Euripides is here not so much pointing out the archer's origins as rather underlining his ἀμαθία, exactly as Socrates had done with Strepsiades in *Clouds*.[67] In this case, the problem is the Scythian archer's lack of musical memories, and consequently his inability to yield to the power of *mousikē*.[68] But Euripides' plots fail also to move Kritylla, one of the women participating in this comic *Thesmophoria*. For this reason, Austin and Olson suggest that the poet's failure is to be explained by the 'immense gap between tragic fiction and what passes within the play for real life'.[69] Without excluding this hypothesis, perhaps we should also consider that Kritylla, as a woman celebrating this particular *Thesmophoria*, could not have been inclined, far from it, to be moved by the re-staged Euripidean plays, even though, in the chosen excerpts, the poet does not mistreat women. As for the Scythian, he is not moved by the tricks of Euripides or the Inlaw because he falls short in dramatic experience.

Whatever the exact interpretation of the details, at the core of this scene are *mimēsis* and dramatic reception. They are closely linked to the training of memory, which in turn goes hand in hand with the dramatic experience or the frequentation of the theatre.

---

[65] Ar. *Thesm.* 1128–32.
[66] Cf. Eur. *Med.* 298, with Austin and Olson 2004: 332.
[67] Ar. *Nub.* 492: 'this man is an ignorant and a barbarian' (ἄνθρωπος ἀμαθὴς οὑτοσὶ καὶ βάρβαρος). On this scene, see Hall 1989: 38–54.
[68] Aristophanes plays with the regular and the technical meanings of δράσω and ἐνδέχομαι, stressing Euripides' craft and the failure of its reception.
[69] Cf. Austin and Olson 2004: 331, on *Thesm.* 1128–9.

2.2   *Musical Training*

The comic poets or their coryphaei, supposedly speaking in their names in the *parabaseis*, emphasize the importance of their civic role as guides, advisers and teachers. Their flattering utterances, the memories they share with the *polis*, cover not only political issues but also poetic ones. And their recollections, as well as those of their characters, are used as a training method to enhance the audience's sharpness and promote a better reception of their plays.

At the beginning of *Frogs*, Dionysus consults Heracles in order to find the shortest and easiest way to Hades: he is determined to descend there and take back Euripides to the Athenian theatre. Asked why he does not choose another poet, he answers that he desires a poet able to enounce lines such as 'Ether the little bedchamber of Zeus' or 'the foot of time', 'the heart does not want to swear by the victims, but the tongue swears aside from the heart'.[70] These are very recognizable allusions to words that Euripides' characters pronounced in his *Melanippe, Alexander* (and then again in *Bacchae*) and *Hippolytus* respectively.[71] Without any doubt, these words revealed to the audience the identity of the poet loved by Dionysus. There is no need, in these lines, to use the vocabulary of recollection because it is clear that he who read with passion Euripides' *Andromeda* is quoting the very best of his favourite poet. But could Aristophanes' public recognize and remember these lines? In other words, was the audience competent enough to recognize a given quotation, the parody of a given plot or of a given scene?

Some answers have been suggested.[72] The ancients' ability to memorize was probably superior to ours; at least part of the audience had served as poets-*didaskaloi*, actors or choruses during the Athenian contests; spectators, such as Dionysus in *Frogs,* could read;[73] the highlights of a drama could be sung, declaimed, performed at banquets[74] and even in the courts[75] and on the streets;[76] reprisals of tragedy or comedy did exist.[77] But in addition, comic poets trained their audiences' memory.

---

[70] Ar. *Ran.* 100–2.
[71] Eur. fr. 487 and 42 Kannicht; *Bacch.* 888; *Hipp.* 612.
[72] Cf. Mastromarco 1997: 530–48 and 2006a: 137–91; Revermann 2006a: 99–124.
[73] *Ran.* 52–4; 145–51; 1109–18. Cf. Mastromarco 2006a: 137–91.
[74] *Daitales* F 234 K.-A.; *Eq.* 529–30; *Nub.* 1354–76; *Gerytades* F 161 K.-A.; *Ran.* 1302; Ephipp. F 16 K.-A. with Lai 1997: 143–8; Imperio 2004: 197–200; Zimmermann 2006: 53–6, Mastromarco 2006b: 265–78.
[75] *Vesp.* 578–87. Cf. Milanezi 2000: 369–96.
[76] *Vesp.* 219–20. Cf. Mastromarco 2006a: 153.
[77] *Vita Aeschyli* (T A1, 48–9 Radt and T Gm 72–7 Radt), Ar. *Ach.* 9–12 and Mastromarco 2006a: 148–9.

In *Women at the Thesmophoria* the Inlaw, before entering the women's assembly in order to defend Euripides, asks the poet he is serving to swear that, if this adventure turns awry, he will save him no matter what.[78] Euripides is not eager to do so, but, finally, he pronounces his oath, which turns out to be a quote from his play *Melanippe*: 'I swear by Ether, the abode of Zeus'.[79] His Inlaw is not satisfied, and, mocking Euripides, he paraphrases and reverses the scandalous line of Euripides' *Hippolytus* (612: 'My tongue swore, but my mind is unsworn') that was used later on as a proof of Euripides' impiety.[80]

The repetition of these lines, first in *Women at the Thesmophoria* and later in *Frogs*, is meaningful. Aristophanes gives pleasure to his audience by appealing to their musical memories, inviting them to join in laughter as they recognize the explicit *psogos* ('blame') turned against Euripides' poetic skills.[81] Audiences certainly acquired musical competence by attending the contests during the Athenian festivals. But the use of musical or dramatic material in the comic poets' plots enhanced the audiences' musical competence. Some Athenians could, it is true, acquire such competence in other ways. But Aristophanes was performing not for a particular group of intellectuals or upper-class citizens, but for all the citizens of Athens and all those visiting the city and able to secure a place in the theatre.

This public instruction offered in the theatre is a comic device whose goal is the delight of the audience. Perhaps this comic device was congenial to comedy; it is at any rate congenial to Aristophanic comedy.[82] Aristophanes often prepares his audience to follow his plays by introducing information in a given scene, which will be developed later on, or even in a comedy to come.[83] This device is adopted in the construction of

---

[78] *Thesm.* 266–79. By raising in advance the possibility that the Inlaw's performance may go awry, and that Euripides will have to intervene, Aristophanes, as Austin and Olson 2004 point out (commentary on 269–76), is preparing the audience for the action that will be developed in the second half of the play.

[79] Ar. *Thesm.* 272 = Eur. *Melanippe Wise* fr. 487 Kannicht; cf. *Ran.* 102.

[80] Ar. *Thesm.* 275–6: μέμνησο τοίνυν ταῦθ', ὅτι ἡ φρὴν ὤμοσεν, ἡ γλῶττα δ'οὐκ ὀμώμοκ', οὐδ' ὤρκρωσ' ἐγώ ('*Remember* then this, that your mind swore, not merely the tongue, nor did I coerce you'). See Arist. *Rhet.* 1416a 28–31, and on the unreliability or implausibility of the tradition concerning legal lawsuits against Euripides and his friends, Dover 1976: 138–51 (= 1988: 135–58); Kloss 2001: 24–8; Austin and Olson 2004: 143.

[81] Compare below, M. Canevaro's chapter, pp. 150–6, for the explicit appeal to the audience's memory in the speeches of the orators, even when the audience is actually unlikely to remember. Here, the appeal to the audience's memory is implicit; see above, Ceccarelli's chapter, pp. 93–5, for how the audience's memory is implicitly called upon to follow the reformulations and variations of the tragic plots.

[82] Other poets could certainly adopt the same device using or adapting a comic common repertoire. See Heath 1990: 152.

[83] On this see Mastromarco 1987: 239–43 and 1997: 534–6.

comic biographies (Cleon, Cleonymus, Socrates, Euripides, Hegelochus, Cinesias),[84] in the use of silent characters later transformed into talkative ones (Hermes in *Clouds*, Peace in the homonymous comedy), in a turn of line that announces a plot,[85] in poetic parodies or quotations, such as those from Euripides that appear in *Women at the Thesmophoria* and *Frogs*. Since at the end of the day the success of the *didaskalos* depends also on the musical memory of his public, he is himself more than eager to help to build and extend such a memory whenever possible.[86]

Some members of the audience will have been sharper than others, their memory being particularly trained thanks also to their affiliation to a musical or theatrical circle. In *Women at the Thesmophoria*, Aristophanes scrutinizes the relationship between Euripides and his Inlaw, whose performances equal that of accomplished *didaskaloi* and actors. Euripides is portrayed as an accomplished poet, an instructor, a stage director, a costumier and even an actor. As for the Inlaw, he is as full of Euripides as an actor should be. His acting skills go hand in hand with his prodigious memory. Nevertheless, as stressed before, the abilities of the various characters vary: the Scythian archer is impervious to theatrical matters. His only reactions to the Euripidean stimuli are annoyance and boredom. His drowsiness is evidence enough of his feelings.

Thanks to the sleep, or the withdrawal, of the Scythian archer, Euripides comes to an arrangement with his enemies, the women celebrating the *Thesmophoria*.[87] Still, his Inlaw must be freed from the archer's grip. So, as an expert *didaskalos*, Euripides produces a new entertainment whose rehearsal is supposed to occur backstage. Re-entering onstage with a dancer and a flute player, Teredon, Euripides instructs the latter to play a Persian tune, while he asks the dancer (Elaphion: Little Deer) to remember

---

[84] Comic poets could also add to their own comic biographies features that another poet had used in his play. On the borrowing comic system, see Heath 1990: 152.

[85] In *Lys.* 283–4, for example, Aristophanes introduces in a line what will become the plot of the *Women at the Thesmophoria*. If the first version of this play dealing with the women's hatred of Euripides went back to 423 BC, as Butrica 2001: 44–76 and 2004: 1–5 has suggested (*contra*, see Austin and Olson 2003–2004: 1–11), Aristophanes' line should be understood as a commentary on this past production. At any rate, in Aristophanes' comedies, the women's anger against Euripides is rooted in the poet's plots, echoing Aphrodite's words at *Hipp.* 13. For other comic uses of Euripides' hatred for women, see Diph. *Synoris*, F 74 K.-A.

[86] He is not the only one to do so: famously, Euripides and Aeschylus in *Frogs* proclaim the excellence of their instruction: Aeschylus has taught the audience how to defend themselves at war, Euripides, excellence in political life by making the audience clever! Dionysus explicitly states that the poet who does not take his 'pedagogical' role seriously must be dead (as Euripides and Aeschylus are, in a different way). For a variation of Euripides' scandalous line (*Hipp.* 612), see *Adespota*, F *832 K.-A.

[87] Ar. *Thesm.* 1160–72.

his instructions (ἃ σοι καθ᾽ ὁδὸν ἔφραζον ταῦτα μεμνῆσθαι ποεῖν).[88] Euripides' new trick, conceived to fit the archer's rusticity, is a great success. In fact, even Euripides' Inlaw cannot recognize the poet when he appears onstage dressed as an old woman, playing the role of a procuress or madam/*didaskalos* and guiding the dancer in her role as a *hetaira*.[89] He almost succeeds in trading the dancer's favours for one drachma.[90]

The performance of the young dancer is so convincing because she acts according to Euripides' instruction, because her memories are transformed into drama. The show procures great pleasure in the Scythian archer. The spectacle is so enticing that he wants to be a part of it, not as an actor onstage, but as an actor in real life.[91] The archer fails to understand that he is being played with, but, with his hands, he plays unrestrainedly, pawing the young Elaphion. Euripides' trick is the invention of a seduction play, highly suitable for a comedy, and particularly so for a 'women's comedy' on women in tragedy, or on women disgusted by a tragic poet who reveals onstage the feminine nature or the most secret tricks of women. Actually Euripides sticks to the promise he had just made to the women: instead of manhandling them, he manhandles men, exposing their petty desires and routines.

This scene is another masterpiece of Aristophanic comedy, a kind of reversal. Aristophanes, who had been mockingly charged by Cratinus with '*euripidaristophanizein*' (F 342), transforms this *psogos* into a comic character. Not only does Aristophanes '*euripidize*', but in his play he makes the comic Euripides '*aristophanizein*'.[92] The tragic poet, introduced in Aristophanes' own comedy, is forced to create a comedy in order to save his Inlaw. But less than the failure of Euripides' craft, tragedy, Aristophanes is stressing the impressive power of his genius. Even though he is mocking Euripides' devices or theatrical machines, ingenious lines and plots, he pays a huge tribute to the poet whose art fills the Athenian theatre and imbues the Athenian minds with wonders. In *Women at the Thesmophoria*, Aristophanes recreates an entire dramatic contest as, in a comedy, he re-stages a tragic tetralogy. In parodying Euripides' plays, he is at the same time inculcating them into the audience's memory, thus contributing to their celebrity. At the same time, he is somehow preparing his audience to

---

[88] Ar. *Thesm.* 1172–5.
[89] See Ar. *Thesm.* 1160–1; 1177–8; 217 and Austin and Olson 2004 ad loc.
[90] Ar. *Thesm.* 1195.
[91] In this case the above mentioned (p. 125) remarks of Austin and Olson 2004 apply perfectly.
[92] See Voelke 2004: 119; 127–34.

receive his comedies to come, in particular the *Frogs*, in which Euripides is one of the protagonists of a new tragic contest within a comedy.

Training and sharpening his audience's memory, Aristophanes, like his rivals, spreads musical memories, paving the way for the audience's reception of his plays. In other words, his comedies are both a bridge between different performances and performances themselves. At the same time, in the competitive context of the dramatic contests, this allows him to emphasize the range of his craft or genius and to call for the reward that he deserves, memory being also the ground in which reciprocity is rooted.

3   Reciprocity, Scorn and Civic Memories

Comic plots often deal with relationships between human beings,[93] or between human beings and gods.[94] In these instances, memory appears as the ground in which reciprocity (*charis*) is rooted.[95] Re-enacted, good memories become rewards; bad memories produce negligence, silence, oblivion and scorn.

Comic characters and even *didaskaloi,* through the voice of the chorus, constantly call for the rewards they deserve in their role of legitimate defenders and advisers of the Athenians. One of the best examples of this poetic pattern, understood by some scholars as literary criticism, by others as the poetics of competition, is the *parabasis* of the *Knights*, in which Aristophanes recalls the endeavours of his ancestors in the comedic craft, and the Athenian audience's poor responses to them. This *parabasis* is not only a way of reproaching the audience for their past mistakes in judging the play within the competition, as they have done with the old poets; it is also a pledge for his future victory, for the just reward of his own poetic endeavour.[96]

If reciprocity is at the core of this *parabasis*, Aristophanes is also constructing a 'memorial', a monument to comedy. As has been recently shown, by evoking a catalogue of his ancestors in craft, Aristophanes is

---

[93] Philocleon claims that he did not receive a reward for his good deeds, and that those who were benefited by his actions are unwilling to remember them anymore. The Paphlagonian is also at pains to obtain the right answer from the Knights, he who was on the brink of proposing a *mnēmeion* of their *andreia* (*Eq.* 268). See also *Eq.* 1052 and *Adespota* F 821 K.-A.

[94] *Eq.* 1166–80; *Pax* 500–2; 734–64; *Plut.* 791–3. But gods can also help Athenians, regardless of their foolishness: *Nub.* 575–94.

[95] For the connection between memory and reciprocity, see Introduction Section 8, as well as Agócs' and Ceccarelli's chapters in this volume.

[96] *Eq.* 518–40 (reproaches); 507–17 and 541–50 (reflexive praise). Something similar is noticeable also in other plays: *Ach.* 628–64; *Nub.* 545–62. See also *Eccl.* 1155–62.

inscribing in the public memory if not the entire history of the comic genre, then at least a part of it.[97] The names of the poets Aristophanes highlights – Cratinus, Magnes, Crates – as well as the title of their plays and the placing obtained at the Dionysiac contests would later appear in the *Didaskaliai*, an Athenian monumental document inscribed in ca. 278 BC.[98] The number of their victories was also inscribed in the Victors' Lists.[99] Furthermore, their names, if they had competed as trainers of their chorus as well, would have also been recorded in the *Fasti*, inscribed by the middle of the fourth century BC.[100] If some of these records were already available and exposed in some form in Athens during the fifth century BC, we may assume that Aristophanes was alluding to what might have been a new practice in Athens, or simply making fun of a para-dramatic Athenian habit. However, no fifth-century fragment of such a document exists. But archons in charge of the *Dionysia* and *Lēnaia* certainly conserved the civic archives pertaining to the dramatic competition; and the theatrical archives of the Rural *Dionysia* in Attica would have been preserved by the *dēmarchoi* dealing with these festivals.[101]

In the *Knights*, then, Aristophanes was sharing with his audience political and poetical knowledge that was not easily accessible to all; he was building a comic memory that he considered worth preserving. Mixing praise and mockery, in the comic *Didaskaliai* of the *parabasis* of the *Knights* Aristophanes creates a monument to the unselfish courage of *komodododidaskalia*. By doing so, he is at the same time preparing the attack against Cleon that figures in the second part of the *parabasis*, in which another monument to courage is built. By honouring the hoplites and rowers who saved their *polis* fighting against the Medes, Aristophanes mocks Cleon and his supporters who, after a single battle, had probably demanded a civic reward.[102]

---

[97] *Eq.* 518–40. On the list reconstructed by Aristophanes in the *parabasis* of *Knights*, see Olson 2007: 382–3; Biles 2011: 116–18. For the Victors' lists, *IG* II² 2325c, see Millis and Olson 2012: 165.

[98] This date concerns the dedicatory inscription of the *Didaskaliai*, *IG* II² 2853; the earliest datable fragment from the monument of the *Didaskaliai* itself (*IG* II² 2319–23a) refers to 421/0 BC (*IG* II² 2319 col. III, tragic victories at the Lenaea); the record continued until at least ca. 140 or 130 BC. See Pickard-Cambridge 1988: 107–11; Ghiron-Bistagne 1976: 27–8; Mette 1977: III A–D; Millis and Olson 2012: 59–121.

[99] *IG* II² 2325c (comic poets victorious at the Dionysia). See Pickard-Cambridge 1988: 112–20; Millis and Olson 2012: 163–70. For the Lenaian Victors, see *IG* II² 2325E; Millis and Olson 2012: 183–92.

[100] *IG* II² 2318; see Pickard-Cambridge 1988: 104–8; Ghiron-Bistagne 1976: 7–26; Mette 1977: I, col. 1–17; Millis and Olson 2012: 5–58.

[101] It is presumably only due to chance that the part of the monument of the *Didaskaliai* concerning the comic productions of the fifth century is lost, while the *Fasti* are badly damaged.

[102] *Eq.* 574–6. The term *mnēmeion* does not figure in these lines, but Aristophanes is clearly referring to the Athenian honorary decrees granting the benefactors of the city the *megistai timai*. The first

Another example of Aristophanes' play on civic memories and archives appears in the *Acharnians*, in a famous comic scene, the visit that Dicaiopolis pays to Euripides:[103] Dicaiopolis needs Telephus' props in order to give a speech that will convince the Acharnians to accept the peace with the Spartans – a peace that he arranged privately – as not only necessary but also fair and just. As is commonly accepted, this scene is a parody of Euripides' tragedy *Telephus*, a parody concerning *rhēsis*, dress and character, and forming a subtext of the comic play.[104] In this comic masterpiece a tragic playwright becomes a comic actor and a wardrobe master, while the peasant Dicaiopolis (or the comic actor impersonating him) becomes a playwright and a tragic actor. Aristophanes achieves thus one of his poetic goals: the construction of a comic Euripides, the resourceful poet whose dramas are filled with beggars and cripples.

At the same time, in *Acharnians* Aristophanes stages the first comic re-performance of a Euripidean tragedy, the *Telephus*, echoing the re-performances of Aeschylus' plays at the *Dionysia* that had been evoked by Dicaiopolis in the prologue.[105] The scene in which Dicaiopolis visits Euripides deserves consideration not only because of its relationship with the *Telephus*; it also represents the first and only catalogue of Euripides' plays given in a comedy.[106] As Dicaiopolis asks for tragic props, Euripides mentions seven of his characters: Oeneus, Phoenix, Philoctetes, Bellerophon, Telephus, Thyestes, Ino. All these characters gave their names to Euripidean tragedies performed at the Athenian *Dionysia* or *Lēnaia*,[107] as Euripides himself stresses by using the verb *agonizōmai*:

> Τὰ ποῖα τρύχη; Μῶν ἐν οἷς Οἰνεὺς ὁδὶ
> ὁ δύσποτμος γεραιὸς ἠγωνίζετο;

> Which ragged garb? Not that in which Oeneus,
> the ill-starred old man, competed? (*Ach.* 418–19)

Athenian honorific decrees are epigraphically attested in the fourth century BC. However, Gauthier 1985: 95–6 observes that in *Eq.* 573–6 we find the first literary attestation of the grant of honours to Athenian citizens and the procedure to follow in order to obtain them. He concludes that Cleon is perhaps the first Athenian to have asked for such honours.

[103] 395–479.
[104] Cf. Voelke 2004: 117–38; Saetta-Cottone 2003: 445–69; Platter 2007: 143–75.
[105] *Ach.* 9–12.
[106] Ar. *Ach.* 418–34. Aristophanes' *Thesmophoriazusae* does not offer a catalogue of Euripides' drama, but rather the reperformance of bits of different dramas in a comedy, as if *Palamedes*, *Helen* and *Andromeda* were part of a tragic trilogy (*Thesm.* 765–84; 850–916; 1015–74). As for comedy, a comic *didaskalia* can be found in *Nub.* 551–9.
[107] For the testimonia and fragments of these plays, see Kannicht, *TrGF* 5.

Aristophanes here mocks Euripides and his factory of characters and plays, manufactured all in a single mould; but in drawing up a list of Euripides' tragedies, he also creates a comic *didaskalia* of the poet's prizes and success.

Admittedly, the list of tragedies fits well in the encounter between Dicaiopolis and Euripides. The awkward confrontation between the peasant and the poet, the blending of fiction and daily life, the theatrical paraphernalia amidst which they interact were certainly enough to promote laughter. Nonetheless it is significant that Aristophanes deals with a poet's career, counting on the audience's competence or memory.

It is certain that the tragedies mentioned in this scene were produced before 425 BC; but the chronology of Euripides' tragedies is not firmly established.[108] Hence our difficulty in ascertaining whether Aristophanes is following a chronological order or arranging the titles as the result of some metrical constraint, or to produce some specific comic effect. We know that in 439/8, under the archon Glaukinus, Euripides' tetralogy – *Cretenses, Telephus, Alcmeon in Psophis* and *Alcestis* – obtained the second prize.[109] In 432/1, Euripides obtained the third prize with *Medea, Philoctetes, Dictys* and the Satyr play *Harvesters*.[110] Scholars believe that the other tragedies mentioned were produced between 455 and 425 BC.[111] If so, Aristophanes was dealing with a theatrical production spanning between 15 and 30 years.

In the *Acharnians*, Dicaiopolis defines the *Telephus* as an 'old drama' (Ar. *Ach.* 415: *palaion drama*), which perhaps is a witty way of flagging up the fact that the *Telephus* had first been produced 15 years earlier. But, as Olson suggests, comparing the terminology used in the *Fasti*, *palaion* can also mean simply 'performed in a previous festival', that is to say, it can refer to a re-performance of a tragedy.[112] Aristophanes/Dicaiopolis might

---

[108] See Harriot 1962: 6–7. The entries concerning Euripides' theatrical activity in the Athenian *Didaskaliai* are lost, and Aristotle's *Didaskaliai* are preserved only in some ancient *Hypotheseis*: cf. Kannicht, *TrGF* 5 T 60–4. Ancient sources suggest that Euripides competed in Athens for the first time around 456/455 BC: *Vita Eur.* 15 and 32. Note however that the Parian Marble, a not very reliable source on theatrical matters, places his début around 442/441 (*FGrHist* A 60; see the list of *testimonia* in Kannicht, *TrGF* 5: T 1 for the 'Life', T 6–9 for catalogues of plays, T 55–9 for his theatrical début). According to the anonymous author of the *Vita Eur.* 16, the poet had produced ninety-two dramas; see also *Suda* ε 3695 Adler (Kannicht, *TrGF* 5 T 1 and 3, respectively).

[109] *Alcestis Hypothesis* b 4–7 (ed. Parker) = Kannicht, *TrGF* 5 T 63. This source matches information pertaining to *Didaskaliai*. But the text is not complete: it lacks information concerning the context of Euripides' drama production, the titles of Sophocles' tragedies and details of the third poet whose name and titles are lost.

[110] Cf. the *Hypothesis* of Aristophanes the Grammarian to the *Medea* (p. 90, 4 Diggle).

[111] For the chronology of Euripides' tragedies, see Jouan and Van Looy 1998: xxii–xxiv.

[112] Olson 2002: 68, with reference to *IG* II² 2318. 202 (first re-performance of an old tragedy at the *Dionysia*, in 386 BC) and 317 (first re-performance of an ancient comedy at the *Dionysia*, in 341 BC), and to *IG* II² 2320. 2, as well as Biles 2011: 68–9, who argues for a recent re-performance of the *Telephus*; on the meaning of παλαιὸν δρᾶμα, see Csapo 2004: 69. From 341 onwards, there were

here have in mind a particular occasion on which Euripides' *Telephus* was re-staged, in Athens or in one of the Attic demes. Besides the comic potential of the Euripidean character, a recent re-staging of this drama would partially explain why Aristophanes chooses it as the core of his play, or, as others have put it, as his 'subtext'.[113] Such a re-staging (if it happened) would have ensured that the play was fresh in the memory of the Athenian audience (as we know to have been the case with his references to Palamedes, Helen or Andromeda in *Women at the Thesmophoria*), helping Aristophanes to win the contest. Given that Dicaiopolis mentions the re-staging of Aeschylus' tragedies in the opening of the play, it is perhaps not absurd to suppose that the expression *palaion drama* alludes to the idiom of official documents – inscribed on stone or preserved in the archon's office – that concerned such re-performances. Unfortunately, the available evidence does not enable us to go beyond speculation in this matter: all the known documents pertaining to the Dionysiac contests in Athens date to the fourth century BC or later. It is, however, suggestive that those official documents we have use the same expression as Aristophanes (*palaion drama*) to designate a drama performed in the past. If so, a comic way of referring to these contests found commemoration in official discourse and thus entered the public memory of the city. In a single scene of the *Acharnians*, Aristophanes thus manages to write a chapter of Athenian theatrical history, perhaps even using what possibly was, and certainly would become, the official language of the *Didaskaliai*, *Fasti* and honorific decrees. Awarding praise and scorn, as his Muses did, he builds up the memory of the Athenian contests.

4 Conclusion

Our examination of ancient Greek comedy confirms that this genre played constantly with memory, be it understood as a disposition to learn, as a form of recollection, or as the foundation of a given relationship. It reveals also the 'musical memory' of a given playwright, that is the consciousness of his role as the instructor of a chorus and of the city. Dealing with

two tragic competitions, one for the new or contemporary tragedies, another for the 'old' ones: *IG* II² 2318 col. xii; Csapo and Slater 1995: 405.

[113] Mastromarco 2006a: 150–1 suggests that if Aristophanes was indeed born around 450 BC, he would have been twelve in 438 BC. This means that the tetralogy of 438 BC was possibly the first that Aristophanes attended (so also Sommerstein 1994: 6 and n. 36): his allusions to, and parodies of, this play suggest a 'sentimental' attachment or a tribute to the spectacle that made him embrace the theatrical life.

musical memories in a competitive context, Aristophanes is spreading past memories and creating new ones, whether real or fictional. In a way, the memorialization of all that pertains to the dramatic contests in honour of Dionysus is a means to control all that escapes the jurisdiction of the poet himself: the attribution of actors and *chorēgos* to the *didaskalos*; the *chorēgos'* choice of the members of the chorus; and other aspects of the fabric of these civic manifestations of piety towards the god. In doing so, the poet is competing with others, enhancing, spreading and fixing the memory of his excellence. Being true to himself, he is spreading the undying memory of his Muse. In a way, as comic poets create a comic *polis*, they also provide the memory that suits it. And their memories were, and still are, used to construct the history of the Dionysiac contests, and thus form an important part of the history of Athens.

CHAPTER 5

Memory, the Orators, and the Public in Fourth-Century BC Athens

Mirko Canevaro

The study of memory in ancient Greece in general and in ancient Athens and the Athenian orators in particular has benefited in recent years from a healthy shift in focus. Previous studies examined the poetical and historical allusions in the speeches of the orators with an eye to their political agenda, to their sources and their education, or to the rhetorical functions of these allusions.[1] More recent studies have pointed out how the orators acted within a definite memory community, and how the memories of the past employed in their speeches, rather than being occasional *topoi* or random selections of facts used for the purpose of persuading their audiences,[2] can be used as windows into the Athenians' understanding of their own past.[3] The funeral orations in particular have been read as representing the 'official' version of Athenian history, one that demands recognition and identification in the audience and that defines the very identity of the Athenian citizen.[4] Concepts such as 'collective memory', 'social memory', 'cultural memory', 'intentional history', borrowed from other disciplines or based specifically on the study of Greek history, have enabled scholars to understand how memories are formed, preserved and changed, and have shed light on the meaning of various civic ceremonies, festivals, traditions and institutions.[5]

[1] For the first approach, see e.g. Perlman 1961. For the second, it is sufficient to quote Jacoby *FGrHist* IIIb Suppl. 1, p. 95: 'Even leaving out of consideration the truly astonishing ignorance of most of the Attic orators and the little use they made of the history of their city ...' For the third, see e.g. Jost 1935 and Nouhaud 1982, in particular 29–133.

[2] See e.g. Buckler 2000 and for a notable example early in the twentieth century, Mathieu 1914.

[3] See e.g. apart from Thomas 1989, Clarke 2008: 245–303 and the extensive studies of Steinbock 2013b and Shear 2011.

[4] See e.g. Loraux 1986; Thomas 1989: 196–237; Parker 1997: 131–41.

[5] Cf. Alcock 2002: 1–35 and, more extensively (but not in relation to the ancient world), Fentress-Wickham 1992 for social memory. For *kulturelle Gedächtnis*, see in particular Assman 1992. For the concept of intentional history, see Gehrke 2001 and Foxhall-Gehrke-Luraghi 2010. For an intelligent discussion of memory in the ancient city and the applicability of Pierre Nora's concept of 'places of memory' (Nora 1984–92) to the Greek world, see Ma 2009. For up-to-date discussions of social memory with an eye to ancient Athens, see Steinbock 2013b: 1–96, Shear 2011: 6–12, 2013.

Moreover, the parameters of the enquiry have widened to include other media: statues, inscriptions and spatial landmarks constructed and fostered memory as a shared and defining feature of a community's identity.[6] At the same time, work on oral traditions has corrected many misconceptions about how memory is transmitted, and provided a counterbalance to the focus on the collective nature of memory, thus helping to avoid essentialist excesses: there is not one memory community (at the level of the *polis*); there are many, connected to particular groups, areas and families, and all preserving their particular versions of the past, transmitted mainly through oral communication.[7] The *polis* is the stage on which these traditions confront one another and are negotiated. If one had to sum up these scholarly developments, one might say that the focus has shifted from the orators to their audiences.[8]

As a result of this shift, the understanding of the orators' uses of memory has also shifted: if the orators were often described in previous works as either ignorant or liars, recently they have come to be portrayed as careful and somewhat circumspect narrators of stories that their public, or sections of their public, already knew, since they were part of the cultural heritage either of a particular memory community or of the community at large.[9] This picture of a public that already remembers most of what it hears, and of orators who have very little space for manoeuvre, needs qualification.[10]

The existence of some shared memories of the past and of distinctive memory communities does determine what an orator can or cannot say,

---

Modern approaches to social/collective memory have their origin in the ground-breaking work of Maurice Halbwachs, on which see Giangiulio 2010, with discussion of modern developments (cf. also Proietti 2012).

[6] See e.g. Csapo-Miller 1998: 87 and *passim*, Boedeker 1998, Alcock 2002, Higbie 2003, Ma 2009, Lambert 2010, Luraghi 2010, Osborne 2011 and Shear 2011: 12–14 for a discussion and *passim* for an example of how these materials can be taken into account.

[7] Cf. Fentress and Wickham 1992: IX, who criticize Halbwachs's excessive focus on the collective nature of memory, and Alcock 2002: 24 n. 37 and Grethlein 2003: 26–7 for other critics and criticism. Giangiulio 2010 on the other hand shows that essentialist excesses are mostly due to misreadings of Halbwachs. For the study of oral tradition, see especially Vansina 1985, and most importantly Thomas 1989 for the implications of this study for ancient Athens.

[8] See Clarke 2008: 245–6 for similar remarks on what the orators have to offer to the study of ancient attitudes toward the past.

[9] See e.g. Perlman 1961 and Nouhaud 1982 for the former assessment, Thomas 1989 and Ober 1989, especially at pp. 177–82, for the latter. Finley 1975: 29 also envisages very tight parameters for what an orator could or could not say about the past. Clarke 2008: 245–303 is right to point out the dual nature of the orators' approaches to their past, which are descriptive (buying into what the audience is familiar with) and prescriptive at the same time.

[10] For an interesting and nuanced analysis of the relationship between orators and masses in the late Roman Republic, which develops and problematises the insights of Ober 1989, see Morstein-Marx 2004.

but it does so according to the attitude towards memory adopted by the orator and his public. This is to say: is the audience's understanding of the reality of their cultural memory (what they should know) an accurate picture of what they actually remember? If it is not, are the orators aware of this? Do they show any signs of using this for their rhetorical purposes? Is it a disadvantage for an orator to allude to historical facts, or to poetry that is unknown to his public? Are there any clear boundaries that determine which memories are considered appropriate, and which are not? This chapter will try to address these, and related, questions. Its aim will be to understand, through the orators' allusions to memories of the past and of poetical texts primarily, but also of laws, recent events and debates, what the audience considered appropriate for an Athenian citizen to remember. It will also assess whether the orators shared uncritically these assumptions, or rather possessed, through reflection and training, a superior understanding of how and what their audience did in fact remember.[11]

When it comes to such questions, in spite of the new understanding of the importance of memory – of laws, of historical facts, of poetry and other cultural artefacts – as key to Athenian identity, an old and widespread contention seems to have gone unchallenged. Scholars still hold that an Athenian orator could remember too much. In other words, it was a disadvantage to demonstrate knowledge beyond that of the average Athenian, which could potentially alienate the audience.[12] Ober in his landmark study 'Mass and Elite in Democratic Athens' discusses the allegedly suspicious attitude of the Athenian *dēmos* toward history and poetry as a notable example of 'the highly ambivalent attitude of the *dēmos* toward the entire subject of rhetoric, rhetorical ability, and rhetorical education'. An Athenian orator, in order to persuade his public effectively, had to be careful not to appear 'a well-educated man giving lessons in culture to the ignorant masses'.[13]

Now, if a 'rhetoric of anti-rhetoric' is clearly to be found in the orators – and it is undeniable that the orators took great pains to present themselves as unskilled, inexperienced speakers and each other as deceitful sophists[14] – it is far from clear how memory of historical facts and poetical texts could

---

[11] By doing this, it will attempt to draw a picture for Athens of the 'set of norms whose function is to regulate the inherent *debatability* of the past' (Appadurai 1981: 201 and *passim*), and therefore in what ways the past in Athens was a 'scarce resource'.

[12] See e.g. Pearson 1941: 212–21; North 1952: 26; Perlman 1964: 135; Ober 1989: 177–81; Ober-Strauss 1990: 250–5; Wolpert 2003: 540; Clarke 2008: 249 n. 14.

[13] Ober 1989: 179.

[14] See e.g. Dover 1974: 25–6; Ober 1989: 170–4 and in particular Hesk 1999 and 2000: 202–41.

be understood as part of a specialist rhetorical education, the province of skilled sophists concerned with deceiving decent Athenians with their craft. Historical instruction and poetical education were in fact part of the intellectual baggage of the average Athenian, provided by the city itself on very public occasions, be it the historical narrative of a funeral speech, the paintings in the Stoa Poikile, an honorary inscription in the Agora, a rhapsodic competition during the Panathenaea or the tragic competition at the Dionysia.[15] If the city itself publicly and relentlessly fostered the memory of the past and a common cultural identity, it is surprising that an orator needed such caution when using historical and poetical examples to argue his point. But did he? To find out whether this view withstands scrutiny it is necessary to reassess the evidence for such an ambivalent attitude of the Athenian *demos* toward memory of the past as well as of cultural artefacts like poetry.

First of all, the orators often introduce historical examples and narratives with a claim that they heard them from their elders. To give only a few examples, Demosthenes at Dem. 20.52 remembers how some brave Corinthians helped the Athenians following their defeat against the Spartans near the Nemean river in 394, and were exiled for this (Diod. 14.83; Xen. *Hell.* 4.2.14–23; Plut. *Ages.* 16.4). He introduces his narrative with the words: 'In describing these events to you, I am obliged to rely on what I have heard from the older men among you.'[16] At Dem. 4.24 he again recalls some facts about the Corinthian War and makes it clear that he knows them because he heard about them. At Dem. 19.277, after mentioning the case of Epicrates, condemned to death following an embassy, Demosthenes once again remarks that he knows from the stories of the elders that Epicrates was a good man and a democrat. In summarizing a speech he delivered in the Assembly, Aeschines (2.75–8) provides examples of errors made by Athenians in the Peloponnesian War and ends his discussion by remarking that he heard these stories from his closest relatives, and in particular from his father. And again Aeschin. 3.191 recalls that the Thirty annulled the possibility of bringing *graphai paranomōn* (public actions against illegal decrees),[17] and seals his account of the episode

---

[15] In fact, as Nouhaud 1982: 109 and Trevett 1990: 419 rightly note, there is no reason to think that history ever was in Athens an element of rhetorical education.

[16] The translations used in this chapter are those of the University of Texas Press 'The Oratory of Classical Greece' series, unless I indicate otherwise.

[17] We know from Thuc. 8.67.2 and [Arist.] *Ath.Pol.* 29.4 that the *graphē paranomōn* was abolished in 411, but Aeschines is our only evidence for 404.

by claiming that he often heard this story from his father, who took part in all the city's struggles.

Pearson interpreted these remarks as evidence that an orator had to fashion his historical examples so as not to give the impression of being 'a scholar or ... a particularly diligent student'. Ober explains them by claiming that 'allusions to the memory of the older citizens or of one's own ancestors allowed the orator to avoid assuming the role of an educated man instructing his inferiors'.[18] But do such remarks necessarily lead us to this conclusion? In fact, what the orators are doing with them is nothing more than using the older members of the audience, or the older members of their family, as guarantors of the trustworthiness of the information they are providing. They are relying on their authority as eyewitnesses to support their statements, and exploiting the reverence the Athenians had for their elders to discourage them from questioning the accuracy of their historical reconstructions.[19] For what all the historical allusions I have listed have in common is that the events alluded to happened too far back for the orator to have been an eyewitness, and they are unlikely to have been matters of common knowledge. To argue that the orators were trying to avoid the risk of sounding like bookish scholars educating their inferiors is to assume what needs to be proven, specifically that the orators were not in fact told about these episodes by somebody, but found (read) about them in some other way, which they had an active interest in concealing.

The orators' use of literary sources, particularly historical works such as those of Herodotus and Thucydides, has been much discussed, and it is now widely recognized that although an orator could occasionally show some awareness of these works (the only two unequivocal cases are Lys. 2.48–53 and [Dem.] 59.97–103),[20] in most cases they did not make use of literary sources. Conversely, Thomas has shown that they did rely extensively on oral traditions and that alternative oral traditions, originating

---

[18] Pearson 1941: 217–8; Ober 1989: 181. Clarke 2008: 249 n. 14 seems to agree with this analysis. See also Worthington 1994: 113–4; Wolpert 2003: 540.

[19] A transparent enunciation of this reverence for the elders is Aeschin. 1.23–4, who attributes relevant norms about the honours to be reserved to the elders in the Assembly to Solon. Ober 1989: 14 and 181–2 recognizes these factors, but fails to draw the implications.

[20] Both passages derive from Thucydides, as noted by Thomas 1989: 202 and 227–9. For Lys. 2.48–53 Walters 1981 argued for an intermediary source, but see Todd 2007: 249–53 and especially 249 n. 57. For [Dem.] 59.97–103, see Trevett 1990 (who believes that Apollodorus had also a second source for the siege of Plataea, cf. pp. 411–5), and Nouhaud 1982: 163–4, Kapparis 1999: 375–88 and Pelling 2000: 61–81 (who believe Thucydides was his only source). It has also been argued, following *Schol. Aeschin. ad* 2.175 (392 Dilts), that the historical narrative of Aeschin. 2.172–6 depends on And. 3.2–9. If Andocides' *De Pace* is an authentic speech from classical Athens, this is certainly the case; but see Harris 2000 who proves that the speech is a Hellenistic forgery.

in different memory communities, often formed the basis of alternative versions of the same historical facts.[21] This is to say, it is possible that the orators' claims that they learnt a particular story from their fathers or from the oldest among the Athenians are in fact more trustworthy than they are given credit for. And even when they are not, they are hardly unusual or surprising as strategies for lending authority to a particular story: Herodotus often asserts the reliability of his accounts by assuring his readers that what he reports, he has heard somewhere (cf. e.g. Hdt.1.20, 2.52: 'I know that … because I heard it at …'). Even Thucydides, while discrediting the value of *akoē* as a historical source (Thuc. 1.20.1, 1.73.2), claims that his account relies either on what he saw himself or on what he heard from those who were present.[22] In this Thucydides is not unlike Demosthenes, who claims that he knows the facts about the Corinthian War not because he was there (he was not yet born) but because he heard the story from older citizens, who presumably were there and saw what happened. So does Lycurgus (1.90) when he mentions the fate of Callistratus, punished for his crimes approximately 25 years before: he assumes that his audience will be aware of these events either because they were there or because they heard about them from those who were. This was in fact the standard way one learned about the past in fourth-century Athens. There is no reason to question the orators' claims that the source of their historical knowledge is what they heard from other citizens. These claims certainly do not indicate that any degree of knowledge of the past was considered excessive.

The orators' strategy in these instances is proactive rather than defensive; they are using the oral testimony of their elders, widely recognized by their public as an authoritative source for the memory of the past, in order to lend authority to their accounts and therefore to their arguments. Those who try to argue against the relevance of the past as guidance for present actions are rather defensive: Demosthenes (19.16) reports to the Athenian judges that Aeschines 'said you should not recall your ancestors or put up with talk of trophies and sea battles but should enact and inscribe a law forbidding you from aiding any Greeks who had not previously aided you'. Demosthenes is alluding to a previous debate in the Assembly about peace with Macedon. His tone is so scandalized that it makes clear that

---

[21] Thomas 1989: 201–2 and *passim*. See also Steinbock 2013b: 21–3. They overstate, however, the extent to which Athens retained the features of an oral society. Writing had a strong impact (cf. Faraguna 2006), that changed substantially the nature of cultural (and oral) transmission. For an example of how writing impacts on oral traditions (in Cyrene), cf. Giangiulio 2001.

[22] On the reference to informers and the fragility of human, psychological memory in Thucydides, and more generally Greek historiography, cf. Darbo-Peschanski's chapter in this volume.

urging Athenians to forget anything of their past was perceived by the audience as preposterous. Demosthenes must have believed this attack against Aeschines to be so effective that he came back to it twice in the rest of his speech: at §307 and again at §311.

Aeschines' answer to this attack (2.63, 75–7) is to claim that he urged the Athenians to remember and emulate the achievements of their ancestors at Marathon, Plataea, Artemisium, in the expedition led by Tolmides into the Peloponnese, but to avoid the mistakes they committed during the Peloponnesian War. Put like this, his words seem sensible. And yet his extensive explanation of what he really meant betrays embarrassment and is defensive;[23] he gives a long account of what he said to contextualize his statements and concludes with the words 'I admit that I urged you to avoid this folly and to imitate the achievements I mentioned just before', at the same time justifying his words and denying that he ever urged the Athenians to forget their past. Making such an argument, however skil-fully, was probably not a good idea, since on such matters as the memory of the city's past it was easy for the audience to become hostile, and easy for an opposing speaker to stir their anger. This example is evidence that for-getting the city's past, exhorting the Athenians to overlook it or even giving the impression of doing so, was a dangerous business, one that could offer an easy target to one's opponents.[24]

Memories of the past had to be somehow substantiated, and the references to the elders were only one of the available strategies. For example, one could use a statue, a monument, or an inscription to corroborate a story about the past. A case in point is the mention by Aeschines (1.182) of the 'place of the horse and girl', the foundations of the empty house where an Athenian father once sealed his daughter, guilty of not having preserved 'her maidenhood honourably'. Aeschines uses the foundations of the building as evidence of the ancestors' 'attitude toward shameful behaviour'. Another interesting example is Aeschines' reference to a statue of Solon in the agora of Salamis. In *Against Timarchus* Aeschines had compared the defendant's wicked character with that of the great statesmen of old, and to provide visual proof of his unworthiness he had pointed out that such great men of the past did not even indulge in the common habit of speaking with the hand outside the clothing, as one could see in the statue

---

[23] Nouhaud 1986 argues that Aeschines was here trying to overcompensate.

[24] Steinbock 2013a argues that this passage is evidence that the prevalent image of the past of the city could be questioned through appeals to alternative family traditions, yet Demosthenes' attack and Aeschines' very defensive reply appear rather to suggest that such a strategy was dangerous and problematic.

of Solon in the agora of Salamis. That statue, Aeschines comments, 'is a representation and a reminder of the posture that Solon in person used to adopt when he spoke to the Athenian people' (Aeschin. 1.25). Conversely, Timarchus just a few days before 'threw off his robe and cavorted like a pancratiast in the Assembly, stripped ...' (Aeschin. 1.26). The statue is used to support Aeschines' statements about a past of which neither he nor any older citizen could have been direct witness.

Rhetorical strategies aimed at highlighting the deficiencies of an opponent's character or actions by pointing out how superior were the practices of the Athenians of old are widespread in the orators and therefore must have been quite effective.[25] They rely however on the correctness of the memory exploited, which must be confirmed through some kind of evidence. Such evidence is in fact the target of Demosthenes' reply to Aeschines' argument: Demosthenes (19.251) does not accuse Aeschines of boring the audience with irrelevant arguments based on the distant past, nor does he blame or ridicule him for showing off antiquarian knowledge of ancient customs. He rather chooses to point out that 'according to the Salaminians, the statue is less than fifty years old, and since Solon lived about two hundred and forty years before, not only was the craftsman who represented Solon in that stance not Solon's contemporary, but neither was his grandfather!' He challenges Aeschines on the ground of historical accuracy. This must have been an effective rhetorical strategy because it suggests that the opponent falsified historical facts to deceive the audience, and qualifies him as a sophist. Yet such a strategy is a viable weapon only in a context in which memory of the past is viewed as desirable and respected.

Such exchanges, with a speaker arguing a point based on the example of the past and the other speaker retorting that his historical information is inaccurate, were not unusual. In his speech *Against Leptines* in 355/4 Demosthenes foresees that Leptines and his *syndikoi* (the advocates elected to defend Leptine's law), in defending a law that abolishes grants of *ateleia* (exemption from liturgies), will point out that 'in the time of our own ancestors, some men who performed good deeds never asked for such a reward but were content to have an epigram inscribed in the district of the Herms' (20.112).[26] Demosthenes' reply, once again, is not that memories of a distant past are irrelevant; he rather proceeds to show that if Leptines is

---

[25] For recent discussions of this strategy and of its ideological and rhetorical implications, see e.g. Grethlein 2010: 127–33 and 140 in particular, and Clarke 2008: 274–82. See also Carey 2005: 77–91.

[26] A similar argument, complete with references to the epigrams in the Stoa of the Herms, is used at Aeschin. 3.183–5 against Demosthenes. See below at pp. 144–5.

claiming that 'these were excellent men who received nothing, he certainly is accusing the city of ingratitude'. Yet 'this charge is not true, not even close'. He shows, through an inscription reporting an honorary decree for Lysimachus moved by Alcibiades,[27] that benefactors of the public were indeed honoured. The honours were different because the city's resources were different, but by no means inferior: Lysimachus received 'twenty-two acres of woodland, the same amount of arable land, and in addition one hundred minas of silver coin, and four drachmas a day'. Demosthenes chooses to prove that the account of the past provided by his opponent is false, but does not argue against the relevance of its use for the present case, nor does he attack Leptines for showing detailed knowledge of the past.[28]

And when an argument similar to that which Demosthenes expects from Leptines is used by Aeschines in a direct attack against Demosthenes himself, with the aim of showing how inappropriate it is to grant him honours when one compares his life and achievements with those of the great men of the past (Aeschin. 3.177–88), the orator still does not dare to dismiss the reference to the past as irrelevant and pedantic. Aeschines keeps clear of sweeping statements that would give Demosthenes an occasion to prove his historical information wrong, and argues his point in painstaking detail; he claims, as did Demosthenes on several occasions (Dem. 23.196–210, 3.23–32 and 13.21–31), that honours and awards have become excessive, while the virtue of the honoured has decreased and almost disappeared. He then proceeds to support his points with examples of great names from the Athenian past such as Themistocles, Miltiades, the exiles from Phyle, Aristides, and urges the judges to compare their achievements with those of Demosthenes. He next quotes a few epigrams from the district of the Herms to show that benefactors were not even allowed to inscribe their names. In his speech *On the Crown* Demosthenes has a hard time refuting this reasoning, and his strategy once again is not that of dismissing any reasoning based on memories of the past: quite the opposite. First of all, at §314, he hastens to say that making references to the great men of the past is commendable (καὶ καλῶς ποιεῖς). His only objection is that, since living men are subject to envy while the dead are not, the comparison is unfair,

---

[27] This inscription was probably a fourth-century forgery. See Davies 1971: 51–2.

[28] Of course Demosthenes does not refrain from using arguments about honours in the past that are very similar to Leptines' when it suits his argument: see e.g. Dem. 23.196–210, Dem. 3.23–32 and Dem. 13.21–31 which I discuss on pp. 146–8. However, his discussion is more nuanced, and he does not deny that honours were granted altogether. He simply claims that the Athenians avoided granting excessive honours and so robbing themselves of their glory. Thus Demosthenes makes sure not to be vulnerable to the same strategy he used against Leptines. The same strategy is used in Aeschin. 3.177–88; see the following paragraph.

and the great men of the past were also objects of slander in their lifetime. The argument is subtle. Demosthenes refrains from dismissing Aeschines' reference to ancestors. In fact, he proceeds to embrace arguments based on the past by claiming that 'anyone who considers it will see that my policies and decisions resemble those made by the eminent citizens of the past and have the same goals as did theirs' (§317). He questions the conclusions Aeschines draws from these memories of the past, but does not question the method. His point is rather that for an Athenian politician who knows the history of Athens, as well as for the Athenian people, fighting Philip was the only honourable choice (§§66–8 and 199–200).[29] Demosthenes thus effectively turns Aeschines' argument upside down: he embraces his reasoning based on the memory of the ancestors, but shows that it supports rather than condemns the award of the crown. Once again the speaker could have accused his opponent of cultural elitism, if this were a viable rhetorical strategy, but chooses to accept the appeal to the memory of the past and make it his own.

In fact, there is to my knowledge no passage in the orators in which a speaker accuses his opponent of elitist erudition or of behaving like a teacher lecturing his inferiors, although the orators often indulge in lengthy historical excursuses, making their educational intent (irritatingly) explicit. The most obvious example of this is Lycurgus' *Against Leocrates*. After reminding the judges of the Ephebic Oath and of the obligations toward the city that it involves (1.75–82), Lycurgus reflects on how Leocrates has betrayed the letter and the spirit of the oath. This provides the occasion for a long series of historical excursuses and poetical quotations, the longest in the orators, running for forty-eight paragraphs (83–130), roughly one third of the speech. This long section of the speech would have irritated the public if the Athenians did in fact hate being lectured about the past (and about poetry).[30] To make matters worse, Lycurgus starts this section of the speech with the remark: 'I want to tell you some brief stories about our past. If you use these as examples, you will make better decisions about both this and other issues.' His self-imposed task seems to be that

[29] Demosthenes' strategy of defending his policies with an argument 'by the burden of the past' is excellently analysed in Yunis 2000.

[30] I am not discussing here funeral speeches, where the historical narratives are even longer, since their role has been extensively analysed and they are representative of a different institution, with different rules, and whose conventions prompt practices that cannot be lumped together with other genres of oratory. I content myself with pointing out that the very existence of these conventions suggests that the Athenians were not prejudiced against being lectured about their past. Indeed, as Milanezi's chapter (above) shows, comic poets would make fun of sophistic teachers (e.g. in Aristophanes' *Clouds*), but also considered themselves as instructors of the city, constructing its (theatrical) memories.

of instructing the judges about the past so that they may be guided in making a decision. Similar remarks are then interspersed throughout the section. At §95 Lycurgus introduces the story about a Sicilian young man who was saved from a stream of fire flowing from Etna as reward for his piety toward his father with the patronising exhortation: 'There is a story, which, even if it is rather fantastic, is suitable for all you younger men to hear.' At §98 the story of Erechtheus is introduced with the words: 'Now pay close attention, for I am not about to turn away from the men of old. Justice demands that you listen to the deeds for which they won respect and take them to heart.' These are hardly the words of a man who is taking pains not to sound too didactic and patronising. And yet Lycurgus almost succeeded in getting Leocrates convicted, despite having a very weak legal basis for his case.[31] In fact, if we were to draw any general conclusion from the speech *Against Leocrates*, we should say that the public did not object to Lycurgus' fondness for telling stories about the Athenian past.[32]

Lycurgus is certainly not an isolated case. Apollodorus in the speech *Against Neaera* goes so far as to provide a ten-paragraph long (§94–104) narrative of all the misfortunes suffered by the Plataeans from Marathon to the destruction of their city in 427 BC in order to make the simple point that it is difficult to acquire Athenian citizenship. In his narrative the orator for once relies on a literary source, Thucydides,[33] and is bold enough to place the Plataeans at Marathon fighting together with the Athenians, against the common practice of the orators of describing Marathon as a solitary Athenian exploit.[34] Yet he does not seem to be worried that the judges might find his long historical excursus pedantic. He wants the judges to learn from his narrative how the law about naturalization originated, and is explicit about his purpose (§93).[35]

Demosthenes too from time to time indulges in lengthy historical excursuses. The most remarkable example is Dem. 23.196–210, where the orator argues that the practice of awarding honours has degenerated in his time, and that the ancestors did not rob themselves of their glory by granting excessive honours like statues to successful generals and politicians, nor did they grant to anyone that whoever might kill him should be arrested;

---

[31] See Harris 2000: 67–75.

[32] For Lycurgus' career and policies, see Faraguna 1992.

[33] See above p. 40 n. 20.

[34] See Walters 1981 and Nouhaud 1982: 149–55 for a discussion of the memory of Marathon in the orators, and the exclusion of the Plataeans. See also Jung 2006 for Plataea as a *lieu de mémoire* for the Athenian *polis*.

[35] Another lengthy historical excursus is found at Aeschin. 2.172–7.

they would rather grant foreigners the honour of citizenship. To show why matters degenerated Demosthenes proceeds with a comparison between the present generation and the ancestors, introduced by a declaration of purpose: 'The responsibility for the situation degenerating so shamefully, if one must frankly speak the truth, men of Athens, lies with none more than you ... Yet consider (καίτοι σκέψασθε) how your ancestors punished those who wronged them and whether you are like them.' And this is why: while the ancestors punished the guilty, now the guilty are too easily acquitted. In the past the private houses of leading citizens like Themistocles and Miltiades were not richer than the average, but public buildings were splendid; now public buildings are 'small and shabby' and private houses ostentatious. The logic of the argument may not be tight (it is not clear how the habit of granting ever-increasing honours to the undeserving could have been caused by Athenian reluctance to punish the guilty), but the very fact of arguing by remembering the past, both the deeds of ancestors and more recent negative examples, seems to lend to the argument enough authority to make it worth pursuing. In fact, the passage was so successful that Demosthenes used it again, with some changes due to different rhetorical needs, on two other occasions: part of it, the comparison, in 349 in the *Third Olynthiac* (3.23–32), and all of it in the speech *On Organisation* (13.21–31).[36]

Thus, references to the memory of the past based on the authority of the elders, a visual landmark, an inscription or the like cannot be taken as evidence of the orators' restraint and reluctance to demonstrate an extensive knowledge of history, but are rather ways in which they claimed authority for their stories. There is plenty of evidence that revealing an accurate and detailed memory of past events was a powerful and effective rhetorical weapon. On the other hand some arguments dealing with poetical knowledge and exhibiting references to poetical texts seem at a superficial reading to suggest that an orator could recall too much poetry and run the risk of sounding like a teacher talking down to his audience. If this reading were correct, then it would prove that a display of excessive awareness of the Athenian and Greek cultural tradition could be perceived as elitist, and therefore alienate the public. By implication, it would be true that the orators did in fact expect their public to have an ambivalent

[36] The authenticity of this speech has been questioned (e.g. by Sealey 1967: 251–3, 1993: 235–7, Badian 2000: 44 n. 70), but the presence in some manuscripts of a total stichometry consistent with that of the other *dēmēgoriai* makes it virtually certain that the speech was part of the original Athenian edition of the Demosthenic *corpus* (see Canevaro 2013: 293–304). The problems found with the text are inconclusive; see Trevett 1994, Lane Fox 1997: 191–5 and MacDowell 2009: 226–7.

attitude toward certain kinds of memory, envisaged as an attribute of the educated elite. Two passages in particular, one at Dem. 19.246–50 and one at Aeschin.1.141, have been used to argue this point.

The first passage is Demosthenes' answer to Aeschines' allegations that he is a *logographos* (i.e., that he writes speeches for others for money) and a *sophistēs*. He refers to Aeschines' quotation and discussion of passages from the poets in his speech *Against Timarchus* (Aeschin. 1.141–54) and points out that Aeschines chose to recite verses from Euripides' *Phoenix* that he never performed as an actor and omitted verses from Sophocles' *Antigone* that he did perform and that would have provided him with good guidance. In Ober's interpretation, excessive knowledge of the poets, and in particular 'to hunt up' quotes from plays that one has no reason to know, is equivalent to sophistry and can be the target of the 'rhetoric of anti-rhetoric' so common in the orators. Remembering too much tragedy, or poetry in general, and showing off this knowledge, could be labelled elitist and ultimately be a disadvantage. According to Ober, there were two kinds of memory, one 'democratic and egalitarian' and one coming from 'specialized research', typical of 'a sophist's training', used 'to trick the average citizens on the jury.'[37] Yet the passage does not warrant this interpretation. Ober translates: 'Oh Aeschines … are you not a logographer … since you hunted up a verse which you never spoke on stage to use to trick the citizens?', yet the Greek is rather different: οὐ σὺ λογογράφος; … ἃ δ' οὐδεπώποτ' ἐν τῷ βίῳ ὑπεκρίνω, ταῦτα ζητήσας ἐπὶ τῷ τῶν πολιτῶν βλάψαι τιν' εἰς μέσον ἤνεγκας.[38] Aeschines should have used Sophocles' verses from the *Antigone* to guide his actions, and he certainly knew them by heart, since he performed them many times. He chose instead to look for different verses that he never performed, and to omit those that were actually useful, for the purpose of damaging his fellow citizens. Demosthenes accuses Aeschines of damaging them (βλάψαι), not tricking them. And this verb is the focus of the expression: he is a sophist because he overlooked what he obviously knew to be appropriate, useful and right and looked for some clever argument for the purpose of damaging his fellow citizens.[39] This is the mark of the *logographos* and *sophistēs* as an irreducibly negative figure antithetical to the democratic ideal. Demosthenes

---

[37] Ober 1989: 173.

[38] 'You are not a speechwriter? … You ignored the verses that you performed many times and knew by heart, but you found verses that you never acted at any point in your life and brought them on the public stage in order to harm a citizen.' Transl. Yunis.

[39] This point against Ober's interpretation is made very effectively by Yunis in his 1991 review of Ober 1989 (*CPh* 86/1: 71).

makes this even clearer at 18.277, where he admits Aeschines' charges of *deinotēs* (cleverness, rhetorical ability) but then claims that 'even if I do have some experience of this kind, you will all find that I always use it … to advance your interests … He, on the other hand, uses his experience in speaking not only to help our enemies but also to harm anyone who has ever annoyed or crossed him; he does not use it fairly or for the benefit of the city.'[40] Thus, the problem with Aeschines' use of poetic quotations is not that he overlooked what he knew from experience and showed off memory coming from specialized research; the problem is that he actively looked for a passage with which he could harm a fellow citizen, and this makes him a sophist. There is no inappropriate, undemocratic memory, only inappropriate uses of memory.

The second passage that seems to suggest a prejudice against displays of excessive knowledge of poetic texts is Aeschin. 1.141. There Aeschines introduces a long series of poetic quotations (the same quotations to which Demosthenes alludes in the passage we have just discussed) with the words: 'But since you remember Achilles and Patroclus and Homer and other poets, as though the jurors are men without education, and represent yourselves as impressive figures whose erudition allows you to look down on the people, to show you that we have already acquired a little knowledge and learning, we, too, shall say something on the subject.'[41] In this passage Aeschines clearly accuses his opponents of posing as men whose superior knowledge and education sets them apart from the judges. The hint of some resentment toward an educated elite seems unmistakable, and the formulation apparently resembles many accusations that one's opponents are skilled *rhētores* (professional orators) and that this gives them an unfair advantage, and therefore the judges should lend the speaker a more favourable ear.[42]

The rhetorical *topos* we find here seems analogous, and therefore exhibited knowledge of poetic texts seems to be liable to attacks very similar to those against rhetorical training. And yet there is a significant difference between the two strategies. All orators rely on the public's mistrust of rhetorical education when they portray themselves as unskilled amateurs fighting

---

[40] See Hesk 2000: 209–19 for an analysis of the irreducibly negative features of the sophist, and where the line must be drawn between a *rhētōr* and a sophist. *Pace* Ober 1989: 187–91.

[41] On Aeschines' quotation techniques, with some texts read out by the clerk and some by himself, see Ford 1999; Olding 2007; Bouchet 2008 with further references.

[42] Some examples are Antiph. 3.2.2, 3.3; Andoc. 4.7; Lys. 19.2; Isoc. 8.5; Isae. 10.1; Dem. 18.6–7, 27.2, 35.40, 37.5, 38.2, 57.1. For discussion, see Dover 1974: 25–8, Ostwald 1986: 256–7, Ober 1989: 170–7, Hesk 2000: 207–9.

against professional rhetoricians. They assume that the audience is, and is proud of being, unskilled in rhetoric, and will not be sympathetic to those who have professional training in public speaking. Professional sophists are in fact considered *ponēroi* (disreputable), as is made clear by Pheidippides in Aristophanes' *Clouds*, against his father's claims that Socrates and his associates are *kaloi kagathoi*, and no Athenian judge would want to be considered one of them.[43] This strategy is very different from what we find at Aeschin. 1.141: the orator here is not relying on the judges' ignorance of poetry, nor is he relying on their mistrust of those who have a poetical education. In fact, he is doing the opposite: he portrays his opponents as questioning the audience's memory of poetic texts, assuming that they will be utterly offended by the insinuation that they do not remember them, and then he rescues the public from this imagined accusation of poetic ignorance by claiming that 'we (καὶ ἡμεῖς) have already acquired a little knowledge and learning, we, too, shall say something on the subject'. It is a cunning strategy that relies on the audience having strong cultural pretentions. This passage therefore, rather than proving that the Athenians were suspicious of extensive poetical education, shows that they aspired to it *themselves*. Aeschines himself recognises this when he states: 'the reason I think we learn by heart the poets' thoughts as children is to make use of them when we are men' (3.135). This presumption of poetic knowledge on the part of the public is due to the fact that poetic ignorance was considered typical of the *ponēroi* (or *kakoi* or *banausoi*: the 'bad', manual labourers).[44] Such a presumption also helps to explain how Demosthenes could pride himself on his impeccable upbringing (Dem. 18.257) and think that his ferocious attacks against Aeschines as an uneducated individual could be effective.[45] Accordingly Aeschines, whose upbringing was certainly not as privileged, strove to prove his status as a *kalos kagathos* (or *chrēstos*, or *gnōrimos*, or *beltistos*: the best, reputable) by showing off his cultural credentials; this is probably why, compared with Demosthenes, he makes particularly intensive use of poetic quotations in his speeches: he has something to prove.[46] The public expected people to participate in the shared cultural and poetical memory, just as they mistrusted those who did not remember the past. Knowledge of poetry was the attribute of the good

---

[43] Ar. *Nub.* 100–25. Additional evidence that the sophists were not considered by average Athenians *kaloi kagathoi* are the remarks of Anytus at Pl. *Men.* 91c, Callicles at Pl. *Grg.* 520a, Laches at Pl. *La.* 197d. Cf. Harris 1995: 28 and 185 n. 30.

[44] Cf. Harris 1995: 17–29.

[45] See e.g. Dem. 18.128, 242, 258. Cf. also Lys. 20.12.

[46] Harris 1995: 28.

and worthy citizen and did not have negative associations, unlike sophistry, which was a trait of the *ponēros*.

Our analysis has shown that as far as memories of the past and poetical knowledge are concerned, there was in Athens a widespread presumption, among both the speakers and the public, that an Athenian should
'remember', and no detectable distinction between appropriate memories
and inappropriate elite education was drawn. Those who did not remember
the Athenian past were attacked for their ignorance. The orators were
aware of this presumption and did not refrain from showing off the extent
of their poetical and historical knowledge, confident that they would thus
strengthen their arguments and enhance their authority. Isocrates (4.9),
the most self-conscious of the orators, makes this explicit: 'For the deeds
of the past are, indeed, an inheritance common to us all; but the ability
to make proper use of them at the appropriate time, to conceive the right
sentiments about them in each instance, and to set them forth in finished
phrase, is the peculiar gift of the wise' (transl. Norlin).

The last step in our analysis, however, is to enquire whether the
Athenians did in fact possess a cultural and historical memory as vast as
they presumed, and expected politicians, to possess. One particular form
of argument may give us a hint; orators often introduce their accounts of
cultural and historical memories with expressions such as 'you all know',
'you all remember', 'let me remind you'. To give only a couple of examples,
in the speech *On the Chersonese* Demosthenes urges the Athenians to take
action against Philip with the words 'You doubtless know that the famous
Timotheus once made a speech before you saying that you should assist
and go to the rescue of the Euboeans ...' (Dem. 8.74). In Demosthenes'
Against Aristocrates the speaker uses the same argument when he asserts
'you certainly know, men of Athens, that you granted Iphicrates the
honour of a bronze statue and the right to dine in the Prytaneion and
other rewards and honours, which were the source of his good fortune ...'
(Dem. 23.130). This rhetorical strategy has often been interpreted as yet
another example of the orators' restraint in displaying historical knowledge.[47] We have shown, however, that there is no detectable trace of such
an attitude, so we must search for another explanation. In fact the *topos* is
found not only in relation to the past, but even more often in relation to
laws, documents and facts about an opponent. Aeschines (1.44) reinforces
his depiction of Timarchus' sexual practices with the statement: 'I find it
very gratifying that my dispute is with a man who is not unknown to you,

---

[47] Cf. Ober 1989: 181; Pearson 1941: 215–19.

and is known for precisely the practice on which you will be casting your vote.' Demosthenes (18.129) slanders Aeschines' mother and then asserts 'everyone knows these things without my having to mention them'. What the orators are trying to do is to imply that the audience should already know whatever they are referring to. The desired outcome is that even those who do not know will assume everyone else does. They will assume that whatever the orator is saying is common knowledge and therefore will accept his statements without questioning them. The orator is playing on the illusion of a face-to-face society where everyone knows everything about everyone else to pass off something he needs his audience to believe as shared knowledge.[48]

That this is what the orators were doing when using this *topos* is confirmed by Dem. 40.53–4. The speaker anticipates his opponent's use of this *topos* and warns the judges that 'if he has no witnesses to prove a fact, he will say that it is well known to you ... This is something which is done by all those who do not have a clean argument ... What anyone of you does not know, let him assume that his neighbour does not know it either ...' Aristotle's explanation of the *topos* (*Rh.* 3.1408a32–6), is no different: 'Listeners react also to expressions speechwriters use to excess: "Who does not know?" "Everybody knows ..." The listener agrees out of embarrassment in order to share in the feelings of all others' (transl. Kennedy).[49] In these cases the orators are relying on the audience's presumption of remembering facts and events. Theirs is subtle misdirection, whose ultimate aim is once again to claim authority for their statements: and the source of the authority this time is the audience themselves. If the audience does not know what the orator is talking about, or does not remember confidently enough to question the speaker, they will assume that everyone else does and accept the speaker's statements. The use of this *topos* in such arguments is evidence that the orators were to some extent aware of the audience's beliefs and presumptions, and they were aware that what their hearers assumed was appropriate for them to know often did not correspond to what they actually did know. The orators used this as a rhetorical loophole to gain the trust of their hearers.

Even more significant is their use of this *topos* in relation to knowledge of the laws of the city, since this knowledge was considered one of the key

---

[48] Finley 1973: 17–18, 1983: 28–9 believed that Athens was indeed a face-to-face society, but see Osborne 1985: 64–5 and Ober 1989: 31–3.

[49] For an excellent discussion of these passages, see Hesk 2000: 227–30. Cf. also Pelling 2000: 28–31, 40–1. Steinbock 2013b: 42–3 recognizes this, but still tries to argue that the 'you all know' *topos* is often used for facts that are well known.

attributes of the Athenian citizen, and was expected in a politician. This is made very clear, for example, at Aeschin. 1.39 when the orator claims that he will leave out of his account any abuse committed by Timarchus when he was a boy, 'but the acts he has committed since reaching the age of reason and as a young man and in full knowledge of the laws, these I shall make the subject of my accusations, and I urge you to take them seriously'. Knowing the laws was not a matter of elite education; it was rather the mark of maturity and citizenship.[50] And the orators use the 'you all remember' *topos* also when referring to laws. To give only a couple of examples, Nicobulus at Dem. 37.18 claims: 'that the laws do not allow a fresh suit to be brought regarding matters that have been thus settled I believe you know even without my telling you'. At Dem. 23.31 the speaker seems to believe that the judges will remember not only the words of an old law about homicide, but also their meaning: 'But how [are they to be arrested]? "As provided in the axon", it says. What does it mean? You all know what it means.' Once again, it is hard to find in such cases an attempt to conceal any special knowledge or education. The explanation for the use of the *topos* in relation to laws is the same as in the case of allusions to the opponents' past; in Aristotle's words 'the hearer agrees, because he is ashamed to appear not to share what is a matter of common knowledge'. But were these appeals to the memory of the judges always justified by what they did remember, or rather, once again, often a subtle form of manipulation? At least in one case, at Dem. 20.18 and 26, we have the answer; the audience did not remember the provision Demosthenes refers to, because that provision did not exist in that form. At §18 the orator claims that 'in regard to the property taxes for war and defence of the city and to the trierarchy the old laws rightly and correctly do not allow for any exemption'. The same law is paraphrased again at §26: 'you are certainly aware that no one is exempt from the trierarchy, nor from the property tax levied for war'. In fact, an inscription proves that *ateleia* (exemption) from the property tax could indeed be granted: in an amendment to a grant of honours to the king of Sidon (*IG* II² 141.29–36), all the Sidonians living in Athens as merchants are declared not liable to the tax for foreign residents, to be appointed as *chorēgoi* (producers of choruses for festivals) and to pay the war property tax. Significantly, when at §27 Demosthenes asks the clerk to read out the relevant law his paraphrase of the provision changes and the property tax disappears: 'even though I think that all of you know that no one is exempt from the trierarchy ... You see, men of Athens, that

---

[50] Cf. e.g. Aeschin. 1.39 and Harris' Introduction in Harris-Leao-Rhodes 2010: 1–7.

the law clearly has stated that no one is exempt except the nine Archons.' He would not run the risk of making up a provision when the judges are about to hear, or have just heard, that any mention of the property tax is missing from the actual law. But he tries to give the impression that the law confirms what he has been claiming all along by reiterating the 'you all know' *topos*. The property tax reappears after a couple of lines, but Demosthenes does not claim this time that exemption from it is illegal.

This example shows that the use of the 'you all know' *topos* by the orators is not only an attempt at lending authority to their statements; it is in fact often (although not invariably) an attempt at lending authority to questionable, and sometimes false, statements, relying at the same time on the presumptions of the hearers and on the deficiencies of their memory. The orators know that their hearers pride themselves on remembering the laws of the city, but also know that in many cases they do not remember, at least not accurately. This allows them to twist the meaning of certain provisions, and in some cases, as we have seen, to lie about their contents (of course at a safe distance from the clerk's reading of the law), at the same time relying on the fact that no one will admit not to remember.

Now that a certain level of awareness of the discrepancy between what the Athenians thought they knew and what they actually remembered has been found in the case of gossip and legal knowledge, it is time to return to the memory of the past. There is no need to interpret appeals to the shared memory of the audience as attempts to conceal elite education. Such appeals can be explained as performing precisely the same function as with gossip and laws; they lend authority to claims, statements and accounts that are often not as widely known as the orator wants the audience to think, and sometimes actually questionable. The orators often claim that 'you all remember' a particular historical fact when chances are the hearers do not. A very common strategy is to introduce some obscure detail useful for their argument as part of a more general historical allusion whose outline the hearers are indeed likely to remember. For example Dem. 15.9–10 brings the case of Timotheus liberating Samos as an example of military action against the Persians, but not against the terms of the Peace of Antalcidas, to support his claim that helping the Rhodian democrats against Artemisia would have no consequences, since it would not violate the terms of the peace treaty. Demosthenes opens his account by claiming that he will remind the Athenians of Timotheus' actions. The audience probably did remember that Timotheus liberated Samos, but could hardly remember the exact diplomatic situation, which was of direct relevance in the present circumstances: the Athenians 'sent Timotheus to help Ariobarzanes, adding to the decree the condition that he was not to break the treaty with the king. When Timotheus saw that Ariobarzanes was clearly in revolt from the King', he decided to liberate Samos instead. Demosthenes adds details that the audience could hardly recall to an event that was indeed shared memory, and this allows him to claim that he is doing nothing more than reminding the audience of what they already remember.

A similar strategy is used at Dem. 22.15, when the speaker argues that the fleet is the most important guarantee of Athenian safety and success, against Androtion who as member of the Council failed to build the legal number of triremes. He refers to the 'last war against the Spartans', presumably the one of 374 over Corcyra. At that time, the speaker says, 'you know what state the city was in when you thought you would not be able to send the fleet out. You remember that even vetches were for sale. But when you did send the fleet out, you obtained the kind of peace you wanted.' The Athenians certainly remembered the war, and in all likelihood remembered that they were forced to eat (and buy!) vetches, but that the reason for all this was the impossibility of sending out the fleet is historical interpretation, not shared memory. This interpretation, however, is necessary to strengthen the argument, and the speaker uses existing shared memories of the past to lend credence to it. Even more strikingly, sometimes the orators use the *topos* to lend the authority of a shared memory to an historical allusion that in all likelihood was hardly remembered by anybody. At Dem. 23.104 the speaker opens an obscure and convoluted account of Thracian politics with the words 'I will remind you about an event in the past that all of you know.' This is very unlikely, but again the orator was confident that the Athenians would assume they should remember those facts, whether they did or not.

To conclude, this chapter has shown that in the Athenian law courts as well as in the Assembly there was no real ambivalence concerning memory. In front of an Athenian audience, no memory, *qua* memory, would have necessarily alienated the hearers.[51] In fact, memory of the past, of the laws, of the culture, even of the day-to-day life of the city was a necessary attribute of the Athenian citizen. The Athenians expected the speakers to show a high degree of cultural, historical and legal knowledge and

---

[51] Of course there were topics that it was painful to recall, such as defeat or civil war, and (derogatory) ways of talking about the past that were considered unacceptable. But the problem also in these cases was not that whoever had alluded to them would be showing off elitist education. The problem was rather that he would be provoking the citizens' pride and would denigrate the city.

memory. They also presumed to know and remember as much. Whatever the topic, in order to please his audience the speaker had to portray them as knowledgeable people who remembered their laws, their poetry, their history and had a good ear for gossip. The Athenians were not receptive to accusations that an opponent was culturally elitist, since they considered themselves a cultural elite.[52] They were therefore inclined to mistrust a speaker if he was caught not remembering enough.

This chapter has also provided evidence that professional *rhētores* were well aware of the audience's expectations. But they were also aware that the Athenians often presumed to remember much more than they actually did. Often they remembered no more than general outlines, or some key elements; sometimes they simply did not know. And yet they were ashamed to admit it. Once this is recognized, so much of the way the orators argue when it comes to memory, history and poetry can be read as a subtle rhetorical game played on the difference between the audience's pretensions of memory, and what they actually remembered. When analysing such arguments, taking into account what the hearers probably did not remember is as important as recognizing, as has been done in recent studies, that the orators acted in specific mnemonic communities.[53] The orators certainly paid attention to the Athenians' shared memories and beliefs, but they were also very careful to detect what they had forgotten or what they did not know. Through strategies like the 'you all remember' *topos* a speaker would exploit such holes in their knowledge, together with their cultural presumptions of remembering, and convince his hearers that they did remember facts, artefacts, laws and the like, when they did not. They used such strategies for the specific purpose of convincing the judges in a law court, but also in political propaganda, as well as in shaping the intentional memory of the city according to their agenda.[54] This was not necessarily a game of deception by clever politicians. It is not clear how much the orators themselves knew and where their information came from. They certainly used different versions of historical facts, opposing memories of the past, coming from different sources, traditions and mnemonic communities (as well as different interpretations of a poem or a legal text),

---

[52] Cf. the proud remarks by Pericles in his Funeral Oration (Thuc. 2.38.1, 40.1, 50.1): 'Further, we provide plenty of means for the mind to refresh itself from business. We celebrate games and sacrifices all the year round, and the elegance of our private establishments forms a daily source of pleasure and helps to banish the spleen ... We cultivate refinement without extravagance and knowledge without effeminacy ... In short, I say that as a city we are the school of Hellas' (transl. Crowley).

[53] See e.g. Thomas 1989 *passim* and Steinbock 2013b: 70–99.

[54] For political propaganda in the orators, see Perlman 1964 and recently Carey 2005. For the creation of the social memory of the city, see e.g. Wolpert 2003 *passim*; Luraghi 2010; Shear 2011 *passim*; 2013.

but they were not passive vehicles for these memories.[55] They would switch versions and interpretations, but they would also modify them, occasionally adding details. They could do this because their audiences forgot, and presumed to know more than they actually did. Therefore their accounts should not be taken at face value as witnesses of oral traditions or particular social memories circulating at a given time, because very conscious alterations and additions were often a viable option, and the orators were masters in understanding when their hearers' memory was feeble enough to be manipulated. But this chapter is not about uses and abuses of social memory. The key point here is rather that the evidence suggests that the orators were well aware of the importance that their audience attributed to memory and knowledge – of all the components of the common identity of the Athenians. Professional orators and politicians knew and studied the audience's attitudes so well that they could exploit them to their advantage, and sometimes, through the loopholes of individual forgetting, even shape new shared memories. As the memory of the individual Athenians, like that of any individual, was more malleable than is usually assumed,[56] and since the Athenians forgot, this constant tampering with what the Athenians believed they remembered, in the long run and following long-term political and cultural trends, would turn individual forgetting into what has been defined as public forgetting, the condition for development and change in social memory.[57]

[55] As Thomas 1989: 201–2 implies.

[56] On the concept of malleability applied to social memory, see Fentress-Wickam 1992: 29; Alcock 2002: 17; Clarke 2008: 316–7; Ma 2009: 255–6; Shear 2011: 7–8. Such malleability, I argue, has its base in the malleability of the individuals' memory.

[57] See Vivian 2010: 1–38 and *passim* for the concept of public forgetting. Shear 2011: 7–8 highlights forcefully the importance of public forgetting. On cases in which the social and 'official' memory of the city did change following political development, see Loraux 2002, Wolpert 2002 and Shear 2011 about the end of the fifth century.

CHAPTER 6

The Place and Nature of Memory in Greek Historiography

Catherine Darbo-Peschanski

The study of the place and nature of memory in Greek historiography involves two fundamental and interrelated sets of questions that scholars have been asking for a long time, and regularly re-propose.

On the one hand, such a study raises questions concerning the very definition and limits of Greek historiography. Is it just a literary genre, is it the product of a kind of knowledge, or is it both?[1] Did historiography arise from changes in the nature of cultural memory?[2] When and how did it arise, and what narratives exemplify it? What is its relation with the contemporary Western historical discipline, characterized, since the nineteenth century, by a precise set of methodological principles and a more or less confessed desire to come as close as possible to the status of science?[3]

---

[1] The claim that history is just a literary genre prevails currently, especially among literature scholars. Historiography is variously dissolved in the broad set of the genres that deal with the past. See e.g. Bowie 1986, 2001; Boedeker 1995, 2001; Marincola 1997, 2001; Dewald 2002; Grethlein 2010. History arises from the narrative of Herodotus' *Histories* (Lateiner 1989: 6), either through the establishment of a dominant narrative schema (the series of conquests leading to the Persian empire and its fall) that integrates and co-ordinates the most diverse accounts (Lateiner 1989), or through the explicit and implicit textual criticism of epic poetry and the use of the past in oratory (Grethlein 2010: 186–203), or through the 'double voice' of the narrator, reporting accounts with one voice, and criticizing them with the other (Dewald 2002: 286). According to other scholars, history is already present in Herodotus' *Histories* and the only question to ask is 'how'. The deployment in the text of the agents' and the informers' multiple and various motivations creates dissonances which involve the readers in the difficulty of historical research and in the widening of historical and narrative themes (Baragwanath 2008). Other historians and anthropologists are more interested in the meaning of the specifically Greek notion of *historiē/a*; they construe it as a cognitive activity, either one that Herodotus shares with *physiologoi* and orators in a similar context (Thomas 2000), or one that partakes in the same structure whatever its contexts of use, and that gives birth to *historia* as a literary genre through the effects of 'discourses' (in Foucault's sense) change (cf. Darbo-Peschanski 2007).

[2] Cf. Assmann 1992 (2011 for the English translation).

[3] At least from Jacoby onwards, and up to 'the narrative turn' and the new historical and anthropological approaches, scholarship tended to ask of the ancient historiographers that they account for their research methods of truth against the standards of 'scientific' history. This trend is fading.

On the other hand, such a study implies a definition of 'memory'. By adopting the different notions of 'intentional memory',[4] 'social memory',[5] 'idea of history'[6] or 'cultural memory', classical scholars have tended to place memory beyond historiography, as a field that somehow includes it, and where historiography encounters myth, ideology,[7] identity and shared experience, both individual and collective.

In this chapter, I do not aim to endorse any specific social or cultural theory of memory in order to find historiography somewhere encapsulated in it.[8] On the contrary, I will proceed by analysing the meaning and the development of *historia* as a native Greek notion,[9] in order to understand what memory patterns different forms or stages of *historia* encapsulate.

But I first want to stress two points about the definition of *historia* and about the history of time patterns in ancient Greece, from the earliest period for which we have textual evidence, up to the Hellenistic age. To put it briefly, in my view Greek *historia* is neither a mere collection of empirical evidence nor self-sufficient empirical knowledge, not even in empiricist approaches.[10] It is rather an initial judgement or collection of judgements made on phenomena by a first authority.[11] First authority,

---

[4] This concept, introduced by Gehrke (2001), forms the premise of the collection of essays edited by Foxhall, Gehrke and Luraghi (2010). Intentional history is defined as 'the projection in time of the elements of subjective, self-conscious self-categorization which construct the identity of a group as a group'; 'Intentional history would then be history in a group's own understanding, especially in so far as it is significant for the make up and identity of a group' (Gehrke 2001: 298).

[5] Defined by Alcock (2002) as 'the shared remembrance of a group experience', this notion is considerably widened by Steinbock (2013b: 7–19). In his view 'it involves personal memories and communal commemorations, active memory politics and unintentional distortions, as well as a group's identity and ideology ... It includes memories ranging from the mythical to the most recent past, memories cherished by the entire *polis* community as well as those shared primarily by the members of a small group.'

[6] Grethlein 2010: 9–15. Grethlein's 'idea of history' is not the same as Collingwood's, but a 'particular arrangement of four commemorative modes in an act of memory': contingency, with its double aspect of contingency of chance and contingency of action; the horizon of expectation and space of experience; the acceptance of chance vs. the continuity, and then the regularity, that lead to the idea of development. He calls this model, in which memory and history look like invariant notions, 'a phenomenological model of the idea of history'.

[7] Steinbock (2013b: 14) borrows this notion from Ober (1989: 38): 'Each member of any given community makes assumptions about human nature and behaviour, has opinions on morality and ethics, and holds some general political principles; those assumptions, options and principles which are common to the great majority of those members are best described as ideology.'

[8] However, I will often refer to Jan Assmann's *Cultural Memory and Early Civilization* (1992, 2011), in my view, the landmark work. As a global theory and, at the same time, a history of memory in early antiquity, its tightly and clearly articulated conceptual framework and descriptions definitely escape the previous reservations.

[9] Cf. Calame 1990 ('Catégorie indigène').

[10] Darbo-Peschanski 2007.

[11] Judgement understood sometimes in the epistemic sense, sometimes in the judicial sense.

because actually this judgement (or these judgements) is (are) in turn the object of another judgement, this time decisive, emanating from a second authority.[12] *Historia* therefore constitutes the first phase, necessary but not autonomous, of a double process that leads to a ruling on the just or the real, and sometimes on both, when they are confused. In the case of Herodotus, the recipient of the work (irrespective of whether hearer or reader) is asked to pass a definitive judgement both on what the inquirer himself or his informants present as their own experiences or as valuable accounts of the past, and on what is presented as worth recounting merely by virtue of its inclusion in the text.

Just before or around Herodotus' age, the 'natural histories' (Περὶ φύσεως ἱστορίαι) that Plato will later reject because they rely on information from the senses,[13] or the theses of the *physiologoi* discussed by Aristotle,[14] deal with natural phenomena.[15] With Herodotus, temporal phenomena (*ta genomena*) are also, although not exclusively, at stake. From a general point of view, this type of interest might be the result of the gradual[16] emergence of a writing culture, as described by J. Assmann.[17] According to him, this emergence changed 'the time-structure of cultural memory'. The 'ontic time' regularly made present by ceremonies and ritual performances, a time that 'always remained at the same distance from the progressive present', gives place to a 'historical time'. From the 'spirit of writing itself' arise practical texts for daily communication, a collection of 'classics' created by copying and quoting, but also an observable and measurable time that divides into past and present, the ancient and the modern. Continuity then gives way to interpretation and critical approach; or rather, the 'dissonant plurality of voices' sets up a kind of continuity different from that guaranteed by the regularity of commemorations and ritual performances:[18] the continuity of culture which consists in a progressive variation. But the question remains to be asked of how this phenomenon occurred in Greece, and more specifically within *historia*. And this is precisely my second point.

---

[12] From the empiricist's point of view referred to above, *historia* provides the physician with what he was or is unable to experience by himself, but does not carry absolute authority. It just provides additional or past phenomenal connections and epilogisms that will be assessed anew.

[13] *Phaedo*, 97b8–99e7; 99d4–e6; *Theaetetus* 184b–186e; *Republic* 521c–525a; 602e–603a.

[14] *De anima* 426a20, for instance.

[15] Aristotle's *Animalium Historia* perfectly illustrates the double structure in which *historia* stands at the first stage. Pellegrin 1986 speaks of an 'apodictic zoology' in which the *Animalium Historia*, that is to say, the material cause, provides the premises.

[16] On this gradual aspect in Greece, cf. Thomas 1989.

[17] Cf. Assman 2011: 74, 77.

[18] Assmann 2011: 261. See Calame's chapter in this volume for a different take on this issue.

Throughout its history, Greek culture brought to the fore several ways of framing the 'historical time'.[19] Like many other ancient cultures, and especially that of the Hittites,[20] the Greeks first patterned[21] time as a requital movement from guilt to punishment, able to encapsulate both human and divine actions. 'The focus is on requital, not on causality' and, 'instead of requital, the sources speak of justice'.[22] Early *historia* (that of Herodotus, but also of Anaximander, for example) is inscribed in such a framework. Precisely named after the judge of the *Iliad* (*histōr*), it organizes time through responses to recurrent offences against human or divine justice. From the Peloponnesian War onwards, however, another conception of time gradually emerges next to the old one, because obviously justice itself cannot any longer balance the offences throughout the world. This new conception is based on the immutability of human nature, which is conceived as something governed by the almost irresistible strength of the passions that cause *kinēseis*, both changes and revolutions, in the world. Finally, from the Roman conquests onwards, in addition to the time of human nature, there appears a time moved by fate or fortune (*tuchē*), understood as a fatal power able to gather together all the regions of the inhabited world around Rome.[23]

All these pattern changes had an impact on the narratives of the past. The Herodotean display of a *historia* (ἱστορίης ἀπόδεξις)[24] which concerns past events can no longer fit a world in which justice does not rule any more. The judicial frame of both inquiry and narrative thus stops being relevant. Not surprisingly, then, Thucydides ostensibly abandons that model of *historia* and adopts another kind of inquiry and narrative: the *suggraphē* ('writing down together').

The classic texts, whatever their nature, have by now become the boundaries that mark out the past.[25] One can rely on them, from Homer up to the

---

[19] Darbo-Peschanski 2007: 232–312.

[20] Assmann 2011: 206–33.

[21] Assmann says 'semiotized'.

[22] Assmann 2011: 209. The connection between memory (of past actions) and reciprocity highlighted in other chapters (Introduction, above, pp. 30–3; Agócs, pp. 79–81; Ceccarelli, pp. 99–111) comes to the fore here.

[23] Thucydides perfectly illustrates the pivotal shift from the time of justice to the time of human nature; Polybius the shift from the latter to the time of fate or fortune.

[24] Herodotus 1.1.1.

[25] Assmann 2011: 255–8 speaks of 'hypolepsis' and 'hypoleptical discourse organization' to mean 'the reference to texts of the past, in the form of controlled variation'. I also used this Greek term (cf. Darbo-Peschanski 2007: 337–55), but in its native meaning, and not in Assmann's sense. The Greek *hupolēpsis* is restricted to poetry, especially epic, and refers to the double movement by which either a hero within the poem or the rhapsodes during the festivals interrupt the previous speaker and extend ahead the *logos* he was putting forward, somehow by 'grasping it from underneath' (*hupo-lambanein*). But the continuity of the texts in the case of historiography breaks with the epic

present. This is why Thucydides begins with the age Homer is supposed to refer to, and why he also comes back to the moment when Herodotus' narrative stops. All his successors will do the same. However, such a textual continuity, which has the function of shaping the continuity of time itself, directly determined the emergence of a new literary genre, named after the first example of inquiry about the past, the Herodotean *historia*: the genre of *historia* as historiography, beyond all the differences of approach. So, later on, the grammarians and the rhetoricians will rank Thucydides himself among the *historiographoi*.

In what follows I shall focus on four of the classic texts that the 'writing culture' has selected as prime examples of historiography. Each of them belongs to one of the three temporal frameworks distinguished above: Herodotus exemplifies the 'time of justice'; Thucydides and Xenophon the 'time of human nature'; Polybius the 'time of fate/fortune'. My aim is to define what kind of memory each of them sets up, and hence to identify specific forms of memory within the broader pattern of cultural memory in classical and Hellenistic Greece.

1 The Fading of Poetic Memory

Herodotus, Thucydides, Xenophon and Polybius almost entirely ignore the product of poetic memory, both epic and lyric: the *kleos*. Jean-Pierre Vernant and Marcel Detienne have shown that in the bard's society epic memory (*mnēmosunē*) does not refer to a psychological faculty, but to a goddess, mother of the Muses who, along with her daughters, presides over the poetic operations.[26] She gets the bard to witness the past and future events he describes in song as if they were occurring in front of him. Because, according to this representation, the past and the future partake in the invisible, such a visual experience guarantees poetic knowledge. Therefore, even though mnemonic techniques can support such a supernatural memory, this memory remains a divine cognitive gift that enables the poet to see the otherwise invisible past and future. Moreover, thanks to the 'eye-caught truth' that the bard regularly performs, and which successive audiences listen to, the heroes' deeds can survive forever. This does not involve any psychological faculty of individual or collective

---

hupolēpsis (the word does not occurs in this context). Henceforth one does not 'carve out' for oneself a part of a *logos*, with its own plot and temporality, but a period of time (*chronos*) about which each *historiographos* elaborates a narrative which has not been already framed.

[26] Vernant 1965: 87; Detienne 1967: 15.

remembrance. The regularity of the eyewitness-singer's performances and the succession of the audiences are enough to create a temporal continuity that requires no remembrance, but only the display of the always-present heroic deeds. In this very specific way these deeds acquire immortal fame (*kleos aphthiton*).

Undoubtedly epic and lyric poetry deeply differ from one another. It is possible, for instance, to contrast the 'rhetorical stances'[27] adopted in each case: the epic poet links his content closely to a traditional form made of anonymity, universality, great consistency of language and compositional rules, a form which looks immutable and timeless and which partakes in a kind of 'poetics of truth';[28] the lyric poet adopts a language just as artificial and unusual, but he displays a greater variation of vocabulary, metre and tone, places himself in a more explicit situational performance, and tends to adapt his account of the past to his listeners, in what has been defined as a 'consumerist approach'.[29]

Undoubtedly, again, the *kleos* was open to contestation from very early on. The Muses of Hesiod may sing the truth, but they can utter lies as well.[30] But even if they are able to inspire ambiguous accounts in the poet, nonetheless they keep inspiring him. Stesichorus upsets the equilibrium of the system more radically when, in his *Palinodes*, he acknowledges that he *himself* has told an untrue *logos* about Helen.[31] In this poem he probably narrated the loss of his eyesight, as well as its recovery following a meeting with a woman (Helen? at any rate, not a traditional Muse) who, having first punished him for his error, forgave him when he recanted.[32] Nevertheless, the poet does not completely break the relationship of his poetry with a superior warrant, even if a different one from the Muses.

Simonides seems to have further modified the pattern of the inspired poet. In his elegy on the battle of Plataea, for instance, he shapes his speaking position by introducing deviations from the Homeric model:[33] he addresses his *chaire* to Achilles instead of an Olympian deity,[34] exactly

---

[27] Graziosi and Haubold 2009: 107.
[28] Finkelberg 1998: 18–27.
[29] Graziosi and Haubold 2009: 107.
[30] Hes. *Theog.* 27–8.
[31] Quoted by Plato, *Phdr.* 243a: 'The story was not true (οὐκ ἔστ᾽ ἔτυμος λόγος οὗτος), and you did not go on the well-benched ships and you did not reach the citadel of Troy' (Stesichorus fr. 192 *PMGF* = 192 Campbell).
[32] Stesichorus fr. 193 *PMGF* (= 193 Campbell) and the testimonia *ibid*; for a recent discussion of the *Palinode*, see Beecroft 2006; Kelly 2007.
[33] Stehle 2001: 107–12.
[34] Fr. 11.19–20 W². Perhaps this is a way of attributing to him the status of cult hero to which Homer never explicitly refers.

as Stesichorus had done towards Helen, and he calls on the Muse to be just his 'auxiliary' (*epikouros*).[35] More generally, Simonides overturns three major features of the epic poet's stance: memory as a divine gift, as a power of escaping time and as a medium of truth. More precisely, he is said to have turned memory into a human technique, mnemonics,[36] that is to say, into an intellectual and profane faculty of remembering which depends on mental images.[37] Aristotle and Simplicius testify that Simonides dealt with the issue of time; he called it 'the wisest, since men become knowledgeable thanks to time'.[38] Finally, he gained a strong disrepute as a deceitful poet.[39] Nevertheless, thanks to the Muse and sometimes to his own skill,[40] the poet remains a master of *kleos*, and all the more a 'master of truth', since he can be deceitful whenever he likes, and sometimes with impunity.

Some references to *kleos* still appear in the works we are going to examine; but *kleos*, when mentioned, is both somehow discredited, or at least weakened, and reduced to a very human glory, neither truer nor more deceitful than any other fame.

In the opening of his *Histories*, for instance, Herodotus seems to borrow the epic manner when he announces that he will care for the *kleos* of deeds that are great and full of wonder, *megala kai thōmasta erga*; yet he makes his announcement through a curiously negative formula. Actually he does not promise anything more than simply preventing an already fading *kleos* from vanishing entirely:

Ἡροδότου Θουρίου ἱστορίης ἀπόδεξις ἥδε, ὡς μήτε τὰ γενόμενα ἐξ ἀνθρώπων τῷ χρόνῳ ἐξίτηλα γένηται, μήτε ἔργα μεγάλα τε καὶ θωμαστά, τὰ μὲν Ἕλλησι, τὰ δὲ βαρβάροισι ἀποδεχθέντα, ἀκλέα γένηται, τά τε ἄλλα καὶ δι' ἣν αἰτίην ἐπολέμησαν ἀλλήλοισι. (Hdt. 1.1.1)

---

[35] Fr. 11.21 W².

[36] Plin. *N.H.* 7.24.89; Cic. *De Fin.* 2.32.104; Longin. *Rhet. App.* I 105–10 Patillon-Brisson (p. 201, 24–202, 3 Spengel-Hammer). For a discussion of ancient attitudes towards mnemonic techniques, cf. Sassi's chapter in this volume.

[37] Cic. *de orat.* 2.86.351–3; Quint. *Inst.* 11.2.11–16. See Sassi's chapter in the present volume.

[38] Simonides 645 *PMG* (= 645 Campbell): Simplicius, *On Aristotle Physics*, 754, 7–17, and Themistius, *On Aristotle Physics* 4, 158.25–159.2, commenting on Arist. *Phys.* 4.13.222b, 16–19; cf. Eudemus fr. 90 Wehrli.

[39] Plut. *Aud. Poet.* 15c.

[40] Simonides fr. 92 W² (= *Anth. Pal.* 13.30) seems in line with Homer when he asks: 'Muse, sing for me of the son of fair-ankled Alcmena. Of the fair-ankled son of Alcmena, sing, Muse, for me.' Similarly Ibycus, S. 151.23 *PMGF* (= 282a Campbell), asserts: 'On these themes the *sesophismenai* muses of Helicon might embark in story, but no mortal man [lacuna: untaught ?] could tell each detail.' However, in the coda of the poem, S. 151.47–8, the latter claims his own power on fame: 'you too, Polycrates, will have undying fame as song and my fame can give it' (Campbell's translation).

This is the display of the inquiry of Herodotus of Thourioi, so that things done by men not be forgotten in time, and that great and marvellous deeds, some displayed by the Hellenes, some by the Barbarians, *not lose their fame*, including among others what was the cause of their waging war on each other.

Afterwards, the *kleos* almost disappears from the *Histories*: the term occurs only four more times, in statements and circumstances that have some epic flavour, such as oracles and ceremonial speeches pronounced by some characters of the narrative:

ταύτῃ καὶ μᾶλλον τὴν γνώμην πλεῖστός εἰμί, Λεωνίδην, ἐπείτε ᾔσθετο τοὺς συμμάχους ἐόντας ἀπροθύμους καὶ οὐκ ἐθέλοντας συνδιακινδυνεύειν, κελεῦσαί σφεας ἀπαλλάσσεσθαι, αὐτῷ δὲ ἀπιέναι οὐ καλῶς ἔχειν· μένοντι δὲ αὐτοῦ *κλέος* μέγα ἐλείπετο, καὶ ἡ Σπάρτης εὐδαιμονίη οὐκ ἐξηλείφετο. Ἐκέχρηστο γὰρ ὑπὸ τῆς Πυθίης τοῖσι Σπαρτιήτῃσι χρεωμένοισι περὶ τοῦ πολέμου τούτου αὐτίκα κατ᾽ ἀρχὰς ἐγειρομένου, ἢ Λακεδαίμονα ἀνάστατον γενέσθαι ὑπὸ τῶν βαρβάρων, ἢ τὸν βασιλέα σφέων ἀπολέσθαι. Ταῦτα δέ σφι ἐν ἔπεσι ἑξαμέτροισι χρᾷ λέγοντα ὧδε· "Ὑμῖν δ᾽, ὦ Σπάρτης οἰκήτορες *εὐρυχόροιο*, | ἢ μέγα ἄστυ *ἐρικυδὲς* ὑπ᾽ ἀνδράσι Περσείδῃσι | πέρθεται, ἢ τὸ μὲν οὐχί, ἀφ᾽ Ἡρακλέους δὲ γενέθλης | πενθήσει βασιλῆ φθίμενον Λακεδαίμονος οὖρος· | οὐ γὰρ τὸν ταύρων σχήσει μένος οὐδὲ λεόντων | ἀντιβίην· Ζηνὸς γὰρ ἔχει μένος· οὐδέ ἕ φημι | σχήσεσθαι, πρὶν τῶνδ᾽ ἕτερον διὰ πάντα δάσηται.' (Hdt. 7.220.2–4)

I, however, tend to believe that when Leonidas perceived that the allies were dispirited and unwilling to run all risks with him, he told them to depart. For himself, however, it was not good to leave; if he remained, he would leave a name of great *fame*, and the prosperity of Sparta would not be blotted out. When the Spartans asked the oracle about this war when it broke out, the Pythia had foretold that either Lacedaemon would be destroyed by the barbarians or their king would be killed. She gave them this answer in hexameter verses running as follows:

'For you, inhabitants of *wide-wayed* Sparta,

Either your great and *glorious* city must be wasted by Persian men,

Or if not that, then the bound of Lacedaemon must mourn a dead king, from Heracles' line.

The might of bulls or lions will not restrain him with opposing strength, for he has the might of Zeus.

I declare that he will not be restrained until he utterly tears apart one of these.' (Transl. Godley)

Note the epic vocabulary of the passage (italicised), which explains Herodotus' mention of the *kleos*.

Moreover, the historical inquirer tends to focus on extraordinary deeds more because of their oddness than because of their consistency with the heroic code. Typically Herodotus considers only exceptionality, even when it is a negative one, as worth noting; as a result, he introduces an ironical and polemical gap between the epic *kleos* and what he recalls. Let us quote just one instance, in *Histories* 8.85, where he chooses to mention nobody but two Samians, two Greeks who fought with the Persians against other Greeks and were rewarded for that with gifts and tyranny over Samos:

Ἔχω μέν νυν συχνῶν οὐνόματα τριηράρχων καταλέξαι τῶν νέας Ἑλληνίδας ἑλόντων, χρήσομαι δὲ αὐτοῖσι οὐδὲν πλὴν Θεομήστορός τε τοῦ Ἀνδροδάμαντος καὶ Φυλάκου τοῦ Ἱστιαίου, Σαμίων ἀμφοτέρων. Τοῦδε <δὲ> εἵνεκα *μέμνημαι* τούτων μούνων, ὅτι Θεομήστωρ μὲν *διὰ τοῦτο τὸ ἔργον* Σάμου ἐτυράννευσε καταστησάντων τῶν Περσέων, Φύλακος δὲ εὐεργέτης βασιλέος ἀνεγράφη καὶ χώρη ἐδωρήθη πολλῇ. (Hdt. 8.85.2–3)

I can list the names of many captains who captured Hellenic ships, but I will mention none except Theomestor, son of Androdamas, and Phylacus, son of Histiaeus, both Samians. I recall[41] only these because Theomestor was appointed tyrant of Samos by the Persians for this feat, and Phylacus was recorded as a benefactor of the king and granted much land.

Finally, even if the *kleos* exceptionally occurs in the *Histories* as a weak or occasional product of recalling the past, it does not provide the matter for the making of *historiē*, namely for knowing what happened (*ta genomena*). While in the epic the truth was inherent in and concomitant with the poetic speech act and its reception, now the very matter of the inquiry, what the inquiry aims for, what it produces and then accounts for,[42] are human *logoi*, whose truthfulness is open to a debate. That debate will be definitively decided and ended when the audience (by now not just an aristocratic circle, but any listener or reader in the city-state) will silently agree, in an act of reception, with the more persuasive version.[43]

As for Thucydides, he also lessens the place of the *kleos*, and refers to it mainly because of its positive ideological aristocratic connotations. Thus, in Pericles' funeral speech, the Athenian city, thanks to the citizens who

---

[41] Μέμνημαι τούτων here; ἐπιμνήσομαι in 1.5.4. What is at stake is simply mentioning the past to the reader or the audience.

[42] *Histories* 1.1.1: Ἡροδότου Θουρίου ἱστορίης ἀπόδεξις ἥδε.

[43] Darbo-Peschanski 1987: 164–88; 2007: 67–82. The display of the inquiry (ἱστορίης ἀπόδεξις) as a kind of trial refers to the judicial origin of *historiē*: the *histōr* of *Iliad* 18. On this, see Darbo-Peschanski 2007: 39–67.

have chosen to die for her, becomes the heroine of a novel kind of epic. *Kleos* also appears when speaking of Sparta, a city of warrior excellence (*aretē*) similar to the Iliadic version, and sometimes in the characters' speeches during political debates, when the speakers invoke the greatness of their past history and ancestors. But Thucydides too denies poetry the capacity for telling the truth about the past by means of the *kleos*. The single aim and power of poetry is the audience's pleasure. That is the reason why finally the *kleos* has to yield to the prosaic *mnēmē* and its monuments (*mnēmeia*).

So, in the 'archaeology', Thucydides uses the memories (*mnēmai*) of wise men to challenge the Homeric account of the Trojan War:

Ἀγαμέμνων τέ μοι δοκεῖ τῶν τότε δυνάμει προύχων καὶ οὐ τοσοῦτον τοῖς Τυνδάρεω ὅρκοις κατειλημμένους τοὺς Ἑλένης μνηστῆρας ἄγων τὸν στόλον ἀγεῖραι. λέγουσι δὲ καὶ οἱ τὰ σαφέστατα Πελοποννησίων μνήμῃ παρὰ τῶν πρότερον δεδεγμένοι Πέλοπά τε πρῶτον πλήθει χρημάτων, ἃ ἦλθεν ἐκ τῆς Ἀσίας ἔχων ἐς ἀνθρώπους ἀπόρους ... (Thuc. 1.9.2)

What enabled Agamemnon to raise the armament was more, in my opinion, his superiority in strength, than the oaths of Tyndareus, which bound the Suitors to follow him. Indeed, the account given by those Peloponnesians who have been the recipients of the most credible *memory* is this. First of all, Pelops, arriving among a needy population from Asia with vast wealth ... (Transl. Crawley, slightly modified)

Elsewhere, Pericles, in almost the same words as Thucydides in the first book, invokes, implicitly against the *kleos*, the Athenian *mnēmeia kakōn kai agathōn*:

μετὰ μεγάλων δὲ σημείων καὶ οὐ δή τοι ἀμάρτυρόν γε τὴν δύναμιν παρασχόμενοι τοῖς τε νῦν καὶ τοῖς ἔπειτα θαυμασθησόμεθα, καὶ οὐδὲν προσδεόμενοι οὔτε Ὁμήρου ἐπαινέτου οὔτε ὅστις ἔπεσι μὲν τὸ αὐτίκα τέρψει, τῶν δ' ἔργων τὴν ὑπόνοιαν ἡ ἀλήθεια βλάψει, ἀλλὰ πᾶσαν μὲν θάλασσαν καὶ γῆν ἐσβατὸν τῇ ἡμετέρᾳ τόλμῃ καταναγκάσαντες γενέσθαι, πανταχοῦ δὲ *μνημεῖα* κακῶν τε κἀγαθῶν ἀΐδια ξυγκατοικίσαντες. (Thuc. 2.41.4)

Rather, the admiration of the present and succeeding ages will be ours, since we have not left our power without witness, but have shown it by mighty proofs; and far from needing a Homer for our panegyrist, or other of his craft *whose verses might charm for the moment* only for the impression which they gave to melt at the touch of fact, we have forced every sea and land to be the highway of our daring, and everywhere, whether for evil or for good, have left imperishable *monuments* behind us. (Transl. Crawley)

Another memory settles down, that of generations of men who receive stories from each other and pass them on as traditions (*akoai*): in short, a memory both psychological and social.

With Xenophon and Polybius, the *kleos* disappears almost entirely. As glory linked to an aristocratic virtue at war, it becomes an object of empty talk, denied by the reality of the fratricidal strife among the Greeks in Xenophon's *Hellenics*, and by the betrayals that mark the retreat of the Ten Thousand in the *Anabasis*. In Polybius' *Histories*, the word *kleos* belongs to laudatory and sometimes theoretical passages about the Roman constitution, especially the funeral rites, and less often to the glorious past of Athens during the Persian Wars (as in 38.2.2–4). Interestingly, Polybius feels the necessity to compensate for the weakening of the term's meaning by the addition of the euphemistic prefix *eu-* in the word *eukleia*:

> πλὴν ὅ γε λέγων ὑπὲρ τοῦ θάπτεσθαι μέλλοντος, ἐπὰν διέλθῃ τὸν περὶ τούτου λόγον, ἄρχεται τῶν ἄλλων ἀπὸ τοῦ προγενεστάτου τῶν παρόντων, καὶ λέγει τὰς ἐπιτυχίας ἑκάστου καὶ τὰς πράξεις. ἐξ ὧν καινοποιουμένης ἀεὶ τῶν ἀγαθῶν ἀνδρῶν τῆς ἐπ' ἀρετῇ φήμης ἀθανατίζεται μὲν ἡ τῶν καλόν τι διαπραξαμένων *εὔκλεια*, γνώριμος δὲ τοῖς πολλοῖς καὶ παραδόσιμος τοῖς ἐπιγινομένοις ἡ τῶν εὐεργετησάντων τὴν πατρίδα γίνεται δόξα. τὸ δὲ μέγιστον, οἱ νέοι παρορμῶνται πρὸς τὸ πᾶν ὑπομένειν ὑπὲρ τῶν κοινῶν πραγμάτων χάριν τοῦ τυχεῖν τῆς συνακολουθούσης τοῖς ἀγαθοῖς τῶν ἀνδρῶν *εὐκλείας*. πίστιν δ' ἔχει τὸ λεγόμενον ἐκ τούτων. (Plb. 6.54.1)

> Besides, the speaker over the body about to be buried, after having finished the panegyric of the particular person, starts upon the others whose representatives are present, beginning with the most ancient, and recounts the successes and achievements of each. By this means the glorious memory of brave men is continually renewed; the *glorious fame* of those who have performed any noble deed is never allowed to die; and the renown of those who have done good service to their country becomes a matter of common knowledge to the multitude, and part of the heritage of posterity. But the chief benefit of the ceremony is that it inspires young men to shrink from no exertion for the general welfare, in the hope of obtaining the *glorious fame*, which awaits the brave. And what I say is confirmed by this fact. (Transl. Shuckburg, slightly modified)

Furthermore, by now the role of the *kleos* as a source of knowledge, and especially of true knowledge, is definitely over: the historical inquirer does not need it to look for what happened in the human world.

2 Herodotus as the Mnēmōn

Even if in Herodotus and his successors Mnemosyne has become *mnēmē* or *memnēsthai* or *epimimnēskesthai*, we do not find in each of them the same use of memory, because memory is involved in different ways of knowing the past.

The lack of any reference to memory as an individual psychological faculty which allows us to grasp the past is an outstanding feature of Herodotus' *Histories*. In Herodotus no one *remembers*; and this applies also to the inquirer (with one exception, in 2.125). Groups (Athenians, Spartans, Greeks, Egyptian priests, Thracians, Persians, and so on) or the inquirer himself put forward *logoi* in which they both tell and explain what happened. Those *logoi* are collected by means of *akoē* or *opsis*; nowhere is this collecting ascribed to memory and its psychological mechanisms. Those *logoi* are most often traditions that prevail here and there, no matter how; as for the inquirer himself, if he has visited some place, he does not say that he remembers having seen it, but only that he saw it.

In fact, the relevant Greek vocabulary for 'memory' here does not mean *to remember* something, but *to recall something to someone*, in this case, to the audience of the Herodotean work. The nuance of 'recall' is evident in especially important places, for example at the end of the *prooimium*, where the inquirer is talking about his entire future *logos*:

> Ταῦτα μέν νυν Πέρσαι τε καὶ Φοίνικες λέγουσι. Ἐγὼ δὲ περὶ μὲν τούτων οὐκ ἔρχομαι ἐρέων ὡς οὕτως ἢ ἄλλως κως ταῦτα ἐγένετο, τὸν δὲ οἶδα αὐτὸς πρῶτον ὑπάρξαντα ἀδίκων ἔργων ἐς τοὺς Ἕλληνας, τοῦτον σημήνας προβήσομαι ἐς τὸ πρόσω τοῦ λόγου, ὁμοίως μικρὰ καὶ μεγάλα ἄστεα ἀνθρώπων ἐπεξιών. Τὰ γὰρ τὸ πάλαι μεγάλα ἦν, τὰ πολλὰ αὐτῶν σμικρὰ γέγονε· τὰ δὲ ἐπ᾽ ἐμέο ἦν μεγάλα, πρότερον ἦν σμικρά. Τὴν ἀνθρωπηίην ὦν ἐπιστάμενος εὐδαιμονίην οὐδαμὰ ἐν τὠυτῷ μένουσαν, ἐπιμνήσομαι ἀμφοτέρων ὁμοίως. (Hdt. 1.5.3–4)

> This is what the Persians and the Phoenicians say. For my part, I shall not say that things happened in this way or another one, but I shall identify the one who I myself know was the first who began unjust deeds against the Greeks, and I shall progress in my account going through small and great cities of men alike. For many states that were once great have now become small; and those that were great in my time were small before. Knowing therefore that human prosperity never remains in the same place, I shall *recall* both alike.

The inquirer's position can be compared to that of the *mnēmones*, magistrates well attested by inscriptions from the beginning of the fifth century until the third century BC at least. The scribe Spensithios, appointed by a Cretan city in a contract engraved in ca. 500 BC,[44] or the magistrates mentioned in the Gortyn Laws around 480–460 BC,[45] provide us with two important examples to understand the role of the *mnēmōn*. He is in charge of keeping records of previous juridical acts: this function does not make of him a kind of clerk of the court,[46] for either he accompanies another magistrate (the *cosmos*) in official acts,[47] or he acts as a substitute of the *cosmos*. The Gortyn Laws let us understand the situation more precisely.[48] The *mnēmōn* and the magistrate who were associated in a first trial may together participate in a second trial about a related cause, but now only as witnesses. One would expect that the *mnēmōn* would keep his role if he was only in charge of recalling the previous case, but as soon as other magistrates hold their office at the new trial, that is to say as soon as he and his colleague are no longer magistrates for the present case, he stops being the *mnēmōn*. Therefore, not only does the *mnēmōn* appear as a *magistrate* of memory, but his memory appears to be an *institutional* one, an *official recalling* very different from the personal remembering he has when he becomes a witness in the second trial.

The *mnēmōn* bears some analogy with the Herodotean inquirer, for two reasons at least. First, because of the judicial tone of the *Histories*: in Herodotus, events appear as injuries against justice (human and divine, individual as well as institutional), or as revenge and punishment out of justice. Second, because of the twofold process of which *historiē* is the first stage, as previously explained. To begin with, the inquirer judges the facts that his sources mention, or gives an opinion when he is personally informing his readers;[49] next, the recipient of the work, located outside of it, is asked to pass final judgement on what has been previously assessed. An indication of this judicial task appears in *Histories* 1.5

---

[44] Jeffery and Morpurgo-Davies 1970: 118–54, 1977: 631.
[45] Willetts 1967. See also the so-called 'Lygdamis inscription' (Meiggs-Lewis 1969 no. 32, ca. 465–450 BC) from Halicarnassus, the native land of Herodotus, on which see Maffi 1988 and Carawan 2008, or an inscription of Iasos (*I.Iasos* 1 = Dittenberger *Syll.*³ 169, ca. 351 BC). For a more detailed analysis, see Darbo-Peschanski 2007: 192–228.
[46] For a different interpretation, see Van Effenterre 1973: 37–9 and 46; Ruzé 1988: 82–94.
[47] *IC* IV 42 B, l. 1–4: *pareinai, suneinai*, 'be beside', 'be with'.
[48] *IC* IV 72 col. IX 24–34, cf. Willetts 1967.
[49] Even if there is no comment on the *logoi*, their selection presupposes the judgement that they are worth mentioning.

(quoted above on p. 169), when the inquirer promises that he will travel (actually or metaphorically) through the great and small cities *homoiōs* and will recall them *homoiōs*, 'alike'. For, in a trial, treating both sides alike (*homoiōs*) or equally (*isōs*) must precede and warrant a judgement consistent with justice.

This first judgement resembles that which the *mnēmōn* displays at the first trial, before a second one in which he will participate as a witness to the facts, with all the other informants. In the *Histories* indeed there is another stage after the first, in which the inquirer selects and judges the *logoi*. It is the stage when the audience of the work, exactly like a new magistrate, is invited to judge what has been first recalled and evaluated and is now brought up again for the final and definitive judgement. That is why, sometimes, the inquirer ends an account with some surprising statements. After having recorded the *logos* of the Egyptian priests about Helen, according to whom she was not present in Troy during the war, for instance, he does not present his own view as the truth, but merely as his opinion:

Ταῦτα μὲν Αἰγυπτίων οἱ ἱρέες ἔλεγον. Ἐγὼ δὲ τῷ λόγῳ τῷ περὶ Ἑλένης λεχθέντι καὶ αὐτὸς προστίθεμαι, τάδε ἐπιλεγόμενος· εἰ ἦν Ἑλένη ἐν Ἰλίῳ, ἀποδοθῆναι ἂν αὐτὴν τοῖσι Ἕλλησι ἤτοι ἑκόντος γε ἢ ἀέκοντος Ἀλεξάνδρου … ἀλλ᾽ οὐ γὰρ εἶχον Ἑλένην ἀποδοῦναι οὐδὲ λέγουσι αὐτοῖσι τὴν ἀληθείην ἐπίστευον οἱ Ἕλληνες, ὡς μὲν ἐγὼ γνώμην ἀποφαίνομαι, τοῦ δαιμονίου παρασκευάζοντος ὅκως πανωλεθρίῃ ἀπολόμενοι καταφανὲς τοῦτο τοῖσι ἀνθρώποισι ποιήσωσι, ὡς τῶν μεγάλων ἀδικημάτων μεγάλαι εἰσὶ καὶ αἱ τιμωρίαι παρὰ τῶν θεῶν. Καὶ ταῦτα μὲν τῇ ἐμοὶ δοκέει εἴρηται. (Hdt. 2.120.1 and 5)

The Egyptians' priests said this, and *I myself believe their story about Helen, for I reason thus*: had Helen been in Ilion, then with or without the will of Alexandros she would have been given back to the Greeks … But since they did not have Helen there to give back, and since the Greeks would not believe them although they spoke the truth – *as I am convinced and declare* – the divine powers provided that the Trojans, perishing in utter destruction, should make this clear to all mankind: that retribution from the gods for terrible wrongdoing is also terrible. *This is what I think, and I state it.*

In another case, he states that he does not believe in the account of the circumnavigation of Africa by the Phoenicians, but asks the audience to pass judgement on the story:

Καὶ ἔλεγον, ἐμοὶ μὲν οὐ πιστά, ἄλλῳ δὲ [δή] τεῳ, ὡς περιπλέοντες τὴν Λιβύην τὸν ἥλιον ἔσχον ἐς τὰ δεξιά. (Hdt. 4.42.5)

There they said (what some may believe, though I do not) that in sailing around Libya they had the sun on their right hand.

Elsewhere, he leaves the audience free to judge among those accounts he has considered worth reporting:

Αἰτίαι μὲν δὴ αὗται διφάσιαι λέγονται τοῦ θανάτου τοῦ Πολυκράτεος γενέσθαι, πάρεστι δὲ πείθεσθαι ὁκοτέρῃ τις βούλεται αὐτέων. (Hdt. 3.122)

These are the two reasons alleged for Polycrates' death; let everyone believe whichever he likes.

In short, the Herodotean *historiē* seems to find in an institutional kind of memory without psychological features, that of the *mnēmones*, a pattern close to its own.

And this is actually the difference between Herodotus and Simonides or Aeschylus, even though they all chose 'historical' episodes as topics of their works, either the whole Persian Wars or some specific battles. It is difficult to argue on the basis of the difference of literary genres,[50] because Herodotus is the first to display a *historiē* about past human events and because *historiē* becomes a genre only after him, when other writers, first of all Thucydides, will narrate the events that followed those he had narrated.[51] Certainly the judicial pattern, especially inasmuch as it concerns memory, is one of the original features by which *historiē* differs from Simonidean poetry and tragedy as well.

3   The Psychological and Epistemic Fragility of Mnēmē

The Thucydidean memory appears radically different from the Herodotean one, because it is fully psychological, and because it is related to *suggraphē* ('gathering through writing down'), and no longer to *historia* ('inquiry'), with its judicial colour.

First of all, Thucydides explicitly links memory (*mnēmē*) with *akoē*, which is not the faculty of hearing, as was the case in Herodotus, but the *product* of people's memory, a synonym of 'tradition'. Sometimes, as in the text about the leadership of Agamemnon, the *akoē* is able to provide acceptable evidence; but this happens only in connection with the Homeric account, and about very ancient data.

---

[50]   Boedeker 2001: 131–2.

[51]   For the recently edited papyrus of Simonides about the battle of Plataea, see Parsons 1992; West 1992; Boedeker and Sider 2001, and especially Sider's commentary (2001); about *Historia* as a literary genre, see Darbo-Peschanski 2007: 335–426.

Elsewhere, and in particular for the more recent past, *mnēmē* appears to be a weak faculty, which selects events, changes and reorganizes the past according to the feelings and emotions of the present. The disturbance and fear experienced by Athenian citizens during the plague shape the past in one way; other conditions would have shaped it differently:

Τοιούτῳ μὲν πάθει οἱ Ἀθηναῖοι περιπεσόντες ἐπιέζοντο, ἀνθρώπων τ' ἔνδον θνῃσκόντων καὶ γῆς ἔξω δῃουμένης. ἐν δὲ τῷ κακῷ οἷα εἰκὸς ἀνεμνήσθησαν καὶ τοῦδε τοῦ ἔπους, φάσκοντες οἱ πρεσβύτεροι πάλαι ᾄδεσθαι 'ἥξει Δωριακὸς πόλεμος καὶ λοιμὸς ἅμ' αὐτῷ.' ἐγένετο μὲν οὖν ἔρις τοῖς ἀνθρώποις μὴ λοιμὸν ὠνομάσθαι ἐν τῷ ἔπει ὑπὸ τῶν παλαιῶν, ἀλλὰ λιμόν, ἐνίκησε δὲ ἐπὶ τοῦ παρόντος εἰκότως λοιμὸν εἰρῆσθαι· οἱ γὰρ ἄνθρωποι πρὸς ἃ ἔπασχον τὴν μνήμην ἐποιοῦντο. ἢν δέ γε οἶμαί ποτε ἄλλος πόλεμος καταλάβῃ Δωρικὸς τοῦδε ὕστερος καὶ ξυμβῇ γενέσθαι λιμόν, κατὰ τὸ εἰκὸς οὕτως ᾄσονται. μνήμη δὲ ἐγένετο καὶ τοῦ Λακεδαιμονίων χρηστηρίου τοῖς εἰδόσιν, ὅτε ἐπερωτῶσιν αὐτοῖς τὸν θεὸν εἰ χρὴ πολεμεῖν ἀνεῖλε κατὰ κράτος πολεμοῦσι νίκην ἔσεσθαι, καὶ αὐτὸς ἔφη ξυλλήψεσθαι. περὶ μὲν οὖν τοῦ χρηστηρίου τὰ γιγνόμενα ἤκαζον ὁμοῖα εἶναι· ἐσβεβληκότων δὲ τῶν Πελοποννησίων ἡ νόσος ἤρξατο εὐθύς, καὶ ἐς μὲν Πελοπόννησον οὐκ ἐσῆλθεν, ὅτι καὶ ἄξιον εἰπεῖν, ἐπενείματο δὲ Ἀθήνας μὲν μάλιστα, ἔπειτα δὲ καὶ τῶν ἄλλων χωρίων τὰ πολυανθρωπότατα. Ταῦτα μὲν τὰ κατὰ τὴν νόσον γενόμενα. (Thuc. 2.54.1–5)

Such was the nature of the calamity, and heavily did it weigh on the Athenians; death raging within the city and devastation without. Among other things which they *remembered* in their distress was, very naturally, the following verse which the old men said had long ago been uttered: 'A Dorian war shall come and with it death.' So a dispute arose as to whether 'dearth' and not 'death' had not been the word in the verse; but at the present juncture, it was of course decided in favour of the latter; *for the people made their recollection fit in with their sufferings.* I fancy, however, that if another Dorian war should ever afterwards come upon us, and a dearth should happen to accompany it, the verse will probably be read accordingly. *The oracle also which had been given to the Lacedaemonians was now remembered by those who knew of it.* When the God was asked whether they should go to war, he answered that if they put their might into it, victory would be theirs, and that he would himself be with them. With this oracle events were supposed to tally. For the plague broke out as soon as the Peloponnesians invaded Attica, and never entering Peloponnese, not at least to an extent worth noticing, committed its worst ravages at Athens, and next to Athens, at the most populous of the other towns. Such was the history of the plague. (Transl. Crawley)

Therefore, when Thucydides himself resorts to his own *mnēmē* as an acceptable means for grasping the past, he dramatically emphasizes how such an exception proves the rule. He is calculating how long the war has lasted:

ὥστε ξὺν τῷ πρώτῳ πολέμῳ τῷ δεκέτει καὶ τῇ μετ᾽ αὐτὸν ὑπόπτῳ ἀνοκωχῇ καὶ τῷ ὕστερον ἐξ αὐτῆς πολέμῳ εὑρήσει τις τοσαῦτα ἔτη, λογιζόμενος κατὰ τοὺς χρόνους, καὶ ἡμέρας οὐ πολλὰς παρενεγκούσας, καὶ τοῖς ἀπὸ χρησμῶν τι ἰσχυρισαμένοις μόνον δὴ τοῦτο ἐχυρῶς ξυμβάν. αἰεὶ γὰρ ἔγωγε *μέμνημαι*, καὶ ἀρχομένου τοῦ πολέμου καὶ μέχρι οὗ ἐτελεύτησε, προφερόμενον ὑπὸ πολλῶν ὅτι τρὶς ἐννέα ἔτη δέοι γενέσθαι αὐτόν. ἐπεβίων δὲ διὰ παντὸς αὐτοῦ αἰσθανόμενός τε τῇ ἡλικίᾳ καὶ προσέχων τὴν γνώμην, ὅπως ἀκριβές τι εἴσομαι· καὶ ξυνέβη μοι φεύγειν τὴν ἐμαυτοῦ ἔτη εἴκοσι μετὰ τὴν ἐς Ἀμφίπολιν στρατηγίαν, καὶ γενομένῳ παρ᾽ ἀμφοτέροις τοῖς πράγμασι, καὶ οὐχ ἧσσον τοῖς Πελοποννησίων διὰ τὴν φυγήν, καθ᾽ ἡσυχίαν τι αὐτῶν μᾶλλον αἰσθέσθαι. (Thuc. 5.26.3–4)

So that the first ten years of war, the treacherous armistice that followed it, and the subsequent war will, calculating by the seasons, be found to make up the number of years which I have mentioned, with the difference of a few days, and to afford an instance of faith in oracles being for once justified by the event. I certainly all along *remember* from the beginning to the end of the war that it was commonly declared that it would last thrice nine years. I lived through the whole of it, being of an age to comprehend events, and giving my attention to them in order to know the exact truth about them. It was also my fate to be an exile from my country for twenty years after my command at Amphipolis; and being present with both parties, and more especially with the Peloponnesians by reason of my exile, I had leisure to observe affairs somewhat particularly. (Transl. Crawley, slightly modified)

We will come back to this text later.

The fact that orators (e.g. generals, political leaders, prosecutors) resort to their audiences' memory in order to push them to fight bravely or to take a specific decision provides another sign of the weakness or fragility of *mnēmē*.[52] *Mnēmē* is actually one of the main instruments of the mechanism of rhetorical persuasion, and sometimes manipulation, because of its strong relationship with feelings and emotions. So everyone appeals to memory, and tries to make use of it to induce present decisions: for example, when Cleon wants the Athenians to punish the Mytileneans for their betrayal, he reminds the former of their past anger toward the latter; Brasidas, to escape a difficult situation, recalls for his soldiers other battles in which they were self-confident.

For all these reasons, but especially because of his theory of passions and emotions as sources of corruption of understanding, decisions and, in

---

[52] See M. Canevaro's chapter in this volume.

short, truth, Thucydides expels memory from his *suggraphē*: he acknowledges it as an important psychological faculty, but denies it any reliable cognitive power.

This appears at its clearest in the famous 'methodological' passage: neither in the case of speeches, nor in that of events, is memory a sufficient foundation to produce a true and precise account, not even the memory of someone who witnessed the speech or event. Thucydides states:

Καὶ ὅσα μὲν λόγῳ εἶπον ἕκαστοι ἢ μέλλοντες πολεμήσειν ἢ ἐν αὐτῷ ἤδη ὄντες, χαλεπὸν τὴν ἀκρίβειαν αὐτὴν τῶν λεχθέντων διαμνημονεῦσαι ἦν ἐμοί τε ὧν αὐτὸς ἤκουσα καὶ τοῖς ἄλλοθέν ποθεν ἐμοὶ ἀπαγγέλλουσιν· ὡς δ' ἂν ἐδόκουν ἐμοὶ ἕκαστοι περὶ τῶν αἰεὶ παρόντων τὰ δέοντα μάλιστ' εἰπεῖν, ἐχομένῳ ὅτι ἐγγύτατα τῆς ξυμπάσης γνώμης τῶν ἀληθῶς λεχθέντων, οὕτως εἴρηται. (Thuc. 1.22.1)

With reference to the speeches, some were delivered before the war began, others while it was going on; some I heard myself, others I got from various quarters; it was in all cases difficult to carry them word for word in one's memory, so my habit has been to make the speakers say what was in my opinion demanded of them by the various occasions, of course adhering as closely as possible to the general sense of what they really said.

Presence does not guarantee an exact account even in the case of deeds: for we cannot understand 'to be actually present at the deeds with both parties' throughout the war, as said in 5.26.3–4, unless we weaken the meaning of 'being present' into something like 'having some direct experience of' – a meaning which immediately excludes an exhaustive memorization of what happened on both sides, because the witness could not have been present there at the same time. Perhaps, as in 1.22.2–3, this necessary presence involves a joint effort of Thucydides and of others actors or eyewitnesses. But then we meet again the fragility of remembrance:

τὰ δ' ἔργα τῶν πραχθέντων ἐν τῷ πολέμῳ οὐκ ἐκ τοῦ παρατυχόντος πυνθανόμενος ἠξίωσα γράφειν, οὐδ' ὡς ἐμοὶ ἐδόκει, ἀλλ' οἷς τε αὐτὸς παρῆν καὶ παρὰ τῶν ἄλλων ὅσον δυνατὸν ἀκριβείᾳ περὶ ἑκάστου ἐπεξελθών. ἐπιπόνως δὲ ηὑρίσκετο, διότι οἱ παρόντες τοῖς ἔργοις ἑκάστοις οὐ ταὐτὰ περὶ τῶν αὐτῶν ἔλεγον, ἀλλ' ὡς ἑκατέρων τις εὐνοίας ἢ μνήμης ἔχοι. (Thuc. 1.22.3)

And with reference to the narrative of deeds, far from permitting myself to derive it from the first source that came to hand, I did not even trust my own impressions, but it rests partly on what I saw myself, partly on what others saw for me, the accuracy of the report being always tried by the most severe and detailed tests possible. My conclusions have cost me some labour from the want of coincidence between accounts of the same occurrences by different eyewitnesses, arising sometimes from imperfect memory, sometimes from undue partiality for one side or the other.

How to get through the difficulty, then? How can Thucydides support deficient memory? On this point his criticism is as harsh as the method he suggests is mysterious. It would seem that one must grasp the general sense of speeches (their *gnōmē* 1.22.1), and labour (*epiponōs* 1.22.3) at cleansing the deeds of the deceptive spell of myth and poetic pleasure, in order to provide useful means of comparing situations and gaining clear knowledge of them. On this point, another famous Thucydidean passage is relevant:

> καὶ ἐς μὲν ἀκρόασιν ἴσως τὸ μὴ μυθῶδες αὐτῶν ἀτερπέστερον φανεῖται· ὅσοι δὲ βουλήσονται τῶν τε γενομένων τὸ σαφὲς σκοπεῖν καὶ τῶν μελλόντων ποτὲ αὖθις κατὰ τὸ ἀνθρώπινον τοιούτων καὶ παραπλησίων ἔσεσθαι, ὠφέλιμα κρίνειν αὐτὰ ἀρκούντως ἕξει. κτῆμά τε ἐς αἰεὶ μᾶλλον ἢ ἀγώνισμα ἐς τὸ παραχρῆμα ἀκούειν ξύγκειται. (Thuc. 1.22.4)

> The absence of romance in my history will, I fear, detract somewhat from its interest; but if it be judged useful by those inquirers who desire an exact knowledge of the past as an aid to the interpretation of the future, which in the course of human things must resemble if it does not reflect it, I shall be content. In fine, I have written my work, not as an essay which is to win the applause of the moment, but as a possession for all time. (Transl. Crawley)

One might thus say that, in the *Peloponnesian War*, the analysis of memory has two functions. First, it implicitly points to the Herodotean *logoi* as *akoai*, unreliable because of their unstable psychological grounds (even if this psychological point of view was in no way Herodotean); on this basis, Thucydides breaks with Herodotus. Second, it dismisses the individual or collective remembrance from research into the actual events. Ideally an authentic *suggraphē* should do without remembrance, and should rely exclusively on actual presence at the events. But the muse no longer helps the *suggrapheus* as she previously did with the poet. The consequence of such a change is that the *suggraphē* deals with the present time and the *suggrapheus* seeks to merge his role with that of a perfectly accurate witness.

4   Monuments and Honorific Accounts

Let us turn now briefly to Xenophon. In the *Hellenica* and *Anabasis*, memory essentially appears in the form of material monuments (*mnēmeia*). All its other types disappear, as well as any statement about the means to retrieve the past. Agents do not act on the basis of their remembrance, nor do they try to get future fame. The historian himself does not resort to remembrance for researching or even telling what happened in the human world; and he never compares his account to a 'recalling'. So memory is neither an important psychological faculty, nor an intellectual instrument of the *historia*, nor one of the aims of the historical narrative. This fits with the main feature of Xenophon's *Hellenica*: they tell what happened *after* the events narrated by Thucydides, without any other principle of organization than a chronological one, the *meta de tauta* by which the 'historian' ties together the episodes of his account. This is not to say that Xenophon does not know how to find such principles. Rather, he chooses to reflect in his narrative the disorganized world he experiences. The absence of memory seems to be, therefore, more a symptom of this disorder than a lack of skill.

Finally, Polybius offers yet another pattern. In Polybius, *mnēmē* loses its psychological features; it is again set at the core of *historia* – but a *historia* henceforth understood as the *narrative* of past events, and not as an inquiry. The recurrent expression *mnēmēn poieisthai* in Polybius' *Histories* does not simply mean 'to recall', but to 'inscribe in memory'. The historical work indeed welcomes only what is worth of memory (*axion mnēmēs*). On account of both ethics and knowledge, it behoves *historia* to give out memory as a prize to those actors of events who have deserved praise. Concerning the ethical point of view, let us read what Polybius writes when he attacks Phylarchus' tragic *historia*:

Χωρὶς τε τούτων τὰς μὲν Μαντινέων ἡμῖν συμφορὰς μετ' αὐξήσεως καὶ διαθέσεως ἐξηγήσατο, δῆλον ὅτι καθήκειν ὑπολαμβάνων τοῖς συγγραφεῦσι τὰς παρανόμους τῶν πράξεων ἐπισημαίνεσθαι, τῆς δὲ Μεγαλοπολιτῶν γενναιότητος, ᾗ περὶ τοὺς αὐτοὺς ἐχρήσαντο καιρούς, οὐδὲ κατὰ ποσὸν ἐποιήσατο μνήμην, ὥσπερ τὸ τὰς ἁμαρτίας ἐξαριθμεῖσθαι τῶν πραξάντων οἰκειότερον ὑπάρχον τῆς ἱστορίας τοῦ τὰ καλὰ καὶ δίκαια τῶν ἔργων ἐπισημαίνεσθαι, ἢ τοὺς ἐντυγχάνοντας τοῖς ὑπομνήμασιν ἧττόν τι διορθουμένους ὑπὸ τῶν σπουδαίων καὶ ζηλωτῶν ἔργων ἤπερ ὑπὸ τῶν παρανόμων καὶ φευκτῶν πράξεων. (Plb. 2.61.1–2)

There is another illustration of this writer's manner to be found in his treatment of the cases of Mantinea and Megalopolis. The misfortunes of the former he has depicted with his usual exaggeration and picturesqueness: apparently from the notion that it is the peculiar function of an historian to *select for special mention* only such actions as are conspicuously bad. But about the noble conduct of the Megalopolitans at that same period *he has not said a word*: as though it were the province of history to deal with crimes rather than with instances of just and noble conduct; or as though his readers would be less *improved* by the *record* of what is great and worthy of imitation, than by that of such deeds as are base and fit only to be avoided. (Transl. Shuckburgh)

As for knowledge, we may quote Polybius' statement following a passage about the Gauls:

ἡγοῦμαι γὰρ τὴν περὶ αὐτῶν ἱστορίαν οὐ μόνον ἀξίαν εἶναι γνώσεως καὶ μνήμης, ἀλλὰ καὶ τελέως ἀναγκαίαν χάριν τοῦ μαθεῖν τίσι μετὰ ταῦτα πιστεύσας ἀνδράσι καὶ τόποις Ἀννίβας ἐπεβάλετο καταλύειν τὴν Ῥωμαίων δυναστείαν. πρῶτον δὲ περὶ τῆς χώρας ῥητέον ποία τίς ἐστιν καὶ πῶς κεῖται πρὸς τὴν ἄλλην Ἰταλίαν. οὕτως γὰρ ἔσται καὶ τὰ περὶ τὰς πράξεις διαφέροντα κατανοεῖν βέλτιον, ὑπογραφέντων τῶν περί τε τοὺς τόπους καὶ τὴν χώραν ἰδιωμάτων. (Plb. 2.14.2)

For the story I think is worth knowing for its own sake, and must absolutely be kept in memory if we wish to understand on what tribes and districts Hannibal relied to assist him in his bold design of destroying the Roman dominion. I will first describe the country in which they live, its nature, and its relation to the rest of Italy; for if we clearly understand its peculiarities, geographical and natural, we shall be better able to grasp the salient points in the history of the war. (Transl. Shuckburgh)

So, by means of memory, *historia* can become the famous teacher of life later celebrated by Cicero.

5 As a Conclusion

In our modern historical discipline, memory, as an individual or as a social faculty of remembering, provides primary sources that historians compare with secondary ones. Memory is an essential auxiliary of history, especially of oral history: it supplies it with a rich and complex body of material. Things work very differently in the texts that we subsume under the genre of Greek historiography. Inquiry into what happened (the *genomena/gegenēmena*) does not rest on memory: (personal) memory is sometimes considered as a psychological faculty potentially misleading and dangerous, and thus to be kept out of the *suggraphē*; or, far from resembling our individual or social phenomena, it is closely associated with institutional processes of justice; or, in other cases, it appears as the personal reward that the *historiographos* gives to some characters of his narrative. Memory is thus a fundamental key for our understanding of how works gathered under the same heading of 'ancient historiography' differ from one another and diverge from our conception of historiography.

CHAPTER 7

Lyric Oblivion: When Sappho Taught Socrates How to Forget*

Andrea Capra

Given the limits of our human nature, oblivion can hardly be excluded from the scene of memory: most of the time, remembering involves a more or less conscious selection, whereby our memories are made possible precisely by our acts of forgetfulness. Yet the polarity between memory and oblivion is as much a cultural as a natural fact. However fascinated by glory and memory as the highest goal of human striving, Plato's fellow Greeks encouraged and praised various forms of forgetfulness. This, I will argue, paved the way for a radical solution, which sees the polarity in terms of a direct correlation that emphasises the positive role of oblivion: in the *Phaedrus*, the highest and best form of memory, that is the metaphysical recollection of the Forms, turns out to be inseparable from an extreme act of forgetfulness, which consists in the erasing of all earthly concerns.[1] I refer to this act as 'lyric oblivion' because it emerges from Plato's hitherto unnoticed reworking of Sappho's 'Ode to Helen', a poem that emphasises oblivion in the context of a pioneering juxtaposition of memory and recollection. Plato, I will argue, shapes his notion of both oblivion and memory through and against Sappho.

* The core of this paper dates back to the Conference 'Greek Memories: Theories and Practice' (Durham University, 27–8 September 2010). I developed some of the original ideas in Capra 2014a, ch. 2, and in a paper entitled 'Plato's Possessors of Beauty (*Symposium*, *Phaedrus*)', which I delivered at the workshop 'Qu'est-ce que le beau? (Homère, Platon, Aristote)', Université Catholique de Louvain – Institut Superieur de Philosophie, Centre De Wulf Mansion, 27 April 2015. After so many years, I have lost track of the many good people who helped me improve this paper: ideally, I thank them all warmly.
[1] I will not address here the inseparability of memory and oblivion as discussed by Diotima in the *Symposium* (207d–208a). Cf. the perceptive discussion by Ledesma 2016, who goes so far as to say that for Plato 'el olvido es inseparable del lenguaje' (107). Cf. also Gonzalez 2007: 288–91. For the way in which the later Platonists, and in particular Plotinus, developed this polarity, see Clark's chapter in this volume.

1 Sappho on the Ilissus

The scene is well known: Phaedrus and Socrates are on the banks of the Ilissus, in what is possibly the most influential *locus amoenus* of western literature.[2] Phaedrus has just finished reading aloud a clever speech by Lysias, who maintains that a beloved boy (*eromenos*) should grant his favours to a non-lover rather than to a lover. Yet Socrates is unimpressed:

{ΣΩ.} Τοῦτο ἐγώ σοι οὐκέτι οἷός τ' ἔσομαι πιθέσθαι· παλαιοὶ γὰρ καὶ σοφοὶ ἄνδρες τε καὶ γυναῖκες περὶ αὐτῶν εἰρηκότες καὶ γεγραφότες ἐξελέγξουσί με, ἐάν σοι χαριζόμενος συγχωρῶ.

{ΦΑΙ.} Τίνες οὗτοι; καὶ ποῦ σὺ βελτίω τούτων ἀκήκοας;

{ΣΩ.} Νῦν μὲν οὕτως οὐκ ἔχω εἰπεῖν· δῆλον δὲ ὅτι τινῶν ἀκήκοα, ἤ που <u>Σαπφοῦς τῆς καλῆς ἢ Ἀνακρέοντος τοῦ σοφοῦ</u> ἢ καὶ συγγραφέων τινῶν. πόθεν δὴ τεκμαιρόμενος λέγω; <u>πλῆρές πως</u>, ὦ δαιμόνιε, <u>τὸ στῆθος ἔχων</u> αἰσθάνομαι παρὰ ταῦτα ἂν ἔχειν εἰπεῖν ἕτερα μὴ χείρω. ὅτι μὲν οὖν παρά γε ἐμαυτοῦ οὐδὲν αὐτῶν ἐννενόηκα, εὖ οἶδα, συνειδὼς ἐμαυτῷ ἀμαθίαν· λείπεται δὴ οἶμαι <u>ἐξ ἀλλοτρίων ποθὲν ναμάτων διὰ τῆς ἀκοῆς πεπληρῶσθαί με</u> δίκην ἀγγείου. ὑπὸ δὲ νωθείας αὖ καὶ αὐτὸ τοῦτο <u>ἐπιλέλησμαι</u>, ὅπως τε καὶ ὥντινων ἤκουσα.

SOC. That's where I shall no longer be able to go along with you; men and women of old, wise people who have spoken and written about the subject, will refute me if I agree as a favour to you.

PHAEDR. Who are these people? And where have you heard better things than there are in Lysias' speech?

SOC. At the moment I can't say, just like that, but clearly I *have* heard something, either – maybe – <u>from the beautiful Sappho, or from Anacreon the wise</u>, or indeed from some prose-writers. On what evidence do I say this? <u>My breast is full</u>, if I may say so, my fine fellow, and I see that I would have other things to say beyond what Lysias says, and no worse either. I am well aware that I have thought up none of them from within *my* resources, because I am conscious of my own ignorance; the only alternative, then, I think, is that <u>I have been filled up through my ears</u>, like a vessel, from someone else's streams. But dullness again <u>has made me forget</u> this very thing, how I heard it and from whom. (*Phaedrus*, 235b–d, transl. Rowe)

As well as providing a nice introduction to our topic in the shape of an allegedly amnesic Socrates, this passage, with its mention of Sappho and Anacreon, can work as a litmus test for Platonic scholarship. In olden days, such references to poetry used to pass unnoticed, or else they were

---

[2] See Hunter 2012.

quickly dismissed as mere embellishments. The first article specifically devoted to this passage dates back to 1966, when a distinguished scholar came up with the suggestion that 'the purpose for naming these poets is to anticipate poetic reminiscences'.[3] These days, such a statement is likely to sound unsophisticated to most readers: the scholarly landscape has radically changed since that time, and Plato has metamorphosed into a master of polyphony à la Bakhtin and as a swift manipulator of metaphors à la Ricoeur.

Despite certain excesses, the consequences for our passage are intriguing: not only are scholars increasingly aware that Plato appropriates Sappho's poems, but 'Plato's Sappho' is at the centre of a lively debate, mostly focused on issues of gender.[4] As for *genre*, Andrea Nightingale has suggested that the *Phaedrus* differs from other dialogues in that 'it abandons the notion that traditional genres of poetry and rhetoric are inherently "un-philosophical" '.[5] In Bakhtin's terms, as adopted by Nightingale, this amounts to 'passive double-voiced discourse': the author 'assumes a passive stance, thus allowing the alien genre to play an active and relatively autonomous role in the text'.[6] As a result, Nightingale considers the genre of lyric poetry as a crucial ingredient of Socrates' palinode.[7]

I shall return to the 'autonomous role' of lyric poetry at the end of the chapter. For the time being, let me note at least four of Sappho's poems that are thought to be echoed in the *Phaedrus*. Ode 31 Voigt is probably a crucial source for the symptoms experienced by the lover at 251a–252e. Sappho 2 Voigt is an important precedent for the setting of the *Phaedrus*, as Sappho's *locus amoenus* has much in common with that of Plato. Sappho 1, the 'Ode to Aphrodite', is possibly echoed twice: at 241a–b, when Socrates describes the lover's flip-flop once his passion is extinguished, and at 246e, where the image of the charioteer is arguably inspired by Aphrodite's divine chariot as described by Sappho.[8] Finally, Sappho 96 possibly influences Plato's imagery when Socrates recounts how the lover grows wings (251b–c). Moreover, scholars have long been looking for thematic and even

---

[3] Fortenbaugh 1966: 108.
[4] See e.g. Burnett 1979, Dubois 1985 and 1995, and Foley 1998.
[5] Nightingale 1995: 133.
[6] Nightingale 1995: 149.
[7] One possible objection is that, as Genette 1979 noticed long ago, in the eyes of Plato's contemporaries there was no such thing as 'lyric poetry', the relevant genre, and its alleged *Weltanschauung*, being a modern construction. The *Phaedrus*, however, comes close to 'inventing' the genre: cf. Capra 2014b. The very notion of palinode, of course, calls to mind Stesichorus' lyric poetry. Cf. Capra 2014a: ch. 1.
[8] See Pender 2007: 21.

philosophical links between Plato and Sappho, given that a long-standing tradition views Sappho as a proto-philosopher, 'concerned' – to quote Bruno Snell's typically grand formulation – 'to grasp a piece of genuine reality: to find Being instead of Appearance'.[9]

2 Plato's Hymn to Memory

As well as alerting the reader to possible poetic echoes, Socrates' mention of Sappho and Anacreon announces something peculiar: he is filled 'with the streams of another', and Phaedrus readily remarks his unusual eloquence (238b). Socrates' speeches are arranged carefully into a climax relating to poetic possession, which he credits not only to ancient poets, but to the inspiring landscape, the local divinities, his own *daimōn* and the 'chorus' of the cicadas.[10] Inspired, Socrates succeeds in beating Lysias at his own game: his first speech proves far superior in force, clarity and inventiveness. At this point, Socrates makes it clear that his inspiration is growing wild: at any time the Nymphs might abduct him in *ekstasis* (238d).

Ekstasis is crucial to Socrates' second speech or 'palinode', which argues for an opposite thesis and opens with the famous distinction between two opposite forms of madness, one good and divine, one bad and human. Here is a major innovation, which has remarkable consequences even for Socrates' vocabulary, now shifting in important ways. The lover is described as ecstatic, the Greek verb being ἐκπλήττω.[11] Along with its cognate ἔκπληξις, which LSJ renders as 'mental disturbance', this verb is a favourite in Plato's vocabulary: it conveys the basic idea that passions overwhelm and dispel human rationality (including memory).[12] Only here and in another poetic and erotic speech, namely Aristophanes' myth in the *Symposium*, does this verb express positive ideas.[13] In both cases, love

[9] Snell 1953: 50 (orig. Hamburg 1948²). Philosophical interpretations of Sappho, although certainly not in such an idealistic and teleological vein, are now common in the Anglo-Saxon literature as well. See e.g. Baxter 2007, who builds on the testimony of Maximus of Tyre (18.9) and Greene-Skinner 2009 on the 'new Sappho' and its philosophical entanglements. Sappho's poems have been rightly described as 'both intensely passionate and resolutely abstract' (Most 1996: 34). For other references, see below (given the vastness of the relevant bibliography, my references to Sappho as a proto-philosopher will be limited to the poem I directly discuss, namely 16). Plutarch provides an important precedent for a philosophical reading of Sappho's poetry (cf. Zadorojny 1999).

[10] For a very useful list of such sources, cf. Cairns 2013.

[11] 250a, 255b, cf. 259b. The 'Platonic' definition of ἔκπληξις is 'fear caused by the expectation of something bad' (φόβος ἐπὶ προσδοκίᾳ κακοῦ; *Def.* 415e).

[12] Cf. e.g. *Phaed.* 66d; *Crat.* 394 b; *Phlb.* 26c; *Prot.* 355b; *Grg.* 523d; *Resp.* 436e; 576d; 577a; 591d; 619a; *Leg.* 659a.

[13] 192b, somehow echoed at 211d. There are some forty instances of the verb in the Platonic corpus.

is described as a storming no less than exclusive passion, obliterating all other concerns.

Memory perfectly fits in the frame of divine madness, in that ἔκπληξις strikes the lover's mind and brings about the recollection of the eternal Forms. The lover is overwhelmed and shocked by his beloved's beauty, which sparks the growth of wings and 'a recollection (ἀνάμνησις) of those things which our soul once saw when it travelled in company with god' (249c). This divine reaction is the hallmark of a philosophical soul, 'for so far as it can it is close, through memory (μνήμη), to those things his closeness to which gives a god his divinity'. In fact, most souls are impeded by oblivion (λήθη) and only few are capable of recollection (ἀναμιμνῄσκω: twice in 249e–250a) and memory (μνήμη, 250a): only these are struck by beauty (ἐκπλήττονται 250e), as if by a lightning bolt (cf. 254a ὄψιν ἀστράπτουσαν), with the result that they are completely beside themselves. This lightning bolt sparks glimpses of their divine past, when they followed their gods dancing through the skies and visited 'the plain of *alētheia*'.[14] This arresting expression invites comparison with, and should be construed in the light of, the 'plain of *lēthē*' mentioned in the myth of Er and elsewhere.[15] In fact, the 'plain of *alētheia*' is where truth as 'non-oblivion' is fully manifest.[16]

Before proceeding to a new topic, namely beauty, Socrates concludes his praise of memory as follows:

Ταῦτα μὲν οὖν <u>μνήμῃ κεχαρίσθω</u>, δι' ἣν πόθῳ τῶν τότε νῦν μακρότερα εἴρηται· περὶ δὲ κάλλους ...

Let this be our <u>farewell/token of gratitude</u> to memory, which has made me speak now at some length out of longing for what was before; but on the subject of beauty ... (*Phaedrus*, 250c, transl. Rowe modified)

The very unusual expression μνήμῃ κεχαρίσθω, '*charis* be given to *mnēmē*', is usually translated more or less as 'thanks be given to memory'.[17] This

---

[14] 248b τὸ <u>ἀληθείας</u> ἰδεῖν πεδίον οὗ ἐστιν.

[15] *Resp.* 621a τὸ τῆς Λήθης πεδίον. Cf. e.g. Ar. *Ran.* 186. Cf. Heitsch 2011: 7 'nun wird ohne Zweifel das Wort ἀληθής von den Griechen der klassischen und späteren Zeit weitgehend im Sinne von wahr verwendet. In der Alltagssprache wird das Wort also nicht mehr als Kompositum mit der Vorsilbe ἀ- verstanden. Ebenso sicher aber ist, daß die Etymologie des Wortes auch wieder aktiviert werden konnte' (besides *Resp.* 621a and *Phdr.* 248b, he cites Antiphon 1.6 and Men. 725 K.-A.).

[16] I leave aside Heidegger's well-known speculation about *alētheia* as *Unverborgenheit*. For a sober assessment of the question, see now Heitsch 2011: 8–11.

[17] Overall, the *TLG* counts six more instances of the form κεχαρίσθω in the whole of Greek literature. Three of them are direct quotations from the *Phaedrus* (Herm. Alex. *in Plat. Phdr.* p. 179.1; p. 179.8; Proclus, *In Plat. rem publ. comm.* 1. p. 205.22), and the remaining three are quite obviously direct imitations (Ammon. *In Arist. de interpr. comm.* p. 186.9; Simplic. *In Arist. phys. comm.*

is fine, yet the verb χαίρω as a device to change subject cannot but recall its usage in hymns: this is a standard way to take leave of a god, and such usage, whereby the verb means 'bid farewell', surfaces in other poetic genres as well.[18] Intriguingly, Socrates refers to his inspired speech precisely as a 'hymn' (ὑμνέω, 247c).[19] Memory, then, emerges as a godlike entity addressed in quasi-cultic forms.

3 Beneficial Oblivion: The Broader Picture

Socrates' 'hymn' extols memory to the detriment of oblivion, which affects the non-philosophical soul and is implicitly conceptualised as the opposite of truth (a-lētheia). One may wonder if this Manichean opposition is consistent with Plato's overall position and, more generally, with his cultural background. As we shall see, the following section of the *Phaedrus*, devoted to beauty, rehabilitates forgetfulness, but before addressing it a quick look at the broader picture may be in order.

In classical Athens there were no doubt a number of social practices that actively encouraged oblivion. Traditionally, a highly praised feature of poetry is its ability to induce, like wine, forgetfulness of cares,[20] and in fact Phrynichus' play on the taking of Miletus was fined precisely because it openly recalled Athens' miseries, rather than ignoring them.[21] When Plato was in his twenties, in the wake of the restoration of democracy in 403 BC, all Athenians became familiar with the political slogan μὴ μνησικακεῖν, which promoted amnesty and discouraged remembrance of past wrongs.[22] A fragment attributed to Plutarch nicely captures a number of comparable attitudes:

> Τῷ Διονύσῳ νάρθηκα καὶ λήθην συγκαθιεροῦσιν, ὡς μὴ δέον μνημονεύειν
> τῶν ἐν οἴνῳ πλημμεληθέντων ἀλλὰ νουθεσίας παιδικῆς δεομένων. ᾧ

---

9 p. 90.21; *Comm. in Epict. enchir.* p. 89.26). The form, then, is virtually a *hapax legomenon*, although no commentary, to the best of my knowledge, makes the point (the phrase μνήμη κεχαρίσθω, in fact, is not even mentioned).

[18] The formula is ubiquitous in the *Homeric Hymns*, often, as in the *Phaedrus*, in connexion with the particle μέν. Non-Homeric examples include Hes. *Theog.* 963–5; Pind. *Isthm.* 1.33; Simon. 11.19 W².

[19] Menander the Rhetorician construes the speech as an early example of prose hymn. See Velardi 2001.

[20] Cf. Eur. *Ba.* 282: wine induces λήθην τῶν καθ'ἡμέραν κακῶν. Poetry itself implicitly acquires an escapist quality in Euripides' late plays. See e.g. Di Benedetto 1971: 239–72. In general, cf. Simondon 1982: 128–31; 248–50.

[21] Hdt. 6.21.

[22] Cf. e.g. Moggi 2009, with further bibliography. Hom. *Od.* 24.485 is a famous antecedent. For some additional notes and references on positive oblivion and amnesty in ancient Greece, cf. the Introduction to this volume, pp. 20–5.

συνᾴδει καὶ τὸ "μισέω μνάμονα συμπόταν." ὁ δ' Εὐριπίδης τῶν ἀτόπων τὴν λήθην σοφὴν εἴρηκε.

> They dedicate the cane to Dionysus and along with it forgetfulness, in the belief that one ought not to remember offences committed while drinking, yet needing the disciplinary action appropriate to children. Consistent with this is the phrase 'I hate a boon companion with a good memory'.[23] And Euripides said that forgetfulness of bad events was wise.[24] (*Moralia*, fr. 128 Sandbach, transl. Sandbach)[25]

Happily, these days few would dispute the pervasiveness of Egyptian and Near-Eastern influences on Greek civilisation, yet the daughters of Memory, the Muses who preside over the song of the poets, 'are, so far as we know, purely Greek creatures, and have no counterpart in the orient'.[26] This probably depends on the Greeks' notional 'youth': the loss of writing after the fall of Mycenean palaces, and the resulting historical oblivion, arguably favoured the rise of an enduring and authoritative oral tradition, which stands in sharp contrast with the markedly scribal nature of Egyptian and Near-Eastern epic and poetry.

Against this background, one may recall the proverbial forgetfulness of the Greeks vis-à-vis the Egyptians as depicted in Herodotus' account of the encounter between Hecataeus and the Egyptian priests (2.143–4) as well as in Plato's refashioning of the story in the *Timaeus-Critias*, where Solon replaces Hecataeus as the inexperienced Greek lectured by an Egyptian priest. With their sacred writing, the Egyptians are no doubt more authoritative in comparison with 'childish' Solon and his fellow Greeks, yet the latter, as is clear from Critias' account, have youth on their side and exhibit prodigious capacity for recollection-like memory to be displayed through oral performance, which is favourably, if implicitly, compared with the Egyptian priest's inability to relate the Atlantis story without the aid of writing.[27] The *Timaeus-Critias* seems to imply that good and creative

---

[23] *PMG* 1002 (*adespoton*).

[24] Cf. Eur. *Or.* 211–14.

[25] Cf. Sandbach 1967: 78 '*128–133 an genuina sint propter hiatus et quod titulo aliena sint dubitat Zie. RE XXI 792. sed hiatus breuiatori adscripserim neque is erat Plutarchus ut ad rem propositam adstricte haereret*'.

[26] West 1997: 180. The etymology of the word 'Muse' is a notorious conundrum. Cf. e.g. Assaël 2006, ch. 1.

[27] Towards the beginning of the story, the priest famously says that the Greeks 'are always παῖδες' and 'νέοι ... τὰς ψυχὰς πάντες' (22b). Their stories, he adds, resemble tales for παῖδες (23b), their memory is limited, they are oblivious to the past (23b–c, cf. μέμνησθε and ὑμᾶς λέληθε). In the end, however, it turns out that Critias the younger has a prodigious capacity for recollection thanks to the lessons of his childhood (26b, παίδων μαθήματα). The fact that he kept questioning Critias

recollection depends on historical oblivion, thus recalling the *Phaedrus* and its famously ambiguous critique of (Egyptian!) writing, which turns out to be a *pharmakon* that affects memory less as a remedy than as a poison.[28]

None of Plato's works is specifically devoted to memory, the earliest on record being those by Aristotle and Xenocrates.[29] Besides discussing recollection in a metaphysical perspective, however, Plato devotes interesting analyses to memory both as an intentional activity (in the *Theaetetus*) and as a process complete with propositional contents (in the *Philebus*).[30] This is understandable, because memory is crucial to human behaviour and is also deemed an important quality for a philosophical soul. At the same time, Plato makes it very clear that no *technē* based on empirical memory can qualify as true knowledge, and he is very sharp in debunking any alleged knowledge based on experience:[31] thus, memory is a typical quality of the cave's inhabitants, who remember the patterns and movements of the cave's shadows and are thus pathetically persuaded to be wise.[32]

The comparison between the prisoner and the philosopher resurfaces in the famous digression of the *Theaetetus*.[33] While forgetfulness is not discussed as such, Socrates uses words related to the stem *lath-/leth-* to describe the philosopher's obliviousness to the tricks and ruses of his fellow citizens.[34] It is precisely this obliviousness that allows him to rise above the city's pettiness and to devote himself to the supreme end, namely spiritual

the elder resulted in the story being stamped in his mind 'like the encaustic designs of an indelible painting' (26b–c). By contrast, the Egyptian priest was unable fully to remember the story (24a). While there are obvious similarities between the two stories, Plato's in a sense runs counter to the moral of Herodotus'. Plato is in fact ambivalent towards the perceived fixity of Egyptian civilisation as opposed to the constant of evolution of Greek performative practices. The question takes centre stage in *Laws* book 2. Cf. Rutherford 2013.

[28] 274e–275b. It is hardly a coincidence that the critique of writing finds place in a dialogue that extols poetic inspiration. Also telling is Plato's choice to opt for the Egyptian Thoth, rather than for the Greek Palamedes, as the inventor of writing, all the more so because 'in contrast to the Greek gods who *inspire* their poets to the heights of literary creativity, Thoth actually *writes* texts and functions as an "author", and does not stimulate people to write. In Egyptian texts, divine authorship occasionally replaces scribal authorship' (Vasunia 2001: 152).

[29] For the latter, cf. D.L. 4.12.

[30] See Cambiano 2007b. On memory in the *Philebus*, cf. also King's chapter in this volume. Whether or not there is such a thing as a Platonic theory of recollection is a much-debated question. See the useful survey (and solution) found in Gonzalez 2007.

[31] *Gorgias* 463a–d is the *locus classicus*. At the other end of the spectrum is 'memorism', promoted by 'empiricists who tried to give an account of technical knowledge solely in terms of perception and memory' (Frede 1990: 248).

[32] *Resp.* 516c–d. The *Theaetetus*, however, arguably provides 'an empiricist account of memory … which is free from hereditary factors, innate ideas and inherited patterns' (Andriopoulos 2015: 135).

[33] 172c–177c. While there are obvious parallels between the cave allegory and the digression of the *Theaetetus* (e.g. Polansky 1992), a number of scholars have questioned their ideological consistency. This is not the place to address this vexed problem.

[34] 173d (λέληθεν), 174a (λανθάνοι), 174b (λέληθεν).

freedom and assimilation to god. Thus, the parable of the cave and the digression of the *Theaetetus* form a diptych that, at least potentially, redresses the balance between memory and oblivion. In fact, memory can be good only insofar as it remembers good things, which rules out memory as an empirical tool in such areas as rhetoric or demagogic politics. Conversely, obliviousness turns out to be a virtue insofar as it allows the philosopher to set aside earthly concerns. Similarly, Plato's ambiguous attitude towards writing in the *Timaeus-Critias* and in the *Phaedrus* seems to suggest that good recollection goes hand in hand with historical oblivion.

4 Recollection and Oblivion

As we have seen, both memory and oblivion have their merits in the eyes of Plato and of his contemporaries. Socrates' unqualified hymn to Memory, with its uncompromising condemnation of oblivion, may therefore seem out of place in Plato's world, but the necessary qualifications are implicit, inasmuch as Socrates refers to a form of memory based on the recollection of the highest and most desirable entities. In fact, such recollection is tantamount to dialectics, as is clear from the extraordinary passage where Socrates first mentions recollection:[35]

> δεῖ γὰρ ἄνθρωπον συνιέναι κατ' εἶδος λεγόμενον, ἐκ πολλῶν ἰὸν αἰσθήσεων εἰς ἓν λογισμῷ συναιρούμενον· τοῦτο δ' ἐστὶν ἀνάμνησις ἐκείνων ἅ ποτ' εἶδεν ἡμῶν ἡ ψυχὴ συμπορευθεῖσα θεῷ καὶ ὑπεριδοῦσα ἃ νῦν εἶναί φαμεν, καὶ ἀνακύψασα εἰς τὸ ὂν ὄντως.

> A human being must comprehend what is said universally, arising from many sensations and being collected together into one through reasoning; and this is a recollection of those things which our soul once saw when it travelled in company with a god and treated with contempt the things we now say are, and when it poked its head up into what really is. (*Phaedrus*, 249b–c, transl. Rowe)

The process of arising and *collecting* things together is an unmistakable reference to dialectics, and such a process is said to be equivalent to *recollection*.[36] As we hear in the *Meno*, 'searching and learning are as a whole

---

[35] The passage is extraordinary also for the imperviousness of the Greek, which has prompted many readings and emendations. A detailed discussion is found in Hoffmann and Rashed 2008, who argue for ἰέναι *pro* ἰόν.

[36] Cf. e.g. Carter 1967: 115. Punning on (re)collection may not be inappropriate, as the Greek possibly contains a comparable pun (συνιέναι ... ἰὸν ... εἰς ἓν, and see *Crat.* 412a for the ambiguity of συνιέναι, which may derive from either συνίημι or σύνειμι). Cf. Hoffmann and Rashed 2008: 56. Their emendation (ἰέναι *pro* ἰόν) would make the word play fully explicit.

anamnēsis' (81d), and dialectics and recollection are, by and large, two equivalent processes.[37] Both require contempt for earthly realities, which are said to be but are not endowed with real existence. If we now turn to the section of the *Phaedrus* that immediately follows Socrates' 'hymn to Memory', we will soon find out that 'contempt' is in fact tantamount to oblivion.

To begin with, we come across a distinction between the corrupt man and the initiated, who has seen much of the Forms in his pre-natal wanderings through the heavens. The former 'does not move keenly from here to there, to beauty itself' (250e), so that the sight of beauty (a handsome youth) makes him 'surrender to pleasure', in a beastly attempt to cover his beloved. On the contrary, the latter is overwhelmed by beauty, resulting in awe, shuddering, sweating, high fever, until he grows divine wings (251a ff.). By fairly general consensus, Plato borrowed the list of symptoms from Sappho 31.[38] We reach here the climax of the entire passage, which I quote in full:

... πᾶσα κεντουμένη κύκλῳ ἡ ψυχὴ οἰστρᾷ καὶ ὀδυνᾶται, <u>μνήμην δ' αὖ ἔχουσα τοῦ καλοῦ</u> γέγηθεν. ἐκ δὲ ἀμφοτέρων μεμειγμένων ἀδημονεῖ τε τῇ ἀτοπίᾳ τοῦ πάθους καὶ ἀποροῦσα λυττᾷ, καὶ ἐμμανὴς οὖσα οὔτε νυκτὸς δύναται καθεύδειν οὔτε μεθ' ἡμέραν οὗ ἂν ᾖ μένειν, θεῖ δὲ ποθοῦσα ὅπου ἂν οἴηται <u>ὄψεσθαι τὸν ἔχοντα τὸ κάλλος</u>· ἰδοῦσα δὲ καὶ ἐποχετευσαμένη ἵμερον ἔλυσε μὲν τὰ τότε συμπεφραγμένα, ἀναπνοὴν δὲ λαβοῦσα κέντρων τε καὶ ὠδίνων ἔληξεν, ἡδονὴν δ' αὖ ταύτην γλυκυτάτην ἐν τῷ παρόντι καρποῦται. ὅθεν δὴ ἑκοῦσα εἶναι οὐκ ἀπολείπεται, οὐδέ τινα τοῦ καλοῦ περὶ πλείονος ποιεῖται, ἀλλὰ <u>μητέρων τε καὶ ἀδελφῶν καὶ ἑταίρων πάντων λέλησται</u>, καὶ οὐσίας δι' ἀμέλειαν ἀπολλυμένης παρ' οὐδὲν τίθεται, νομίμων δὲ καὶ εὐσχημόνων, οἷς πρὸ τοῦ ἐκαλλωπίζετο, πάντων καταφρονήσασα δουλεύειν ἑτοίμη καὶ κοιμᾶσθαι ὅπου ἂν ἐᾷ τις ἐγγυτάτω τοῦ πόθου· πρὸς γὰρ τῷ σέβεσθαι <u>τὸν τὸ κάλλος ἔχοντα</u> ἰατρὸν ηὕρηκε μόνον τῶν μεγίστων πόνων. τοῦτο δὲ τὸ πάθος, ὦ παῖ καλέ, πρὸς ὃν δή μοι ὁ λόγος, ἄνθρωποι μὲν ἔρωτα ὀνομάζουσιν ...

... the entire soul, stung all over, goes mad with pain; but then, <u>remembering the beautiful</u>, it rejoices again. The mixture of both these states makes it

---

[37] Cf. e.g. Trabattoni 2012: 313–4. This of course does not mean that there are no 'phenomenological' differences: whereas recollection, in the *Phaedrus*, is a dramatic process brought about by the shock of beauty, which is the only Form to be somehow visible on earth, dialectics, as sketched in the *Republic* and in other dialogues, is a long and painstaking procedure. Cf. Scott 1995: 80–5, whose arguments support the equivalence between recollection in the *Phaedo* and the painful acquisition of knowledge depicted in the parable of the cave.

[38] Cf. e.g. Yunis 2011: 152. Even the medical twist implicit in Socrates' words seems to evoke Sappho, who arguably describes a panic attack, with a vocabulary that is intriguingly paralleled in the Hippocratic Corpus: see Ferrari 2010: 171.

despair at the strangeness of its condition, raging in its perplexity, and in its madness it can neither sleep at night nor keep still where it is by day, but passionately runs wherever it thinks it will see the possessor of beauty; and when it has seen the possessor and channelled desire in to itself it releases what was pent up before, and finding a breathing space it ceases from its stinging birth-pains, once more enjoying this for the moment as the sweetest pleasure. This it does not willingly give up, nor does it value anyone above the one with beauty, but quite forgets mother, brothers, friends, all together, not caring about the loss of its wealth through neglect, and with contempt for all the accepted standards of propriety and good taste in which it previously prided itself it is ready to act the part of a slave and sleep wherever it is allowed to do so, provided it is as close as possible to the object of its longing; for in addition to its reverence for the possessor of beauty, it has found him the sole healer of its greatest sufferings. This experience, my beautiful boy, men term 'love'. (*Phaedrus*, 251d–252b, transl. Rowe modified)

Remarkably, both the subject and the object of love are presented as abstract, hardly individual entities, whereas certain overtones cannot but evoke erotic intercourse. Moreover, the lover's contempt for earthly things, which is of course a result of the lover's recollection of the Forms, brings about a turning of values upside down, which takes the form of oblivion, thus making explicit the case for a good form of forgetfulness.[39]

5 In The Name of Helen

Plato's true lover, it turned out, is someone who forgets everyday values – mother, brothers, friends, riches – only to devote himself to what Plato refers to as 'the possessor of beauty'. What is the source of this dramatic change? Sappho's 'ode to Helen' may help answer this question:[40]

> [o]ἰ μὲν ἰππήων cτρότον οἰ δὲ πέcδων
> οἰ δὲ νάων φαῖc' ἐπ[ὶ] γᾶν μέλαι[ν]αν
> [ἔ]μμεναι κάλλιcτον, ἔγω δὲ κῆν' ὄτ-
> τω τιc ἔραται·
> [πά]γχυ δ' εὔμαρεc cύνετον πόηcαι   (5)
> [π]άντι τ[ο]ῦτ'· ἀ γὰρ πόλυ περcκέθοιcα

---

[39] For the key role of forgetfulness in the educational path of Plato's philosophical dialectic, see also Wygoda's chapter in this volume.

[40] Fr. 16. I reproduce the text provided by Obbink 2016, which makes use of the most recent papyrological finds, but I add the supplement [οὐδέ θέλοι] at line 12, which is most likely on palaeographical grounds: hardly any other supplement is compatible with the trace of a grave accent at the beginning of the line (see Martinelli Tempesta 1999). It is not certain that the poem ended at l. 20: cf. e.g. Lardinois 2009.

κάλλος [ἀνθ]ρώπων Ἐλένα [τ]ὸν ἄνδρα
τόν[...]ιϲτον
καλλ[ίποι]ϲ’ ἔβα ’ϲ Τροΐαν πλέοιϲα
κωὐδ[ὲ πα]ῖδοϲ οὐδὲ φίλων τοκήων   (10)
πά[μπαν] ἐμνάϲθη, ἀλλὰ παράγαγ’ αὔταν
[οὐδὲ θέλοι]ϲαν
[.....γν]αμπτον γὰρ [.....]ϝόημμα
[....]... κούφωϲ τ[......]ϝοηϲηι.
[..]με νῦν Ἀνακτορί[αϲ] ὀνέμναι-   (15)
[ϲ’ οὐ] παρεοίϲαϲ,
[τᾶ]ϲ κε βολλοίμαν ἔρατόν τε βᾶμα
κἀμάρυχμα λάμπρον ἴδην προϲώπω
ἢ τὰ Λύδων ἄρματα κἀν ὄπλοιϲι
[πεϲδομ]άχενταϲ.   (20)

Some say an army of cavalry, others of infantry,
and others of ships, is the finest thing[41]
upon the black earth – but I say it is whatever
    one is in love with.
And it is totally easy to make this plain
to all, for even she who far surpassed
everyone in beauty, Helen, abandoned
    the [best?] of men, her husband,[42]
when she departed for Troy by sail,
giving no mind to her child
or beloved parent, led astray
    – *far from willing* –
for (in)flexible … thought
    lightly … thinks
brings to my mind now Anaktoria,
    who is gone
her beloved step, the bright spark
of her face, I would rather see
than the chariots of Lydia, than any march
    of soldiers at arms.

[41] Konstan 2015 emphasises the crucial semantic distinction between the adjective καλός ('fine') and the noun κάλλος ('beauty'), which in archaic poetry 'is primarily ascribed to good-looking youths, or to adults … who are noted for their seductiveness' (22). In fr. 50 Sappho explicitly toys with the meaning of the adjective ('fine' in its ordinary meaning but 'beautiful' or 'handsome' when in conjunction with ἴδην 'gazing'). I believe that a comparable shift is at work here: by the end of the poem, with the mention of κάλλος and ἴδην, the adjective is retrospectively re-defined. Fr. 50 explicitly argues that whoever is good is also handsome; fr. 16 argues that what is truly beautiful, i.e. displays κάλλος and induces love, is finer than (what people take as) the finest things, at least in the eyes of a lover. Sappho's intention to toy with the meaning of the word(s) is also signalled by the pun κάλλος/καλλίποισα (9).

[42] I translate ἄνδρα as 'the [best?] of men, her husband' because the Greek word is used for both (male) men and husbands, and the context seems to require both meanings.

In the extant fragments, this is the only time in which Sappho tries to 'demonstrate' a general thesis to 'everyone'.[43] This gives the ode a curiously proto-philosophical turn.[44]

As in Socrates' speech, the poem may be taken to entail a full '*Umwertung aller Werte*',[45] in what looks like an inquiry into the ultimate object of love (compare Sappho's ὄττω τις ἔραται and Plato's ἐρᾷ μὲν οὖν, ὅτου δὲ ἀπορεῖ). Sappho's Helen, who is referred to as the 'hyper-possessor of beauty' (6–7),[46] *forgets* her parents, daughter and excellent husband. At the same time, Helen's story reminds Sappho of Anactoria.[47] Beside an interesting dialectic between memory and oblivion, we may note the juxtaposition between the verb μέμνημαι, 'remember', and ἀναμιμνήσκω, '(cause somebody to) recollect', which is no doubt exceptional and, again, may sound 'proto-philosophical'.[48]

Points of context – Socrates' speech is compared to a palinode to Helen, and love symptoms have just been described in Sapphic tones – enhance Plato's echoing of this often echoed poem.[49] Sappho is a model for the reversal of values brought about by the shocking experience of falling in love, and, more specifically, for the oblivion this brings about: lovers forget their relatives and pursuits and cannot but recall love. In both cases, the evocation of the beloved has a shining quality (compare Sappho's κἀμάρυχμα

---

[43] Cf. e.g. Bouvrie Thorsen 1978: 13.

[44] Accordingly, scholars have labelled Sappho's stance as sophistic (e.g. Race 1989–90, who stresses Sappho's arguments for subjective and emotional choices), aesthetic (e.g. Koniaris 1967, who takes τὸ κάλλιστον as the pivotal element of the ode), relativist (Zellner 2007, arguing that the poem is an instance of Inference to the Best Explanation), political (Svenbro 1984, arguing for a feminist interpretation), logical/rhetorical (Most 1981, who interprets the poem in the light of Arist. *Rhet.* 1398b19–1399a6), pedagogical (Johnson 2012, who compares the unusual pedagogy of Sappho with that of Socrates). To be sure, other scholars have resisted the temptation of interpreting 16 Voigt in a philosophical perspective, either by claiming that the poem is obscure (e.g. Page 1955: 53) and discontinuous (Fränkel 1955: 92) or by stressing its religious (e.g. Privitera 1967), performative (e.g. Dodson-Robinson 2010) and ritual (e.g. Bierl 2003, who also offers a good survey of previous interpretations) dimension. I would opt for a middle ground: ancient readers, as is the case with recent scholars, could have found in the poem 'the seeds of a variety of arguments that claim it for philosophy' (Foley 1998: 62).

[45] So runs the title of Wills 1967, who stresses the strongly assertive tone of Sappho's poem. Plato *may* have understood the poem in this way.

[46] Of course περσκέθοισα κάλλος (6–7) entails an accusative of relation and not an object complement, but such a distinction could hardly be available or interesting to either Sappho or Plato.

[47] Cf. Dane 1981.

[48] Before Plato, there seems to be just one more instance in another poem by Sappho (Sappho 94.10, cf. Burnett 1979, 18), and one in Sophocles (*OT* 1133).

[49] The poem was no doubt famous. Cf. Calder 1984 (on Aesch. *Ag.* 403–19); Casali 1989 (on Eur. *Bacch.* 881); Di Marco 1980 (on Eur. *Cyc.* 182–6); Scodel 1997 (on Eur. *Hyps.*, *Phoen.* 88–177, *IA* 185–302); Tulli 2008 (on Isoc. *Hel.* 1).

λάμπρον ἴδην προσώπω with Plato's κάλλος ἰδεῖν λαμπρόν, 250b, and θεοειδὲς πρόσωπον ἴδῃ, 251a) but perhaps the two texts are even closer.

André Lardinois (2008) has convincingly shown that, in Sappho's extant poetry, whenever a character longs for her beloved she evokes a moment of performance, namely dance and music as practised by Sappho and her companions. This is very clear in some cases, and Lardinois argues that it is implicit in our poem: Sappho remembers Anaktoria's 'lovely step', which by itself may evoke dance, and even the 'shining spark of her face' seems to suggest movement, in that in early Greek poetry ἀμάρυγμα and its cognates are used either for glittering gestures or as an epithet of the Graces, who are of course dancing goddesses.[50]

These 'choral' traits resurface in the *Phaedrus*. When struck by the youth's beauty, the lover remembers the time when he followed his god as a χορευτής, that is a member of a chorus (252d). After the end of the palinode, as a symbol for the uncompromising pursuit of philosophy, he chooses 'choral' (cf. 230c) cicadas.[51] The cicadas were once humans who, carried away by music, were oblivious to primary needs and died without realising (ἠμέλησαν σίτων τε καὶ ποτῶν, καὶ ἔλαθον τελευτήσαντες αὐτούς, 259c). Accordingly, the Muses turned them into cicadas and granted them the gift of song,[52] which in turn recalls Sappho's longing for the hereafter in the form of perennial song and dance.[53] So here is Sappho's lesson for Socrates, one of both memory and oblivion: forget earthly things, remember beauty in the divine sparkle of a dancing movement.[54]

6 The 'Mother of the Speech' and the 'Possessor of Beauty'

As I mentioned at the beginning of my paper, 'Plato's Sappho' has recently sparked a lively debate, which is in fact a very old one, if we only think that Maximus of Tyre went so far as to equate Sapphic and Platonic love, further claiming that Sappho must be recognised as the 'mother' of Socrates' palinode in the *Phaedrus*.[55] Maximus' words deserve serious consideration, as Plato, in the words of one critic, 'draws directly on the poetic language of the lyric

---

[50] On *amarugma*, cf. Brown 1989.

[51] A number of scholars take Plato's cicadas as a negative paradigm. I believe that this is demonstrably wrong: see Capra 2014a: 106–9.

[52] The story is modelled on scenes of poetic initiation such as that of Hesiod in the *Theogony* and Archilochus in Mnesiepes' inscription. Cf. Capra 2014a: ch. 3.

[53] See Lardinois 2008.

[54] Intriguingly, Sappho 95 perhaps implied, or at least could suggest to later readers, a reference to cicadas (cf. Rawles 2006 and Pataki 2015). For Sappho's fascination with the radiance of the sun, see Nagy 2009.

[55] Max. Tyr. 18.9. Unlike Parker 1996, Foley 1998 and Johnson 2012 take Maximus' claim seriously.

poets' while at the same time setting against them 'a need for self-control to redirect the soul's energy from physical beauty to the Forms', which means that unlike Sappho he turns to memory 'not as a consolation but as a spur to further effort'.[56] Yet what makes it truly attractive to Plato is its erasing effect, resulting in the severing of all ties that bind us to our everyday life.

While memory and oblivion are two sides of the same coin in both the *Phaedrus* and the poem, it is memory, rather than oblivion, that opens a gap between Plato and Sappho. In the 'Ode to Helen,' as in other nostalgic poems, Sappho's memory is obsessed with single details: she magnifies the light shining on the face of a dancer, a hand playing a lyre and so on.[57] Sappho, in sum, makes a fetish of her beloved ones;[58] Plato could not possibly agree: in *Republic* 10 (604d) he attacks poetry precisely because it indulges in 'recollections of *pathos*' (ἀναμνήσεις τοῦ πάθους) and 'lamentations' (ὀδυρμούς). Unlike Sappho and ordinary people, Plato's lover 'treats the sensibles as reminders of the vision, not as objects of desire in themselves'.[59] Unlike Sappho's beloved ones, in turn, Plato's are abstract creatures, 'possessors of beauty', with no names, quirks or individual traits other than their affinity with the god. Remarkably, this parallels the gap between Diotima's eros and that of Aristophanes: the latter resembles Diotima's qua 'ecstatic' and oblivious, but is criticised for its inability to transcend the individual.[60] So here is a consistent (dis)similarity between 'philosophical' and 'poetic' love.

Through what Socrates refers to as 'enthusiasm through memory' (253a), Plato's lover transcends earthly beauty as described by poets. He aims his gaze at the metaphysical realm behind the divine face of the 'possessor of beauty', as if his radiant face were an iconic window open to the relevant Form.[61] Plato's phrase 'possessor of beauty' (ὁ τὸ κάλλος ἔχων), repeated twice at 251d–252b, is in fact exceptional: with the very telling exception of Isocrates' *Helen*,[62] to the best of my knowledge it is found nowhere

---

[56] Pender 2007: 54. Cf. Pender 2011.

[57] Discussions of Sappho's 'memory' include Burnett 1979, Jarrett 2002, Rayor 2005, Lardinois 2008. Cf. also Catenacci 2013, who argues that Sappho's nostalgic poems inspired the representation of Sappho by the Tithonus Painter: the relevant vase (Kunstsammlungen of Ruhr Universität Bochum, inv. S 508, ca. 480 BCE) depicts Sappho and a girl in what is perhaps a moment of sad farewell.

[58] And so does Anacreon, who went so far as to maintain that 'Boys are my gods' (test. 7 Campbell = Schol. Pind. *Isthm.*2.1b (iii 213 Drachmann)). This may have inspired *Phdr.* 251b.

[59] Scott 1995: 76–7.

[60] *Symp.* 205e and 212c.

[61] This cannot but recall Diotima's *scala amoris* in the *Symposium*. Diotima *does not* mention recollection, yet her discussion provides 'un esempio e un'illustrazione concreta delle diverse tappe del percorso che deve essere intrapreso dagli uomini in virtù della ἀνάμνησις, con l'orientamento epistemologico verso le idee che la reminiscenza determina' (Fronterotta 2001: 98).

[62] 'Further, we show such pious respect and consideration for this *idea*, that we hold the possessors of beauty (τῶν ἐχόντων τὸ κάλλος) who make a profit of it and counsel ill in regard to their youth in greater dishonour than those who violate the persons of others' (58, transl. Freese modified).

else in the classical age.[63] While possibly pointing to Sappho's Helen as the archetypal 'hyperpossessor of beauty', the phrase is arguably borrowed from the old epic formula 'possessing beauty from the gods/Graces', which Plato could take as meaning that all beauty is divine in origin.[64] In other words, the language of the Forms is the result of Plato's poetic memory and emerges in and against the poetic tradition. Socrates' claim that no poet has ever succeeded in singing the hyperouranian world (247c) could hardly be more appropriate.

Sappho is fond of close-ups, she likes to blow up poignant details of the past. By contrast, Plato's eye captures no less poignant and breathtaking views from the metaphysical, pre-natal world with an extreme long shot. Both views, however, require the severing of ordinary memories, that is they require what I have labelled 'lyric oblivion', resulting in a direct, rather than inverse, correlation: the more one forgets, the more – and the better – one remembers. To this extent, both Nightingale and Maximus are right: the lyric voice of oblivion stays 'autonomous' and Sappho is truly 'the mother of the speech'.

---

[63] Pl. *Crit.*, 117b is only partially comparable. The phrase resurfaces in one of Aristides' *Sacred Tales* (2.300.4–7). Cf. also *App. Anth. Epigr.* (Cougny), ii 191.7–8.

[64] Cf. Hom. *Od.* 6.18 Χαρίτων ἄπο κάλλος ἔχουσαι; *Od.* 8.457 θεῶν ἄπο κάλλος ἔχουσα; Hes. Fr. 171.4 θεῶν ἀπ]ο κάλλος ἔ[χουσαν; Hes. Fr. 215.1 Χαρίτων ἄπο κάλλος ἔχουσα, *Hy. Ven.* 77 θεῶν ἄπο κάλλος ἔχοντα.

CHAPTER 8

Socratic Forgetfulness and Platonic Irony

Ynon Wygoda

1 Introduction

Perhaps because of the centrality of the theory of recollection in the traditional conception of Plato's thought, it has seldom been remarked that there also exists a veritable *leitmotif* of Socrates' forgetful image in the Platonic corpus. After all, how can we square the image of Socrates as the promoter of the 'learning as recollection' theory, thrice repeated in the *Phaedo*, the *Meno* and the *Phaedrus*,[1] with his portrayal as someone who is forgetful? And yet expressions of this forgetfulness are strewn across the Platonic corpus, taking the form both of offhand Socratic confessions of having forgotten this or that detail and of personal proclamations of having a forgetful character. Such is Socrates' declaration in the beginning of the *Phaedrus*: because of the dullness of his mind he has forgotten (ὑπὸ δὲ νωθείας αὖ καὶ αὐτὸ τοῦτο ἐπιλέλησμαι, 235d) from whom he had once heard a better speech than the one just read out to him. And such are his avowals to Meno and Protagoras: 'I am hardly memorious, Meno' (Οὐ πάνυ εἰμὶ μνήμων, ὦ Μένων) (*Men.* 71c);[2] and 'Protagoras, I find that I am a forgetful sort of person' (Ὦ Πρωταγόρα, ἐγὼ τυγχάνω ἐπιλήσμων τις ὢν ἄνθρωπος) (*Prot.* 334c).[3]

The picture is further complicated by the fact that these declarations are both implicitly and explicitly belied by Socrates' proof of the contrary, as well as by unequivocal opposing testimonies. Thus we find that Socrates actually scolds Agathon with the words: 'Agathon! ... how forgetful do you

---

[1] For considerations on whether to include the *Republic* in this group, see Scott 1995: 80–5. For some remarks on the theory of recollection, cf. the Introduction to this volume, pp. 12–13, 26–7, and Capra's chapter.

[2] All references to Plato's works in Greek are to Burnet's *OCT* edition of the text, except for the *Meno* for which I use Bluck's 1978 edition. Translations are mine except where otherwise stated. For my use of the adjective 'memorious', here and elsewhere, see the parallel with Borges' character 'Funes the memorious' below, p. 200.

[3] Notice that the same formula is used in the *Phaedrus* (οὐ πάνυ μέμνημαι, 263d).

think I am?' (ἐπιλήσμων μέντ'ἂν εἴην, ὦ Ἀγάθων, εἰπεῖν τὸν Σωκράτη) (*Symp.* 194a), and to Hippias' query about whether he remembers the original question of their discussion he resolutely answers 'Certainly!' (Ἔγωγε!) (*Hipp. Mai.* 289c). This kind of rhetorical response, assuring his interlocutors of the dependability of his memory in remembering the train of arguments in their discussions, fits well with Socrates' standard demand that his interlocutors remember their past arguments, scolding them if they fail to do so. This occurs, for example, with Polus, whom Socrates reprimands: 'Why, at such a young age, Polus, have you no memory?' (ἀλλ' οὐ μνημονεύεις τηλικοῦτος ὤν, ὦ Πῶλε;) (*Grg.* 466a).[4] The same is also the case in the *Republic* (486d), with its programmatic educational tone, where this requirement is set in stone by Socrates' statement that those who cannot provide proof of a memorious soul (ἐπιλήσμονα ψύχην) must not be accepted into the ranks of the pursuers of knowledge and wisdom (φιλόσοφοι), for they will not be able to make the necessary effort for a life of inquiry.[5] While Socrates' insistence on a capable faculty of memory as a prerequisite for a life of inquiry such as his own[6] and the testimonies to his capacity to retain previous arguments undercut the frankness of Socrates' confession of forgetfulness only implicitly, Alcibiades' declaration in the *Protagoras* makes the point explicit: 'For Socrates, I assure you, will not forget (μὴ ἐπιλήσεσθαι), though he jokes and calls himself forgetful' (ἐπεὶ Σωκράτη γε ἐγὼ ἐγγυῶμαι μὴ ἐπιλήσεσθαι, οὐχ ὅτι παίζει καί φησιν ἐπιλήσμων εἶναι) (*Prot.* 336d).

In the light of this, a question looms large: how can we reconcile the recurring incongruence concerning Socrates' forgetfulness in Plato's oeuvre? It is my claim that the inquiry into Socrates' forgetfulness is in fact an inquiry into a fascinating case of Platonic irony. At times, this irony

---

[4] Cf. *Euth.* 15c, *Prot.* 332e, *Men.* 94c, *Resp.* 350d, *Phlb.* 31a, *Resp.* 374a. See too *Hipp. Min.* 371d, *Ion* 539e where Socrates scolds Ion for being forgetful when, surely, forgetfulness is unbecoming of a rhapsode (ἢ οὕτως ἐπιλήσμων εἶ; καίτοι οὐκ ἂν πρέποι γε ἐπιλήσμονα εἶναι ῥαψῳδὸν ἄνδρα).

[5] In contemplating the necessary qualities of a good student, Socrates describes him as having a quick and good learning ability (εὐμαθής), alongside a nimble faculty of memory (μνήμων) (*Republic* 494b, *Charmides* 159e–160a and *Laws* 709e; this aspect of Socratic teaching had been clearly perceived already by Aristophanes: see below, pp. 209–10, as well as Milanezi's chapter, pp. 120–3). In fact, in both Plato's dialogues and Xenophon's memoirs (*Mem.* 4.1.2), this emphasis on the importance of memory appears to have been quite a standard Socratic request, and indeed a necessary condition for all scholarly ventures. For not only does an improved faculty of memory enable and facilitate the tasks of comparing and evaluating various pieces of information, crucial to deductive reasoning (cf. Aristotle, *Metaphysics* 1.7.988a30); it enables the securing of these retained pieces of information once amassed and prevents them from exiting one's soul. For the importance of 'natural memory' in Plato, see also Sassi's chapter in this volume.

[6] Cf. e.g. *Apol.* 28e, 29d.

finds its expression in the words attributed to Socrates in his interaction with a single interlocutor within a given dialogue. At other times it appears on a meta-dialogical level, deriving its sting from the larger Platonic literary composition and targeting the readers rather than the dialogue's *dramatis personae*. As in all cases of irony, Socrates' forgetfulness involves a certain degree of playfulness that challenges both his interlocutors and ourselves, as readers, to attempt to resolve the discrepancy between the ironist's intentions and the common understanding of his words.[7] In the case of Socrates' forgetfulness this discrepancy between his intention and others' understanding of it corresponds to the distinction between two meanings of the verb 'to forget': on the one hand, forgetting in its primary sense, as lack of remembrance – to which I shall refer as the *privative model*; on the other hand, forgetting in its secondary meaning, denoting inattention or disregard – to which I shall refer, following Nietzsche, as the *active model*.[8]

Admittedly, as Goethe has already remarked, when dealing with such a masterful writer as Plato any claim as to the presence of irony is extremely difficult to prove, since one is never quite sure whether to read the argument in earnest or in jest, as an avowal of conviction or as an elenctic device.[9] Indeed, since the edge of verbal irony is dependent on the incongruity between one's speech and one's intention, some degree of certainty as to the speaker's position must first be reached to understand whether irony is in play. Yet, as is well known to all readers of Plato, and as has in fact been declared by Socrates' interlocutors, it is precisely this apprehension of Socrates' own position that is often so tantalizingly difficult due to the dialectical nature of his argumentation. What is more, since it is in the

---

[7] For the basic definition of Socratic irony that hints at a hidden message but does not reveal it at once, cf. Cicero's classic formulation (*De oratore* 2.67.269–70): 'Ironical dissimulation (*dissimulatio*) is agreeable (*urbana*) when what you say is quite other than what you think … In this irony and dissimulation Socrates, in my opinion, far excelled all others in charm and humanity. It is an elegant kind of humour, seasoned with gravity.' For the existence *avant la lettre* of such Attic *urbanitas* in the image of its Roman offshoot, as well as in its description of the ἀστεῖος (literally the 'urban' type), cf. Lammermann 1936: 25. I am grateful to Katja Machill for her assistance in procuring this text. On the scholarly debate on how to interpret the nature of this Socratic irony, cf. Vlastos 1991: 21–44 and Nehamas' criticism (1999: 46–100). See further below n. 28.

[8] 'Forgetfulness is no mere *uis inertiae* as the superficial believe, but rather an active, and in the strict sense of the term, positive capacity of inhibition (ein aktives, im strengsten Sinne positives Hemmungsvermögen) … a little quietude, a little tabula rasa of the consciousness, so as to make room for the new, and above all for the more noble functions and functionaries … This is the usefulness, as said, of active forgetfulness (aktiven Vergesslichkeit).' Nietzsche 1980: 291 (my translation).

[9] See Goethe's concluding sentence in 'Plato als Mitgenosse einer christlichen Offenbarung' (1796) quoted by Friedländer 1958: 137.

nature of irony to invite its addressees into a dance-of-veils of meanings and intentions, its message is not always meant to be discovered by all, or so quickly. Taking Vladimir Jankélévitch's lead, one could say that the ironic mask does not resemble the mask of the robber attempting to disappear without a trace, but rather that of the coquette in the masked ball, tantalizing her suitors with her evasiveness, while making sure to drop her glove behind her. Irony is first and foremost a game, and as a game it is never a 'mere swapping of a yes for a no',[10] which would annul its playful call for discovery. Nor can irony, for the very same reason, be meant to address a gullible crowd which would accept its message at face value; nor can it intentionally desire to remain completely ungraspable, if its aim is to point back to the incongruity that underlies it. Hence, if Socrates' declaration of forgetfulness is indeed ironic, its first signs of playfulness should arouse our attention, but further clues must be sought and further proofs must be uncovered in order to verify the existence of its hidden message and to inquire after its possible cipher in light of the particular interlocutor involved. Furthermore, since the enigmatic figure of Socrates the forgetful is equally the fruit of a meta-dialogical process, an attempt should be made to decipher the logic behind the use of this image with all its varied resonances beyond the concrete dialogical circumstances. Thus I suggest that Socrates' forgetfulness is to be evaluated in its particular expression vis-à-vis interlocutors such as Theaetetus and Meno, with whom the question raised is that of the understanding of the learning process; knowledgeable sophists such as Protagoras, Gorgias, and Hippias, whom Socrates confronts about the nature and effects of their teaching methods; and masterful mnemonists such as Ion and Hippias himself, with whom the nexus between memory and understanding is brought to the fore.

In what follows, I propose to begin to undertake this task by reviewing and comparing two instances in which Socrates' forgetfulness appears: once in the *Meno*, which will serve as the main focus of this chapter, where Socrates' forgetfulness displays its pedagogic quality as it is presented in opposition to the figure of the memorizing student, drawing upon the more prevalent privative understanding of forgetfulness; and once in the *Protagoras*, which exemplifies the polemical qualities of the active sense of forgetfulness by contrasting it with the figure of the masterful and eloquent sophist.

---

[10] The expression is Jean Paul's (Friedrich Richter), quoted by Friedländer 1958: 137. On the notion of pseudo-irony, cf. Jankélévitch 1964: 61–5 *et passim*.

2 The Privative Model of Forgetfulness

When Herodotus, the 'father of history', declared that the aim of his *Historiae* (1.1) was to save the Greek and Barbarian feats from fading away into the oblivion of time (ἐξίτηλα γένηται τῷ χρόνῳ), he propounded the writing of history as a human tool in the battle against its all-devouring adversary, time.[11] In other words, he proposed memory to counter forgetfulness in its primary lexical sense: as the state of forgetting, of being apt to forget, or of being forgotten. Thus, memory (through writing) was presented as a counter to the state of lack of memory. Yet, Herodotus' imagery of the fading imprint of heroic human deeds, or literally their exit (from ἐξ-εῖναι) or departure from the pool of retained memories, further suggests an insight into the nature of forgetfulness. It represents forgetfulness as the nullifying chaos that lies beyond the contours of memory, and defines it by contrast.[12] How this contour is defined, and what exactly it entails, remains unstated, but the imagery used by Herodotus is that of a binary opposition. It is presented as an inside-outside opposition denoting that one either possesses memory or one does not, thereby excluding all intermediate stages and laying the defining emphasis entirely on memory's side, while assigning to forgetfulness the role of its converse.[13]

This Herodotean image and terminology – which linguists have suggested may belong to a rather popular understanding of the concept of forgetfulness[14] – was echoed by Plato in his description of forgetfulness as 'the departure of memory' (λήθη μνήμης ἔξοδος).[15] Taking the soul to be the

---

[11] Cf. Asheri et al. 2007: 73. On alternative ways of reading this term, cf. Moles 1999: 27–69.

[12] Note the presence of the Greek term for chaos (χάος) at the basis of later Greek verbs such as ξεχάνω or ξεχνῶ denoting forgetfulness, cf. Buck 1920: 39. For a discussion of memory in Herodotus, and for a different reading of the Herodotean passage, see Darbo-Peschanski's chapter in this volume.

[13] The single equivalent to this proemial expression in Herodotus' work, describing the danger that a certain dynasty will cease to exist (γενέσθαι ἐξίτηλον) (5.39.2), renders the *exitus* image even clearer, but also emphasizes the possible definitiveness of the verb 'exit'. Cf. Chantraine 1968–80: 322 s.v. εἶμι; Pelliccia 1992: 74–80; Asheri et al. 2007: 73. Memory and forgetfulness are thus structurally likened to existence and nonexistence: in both pairs the latter term is defined as the negation of the former. In the background of this parallel lies the mythic imagery of the convergence of the two opposite pairs into the single mythical opposition marked by the river Lethe (Forgetfulness) separating the land of the living from the land of the dead, by the contrast between those filled with memories and those 'gorged with forgetfulness', as Plato says in the *Phaedrus* (248c). On further structural parallels between life and death, forgetfulness and memory, cf. Eliade 1963: 329–44.

[14] This could be inferred from the extensive linguistic use of the inversive prefix and from a variety of words for the verb 'to remember', from the Sanskrit 'vi-smr' to its colloquial nineteenth-century English equivalent 'to dis-remember'. Cf. Buck 1920: 39–40.

[15] *Phlb.* 33e. Cf. *Symp.* 208a 'forgetfulness is the departure of knowledge' (λήθη γὰρ ἐπιστήμης ἔξοδος). For the image of the soul as a container or a vessel (ἀγγεῖον), cf. *Prot.* 314a, and *Tht.* 197e (the famous aviary simile). For a more comprehensive look at the distinctive and complex ways in which later dialogues, especially the *Philebus* and the *Theaetetus*, depict the soul and memory in

seat of memory (cf. e.g. *Men.* 88a), Plato has Socrates remark to Simmias in the *Phaedo*: 'Is this not what we call forgetfulness, Simmias: the loss of knowledge?' (ἢ οὐ τοῦτο λήθην λέγομεν, ὦ Σιμμία, ἐπιστήμης ἀποβολήν) (*Phaed.* 75d). Yet, by so relating memory and knowledge to forgetfulness, Plato seems to add another element to be considered in defining the concept. For if it is in the capacity of the mind or the soul that memories be gotten (in the sense of retained), it is also in its capacity that they be for-gotten (in the archaic sense of forsaken) if the required effort to retain them is not made. Thus the lack of accumulated knowledge is seen as a loss of knowledge, and this emphasizes forgetfulness as the result of the lack of effort required to retain knowledge. Consequently, the forgetful soul (ἐπιλήσμονα ψυχήν) is described by Plato as 'lethargic' (λήθαργος), a term whose meaning in Greek later shifted to both 'lassitude' and 'forgetfulness'.[16] Socrates' staunch opposition to such lethargy and idleness (ἀργός) (*Meno* 81d; 86b) is therefore consistent with his above-mentioned standard expectation that his interlocutors remember what was previously said,[17] as well as his rejection of those who could not provide proof of a memorious soul (μνημονικὴν ψυχήν) from the ranks of the potential pursuers of knowledge and wisdom.

3   Facing the Memorious Meno

When we turn to the *Meno*'s introductory paragraph we realize that it corroborates the privative model of forgetfulness through its very structure, by presenting the two protagonists as the positive and negative embodiments of memory. Keeping the character of Jorge Luis Borges' 'Funes el memorioso' ('Funes the memorious') in mind, one may say that Socrates introduces Meno in the dialogue as 'Meno the memorious', as suggested by the play on words between his name (Μένων) and the participial form of the verb 'to remember' (μνήμων).[18] Socrates expressively positions himself in contrast, as the privative image of his interlocutor,

comparison with Plato's earlier and early middle dialogues, cf. Klein 1989: 108–72. For memory and recollection in the *Philebus*, see also King's chapter in this volume.

[16] Cf. Chantraine 1968–80: 636 s.v.

[17] E.g. *Ion* 539e, *Euthd.* 287b and *Grg.* 466a, where the formula is close to that of the *Meno* (ἀλλ' οὐ μνημονεύεις τηλικοῦτος ὤν, ὦ Πῶλε).

[18] In the background there might be the fact that μνήμων was also the title given to the individual responsible for functioning as a living 'recorder' of legal decisions before writing was available, especially since, as Vernant remarked, following Gernet, the use of the term extended beyond the legal context (Vernant 1983: 96 n. 4; see also Darbo-Peschanski's chapter in this volume, and pp. 14–15 of the Introduction). On Plato's word-play with Meno's name, see further n. 25 below.

i.e. as a forgetful character: 'I am hardly memorious, Meno' (Οὐ πάνυ εἰμὶ μνήμων, ὦ Μένων) (71c). In fact, if one considers the abrupt manner in which Meno poses his question concerning the possibility of teaching ἀρετή (70a) at the very beginning of the dialogue, and Socrates' call upon Meno's memory to remind him of Gorgias' definition of ἀρετή (ἀνάμνησον οὖν με) (71c), at its end, the opening of the *Meno* might seem to present Meno as just the sort of memory-capable, eager student sought after by Socrates.[19] Yet Meno's embodiment of memory only heightens our surprise in finding Socrates himself as his immemorious antipode, who negates what is affirmed by his memorious counterpart. Thus, Socrates denies possessing any definition of ἀρετή at all (τὸ παράπαν) (71a), contrary to the memorious Meno who is capable of reproducing from memory Gorgias' authoritative opinion on the matter (71e–72a, 73c). Declaring his forgetfulness (rather than his criticism) of Gorgias' opinion, which he admits to have heard but of which he apparently retained no memory, Socrates asks Meno to remind him of what seems to have slipped from his mind. As a result, Socrates' declaration corresponds to the privative model in its binary nature: complete knowledge and memory, on the one side, and complete lack of knowledge and utter forgetfulness, on the other.

The stark contrast between the two interlocutors in the *Meno* is not only emphasized by the structure of Socrates' statement but by his very choice of terms. For unlike Socrates' confession in the *Protagoras* that he is a forgetful character (ἐπιλήσμων τις) (334c, 334d) or his habitual declaration of being forgetful (ἐπιλήσμων) to which Alcibiades testifies in the same dialogue (336d),[20] Socrates' declaration in the *Meno* does not make use of the common Greek verb for forgetting (ἐπιλήθομαι), but rather recurs to the periphrastic 'being im-memorious' (Οὐ πάνυ … μνήμων).[21] This

---

[19] The abruptness with which the dialogue begins and which characterizes Meno's question has given rise to several interpretations that unfold along the course of the dialogue. Some see Meno's question as an expression of eagerness on the part of a student, who in his encounter with the renowned Socrates during his short stay in Athens (76e) wishes to quickly become an authority on the topic of his inquiry (cf. Scolnicov 1988: 51; Scott 2006: 12). Other more critical views interpret his abruptness as a belligerent question aimed at seeing what Socrates would answer only to refute it, and then report Socrates' downfall back home (71b–c). This second view has been associated by some with the ancient evidence on Meno's historical figure according to which he had no interest in virtue at all (cf. Klein 1989: 38–9, 189).

[20] Cf. also *Symp.* 194a, where Socrates implicitly denies this attribute: ἐπιλήσμων μεντἂν εἴην, ὦ Ἀγάθων … On the chronological order of the dialogues and the relationship between the *Meno* and the *Protagoras*, cf. Hoerber 1960: 79–82; Bluck 1978: 109.

[21] My reading rests on the *double entendre* present in the οὐ πάνυ which could be interpreted as a weak ('not quite' or 'not very') or a strong ('not at all!') negation. Cf. LSJ πάνυ 1.3, Riddell 1877: §139, Ademollo 2011: 80. See further below n. 43.

detail is of some importance. For whereas the verb ἐπιλήθομαι is open to a broader semantic spectrum than the strict binary structure of the privative definition of forgetfulness, and may indeed even stand alongside the capacity of memory, the formula used in the *Meno* allows no such alternative interpretation. For to declare that one is *im*-memorious is to negate, by the principle of contradiction, any simultaneous trace of memory, and to place, in addition, the two interlocutors irreconcilably at odds.[22]

Yet, if the privative model portrayed in the *Meno* raises the question of the significance of Socrates' counter-position, it also offers the key to its explanation. Since according to that model forgetfulness is defined entirely in opposition to memory, and the character of Meno is introduced as memory's representative, in order to understand what it is that Socrates so starkly negates one must first inquire after the nature of Meno's memory.[23] A careful reading of the introductory paragraph reveals that the key to Meno's memory lies with the figure of the absent (71d) – yet very much present – Gorgias, whose teachings Meno committed to memory. For it is through the introduction of the figure of Gorgias that Meno-the-memorious is portrayed as Meno-the-student, who carries the imprint of his master's teachings in his manner of speech; Meno equates his own opinions with those of his master, relying on his ability to reproduce them from memory upon demand.[24] In fact, Meno's attitude towards

---

[22] Cf. *Prot.* 332e, where Socrates presses Protagoras to admit that folly (ἀ-φροσύνη), which through its alpha-privative literally signifies 'non-wisdom', is the opposite of wisdom (σωφροσύνη), and that every opposite (ἐναντίον) has but one opposite.

[23] Note the interesting homophonic parallel between Socrates' cry to Meno Οὐ πάνυ εἰμὶ μνήμων, ὦ Μένων (*Meno* 71c) and his cry to Polus ὦ Πῶλε, οὐκ εἰμὶ τῶν πολιτικῶν (*Grg.* 473e), a similitude that further emphasizes the oppositional forces present in each case while facing these two students of Gorgias. Countering Polus, who represents the thinker-turned-politician who believes that politics is everything, Socrates presents himself as one who does not belong to the number of the politicians. Facing the memorious Meno, for whom memory is the quintessence of the learning process, Socrates presents himself as immemorious. In both cases, the irony of Socrates' initial statement is revealed by a second statement to have targeted his interlocutor's position. Thus, in the *Gorgias*, after having claimed not to be a politician, Socrates later in the dialogue presents himself as the *only* true practitioner of the art of politics (*Grg.* 521d), thereby emphasizing the difference between his and Polus' understanding of the essence of politics. In the *Meno*, Socrates' later exposition of the theory of recollection, as will be seen below, will unveil a discussion revolving around the nature of memory and its role within the learning process that is meant to counter Meno's equation of learning as memorization.

[24] Plato's subtle irony is revealed in the juxtaposition of the two elements learned from Gorgias: the rhetorical ability and the definition of ἀρετή. At first, in his (mock) exhortation at the beginning of the dialogue, Socrates claims that the Thessalians owe all their knowledge to Gorgias' teachings (70b), leading us to believe that they acquired knowledge from him. This fact is later confirmed by Meno's testimony that he had been able to make well-received speeches on virtue. The claim ultimately reveals itself, however, to signify that what Gorgias' students actually acquired was only the rhetorical ability to make successful speeches, which indeed is, as Meno remembers at the end of the dialogue, all that Gorgias actually ever claimed to teach (95b).

the learning process is not only represented in his reliance on a pool of memorized doctrines, it is depicted in a way remarkably similar to the type of all-or-nothing memory he embodies within the privative model announced by Socrates. For if knowledge is the memorization of authoritative doctrines, one either knows, that is, remembers, or one does not. There is no middle possibility. As a result, Meno's memory is consistent with Meno's persistent equation, announced in his opening question and restated throughout the dialogue, of that which can be learned (μαθητόν) with that which can be taught (διδακτόν), i.e. that which is to be taught *by others*. Hence his recurring request that Socrates teach him (ἔχεις με τοῦτο διδάξαι) what he says is true (70a, 81e, 86c), a request that frustrates all of Socrates' attempts to convince Meno to jointly inquire after the answer, rather than seek from others an answer to be stored in his memory. It is this insistence on being taught that contributed to Meno's famous paradox on the impossibility of conducting any inquiry if one does not know at all (τὸ παράπαν) what it is that one is searching for (80d), and gained him his reputation of being an uncooperative, lazy, and disputatious interlocutor. However, seen through the all-or-nothing perspective Meno represents, Meno's behaviour should not be attributed to character traits, but should rather be seen as stemming from the natural impasse he reaches after having failed to defend Gorgias' ideas upon which he had previously completely relied.[25] He is simply left without any way at all (τὸ παράπαν) to start anew without returning to Socrates as an alternate source of authoritative teachings. Moreover, one may understand Meno's plight to an even greater extent considering the fact that Gorgias himself, whose doctrines he is portrayed to have memorized, is presented by Plato as an influential teacher 'who never leaves a question unanswered' (70c). Thus, Meno is presented as the student whose knowledge completely rests on his master's knowledge, and his master's knowledge is supposed to be complete. Accordingly, we can understand the feeling of perplexity and paralysis that Meno describes with the stingray analogy, resulting from his inability to defend his appropriated authoritative notions in the face of Socrates' persistent questioning (79e–80b).

Both Meno's good memory thus understood as the very cause of his paralysis and Socrates' feigned adoption of the counter-position of being

---

[25] The portrait of Meno as an unyielding, stubborn character may also be reinforced by the fact that his name also happens to coincide with the participle form of μένειν, signifying 'to remain' or 'to stay in place'. Plato's word-play might allude to the fact that Meno does not budge in his conversation with Socrates exactly because of the memories lodged within his soul.

immemorious can now be explained as an attempt to draw Meno away from the authoritative doctrines he has memorized, as well as from his educational paradigm of learning-as-memorizing. In its place Socrates attempts to introduce him to the benefit of inner recollection and its elucidation through joint inquiry (κοινῇ ζητεῖν) (86c). Yet, the dilemma presented in the *Meno* is how a student such as Meno, who is so ensnared by the binary conception of memory and knowledge, can accomplish this task. How does one convince a student that a complete re-evaluation of his position is needed when the student himself is convinced of the truthfulness of his master's doctrines and of his own means of obtaining those truths? How does one convince him that a complete turning of the tables is required on the content of his memory and on the educational paradigm of learning as memorizing? A simple rejection of his master's views would not suffice, since it would not alter the student's educational paradigm, nor would it lead to further discussion. For either the faithful student would refuse to begin a discussion with one who does not recognize the authority of his master; or, alternatively, should he choose to enter the discussion in defence of his master's position, any failure on his part could be attributed to nothing else but his own inability to remember it well enough (as is seemingly the case in the first part of the dialogue)![26]

What the *Meno* makes clear is that when one only recites from memory, indeed when one equates understanding with memorization and declamation of authoritative doctrines, no true dialogue can be generated, since no true interlocutor is present. The crux of the problem lies in the lack of an interlocutor with whom the premises and implications of the opinions could be critically examined: for the acclaimed authors of the opinions quoted are never present during the discussion – hence the passing remark made in the dialogue about Gorgias' absence (71d) – and the interlocutors at hand do not possess the ability to abandon the authoritative opinion they represent, but can only make show of their misunderstanding or imperfect memory of it. The cited authoritative opinion itself, however, remains unquestioned and unquestionable, and as such threatens to continuously cast a long shadow on the mind of the memorizer, making him unable to free himself from its message.

---

[26] For the belligerent option, cf. Meno's question (71c) which Socrates sidestepped by declaring his lack of memory; the ill-memorized option is accentuated by Socrates' attempt to first convince Meno to define or defend *his* (acquired and) remembered answer concerning the nature of ἀρετή (71d, 73c, 76b), only to end up accusing him of not remembering what Gorgias said on the topic (76b) after his repeated failures to defend the thesis.

In the face of the threat of the inability to inquire due to the reliance on memorized doctrines, the importance of Socrates' declaration of forgetfulness in the *Meno* becomes all the more apparent. Serving as a mirror image to Meno's memory, it is an attempt to both debunk Meno's conception of learning as memorization as well as to offer him an alternate source of truth via recollection from within. And, as a mirror image, it is used by Socrates as a subtle tool to provide Meno with a reflection of his own conception of the learning process via memory, all the while hinting at the existence of a diametrically opposed alternative. Thus, Socrates' confession of forgetfulness at first feigns to be nothing but an inconspicuous declaration of a faulty memory, only to later reveal its advantages as a tool used to begin a discussion. Yet, it should be noticed that the discussion it generates does not target Gorgias' position, but rather the figure of the student ensnared by authoritative memory.[27] As such, Socrates' forgetfulness, presented as a mere lack of memory, is a dialogical tool enabling a discussion on the interlocutor's own terms, much like his famous disavowals of knowledge (e.g. *Resp.* 337a, *Apol.* 21d). At the same time, it also serves as a tool of pedagogical irony, particularly apt for such an authority-bound student, as it is meant to allow the student to discover of his own accord and through his own perplexity what Socrates refuses to teach him.[28] The stimulus of self-propelled inquiry, rather than reliance on memory, is therefore fittingly announced by a word-play (Οὐ μνήμων, ὦ Μένων), which suggests that irony is at play, and invites the interlocutor as well as the reader to inquire after its meaning.[29] Indeed, the genius of the word-play is that it enables Socrates to lead Meno through various stages of interrogation where Meno could realize by himself that something is fundamentally wrong with his educational perspective, without having to be told as much, or having the

---

[27] The dialogue ultimately denies that Gorgias ever had a position to teach on the matter (95c).

[28] There is no contradiction in claiming that Socrates uses both such pedagogic irony and his famous disavowal of teaching. On this I agree with Vlastos' position: 'In the conventional sense, where to "teach" is simply to transfer knowledge from a teacher's mind to a learner's mind, Socrates means what he says: that sort of teaching he does not do. But in the sense that *he* would give to "teaching" – engaging would-be learners in elenctic argument to make them aware of their own ignorance and enable them to discover for themselves the truth the teacher had held back – in that sense of "teaching" Socrates would want to say that he *is* a teacher, the only true teacher' (1991: 32). Indeed, as portrayed in the *Meno*, Socrates' forgetfulness could be viewed as an additional example of what Vlastos named 'complex irony'. I do not mean to claim, however, that Socrates' ironic forgetfulness is restricted to a pedagogic function alone, as this is not the case, in my opinion, in its appearances vis-à-vis the sophists and the rhapsodes.

[29] To the informed reader, there are additional levels of irony that are of a more historical nature. On these, cf. Klein 1989: 35–8; Sharples 1985: 125–6.

alternative dictated to him. In other words, it enables Socrates to refrain from becoming another authoritative figure for Meno.

Socrates' statement is tailored to Meno's own beliefs, and can only be interpreted differently by Meno and the readers as Socrates' position vis-à-vis Meno's grows clearer. At first, the opposition between the memorious and im-memorious interlocutors does not question the premise that knowledge is memory and memory is knowledge. Rather Socrates uses this premise to lead Meno to the despairing conclusion that he is bereft of any valid and defendable memory of a thesis on which he can rely, as well as of an authoritative figure to whom to turn.[30] At this stage, however, Meno's educational paradigm of learning-as-memorization and his binary conception of knowledge remain undisturbed. Accordingly, Socrates does not simply refute this model; he allows Meno to retain the binary opposition, but leads him toward a reconsideration of the source of this knowledge through the exposition of the theory of recollection. In fact, the recollection thesis itself replaces both Meno's source of authority and his conception of learning, without explicitly presenting itself in contradiction to Meno's previous position. Thus Socrates suggests replacing Meno's attitude, turning towards his all-answering master (70c), with an inward turn towards the all-knowing soul (μεμαθηκυίας τῆς ψυχῆς ἄπαντα) (81d), and to replace the memorization of authoritative theses with what he calls 'to recollect by and within one's self' (ἀναλαβὼν αὐτὸς ἐξ αὐτοῦ τὴν ἐπιστήμην) (85d) through a question-and-answer process that elucidates what lies hidden within.[31] What shifts in the process is the very parameter of truth: from an agreement with an authoritative opinion that has to be

---

[30] Hence Meno's initial response to Socrates' introduction of the theory of recollection: 'what is it and who are the people saying it?' (τίνα τοῦτον, καὶ τίνες οἱ λέγοντες, 81a). The remaining option, i.e. the possibility that the authority who voiced the original thesis would come and defend the thesis from Socrates' attacks, does not come up, and rightfully so. It does not come up because even if an answer had been given by Gorgias, for example, it would not have altered the fact that facing the next set of difficulties Meno would have been left alone again. And the emphasis of the dialogue, as said above, is placed on Meno and his memory. The problem is thus essential and non-contingent to any particular view or argument for which any particular criticism could be or has been made.

[31] In the words of Hoerber (1960: 91): 'According to the pedagogy of Plato μαθητόν implies an understanding of the basic principles involved, an inward learning, a personal participation in "research", an active process of personal thought; while διδακτόν means a learning "by heart", a teaching from the outside ... a mere transmission from one person to another.' Hoerber further suggests that the mentions of Prodicus, the specialist in semantic discriminations between synonyms, at 75e and 96d underline the necessity to differentiate and define the various terms (89). What Socrates glosses over, however, in his attempted lexical accuracy, is the existence of a double meaning of the verb μανθάνειν, which signifies both 'learning', in the sense of acquiring knowledge one does not possess, and 'understanding', in the sense of examining a piece of knowledge one already possesses (cf. Euthd. 277e–278a). On this point, cf. Klein 1989: 91–2.

memorized, i.e. poured into one's soul and then retained, to the unveiling through recollection and inquiry of an existing truth that lies within.[32] What is fascinating to note is that, despite the fundamental changes involved in the process, Socrates is able to lure Meno into agreeing with the thesis by appealing to his mnemonic weak spot, that is, with the promise of unveiling what could be translated as 'unforgettable opinions' (ἀ-ληθεῖς δόξας, emphasizing the alpha privativum) (85c; 86a).[33] The implicit contrast is clearly between these opinions, which are truly unforgettable as they are found in himself and could be retrieved out of himself (ἐξ αὑτοῦ) (85d), and those taken over from his master, which Meno was unable to defend, i.e. to remember. But the main point of Socrates' argument lies in the manner by which these opinions are to be made truly unforgettable, to wit, by reasoning out explanations through joint inquiry. Solely by inquiry, in direct contrast to memorization, can the opinions one holds to be true become pieces of knowledge (ἐπιστῆμαι) that are stable (μόνιμοι) and unable to exit the soul (δραπετεύουσιν ἐκ τῆς ψυχῆς) (98a).

By presenting his argument in this ironic way, returning in the end to the privative model from which it had begun, Socrates seems to convince Meno to overcome his resistance towards inquiring after what he does not yet know, that is, what he has no externally acquired knowledge of. Moreover, he is able to lead Meno to agree with the necessity to direct one's energy to the incessant inquiry and reflection that are needed to

---

[32] For the contested view, cf. Agathon's claim in the *Symposium* (175d) that wisdom can be poured from the fuller glass to the less full. In the *Protagoras* Socrates voices a similar warning concerning the lasting effect that accepted doctrines could exercise on the souls of eager students. For the soul, Socrates warns the young Hippocrates who is drawn to Protagoras' wisdom, is like a container or a vessel (ἀγγεῖον), whose content is unlike any other as it cannot be removed and transported away, and should therefore be handled with the utmost care (*Prot.* 314a–b). After a doctrine enters one's soul by means of learning, the soul will either be benefitted or be damaged by it, but (as I argue could be seen in the the *Meno*) the doctrine is sure to leave an indelible mark. This fact should greatly influence our decision of who to accept as our teachers, entrusting our soul only to someone who is an expert in its care (313e).

[33] The argument for the translation of ἀληθεῖς δόξας not only as 'true opinions' but as 'unforgettable opinions' is supported by the contrast λήθη/ἀ-λήθεια that is further developed and demonstrated to exist in Plato's works (e.g. *Phdr.* 248b, 275a; *Resp.* 621a) by Rankin 1963: 51–4; Heitsch 1962: 24–33, 1963: 36–52; and Grondin 1982: 551–6. The contrast is explicitly applied by Klein (1989: 157, 176) to the use of ἀληθεῖς δόξας in the *Meno*, which he argues should be seen as 'unforgotten or even unforgettable opinions'. Indeed the link between truth and un-forgetting, or the un-forgettable, may also be found in Hesiod's *Theogony* (233–6). Etymologically speaking, the derivation of the term ἀλήθεια from λήθη, λήθομαι may be questioned in favour of the derivation from λήθω, λανθάνω as argued by Luther (1935: 7–13) and subsequently Beekes (2010: 66). However, as Luther admitted, it is the former derivation that is commonplace among ancient etymologists and the debate for the latter derivation was rekindled following Heidegger's suggestion (1998: 155–82) that ἀ-λήθεια is to be translated as the 'unhiddenness of Being'. For a criticism of Heidegger's position, see Friedländer's 1958: 221–9.

ensure that the true opinions existing within one's soul not escape the soul and be forgotten, unlike the authoritative opinions placed therein.[34] Yet, what the figure of Meno ultimately demonstrates, as does the dialogue as a whole, is the *difficulty* involved in attempting to overcome one's acquired authoritative opinions and one's acquired vocabulary, because of the depth of the mark left on one's soul by their memory. This is made clear by the dialogue's central breaking point, marked by Meno's return to the binary model when he reiterates his original question of whether ἀρετή could be obtained by teaching (διδακτῷ) or not (86c). This immediately follows, and denies, his supposed agreement with Socrates on his own lack of memory and knowledge, and his admission that it is necessary to engage in common inquiry (κοινῇ ζητεῖν). The *Meno* thus ultimately marks the failure of the educational project of Socrates-the-forgetful vis-à-vis Meno as the embodiment of the dangerous spell of memory (μνήμη), and reveals this character – both as a *dramatis persona* and as a representative of memory – to be stagnant and incapable of change (μένειν), trapped in his own starting point, and stubborn in pursuing the question of the teachability of ἀρετή.[35]

Quoting Francis Bacon, Jorge Luis Borges once remarked with respect to the Platonic doctrine presented in the *Meno*, that 'if to learn is to recollect, to ignore is to learn how to forget'.[36] Indeed, it seems that Socrates' ironic lack of memory aims to indicate to Meno precisely that: he must first forget all that he has retained from Gorgias until, much like Socrates (and the slave), he gains the awareness of his lack of knowledge. Then, and only then, will he find that the state of non-memory and non-knowledge is actually a catalyst, rather than a numbing shock, that enables him to engage in the process of further inquiry (cf. 84a–b). Should he realize this, Meno would also realize that the truly petrifying position for a student

---

[34] For the conception of knowledge as superior to true opinions, see Socrates' famous analogy of true opinions with Daedalus' statues (97e–98a). Notice that the very idea of an escape from the soul of true opinions seems paradoxical in itself, since they are said to be opinions that are always in the soul (86b: ἀεὶ … ἐν τῇ ψυχῇ), but as Klein has noted (1989: 176) Plato refrains in the *Meno* from addressing the paradoxical nature of this claim.

[35] On Gorgias' responsibility for this failure, as one who has claimed to know it all, cf. Klein's remark (1989: 89–90) regarding Socrates' double derogatory accusation towards Meno of being a rogue, a rascal or a knave (πανοῦργος) (80b8, 81e6). Klein suggests that this accusation retains the same hue of the all-or-nothing attitude towards knowledge which Gorgias represents, and further emphasizes Gorgias' imprint on Meno; for the term πανοῦργος literally means a ready-to-do-all (from πᾶς + ἔργον), and was used as a pejorative name given to the sophists (cf. *Soph.* 239c6, and Arist. *NE* 6.1144a23), complementing their claim that they know everything (cf. *Soph.* 233d: ποιεῖν καὶ δρᾶν μιᾷ τέχνῃ συνάπαντα ἐπίστασθαι πράγματα).

[36] Borges 1985: 96.

such as himself is to rely upon the memorization of the 'gorgon-like' teachings of a master,[37] and would no longer believe that it is the lack of memory, and the subsequent call for inquiry, that benumb him, as he had first claimed (80a–b).

4   Facing Protagoras: Socrates' Active Forgetfulness

The *Meno*'s contrast between two protagonists who represent memory and forgetfulness has a striking parallel in Aristophanes' *Clouds*. This may help us understand the precise way in which Plato crafted the image of Socrates' forgetfulness. I suggest that, through the use of specific terms that would have been familiar from Aristophanes' play, Plato attempted to draw the attention of his scholarly readers and induce them to reflect on the differences between his own description of Socrates' forgetfulness and the one made by Aristophanes.[38] What a careful reader will discover is that analogies with Aristophanes' language of forgetfulness can be identified in two Platonic dialogues, the *Meno* and the *Protagoras*; but what appears in the *Clouds* as a single description was split by Plato into two distinct notions of forgetfulness, and this suggests that these notions should be analyzed separately.

Memory and forgetfulness are first introduced in the *Clouds* through a reference to Socrates' requirement that prospective students have a nimble faculty of memory,[39] which is also attested in Plato and Xenophon.[40] As soon as the slightly senile Strepsiades, who wishes to be admitted as Socrates' student, declares that he once forgot to make a slit in the sacrificial

---

[37] On the gorgon-like effect of Gorgias, whose teachings Meno commits to memory, cf. *Symp.* 198c.

[38] Given Aristophanes' lampooning depiction of Socrates' person and teachings, such parallels may at first seem surprising. However, the importance of Aristophanes' play, which was first staged in 423 BC, in determining Socrates' public image is already attested in the *Apology* 19c, and it seems that the *Clouds* was in fact a common source of reference for Plato, whether as an attempt to combat the views attributed by Aristophanes to Socrates, to ironize its images, or to usurp its phrases, images and even specific expressions for his own purposes as a scholarly nod towards those familiar with the play. Be it as it may, one can find direct quotations from the play (*Symp.* 221b quoting *Nub.* 362) as well as playful allusions to famous images within the *Clouds* 218–34, such as Socrates 'walking on air' (*Apol.* 19c, 23d), or 'hung up on high' (*Tht.* 175d). Passing references are made to 'the comic poet' (κωμῳδοποιός) and his accusation of verbiage (ἀδολεσχίᾳ) and of being a 'stargazer' (μετεωροσκόπον) of which he accuses Socrates (*Phdr.* 70c, *Resp.* 488e and *Nub.* 333, 1480), etc. A short list was compiled by Tarrant 1988: 122 n. 24, but several studies since have shown the extent of Aristophanes' presence within various dialogues. Thus, Capra 2001: 59–86 on the *Clouds* and the *Protagoras*; Baracchi 2001: 151–76 on the influence of the *Clouds* on the first book of the *Republic*; and most recently Moore 2015: 545–51 on the *Clouds* and the *Phaedrus*.

[39] For a larger contextualization of this passage in the *Clouds* and within Aristophanes' oeuvre, see Milanezi's chapter in this volume.

[40] Cf. *Nub.* 412 and nn. 4–5 above.

offering, which resulted in its splattering, the chorus jumps up and chants that being memorious (μνήμων) is the first of a long list of qualifications required of a student (412–9). Socrates then explicitly asks his would-be student whether he has indeed a sound memory (μνημονικός). To which Strepsiades replies, in the two lines that I suggest were in the back of Plato's mind while writing both the *Meno* and the *Protagoras*:

> δύο τρόπω νὴ τὸν Δία· ἢν μὲν γὰρ ὀφείληταί τί μοι, μνήμων πάνυ· ἐὰν δ' ὀφείλω, σχέτλιος, ἐπιλήσμων πάνυ. (483–5)
>
> Yes, in two ways, by Zeus! If anything is owed to me, I am quite memorious; but if, miserably, I owe, I'm quite forgetful.[41]

Both elements of Strepsiades' statement have parallels in Plato's own description of Socrates in those dialogues, but with two major differences.[42] Whereas Strepsiades claims to be quite memorious (μνήμων πάνυ), Socrates denies the very same claim in the *Meno*, all while retaining the same formulaic phrase (οὐ πάνυ ... μνήμων).[43] And when Strepsiades adds to this memoriousness a claim of forgetfulness, he uses the term ἐπιλήσμων, which Plato does not use in the *Meno*, but uses repeatedly in the *Protagoras* with reference to Socrates (334c, 334d, 336d). Therefore, what is highlighted through this comparison with Aristophanes is the distinctiveness of the turn of phrase used in the *Meno*, as well as the question of the specific significance of the term ἐπιλήσμων.

To understand the purpose of Plato's complex allusion to Aristophanes, it should be noticed that in the *Clouds* it is one and the same man, Strepsiades, who is portrayed as being both forgetful (ἐπιλήσμων) and memorious (μνήμων), depending on convenience. His forgetfulness is not a form of *vis inertiae*, but rather an intentional disregard of information *that feigns a lack of knowledge or memory.*[44] Thus I would argue that Plato's

---

[41] Translation by West and West 1984 (slightly modified).

[42] On the fact that Plato's Socrates assumes in part Strepsiades' position in the *Clouds*, see Capra 2001: 79.

[43] The adverbial πάνυ appears in both statements. Yet in Plato's version Socrates' statement first seems to mean that he is hardly, or 'not all that', memorious, so as to enable him to present the slip-of-the-mind excuse in his answer to Meno's question on his position concerning Gorgias' definition. In Aristophanes' text an alternative use of the adverb surfaces, known in classical rhetoric as a litote, or emphatic negation, and which consequently reads as 'not at all!' What the allusion to the *Clouds* suggests is that what first appears to be a meek declaration on Socrates' part apologizing for his being hardly memorious should be reread as expressing a more emphatic opposition to Meno's memory, declaring Socrates to be 'not memorious at all' or 'completely unlike Meno'.

[44] The fact that such a model of active forgetfulness is attached to the term ἐπιλήσμων might be, interestingly, further supported by Herodotus, who twice in his *Historiae* uses the verb when he comments that, although he knows someone's name, he deliberately chooses to omit it (τοῦ ἐπιστάμενος τὸ οὔνομα ἑκὼν ἐπιλήθομαι) (4.43.7, 1.51.1).

abstention from using the term ἐπιλήσμων in the *Meno* and his choice of using it repeatedly in the *Protagoras* are intentional ways of differentiating two forms of forgetfulness: Socrates' active and polemical forgetfulness vis-à-vis the spell-binding speeches of the sophist in the *Protagoras*, where Socrates' forgetfulness is not put in contrast with his interlocutor's mnemonic capacity; and Socrates' privative form of forgetfulness in the *Meno*, where he tries to convince the memorious Meno to relinquish his equation of learning and memorization.

We find the term ἐπιλήσμων used by Socrates as a reaction to one of Protagoras' long digressions:

> ὦ Πρωταγόρα, ἐγὼ τυγχάνω ἐπιλήσμων τις ὢν ἄνθρωπος, καὶ ἐάν τίς μοι μακρὰ λέγῃ, ἐπιλανθάνομαι περὶ οὗ ἂν ᾖ ὁ λόγος. ὥσπερ οὖν εἰ ἐτύγχανον ὑπόκωφος ὤν, ᾤου ἂν χρῆναι, εἴπερ ἔμελλές μοι διαλέξεσθαι, μεῖζον φθέγγεσθαι ἢ πρὸς τοὺς ἄλλους, οὕτω καὶ νῦν, ἐπειδὴ ἐπιλήσμονι ἐνέτυχες, σύντεμνέ μοι τὰς ἀποκρίσεις καὶ βραχυτέρας ποίει, εἰ μέλλω σοι ἕπεσθαι. (334c–d)

> Being, as it happens, a rather forgetful sort of person, Protagoras, I tend to forget, faced with a lengthy statement, the original point of the argument. Now, suppose I happened to be hard of hearing: if you meant to hold a conversation with me, you would think it necessary to speak more loudly than normal; so now that you are faced by a man with poor memory, please cut your answers down and make them short enough for me to follow.[45]

Supported by the analogy between hearing and memory impairment, Socrates uses his alleged forgetfulness as a means to advance his typical demand that the sophists limit themselves to short answers and refrain from drawn-out speeches and extensive expositions in order to enable him to follow their arguments.[46] It is his forgetfulness that enables him to request what may indeed be seen as a minor concession from someone, Protagoras, who is said to be capable, and indeed unbeatable, both in prolonged speech (μακρὰ λέγειν) and in short arguments (βραχυλογία) (329b; 334d–e).[47] In truth, however, the demand that Protagoras shorten his answers due to Socrates' feigned mnemonic weakness affects the very foundations of the rhetorical brilliance that underlies his sophistic know-how, and

---

[45] Translation by Hubbard and Karnofsky 1982.

[46] For the use of a similar strategy to shorten his interlocutor's responses, cf. *Hipp. Min.* 373a, *Grg.* 449a–d. Compare this with the image of Thrasymachus pouring quantities of water down his listeners' ears with his arguments (*Resp.* 344d).

[47] Cf. also Gorgias' claim, happily agreed with by Socrates, that no one can speak in fewer words than himself (*Grg.* 449c).

could be compared to asking one's opponent to wrestle with his hands tied behind his back. The agonistic image is quite fitting, since Protagoras is represented as spoiling for a fight (ἀγωνιᾶν) (333e), and a regular participant in verbal competitions (ἀγῶνα λόγων) (335a).[48] In fact much of the discussion between Socrates and Protagoras assumes the characteristics of a spectator sport (317d–e; 335d–336a, 339e), with its need for an arbiter (337e, 338a–b), and the vivid imagery it offers of the knockout effect of sophistic speech (339).[49] In this context Socrates' declared inability to retain what was said in the course of a long rhetorical exposé is to be seen as a means to undercut and disregard his opponent's rhetoric, as well as to goad him to agree to an exchange of concise questions and answers. That Socrates' declarations of forgetfulness are indeed only feigned is stated later in the dialogue by Alcibiades:

ἐπεὶ Σωκράτη γε ἐγὼ ἐγγυῶμαι μὴ ἐπιλήσεσθαι, οὐχ ὅτι παίζει καὶ φησιν ἐπιλήσμων εἶναι. (336d)

For Socrates, I warrant you, will not forget, despite his jesting way of calling himself forgetful.[50]

And yet, much like in the *Meno*, Socrates' declaration of forgetfulness serves a larger purpose than just working as a polemical tool to coax the sophist into what Socrates conceives as the only proper form of dialogue, or as a means to diminish the glamour of the sophist and his art for the benefit of the audience (335b–d). In both dialogues Socrates' forgetfulness enables him to pinpoint a major flaw in his interlocutor's understanding of the process of learning and teaching: memorization of authoritative opinions on the part of the student in the *Meno*; and neglect of the needs of one's pupils, which prevents their further inquiry in favour of rhetorical brilliance, on the part of the sophist in the *Protagoras*.

Much like in the *Meno*, Socrates' forgetfulness had already appeared at the very beginning of the *Protagoras*, thus providing a hint of its meaning and *raison d'être*. In the opening scene Socrates claims that he had paid no attention to, and indeed had often forgotten (οὔτε προσεῖχον τὸν νοῦν ἐπελανθανόμην τε αὐτοῦ θαμά) (309b) the youth by his side because of

---

[48] On Protagoras as a teacher of eristic techniques and the first to institutionalize debating contests (λόγων ἀγῶνας), cf. Diogenes Laertius 9. 52–3 and Klosko 1979: 125–42.

[49] Cf. *Euthd.* 276c, 303a–c.

[50] I prefer Lamb's translation of these two lines to Hubbard's and Karnofsky's ('I have a suspicion he won't forget, in spite of his little joke about having a poor memory') since they completely miss the assurance and the pledge (hence the verb ἐγγυάω) that Socrates will not forget, which emphasizes the irony of Socrates' claims of forgetfulness.

the overwhelming effect of the sophist's power of speech.[51] Ironically, the youth in question is none other than the beautiful Alcibiades, Socrates' most (in)famous companion and disciple.[52] Because of Socrates' known fascination with this youth, with which the dialogue opens (309a), his claim of forgetfulness is striking, and not only serves as a powerful acknowledgement of Protagoras' mesmerizing rhetorical skill, but simultaneously draws the reader's attention to the relationship between the sophist's power of rhetoric and his consequent neglect or forgetfulness of his students. Tellingly, Socrates' forgetfulness will be declared to be ironic by none other than Alcibiades, who, as mentioned above, reappears later in the dialogue and claims that Socrates' forgetfulness is not to be believed (336d). If Alcibiades' warning is meant to alert us to the fact that Socrates' claim to forgetfulness is ironic, then Socrates' confessed neglect of young Alcibiades' presence actually may be meant to highlight the real, yet unprofessed, neglect, on Protagoras' part, of the young Hippocrates who, at the beginning of the dialogue, wishes to receive the sophist's instruction despite Socrates' warnings (310a–314c).[53] Having failed to prevent Hippocrates from entrusting his impressionable soul into the hands of the sophist, Socrates' ironic forgetfulness is a way to reveal, at least to the readers, Protagoras' empty educational pretence: the sophist had promised that Hippocrates would continuously improve, and finally leave as a better man, if he were to associate with him (318a), but Protagoras clearly forgets about him for most of the dialogue. Plato's irony, and the significance of drawing our attention to the figure of the neglected student, are only revealed after Protagoras' Great Speech on the teachability of ἀρετή, which spans over eight Stephanus pages (320d–328d). The speech, supposedly

---

[51] Cf. Taylor's remarks (1991: 103) on how Plato often likens the sophists to wizards (*Soph.* 235a, *Pol.* 291c) and to magicians (*Soph.* 235b, 268d), thereby colouring the seemingly laudatory description that they can make enchanting speeches with hues of trickery, charlatanism, and showmanship. In the *Meno* similar accusations of wizardry (γοητεύειν), beguilement, and the casting of spells are voiced by Meno against Socrates (80a–b). On the image of Socrates in the *Clouds* as γοής, cf. Bowie 1993: 112–24.

[52] On the old quarrel as to whether we should view Alcibiades as Socrates' disciple or not, and the implication of the issue of the accusations raised against Socrates of corrupting the youth, cf. Guthrie 1987: 383 n. 1. Xenophon calls Alcibiades Socrates' ὁμιλητής, meaning both associate and disciple (*Mem.* 1.2.47–8). On the relationship between the two figures, see Ellis 1989: 20–7.

[53] Cf. n. 32 above. I am entirely in agreement with Beversluis (2000: 255) who discards Guthrie's and Coby's contention that Hippocrates' enthusiasm for Protagoras simply abates after Socrates' severe warning. And I disagree with Kitto's proposal, cited by Beversluis (255), of the 'literary error' made on Plato's part of requiring excessive imaginative powers on the reader's side which would make the dazzle-eyed youngster's repeated consents simply superfluous. Rather, to put it in Sherlock Holmes' terms, I am inclined to believe that the key to the mystery lies in the curious incident of Hippocrates' present non-presence ...

proposed for the benefit of the young Hippocrates, is said to have left
Socrates absolutely spellbound (κεκηλημένος) (328d) and unable to recall
the original subject of discussion for two reasons: the sheer length of the
masterful exposé, and Socrates' own forgetful character (ἐπιλήσμων τις)
(334c). Thus, bracketed between Socrates' two declarations of forgetfulness, the reason for the disappearance of Hippocrates and for Socrates' use
of irony is revealed: they both highlight the fact that the sophist's rhetorical
brilliance relegates his whole audience, including his pupils, to the mere
role of astounded listeners, preventing them from questioning his theses
and rendering their own intellectual stances meaningless.[54]

The unquestionability of memorized doctrines, of which Socrates
attempted to warn Meno through his own forgetful self-portrayal, is thus
taken up again in the *Protagoras*, where it is presented as the result of the
unquestionable nature of the sophists' rhetoric. This is why Socrates likens
the sophist's long speeches to (quotable) books that can express opinions,
but cannot be questioned or pose questions of their own (329a).[55] In the
Meno this unquestionability depended on the absence of the father of the
opinion, who could have clarified its intended meaning and thus enabled
its scrutiny had he been present, excluding any fear that emerging problems
may just depend on someone else's garbled memory or understanding.
In the *Protagoras* the unquestionable nature of the thesis depends on the
absence of a questioning student. For someone unable to engage with
the argument at any stage, as a result of the way in which his sophistical
teacher speaks, is likened to an individual who cannot express himself or
be mindful of his own position. Such a student can be mesmerized, but
cannot properly advance in his intellectual inquiries and, what is worse,
may actually be harming his soul by accepting his teacher's theses without
questions (313a–314b). Just ask Meno, Socrates would say.

5   Conclusion

'Difficult though it might be to detect it,' Goethe once remarked, 'a certain polemical thread runs through any philosophical writing. He who

---

[54] Note that the gathering of sophists which Socrates and Hippocrates encounter upon entering
Callias' house is described by Plato in terms borrowed from Homer's account of Odysseus' journey
to Hades and his entrance to the netherworld beyond the river or the plains of Lethe (cf. *Republic*
621a). Two direct quotations from Homer contribute to this effect in the *Protagoras*: 315b, from
Od. 11.601; and 315c, from *Od.* 11.582. See further Segvic 2006: 255–7 and Capra 2001: 67–71. The
imagery of the study hall as the netherworld is also suggested in Aristophanes' *Clouds* (184–7), where
philosophy students are made to look like the dispirited dwellers of Tartarus.

[55] Cf. *Phdr.* 275d.

philosophizes is not at one with the previous and contemporary world's way of thinking of things. Thus Plato's discussions are often not only directed to something but also directed against it.'[56] It is, indeed, in this sense that I have attempted to outline the seldom noticed Platonic *topos* of Socrates' forgetfulness,[57] and to show that it functions in the twofold manner described by the great German poet. For the declaration of forgetfulness can be seen as a strategy which Socrates uses with his various interlocutors – be they memorizing students, insecure youngsters making their debut in the field of learning, loquacious sophists, or professional rote learners – in support of his constant attempt to lure them all into philosophical inquiry despite their reluctance to do so. Simultaneously, however, Socrates' forgetfulness is also directed against these interlocutors' various (mis-)understandings of the role of memory within the learning process, which Socrates saw as a threat for the very existence of the one belief he was absolutely convinced was worth fighting for: the belief in the duty to inquire (δεῖν ζητεῖν) (*Meno* 86b). Therefore, if we now return to Alcibiades' cautionary call not to believe Socrates' jesting claim that he is forgetful (παίζει καί φησιν ἐπιλήσμων εἶναι) (*Prot.* 336d), which we may now justly deem to be shrouded in irony several times over, we must not forget to bring to mind Socrates' declaration to the jury in *Apology* (20d): although he may seem to be jesting (παίζειν), he speaks nothing but the truth.

---

[56] Goethe, 'Plato als Mitgenosse einer christlichen Offenbarung', cited by Gadamer 1980: 39.
[57] For the same *topos* in a different Platonic context, see also Capra's chapter in this volume.

CHAPTER 9

Memory and Recollection in Plato's Philebus: *Use and Definitions*

R. A. H. King

1 Introduction

In the *Philebus*, Plato's Socrates argues that human life is best lived as a mixture of pleasure and knowledge. Human life is lived in time, so we have to remember what we have done and undergone, as well as harbour expectations, based on reckoning of what will happen. The treatment of memory is arguably the most elaborate in Plato, embedded as it is in a sophisticated psychology. Naturally, as in *Meno, Phaedo, Phaedrus*, and *Theaetetus*, memory serves knowledge. Yet, insofar as it makes sense to contrast the interests of knowledge with its practical application in Plato, memory is here harnessed directly to living well. For it allows us memory of pleasure, indeed as a kind of pleasure that the soul can have on its own. Apparently, the doctrines of the soul's prenatal existence – which are so important in *Meno, Phaedo*, and *Phaedrus*, and which then require recollection of the soul, if it is to acquire knowledge – retreat into the shadows in the *Philebus*, although nothing said here by Socrates precludes the soul's immortality. As has often been observed, the *Philebus* appears to be close to Aristotle's treatment of memory in *De Memoria* (e.g. Carpenter 2010). However, in place of the seal and wax block of the *Theaetetus*, with its affinities to Aristotle, and other treatments of memory in the period, we have the image of a soul populated by workmen, a scribe, and a painter, whose work is memory and expectation. This image provides the reader with scope for thought and interpretation. Here, I take up this challenge.

The *Philebus* ends (67B11–13) with Protarchus reminding Socrates of unfinished business he wishes to go on to discuss (ὑπομνήσω δέ σε τὰ λειπόμενα). And Socrates and Protarchus remind one another elsewhere in the dialogue of what has been said, and what has to be discussed; dialectic takes time, and the earlier and later are connected – woe betide the forgetful participants! And speakers remind one another; reminding is a part of what we do to one another, apparently, even something the gods can do to us (20B3), as well of course as something we may do to ourselves. Thus memory serves the (successful) conduct of the dialogue. It contributes to, and in fact forms part of, the work of reason. But Plato also defines what memory itself is in order to contribute to answering the main question of the dialogue, what the good life for humans is. Principally, memory is a constituent of the good life, belonging, with knowledge, right judgement, true calculations, and intellect,[1] to those elements we need to appreciate pleasure.[2] Thus memory also serves the (successful) conduct of human life. Now, the *Philebus*, in arguing about the good life for humans, tells us how to research, learn, and teach (16E3–4) about the practice of theory, and one may wonder if the definitions of memory and recollection proposed and accepted by the interlocutors in fact can, or even should, be used to understand the use of memory in the conduct of the dialogue itself.

Memory and recollection are natural bedfellows; but just what is the nature of their liaison? The *Philebus* gives the earliest account of the affair. No memory without recollection, no recollection without memory. They belong together naturally; but still they need bringing together (neither are they identical, nor is their relationship simply necessary). The question arises naturally of how they are connected, how they, in fact, form a unity. In this paper I wish to show how this can be done.

In the course of trying to analyze pleasure – in fact, false pleasure – in the *Philebus*, Plato has to give an account of psychic activities, above all, desire, and he analyses memory (μνήμη) to explain desire (ἐπιθυμία); crudely put, animals do not desire what they now have, but they must know what they do not have, viz. from memory, so desire requires memory. This is a striking use of the concept, first because of its practical slant and second because of the questions it raises about Phileban psychology; for the argument continues to show that the soul, not the body, is the principle of what living things do (35D1–3), in that desire, relying on memory, is the principle of their behaviour.

The first argument touching upon memory works with definitions of memory and recollection (ἀνάμνησις). A second argument is also to be found which, at least at first blush, forms a completely new stage in the discussion of the truth and falsity of pleasures. One way pleasures may deceive us, and so can be false, is when we take pleasure in things to come. So we have to be able to give an account of expectations, and, as a first step towards doing this, Plato gives an account of sensory judgement using

---

[1] 11B7–8, similar lists in the texts in the next note, and 21D9–12.
[2] 21B6–7, 21C1–6.

memory and sensation.[3] This argument about sensory judgement provides a way of showing that 'images' (εἰκόνες) in judgement, expectation, and memory are secondary to what we believe in these operations. The truth of the 'images' fits the truth of the judgements, and not the other way round. This second argument using memory depends on the former at least in that some use is made of memory, in the sense that has already been defined. Just how memory and sensation come together or co-operate needs to be clarified. But the account of sensory judgement does allow one to deny that Plato has a theory of memory that is based on imagination, since the 'images' are derivative. It is only a slight exaggeration to say that memory, while it is the preservation of sensation, is an intellectual activity and capacity, since it consists in having judgements; and these are not provided by sensation. Sensation is dumb; it says nothing.[4]

Let us turn, then, to the account of memory.

2 Memory

Memory (μνήμη) is defined as σωτηρία αἰσθήσεως (34A10), the preservation of sensation. One reason why this definition is difficult to deal with is that it is just posited; little is given by way of reasoning to help understand why we should accept it as uncomplainingly as Protarchus does (34B1). Background is provided by the observation that sensation will have to be defined first; but why this is so, is not clear. When Protarchus reminds Socrates of what has been said, and of what is to be done, this clearly relates in some way to sensation; after all, we hear, or read, what is said. But equally clearly the relation between remembered utterances and what is conveyed by the utterances requires careful handling. Sensation has previously been defined as a 'change which changes body and soul in common with one affection' ('undergoing', πάθος, 34A3–5). I use 'change' to translate κίνησις in preference to 'motion' or 'movement', since change is broader than simply moving from place to place; while sensation may involve locomotion within the body, it would be strange to say that it is locomotion, as though sensation were a bodily bumping from one place to another. And it is of course difficult to say in what way the soul is somewhere at all. There are indications, it must be admitted, that sensation,

---

[3] αἴσθησις is not perception, that is, a form of cognition, in the *Philebus*; it does not belong with the forms of cognition contributing to the good life in the texts listed above.

[4] Cf. *Tht.* 184B–186E, especially 186e1–6. Perception is passive, and so does not include the activity of forming a judgement. See Burnyeat 1976, Frede 1987, and Lee 2008. I see no reason to attribute a change of view of sensation to Plato between *Tht.* and *Phlb.*

shaking body and soul together, is conceived of as a localized change. The possibility has been allowed for that the body may be changed without the change penetrating into the soul (33D2–6). When the bodily 'disturbance' reaches the soul then there is sensation; if the disturbance does not reach the soul, then there is ἀναισθησία. This does sound local. But, of course, change may occur in a place without being change of place.

Many questions arise from this brisk treatment of sensation, which we cannot go into here.[5] Sensation is at any rate a change; and this change is preserved in memory. Now, we are not told much about change in the *Philebus*, although it (in the form of 'genesis') is a key player.[6] So, for example, we are not told what makes a change *one* change. The identity of a change is relevant to the theory of memory in different ways, depending on how one conceives of the preservation of change. If one thinks that the preservation of a change, such as sensation, means that this change continues, then we are left asking how we know that, and what it is for a change to continue, in other words to be one and the same change. And if one thinks that the preservation of a change means in fact that the preserved change is then another one, then we have the rather more complicated task of explaining what makes one change the preservation of another change. The point is that preservation might either mean that one thing continues in existence, or that another item in fact constitutes the preservation of it; in being preserved, the sensation itself could be modified, for example, growing weaker, or it might be preserved by being represented by something else. What I mean will become clear when applied to memory. For one might think that the memory of seeing something occurs when the seeing has stopped. I see Theaetetus, then I stop seeing Theaetetus, and I remember Theaetetus. So, supposing that memory is a change,[7] then it is a different change from the change that was seeing. Then we should ask why the memory-change is the preservation of the seeing-change. It may be merely the seeing, but weaker, or else it may keep the seeing by representing it.

What about memory itself? It seems that this is a very restrictive account of memory. Surely we do not remember, or say that we remember,

---

[5] See King 2016.
[6] 26D8–9, 54A5, 60D7.
[7] Plato does not actually say that memory is a change. This is, however, a reasonable assumption: the preservation of an X must be itself an X. Cf. *Laws* 10.896c–d: memories are listed, along with manners, characters, wishes, calculations, correct judgements, and diligent acts of caring as belonging to the soul, and so being prior to the attributes of the body (length, breadth, depth and strength). Here too we are not told that these attributes of the soul are changes, but again it is sensible to think so.

only sensations.[8] And apparent examples of a more encompassing view of memory can be gleaned from the dialogue itself. In summing up the positions of Philebus and Socrates, Protarchus remarks of each candidate for the best human possession that the speakers 'remind themselves of them often, quite rightly, so that they can be tested while lying to hand in memory' (19C5–D3). One way out of this impasse may be to say that we can remember the things we have sensations of. So, clearly, these candidates (e.g. pleasure and knowledge) have been mentioned often in the dialogue, and there is a connection between these mentions and the ability of the speakers to remind themselves, not of the utterances, but of the things mentioned. While one can remember the one without the other (I can remember what you said, without remembering your saying it), that you said *this* when you spoke is necessary, in some sense, for my memory. And the repeated recall of these things, pleasure and knowledge and the parts that make them up, keeps them before the mind, so that they can be examined.[9]

Another strategy is to suggest[10] that Plato is restricting his attention to sensation because of the importance of pleasure. Clearly, pleasures are among the things one can remember; this is the part of the argument for rejecting a life of pleasure alone (21C1–4), but this manoeuvre makes the definition very loose, saying, as it were, that memory is, *inter alia*, such and such. A weak definition, which does not sit well with an investigation that kicks off with a problem of the one and the many (14D4–15C3). For if the problem of the dialogue (what is the human good?) is conducted by asking which parts of pleasure and which parts of intelligence make up a good life, then one would hope that, to begin with, we have an account of memory as a whole, and we then proceed to divide it up. This is where

[8] For a similar issue in Aristotle, see Castagnoli's chapter in this volume.
[9] Socrates' expression here is interesting for another reason. He says that the various candidates, such as pleasure and knowledge, are 'lying to hand in memory': here at least memory looks to be actual, but it is conceivable that what is referred to here is lying in memory, that is, lying ready to be realised. One question is if this contrast between modalities, if one may use the term here, should carry over into the understanding of memory in the official account. Is the contrast between actuality and capacity relevant at all for the business of the dialogue? And the importance of memory for examining things is dwelt on elsewhere. Later in the dialogue, repetition of the four genera of being (the unlimited, the limited, the mixture of the two and the cause of the mixture) is deemed necessary 'for the sake of memory' (27B5), and the memory served may be either the capacity to remember, or actual memory. We repeat them either to improve our capacity to recall them later, or to have them in mind now. In either case, what is being remembered is not the audible utterances, but the genera themselves. But the utterances are the way the genera are remembered. Quite how this happens is obscure; and Plato gives us here almost no help in working out his view of it. As Luca Castagnoli reminds me, this is reminiscent of Aristotle's accidental memory (*Mem.* 1, 450a13–14), although of course the relation between utterance and the genera in the *Phlb.* is not the same as that between the *phantasmata* and the intelligibles in Aristotle.
[10] Delcomminette 2006: 321.

we find recollection, for there are various ways of remembering, as we shall see. Not only does the account of recollection include the possibility of remembering knowledge (μαθήματα) (a good thing surely if memory is to count among the kinds of cognition), but also any hopes of understanding the marked use of memory in the dialogue would vanish if memory was narrowly focused on sensation.

Of course, interpreters have denied that large stretches of the dialogue do in fact conform to the method or methods sketched towards the beginning.[11] And there may seem to be ferocious difficulties for anyone claiming that the methods are used, especially as far as the role of numbers is concerned: they play an important role, or important roles, in these methods (cf. especially 16C3–7), while the account of memory we are looking at seems entirely inno-cent of numbers. At best, one can point to the fact that first the whole of memory is defined, and then all its parts. And perhaps there are also signs that Plato thought that remembering when something happened is part and parcel of memory, even if the point is not developed in the accounts we are given: when something happens may be measured, and so requires counting.[12] A consideration that goes in favour of viewing the present investigation as falling under the method is, of course, that this method is set up as entirely general. To some readers, it beggars belief that a method should be described and then, as if to tease the reader, *not* used.

Further problems relate to what one might call the modality of memory here, which we have already touched on briefly. Are we talking of a cap-acity or an actuality here, or both?[13] Or is this distinction in fact irrelevant? Both verbal and nominal forms of Greek terms for memory and recollec-tion are used; but it is well to note that there is, of course, no easy mapping of this grammatical distinction onto any contrast between capacity and actuality. And perhaps Plato's own usage does not force us into an analysis in terms of actuality and capacity.[14] After all, on the surface the distinction

---

[11] See especially Striker 1970.

[12] Cf. Arist. *Mem.* 2, 452b7–453a4 for a very tricky account of how one may work out when something occurred (on which, cf. King 2004: ad loc.). As Aristotle says, it is possible to remember without remembering when something occurred or was perceived.

[13] The birdcage in the *Theaetetus* 196D1–200C6 is of course an ample source for this line of thought; but it is moot how exactly it fits with the Phileban method or methods.

[14] μέμνημαι is an important term in this connection; while it may indeed be a matter of memory, it can mean simply 'to be made to think of something', or, indeed, to bear something in mind; either of these last two uses may, but need not, imply a previous occasion or assertion which is being remembered. All but one case of μέμνημαι in the dialogue are clearly memory uses – 11B7, 21C1, 25A4, 31B1, 59A10 – the last three apply to actual memory; 21C1 may be a capacity as well as actuality, as may 11B7. At 25A1–5, Socrates is asking Protarchus if he remembers that they must collect the genera together and give them a single mark, as required at 23E4–5 (and cf. 15B4–5). The

between actuality and capacity is not part of the theoretical framework of the dialogue.[15] And their introduction gives rise to a large number of questions. Is memory the actual preservation of a sensation, or the capacity to remember the sensation preserved? The bare statement of the definition does not allow one to adjudicate the issue here; for one thing, no example is given. Another issue is the difficulty in explaining just what the relations are between actual remembering and the capacity to remember.[16]

3 Recollection

Now that we have the definition of memory, we can turn to that of recollection (ἀνάμνησις). It is defined in two ways, which I call recollection (a) and (b). The first one may be translated as follows:

> (a) If the soul, on its own, grasps anew (ἀναλαμβάνῃ) as far as possible that which soul and body once underwent together, without the body, then we say it recollects (ἀναμιμνῄσκεσθαί). (34B6–8)

Notably, verbal forms are being used here, and it seems correct to suppose that an act (rather than a state or capacity) is being defined. The phrasing in no way suggests that what is at stake here is what we *can* do. There is a distinction between the time of the original experience and the time of recollection (34B6, 8 ποθ' ... τότε). Most notably, no mention of memory is made in this definition of recollection. What is recollected is not memory. Rather it is sensation that is recollected (but surely one may object: *preserved* sensation, hence memory is what is being discussed). Recollection is being restricted here to sensory recollection, for only sensation is common to body and soul: this is what they undergo in common.[17] What performs the act of recollecting, in contrast, is the soul on its own.

genera that thought and pleasure belong to are fixed at 28A1–7 and 30D10–E1 and referred back to as remembered at 31B1. The one problematic case is 33A3–6, where Socrates draws Protarchus' attention, for the first time, to a third state besides having pleasures or pain, and says he should μεμνῆσθαι it, since μεμνῆσθαι is important for discerning pleasure; whether or not one thinks memory is involved here is a nice question. Contrast Dorothea Frede's translation (1997) with those of Schleiermacher (1991), Gosling (1975), and Taylor (1956) (Gosling has for the first, 'bearing in mind', for the second, 'keep in mind', perhaps merely for the sake of style; Taylor has 'keep in mind', for the first, 'recollection' for the second). The question is whether keeping something present to one's attention counts as memory, when the past occasion in which the thing has been mentioned is not part of what one has in mind. Of course, what Socrates is *doing* in this passage is calling the third state to mind. This is the first passage where the third state is mentioned. At 42E–43C where it recurs, there is, however, no reference to the earlier passage. Have they both forgotten?

[15] But note the use of δύναμις at 24C2, 32A1, 47C7, 57E7, 63C3, 64E5, 67A8, 15. The contrast with actuality is arguably not present in these cases.

[16] For some ways in which capacities can relate to activities, cf. Makin 2006.

[17] See 34A3–5.

Why grasping 'as far as possible' (ὅτι μάλιστα)? Obviously, the qualification governs 'grasps anew'.[18] Now, it may be that recollection (a) is meant to be a form of reliving the original experience, and clearly this is not *literally* possible. On this reading, 'as far as possible' would just be marking the fact that recollection always falls short of the original. One alternative is that the qualification should help us to decide how good recollection has to be to qualify as recollection. But actually it does not; for what is possible in any case has not been determined. So the text remains indeterminate on a test of recollection. 'As far as possible' obviously gives us no practical indication of when the recollection is reliable or successful. This is a problem insofar as there are cases when the soul 'grasps anew what one has undergone with body and soul together' which should not count as successful recollection: deceptive or imperfect recall is, alas, all too possible.

Another line of thought is that, in fact, the sensation itself is not recalled. In fact what is recalled is necessarily what one believed as the result of the sensation. What Socrates and Protarchus remember in discussing the four genera is not the utterance, but the belief the utterance gave rise to; and that is what is preserved. This line of thought offers help in tackling a paradox in two aspects of memory in the *Philebus*. On the one hand it is connected to intellect, calculation, and true belief, and on the other hand it is the preservation of sensation. And one may well wonder how the mere preservation of sensation produces a psychic item of the same dignity as intellect. The answer would be to see that memory – in preserving sensation – in fact also transforms it into something capable of truth and falsity. Thus the preservation of sensations is not their prolongation, as though memory was a lasting look, but a transformation of sensations into something propositional. When we remember, we say something.

What about the second form of recollection?

> (b) After [the soul] has lost memory (μνήμη), whether of a sensation or of some knowledge (μάθημα), [the soul] again (αὖθις) brings up [the memory] in turn in itself as in the first case (πάλιν); all these things we call recollections and memories. (34B10–C2)

Like recollection (a), recollection (b) sounds like a performance, not a capacity. The soul is doing something. This may be clear; what is not clear, as already noted, is the relevance of this observation for the understanding of

---

[18] ἀναλαμβάνειν is of course a term which is important in Plato's accounts of memory, in the *Phaedo* (75E4,6), the *Meno* (85C), and in our dialogue (33C8); but it need not be a memory term in itself, which would vitiate the definition here by making it circular; cf. the phrasing at *Pol.* 294D and *Tim.* 26A.

memory words in the *Philebus*. In fact we will see that there is a very good argument for thinking that the contrast between memory and recollection is not that between capacity and activity.

If we have two forms of recollection, there must be properties that distinguish them. And there are two that recollection (b) possesses and recollection (a) does not:

i) memory *must have been lost* before recollection (b) can occur;
ii) the object of the memory recollected is either sensation *or knowledge*.

i) precludes recollection (b) being the exercise of the capacity of memory.[19] This recollection cannot be the exercise of the capacity of memory, if memory, that is, the capacity for memory, has been lost (forgetting is memorably defined as the 'exit of memory' at 33E3). Lost capacities cannot be exercised. And it is memory which is recovered; whether or not recollection revives the capacity for memory, depends on what you mean by the capacity for memory. If recollection brings back a memory, and we are looking at memory in terms of actuality and capacity, then it seems that what recollection primarily gives us is the actual memory. Secondarily, as the result of an act of recollection (b) one may then be able to remember the thing, and remain able to remember. In this way recollection may give us back memory; in fact what it then gives us is recollection (a), which may, as a form of memory in act, be called 'memory'.

The fact that here memory is said to be of sensation or knowledge may cause surprise. For if memory is the preservation of sensation, the natural assumption is that what is remembered is the sensation. Yet it is clear, I think, that more is happening in preservation than mere continuance; the preservation of a belief attaching to the sensation must be included. It becomes clear later in the dialogue, as we will see, that in the work of the scribe, and thus in that of the painter, an element of belief must be added to sensation, despite its complete absence so far in the account of memory and recollection. If the sensation is of someone talking, or of diagrams drawn in the sand, then this memory could be of something learnt as well. And this promises to allow us to see the use of memory in the dialogue as meshing well with the definitions we are currently considering. Remembering the four genera of being (27B5) is surely remembering a μάθημα. Here, the term used is μνήμη and we are faced

---

[19] Gosling (1975: 103) thinks the sensation (he also calls it 'perception') or the piece of knowledge, not the memory, is lost; but ταύτην at 34B11 surely refers to μνήμην in the previous line.

with the choice: either we take the preservation of sensation in a subtle enough sense to understand it here (recollection is a form of memory, and the preservation of sensation preserves also what we think along with the sensation), or else we have to say that it escaped Plato's notice that the uses of memory terms he presents in the dialogue do not fit the concept of memory he defines.

James Warren (2014: 47ff.) uses the second view of *anamnēsis*, recollection, at 34A10–C2 to explain the re-actualisation of knowledge by the philosopher kings throughout their lives, along the lines of Aristotle's distinction between grades of capacity and actualisation in *De anima* 2.5: it is one thing to move from ignorance to knowledge of something, and another to move from acquired knowledge to its actualisation. The schoolchild ignorant of geometry is one thing, the trained but sleeping Archimedes another. The latter does not re-learn his stuff every time he settles down to prove something in the sand. He does not, however, sit easily with the second kind of recollection in the *Philebus* in that he has not lost the memory (34A10), while asleep or in the bath.

Let us begin with perhaps the most striking difference between the two forms of recollection. What does it mean to say that memory has been lost? I think that Plato is making a distinction between immediately available memories, that is, ones that are present without a search, and ones that have to be looked for.[20] Here, we can use the fact that recollection (a) and (b) are, on my interpretation, kinds or species of memory. Immediately available memories are cases of recollection (a). Thus in recollection (b) the immediate memory, i.e. recollection (a), has been lost. What then happens in recollection (b) is that we reacquire the memory. Significantly Plato uses the word ἀναπολεῖν, not ἀναλαμβάνειν. In recollection (b) something is not just grasped again, as it were, with no barrier to doing so: the soul has to bring it back to the surface. The second case allows for a break between recollection and the original perception: memory, in the sense of recollection (a), is lost. So much for the relation between recollection (a) and (b).[21]

---

[20] Gosling 1975: 103 ad 34b2: 'The "retention of sensation" referred to in the definition of memory at 10–11 refers presumably not to, or not merely to, the capacity to know what we have been perceiving in preceding moments. According to b10–c2 [i.e. recollection (b)] it is possible to regain memory.' One thing that Gosling appears to be saying is that not only the objects of 'perception', i.e. αἴσθησις, are the objects of memory. Another is that actual retention can be interrupted. Cf. also Gadamer 2000: 112.

[21] This resurfaces again (αὖθις), as in the first case. πάλιν in line 11 signals a repetition of the phrase αὐτὴ ἐν ἑαυτῆ from the first case in line 7.

4   Memory and Recollection

Now let us turn to the relation between memory and recollection. Two basic models for the relation are

- the capacity of memory is actualised in acts of recollection;
- the genus *memory* can be divided into two kinds of recollection.

The first model has an Aristotelian ring to it, using as it does the terminology of actuality and capacity, and is popular with readers.[22] The second also has its friends,[23] and it would appear to fit better with the general Phileban preoccupation with dividing wholes. My suggestion is that the second model is the correct one. This suggestion will be confirmed when we turn to an important textual difficulty. At the end of his account of recollection (b), Socrates comments that 'all these things we call recollections *and memories*', according to the MSS reading at 34C1: ἀναμνήσεις καὶ μνήμας. In a context where there is a distinction between μνήμαι and ἀναμνήσεις (34B2) it seems unhelpful to be told that 'all these' (ταῦτα σύμπαντα) are both memories and recollections. Hence the editors emend the text either by bracketing καὶ μνήμας (Gloel) or by adding οὐ before μνήμας (Diès).[24]

An obvious option for interpreting the relation between recollection and memory is, as already indicated, to see the two forms of recollection as two parts of a genus (in a loose sense: determinates of a determinable), and presumably the only ones. Either preservation is interrupted or it is not. In other words, a differentiation between kinds of memory is established by means of a contrariety. This option enables one to identify the 'is' in 'recollection is memory' as that of class inclusion, and not identity. Memory, it is agreed, differs from recollection (34B2, again, a loose sense of 'differ'). Thus the two cases of recollection are cases of recollection, trivially, and of memory as the class they are included in. In this way memory, either as recollection (a) or as recollection (b), may explain desire; and either may be referred to by the generic term. This explains the fact that the

---

[22] Gosling 1975: 103 ad 34b2, 'It seems that "memory" refers to the capacity to recall, "recollection" to the occasions of recall.'

[23] Delcomminette (2006: 325–6) uses both language of capacity and actuality as well as the talk of species.

[24] Delcomminette (2006: 324) sees the two forms of recollection as two 'modalities', apparently without one kind encompassing both. In what I am calling recollection (b), he thinks that memory is recovered; in this way he wishes to keep the MSS text: these are all 'recollections and memories', because recollection recovers memory. This would not appear to fit with my recollection (a).

term 'recollection' is never used to explain desire.[25] And the text of the MSS at 34C1 may be kept. So, it is just as well if recollection in some way be equated with, or, equivalently, fall under memory, insofar as the pleasure we are dealing with only requires memories. Plato is not indulging in a definitional orgy, producing unnecessary definitions. If memory divides exhaustively into two forms of recollection, we no longer have this problem. For saying that memory explains desire will cash out into an explanation in terms of one of the two forms of recollection.

One might object that this is a very artificial way of accounting for the fact that recollection is never used to explain desire: the simple point is that one needs to have memory of what it is to be full in order to desire to eat, but no act of recollection is needed. In English, this may be right, although one may indeed wonder about the use of memory to describe the way in which being full is present to the soul: in the case of hunger 'the soul touches filling, obviously by means of memory' (35B11–C1). What kind of memory is that? I think that one reason this sounds odd to our ears is that we might think it is the nature (structure, biology) of the organism that determines when it is hungry or not.[26] But Plato thinks that it is the soul of an animal which is the principle of this determination. So he is looking for something that souls do to account for the processes undergone by the animal. In Phileban Greek, the 'memory' involved in having a past state of satiety present is recollection (a).

A final point may be made here about the status of knowledge. If recollection (b) is a form of memory, and memory is restricted to sensation, then so is recollection (b). So the knowledge recollected in (b) is the sensation of being told something, or watching a demonstration, or reading something.[27] We will see when we turn to the famous scribe and

---

[25] For the explanation of desire and certain kinds of pleasure using memory, see 33C6, 10, 35A7, C1, 13, D2; cf. also 38B12. μνήμη is used in a broad sense (to cover all memory phenomena?) at 21B6, D10; at 21C1–5 it is not the capacity for an actuality; nor at 20B3, or 19D1–2. On desire, the soul's potential authority over us, see Harte 2014. She argues that memory 'fastens onto' the object of desire, by a representative likeness, in this reconstruction relying on a reading of Aristotle's theory in *Mem*. As will be clear, I disagree that 'representative likeness' is essential to Phileban memory. In King 2016 I argue that the function of aesthesis is to pick out, point at things – and it is this that memory preserves. Whilst Harte sees aesthesis as 'perceptual awareness', it is not a form of cognition in the *Philebus*, and so is, in my view, better seen as sensation.

[26] In fact there is one passage in the *Phlb.* that looks very much as though Plato also is thinking in terms of the οὐσία of a living thing when explaining pleasure and pain: 32A6–B4. This is not incompatible with the view that it is the soul that gives the proximate explanation; one also would need to work out the relation between soul and 'the living form which has come to be naturally out of the unlimited and the limited' (32A9–B1). For a different, 'prospective' and performative way in which the memory language can be connected with physiological necessities like eating and drinking ('memory of action'), cf. the Introduction above, p. 4 and nn. 8–9.

[27] For discussion of the question of the objects of memory in Aristotle, see Castagnoli, this volume.

painter simile in the next section that the crucial aspect in memory is what we believe. Thus some of the uses of memory in the dialogue can be captured, explicitly, at least by recollection (b). A question may remain about recollection (a) and learning; for surely we remember some bits of learning without calling them to mind. Perhaps the point lies in the grasping anew that is part of recollection (b); merely recalling what one learnt is not enough. Learning requires understanding, as the Greek term μάθημα suggests. In contrast, a sensation may be preserved without understanding. Just how Plato conceives of the transmission of learning by sensation remains unclear, and hence also how recollection, rooted in sensation, can be a route back to forgotten knowledge.

Now that we have dealt with the definitions of memory and recollection, and the relations between these concepts, we can move on to the second key discussion involving memory in the *Philebus*. It will confront us with problems in interpreting the models of memory just described and fleshing out the theory.

5 The Scribe

In pursuing the argument that some pleasures can be true and some false, Socrates gives an account of sensory judgement (δόξα), as a preparation for an account of expectations about the future. Some expectations are, or provide, deceptive pleasures. The crucial point, it seems, is that we are full of expectations (39E5–6), and these present themselves as images, but in fact it emerges from Plato's account that the images are secondary; they depend on the judgements we have about the future, just as they do in the case of sensory judgements, relating to the present, and memory, relating to the past. The analysis of sensory judgements provides grounds for thinking that the images are secondary to the judgements.

Socrates explains that judgement (δόξα), or attempts at confirmed judgement (διαδοξάζειν), come about on each occasion from sensation and memory (38B12), and provides the following example. Suppose you ask yourself: 'What is that thing appearing there, standing by the stone under the tree?' (38C12–D1), and then you give yourself an answer: 'It's a man', or 'It's a statue'. This is δόξα, and if you said this aloud it would be a statement (λόγος) instead of a judgement. This is an example of a sensory judgement which may be right or wrong. Our next task is to see how memory is involved in the production of such judgements. So let us turn to the genesis of δόξα:

Memory, coinciding with sensations in respect of the same thing (εἰς ταὐτὸν), and those affections (παθήματα) associated with these [i.e. with sensations, with memory] appear to me, as it were, to write reports (λόγοι) in our souls. And when this affection writes true things, then judgement and statements come about in us that are true. And when this scribe writes false things in us, then they turn out to be opposite to the true things. (39A1–7)

At first blush, this seems clear enough. What is being accounted for is a present sensory judgement which requires a past sensation preserved by memory, and a present sensation. When forming a judgement about what this thing here is, I must look at it and I must have some relevant memory. Memory and sensation combine in some way to produce a unitary judgement. In the metaphor of the scribe, we are told that memory, along with sensations, and other undergoing 'affections' concurrent with them, 'writes reports', as it were, in the soul. Despite any superficial clarity, three problems have arisen in attempts to make sense of the genesis of sensory judgement:

(1) First, we have to ask what the role of memory is. Is it a provider of the concepts to be used in forming a sensory judgement, as some interpreters have thought? Or does it merely provide a comparison which the present experience can fit or not?

(2) Second, we need to identify the 'affections' that are connected to sensation and memory. Different suggestions have been made: an interior dialogue (e.g. Delcomminette 2006: 365), feelings (i.e. emotions, e.g. Hackforth 1945: 72, 74, 75 n.1), the feelings of replenishment and depletion from 32C ff. (e.g. Gosling 1975: 110–11).

(3) The third problem is: why is this multifarious combination of memory, sensation, and affections from the first sentence referred to as *an* affection, in the singular, in the second sentence (39A4: 'this affection')? Badham, followed by Burnet in his Oxford Classical Text edition, brackets these words, but Gosling argues they may be kept, in my opinion correctly.

I will say nothing more about the third problem, except for the general remark that the point of the ingredients in 39A 1–2 is that they have to form a unity, in some sense, if a judgement is to arise from them.[28] So the singular is not so odd; as others have noted, it prepares the way for the *single* scribe operating in the soul.

---

[28] The real problem is that forming a judgement is something we do rather than undergo; but this may be alleviated by the sensory undergoing that provides the occasion for forming the judgement.

As to the second problem, the present example of the man or statue seen from a distance does not fit Gosling's reading, since it has nothing to do with the previous account of pleasure and pain. Gosling sees a close connection between this passage and the account of desire using memory (34–5): the undergoings are the past replenishment and the present depletion. It is unclear why desire should be connected to the genesis of sensory judgement. The question here is surely what I should think, given the deliverances of my senses, not what I should think, given my desires. Delcomminette's suggestion of an interior dialogue is clearly possible, but hardly necessary. Of course a dialogue is suggested by the little story Socrates tells of someone wondering within himself about what he is seeing in the distance (38C5–E4); but this is not the only way in which a sensory judgement can be formed, and indeed it only needs to apply to cases in which things are unclear (38C5–6). At a fundamental level, the deliverances of sensation and memory are immediate (and, I suppose, those of hopes as well). Normally, I need not debate internally whether it is Theaetetus that I see, or Theaetetus that I remember; I know him well, and here he is shaking my hand. In the case of memory, that corresponds to what I have called recollection (a).[29] The same problem applies to Hackforth's proposal: emotions may be concomitant, but they are not necessary for the explanation of all sensory judgements.

I have another suggestion as to what the παθήματα are. Consider what happens when we make a sensory judgement. I think we are dealing with changes that we undergo: on the one hand bodily changes, for it is clear enough that sensation is accompanied by undergoing changes, namely of the body and soul in common (see 33D2–10, 33A3–5); and on the other hand memory is accompanied by undergoings of the soul, namely consisting of grasping anew (recollection (a)) or a resurfacing (recollection (b)) of memory. This heterogeneous group comprises my candidates for the παθήματα in line A2.

The question to which I wish to devote a little more time is the first one; in this connection, I want to concentrate especially on the meaning

---

[29] Not only may there be an interior dialogue, as Delcomminette suggests; also the use of association, as in the *Phaedo*, is not precluded, in the case of recollection (b). Thein (2012: 123), who does not try to connect the two passages on memory, and who hence does not worry about the distinction between memory and recollection, sees in the account of the formation of sensual judgement an associative process at work, as in the *Phaedo* 73–4. Two brief comments. The *Phaedo* does not distinguish *in its theory* between memory and recollection; and we can distinguish between cases when recollection (a) is needed in forming sensory judgement, and when recollection (b) is needed. Clearly, I do not need to recollect by rummaging in my memory to ascertain that what I see is a man; but I may well do to ascertain that what I see is Theaetetus.

of 'coincide' (συμπίπτειν). Let me begin by making two introductory comments. First, it is not an interaction (as Gosling translates) between memory and sensation, at least if interaction is always causal and physical. Rather, they must occur together, in fact *co-operate* to be able to write the reports. Writing is a purposeful activity in which various factors work together. I think that in Phileban psychology activities of the soul serve purposes. This can be seen from the use of the simile of the two workmen in the soul (39B3–7), the scribe and the painter: each has a job to do, a function.[30] It is clear that in the *Philebus* the soul and its activities can achieve certain ends. Whether the end is achieved or not depends on the co-operation of the various elements in the soul. So too here; our success in forming a judgement on what we see depends on just how memory and sensation co-operate. Second, no sign is apparent that sensation offers only the raw material to which the concepts of memory are applied. For memory just is the preservation of sensation, if we stick to the definition of memory already presented. We would have an obviously vicious circle, if memory were needed for a sensory judgement.

Plato says συμπίπτουσα εἰς ταὐτόν.[31] I suspect that most translators, interpreters and readers think that these words form a unit. Memory coincides with sensations, and that is it.[32] But just what is this coincidence – what coincides with what? Three forms of coincidence suggest themselves at once:

(a) we must assume that there is coincidence of the person, that is, here, soul, in whom memory and sensations take place (as in 48E8);
(b) memory and sensation must coincide as far as time is concerned;
(c) the content of sensations and memory must be related to one another: seeing Peter and remembering Paul would not be much good. Or seeing a statue and remembering *human*.

Yet exactly how they are related, and how sensation and memory 'coincide' or come together to produce judgements, is hard to say. Coincidence cannot produce truth here; for otherwise we could not deal with false

---

[30] And, more fundamentally, if more controversially, the scheme of the four genera posits *nous*, intelligence, as the cause or maker. The relevance of this to our passage may be disputed; and it is not easy to map the various factors at work in the accounts of memory and sensory judgement onto the four genera (esp. 26E6–27B2).

[31] The form of words we have here can be used for a wide range of relations in Plato: συμπίπτειν with εἰς ταὐτόν of sensation and knowledge in *Tht.* 160d6 (be identical) of political science and philosophy; in *Resp.* 473D3 (coincide). It is not a grammatical triviality that εἰς ταὐτόν is inserted; in *Phlb.* e.g. 41A3, 47D3 συμπίπτειν is used without any such addition (in contrast, cf. e.g. *Leg.* 712A).

[32] For example, Dorothea Frede's German translation offers 'übereinstimmen'.

judgements, and there is no suggestion that we are only dealing with true ones here.[33] Indeed, Plato emphasises that the reports can be either true or false, depending on how successful the scribe is at his work. A minimal interpretation would be to say that (the content of) the previous sensation (memory) and the present sensation coincide in that they are similar. No 'concepts' are needed to establish those relations, and so no concepts are needed for sensory judgements. The restriction in scope to sensory judgements excludes any form of inductive picture of concept acquisition or indeed of the development of innate concepts in experience. What is at stake here is not learning, but simply forming a sensory judgement, for example on the occasion of seeing something. Given that the sensation happens in the context of an interior dialogue, even when the sensation is clear, what appears to happen is that memory allows for the assignment of the present sensation to a past one; and it is assumed that in fact the past one is verbalised, while retaining something of its sensual character.

Let me briefly sum up my interpretation of the scribe passage. True or false reports about what one sees arise in the soul on the basis of previous sensations, preserved in memory, combining with a present sensation. A simple report is then roughly: what I see is what I remember.[34] Both sensation and memory are accompanied by occurrences, undergoings in body-and-soul and soul respectively. All that memory provides is a preserved sensation which can then be compared with the present one. Memory deliverances and sensory deliverances have the same status; nowhere is there any talk of abstraction. All one needs is, as Plato says, the coincidence of a memory with the present sensation, for the scribe to write his report. This coincidence is of person, time, and content.

---

[33] This point was made in Dublin by Jessica Moss. One problem is that we are not told how it is possible – even with coincidence – that also false judgements come about. For it would be an obvious thought, at least for someone remembering the *Theaetetus*, to think that it is not coincidence of my memory and my sensation that explains the falsity of a judgement. This might provide an argument against using the *Theaetetus* straightforwardly to interpret the *Philebus*. It is by no means easy to translate the terms of the wax block model into those of the painter and the scribe; perhaps that is a work of abstraction and interpretation we are meant to do, but I cannot do it here. It seems worth remembering that the wax block does not work, and that it allows for the memory of thoughts (191D); but, perhaps, cf. recollection (b) above). Finally, Phileban 'coincidence' cannot be the same as Theaetetan putting the right shoe on the right foot (cf. 193C) – that is, having a true belief, fitting perception and imprint to one another correctly – if the present interpretation of coincidence is right; for any sensory judgement, both true and false, requires co-operation of memory and sensation. For an attempt to make *Tht.* and *Phlb.* compatible, see the next footnote.

[34] Sedley (2004: 137) suggests that the Phileban workmen are compatible with the wax tablet of the *Theaetetus*. The workmen can account for mistakes since the perceptual description 'the thing I see' (38D9–10) makes misidentification possible.

6 The Painter

After the scribe, Plato introduces another workman in the soul, a painter:

s.: When someone removes (ἀπαγαγών) from a sight or some other sensation what is believed or said at that time, he sees in himself images (εἰκόνας) of what was believed and said. Is that not what happens in us?
p: Absolutely.
s.: So the images of true judgements are true, and the images of false judgements and statements are false. (39B9–C5)

As Gosling puts it (1975: 111), 'the painter is established as a distinct operator whose role comes after judgement'. The judgement (*doxa*, *logos*) of the scribe is clearly primary. The next puzzle is the meaning of the statement that judgements and statements are removed (ἀπάγειν; Gosling: 'isolates');[35] what are they removed from? Is this taking away something that one does, or something that occurs in the natural course of events? A natural thought is that they are removed from the original experience (a notion that is perhaps not easy for Plato to express; the original πάθος seems to me both broader and to have different connotations). The assertion can as it were be abstracted, leaving an after image, or memory image from that experience. The idea is that we primarily have an experience, and that the report written by the scribe is removed from it leaving a painting representing the report. Take the *Iliad*, illustrate it and then tear out the text, leaving a picture book.

As to the primacy of judgement: Plato is using figures or *homunculi* in the soul to represent activities of the soul; how they are to be cashed out is not clear. For example, the fact that they are *two* workmen suggests that they are strictly independent of one another, thus making it possible to have writing without pictures. But the extent to which, and in which sense, the painter is dependent on the writer (first the 'annalist', then the illustrator)[36] is problematic if taken as the narrative of events, and not as an analysis of the structure of the events. The writing might be logically, and not temporally, prior to the painting. For one may think of cases where,

---

[35] Thein (2012) argues for a more considerable role for images in Phileban psychology. To do this he argues against the (obvious) point that the painter is a simple illustrator, by suggesting that the work of the painter is no less 'propositional' than that of the scribe. Whatever exactly is meant by 'propositional', this reading is hard to square with ἀπάγειν at 39B10. His account of what this verb means here is complicated, and involves some kind of 'abstraction' in which the painter has a role to play (for the verb he compares *Phaed.* 97B3). He identifies the scribe (sic!) with the φαντασία of *Soph.* 264A–B, which is said there to be a combination of perception and judgement.

[36] 39B6. Note, however, the rather more compendious temporal indication at B4.

as a matter of fact, while seeing something one formed no judgement at all; only later does one form a judgement. I see a Chinese pine, but do not think this, because at that stage I do not know what a Chinese pine is. Nonetheless, the report is, in Plato's theory, logically prior to any painting ('image') of it.

So what function do images have in Plato's theory? The real work is done by reports, judgements: these are primarily true and false. The truth and falsity of images is derivative. The two workmen at work in our book-like soul are in fact a rather theatrical manner of suggesting the fundamentally propositional nature of sensual judgement. In terms of the argument at this point in the dialogue, they are important for Socrates to persuade Protarchus that pleasures can be false, and indeed, can be false without judgement. 'Images' are presumably also meant to form familiar features of our forming sensory judgements, and presumably sensory memories; so Plato has to give an account of them. They do not appear necessary to the formation of such judgements, even if they are one way in which memories, expectations, and indeed sensual input are present to us; the crucial idea in Plato's view is their derivative nature. They serve no ineliminable function in their own right. They are merely side effects of the reports, rather than structural factors in the production of sensory judgement, expectation, or memory. Socrates asks, after introducing the painter: is that not what happens in us? (39C1–2) And Protarchus is enthusiastic in his affirmative answer. A very straightforward point is being made. Images are an obvious phenomenon in our experience of memory which has to be accounted for, at least mentioned, in a theory, even if in the last analysis they need contribute nothing to the functioning of memory. Plato is far from being a proponent of a theory of memory based on imagination. That accolade, as far as our evidence goes, must be accorded to Aristotle.[37]

7 Conclusion

In conclusion, I would like to add a few remarks about the Phileban theory of memory as a purely psychic phenomenon. I suspect that one reason it is purely psychic is that memory is a form of cognition and so a good in the *Philebus*, one of the things that go into the mix of the best life.

In the texts we have looked at, the only notions which involve the body are those concerned with sensation. Yet it seems to be the point of this

---

[37] By this I do not mean that Aristotle bases his view of memory on 'mental images'. For the propositional nature of Aristotelian memory, see King 2009.

conception of memory that once a sensation has been had, all connection with the body can be left behind. This is clear from the definition of recollection (b). And in the account of sensory judgement neither the scribe's report nor the painter's image are bound to the body. It remains hard to understand, however, how a report can be written without a block to write on, or a painting painted without wood or plaster. In other words, the terms of Plato's images suggest something he does not want, namely the need for a material basis for memory.[38] One striking omission from the account of the activities of the soul in the *Philebus* is an account of the soul. Sure, as we noted at the start of this paper, the dialogue ends with Protarchus reminding Socrates of things still to be discussed, and begins in dramatic fashion *in medias res*; the work is dramatically and philosophically a fragment of dialectic. One avenue some readers may find attractive is to take the definitions of the soul from the *Phaedrus* and the *Laws* to stop this gap.[39] And if we do this, then we might also think that because the soul both originates change and undergoes it, is both passive and active; no body is necessary for the soul to have 'scribes' and 'painters' in it. Thus, it is quite conceivable that the soul alone has memory, even if memory necessarily includes 'affections'. Even if this does not strictly imply the existence of a soul independent of the body,[40] it does suggest independent activity and passivity on its part. The soul is the subject of memory, even when coupled with the body. But of course, sensation is necessary, at some point in the soul's trajectory, if it is to have memory, and memory is the preservation of sensation, even if memory in fact preserves what we learn in sensation, not the sensation itself. That this is so is suggested by the *uses* of memory and memory terms in dialectic. In this way the definition of memory in the *Philebus* accounts for part of the conduct of the dialogue.[41]

---

[38] Some readers, perhaps constructing a coherent picture of memory from Plato's dialogues, have felt that the scribe and painter can, and indeed should, be seen in the context of the wax block of the *Theaetetus*. Sedley suggests that the scribe and painter model does better than the wax block (see above note 34).

[39] *Phdr.* 245D-E, *Leg.* 896A. Delcomminette (2006: 317) makes use of these two (distinct) accounts of the soul.

[40] This point was made by Dorothea Frede in response to my paper in Dublin.

[41] The editors of this volume deserve rich thanks for pursuing this project to completion, and also for many improving suggestions for this piece. Audiences in Dublin, Durham, Glasgow, and St Andrews all nudged me in various ways to clarify and even modify my views: many thanks!

CHAPTER 10

Is Memory of the Past?
Aristotle on the Objects of Memory

Luca Castagnoli*

In memoriam Pietro Castagnoli

Shortly after the opening of his treatise *On Memory and Recollection* (hereafter, *De Memoria*) Aristotle writes:

> Τι πρῶτον μὲν οὖν σκεπτέον ποῖά ἐστι τὰ μνημονευτά· πολλάκις γὰρ ἐξαπατᾷ τοῦτο. οὔτε γὰρ τὸ μέλλον ἐνδέχεται μνημονεύειν, ἀλλ' ἔστι δοξαστὸν καὶ ἐλπιστόν (εἴη δ' ἂν καὶ ἐπιστήμη τις ἐλπιστική, καθάπερ τινές φασι τὴν μαντικήν), οὔτε τοῦ παρόντος, ἀλλ' αἴσθησις· ταύτῃ γὰρ οὔτε τὸ μέλλον οὔτε τὸ γενόμενον γνωρίζομεν, ἀλλὰ τὸ παρὸν μόνον. ἡ δὲ μνήμη τοῦ γενομένου· τὸ δὲ παρὸν ὅτε πάρεστιν, οἷον τοδὶ τὸ λευκὸν ὅτε ὁρᾷ, οὐδεὶς ἂν φαίη μνημονεύειν, οὐδὲ τὸ θεωρούμενον, ὅτε θεωρῶν τυγχάνει καὶ νοῶν, ἀλλὰ τὸ μὲν αἰσθάνεσθαί φησι, τὸ δ' ἐπίστασθαι μόνον.[1] (*Mem.* 1, 449b9–18)

First, then, one must consider what sort of things the objects of memory are; for often people are in error about this. For it is not possible to remember the future, but this is an object of opinion and expectation (and there might even be a science of expectation, as some people say divination is), nor is [memory] of the present, but perception [is]; for by this we cognise neither the future nor the past, but only the present. *Memory is of the past*; no one would say he remembers the present when it is present, e.g. this white thing when seeing it, nor [would anyone say he remembers] what is contemplated when he happens to be contemplating and thinking it; but one says only that he perceives the one, and knows the other.

The view that memory (μνήμη) is 'of the past' (τοῦ γενομένου), that is, the *only* object of memory is the past, or, more precisely, the *objects* of

---

* Many thanks for generous feedback to many friends and colleagues who over the years have commented upon various drafts of this chapter, including audiences in Durham, Gothenburg, Cambridge, Oxford. Special thanks to Rachel Parsons for her comments, and for allowing me to read her dissertation. Although it reached me too late for me to make substantial changes to the chapter, I learnt much from it.

[1] Unless otherwise stated, the edition of the *De Memoria* used is Ross 1955; all translations are mine.

memory (τὰ μνημονευτά: 'the things remembered', or 'the things that can be remembered') are past, sounds like a platitude.[2] *Of course* memory is directed towards the past: we cannot remember the future[3] and we do not need to remember what is present.[4] I will aim to demonstrate that when we unpack this apparent Aristotelian platitude, several exegetical and philosophical questions come to the fore. Let us start from Richard Sorabji's (1972: 13) remarks in his seminal study of the *De Memoria*:

> Aristotle says (449b10–15) that the object of memory is the past (or, perhaps, what is past). This view is understandable and is widely shared. But in fact there are many cases where it is not at all clear that the view is true. For example, one can remember a fact, how to do something, a number which one has memorized, the flavour of honey, to feed the cat, the way from A to B, the strokes in swimming, the Queen's presence, tomorrow's appointment or meeting, a character in a fiction, the incommensurability of the diagonal and the side of a square ... it is true that a good many of these examples can be relegated to the categories of remembering that something is the case, or remembering how to do something ... It may be thought that at least there is a *type* of memory of which the view is true. And perhaps there is. But if so, it is important to be able to spell out what the type is. And this is not so easy a task as one might suppose. For the present purposes, it is enough to say that at least Aristotle is not in a position to defend his view that the thing remembered belongs to the past. For in several of the examples which he actually discusses [e.g. objects of scientific knowledge, persons, names, the last member of a list, mathematical objects, objects of thought], the view is not true.

There are three distinct reasons why Aristotle's claim that memory is of the past is problematically interesting. Two of these are reflected in Sorabji's comments:

---

[2] For the same point, cf. *Top.* 111b26–31.

[3] On τὸ μέλλον, cf. King 2009: 27: 'what is going to happen, above all what one is going to do ... thus it does not have to happen, in contrast with that which will be'.

[4] Aristotle's preliminary claim that '*no one would say* he remembers the present when it is present' reflects Aristotle's typical endoxic procedure (cf. King 2009: 30). A Greek, on seeing someone he has met before, would not say: 'I remember him', but 'I recognise him' (ἀναγνωρίζειν). Sorabji (1972: 66) notices the point, but he does not draw its consequences for the way in which *we* should approach the question of the objects of memory: the fact that in English we can say 'I remember him' or 'I remember that 2 + 2 = 4' should not lead us to *assume* that the person we are currently perceiving and recognising, or the results of mathematical calculations, are objects of memory. G. R. T. Ross (1906: 245) makes the different (but possibly complementary) point that 'one might remember, while he was looking at a white thing, that he had seen it before; but he cannot remember that it is now present'.

(1) To begin with, Aristotle's claim raises a broad *philosophical* question: is this too narrow a conception of memory? To use modern jargon, it seems to exclude not only *procedural* or *habit* memory, that is remembering *how* to do things, but also part of what we call *semantic* or *propositional* memory, namely remembering *that* – for example that a certain word has a certain meaning, or that Paris is the capital of France, or that 2 + 2 = 4.[5] One could object that whereas *some* memories are of the past, or – with Sorabji – that a *type* of memory has the past as its object, memory as a whole is a heterogeneous phenomenon with much broader scope. And, first of all, what counts as a 'past object' of memory anyway? What do *we* mean, *exactly*, when we accept, unreflectively, that memory is of the past?

(2) The second source of interest lies in an *exegetical* question, that of the intrinsic consistency of Aristotle's position: is the view that memory is (only) of the past compatible with what he himself says about memory, its objects, its workings and its function in the *De Memoria* and elsewhere? Sorabji believes that Aristotle is not consistent, because he uses reasonable examples of objects of memory in the course of his treatment in which actually what we remember is not 'past' in any recognisable sense. What did *Aristotle* mean, *exactly*, when he claimed that memory is of the past, then?[6]

The third reason why T1 makes a more interesting point than it might appear, and which does not emerge from Sorabji's comments above, is a broader *historical* one:

(3) How obvious would this view have sounded at Aristotle's time? My suggestion is that Aristotle's claim represents an original departure from one important thread of the Greek cultural tradition. Memory was central to Greek culture and education from very early on. This is reflected, for example, by the position of Mnemosyne, the memory goddess, in the Greek pantheon. In Hesiod's *Theogony* Mnemosyne is an early, pre-Olympian deity, daughter of Gaia and Ouranos; significantly, she is the sister of Kronos[7] and the *mother of the Muses*.

---

[5] For an introduction to modern taxonomies of memory, see pp. 2–5 in the Introduction to this volume.

[6] For an analogous question raised by Plato's definition of memory as 'preservation of sensation' in the *Philebus*, see King's chapter in this volume.

[7] For the ancient association between Kronos and Chronos (Time), see Plutarch (*Is. Os.* 32), according to whom some Greeks 'say that Kronos is but a figurative name for Chronos'; Cicero had called this

In fact there is another tradition which made of Memory herself one of three Muses, under the name 'Mneme'. It is clearly in virtue of their kinship with memory and time that the Muses represented *omniscient* sources of super-human *knowledge* (cf. e.g. Homer *Iliad* 2.484–7; Hesiod *Theogony* 22–33; Pindar *Paean* 7), which human beings can attain only through the medium of inspired poetry and art; but this memory-related knowledge concerns not only the *past*,[8] but also the *present* and the *future*.[9] Plato was engaging critically with this tradition, appropriating and transforming it at the same time, when he chose ἀνάμνησις, 'recollection', as a way of describing our access to a-temporal, intelligible, divine truths (cf. especially the *Phaedo* and the *Phaedrus* – although the cognate ἀνάμνησις is Plato's preferred term, μνήμη is also used in that context).[10] To put it crudely, by arguing that memory is *only* of the past Aristotle brought μνήμη down to earth, 'humanising' it.[11]

The analysis of the role which memory played in ancient reflections on knowledge and learning, philosophical theories, practices of inquiry, and teaching cannot be pursued in this context.[12] I will focus here on the second, exegetical question I have identified above, with some remarks on the philosophical dividends which come from our reading of Aristotle with relation to the first, philosophical question.

---

idea an 'ancient belief' (*ND* 2.64). For earlier evidence of this association, see the Introduction to this volume, pp. 5–6 n. 14.

[8] Heroic or cosmogonic: cf. Vernant 1983, and the discussion of this form of memory in Darbo-Peschanski's chapter in this volume.

[9] For the role of Mnemosyne at the Lebadeia oracle, cf. Pausanias 9.39.3 and p. 18 in the introduction. On the relationship between memory and the Muses, see also the introduction to this volume (pp. 9–12).

[10] Cf. e.g. *Phdr.* 253a3, 254b5.

[11] Of course there had been important antecedents for this, including Plato himself, especially in the *Philebus* and the *Theaetetus* (see below). Sorabji (1972: 65) refers to *Philebus* 39d–e as a clear antecedent of Aristotle's view that memory is of the past (and perception of the present, prediction of the future), but this does not seem to be warranted by Plato's text. In fact Plato never claims that memory 'is of the past' in the *corpus*, but posits as a necessary condition for memory and recollection the existence of some past experience (cf. PCVM below).

[12] See some notes in the Introduction to this volume, especially section 6. For a wide-ranging study of archaic and classical Greek views of memory until the late fifth century BC, cf. Simondon 1982; for an overview of ancient philosophical theories of memory, until Augustine, cf. Coleman 1992: 1–112. For discussion of the role which memory plays in learning in the Greek philosophical tradition, including Aristotle, cf. also Sassi's chapter in this volume.

1 Memory, Images and Likenesses

What did Aristotle mean, then, by claiming that memory is of the past? And was he in a position to consistently say what he meant? Let us read how he continues after T1:

> **T2** ὅταν δ' ἄνευ τῶν ἔργων[13] σχῇ τὴν ἐπιστήμην καὶ τὴν αἴσθησιν, οὕτω μέμνηται, τὸ μὲν ὅτι ἔμαθεν ἢ ἐθεώρησεν, τὸ δὲ ὅτι ἤκουσεν ἢ εἶδεν ἢ τι τοιοῦτον· ἀεὶ γὰρ ὅταν ἐνεργῇ κατὰ τὸ μνημονεύειν, οὕτως ἐν τῇ ψυχῇ λέγει, ὅτι πρότερον τοῦτο ἤκουσεν ἢ ᾔσθετο ἢ ἐνόησεν. ἔστι μὲν οὖν ἡ μνήμη οὔτε αἴσθησις οὔτε ὑπόληψις, ἀλλὰ τούτων τινὸς ἕξις ἢ πάθος, ὅταν γένηται χρόνος. τοῦ δὲ νῦν ἐν τῷ νῦν οὐκ ἔστι μνήμη, καθάπερ εἴρηται, ἀλλὰ τοῦ μὲν παρόντος αἴσθησις, τοῦ δὲ μέλλοντος ἐλπίς, τοῦ δὲ γενομένου μνήμη· διὸ μετὰ χρόνου πᾶσα μνήμη. ὥσθ' ὅσα χρόνου αἰσθάνεται, ταῦτα μόνα τῶν ζῴων μνημονεύει, καὶ τούτῳ ᾧ αἰσθάνεται. (*Mem.* 1, 449b18–30)

(a) But when someone possesses knowledge and perception without the activities, thus he has memory, in one case that[14] he learnt or contemplated, in the other that he heard, or saw or something of this kind; for always when someone actualises his remembering he says in his soul in this way that he heard or perceived or thought this before. (b) Thus memory is neither perception nor thought, but having one of these or an affection from one of these, when time elapses. (c) There is no memory of the now in the now, as has been said, but of the present there is perception, of the future expectation, of the past memory. Therefore all memory occurs with time. (d) So only those animals that perceive time remember, and by means of that with which they perceive [time].

This initial and provisional account of memory as something which results in our soul from a previous perception (αἴσθησις) or 'thought' (ὑπόληψις)[15] *after some time elapses* provides a first suggestion as to why memory is of the past (we will discover shortly what this 'something', described here as an ἕξις or πάθος, is).[16] But we should be clear about the implications of this

---

[13] Following the majority of the MSS, with Ross 1955 and Bloch 2007; King 2009: 30–1 n. 93 has ἐνεργειῶν.

[14] For an alternative translation of this and the following ὅτι, cf. Bloch 2007: 25 n. 2: 'he recalls, in the case of knowledge *because* he has learned or contemplated it, in the case of sensation *because* he has heard or seen it or sensed it in some other way'. The translation, although possible, seems unlikely, given the parallel use of ὅτι to introduce a declarative clause in the following lines.

[15] According to *An.* III 3, 427b24–6, ὑπόληψις (often rendered as 'conception' by translators) includes δόξα ('opinion'), ἐπιστήμη ('knowledge') and φρόνησις ('practical wisdom').

[16] Sorabji (1972: 69–70) takes πάθος to refer to a transient memory-image (see below), and ἕξις to a more stable state, or a disposition to form a certain memory-image ('memory is ... a state or affection connected with one of these [sc. perception or thought]'). For a different suggestion, cf.

account. In itself, this is compatible with what Sorabji (1972: 13) calls the 'past-cognition' view of memory:

> (PCVM) **Past-Cognition View of Memory:** if I remember X at time t, then I must have perceived, thought or otherwise experienced X at some previous time t_{-n}.

I look at the white paper in front of me, and I see something; this is perception, and not memory. Suppose I retain something of this experience while I am no longer perceiving the white paper, and after some time has elapsed; then I have memory of the white paper. What is past is not the thing remembered (the white paper), that can still exist, but the *cognitive act* which produced the memory of it, which is now present.

Was Aristotle committed to something as uncontroversial as PCVM?[17] Or was he wrongly committed, as Sorabji complains, to a philosophically dubious 'past-object' view?[18]

> (POVM) **Past-Object View of Memory:** if I remember X at time t, then X must be *something past*: it must have existed at some previous time t_{-n}.[19]

The innocuous PCVM is not, I will argue first, all that Aristotle had in mind. Two clues already occur in T2:

(1) Aristotle's commitment to PCVM would explain why a time lapse from the original experience is a necessary condition for memory, but not why the *perception* of the time lapse is, and why those animals that have memory must have a sense of the passing of time (T2d);

---

n. 41 below. For a translation similar to mine, cf. Bloch 2007: 27: 'the state of having one of these or the affection resulting from one of these'.

[17] Cf. e.g. Shoemaker 1967: 265: 'It is true in general that remembering involves having *previously* learned or acquired knowledge of what one remembers'. For an ancient formulation of the idea, cf. Pl. *Phaed.* 73c1–2: ὁμολογοῦμεν γὰρ δήπου, εἴ τίς τι ἀναμνησθήσεται, δεῖν αὐτὸν τοῦτο πρότερόν ποτε ἐπίστασθαι. For two medieval readers of Aristotle who attributed to him PCVM, cf. Thomas Aquinas, *Sententia de memoria et reminiscentia, lectio I, 308* and Peter of Auvergne, *Quaestiones super de memoria, quaestio 4*.

[18] King (2009: 29 n. 83) objects that Sorabji's reconstruction of Aristotle's point is incorrect, and that actually Aristotle shared PCVM. What King ultimately attributes to Aristotle, however, is a narrow conception of Aristotelian μνήμη as episodic memory which comes very close to POVM (see below).

[19] According to Sorabji 1972: 14, 'a great advantage of accepting the past-cognition view is that it enables one to explain why the past-object view was so tempting. In many cases, cognition and thing cognised are contemporary with each other. In all these cases, if the cognition is past, as it is when one remembers something, the thing cognised, and hence the thing subsequently remembered, will also have existed in the past.' Notice that both PCVM and POVM express *necessary*, and not *sufficient* conditions for memory.

(2) Moreover, it would be sufficient to explain why whatever I remember must have been previously experienced by me, but not why whenever I remember I *must* say to myself, or somehow be aware, that I have previously experienced what I am now remembering (T2a).[20]

The insufficiency of PCVM to fully capture Aristotle's claim that μνήμη is of the past becomes more evident as we proceed in our reading of the *De Memoria*. I will limit myself to summarising the main lines of the development of Aristotle's argument, focusing on those details that are more relevant to our present question. At 449b30–450a14 Aristotle argues, through a complex argument that has been the object of extensive philological and exegetical debate,[21] that memory must belong to the 'primary perceptive part' of the soul, on the grounds that memory involves time, as we have just seen, and 'images' (φαντάσματα):

(1)	Magnitude is cognised by means of images	(450a1–7)
(2)	Magnitude, change and time are cognised by the same means (since they are all related continua)	(450a9–10)[22]
(3)	An image is an affection of the 'common sense'	(450a10–11)[23]
(4)	<Common sense is (a part or function of) the primary perceptive part>	(unstated premise)[24]

---

[20] There is a further complication here, because Aristotle says that some animals have memories, because they perceive time, but according to Aristotle animals are incapable of propositional thought, and thus, strictly speaking, cannot *say to themselves* that they have previously experienced what they now remember. Later at 450a15–22, when he repeats the point that some animals too have memory, exactly to support his claim that memory does not belong to the thinking part of the soul, Aristotle says that 'when someone is actively engaged in memory, he *perceives in addition* (προσαισθάνεται) that he saw this, or he heard this, or learned this earlier'. This kind of internal perception or awareness need not be propositional, and thus could apply to animals too.

[21] The reconstruction offered below is indebted to Sorabji 1972: 74–5. For different reconstructions of the text and the argument, cf. Ross 1955: 237–8; Gregoric 2007: 99–111; King 2009: 42.

[22] μέγεθος δ᾽ ἀναγκαῖον γνωρίζειν καὶ κίνησιν ᾧ καὶ χρόνον. Time is a measure of change, 'the number of change with respect to before and after' (*Phys.* IV 11, 219b1–2). On Aristotle's theory of time, cf. Coope 2005 and Roark 2011.

[23] τὸ φάντασμα τῆς κοινῆς αἰσθήσεως πάθος ἐστίν. From the only two other occurrences in Aristotle we learn that 'common sense' (1) apprehends images and (2) the sense-objects common to more than one sense, e.g. size, which is common to sight and touch (*An.* III 1, 425a27). On 'common sense' in Aristotle, see Gregoric 2007 and Marmodoro 2014.

[24] On the relationship between the primary perceptive part or capacity of the soul and common sense here, cf. Sorabji 1972: 75–6; Gregoric 2007: 108–9. Aristotle is reticent about the physical location and constitution of the organ of the primary perceptive part. Elsewhere he says that it is located in the region of the heart – or the analogue of the heart in other animals (*Juvent.* 3, 469a5–12; *GA* II 6, 743b25). Incidentally, in the *Theaetetus* the wax block of memory was called 'the heart of the soul' (194c).

(5)	Thus the cognition of magnitude, change and time belongs to the primary perceptive part	(450a11–12, from (1), (2),(3),(4))[25]
(6)	Memory (even memory of intelligibles) always involves images	(450a12–13)[26]
(7)	Therefore, insofar as it involves time and images, memory belongs in its own right to the primary perceptive part	(450a13–14)[27]
(8)	Therefore, some animals too have memory	(450a15–22)

The concept of φάντασμα takes centre stage now: what is in the soul after the original 'perception or thought' has ended and we have a memory of it is a φάντασμα. Only those things of which there is φαντασία, i.e. those things which can be 'imagined', in the literal sense that the faculty of 'imagination'[28] can form images of them, 'are objects of memory in their own right' (450a23–4: καί ἐστι μνημονευτὰ καθ᾽ αὑτά[29] μὲν ὧν ἐστι φαντασία). I have adopted here the traditional translations 'images' and 'imagination', with full awareness that φαντάσματα should not be conceived narrowly as *pictorial* images (we have φαντάσματα of sounds, smells, flavours …), despite the fact that Aristotle uses, as we will see shortly, the metaphors of 'imprints' and 'paintings' to illustrate the workings of φαντάσματα (see T3 below).[30]

Aristotle next clarifies the nature of the affection, change or image[31] generated when some memory is formed:

> **T3** δῆλον γὰρ ὅτι δεῖ νοῆσαι τοιοῦτον τὸ γιγνόμενον διὰ τῆς αἰσθήσεως ἐν τῇ ψυχῇ καὶ τῷ μορίῳ τοῦ σώματος τῷ ἔχοντι αὐτὴν οἷον ζωγράφημά τι οὗ φαμεν τὴν ἕξιν μνήμην εἶναι· ἡ γὰρ γιγνομένη κίνησις ἐνσημαίνεται οἷον τύπον τινὰ τοῦ αἰσθήματος, καθάπερ οἱ σφραγιζόμενοι τοῖς δακτυλίοις. (*Mem.* 1, 450a27–32)

> For it is clear that one must think of what is so generated by means of perception in the soul and in the part of the body which contains it as a sort of picture, the having of which we say is memory; for the change that occurs

---

[25] ὥστε φανερὸν ὅτι τῷ πρώτῳ αἰσθητικῷ τούτων ἡ γνῶσίς ἐστιν.

[26] ἡ δὲ μνήμη, καὶ ἡ τῶν νοητῶν, οὐκ ἄνευ φαντάσματός ἐστιν.

[27] ὥστε … ἂν εἴη, καθ᾽ αὑτὸ δὲ τοῦ πρώτου αἰσθητικοῦ. I will return to the import of the qualification καθ᾽ αὑτὸ below.

[28] On imagination and images in Aristotle, cf. especially Wedin 1988, Caston 1996, Scheiter 2012.

[29] I will return to the import of the qualification καθ᾽ αὑτὰ below.

[30] For criticism of Aristotle's too pictorial conception of φαντάσματα, cf. Sorabji 1972: 2–8; for the view that Aristotelian φαντάσματα are to be intended, more broadly, as 'representations', cf. King 2009: 43–62.

[31] A difficult problem, which I cannot tackle here, is that of the exact relationship between *pathos*, *phantasma* and *kinēsis* throughout the treatise. For some introductory remarks on the problem, cf. Sorabji 1972: 14–17.

marks in a sort of imprint, as it were, of the percept, as people do who seal things with signet rings.

The adoption of the similes of a picture (ζωγράφημα) and an imprint (τύπον) is Aristotle's own fusion of two late Platonic models for μνήμη, in the *Philebus* (38c–39d: the scribe and the painter in the soul)[32] and in the *Theaetetus* (191b–195c: memory as a wax block).[33] Having a memory is *something like*[34] having a picture in the soul which has been drawn or imprinted by a 'percept' or 'sense-image' (αἴσθημα),[35] which was in turn the causal effect of the interaction between a certain sense-object and our senses:

Sense-object (αἰσθητόν) → Percept (αἴσθημα) → Image (φάντασμα)

At 450a32–b11 Aristotle explains how differences in mnemonic capacities of individuals can be accounted for on the basis of the condition of the substrate receiving the imprint, again along the lines of the Theaetetan wax block.[36] Next he explores an *aporia*: how is it possible that when only the image is present in the soul, but what produced it is absent, we remember what is not present?[37] When we remember, do we remember the image in the soul, or the thing by which it was produced? Both horns of the dilemma appear to be problematic: 'if the former, we would remember nothing absent' (which clashes with the initial intuition that memory is of the past, and not of what is present); but if the latter, the question remains of how to explain why attending to a present image in the soul should count as remembering *something else*, which is absent and which we are

---

[32] For the treatment of memory in Plato's *Philebus*, and for a deflationary account of the role which images play in memory, cf. King's chapter in this volume.

[33] For a discussion of the way in which the introduction of writing influenced the way in which the Greeks conceptualised memory and its workings, see the remarks and references in the Introduction to this volume (especially Sections 2 and 3), and Agócs' chapter.

[34] Notice Aristotle's caution in emphasising the non-literal use of the ideas of pictures and imprints: οἷον ζωγράφημά τι … οἷον τύπον τινά.

[35] On the concept of αἴσθημα, cf. Sorabji 1972: 82–3; Wedin 1988: 36–9; Everson 1997: 174–7; King 2009: 70–1.

[36] Young and old people have poor memories because of their physical constitution, i.e. their process of rapid change and decay: imprints are not formed because the surface is either too fluid or too hard (the point will be repeated at 453a31, with the addition that those who are 'dwarf-like' also have bad memories because they have too much weight resting on their central perceptive organ). Those who are too quick or too slow have bad memories for the same reason: the former are too moist (the imprint does not remain), the latter too hard (the imprint does not take hold).

[37] The puzzle was first formulated before T3, at 450a25–7: ἀπορήσειε δ᾽ ἄν τις πῶς ποτε τοῦ μὲν πάθους παρόντος τοῦ δὲ πράγματος ἀπόντος μνημονεύεται τὸ μὴ παρόν. Note the shift, here and below, in the use of τὸ (μὴ) παρόν, from its purely *temporal* sense in T1 (where the present is opposed to the past and the future) to the more general sense of what is not present *to us*.

not perceiving (*Mem.* 1, 450b11–20).³⁸ Aristotle's solution consists in clarifying that just as a painted figure (γεγραμμένον ζῷον) is at the same time a figure (ζῷον), in its own right, and a likeness or representation (εἰκών) of something else, and can be looked at either *as a figure or as a likeness* (ἔστι θεωρεῖν καὶ ὡς ζῷον καὶ ὡς εἰκόνα), so we can regard the image in us (τὸ ἐν ἡμῖν φάντασμα) by itself (καθ' αὑτό), or relatively to something else, e.g. as a likeness (εἰκών) of something else³⁹ (what produced it), and thus as a *memory-image*, a 'reminder' (μνημόνευμα) of it (450b20–451a2).⁴⁰ Aristotle shows the explanatory power of the distinction in the account of some familiar memory phenomena (451a2–14), including extreme cases of false memories: certain φαντάσματα created by our faculty of imagination, which are not likenesses of something past, are 'looked at' by deranged people as if they were likenesses, and thus as memories. That distinction also allows him to reach the final definition of memory:

> **T4** τί μὲν οὖν ἐστι μνήμη καὶ τὸ μνημονεύειν, εἴρηται, ὅτι φαντάσματος, ὡς εἰκόνος οὗ φάντασμα, ἕξις, καὶ τίνος μορίου τῶν ἐν ἡμῖν, ὅτι τοῦ πρώτου αἰσθητικοῦ καὶ ᾧ χρόνου αἰσθανόμεθα. (*Mem.* 1, 451a14–17)
>
> We have said, then, what memory and remembering are, that is having an image regarded as a likeness of that of which it is an image, and to what part in us <they belong>, that is the primary perceptive part and that with which we perceive time.

Memory is defined as having images present to us. For a certain image to count as a memory, as opposed to a mere figment of imagination, it must be the result of some past experience (it was imprinted by an earlier perception as some kind of copy). If Aristotle had stopped here, his theory would be fully captured by PCVM. But he adds a further condition: the image must

---

³⁸ ἀλλ' εἰ δὴ τοιοῦτόν ἐστι τὸ συμβαῖνον περὶ τὴν μνήμην, πότερον τοῦτο μνημονεύει τὸ πάθος, ἢ ἐκεῖνο ἀφ' οὗ ἐγένετο; εἰ μὲν γὰρ τοῦτο, τῶν ἀπόντων οὐδὲν ἂν μνημονεύοιμεν· εἰ δ' ἐκεῖνο, πῶς αἰσθανόμενοι τοῦτο μνημονεύομεν οὗ μὴ αἰσθανόμεθα, τὸ ἀπόν; εἴ τ' ἐστιν ὅμοιον ὥσπερ τύπος ἢ γραφὴ ἐν ἡμῖν, ἡ τούτου αἴσθησις διὰ τί ἂν εἴη μνήμη ἑτέρου, ἀλλ' οὐκ αὐτοῦ τούτου· ὁ γὰρ ἐνεργῶν τῇ μνήμῃ θεωρεῖ τὸ πάθος τοῦτο καὶ αἰσθάνεται τούτου. πῶς οὖν τὸ μὴ παρὸν μνημονεύσει; εἴη γὰρ ἂν καὶ ὁρᾶν τὸ μὴ παρὸν καὶ ἀκούειν.
³⁹ For some of the background and implications of Aristotle's adoption of the εἰκών language here, cf. Sorabji 1972: 2–5.
⁴⁰ οἷον γὰρ τὸ ἐν πίνακι γεγραμμένον ζῷον καὶ ζῷόν ἐστι καὶ εἰκών, καὶ τὸ αὐτὸ καὶ ἓν τοῦτ' ἐστὶν ἄμφω, τὸ μέντοι εἶναι οὐ ταὐτὸν ἀμφοῖν, καὶ ἔστι θεωρεῖν καὶ ὡς ζῷον καὶ ὡς εἰκόνα, οὕτω καὶ τὸ ἐν ἡμῖν φάντασμα δεῖ ὑπολαβεῖν καὶ αὐτό τι καθ' αὑτό εἶναι καὶ ἄλλου. ᾗ μὲν οὖν καθ' αὑτό, θεώρημα ἢ φάντασμά ἐστιν, ᾗ δ' ἄλλου, οἷον εἰκὼν καὶ μνημόνευμα. ὥστε καὶ ὅταν ἐνεργῇ ἡ κίνησις αὐτοῦ, ἂν μὲν ᾖ καθ' αὑτό ἐστι, ταύτῃ αἰσθάνεται ἡ ψυχὴ αὐτοῦ, οἷον νόημά τι ἢ φάντασμα φαίνεται ἐπελθεῖν· ἂν δ' ᾖ ἄλλου καὶ ὥσπερ ἐν τῇ γραφῇ ὡς εἰκόνα θεωρεῖ καί, μὴ ἑωρακὼς τὸν Κορίσκον, ὡς Κορίσκου, ἐνταῦθά τε ἄλλο τὸ πάθος τῆς θεωρίας ταύτης καὶ ὅταν ὡς ζῷον γεγραμμένον θεωρῇ, ἕν τε τῇ ψυχῇ τὸ μὲν γίγνεται ὥσπερ νόημα μόνον, τὸ δ' ὡς ἐκεῖ ὅτι εἰκών, μνημόνευμα.

be 'looked at' in a particular way, *as* a likeness or representation of something different from itself.[41] This idea that the *modus spectandi* is fundamental to identify a certain mental occurrence as a memory is, I suggest, a different way of cashing out the earlier condition that some awareness of the temporal dimension, a 'sense of the past', is a necessary condition for memory; to perceive that the φάντασμα I am attending to is a likeness of something else, which produced it and is not currently present to me is to have some awareness that I have experienced that thing at some earlier time.[42]

Let us be clear on why, in the light of this, PCVM is too weak to capture Aristotle's view that memory is of the past. PCVM is compatible with any model of memory according to which memory is the retention of acquired information, and remembering the retrieval of it. Anything that came to be in your mind in the past, and somehow 'is still there' and can be accessed, counts as 'memory' on this familiar model. From this point of view, all kinds of semantic or propositional knowledge would be included under the heading of memory. This model resembles the *Philebus* view of memory as 'preservation of perception' (34a10–11: Σωτηρίαν τοίνυν αἰσθήσεως τὴν μνήμην λέγων ὀρθῶς ἄν τις λέγοι κατά γε τὴν ἐμὴν δόξαν), and the two *Theaetetus* models of the aviary and wax block (191b–198c). But, I have argued, this is a model that Aristotle, despite his extensive borrowing of Platonic imagery,[43] does not share.[44]

---

[41] This seems to apply to *acts* of remembering only; to have a memory in us without using it should be, *mutatis mutandis*, to have an image which *can* be 'accessed' as a representation of something else. For the different view that Aristotle's theory does not account for 'memory acts', cf. Bloch 2007. Interestingly Aristotle criticises a dispositional definition of memory as a ἕξις in *Topics* IV 5, 125b17–19: ὁμοίως δὲ καὶ εἰ τὴν μνήμην ἕξιν καθεκτικὴν ὑπολήψεως εἶπεν· οὐδεμία γὰρ μνήμη ἕξις, ἀλλὰ μᾶλλον ἐνέργεια. I suggest that in the De Memoria Aristotle's use of ἕξις might be influenced by the Platonic distinction between ἕξις ('having') and κτῆσις ('possession') in the aviary (*Theaetetus* 197b–d), where ἕξις corresponds to the actualisation and use of stored (i.e. possessed) knowledge. For a much more developed suggestion along the same lines, backed up by detailed philological and textual considerations, see Parsons 2016.

[42] This awareness is explained by Aristotle in terms of the co-occurrence in the soul of the memory image and an associated 'change connected with the time' at *Mem.* 2, 452b7–453a3. The proposal is unclear and problematic, and I cannot examine it further here. For a modern account of memory strikingly in line with Aristotle's, cf. Russell 1921: 175–6: 'Memory-images and imagination-images do not differ in their intrinsic qualities, so far as we can discover. They differ by the fact that the images that constitute memories, unlike those that constitute imagination, are accompanied by a feeling of belief which may be expressed in the words "this happened." The mere occurrence of images, without this feeling of belief constitutes imagination; it is the element of belief that is distinctive in memory.' This account is in turn reminiscent of John Locke's view of memory as the power of the mind 'to revive Perceptions, which it has once had, with this additional perception annexed to them, that it has had them before' (*An Essay Concerning Human Understanding* II 10).

[43] For a short study of Aristotle's appropriation of, and reaction to, Platonic ideas and language in this area, cf. Lang 1980.

[44] Cf. Ross 1906: 34: 'Memory (μνήμη) is used in a very restricted sense, one much narrower than that assigned to it in modern psychology. It does not comprise retention: that rather is an element

Does this mean that Aristotle endorsed the narrow POVM, as Sorabji and others believe? As a consequence of his emphasis on the past, and our awareness of it, in his account of μνήμη, several scholars have maintained, in different ways, that Aristotle's conception of memory is indeed very narrow, and have identified Aristotelian μνήμη with what is variously called nowadays 'episodic', 'personal', 'recollective' or 'experiential' memory.[45] According to Julia Annas (1992: 301), for example, 'it won't be true that I remember the white thing unless I remember *seeing* the white thing', and (304–5) 'it is surely clear that what the image represents is one's past experience of the object, not just the object'; Tony Roark (2011: 145) has claimed 'what one remembers, for instance, is that (ὅτι) one witnessed the falling of the Berlin Wall, rather than simply remembering the Wall itself or the event of which it was a constituent'.[46] If this were correct, the POVM would be correct too: since my original experience is the object of memory,[47] and that experience occurred in the past, memory is only of the past in the narrow object sense. But this seems to me a counter-intuitive reading, philosophically dubious and not required by Aristotle's words. Of course we remember things as we have perceived them – or, more precisely, *as a consequence of how we have perceived them*, since there might be some lack of accuracy in our memories; but the object of my memory is not thereby my perception of the thing, or my perceiving the thing, but the thing itself.[48] Otherwise it would not even be possible to say that two people remember the same thing or event, and to compare how accurate their memories are: we would fall into a form of memory solipsism. It is true that the image in the soul was imprinted by an αἴσθημα, and not directly by the sensible object; but the most natural reading of Aristotle's dilemma 'do we remember the image or what it is an image of?' is that

present in the general faculty of Imagination, of which Memory is a special determination'; Bloch 2007: 118–9; King 2009: 25, 30.

[45] For an introduction to modern discussions of memory in philosophy and cognitive sciences, with extensive bibliography, cf. Sutton 2010 and Michaelian and Sutton 2017.

[46] Cf. also Sassi 2007: 43–4: 'una restrizione della nozione di memoria alla capacità e attività di ricordo di eventi della vita personale passata'.

[47] Or at least a *part* of the object of memory, as Annas qualifies her view (1992: 301 n 10). For although Annas claims, as we have seen, that the memory-image represents our experience of *p*, and not *p*, she takes a memory claim such as 'I remember (that) *p*' as *implying* some *other* claim, such as 'I remember (my) *F*ing (that) *p*' (1992: 299), and not as *equivalent* to it.

[48] For a similar view, cf. Bloch 2007: 83: 'remembering the experience precisely as a personal encounter with the content of one's present memory simply is not required'. I do not agree with Bloch's suggestion, however, that this follows from the fact that, for Aristotle, I can remember something with a completely indeterminate awareness of when the experience occurred (452b29–453a4): I can have a very vivid personal episodic memory even if I am unable to date the remembered episode with any precision.

the latter is whatever, through the senses and their αἴσθημα, produced the φάντασμα.[49] Consider also the idea, in T2, that when we remember X we say to ourselves: 'I have seen X' or 'I have heard X before'. Clearly we do not see and hear our own perceptions of trees and birds; we see and hear trees and birds (to accept the contrary would be, again, a form of solipsism, towards which we have no reason to think that Aristotle would have had any sympathy).

If we avoid a too narrow interpretation of the sense in which Aristotelian μνήμη is 'episodic', 'personal' or 'experiential' memory, we avoid the Scylla of POVM, having realised that Aristotle wanted to sail safe from the Charybdis of a too lax view of memory as mere retention (according to which PCVM expresses a *sufficient* condition for memory). Aristotle's position is thus an interesting third way which could be labelled '*as-past* cognition view of memory':

> **(A-PCVM) As-Past Cognition View of Memory:** if I remember X at time t, I have an image of X which I regard as a likeness of X, i.e. I have an image of X with the additional awareness that this is a representation of something else, which produced it and which I experienced at some past time t_{-n}

2   Memory of Intelligible Objects

There is another dimension of Aristotle's discussion of the objects of memory which requires analysis. The obvious counterexample to the view that the objects of memory are themselves past, in accordance with the narrow POVM, is represented by abstract intelligible objects, such as the definition of triangle, the proposition '2 + 2 = 4', or a set of propositions such as Pythagoras' theorem. These are non-temporal[50] (or at best omni-temporal) items and truths. I have argued in the previous section that POVM does not reflect Aristotle's position. This does not mean, however, that his account is broad enough to admit these as *proper* objects of memory – his reasons for such an exclusion are independent, however, of the fact that these objects are not 'past', and prior to it. I will now attempt a reconstruction of these reasons.

---

[49] *Contra* King 2009: 80: 'In taking the representation to be the image of the past perception we remember that perception'. For the implication that the 'object' of memory is the image, cf. Bloch 2007: 89.

[50] According to Arist. *Phys.* IV 12, heavenly bodies and objects of mathematics are not 'in time'. For a reference to things 'not in time' which cannot be thought of 'without time', cf. also *Mem.* I, 450a7–8.

As we have seen above, Aristotle used the thesis that memory of intelligibles could not occur 'without an image' (*Mem.* 1, 450a12–13) to conclude that memory 'belongs to the same part of the soul to which imagination belongs', namely the 'primary perceptive' part (450a9–12). And that thesis was a corollary of the more fundamental tenet that 'it is impossible to think without an image' (449b31–450a1: νοεῖν οὐκ ἔστιν ἄνευ φαντάσματος): any thought, even one at a high level of abstraction, for example in geometry, must be accompanied by a φάντασμα.[51] For example, it is not possible to think of Pythagoras' theorem without visualising – in front of the 'eye of the mind', we might say – the image of a certain triangular shape, on which our thought operates by abstracting from certain features (e.g. the relative length of the sides, or the particular ratio of the angles) and focusing exclusively on the relevant ones.[52] This Aristotelian idea is influential, but not uncontroversial. While the use of images and diagrams, both drawn and mental, is certainly a useful aid to, for example, geometrical thinking, the idea that it is *necessary* in all cases for us to think of intelligible objects makes Aristotle diverge not only from Plato (cf. the fourth segment of the Divided Line in the *Republic*),[53] but also from our common awareness of our own mental processes.

We learn a bit more about Aristotle's idea from a passage in the third book of *On the Soul*:

> **T5** ἐπεὶ δὲ οὐδὲ πρᾶγμα οὐθὲν ἔστι παρὰ τὰ μεγέθη, ὡς δοκεῖ, τὰ αἰσθητὰ κεχωρισμένον, ἐν τοῖς εἴδεσι τοῖς αἰσθητοῖς τὰ νοητά ἐστι, τά τε ἐν ἀφαιρέσει λεγόμενα, καὶ ὅσα τῶν αἰσθητῶν ἕξεις καὶ πάθη. καὶ διὰ τοῦτο οὔτε μὴ αἰσθανόμενος μηθὲν οὐθὲν ἂν μάθοι οὐδὲ ξυνείη, ὅταν τε θεωρῇ, ἀνάγκη ἅμα φάντασμά τι θεωρεῖν· τὰ γὰρ φαντάσματα ὥσπερ αἰσθήματά ἐστι, πλὴν ἄνευ ὕλης. ἔστι δ' ἡ φαντασία ἕτερον φάσεως καὶ ἀποφάσεως· συμπλοκὴ γὰρ νοημάτων ἐστὶ τὸ ἀληθὲς ἢ ψεῦδος. τὰ δὲ πρῶτα νοήματα τί διοίσει τοῦ μὴ φαντάσματα εἶναι; ἢ οὐδὲ τἆλλα φαντάσματα, ἀλλ' οὐκ ἄνευ φαντασμάτων. (*An.* III 8, 432a3–14)

> Since nothing is separate besides the sensible magnitudes, as it seems, the objects of thought are in the sensible forms, both the abstract objects and all the states and affections of sensible things. And for this reason no one

---

[51] In Aristotle the phrase οὐκ ἄνευ typically signals a strong link of dependence: if A is 'not without' B, then B is a *necessary condition* for A. This link does not amount, however, to an identity.

[52] Cf. *Mem.* 450a1–7. For the relation between imagination and thought in Aristotle, cf. e.g. Wedin 1988: 100–59; Caston 1996; Cohoe 2016.

[53] Dialectical, 'noetic' thought, unlike geometrical, 'dianoetic' thought (*Resp.* VI, 510c–511a), eschews the use of sensible images and hypotheses (*Resp.* VI, 511b–c).

can learn or understand anything without perception, and when one is contemplating anything one is necessarily contemplating some image along with it; for images are like percepts, except in that they are without matter. Imagination is different from assertion and denial; for what is true or false is a weaving of thoughts. But in what will the primary thoughts differ from images? Not even these other[54] thoughts are images, but they do not occur without images.

Intelligible objects (νοητά), for example geometrical or mathematical entities, which are obtained through 'abstraction' (ἐν ἀφαιρέσει), or those universals that correspond to the properties of sensible objects, whether essential or contingent (e.g. the universals man and whiteness), are (Aristotle does not explain how) 'in the sensible forms' (ἐν τοῖς εἴδεσι τοῖς αἰσθητοῖς). These are in turn contained in the αἰσθήματα which are produced through our perception of some sensible object, and which persist in the soul until the perception lasts.[55] These sensible forms are then preserved in the soul as φαντάσματα.[56] This is why any thought must be accompanied by an image: 'the intellect thinks the forms *in* the images' (*An.* III 7, 431b2: τὰ μὲν οὖν εἴδη τὸ νοητικὸν ἐν τοῖς φαντάσμασι νοεῖ), that is, can think the intelligibles only where they can be 'contained', in the images of the senses, whether present or imprinted in the soul. Thoughts (νοήματα) of any degree of complexity are possible only thanks to the presence of images, because their objects (νοητά) are contained in those images which are their 'vehicles', and from which they can be abstracted (geometrical and mathematical items) or 'extracted' in some other way by our *nous*. Aristotle is adamant in clarifying that the φαντάσματα are neither thoughts (νοήματα) nor thought-contents (νοητά). Thought does not think images, or *through* images; thought thinks thoughts about intelligibles.

This has important consequences for Aristotle's position on the relation between memory, thought and intelligible objects. As we have seen (T4 above), a necessary condition for something to be a possible object of memory is that we can form an image of it. The key point is not that νοητά are not φαντάσματα;[57] not even sensible objects like colours, sounds, trees

---

[54] For a defence of the MSS reading τἆλλα, emended into ταῦτα by Torstrik and Ross on the basis of Themistius' commentary, cf. Hicks 1907: 547–8 and Polansky 2007: 499.

[55] In some cases, they can persist briefly as after-images when the external object of perception is no longer present (cf. *Insom.* 460b2–3).

[56] The idea that φαντάσματα are like αἰσθήματα, but 'without matter', might appear problematic, since the sense organs already receive the form of the sensible object 'without matter' (cf. *An.* III 2, 425b23–4). According to Wedin (1988: 121–2), Aristotle's point is that φαντάσματα are already at a higher degree of abstraction than αἰσθήματα.

[57] *Pace* Castagnoli 2006b.

and birds are, but we can remember them, because we can form images of them. The problem is that there cannot be φαντάσματα of νοητά, in such a way that the νοητά are remembered through the proxy of their images in the same way in which the αἰσθητά are remembered. T5 states that φαντάσματα are 'impoverished copies' *of percepts* (αἰσθήματα), without hinting at any possible alternative non-sensible origin.[58] In T3 the affection or change in the soul was described as an imprint *of the percept* (τύπον τινὰ τοῦ αἰσθήματος) and as a product *of perception* (τοιοῦτον τὸ γιγνόμενον διὰ τῆς αἰσθήσεως). The same point is confirmed by Aristotle's later observation at 451a3–4 that 'such changes in our soul derive from a previous *perception*' (ἐγγινομένων ἡμῖν ἐν τῇ ψυχῇ τοιούτων κινήσεων ἀπὸ τοῦ αἰσθέσθαι πρότερον).[59]

That Aristotle was not confused when he adopted views that entailed the impossibility of having memory of intelligibles, but *consciously* constructed his theory this way is confirmed by a key passage which I introduced only partially above on p. 243:

> **T6** καί ἐστι μνημονευτὰ καθ' αὑτὰ μὲν ὧν ἐστι φαντασία, κατὰ συμβεβηκὸς δὲ ὅσα μὴ ἄνευ φαντασίας. (*Mem.* 1, 450a23–5)
>
> And only things of which there is imagination are objects of memory in their own right, whereas those things that are not without imagination are objects of memory by accident.

As we have seen, the things which 'are not without imagination' are intelligible objects (τὰ νοητά). Unlike sensible objects, of which we can form images, these will be objects of memory *only by accident* (κατὰ συμβεβηκός).[60] But what does Aristotle mean by this qualification? A passage about accidental sensibles from *On the Soul* will come to our aid:

> **T7** κατὰ συμβεβηκὸς δὲ λέγεται αἰσθητόν, οἷον εἰ τὸ λευκὸν εἴη Διάρους υἱός· κατὰ συμβεβηκὸς γὰρ τούτου αἰσθάνεται, ὅτι τῷ λευκῷ

---

[58] In the wax block model, on the contrary, Plato had allowed for the possibility of imprints of objects of thought: Δῶρον τοίνυν αὐτὸ φῶμεν εἶναι τῆς τῶν Μουσῶν μητρὸς Μνημοσύνης, καὶ εἰς τοῦτο ὅτι ἂν βουληθῶμεν μνημονεῦσαι ὧν ἂν ἴδωμεν ἢ ἀκούσωμεν ἢ αὐτοὶ ἐννοήσωμεν, ὑπέχοντας αὐτὸ ταῖς αἰσθήσεσι καὶ ἐννοίαις, ἀποτυποῦσθαι, ὥσπερ δακτυλίων σημεῖα ἐνσημαινομένους (*Tht.* 191d3–7).

[59] A different and difficult question is whether Aristotle's theory allows for the possibility of φαντάσματα of νοήματα, and thus for the possibility of remembering our *thinking acts or processes* (the possibility of remembering having thought something is explicitly admitted by Aristotle at *Mem.* 1, 449b18–21: see T1 above). As we have seen, not even νοήματα are φαντάσματα; but since our thoughts must always be accompanied by certain successions and combinations of images, we might conjecture that memory could preserve these, that is φαντάσματα of φαντάσματα. For discussion of a similar problem in Plotinus, see Chiaradonna's chapter in this volume.

[60] For an attempt to downplay the point, cf. Sorabji 1972: 71–2.

συμβέβηκε τοῦτο, οὗ αἰσθάνεται· διὸ καὶ οὐδὲν πάσχει ᾗ τοιοῦτον ὑπὸ
τοῦ αἰσθητοῦ. (*An.* II 6, 418a20–4)

We speak of an accidental object of sense, for example, if the white object
is the son of Diares; for this [*sc.* the son of Diares] is perceived accidentally,
because what is perceived is an attribute of the white object; hence we are
not at all acted upon by the <accidental> sensible as such.

Diares' son is not an object of perception in his own right: his particular
sensible qualities, e.g. the colour of his skin, the shape of his face and
body, or the sound of his voice, are objects of our senses in their own
right (proper qualities such as colours and sounds are perceived by a single
sense, common qualities such as shapes by more than one sense). We do
say that we perceive (see, hear, touch) Diares' son, but only because we
perceive some sensible quality, e.g. whiteness, of which he happens[61] to be
the bearer.[62] Analogously, the intelligible triangle, as such, is not an object
of memory: it is only this or that particular triangular shape or object
that can be remembered in its own right (when the retained φάντασμα
is considered as a likeness of something experienced in the past). It is not
sight alone, or primarily, that tells us that the white thing approaching
is Diares' son (imagination and thought seem to be fundamental to the
process). Similarly, it is not memory alone, or primarily, that allows us
to think of the intelligible triangle; it is the intellect that grasps the universal essence of a triangle in the images of triangular objects stored in
our memory.[63] Sight presents us with something white, which happens
to be Diares' son; memory preserves in us an image, which happens to
be the image of something triangular, and thus 'contains' the intelligible
form of triangle. Without perceiving his sensible qualities (colour, shape,
sound of voice) we would not come to know, and subsequently recognise,
Diares' son (even if, of course, for Aristotle a person is not a bundle of
sensible qualities); in the same way, without perceiving triangular objects
and retaining their images in our souls we could not grasp the essence of a

---

[61] As Hicks (1907: 363) remarks, 'though it is more usual to call the quality whiteness a συμβεβηκός of
the substance, we have a perfect right to call the thing or substance a συμβεβηκός of the quality, and
this A[ristotle] occasionally does'.

[62] For the same point, cf. *An.* III 1, 425a24–7: εἰ δὲ μή, οὐδαμῶς ἂν ἀλλ' ἢ κατὰ συμβεβηκὸς
ᾐσθανόμεθα οἷον τὸν Κλέωνος υἱὸν οὐχ ὅτι Κλέωνος υἱός, ἀλλ' ὅτι λευκός, τούτῳ δὲ συμβέβηκεν
υἱῷ Κλέωνος εἶναι. On accidental perception, cf. Cashdollar 1973; Polansky 2007: 259–61; Scheiter
2012; Marmodoro 2014.

[63] As Rachel Parsons suggested to me, and in Parsons 2016, the faculty of *phantasia* could be taken to
be more directly relevant to (and sufficient for) our thinking, since normally we do not need to use
the images in us as memories (i.e. with an awareness of their temporal dimension) in our acts of
thinking. For a similar issue in the case of *empeiria*, see note 66 below.

triangle (even if, of course, for Aristotle the universal triangle is not a set of triangular objects). But this does not mean that Diares' son is, in his own right and essentially, an object of perception, or that the universal triangle is, in its own right and essentially, an object of memory.[64]

Dorothea Frede (1992: 293) observed that, for Aristotle, 'we only remember when and how we first learned Pythagoras' theorem, but not the theorem itself'; the point is slightly overstated, but the intuition is correct. On the basis of Aristotle's theory of memory, we can remember, *in their own right*, past episodes in which we have exercised our thought on Pythagoras' theorem (not necessarily the first such episode); or the diagrams drawn on those occasions. Or, although Aristotle does not make the point, we must be able to remember, 'by heart', the wording of Pythagoras' theorem which we learnt at school (in a certain language): but remembering a sequence of signs seen on paper or of sounds heard is not the same as remembering Pythagoras' theorem, because those signs and sounds are not the theorem.[65]

One could object, with Sorabji, that Aristotle's restriction is unacceptable, since it clashes with our intuitions concerning the scope of memory: certainly I do remember what a triangle is, or that 2 + 2 = 4, or Pythagoras' theorem![66] Aristotle would have replied that when you say that you remember these things, what you actually mean is that you *know* what a triangle is (you grasp its essence), you *know* that 2 + 2 = 4 (you are able to

---

[64] Just in the same way as universals are not, in their own right, objects of perception, although we can say that we perceive universals accidentally (cf. e.g. *Metaph.* XIII, 10, 1087a19–20: by seeing a particular colour, e.g. white, we are seeing accidentally the universal colour).

[65] It is exactly for this reason that it makes sense to say that someone 'remembers' the theorem, but he does not *really* know it, if he is able to repeat the words of the theorem by heart, but without understanding the theorem itself, i.e. without fully grasping its meaning and how it works. For a similar idea cf. *EN* VII 3, 1147a17–24: 'It is obvious, then, that we should say that incontinent people have knowledge in a similar way to these people. The fact that they use words that have their origin in knowledge proves nothing. For people under the influence of these feelings even recite proofs and verses of Empedocles, and those who have just begun to learn can string words together, but do not yet know; it must grow into them, and this takes time. So we must suppose that incontinent people speak just like actors.'

[66] Annas (1992: 301) too suggests that there is a very serious objection to the view that memory is only of the past, exactly because 'if this is so Aristotle can give no account of memory of timeless truths, such as that 2 + 2 = 4, or that the interior angles of a triangle add up to two right angles'. She assumes that we *must* be able to say that there is, properly speaking, memory of intelligible objects, finding 'outrageous' the idea that we can remember objects of thoughts only accidentally (1992: 305–6), in so far as we can represent them to ourselves through images. Therefore, she identifies that kind of non-personal memory in Aristotle's ἀνάμνησις ('recollection'), but to do so she has to adopt a strained reading of the difference between μνήμη and ἀνάμνησις in the *De Memoria*. I cannot examine Aristotle' account of ἀνάμνησις here. Although recollection is a more 'intellectual' process than memory, which requires deliberation and thought (animals do not possess the faculty of ἀνάμνησις), its double link with (1) mental images (*Mem.* 2 453a15–16), and thus primarily with perception, and with (2) the awareness of the temporal gap (*Mem.* 2 453a10–14) suggest that

make this and similar calculations, because you have learnt mathematics), and you *know* Pythagoras' theorem (you are able to provide a demonstration of it, which involves the capacity for thinking of a set of propositions about intelligibles and understanding their logical interconnections).[67] These intelligible objects are the domain of your faculty of thought (cf. the last sentence of T1 above); but memory, which does not require that faculty (some animals have it) is, essentially and properly speaking, memory of what you have experienced in the past through your senses. We can still say that we remember what a triangle is, or that 2 + 2 = 4, or Pythagoras' theorem, just as we can say that we see Diares' son approaching: Aristotle had no intention to overthrow *endoxa*, and to reform ordinary parlance.[68] What he aimed to clarify is a key point about human psychology: what faculties of the soul are directly and primarily involved in the different cognitive processes, and what their objects are and their division of labour.[69]

Further confirmation of this interpretation might come, I suggest, from Aristotle's remark in the second chapter of the *De Memoria* that 'nothing prevents from also remembering, accidentally, some of the things we know'

Aristotelian recollection, like memory, has, properly speaking, a narrow domain. For a different view on the scope of ἀνάμνησις, see Parsons 2016. Sassi notices (2007: 45–6) that Aristotle has room for non-personal memory in his theory, not in ἀνάμνησις, however, but in the situation in which one considers a φάντασμα by itself, and not as a likeness of something experienced in the past. This is right, but it is important to stress that this should not be described as 'memory' (μνήμη) from Aristotle's perspective in the *De Memoria*. Bloch (2007: 89) suggests that the retrieval and use of φαντάσματα without awareness that they are 'from the past' was consistently labelled by Aristotle in the *De Memoria* through the verb μεμνῆσθαι, as opposed to the verb μνημονεύειν: 'both μνημονεύειν and μεμνῆσθαι would reasonably be called forms of "remembering" in modern terminology (and, admittedly, in ordinary Greek parlance)'. It is an interesting question, which I cannot discuss here, whether the retention of φαντάσματα is sufficient for ἐμπειρία, 'experience' (cf. e.g. Sassi 2007: 43–4; Scheiter 2012: 262), or whether actually the temporal dimension associated with μνήμη in A-PCVM is fundamental for the formation of an 'experience' (cf. e.g. King 2009: 88–90). If the first option were the case, Aristotle would not be consistent with his own *De Memoria* theory of μνήμη when he claims, elsewhere, that ἐμπειρία derives from μνήμη or μνῆμαι (*Metaph.* I 1, *APo.* II 19, 100a3–9: Ἐκ μὲν οὖν αἰσθήσεως γίνεται μνήμη, ὥσπερ λέγομεν, ἐκ δὲ μνήμης πολλάκις τοῦ αὐτοῦ γινομένης ἐμπειρία· αἱ γὰρ πολλαὶ μνῆμαι τῷ ἀριθμῷ ἐμπειρία μία ἐστίν).

⁶⁷ King (2009: 39) correctly emphasises Aristotle's 'exclusion of universals from memory'; 'nothing prevents one from remembering concepts, in Aristotle's view, but one only remembers them accidentally. For as such they are not temporally marked. One might instead remember (the circumstances surrounding) learning a concept, or perceiving an instance falling under a concept. Possession of a concept is not, as we have seen, a matter of remembering it; but of having learnt it.' I fully agree with these remarks, with the exception of the clause 'for as such they are not temporally marked'; as I have explained, the ontological and epistemological status of the intelligibles, and not the fact that they are not 'past', is the main reason why there cannot be memory of them in the proper sense.

⁶⁸ There is one case in the *De Memoria* in which Aristotle speaks of 'memory of the objects of thoughts' (*Mem.* 1, 450a12–13) without introducing the qualification 'accidentally'.

⁶⁹ Cf. also 450a14–15: ὥστε τοῦ νοῦ μὲν κατὰ συμβεβηκὸς ἂν εἴη, καθ' αὐτὸ δὲ τοῦ πρώτου αἰσθητικοῦ.

(*Mem.* 2, 451a28–9: οὐθὲν δὲ κωλύει κατὰ συμβεβηκὸς καὶ μνημονεύειν ἔνια ὧν ἐπιστάμεθα). If it is *also* possible to remember, if only by accident, *some* of the things we know, then there must be *some* other things that we know but do *not* remember, not even accidentally.[70] This is coherent with the framework of a theory of memory according to which not everything that is in our soul, or mind, as the result of previous experience, thought or learning is correctly described as a memory.[71] To have learnt a science like geometry, for example, is not to have stored certain memories in our soul (although the former requires the latter); it is rather to have acquired a certain intellectual *capacity* for performing certain intellectual operations on images: 'science is a disposition to demonstration' (*NE* vi 3, 1139b31–2).

3 Conclusion

In T1 Aristotle claims that people are *often* mistaken about the objects of memory, and immediately clarifies that memory is of the past. Sorabji (1972: 65) remarks that this comment does not specifically focus on memory, but expresses the more general point that 'mistakes about the objects of an activity often lead to mistakes about the activity itself'.[72] This suggestion is unwarranted by Aristotle's Greek wording, and unduly downplays the historical significance, and the philosophical distinctiveness, of Aristotle's proposal that memory is only of the past. As we have seen, the definition of the domain and status of the objects of memory is very far from being clear,[73] and Aristotle's nuanced reflection in the *De Memoria* has the merit of helping us to appreciate that.

---

[70] Sorabji suggests that remembering something we know 'will involve simply thinking of the proposition itself, without deriving it from reasons' (1972: 90). But, as I have argued above, the propositions *themselves* which are part of a body of knowledge are not possible objects of imagination and memory, even if considered in isolation, unless by 'propositions' we intend linguistic tokens (signs and sounds) and not the intelligibles which these signify.

[71] *Contra* Senor 2009: 'that most of our knowledge is in memory at any particular time is a given'; 'virtually all of what we know (or are justified in believing) at any given time resides in memory'.

[72] This is not to deny the different point that the reason why first we must consider τὰ μνημονευτά is that *in general* the correct way to proceed in the analysis of an activity is first to identify what its objects are (cf. *An.* 415a20–2, 418a7–8). According to Annas (1992: 301), the common mistake to which Aristotle is referring is that people do not recognise that memory (i.e. personal memory) is of the past, whereas recollection (non-personal memory) is not. Apart from other reservations concerning Annas' distinction (see n. 66 above), however, it should be noticed that there is no discussion or even mention of ἀνάμνησις in T1.

[73] A source of error might be the confusion, discussed later in the *De Memoria*, between the past objects of memory and their present proxies in our souls, i.e. memory images (see pp. 244–5 above; cf. also, possibly, Pl. *Tht.* 166b).

Hellenistic Configurations of Memory

PART III

Hellenistic Configurations of Memory

Hellenistic Cultural Memory: Helen and Menelaus Between Heroic Fiction, Ritual Practice and Poetic Praise of the Royal Power (Theocritus 18)

Claude Calame*

Every society holds a store of texts, images, and rituals which allow it, through repeated use, to normalize and convey an image of itself, an image based in particular on a shared knowledge of the past. Embedded in collective memory, this knowledge is the foundation upon which a group develops its sense of unity and distinctiveness. Such is the approximate definition of the concept of 'cultural memory' that the Egyptologist Jan Assmann introduced and developed in several comparative studies of the historiographic and religious traditions of ancient societies.[1] Assmann begins by borrowing Maurice Halbwachs' concept of collective memory. He notes that beyond its biological and neuronal foundation, which is unique to each individual, memory has both a social and a cultural dimension; this does not mean that culture has its own memory, but rather that the inner world of the individual is dependent on the emotional and social frameworks (*Rahmenbedingungen*) of memory in general.

Contrary to the implications of Halbwachs' distinction between lived memory and tradition, social memory is understood by Assmann to be anchored in tradition; as such, it is dependent on a combination of vertical processes of communication (between generations) and horizontal processes (synchronic and interactive). But the dependence of collective memory on tradition means that we must ask how a cultural memory may be created and preserved, a question that we shall examine with reference in particular to the Greek culture of the Hellenistic period. For his part, Assmann identifies two central factors: ritual practices and textual manifestations. In this context, he takes over Claude Lévi-Strauss' famous distinction between 'cold' and 'hot' societies, the former referring to societies that do not know writing and whose

---

* Translation by Amanda Iacobelli, reviewed by the editors.
[1] Cf. Assmann 1992: 19–25.

tradition is entirely oral, the latter corresponding to societies in which the
spoken word is systematically transcribed and graphically communicated.
Implicitly, Assmann inserts the concept of cultural memory into the 'Great
Divide', or 'Great Dichotomy', that was condemned yet swiftly replicated by
Jack Goody.[2]

Preliterate or 'cold' societies with no written history are thus seen as having
a 'connective' form of memory (what Assmann calls *Bindungsgedächtnis*):
collective memory *par excellence*, this memory, lasting for a period of 80 to
100 years, is based on the iteration of a ritual whose purpose is to recreate
the immutability of the cosmos. In contrast, 'hot' societies with access to a
system of graphic transcription are supposed to internalize (*verinnerlichen*)
history. Invigorated by this process, these societies have a historical and
truly cultural 'formative' memory (*Bildungsgedächtnis*), which could last
for up to 3,000 years. This dichotomy between *Bindungsgedächtnis* and
Bildungsgedächtnis is both structural and evolutionary, and brings to
mind the romantic German distinction between *Zivilisation* and *Kultur*.
In terms of religion, it evokes the corresponding opposition between
Stammeskulturen, or tribal cultures, on the one hand, and the great
civilizations founded on a religion of the book (and of a normative text),
on the other. Within this dichotomous perspective, writing is conceived
as a liberating tool, ensuring 'the free life of the spirit': *das freie Leben des
Geistes*, placed under the explicit authority of Hegel ...[3]

Does the transition from an oral culture based on the tradition of the
Homeric poems to the literate culture of the Hellenistic period reflect a shift
from connective to historical formative memory? In what follows, I would
like to challenge two persistent misconceptions on the subject of historical
collective memory in ancient Greece. First, the use of writing in composition,
communication, and tradition does not imply any loss of pragmatic dimension, nor a transition to literature in the modern sense of the term.[4] Second,
regardless of the presence or absence of writing, the *arkhaîa* corresponding to
the heroic past and the ancient history of a community (those stories which
we refer to as 'myths', to associate them with traditional societies) are an integral part of that community's historical collective memory:[5] the distinction

---

[2] Goody 1977: 146–62.
[3] Assmann 2000: 32–4 and 42–4.
[4] On the subject of auxiliary uses of writing in Greek poetry of the classical period, see Ford 2003, esp.
in reference to Rosalind Thomas' two standard works on orality and literacy in Ancient Greece, and
Athens in particular.
[5] On the native designations of the heroic past which for us belongs to the domain of the 'myth', see
Calame 2015: 24–30.

between *Bindungs-* and *Bildungsgedächtnis* is not a pertinent one. This is what I would like to exemplify through the analysis of Theocritus' *Idyll* 18, a poem composed in Homeric diction at a time when the Alexandrian culture of poetic writing was developing. To follow the narrative movement of the Panhellenic 'mythic' action staged in *Idyll* 18 means to highlight the role which the poetic form plays in giving a new meaning, as well as a new function in the changed political and religious context of Hellenistic Greece, to an episode of the heroic past inscribed in the Greek collective and cultural memory.

1 Helen and Menelaus: a Paradigmatic Couple

If heroic episodes were ever etched into the collective and cultural memory of the Greeks, the union of Helen and Menelaus was certainly one of them. In the fourth book of the *Odyssey*, Menelaus reigns absolute over Sparta. When Telemachus and his companion Pisistratus enter his court, they find 'glorious Menelaus' sitting at a banquet enhanced by the song of an *aoidos*: he celebrates the wedding of his daughter Hermione, the only child the gods bestowed upon his wife Helen. There he receives the travellers. Yet before he is even able to inquire after their identity, Helen appears out of the bridal chamber, similar to Artemis. Helen, the daughter of Zeus, shall lace the guests' wine with drugs to alleviate their suffering. In a scene whose interpretation is controversial, Helen mentions Zeus's discretionary power before narrating, in a detailed *mûthos*, Odysseus' dangerous mission to Troy. The support she secretly gave to the Greek hero allows Helen to exonerate herself and transfer onto Aphrodite the burden of blame for the blindness that led her to abandon her country, her daughter, her bridal room and her irreproachable husband. Having made of Helen and Menelaus the ideal couple, the scene ends in this very spirit, with the couple retiring from the banquet to share their marital bed.[6] In this Odyssean version of the Trojan War, Menelaus, as Helen's husband and, by extension, Zeus's

---

[6] Homer, *Odyssey* 4.219–305; cf. Bettini and Brillante 2002: 98–102, and my own discussion (2009b) of Helen's complex character and the different facets it takes on depending on the narrative context in which she appears; see in particular Sappho fr. 16 Voigt on the subject of Aphrodite's intervention in bringing about Helen's amorous misguidance (with my commentary of this poem in 2005: 107–30 and the study by Thévenaz 2015). For a discussion of the dialectics of forgetting and remembering in this poem, see also Capra's chapter (above, pp. 189–92), as well as L. G. Canevaro's chapter (above, pp. 54–6, 66–7) on Helen's weaving in the *Iliad*.

son-in-law, will enjoy in the Elysian fields a destiny known only to the blessed.[7] Thus was Sparta's ruler immortalized.

From the *Odyssey* to Euripides, by way of Sappho, Alcaeus or Stesichorus, very few among the great poets did not dedicate one of their works to this royal couple, or to the heroic (in our terms, mythical) age of the Trojan War. The same goes for the orators, such as Gorgias and Isocrates, the latter falling squarely within the fourth century BC. At the beginning of the Hellenistic period, Theocritus could not have missed the call. In *Idyll* 18, the Alexandrian poet re-elaborates a version of the heroic story found in the *Odyssey*, to make it conform to the ritual hymenaios song.[8] The hymenaios, or rather epithalamium, if we take the latter term in its etymological sense, is a wedding song performed by a choral group composed of close relations of the bride, probably including both sexes, in front of the *thálamos*; on the nuptial threshold, this melic song ritually initiated the couple's wedding night.[9] Just as the hymenaios is traditionally centred around the young bride or *númphe*, so is Theocritus' *Epithalamium* focused on Helen, both in terms of the actual qualities attached to each of the spouses and from the point of view of the laudatory procedures that characterize the hymenaios genre.

Thus, Helen and Menelaus are endowed by the Alexandrian poet, in a traditional manner and often through the reworking of Homeric expressions, with the qualities attributed to exemplary newlyweds. Both of royal lineage, Helen as the daughter of Tyndareus and Menelaus as the son of Atreus, the young couple's union, in the aftermath of the traditional competitive courtship of suitors, generates a matrilocal alliance between Sparta and Argos.[10] But Helen and Menelaus, even though mortal, belong to the world of heroes: Helen is also the daughter of Zeus, benefiting from

---

[7] According to Proteus' prediction: Homer, *Odyssey* 4.561–9. The heroic couple's conjugal love was undoubtedly alluded to in Stesichorus' *Helen*: cf. fr. 187 *PMGF* = fr. 88 Davies-Finglass; see the commentary by Davies and Finglass 2014: 326–9.

[8] According to the *argumentum* of the *scholia* to *Idyll* 18 (p. 331 Wendel), Theocritus drew part of his inspiration from the first book of the (citharodic) poem dedicated to Helen: Stesichorus fr. 189 *PMGF* = fr. 84 Davies-Finglass (see also fr. 187 *PMGF* = fr. 88 Davies-Finglass).

[9] In the Alexandrian period, the *hymenaioi* composed by Sappho were assembled into a book titled *Epithalamia*: evidence for the expanded meaning of a Hellenistic term that is ultimately used in a generic sense to describe any form (poetic or rhetorical) of hymenaios; see Muth 1954: 23–37 and 44–5, as well as Contiades-Tsitsoni 1990: 30–2. Like the paean, the *hymenaios* can be recognized by its invocatory refrain; it is one of the rare genres of sung and ritual melic poetry that immediately enjoyed a precise designation and practical definition: cf. Calame 1998/2008: 96–100.

[10] In Hesiod's *Catalogue of Women*, it is the number of suitors and the importance of the gifts offered that confers upon Helen her exceptional status (cf. Hesiod frr. 198–204 Merkelbach-West, with commentary by Cingano 2005: 124–33); the scene is also the focus of Stesichorus' *Helen* (fr. 190 *PMGF*).

the same dual paternity claimed by famous heroic figures such as Heracles and Theseus. Henceforth the poem focuses on the young and divine bride, portraying her in a fully realized beauty which signifies fecundity: in the whole Greek poetic tradition, Eros and Aphrodite have a fundamental role in stimulating by means of erotic desire the reproductive fertility of the earth, animals, and humans.[11]

But let us follow the narrative and enunciative flow of the poem, which belongs to a ritual style of poetry, in which first the groom must be addressed, and then the young bride evoked.

1.1 An Outstanding Husband's Happiness

Let us then begin with the young husband, Menelaus. Twice addressed as *gámbros* (verses 9 and 16), the young son of Atreus is portrayed through a lens that is angled toward his role as 'husband of'. From the outset, through the use of the term *gámbros*, which implies the double meaning of 'son-in-law' and 'husband', his status is defined in relation to that of Helen, Zeus's daughter; the term recurs through the various iterations of the hymenaios that ritually mark the phases of the marriage ceremony. In accordance with the customary rules of this ritual poetic genre, the choral group's song makes the young husband the object of the kind of derisive allusions that the occasion of a first wedding night engenders: a fiancé blamed for his passivity as he falls victim to sleep or drunkenness, his wife neglected, with no option but to continue playing games with her friends, her mother at her side. In other words, accusations directed at a groom whose actions condemn his young bride to remain in her adolescent status (*paísdein*, verse 14).[12]

Yet, such lewd references exist only to draw attention to the bride and to introduce a second address to the young husband who, in the wake of this transition from poetic blame to poetic praise, is now cast as a fortunate man. Even the turn of phrase is traditional. One of the rare extant fragments of Sappho's *Epithalamia* opens with it: 'Happy husband, your marriage has taken place as you had wished it, you possess the young girl that you desired ...'; the poem moves on to praise the girl's beauty, the softness of her gaze, the intense eroticism emanating from her face, the

---

[11] Cf. Calame 2002: 140–5, on Aeschylus fr. 44 Radt.

[12] By describing Helen and her companions as *paídes* (verse 14), the poem clarifies, through etymological reference, that the verb *paízein* refers to adolescent games: ball games, dance etc.; on the 'pedagogic' value of these practices, cf. Calame 2001: 222–45.

exceptional honors bestowed upon her by Aphrodite.[13] Theocritus' poem
18 follows the same progression; it is because of the very qualities of his
young wife that Menelaus is now described as fortunate, for it is on their
account that he is distinguished among other eminent heroes. Indeed, as
daughter of Zeus, Helen is of incomparable value among Achaean women,
and cannot but provide her husband with a child equal to the mother.[14]
In the classical Greek understanding of legitimate matrimony, the erotic
charms of feminine beauty lead to a wholly fulfilled maternity.

1.2   A Young Bride's Diaphanous Beauty

The two traditional references to the husband as *gámbros* (verses 9 and
16) lead thus to the subject of his wife: first in relation to her former adolescent status, then to her present qualities as a young wife (through the
use of verbal deixis: *teà nuòs hade*, 'this new bride of yours', verse 15), and
finally as a potential mother. It is now the responsibility of the choral 'we'
to accomplish the transition from Menelaus to Helen.

A sequence of dense metaphors and comparisons, organized in a double
ring-composition, is used to describe the qualities that distinguish Helen
from all the young girls in her entourage. The radiant light that emanates
from 'golden Helen' is compared to the glow that dawn has in the spring.
The use of the verb *diaphaínein* at the beginning of the second colon
(an enoplion) in each of the two hexameters that respectively introduce
and close the comparison serves to focus the attention on the splendor
of this beautiful Spartan woman's face. These three verses implicitly conjure up two female characters whose praises are sung in Alcman's Mariette
Partheneion: Agido and Hagesichora – the one appearing (*phaínen*) like
the sunrise in all her splendor, the other showing a silver-hued face whose
luminosity the choreutai singing the poem renounce to describe, so
imposing is the choregos' presence. And if wheat is the adornment of a
field, as a cypress is of a garden, and a Thessalian horse of a chariot, then
'rosy-cheeked Helen is the jewel (*kósmos*) of Lacedaemonia' (verse 31). In
Alcman's poem, sung as part of a female initiation ritual, Hagesichora is,
in Homeric fashion, not only compared to a sublime racehorse amid a

---

[13] Sappho fr. 112 Voigt; cf. also fr. 111 Voigt. The *topoi* of the *hymenaios* genre, from the ironic criticism of the groom to the praise of the bride's attractions, are listed by Muth 1954 and discussed by
Contiades-Tsitsoni, 1990: 68–109.
[14] On this other *topos* of the Greek matrimonial relationship, cf. Hesiod, *Works* 182. Among the fragmentary verses of Sappho's *Epithalamia*, fr. 113 Voigt probably also insisted on the incomparable
character of the young bride; see also Homer, *Odyssey* 21.106–7, on Penelope.

grazing herd, but also becomes, in her athletic beauty, a Lydian steed.[15] In fact, focused as it is on the persona of a young girl in her role as choregos or chorus member, Theocritus' *Idyll* 18 resonates with echoes of Alcman's ritual poems, mirroring even the Dorian poetic dialect which the poem includes and thematizes, in contrast to its overall Homeric diction: the aetiological conclusion of the poem has Helen's tree speak in 'Dorian' (*doristi*, verse 48)![16] Incidentally, Helen's choral activity was engraved in Athens' cultural memory about Sparta: both Aristophanes and Euripides allude to her in a choral song which, in comedy as in tragedy, replicates the Lacedaemonian style of ritual melic song.[17]

In addition to the young girl's beauty, Theocritus extends his praise to include her skill in the duties expected of an adult woman: spinning wool, weaving fine textured fabrics, singing to the rhythm of the lyre. We are reminded here of the Iliadic scene where Helen, as Paris' wife, weaves a double cloak on her loom; on it she portrays the hardships endured by Achaeans and Trojans alike under the grip of Ares.[18] The extreme ambivalence of Theocritus' Helen emerges again in the lines which follow her praise by her companions. 'Of the same age', these young girls (*kórai*, verse 24) are assembled in a group reminiscent of the *agéla* of young Laconian girls mentioned in a very fragmentary verse of Pindar; this 'herd' exhibits the feature of *communitas* which the anthropologist Victor W. Turner attributes to ritual and initiation groups of adolescent girls or boys.[19] On the one hand, Helen does indeed resort to the charms of the Muses' arts in order to sing, like no other, of Artemis and Athena, the virgin goddesses par excellence; on the other, the gaze of the Spartan heroine, more than any other, carries with it the imperative erotic desire that is *hímeros*.[20]

[15] Alcman fr. 1.39–43 and 55–6 *PMGF* (cf. Homer, *Iliad* 2, 489–95), with the commentary I gave on these verses in 1983: 327 and 331. On these striking cross-references, see also Hunter 1996: 152–3.

[16] This dialectal echo is identified and discussed by Hunter 1996: 153–5, who notes that the Laconian features of the Alexandrian edition of Alcman's poems are not found in Theocritus' poem.

[17] Aristophanes, *Lysistrata* 1248–50 and 1296–315; for an analysis of a melic intervention imitating Spartan choral songs, cf. Calame 2004: 169–72. In the tragedy's last stasimon, the chorus of Euripides' *Helen* (1465–75) also evokes Helen's choral activity in the context of cults dedicated to the city gods: cf. Calame 2001: 191–9.

[18] Homer, *Iliad* 3, 125–8, with the commentary by Rousseau 2003: 27–43. On the weaving theme in Homer, and its connection to memory, see L. G. Canevaro's chapter in this volume.

[19] Pindar fr. 112 Maehler; on the characteristics of the age group and initiation group represented in the Greek choral group in Sparta in particular, see Calame 2001: 30–4 and 214–9, as well as 2009a: 281–4 (with bibliography).

[20] The eroticized charm of (melic) poetry and the gaze as conveyor of eros are constant features in the Greek poetics of love; cf. Calame 2002: 30–52, and 2016.

It is for this reason that, in the introduction to the ritual part of the poem, the choral singers staged by Theocritus can address Helen both as a 'beautiful and charming young girl' (*kóra*, once again, in verse 38) and as the 'mistress of the house' (*oikétis*). And for this reason again, at the end of an aetiological passage to which we shall return, the young woman is invited to rejoice alongside her young husband: he as *gambrós*, and she as *númphe* (verse 49), in a transitory but well-defined matrimonial status, which replicates from a sexual standpoint the ambivalence of the heroine's praise. The young bride is indeed a *númphe* before the birth of her first child, in a position of transition between her status of adolescent, single, and 'virgin', and that of an adult woman, wife, and mother.[21] Indeed, in the concluding section of the matrimonial praise maternity is most important. It is protected not only by Leto Kourotrophos, the goddess of beautiful offspring, but also by Cypris, who promotes equal love in reciprocity (*íson érasthai allálon*, verses 51–2), as well as Zeus, son of Kronos, who ensures the renewal of a perpetually aristocratic progeny through enduring prosperity.[22] From now on, the hero and the heroine are referred to by the plural *you*, and associated in equal measure with the same poetic blessings.

2   Enunciative Movements and Narrative Procedures

Thus are the married couple's qualities praised and recorded in Theocritus' poetic epithalamium. Yet, the enunciative movement that carries a seemingly choral praise of the two Homeric heroes holds two significant surprises in store if one compares its flow to the traditional form of a ritual hymenaios. On first read, the enunciative structure of the poem seems linear: two addresses to the groom for the sake of a short ironic accolade and in order to subordinate his happiness to his fiancée's qualities, centred on maternity (verses 9–21); then, extensive praise of the bride in a series of comparisons leading to a direct address that brings attention to her intermediary status, between maiden and mistress of the house (verses 22–38); next, a double address, directed in equal terms to the *númphe* and the *gambrós*, to wish them an everlasting line of descendants, placed under the aegis of Leto, Aphrodite, and Zeus (verses 49–53); and, finally, wishes for a night of reciprocal love and erotic desire (*philótata pnéontes kaì póthon*, verses 54–5), and the announcement of the forthcoming waking song

[21] On this singular status, see also references provided in Calame, 2002: 140–5.
[22] In connection with the eugenic tendencies of the Spartan laws established by the legendary Lycurgus, the importance of the *euteknía* mentioned in verse 51 is well emphasized by Hunter 1996: 161–3.

(verses 56–7) just before the epithalamium ends with the nuptial song's traditional refrain (verse 58). Attested in particular in Sappho's *Epithalamia*, the double invocation of the refrain ('Hymen, o Hymenaios') associates the figure of Hymen to that of Hymenaeus; through the rhythmic call peculiar to cultic song, the appeal actuates the presence of this hero of matrimony at the moment of the poem's performance.[23] Shouldn't we then think of 'connective' memory?

2.1   *The Choral* We *and the Written Voice*

In an auto-referential movement frequent in the various forms of melic poetry, the choral *we* representing the 'instance d'énonciation' (*ámmes* at the beginning of verse 22) stands opposite to the singular and then plural *you* that refer to the interlocutors and addressees of the poetic song. This poetic *we*, which corresponds to the '*I*-locutor', begins by giving itself an identity: young girls of the same age, who understand themselves in terms that are similar to the concept of *communitas*. This type of egalitarian association suggests to the anthropologist the participation of a certain age class in a ritual of tribal initiation. As pointed out earlier, these adolescent girls (*kórai*, verse 24) are gathered on the occasion of athletic activities that bring to mind the race between Agido and Hagesichora in Alcman's *Partheneion*; they are assembled into a female faction reminiscent of the initiation group of the *agéla*, though its division into four sections of sixty young girls remains a mystery.[24] From a spatio-temporal perspective, the lack of any conjugated verb in these verses leaves a shadow of doubt as to whether this athletic scene temporally coincides with the performance of the hymenaios. Admittedly, the reference to the Eurotas indicates a spatial discrepancy which is later confirmed from a temporal standpoint by the use of an imperfect form (*diephaíneto*, verse 28) to describe the radiance of Helen's face amid the other young girls (who are once again referring to themselves as *we*). Nevertheless, the proximity of the spatio-temporal and enunciative parameters of the previous scene to the *hic et nunc* of the poem's musical performance is accentuated in this context by the

---

[23] In contrast to the pederastic relationships of homophilia, 'heterosexual' love between two adults in Greece is characterized by reciprocity, leading in turn to the creation of beautiful children: cf. Calame 2002: 53–8 and 131–4. On the refrain of the hymenaios, cf. Sappho fr. 111 Voigt, and Aristophanes, *Birds* 1736, Euripides, *Trojan Women* 314 and 331, and further references in Muth 1954.

[24] The numbers of 4 x 60 are discussed by Hunter 1996: 159–62, who ends up adopting the thesis of an 'antiquarian tradition', without providing a more precise explanation; cf. also note 31 below.

invocation of powerful Night; like the use of the form *we*, this invocation recalls the moment of the current musical performance.

The transition in verse 39 from the praise of Helen's beauty and excellence to a second auto-referential description is marked by the same shift from the singular *you* of the 'interlocutor' (and addressee of the poem) to the *we* of the 'speaker' (and performer of the song). In shifting from a direct address to the young wife, who is described with all the appeal of a beauty that calls forth her qualities of both maiden and mistress of the house, to a *we* accompanied by the double form of the future intentional (*herpseûmes drepseúmenai*, 'we are getting ready to go pluck ...'; verse 40), the choral singers describe the establishment of the ritual while at the same time performing it for Helen. Thus, everything happens as if the ritual acts that are described ultimately refer to the *hic et nunc* of the poem's performance; this is even more so when words are eventually attributed to the plane-tree that now belongs to Helen. By means of the letters inscribed on its trunk, and therefore through the intermediary of the voice of the reader who is worshipping it, the tree declares: 'Worship me: I am Helen's tree' (verse 48). Thanks to the conceit of written orality, an oxymoron typical of the 'well-read' Alexandrian Muse, the passerby is summoned to reiterate orally the written statement; the latter is put in the mouth of the object which carries it, following the tradition of many a dedicatory inscription.[25] In giving a written voice to the tree of Helen, and thus in turn to any faithful worshipper, the transition is made from the founding act to ritual repetition. Here, 'connective' memory coincides with writing-based memory, in one single act of ritual and cultural memory!

2.2   Poetry and Ritual Celebration

Thus, in *Idyll* 18 the subtle enunciative strategies of a poetic description that has taken on a 'performative' turn contribute to entangling the different levels that are usually distinguished in the context of an aetiological account: first, at the level of the 'récit', we find a narrative action in the past that leads to the establishment of ritual practice; then, at the level of the 'discours', the ritual act is referred to the moment of the poem's delivery. According to the parameters of the 'formal apparatus of enunciation' (Emile Benveniste),[26] we have first a narrative action as *he*, in

---

[25] For the latter, cf. the insightful analysis proposed by Meyer 2005: 20–52 and 233–5.

[26] Regarding the function of aetiological narrative in its poetic form and its related pragmatics, see especially Calame 2006a, as well as Delattre 2009.

the past and in a distant place, then the discursive action as *I/You* (plural), right here and now. We are here, in some way, at the core of the supposed distinction between *Bildungs-* and *Bindungsgedächtnis*.

In Theocritus' poem however, the narrated actions are situated in the very near past: Menelaus and other princes arriving in Sparta as would-be suitors; maidens racing, among whom Helen shone in all her glory. Furthermore, in the epithalamium, the young Spartan women sing of an intentional and near future into which they project the ritual practice which results from the narrative action; as for the *hic et nunc* of the choral performance celebrating Helen's marriage, the tree ritual established by the young singers could be interpreted as a cultic act meant to recall Helen's paradigmatic wedding, rather than as a pre-matrimonial ritual. Does this mean that, paradoxically, Theocritus' *written* poem is entirely situated on the side of connective (ritual) memory?

In terms of the ritual act itself, in this second descriptive passage the young girls' race, first mentioned within the joint praise of Menelaus and Helen (verses 22–4), is aetiologically replaced by the weaving together of lotus garlands, an act that could be construed as equally generic.[27] The presence of the plane-tree directs us to the first of the two Lacedaemonian cults dedicated to the heroized and then deified Helen. For Pausanias alerts us to the proximity between the Dromos, where young men (*néoi*) raced under the aegis of the Dioscouri and beside which one could see a 'house of Menelaus', and an area known as *Platanistas*; lined by plane-trees and surrounded by a canal that made of it an island, this shaded area accommodated the ephebic fights supposedly instituted by the legendary legislator Lycurgus. Near the *Platanistas* were several sanctuaries erected for the hero sons of Hippocoon, but also to honour both Heracles and Helen. Incidentally, Alcman's tomb was located beside this undoubtedly heroic sanctuary of Helen. His *Partheneion*, discussed earlier, tells the story of a feud between the Tyndarids, who were supported by Heracles, and the Hippocoontids on a matter of matrimonial rivalry: a poetic narrative that belongs to the common cultural memory of Sparta and is here adapted to the young girls singing the poem. There is every reason to believe that the divinity mentioned in Alcman's choral poem under the epicleseis of Orthria (goddess of the Morning) and Aotis (goddess of Dawn) corresponds to Helen; Helen as a young girl reaching maturity, like Hagesichora,

---

[27] As suggested by Gow 1950: 359, the lotus should be identified with the sweet clover used to weave the crowns mentioned by Cratinus fr. 105.7 K.-A. and by Pherecrates fr. 138.2 K.-A., with undoubtedly erotic connotations.

the choregos whose radiant beauty arouses the erotic desire of the young singers performing Alcman's ritual poem.[28]

At Therapne, moreover, in the sanctuary that stood above the Eurotas on the ruins of a Mycenaean building, Helen and her husband Menelaus enjoyed a divine cult; Helen was worshipped as an adult woman who, under the auspices of Aphrodite, could bestow upon young girls the beauty that marks admission to puberty, marriage, and maternity.[29] Thus, the dual cult enjoyed by Helen in Sparta presents the same oscillation as the seemingly ritual poem by Theocritus: on the one hand are the qualities of a young girl ready to face matrimony; on the other, a bride characterized by the charms of fulfilled feminine beauty. As for the ritual acts described in *Idyll* 18, they are not attested elsewhere other than in Pausanias' allusion, in relation to Helen's cult at Therapne, to a sanctuary in Rhodes dedicated to Helen Dendritis. Additionally, Pausanias visits another Dromos in Elis that is characterized by the presence of a plane-tree; finally, in Arcadia he points to a plane-tree worshipped near a spring named after Menelaus.[30] These are most evident examples of the existence of cultic sites of local heroic and cultural memory.

2.3   *Poetic Enunciation and Narrative Fiction*

Regardless of the reality of the ritual practices mentioned in Theocritus' poem, the poem's strategic use of enunciative temporality tends to synchronize the moment when the pre-matrimonial ritual is established with the actual wedding celebration and, consequently, with the *hic et nunc* of the epithalamium's performance. Moreover, the time of the account found in Theocritus' epithalamium, a period that corresponded in classical Greece to the age of heroes and that for us belongs to the realm of myth, practically coincides with the time of the discourse, i.e. the time of the poem's ritual enunciation. The ambiguity, both semantic and enunciative, between pre- and post-matrimonial somewhat deprives the aetiological progression in the second part of the poem of its temporal

---

[28] Pausanias 3.14.6 and 8, as well as 15.1–3: bibliographic references can be found in Calame 2001: 193–6; concerning the purpose of Alcman's 'first Partheneion' (fr. 1, 61 and 87 *PMGF* = fr. 3, 61 and 87 Calame), cf. Calame 1983: 333 and 343, as well as Luginbill 2009. These connections suggest to Hunter 1996: 158 that 'the geography of Idyll 18 is therefore the sacred geography of Old Sparta'.

[29] See again Pausanias 3.19.9–10, as well as Alcman himself, fr. 7 *PMGF* = 19 Calame; other testimonia on this Spartan cult of Helen are discussed by Calame 2001: 193, 196–8, and 200–2; see also Bettini-Brillante 2002: 43–65.

[30] Pausanias 3.19.10; 6.23.1 and 8.23.4–5. For Hunter 1996: 166, Theocritus' poem represents 'a (sophisticated) form of cultural rescue-archaeology'.

aspect. Everything happens as if the wedding of a now adult Helen and the ritual celebration of her memory as a young girl coincided in performative fashion with the song of the Spartan choreutai. The heroic past is somehow turned into ritual, in a strong interaction between 'formative' and 'connective' memory.

And yet, the poem opens on a scene located from the very beginning in an indeterminate past, through the use of the adverb ποκ᾽ (*pote*, verse 1), 'once'. It is thus in the past and from a *he/she* perspective that the eight introductory verses describe the stage setting of the hymenaios occasioned by the union of Atreus' youngest son and Helen. The young choreutai, limited to a group of twelve representing the city's elite, 'sang (ἄειδον) united in one voice (ἐς ἓν μέλος), whipping the ground with woven steps; and all around the house rang to the cadence of the hymenaios' (verses 7–8).[31]

Thus, in lieu of the invocation to the Muse that one might expect in any melic poem, and in lieu of the opening ritual address to the hero Hymenaios which the bridal song calls for, Theocritus' epithalamium begins with a prelude surprisingly delivered in the narrative mode, which offers all the enunciative features of the 'récit': a past time (use of aorist forms), an elsewhere (in Sparta), and third persons (Helen, Menelaus, and the Lacedaemonian chorus members). Instead of being the object of the various forms of verbal deixis whose function is to describe what the audience is seeing, the performance context of Theocritus' epithalamium is the object of a narrative *mise-en-scène*. From the start, the narrated action is placed under the double sign of erotic seduction (hair crowned with scented hyacinth flowers) and choral singing. This description, in its narrative mode, seems to cut off the enunciative poetic context from any spatial or temporal relationship to the moments of composition and reception of the poem. The narrative character assumed by the entire poem is confirmed by the choice of poetic style: not the rhythmic singing and dancing of a melic poem qualified as song, but rather the dactylic hexameter that refers back to the epic accounts of the time of heroes. Do we then have here a written poetry, belonging to a literature (in the etymological meaning of the word) created by learned poets rather than to cultural memory?

---

[31] In connection to the four groups of sixty young girls involved in the race (verse 24) that could represent an age class divided into four 'companies', the group of twelve choreutai is supposedly composed of Helen's close aristocratic friends; see Hunter 1996: 158–60. The numbers provided agree with the idealized portrait that was painted of traditional Spartan culture in the Hellenistic period: cf. note 24 above.

3 Celebration of Sovereigns and the Pragmatics of Poetic Memory

Does this imply that Theocritus' poem is auto-referential not in the performative sense, but inasmuch as it creates an entirely fictitious world, in a purely poetic *hic et nunc*? Is it providing an entirely poetic reconstruction of its conditions of enunciation, with no pragmatic consequence? Does it correspond to a specific type of fiction, playful pretence ('feintise ludique'), with no impact on the cultural memory that could be sustained by invoking the paradigmatic couple of Helen and Menelaus?

3.1 *Poetic Praise of the Ptolemies and the Deification of Rulers*

The erudite readers of *Idyll* 18 have rightly questioned the function of the connector *ára* which accompanies *pote* at the very beginning of the poem ('In Sparta once', Ἐν ποκ᾽ ἄρα Σπάρτᾳ, verse 1). As a narrative incipit, this initial 'once upon a time' seems to clash with the typical function of the connective word *ára* that temporally and logically refers back to what precedes. Theocritus' choice of presenting the narrative *mise-en-scène* of his introductory verses as a logical consequence of a preceding event is usually explained either as a link to a missing prelude (the invocation to the Muses), or as a reference to an external circumstance.[32] A comparison with other more referential poems by Theocritus alerts us to an indirect allusion to historical reality: the epithalamium addressed to Menelaus and Helen alludes to the ideal and deified couple embodied, at the time of the poem's composition in Alexandria, by King Ptolemy Sôter and his Macedonian wife Berenice.

Theocritus had in fact dedicated a laudatory poem to the woman who had been first the mistress and then the third wife of Ptolemy. Known to us through only one citation and one fragment, this poem's diction belongs to the epic type; its title was 'Berenice', i.e. the name of the woman who became the mother of Ptolemy II Philadelphos and Arsinoe, the sister and future wife of this same Ptolemy II.[33] But there is more. Theocritus'

---

[32] On the introductory use of the connector *ára*, see the parallels provided by Gow 1950: 349; for its classic meaning and function, cf. Humbert 1972: 380–1.

[33] A fragment of a poem by Theocritus with the title of *Berenice* (fr. 3 Gow) is indeed cited by Athenaeus 7.284a; cf. Weber 1993: 253–4 (with an exhaustive bibliography) who, for chronological reasons, supports Berenice I. It is indeed unlikely that Theocritus' lost poem may have concerned Berenice, daughter of Magas, who married Ptolemy II Evergetes and whom Callimachus celebrated in his elegy dedicated to *Berenice's Lock* (fr. 110 Pfeiffer); cf. Gow 1950: 326, who refers also to *Idyll* 14.

poem 15 ('The Syracusans, or the women at the Adonis festival') is set in Alexandria and describes a cultic festival explicitly organized by a queen, who can be none other than Arsinoe. As a dialogue dramatized on the occasion of the festival dedicated to Adonis, the young man loved by Aphrodite, this poem, written in dactylic hexameter, makes an equally explicit allusion to the deification of Arsinoe's mother, Berenice. Indeed, we know that Ptolemy II married his sister Arsinoe around 278 BC, and that their mother, Berenice, was deified soon after the wedding, which in principle takes us as far as 270 BC, the year of Arsinoe's death; moreover, the *Papyrus Hibeh* II 199 allows us to date the institution of the cult of the *Theoi Adelphoi* in Alexandria to 271 BC.[34]

Thus in poem 15, in the etiological style common to Hellenistic poetry, Theocritus portrays Arsinoe's cultic celebration of Aphrodite's young lover as a ritual act of gratitude to the goddess for a past action; according to the *mûthos* recounted by men, Cypris, herself the daughter of Dione, is said to have immortalized Berenice by pouring drops of ambrosia into her heart. In the context of the ritual honors offered to Adonis and Aphrodite, Theocritus explicitly compares Arsinoe, the daughter of divine Berenice, to Helen[35] – this for the ritual reconstructed in the poem. As for Berenice, she seems to have been assimilated to her benefactor, Aphrodite, in the ritual honors bestowed upon her; an epigram attributed to Asclepiades or Posidippus may well attest to this. Be that as it may, Aphrodite, worshipped as the goddess of marriage, personified in Alexandria the exceptional power of royalty.[36]

Furthermore, in his poetic praise of Ptolemy II Philadelphus (*Idyll* 17), Theocritus does not hold back in boasting the sanctuaries, the statues of gold and ivory, and the ritual honours bestowed by the King of Egypt upon his parents. Then poem 17 praises the reciprocal conjugal love that unites Ptolemy Sôter and Berenice, brother and sister, a couple whose only

[34] Regarding the historical circumstances of *Idyll* 15, surely to be dated to 272 BC, cf. Gow 1950: 265 and 294, as well as Fraser 1972: 197–8 (who includes epigraphic attestations of Arsinoe's promotion of Egyptian cults for Aphrodite) and Hunter 2003a: 24–46; on a hymn to Aphrodite that was possibly intended for a Cypriot cult of Arsinoe, cf. Barbantani 2005: 142–59.

[35] Theocritus 15.23–4 and 106–11; on the relationship between the celebration of the Adonia and the honours given to Arsinoe II in this context, cf. Gow 1950: 262–5; on the assimilation of Arsinoe and Aphrodite in the context of the yearly ritual evocation of Adonis, and on the suggestive analogies between Berenice's immortalization and the special treatment given to the body of Patroclus or Hector in the *Iliad*, cf. Hunter 1996: 129–34.

[36] Asclepiades, *Epigram* 39 Gow-Page (= *Anthologia Palatina* 16.68); cf. Gutzwiller 1992: 363–5 as well as Weber 1993: 254, and Caneva 2014: 8 n. 39; on the subject of the cultic assimilations with Aphrodite of Berenice I and (later) Arsinoe II, cf. Fraser 1972: 239–40.

equivalent are Zeus and Hera, both children of Rheia.[37] The poet begins
by describing the divine symposium in which Ptolemy, seated alongside
Alexander and Heracles on a throne offered by Zeus, is invited to share in
the nectar; then, Ptolemy and Alexander accompany their heroic friend
to the bridal chamber, occupied by his wife, the eternally youthful Hebe.
This as a pretext to sing of famed Berenice, who enjoys the attentions of
the Cyprian goddess, and to evoke the desire that the queen arouses in
Ptolemy, in the context of a reciprocal conjugal love from which beautiful
children are born. Here again is an occasion to recall the deification of
the queen through the will of Aphrodite, who, the poet says, prevented
Berenice from crossing the Acheron, bringing her instead to her temple,
where the queen would share in the cultic honours of the goddess.[38]

The parallel between the pomp and power conferred upon Ptolemy by
Zeus, and the divine aura bestowed on his wife Berenice by Aphrodite, is
striking. The account of Ptolemy's banquet with his father Zeus, and of
his visit to the bridal chamber shared by Heracles and the divine Hebe,
assumes somehow the role of *aition* for the ritual honors granted to the
two ruling saviors. This account is set in a timeless present, since, just as
the gods, deified heroes too are exempt from the ephemerality of mortals.
It is followed by the sacrificial rites for the king and queen, who had
been deified through Ptolemy II Philadelphus' founding act. Hence the
poet's use of the formulaic 'rejoice' (*khaîre*, verse 135) in his final address
to Ptolemy II, in the very manner that one would address a divinity at the
end of a cultic hymn; hence a concluding evocation of a poetic memory
that will make of the ruler a demi-god, forever; and hence, a probable
convergence with the ideology of the cult of Egyptian pharaohs.[39] Thus a
transition occurs, from ritual in the poem to the poem as ritual, all within
a performance that one might imagine as taking place on the occasion of a
banquet;[40] the poem is intended as a religious and cultural memory, both
connective and formative.

---

[37] *Idyll* 17.121–34, at the conclusion of the poem. This two-sided scene of filial devotion to a deified
mother and divine conjugal love has been discussed by Hunter 2003a: 188–95; on the controversial
question of the poem's date (between 275 and 270?), cf. Hunter 2003a: 3–8.

[38] Theocritus 17.26–52; on this scene's paradigmatic nature in its reference to the Homeric couple of
Alcinous and Arete, or to that of Amphitryon and Alcmene, see Hunter 2003a: 128–30, as well as
the commentary by Caneva 2014, including numerous complementary bibliographic references.

[39] Theocritus 17.135–7; see also 112–7: the stakes of the poetic celebration amount to universal *kléos*; cf.
Hunter 2003a: 195–9. On the significance of the hymnic *khaîre* in engaging the summoned deity
into a *do ut des* relationship, cf. Calame 2005: 54–60. On the influence of pharaonic ideology, see
the conclusions of Heerink 2010: 402–3.

[40] For an internal reference to a performative context, cf. Pretagostini 2009: 27.

3.2 Poetic Performance, Referential Fiction, and the Pragmatics of Memory

From Sappho of Lesbos to Himerius of Prusa, other types of bridal songs are also attested. While they do not exhibit the same enunciative traits as ritual songs, their pragmatic dimension is no less strong.

The best preserved part of Sappho's fr. 44 Voigt is the long account of Hector's and Andromache's wedding. Homeric diction is evoked in the poem, not only through its lexical choices and its use of traditional formulas, but also in its recourse to direct discourse and to an Aiolo-dactylic metrical rhythm for its verses, which are not organized into strophes. The messenger's account of Hector's return to Troy from Thebes with the charming Andromache at his side, and his description of the bridal procession's preparations are situated in the bygone age of heroes; the procession advances to the sound of the aulos, cithara, and castanets, leading to the maidens' pure song (*mélos*), and then to the adult men's performance of a paean; accompanied by the rhythmic shouts of women, the song invokes the god Apollo while at the same time singing (*úmnen*) ... Hector's and Andromache's wedding![41] In the absence of any of the distinctive traits of the singing and ritual performance that characterize the hymenaios genre, this song does not necessarily correspond to a ritual wedding song.[42] However, its melic meter is certainly intended for a sung performance (probably choral) in the context of a group led by Sappho. Its collective musical and no doubt choreographic performance certainly contributed, with its physical expression of poetic seduction and its oral description of the ideal heroic marriage, to the initiatory education into a state of fulfilled beauty, conferred by frequenting a group of young girls destined for aristocratic marriage. Moreover, as is the case also in the few surviving fragments of Sappho's hymenaioi, numerous expressions of this collective manifestation of poetic and cultural memory vis-à-vis the heroic tradition find parallels in Theocritus' poem 18.[43]

Ten centuries later, Sappho and her hymenaic songs inspired the rhetor Himerius. His *Epithalamium of Severus* is based on a model of nuptial

[41] Sappho fr. 44 Voigt; see the commentary by Aloni 1997: LXI–V and 80–3.
[42] Rösler 1975: 279–85 has proposed to see in Sappho's poem an implicit relationship to the performance of a hymenaios. However, as noted by Hunter 1996: 152, Sappho's poem is 'stichic' (and not strophic), as is, incidentally, Theocritus' *Epithalamium*.
[43] As to this initiatory educational function assumed by Sappho's 'group', cf. Calame 1996 (also 2002: 103–12), with numerous bibliographic references. A linguistic comparison between the fragments of Sappho's poetry and *Idyll* 18 has recently been conducted with great acumen by Acosta-Hughes 2010: 31–6, subsequent to Dagnini 1986.

speech described, among others, by Menander Rhetor (who calls it an *epithalámios* or *gamélios logos*);[44] it was no doubt intended to be orally delivered during the bridal banquet. This rhetorical declamation served probably as an introduction to the melic performance of the actual hymenaios. At any rate, this is what is suggested to the modern reader by the fact that the end of Himerius' bridal speech coincides with the choral and ritual song of the hymenaios.[45]

Such is also the hypothesis suggested by the enunciative behaviour of Theocritus' poem 18, oscillating between its narration of the heroic past and its auto-referential performance: a sung declamation, performed either during Ptolemy's and Berenice's wedding ceremony, or at least, as a song of praise, on the occasion of the ritual celebration of the power of Alexandria's rulers.[46] The narrative distancing that initiates the poem is equivalent to the 'framing' procedures identified in Theocritus' pastoral poems and his poems of praise; through discursive distance, they allow for the creation of a more complex relationship with the social context of life under the power of Alexandria's sovereigns.[47] Through dramatization, in the poem featuring women at the Adonia, and through the reformulation of encomiastic poetry, in the *Encomium of Ptolemy*, the voice of the poet acquires a new pragmatic meaning; so too in the *Epithalamium of Helen*, where epic narration is revisited in terms of ritual aetiology and of the performance of a traditional song. In referring to the heroic Greek past and to the rituals that prompt their memory, poetic fiction maintains its pragmatic dimension.[48]

It is probably not a coincidence that Himerius credits Sappho for the address to the graceful maiden, sung to attract the fiancé into the bridal chamber and marking the final portion of Theocritus' *Epithalamium to Helen: Ô kalá, ô kharíessa kóra* (verse 39).[49] Ultimately therefore, the enunciative movement that runs through Theocritus' unusual poem 18 takes us from the heroic age, placed at a distance by the 'one day'/'once' of the

---

[44] Menander Rhetor 399.11–15, a genre contrasted to the *kateunastikòs lógos* (405.15–19), an exhortation to sexual intercourse addressed to the bridegroom.

[45] Himerius, *Speeches* 9.20–1; cf. Gow 1950: 348 and 358.

[46] The different performative contexts that can be gleaned from Theocritus' poems are discussed by Pretagostini 2009: 14–29 (who does not mention *Idyll* 18). As to the form of the idyll that simply evokes the 'petit genre' understood in the sense of its variety, see Gutzwiller 1996: 129–33.

[47] Goldhill 1991: 223–83 (esp. 272–82). As to the 'presentification' of fictional worlds created within pastoral poems by means of internal dramatization, see Payne 2007: 49–91.

[48] On this subject, see Calame 2010.

[49] Himerius, *Speeches* 9.19, citing Sappho's songs of praise (cf. fr. 108 Voigt), perhaps in reference to Theocritus 18.38.

'mythical' narrative, to the apparent *hic et nunc* of a choral performance that is sung and danced in the traditional manner of a ritual wedding song. This learned manipulation of enunciative and temporal dimensions by way of aetiology corresponds to a poetic encomium of the power of Ptolemy and Berenice, who have become deified rulers, as Menelaus and Helen.[50] The poetic praise is placed under the auspices of Zeus and Aphrodite, but also of Leto, the mother of Apollo: we have to remember that the paradigmatic scene of the *Odyssey* which I have mentioned in the introduction celebrates the marriage of Hermione, the only daughter of the two Spartan rulers on the verge of being deified.

4 Conclusion

Not only is the memory of a central episode of the Trojan war's heroic past resurrected in Ptolemaic Alexandria through narrative means that recall those of epic poetry; this Greek cultural memory is also connected to present circumstances which it is called upon to legitimate. The importance of the use of writing is undeniable in the context of Hellenistic poetic composition.[51] However, the transmission of cultural memory is always entrusted to poetic or rhetorical forms that offer a strong pragmatic dimension – a dimension that reflects public and ritualized contexts of enunciation, in an unmistakable combination of *Bindungs-* and *Bildungsgedächtnis*, if these two concepts are to be retained.

A particularly important role is played by the body's participation in the rhythmic transmission, poetic or rhetorical, of a legacy of *arkhaîa* created by poets to be inscribed in collective memory. Certainly, in the process of Alexandrian urbanization and exportation of the cultural memory of small classical Greek states, divided in reticular manner between local and pan-Hellenic traditions, cultural memory will tend to diversify and fissure. It is nevertheless the case that the 'myths' that compose Hellenic collective and cultural memory owe their tradition and cultural impact to discursive forms; without the ritual performance they imply, this heroic past would not exist. Greek cultural memory, in its dynamics and diversity, is a po(i)etic memory.

---

[50] Differently Griffiths 1979: 86–91, who suggests that Menelaus and Helen be likened to the 'Philadelphian gods', inasmuch as Ptolemy ΙΙ and his sister, like the heroic couple, escape from the mortal condition through the intermediary of deification; see, in the same terms, Stephens 2003: 27–8 and Acosta-Hughes 2010: 37.

[51] On the question of the impact of writing on poetic composition, see the study by Hunter 2003b, on the specific subject of Theocritus' poems, particularly *Idyll 7*.

CHAPTER 12

Physiologia medicans: *The Epicurean Road to Happiness*

Emidio Spinelli*

This chapter aims to examine the central role of memory within (and for) the communicative strategies of Epicurus' philosophy, by paying special attention to the interrelation between his physics and ethics. The overall structure of the Epicurean doctrine shows the systematic links between a coherent and precise physical account of the world and the moral flavour of a goal (*telos*) which is really available to human beings. Behind such a global structure one can detect the necessity of a special transmission linked to the basic use and application of 'mnemotechnic' devices, indispensable for fixing in memory and remembering the most relevant points of a well-grounded atomistic theory, as well as for guaranteeing the efficacy of a reliable communication of such doctrines.[1] The final step of all these efforts is undoubtedly placed in the ethical message of the 'Epicurean gospel', which intends to guarantee tranquillity and absence of anguish with respect to any alleged difficulty in our life.

1 A Clear Philosophical Message

Let us begin from some biographical and 'doxographical' data. A first and safe starting point, concerning Epicurus' communicative skills, is that he was certainly a great writer. Not only 'has our philosopher abundance of witnesses to attest his unsurpassed goodwill to all men',[2] but in particular his stylistic qualities were appreciated. As we read in Diogenes Laertius, 'the terms he used for things were the ordinary terms, and Aristophanes

---

* A shorter version of this paper was read at the 10th International Society for Intellectual History Conference '*Translatio Studiorum*. Ancient, Medieval, and Modern Bearers of Intellectual History' (Verona, 25–7 May 2009): see Spinelli 2012. My warmest thanks to Francesco Verde, who offered useful, in many cases invaluable, comments on a first draft of this paper.

[1] For discussion of artificial and natural mnemonic techniques in antiquity, cf. Sassi's chapter in this volume.

[2] Diogenes Laertius, 10.9 (transl. Hicks 1972: II 537).

the grammarian credits him with a very characteristic style. He was so lucid a writer that in the work *On Rhetoric* he makes clearness the sole requisite.'[3]

Nor can we underestimate, beyond the powerful quality of his writings, the quantitative significance of his works, since 'Epicurus was a most prolific author and eclipsed all before him in the number of his writings: for they amount to about three hundred rolls, and contain not a single citation from other authors; it is Epicurus himself who speaks throughout.'[4]

The quality and quantity of Epicurus' philosophical production satisfy the need for efficacy in scientific communication, as well as the desire to avoid any empty or idle talk about the most important aspects of our existence. Underlying such philosophico-linguistic guidelines there is a strong theoretical premise, clearly expressed in a famous passage of his *Letter to Herodotus* (37–8):

> In the first place, Herodotus, you must understand what it is that words denote, in order that by reference to this we may be in a position to test opinions, inquiries, or problems, so that our proofs may not run on untested ad infinitum, nor the terms we use be empty of meaning. For the primary signification of every term employed must be clearly seen, and ought to need no proving; this being necessary, if we are to have something to which the point at issue or the problem or the opinion before us can be referred.[5]

Epicurus' need is here unequivocal, first of all from an epistemological point of view, since he maintains the possibility of inquiry (against Meno's paradox)[6] by assuming foundational criteria of truth, which do not require any further justification (i.e. *aisthēsis* and *prolēpsis*). In addition, linguistic clarity and efficacy represent a sort of propaedeutic mean with respect to

---

[3] Diogenes Laertius, 10.13 (transl. Hicks 1972: II 543); for a different (and maybe excessively critical) condemnation of Epicurus' style of composition, see however Podolak 2010: 44 and 72. At any rate, we find a similar strong appreciation of *saphēneia*/clearness also in Zeno of Sidon: see Diogenes Laertius, 7.35 = fr. 1 Angeli-Colaizzo, as well as Cic. *ND* 1.59 = fr. 6 Angeli-Colaizzo. (On *saphēneia*/ clearness, see e.g. Milanese 1989 as well as Erler 1991, especially in Philodemus, and Beer 2009: 337–42; Arrighetti 2010: 20–1; for Lucretius' *lucida carmina* 'as a response to Epicurus' demand for clarity' and as a 'counterpart' of the bright truth of Epicurus' teachings, see Asmis 2016.) On the basis of this attention towards *saphēneia* we can also better understand Epicurus' preference for the *syggrammata* and his critique against any philosophical value attributed to poetry: see Arrighetti 2006: 322–4.

[4] Diogenes Laertius, 10.26 (transl. Hicks 1972: II 555). For a useful survey on the books written by Epicurus and his followers, see Dorandi 2007.

[5] Epicurus, *Letter to Herodotus* 37–8 (transl. Hicks 1972: II 567). For a useful survey on this important passage, see Verde's clear commentary in Spinelli-Verde 2010: 77–80; useful comments also in Beer 2009: 106–17.

[6] See Fine 2014: ch. 7 and Verde 2016: 351 n. 2; *contra*, but unconvincingly, see Cornea 2011–2012.

all the contents which Epicurus wants to summarize.[7] In principle, therefore, one has to agree on what underlies any term: if, and only if, the basically empirical content of each verbal expression is clear to us, will it be possible for us to advance in any kind of research. It seems that Epicurus is here proposing a sort of 'zetetic methodology' founded on the firm basis of a language free of any ambiguity.[8] This is the only way in which we can 'discriminate' things and at the same time eliminate any risk that our demonstrations (*apodeixeis*) be condemned to an empty *regressus ad infinitum*. In order to reach such a goal, the content of our verbal expressions must be absolutely certain; and – as Conche rightly points out[9] – what guarantees certainty and avoids any possible ambiguity is the 'basic notion' or, more technically, the second Epicurean criterion, namely *prolēpsis* ('pre-conception'), which is defined as 'a recollection/memory (*mnēmē*) of an external object often presented'.[10] It is empirically formed,[11] without unnecessary additions by our opinions and/or judgements; but exactly because it results from repeated acts of perceptual contact with the external world and determines accordingly the constitution of the rich warehouse of our memory, it is significantly different from mere sensation or *aisthēsis*, which on the contrary 'is devoid of reason and incapable of any memory (ἄλογός ἐστι καὶ μνήμης οὐδεμιᾶς δεκτική)'.[12]

By individuating such a philosophically secure linguistic form and by sharing it with other people who are equally convinced of its efficacy, Epicurus establishes the methodological presuppositions of the development of his doctrine.

---

[7] On the possible role played in this case by the Peripatetic Praxiphanes (a teacher of Epicurus, at least according to Diogenes Laertius, 10.13 = *Prax.* 6 Matelli), see Capasso 1984 and Matelli 2012: 51, nn. 1 and 31. In addition, the Epicurean appeal to clarity in any 'linguistic game' should be linked to the refusal of new expressions or nouns (see e.g. Epicurus, *Letter to Herodotus* 72 and some passages in his *Peri Physeōs*, book XXVIII, esp. 17 1–11 Sedley = 31.11–2 Arrighetti): on this topic, see also Sedley 1973: 17–34 and Tepedino Guerra 1990. On Epicurus' terminology, in addition to the invaluable lexicographic tool offered by Usener 1977 and Thyresson 1977, see some useful considerations in Kleve 1963 and (esp. on relevant stylistic features) Brescia 1955.

[8] On Epicurus' account of language, see e.g. Everson 1994; Verlinsky 2005; Atherton 2009; O'Keefe 2010: ch. 6; Verde 2013a: 136–46.

[9] See Conche 1987: 127; see also Striker 1990: 147–8; Milanese 1996; for a very original solution, see Long 1971, criticized however by Glidden 1983; Morel 2007 as well as the following discussion in Konstan 2007; finally, and from a different perspective, the very useful and clear Hammerstaedt 1996.

[10] Diogenes Laertius, 10.33 (transl. Hicks 1972: II 563, slightly modified).

[11] For a survey on the difficult and very complicated question of the empirical *versus* conceptual nature of the Epicurean *prolēpsis*, see e.g. Manuwald 1972: 16–39; Asmis 2009: 84–90; Gavran Miloš 2012; Verde 2016; and Tsouna 2016.

[12] Diogenes Laertius, 10.31 (transl. Hicks 1972: II 561). On the special relation between the 'criterial' pair *aisthēsis/prolēpsis* and *mnēmē*, see also some correct considerations in Frede 1990: 240–2.

In order to fulfil the requirements just highlighted, he decides to adopt a 'double register' of communication. Since he wants to enlarge the actual target of his philosophical message, letting it reach indistinctly *all* human beings, without differences of gender, social status, political position and so on, he makes use of two different types of writings. On the one side, we find the thirty-seven books of his *On Nature*: they were very technical treatises on many general and specific physical themes, and circulated only inside the group of a limited number of disciples. On the other side, Epicurus adopts a completely different approach and employs new, or at any rate distinctive, literary genres (letters, sentences, summaries, and so on),[13] thanks to which he can disclose the 'secrets' of his atomistic theory and of his ethical tenets *also* to all other people, who do not need any technical knowledge of those philosophical matters, but need in fact elementary and reliable notions useful for guiding their life towards the final goal of human happiness.

2 Memory: Its Physical Status and Its Revolutionary Aim

It is at this point and stage of arrangement of the communicative goal of Epicurus' philosophy that we can appreciate the unique function he attributes to memory.[14] His strategy of a double plan of composition is decisive not only from a formal point of view, but also from a moral (and even 'political') perspective. Epicurus does not want to exclude *anyone* from taking advantage of his scientific doctrines, which are explicitly presented not as the final step of vain theoretical leisure, but rather as a concrete tool for reaching the best condition with respect to everyday life and its troubles.

Such a 'revolutionary' approach and the crucial tool therefore represented by any correct effort of memorization are vividly attested at the very beginning of Epicurus' *Letter to Herodotus* (§§35–7):

> Epicurus to Herodotus, greetings. For those who are unable to study carefully all my physical writings or to go into the longer treatises at all, I have myself prepared an epitome of the whole system, Herodotus, to preserve in the memory enough of the principal doctrines, to the end that on every occasion they may be able to aid themselves on the most important points, so far as they take up the study of physics. Also those who have made some

---

[13] For useful information about the special role played by private letters among Epicurean groups, see Tepedino Guerra 2010.
[14] On this point, see especially Masi 2014a, and more generally Vatri 2015.

advance in the survey of the entire system ought to keep in their minds the
mark of the principal headings in which an elementary outline of the whole
treatment of the subject is summarized. For a comprehensive view is often
required, the details but seldom. To the former, then – the main heads – we
must continually return, and must keep in our memory a degree [of doc-
trine] sufficient to get a capital application [of our reflection] to the facts, as
well as the means of discovering all the details exactly when once the principal marks are rightly understood and remembered; since it is the privilege
of the mature student to make a ready use of his conceptions by referring
every one of them to elementary facts and simple terms. For it is impossible to gather up the results of continuous diligent study of the entirety
of things, unless we can embrace in short formulas and hold in mind all
that might have been accurately expressed even to the most minute detail.
Hence, since such a course is of service to all who take up natural science, I,
who devote to the subject my continuous energy and reap the calm enjoy-
ment of a life like this, have prepared for you just such an epitome and
manual of the doctrines as a whole.[15]

The passage helps to identify some key features of Epicurus' intention.[16]
First of all, he wants to reach a widespread audience: *all people* (although
at different levels of specificity) are placed in the position of understanding
his message and benefitting from it. His 'Garden' does not have any entry
requirement, nor does it foster or presuppose any prejudice, since it is open
even to slaves and women.[17] The way to accomplish the task just described
is clearly propounded at the beginning of his *Letter to Herodotus*: disciples,
at any level but with different aptitudes, have to pay attention to Epicurean
physical tenets and especially keep them actively alive in their memory, so
that they can recall and apply them, if and when they need.

This kind of strong encouragement to make use of memory as the best
instrument for securing the help of Epicurus' doctrine in everyday life and in
front of existential worries can be safely confirmed by further, equally strong
and, once again, biographical evidence. According to Diocles, Epicurus

---

[15] *Letter to Herodotus* 35–7 (transl. Hicks 1972: II 565 and 567, slightly modified); see also Angeli
1985: 67–9.
[16] On this question and on the different kinds of 'summaries' typical of the Epicurean tradition, see
especially Angeli 1986 and 1988; see also Hadot 1969; Erler 1994: 88–9; Tulli 2000: III; Gordon 2013.
More generally on the so-called *Kompendienliteratur*, see Untersteiner 1980: 51–3 and 92–7; Asper
2007: 222–36 and 316–23; Arrighetti 2013; De Sanctis 2015; Damiani 2015 and 2016.
[17] See again Diogenes Laertius, 10.6–7 and 21; about Leontius, see also frr. 19 and 28 Usener (along
with frr. 436, 30, and 227a Usener); for other relevant bibliographical references, see Schmid
1961: 723–6; Festugière 1968: 29 and 36–42; Erler 1994: §24; Heßler 2012 (on the presence of slaves
in the Garden); finally, on letters specifically written by Epicurean women, see Campos Daroca-
López Martínez 2010.

'used to train his friends in committing his treatises to memory',[18] a piece of information confirmed by a passage in book xxviii of *On Nature*: 'And you others, try then to memorise what I and Metrodorus here have just said'.[19]

In addition, one should not forget an exceptional feature, namely that Epicurus' works can be dated thanks to the mention of the eponymous archon and that, as Diskin Clay rightly points out, 'we possess nothing like these dates for the writings of any other Greek philosopher'.[20] This means, as Clay underlines again, that 'at some time after his settlement in Athens, and possibly as early as 307/6 BC, Epicurus decided to preserve his writings in an authoritative and unalterable form and on the same footing as the laws and decrees of the *polis* of Athens. To this end he deposited them in the Metroon where they were kept under the year of the archon in which they were written.'[21] Such a complex and official procedure cannot but reinforce the impression that Epicurus deliberately aimed at 'perpetuating' the precious 'memory' of his own writings.

It is therefore reasonable to suppose that Epicurus was convinced that the members of the Garden could possess and show a strong memory, as attested even by a hostile source like Plutarch.[22] Hermippus too, while describing Epicurus' death, emphasizes the final and decisive appeal to the memorization of the crucial Epicurean doctrines: 'Hermippus relates that he entered a bronze bath of lukewarm water and asked for unmixed wine, which he swallowed, and then, having bidden his friends remember his doctrines, breathed his last.'[23] This final recommendation is perfectly at

---

[18] Diogenes Laertius, 10.12 (transl. Hicks 1972: II 541). On this 'mnemotechnic training' inside the Garden, see Clay 1973 as well as some interesting considerations in Schmid 1961: 743–5 and in Wolff 2000: ch. VIII. As for the 'devotional cult' towards Epicurus, well and constantly attested by many and different sources (see *e.g.* Sen. *Ep.* 25.4–5), see Schmid 1961: 745–55 (with other textual references) and also Clay 1986; Capasso 1987: 25–37; Erler 2002.

[19] For the permanent value of memory and memorization inside the Epicurean school, see also what Cicero writes about Virgil's teacher, the Epicurean Siro: *omnia meminit Siron Epicuri dogmata* (Cic. *Luc.* 106 = fr. 4 Gigante 1990). On the permanent value of the Epicurean 'power of memory' as attested in two fragmentary *uolumina Herculanensia* (*PHerc.* 1040 and 1041), see also Capasso 1988. The Epicurean approach to the memorization of authoritative doctrines can be contrasted with the Platonic criticism of the dangers of a memorizing approach, embodied for example by Meno in the homonymous dialogue (see Wygoda's chapter in this volume).

[20] Clay 1982: 18.

[21] Clay 1982: 18–19; for some useful qualifications, see however Verde 2011: 50.

[22] See Usener fr. 579.

[23] Diogenes Laertius, 10.15–6 (transl. Hicks 1972: II 543–5). It is worth noting that also Diogenes Laertius, in his epigram about Epicurus' death, insists on the central role of a strong memorization for the members of the Garden: see again Diogenes Laertius, 10.16 (= *Anth. Pal.* 7.106). For a parallel Philodemean description of the death of a later Epicurean thinker, Dionysius of Heraclea ('the Renegade'), see Erbì 2013; this description seems to be faithful to the standard Epicurean treatment of biographical data: see De Sanctis 2016 on the Epicurean 'biographical methodology'.

home with Epicurus' more general praise of the real, indisputable pleasure one can get from the memory both of a dead friend and of deep philosophical discussions, that can be (and indeed were for him) of great help against physical pains, even in the last, terrible moments of his life, as attested by his *Letter to Idomeneus*.[24]

Against the background of such episodes (or even, thanks to them), one can perhaps better understand the philosophical relevance of Epicurus' argument at the very beginning of his *Letter to Herodotus*. We have there two different but interrelated claims: the Epicurean philosopher has to be able to 'seize the day' (*carpe diem*), to intercept the *kairos*, for example in a situation of alleged embarrassment or puzzlement, but he can do that only if and because he is able to find out in the well-ordered warehouse of his memory the appropriate doctrine or principle for obtaining the right answer and attaining what Epicurus defines *galēnē*, namely 'stillness of the sea', that is, out of metaphor, calmness of life (i.e. a stable condition of one's own atomic structure). The doctrinal focus lies in this case, once again, in a double sense, both in a special function attributed to *theōria*, which must be intended as proper observation of nature and its features, and in a form of concrete *boētheia*, i.e. in a substantial help based on the exercise of memory.[25]

One cannot forget, in addition, that when the Epicureans speak of memory they perhaps refer to a thoroughly materialistic process, as confirmed by the use of the technical term *typos*, the mark impressed in the atomic cluster of our mind/soul.[26] The fact that 'Epicurean students and scholars' pay all their attention to the most important tenets put forward by their master does not imply only that they become able – from an abstract point of view, so to speak – to manage and properly use the conceptual framework of that philosophy. Rather, and more fundamentally, we have here the description of a physical process and of a material

---

[24] See respectively Usener fr. 213 and fr. 138; on the *Letter to Idomeneus* and especially on the stimulating construal of this text by André Laks, see Sedley 2017: 96.

[25] For useful observations on this question, cf. Diano 1974: 289–90; see also Morel 2011: 27–8.

[26] See Diano 1974: 283–4 and Morel 2011: 129, n. 2. For a different explanation of the Epicurean notion of *typos*, see however Lembo 1981–1982: 17–58. For a philosophical antecedent, apart from some significant occurrences in Plato's *Timaeus* (50c5 and 71b4), see the example – although admittedly used neither in a materialistic nor in a physiological sense (see Cambiano 2007b: 5–17; for a different view, see however Adalier 2001) – of the tablet of wax in Plato's *Theaetetus* (191c–192d), discussed also by Aristotle in his *De anima* and *De memoria et reminiscentia* (on some key notions of the latter, see Sassi 2007 and Castagnoli in this volume) and re-proposed by ancient Stoicism, especially by Cleanthes in order to account for the materialistic mechanism of apprehension (see at least *SVF* I 484 and II 58 and more generally Ierodiakonou 2007).

modification.[27] When, as Epicureans, we study and especially memorize Epicurus' *dogmata*, we are going to submit ourselves to an effective alteration of the atomic structure of our mind/*dianoia*. After accepting and repeating all those doctrines, the arrangement of our atoms will change and transform into a firm and stable configuration or disposition (a *diathesis*),[28] which will be available as soon as we need philosophical medicines for our life. Memory, therefore, is not an abstract faculty, but rather a physical *status*, according to a 'reductionist' view, that seems to be similar, *mutatis mutandis*, to some contemporary neuro-physiological theories about the complex functioning of the human mind. A general, but very useful observation by Mary Carruthers might help us to clarify Epicurus' position better than any other explanation (taking for granted, of course, the differences between ancient atomistic speculations and contemporary, more refined theories, and apart from the more 'functionalist' or 'cognitive' tone of the second part of her statement):

> The structures which memory stores are not actual little pictures, but are *quasi*-pictures, 'representations' in the sense that the information stored causes a physical change in the brain that encodes (the modern word) or moulds (the ancient one) it in a certain way and in a particular 'place' in the brain. This 'sort-of' image is then used as the basis for cognition by a process (intellection) which understands it to be a configuration standing in a certain relationship to something else – a 'representation' in the cognitively functional sense, as writing represents language.[29]

3 Philosophy for Everyone

It is in order to reinforce the complicated process which I have just attempted to describe that Epicurus offers to his students the new device of his own *epitomē*, restricted to the main aspects of his physics, but useful also for penetrating other, more specific questions related to the complete clarification of the world make-up.[30] Epicurus' *Letter to Herodotus*, therefore, seems to be of much greater interest not only for the beginners and 'poor' people, but also for advanced scholars, since thanks to it they will be able to keep together both the details of the physical doctrine and the

---

[27] On such a crucial process, see especially Asmis 1984: 61–80 and again Asmis 2009. Also the peculiar expression *katholikē noēsis enapokeimenē* – attested in Diogenes Laertius, 10.33, and accepted, I suppose, *both* by Epicurus *and* by later Epicureans – should be perhaps read in the same 'materialistic' way (*pace* Diano 1974: 161–2): more details on this difficult passage in Verde 2016.

[28] On the purely materialistic meaning of this term, see Grilli 1983.

[29] Carruthers 1990: 23.

[30] See also Angeli 1988: 45.

general framework of the systematic account, praised by Epicurus as the best assurance against any risk of *kenodoxia* ('vain opinion').

In addition, it is easy to conclude that its audience cannot be identified with a single, limited readership. By adopting the literary form of the summary and by insisting on the necessity of using the same communicative strategy guaranteed by the safe tool of *mnēmē*, Epicurus tries to address his message to different listeners and readers. Epicurean 'students' do not all have the same philosophical background and intelligence; nonetheless a faithful and precise summary, aptly preserved in the secure storage of memory, can reach (and help) at least three different categories:[31]

1. those who master the most difficult technicalities of the Epicurean system in all their atomistic and materialistic features;
2. those who are *proficientes*, but still 'on the road' while attempting to learn the central elements of that scientific picture of the world;
3. those who are really at the beginning of the difficult training inside the Garden and need therefore only introductory notions.

The summary offered by Epicurus can be handled by all these categories of people according to their different and flexible capacity to have it (more or less immediately) in mind and to apply its essential content to disparate situations and events. What guarantees a positive and successful result, at any rate, is the fact that Epicurus' *epitomē* does pursue the highest level of exactness or *akribeia*, so that there is no risk of banalities or even distortions as to the explanation of the real nature of things. The vocabulary of *akribeia* seems indeed to distinguish the main passages of the *Letter to Herodotus*[32] and at the same time induces immediately (and will induce later) many disciples inside the school to pay careful attention to the philological details, in order to avoid any dangerous innovation.[33]

4 Towards the Ethical Goal of *Ataraxia*

Apart from the opening passage of the *Letter to Herodotus* and from what Epicurus repeats at the end of the same work,[34] we can therefore

---

[31] On this tripartition, see also Seneca's testimony (*Ep.* 52, 3–4 = fr. 192 Usener) as well as Angeli 1988: 38–40 and Tulli 2000: 111; on the happy condition of the *proficiens* (to be distinguished from the *progrediens*, who carefully proceeds in the science of nature: see Schiesaro 1989), see also Erler 2009.

[32] Angeli 1985 is very useful on this topic.

[33] On this peculiar form of *philologia medicans*, see Erler 2003; for useful observations, see also Arrighetti 2006: 391–5.

[34] 'Here then, Herodotus, you have the chief doctrines of physics in the form of a summary. So that, if this statement be accurately retained and take effect, a man will, I make no doubt, be incomparably

broaden our perspective and contend that Epicurus' goal is not exclusively the exhibition of the strongest accuracy in the scientific treatment of his *physiologia*. He aims rather – also, if not especially thanks to the materialistic 'bridge' of his specific notion of memory – at leading his disciples and readers towards a higher goal, namely the ethical end of *ataraxia* along with the confidence or *pistis* in its achievement.[35]

This overall perspective and this methodological effort are clearly stated also at the beginning of his *Letter to Pythocles*,[36] where Epicurus seems to confirm the undeniable interrelation between a global approach to any scientific or philosophical question, acquired and safely retained through the modification of our memory, considered as a reliable 'hardware', and a minute analysis of its details:

> Epicurus to Pythocles, greeting. In your letter to me, of which Cleon was the bearer, you continue to show me affection which I have merited by my devotion to you, and you try, not without success, to recall the considerations which make for a happy life. To aid your memory you ask me for a clear and concise statement concerning celestial phenomena; for what we have written on this subject elsewhere is, you tell me, hard to remember, although you have my books constantly with you. I was glad to receive your request and am full of pleasant expectations. We will then complete our writing and grant all you ask. Many others besides you will find these reasonings useful, and especially those who have but recently made acquaintance with the true story and those who are attached to pursuits which go deeper than any part of ordinary education. So you will do well to take them and, holding them in your memory, get them up quickly along with the short epitome in my letter to Herodotus.
>
> In the first place, believe that, like everything else, knowledge of celestial phenomena, whether taken along with other things or in isolation, has no other end in view than peace of mind and firm conviction.[37]

better equipped than his fellows, even if he should never go into all the exact details. For he will clear up for himself many of the points which I have worked out in detail in my complete exposition; and the summary itself, if borne in mind, will be of constant service to him. It is of such a sort that those who are already tolerably, or even perfectly, well acquainted with the details can, by analysis of what they know into such elementary perceptions as these, best prosecute their researches in physical science as a whole; while those, on the other hand, who are not altogether entitled to rank as mature students can in silent fashion and as quick as thought run over the doctrines most important for their peace of mind' (*Letter to Herodotus* 82–3, transl. Hicks 1972: II 611 and 613). On this point, for a different textual reconstruction, see Bredlow Wenda 2008 and Spinelli/Verde 2010: 229–30.

[35] For some recent works on the difficult topic of the Epicurean concept of *ataraxia*, see at least Held 2007: ch. 3 and Woolf 2009.

[36] On the authenticity of this *Letter*, see Dorandi 2007: 30; see also Arrighetti 1973: 691–705 and Erler 1994: 78; *contra* see however Podolak 2010. On the content of the *Letter*, useful observations in Bénatouïl 2003 and more generally in Taub 2009; see also Tulli 2014. On its opening section, see especially De Sanctis 2012.

[37] *Letter to Pythocles* 84–5 (transl. Hicks 1972: II 613 and 615, slightly modified).

This *Letter*, in its function as a doctrinal *epitomē* about celestial and atmospheric phenomena, is effective because it summarizes and simplifies important questions treated in other, surely more difficult Epicurean works. In this way, it can more easily and forcefully cause a change in the atomic cluster of our mind and so 'encode' it – to use again Carruthers' contemporary jargon – according to the best possible accommodation for our memory. Such a strengthened use of memory can at this point offer a precious aid not only to all those disciples who do not have technical or detailed knowledge about those topics and are also too 'swamped' by everyday problems and troubles, but also to those *proficientes* or even mature Epicureans who can safely master the more specific and scientific contents of Epicurus' doctrine.

Also his *Letter to Pythocles* – as well as the rest of the *corpus* attested in Diogenes Laertius, book x – can be therefore considered as an indispensable 'mnemotechnic' tool. It works if and only if we always keep in mind and remember the method of plural explanations;[38] and thanks to it we can avoid any empty dispute on abstract topics and give the right direction to our everyday life. The final goal of this and other tools, in fact, is not restricted to the domain of theoretical knowledge or 'pure' scientific satisfaction, but extends immediately to the conduct of life. It represents – if we apply to the Epicurean case a famous hermeneutical category put forward by Pierre Hadot – the core of 'spiritual practices or exercises', strongly recommended to reach the safe harbour of a genuine *ataraxia*, and assumes accordingly the ethical weight so evidently pursued by Epicurus and his school.

5   Easy Memorization and Epicurus' Philosophical System

Despite the richness and epistemological appeal of Epicurus' complex *physiologia*, we are not allowed to consider it as the final step or even the highest point of his philosophical system. Epicurean physics must be evaluated by comparison with other aspects, and therefore considered in its genuine function. The system of thought proposed by Epicurus has undoubtedly different parts, but they are not on the same level, nor reciprocally interwoven in the 'holistic' way characteristic of the Stoic system.[39]

---

[38] See also here, §116. On the *pleonachos tropos*, see e.g. Verde 2013b; Masi 2014b; Bakker 2016: ch. 2; Verde, forthcoming, especially on the problem of the (alleged) Theophrastean origin of this method.

[39] See Diogenes Laertius, 7.40 and also some important comments in Goldschmidt 1979: 64–7; on the role of Zeno for this systematic Stoic approach, see at least Mansfeld 2002, while for other details, see Spinelli 2007 and Verde 2013a: 43–51.

In Epicurus – despite some obvious cross-references among the different elements of his doctrine – one can detect a clear 'direction', and consequently an increasing degree of importance, with regard to the traditional parts of philosophy admitted by the Hellenistic schools.[40] First of all we find the gnoseological/epistemological section – the so-called 'canonic', the theory about our standards or criteria of truth – which provides reliable tools both to investigate the realm of nature and to determine any kind of choice and avoidance. Then we have the 'physiological' section, which supplies the principles indispensable to understand the materialistic framework of nature.

If Epicurus' followers, at any level, are able to hold firmly in their memory the basic tenets of both the epistemological and the physical parts of the system, they will easily find the way towards the third part of it, i.e. the ethical one. It is here that we should locate the culmination of Epicurus' doctrine, since it represents the actual *telos* of his philosophy as a powerful therapy against any kind of psychological evil.[41]

To appreciate the real meaning of this therapeutic turning point we can read the *Key doctrines* 11 and 12. They describe the functional relationship of subordination of physics to ethics, and confirm that correct understanding of the constitution of reality is necessary for obtaining happiness, understood as pure pleasure due to the absence of pain in the body (*aponia*) and of trouble in the soul (*ataraxia*):

> 11. If we had never been molested by alarms at celestial and atmospheric phenomena, nor by the misgiving that death somehow affects us, nor by neglect of the proper limits of pains and desires, we should not have had any need to study natural science.
>
> 12. It would be impossible to banish fear on matters of the highest importance, if a man did not know the nature of the whole universe, but lived in dread of what the legends tell us. Hence without the study of nature there was no enjoyment of unmixed pleasures.[42]

Epicurus' argument is shaped in hypothetical form, but wants to be strongly prescriptive. The Epicurean philosopher does not turn his mind towards nature with a purely theoretical approach. Rather, he devotes himself to the study of reality only because he knows that this is necessary to erase the roots of our troubles and puzzles. After coping with the consistent

---

[40] And even by Xenocrates before: see S. E. *M* 7.16 = *Xen.* fr. 82 Isnardi Parente = F 1 Isnardi Parente.

[41] See paradigmatically fr. 221 Usener; on the role of the *philosophia medicans* as an Epicurean *topos*, see e.g. Gigante 1975.

[42] Epicurus, *Key doctrines* 11–12 (transl. Hicks 1972: 11 667); on the 'cathartic' and 'didactic' function of Epicurus' *physiologia*, see also Manolidis 1987: 104–13.

explanation of our world (as well as of other infinite worlds around us) any motive of anxiety will disappear and we will live more and more in conformity with nature.[43] No dangerous role of gods,[44] no negative or terrifying value of our death,[45] no unbearable level of pain,[46] no prospect of unattainable pleasures[47] will hold in check our everyday life.

This is the confident announcement of the so called *tetrapharmakos*, explicitly illustrated in the rich argumentative texture of Epicurus' *Letter to Menoeceus*. It is shortly repeated in the first four *Key doctrines* and also laconically abridged – evidently, in both cases for the sake of easier memorization – by Philodemus, thanks to a formula immediately available in our memory and really helpful for everyone (slaves and women included, one can suppose): 'God presents no fears, death no worries. And while good is readily attainable, evil is readily endurable.'[48]

6 Living Simply, Also Thanks to Memory …

In order to secure happiness it is sufficient to meditate on the main precepts of the Epicurean message, to keep them in one's own memory, to exercise oneself and use them at the right moment in order to live 'as a god among men'.[49] Happiness does not reside too far; it is rather here, for us, for all of us, at hand. The core of the Epicurean ethical perspective is characterized by a continuous tension towards a simple life, or better towards the reduction to a sort of 'ground zero' with respect to every desire and its satisfaction. Pointing to the idea of philosophy as a *technē peri ton bion* ('art of

---

[43] On this question, see Morel 2003 and 2009: 161–206.

[44] They do not have indeed any 'providential' function, any positive or negative interest in human affairs, since they live completely undisturbed and happy in the *intermundia*, as attested by later sources: see e.g. Cic. *ND* 1.18; *fin.* 2.75; *diu.* 2.40; Philodemus, *De dis* 3.8.31. For a survey on this difficult topic, see Santoro 2000: 43–65; Wifstrand Schiebe 2003 and Kany-Turpin 2007; more generally see also Essler 2011; Konstan 2011; Sedley 2011, and now Piergiacomi 2017.

[45] Since it is absolutely nothing within the radically materialistic framework of the Epicurean doctrine: on this topic, see at least Warren 2009; more in detail, on the Epicurean notion of death, see also Warren 2004 and Tsouna 2006 (esp. on Philodemus' position).

[46] On this specific topic, see also Laurand 2003.

[47] On this question, see now Woolf 2009.

[48] Philodemus, *To the school-fellows* (*PHerc.* 1005 col. 5.9–13 ed. Angeli), transl. Long-Sedley 1987: 1.156; for a useful comment on this passage, see Angeli 1988: 261–70 and 50–61; for a new, different reconstruction of the title of this Philodemean work (*Pros tous phaskobybliakous*), see however Del Mastro 2014: 185.

[49] Epicurus, *Letter to Menoeceus* 135 (transl. Hicks 1972: II 659); see also Epicurus, *Letter to Pythocles* 116. On this peculiar (and consciously anti-Platonic?) form of 'assimilation to god', see especially Erler 2002 and 2014.

life') and as a source of invulnerability,[50] the central grammar of Epicurus' ethics does not need special adjectives. What is important is the easy and easily graspable *zēn*, existence in its simplest forms, and not any theoretically articulated concept of *eu zēn* ('living well') recommended by other philosophical schools. As we read in Epicurus' *Vatican Sayings* 33:

> The flesh's cry is not to be hungry or thirsty or cold. For one who is in these states and expects to remain so could rival even <Zeus> in happiness.[51]

Apart from the inquiry about possible polemical targets – interesting both from a historical point of view and for the proposal of a *Weltanschauung* radically oriented towards the things of this world – a conclusive remark is needed: the undisturbed condition of such a simple life, which means at the same time living simply,[52] is the final stage of a long and careful process, at the beginning of which Epicurus puts the exact transmission of his scientific theories, the never-ending effort to retain them in memory and the powerful impact of memory on the conduct of our life.

---

[50] One of the best surveys of the main points of Epicurus' ethics is still Mitsis 1988; see also Annas 1993: ch. IV.16.

[51] Transl. Long-Sedley 1987: 1.116.

[52] See the Epicurean praise of frugality (e.g. fr. 182 Usener), based on a strict concept of self-sufficiency (see paradigmatically *Vatican Sayings* 68).

PART IV

The Imperial Period: Continuity and Change

CHAPTER 13

Claudius Aelianus: Memory, Mnemonics, and Literature in the Age of Caracalla

Steven D. Smith

Claudius Aelianus (hereafter, Aelian), a Roman writer of the early third century AD, boasted never to have left the shores of Italy in his life, but he wrote Greek like a native from the heart of Attica, according to Philostratos (*VS* 624). His surviving literary compositions include twenty fictional letters by characters from the Attic countryside, the *De natura animalium* (*NA*), the incomplete *Varia historia*, and numerous fragments; all are compelling examples of the aesthetic tendencies of his age, part of the renaissance of Greek rhetoric in the Roman empire that began a century before.[1] Rejecting radical innovation, Aelian's literary persona is that of the conservative scholar, a bibliophile committed to the exploration and preservation of Greek learning, which he transmits to posterity in his favoured form, the literary fragment. We might profitably consider Aelian's fragments not as a sign of intellectual deficiency or as evidence of the decline of classical culture, but rather as the molecular building blocks of a classical culture that have been recombined and newly configured in ways relevant to a post-classical context.[2] Aelian's approach to the memorialization of Greek culture is therefore not just curatorial, but also creative; Aelian is keenly aware that the act of re-membering the fragmentary remains of Greek culture is a matter of art, and it is telling that in the epilogue to the *NA* he declares his wish to be ranked among the poets, natural philosophers, and historians of classical antiquity (*NA* ep., p. 430, lines 19–21).[3]

Given Aelian's interest in the relationship between his own literary composition and cultural memory generally, it is perhaps not surprising

---

[1] For a complete assessment of Aelian's works and his place in Severan literary culture, see Smith 2014. Other recent valuable studies include Campanile 2006, Kindstrand 1998, Prandi 2005, Rink 1997, Schettino 2005, Stamm 2003, and Whitmarsh 2007.

[2] On the fragment and literary *poikilia*, see Smith 2014: 5–6, 47–66; Parker 2008: 116, influenced by the work of Roland Barthes; Goldhill 2009; and DuBois 2010: 40.

[3] The text of the *NA* is from García Valdés et al. 2009. All translations are my own unless otherwise indicated.

that memory recurs frequently as a topic of discussion in the *NA*, his best known work. I will consider the relevance of the topic in three ways: first, on the level of content, by surveying those narratives in which Aelian eulogizes the natural memory of animals; second, from the perspective of the contemporary discourse on mnemonics, that is, the degree to which memory is a product of nature (*phusis*) or art (*tekhnē*); and third, from the political perspective, taking into consideration Caracalla's explicit manipulation of public memory after the murder of his brother and co-emperor Geta in 211. It will be seen that Aelian is not the scholarly recluse that he may sometimes appear to be, but rather a man of his times and a literary artist engaged in the much contested authorization of the past.

To begin, it is worth noting the various creatures that Aelian says are endowed with memory. Hoopoes, for example, are highlighted for their misanthropic savagery, building their nests in desolate places, and deterring strangers by smearing their nest with human excrement. All this they do, according to Aelian, because they 'seem to have a recollection of their formerly human qualities and especially a hatred for the race of women' (δοκοῦσι τῶν προτέρων τῶν ἀνθρωπικῶν ἐν μνήμῃ καὶ μέντοι καὶ μίσει τοῦ γένους τοῦ τῶν γυναικῶν, 3.26, p. 65, lines 9–11). Aelian here alludes to the myth of Tereus, who was transformed into a hoopoe for his savagery, while the Athenian sisters Prokne and Philomela, who together murdered Tereus' son, were transformed into a swallow and a nightingale.[4] The behavioural traits of the hoopoe, then, are interpreted by the author not according to the requirements of nature, but according to the expectations of culture. The creature, in other words, is conceived of as being mindful of its own mythological past.

Regarding the domesticated bull, Aelian writes that the creature will never forget anyone who strikes or punishes him, even if he must wait patiently to avenge himself (οὐκ ἄν ποτε λήθην λάβοι, 4.36, p. 88, lines 12–13). The bull will patiently endure the plough and his fetters, but as soon as he is free, he will lash out at the herdsman who wronged him. The narrative rationalizes the violence of the bull, basing it upon an innate understanding of justice, though this is only implied in the text. But Aelian also anthropomorphizes the bull, writing that so long as he is under the yoke and restrained, 'he is like a prisoner and is tranquil' (ἔοικε δεσμώτῃ καὶ ἡσυχάζει, 4.36, p. 88, line 15). The simile makes the bull's memory

---

[4] A very well known myth, alluded to already in the *Odyssey*, 19.518–24, brought on the scene in both tragedy and comedy (e.g. Sophocles' *Tereus*, Aristophanes' *Birds*), narrated by Ovid (*Met.* 6.424–674), and present in mythological summaries such as Apollod. *Bib.* 3.14.8.

of the injustice committed against him comprehensible within a human context that supposes slaves are naturally disposed to accept their captivity, whatever memory of freedom they may harbour privately within their minds. Elsewhere, however, Aelian shows that humans and non-human animals do not always peacefully accept their status as chattel. The famous story of Androklēs and the lion, for example (7.44, discussed below), recounts how a slave runs away from his Roman master. A fragment preserved in the *Suda* likewise recounts how a man from Aigina once broke free of his shackles and ran away from his wealthy captors to seek sanctuary in the temple of Demeter; finding the temple locked, the man clung so tightly to the door handles when his captors came to retrieve him that they could only remove him by cutting off his hands (fr. 51 Hercher; fr. 54a–c Domingo-Forasté). Non-human animals, too, resist captivity. The Indian elephant, when it is caught and shackled, 'becomes murderous, longing for its freedom' (τὴν ἐλευθερίαν ποθῶν φονᾷ, 12.41, p. 304, line 14); it does not quietly plot revenge like the bull, but 'is kindled to anger and does not endure to be a slave and a prisoner' (ἐς τὸν ἐξάπτεται, καὶ δοῦλος εἶναι καὶ δεσμώτης⁵ οὐκ ὑπομένει, lines 15–16). Such narratives of the impulsive will to break free of the shackles of slavery contrast sharply with the story of the bull, whose memory of his own freedom and his dissimulation before his captors sets him apart from the 'irrational creatures' (ἄλογα ζῷα) that act on instinct.

Given the special status of dolphins in Greek lore, it is not surprising that these creatures receive equally special treatment by Aelian. Aelian opens a particularly elaborate narrative with the programmatic statement: 'And indeed dolphins are mindful also of their dead and in no way do they betray their fellows in the herd even when they have departed from life' (Ἦσαν δὲ ἄρα δελφῖνες καὶ νεκρῶν μνήμονες καὶ τῶν συννόμων καὶ ἀπελθόντων τοῦ βίου οὐδαμῶς προδόται, 12.6, p. 283, lines 5–6). Aelian explains, citing the authority of Aristotle,[6] that dolphins will lift up one of their dead out of the water and entrust it to humans to bury on land, providing even a kind of funeral procession. Humans, in turn, respect the charge that has been entrusted to them by the dolphins, but only, according to Aelian, those humans who live just lives and who love music: 'But those who are both without the Muses, they say, and without the Graces, they have no care for them [dolphins]' (οἱ δὲ ἀπό τε Μουσῶν, φασίν, ἀπό τε Χαρίτων ἀκηδῶς αὐτῶν ἔχουσι, 12.6, p. 283, line 13–14). As he does so

---

[5] I accept Hercher's emendation; García Valdés et al. 2009 print δεσπότην, attested in the manuscripts.
[6] Arist. *HA* 631a15; fr. 270.37 Gigon.

often in the *NA*, Aelian then contrasts the naturally endowed nobility of
animals with the savagery of putatively civilized humans, here addressing
dolphins directly and asking them to forgive humans for their wicked-
ness. Aelian summons three historical *exempla* illustrating humankind's
inability to respect the memory of our dead. The Athenians cast out the
body of Phōkiōn, their distinguished *stratēgos* and fellow assemblyman,
decreeing that it remain unburied (318 BC);[7] similar treatment was shown
even to Olympias, the mother of Alexander the Great, when she died in
316 BC, despite the fact that she had boasted to have given birth to the
son of Zeus. Finally, Pompey the Great was treacherously murdered by
the Egyptians upon his arrival at Alexandria in 48 BC and left, headless,
upon the shore. Aelian concludes the narrative by lamenting that humans
dare to consume creatures like cicadas[8] and dolphins: 'they have forgotten themselves in committing these acts that are hateful to the Muses,
the daughters of Zeus' (σφᾶς αὐτοὺς λελήθασι ταῖς Μούσαις ταῖς Διὸς
θυγατράσι ταῦτα ἀπὸ θυμοῦ δρῶντες, 12.6, p. 284, lines 1–2). Aelian
therefore constructs a sophisticated relationship between respecting and
preserving the memory of the dead on the one hand and, on the other
hand, the privileged connection that a whole class of creatures, including
humans, have with the Muses. But whereas creatures such as dolphins
seem to be forever mindful of their natural nobility, human savagery is
conceptualized by Aelian as a failure of memory, a crucial forgetting of
our special relationship with the Muses that is reflected in transgressions
against the dignity of fellow humans and dolphins alike, even in death.[9]

Two animals associated with kingship and authority, namely the eagle
and the lion, also possess memory. In a short narrative about the eagle,
Aelian recounts a reciprocal emotional bond between the bird and an
anonymous boy; Aelian likens the relationship to that between brothers or
even between an *erastēs* and *erōmenos* pair.[10] The intensity of their love for
one another was achieved especially by the progress of time (προϊὼν δὲ ὁ
χρόνος εἰς φιλίαν αὐτοὺς ἐξῆψεν ἀλλήλων ἰσχυράν, 6.29, p. 144, line 8).

---

[7] Cf. Plut. *Phoc.* 37.
[8] On the relationship between the cicada and the Muses, see Aelian *NA* 5.13, alluding to Pl. *Phdr.*
258e6–259d8; cf. also Capra's chapter above, p. 192.
[9] The Muses clearly are present here as daughters of Mnemosyne, 'Memory', as preserved in song
and poetry; as for the Charites, they have to do with *mousike*, but they may here also allude to the
obligation of reciprocity which is an important element of the conception of (political and ethical)
memory (see below, as well as Ceccarelli's chapter in this volume).
[10] On human–animal romances in the *NA* and on the political symbolism of the eagle in Aelian's literary thought, see Smith 2014: 198–213, 238–46; the myth of the love of Zeus and Ganymedes may
also lie behind this story.

When the boy became ill, the eagle remained steadfastly by his side and took care of the one who had tended him for so long. Finally, when the boy died, 'the eagle too followed him all the way to the tomb, and when he was being consumed by fire, he threw himself upon the pyre' (ἠκολούθησε καὶ ὁ ἀετὸς μέχρι τοῦ μνήματος· καιομένου δέ γε, ἑαυτόν[11] εἰς τὴν πυρὰν ἐνέβαλεν, lines 12–14). Aelian effectively reinforces the eagle's lasting memory for the boy by referring to the boy's tomb with the word μνῆμα, which in turn lends a unity to the whole narrative, as Aelian introduced the passage by citing his third century BC literary source: 'Phylarkhos recalls that …' (Φύλαρχος μέμνηται, line 3). Memory therefore ties together the whole of the fragment, and Aelian suggests a thematic connection between the eagle's natural devotion, enhanced by the passage of time, and the capacity – if not the *responsibility* – of literature to memorialize for humans what is considered ideal in the natural world.

The other animal associated with human kingship and authority is of course the lion, and Aelian illustrates this creature's capacity for memory through the famous story of Androklēs and the lion, in which, after an act of kindness on the part of the runaway slave Androklēs, the lion eventually encounters and recognizes Androklēs in the arena at Rome and intervenes to save the life of the condemned man. While it is not possible here to consider this elaborate narrative in detail, it is worth noting that Aelian introduces the tale with a programmatic statement: 'And that memory is a constant attribute even of animals … the following things also prove' (Μνήμην δὲ παρακολουθεῖν καὶ τοῖς ζῴοις … τεκμηριοῖ καὶ ἐκεῖνα, 7.44, p. 188, lines 16–18). The narrative that follows, however, and similar narratives wherein animals return a favour to a human benefactor after a long period of time, such as the tale of the stork and the woman of Tarentum (8.21),[12] or the tale of Pindos and the giant snake (10.48)[13] – these tales are hardly irrefutable proof that animals possess memory: Aelian's approach to natural phenomena is not that of the scientist. On the contrary, according to a recent interpretation by Catherine Osborne, the Androklēs story 'is actually rather better as a proof that the things that count in moral evaluation are not, as it happens, matters of that sort at all: they do not have

---

[11] I follow here the suggestion of Aelian's earlier editors: Gesner (1556), Jacobs (1832), and Hercher (1864). The editors of the recent Teubner edition of the *NA* preserve the reading of the manuscripts (αὐτόν), but the reflexive pronoun is clearly preferable. It strains belief to imagine the eagle throwing the boy's body upon the pyre; furthermore, the boy is already represented by the genitive participle (καιομένου).

[12] χάριτος δὲ ἀπομνησθῆναι τὰ ζῷα καὶ κατὰ τοῦτο ἀγαθά (8.21, p. 203, line 23–4).

[13] ἴδιον μὲν δὴ τῶν ζῴων ἐκτίνειν χάριτας τοῖς εὐεργέταις, ἥπερ οὖν καὶ ἄνω λέλεκται, καὶ νῦν δὲ οὐχ ἥκιστα (10.48, p. 256, lines 10–12).

to do with intelligence, memory, consciousness, or linguistic abilities, but rather deeds and motives of a more practical nature – good will, loyalty, friendship, kindness, gratitude, generosity, and hospitality.'[14] The question of whether non-human animals possess memory or not turns out to have been a distraction from the fact that the morality of human beings has always been judged in part by the way in which we relate to non-human animals.[15]

If therefore Aelian seeks to illustrate and idealize the natural memory of animals, it is to show that memory reinforces the entire network of human morality. We learn, for example, that the mare is a good mother because she is 'able to remember the foal to which she gave birth' (τοῦ πώλου τοῦ ἐξ αὐτῆς μεμνῆσθαι δεινή, 6.48, p. 151, lines 23–4), and Aelian even provides an historical exemplum, relating how Dareios, defeated by Alexander, fled from the battle of Issos by mounting a female horse: 'And she, indeed because of the recollection of what had been left behind [her foal], is celebrated, as her will and the strength of her feet allowed, for having snatched her master out of the climactic moment of the dangers that were threatening' (ἡ δὲ ἄρα τοῦ καταλειφθέντος μνήμῃ, ὡς εἶχεν ἐπιθυμίας καὶ ποδῶν, τὸν δεσπότην ὑμνεῖται τῆς ἀκμῆς τῶν ἐπικειμένων κινδύνων ἐξαρπάσαι, 6.48, p. 151, line 30–p. 152, line 2). This charming anecdote about the mare's maternal instinct is paralleled by a more elaborate narrative about the devotion of elephants as they protect their young in a variety of ways (7.15).

The examples of the mare and the elephant are, however, to be contrasted with the figure of the wicked Laenilla, a woman of the senatorial class whom Aelian knew as a boy, who treacherously informed against her own children, alleging that they were conspiring to murder the local magistrate, and so successfully had them put to death. What is most appalling to Aelian is that Laenilla became an enemy to her own children because she could not endure their outrage that she was involved in a sexual relationship with her own slave. Unlike the mare and especially unlike the elephant, which is mindful of sex only once in its life, and then only for procreation, the Roman woman Laenilla 'placed lust before her own sons' (τὸν ἔρωτα ἐπίπροσθεν τῶν υἱέων ποιησαμένη, 7.15, p. 172, lines 10–11). The author concludes by expressing his moral indignation with a rhetorical question: 'Oh gods of our fathers and Artemis of

---

[14] Osborne 2007: 138.

[15] For a fuller treatment of the stories of Androklês and the lion, the woman of Tarentum, and Pindos and the snake, see Smith 2014: 133–44, 229–33.

Childbirth and Eileithuiai, daughters of Hera, why would we still mention Medea of Kolchis or Attic Proknē, when we call to mind things that have happened recently and in our own time?' (ὦ πατρῷοι θεοὶ καὶ Ἄρτεμι λοχεία Εἰλείθυιαί τε θυγατέρες Ἥρας, τί ἂν ἔτι Μήδειαν εἴποιμεν τὴν Κόλχον ἢ Πρόκνην τὴν Ἀτθίδα, τῶν ἔναγχός τε καὶ καθ' ἡμᾶς παθῶν μνημονεύσαντες; 7.15, p. 172, lines 16–19).[16]

Contemplating the natural memory of elephants as a basis for their devotion to their young leads Aelian to consider further not only the contemporary moral failings of his own society but equally the failure of myth to offer moral instruction by means of terrifying negative examples. The whole of the narrative is structured around the concept of τὸ μνημονεύειν, being mindful, continually and actively remembering one's moral responsibilities.[17] Aelian reveals over the course of the *NA* that τὸ μνημονεύειν, mindfulness and remembering, is the thread that holds together the fabric of Greco-Roman society; it is the basis of parents' love for their children (*philoteknia*), justice (*dikē*), the performance and repayment of favours and acts of charity (*kharis*), and even sexual continence (*sōphrosunē*) – in short, τὸ μνημονεύειν is the mental activity that supports the whole of Greco-Roman culture.

Aelian's valorization of the natural memory of animals is to be contrasted with his criticism of the various technologies of memory developed by humans. In one narrative, Aelian states outright that 'animals remember what they experience, and they have no need of the artifice pertaining to memory, not that of Simonides, not that of Hippias, not that of Theodektēs, not that of anyone else of those who have been extolled for their profession and for this particular skill' (Μέμνηται δὲ ὧν πάσχει τὰ ζῷα, καὶ δεῖταί γε τέχνης τῆς ἐς τὴν μνήμην οὐ Σιμωνίδου, οὐχ Ἱππίου, οὐ Θεοδέκτου, οὐκ ἄλλου τινὸς τῶν ἐς τόδε τὸ ἐπάγγελμα καὶ τήνδε τὴν σοφίαν κεκηρυγμένων, 6.10, p. 134, line 29–p. 135, line 2). A similar claim is made in the preface to the story of Androklēs and the lion, where Aelian writes that memory is a particular quality of animals 'without the

---

[16] See also Smith 2014: 88–9.

[17] Aelian treats the memory of elephants also in 7.6, 8.16, 11.14, and 13.22. But this point emerges also in discussions of other animals: for instance, in pointed and explicit contrast with human beings, Egyptian Cats, Ichneumons, Crocodiles, and the Hawks 'when well-treated they are good at remembering kindness' (εὖ παθόντα ἀπομνησθῆναι τῆς εὐεργεσίας ἐστὶν ἀγαθά); 'they would never set upon their benefactors once they have been freed from their congenital and natural temper; Man however, a creature endowed with reason, credited with understanding, gifted with a sense of honour, supposed capable of blushing, can become the bitter enemy of a friend and for some trifling and casual reason blurt out confidences to betray the very man who trusted him' (*NA* 4.44).

artifice pertaining to it and the skill that some people who talk marvels boast to have invented' (χωρὶς τῆς ἐς αὐτὴν τέχνης τε καὶ σοφίας, ἣν τερατευόμενοί τινες ἐπινοῆσαι κομπάζουσι, 7.44, p. 188, lines 17–18). The mnemonic theories criticized by Aelian here were well known in antiquity, though we are today uncertain regarding the specifics of the theories of Theodektēs and Hippias. Simonides, however, is said to have theorized that memory could be stimulated by the mental conjuring of some actual or imagined edifice or geographical space. Such use of the imagination is perhaps what inspired Aelian to refer to the theorists of mnemonic systems as 'those who talk marvels' (τερατευόμενοι), likening Simonides and his ilk to archetypal fabricators like Odysseus, whom Lucian, using the same verb (ἐτερατεύσατο, VH 1.3), describes as having duped his Phaeacian audience with tales of his imaginary journeys.[18]

But Aelian's suspicion of artificial mnemonic systems was by no means unique in Severan Rome, as the Platonic debate surrounding memory[19] found renewed relevance in the sophistic milieu of the second and third centuries. Aelian's interest in memory is paralleled, for example, in the writings of his contemporary Philostratos. The theme recurs several times in the novelistic *Life of Apollonios of Tyana*, as when Philostratos eulogizes his subject's philosophical silence: Apollonios 'held his tongue, but his eyes and his mind read very many things and stored very many things in his memory. In fact when he was a hundred years old, the strength of his memory even surpassed that of Simonides. And he used to sing a hymn to Memory, in which he says that all things waste away because of time, but that time itself is ageless and immortal thanks to memory' (*VA* 1.14.1).[20] The praise of the natural memory of Apollonios of Tyana is to be contrasted with Philostratos' criticism of the art of memory espoused by the second-century sophist Dionysius of Miletus. Philostratos writes that 'arts of memory do not exist, nor would they exist, for memory gives us the arts, but memory itself is not taught and it cannot be grasped by any art, for it is a gift of nature or something that has been apportioned to the immortal soul. For things that come from human beings would not be considered immortal, nor would what we learn be considered to be taught, unless memory were dwelling within men' (*VS* 522.25–524.4). The argument seems to be based on the theory of *anamnēsis* described

---

[18] For ancient discussions of the importance of natural memory and its superiority over artificial memory, see Sassi's chapter in this volume.

[19] Pl. *Meno* 81c–d, *Hipp. Min.* 368d–369a. For discussions of memory in Plato and the Platonic tradition, see the chapters of Capra, Wygoda, King, Chiaradonna, Clark, and Sassi in this volume.

[20] Cf. Philostr. *VA* 3.16.4, 3.43; on time and memory see also the Introduction, above, pp. 5–8.

by Socrates in Plato's *Meno*: there the philosopher posits that no human knowledge is learned, but that the virtues and all knowledge reside always in the immortal soul, and that what we think of as learning is really the recollection of what the soul at one time forgot (86d–87c).[21] Philostratos modifies this idea and claims that memory, too, resides in the soul – it *must*, if knowledge and virtue are to be *remembered* – and his views reflect also those of Aelian. But whereas Philostratos projects idealized natural memory onto a quasi-fictitious philosophical hero from the past, Aelian projects idealized natural memory onto non-human animals that live in harmony with nature. Both authors also associate natural memory with the immortal, the transcendent, and the divine: this is explicit in the passage of Philostratos just quoted, but can also be gathered from Aelian's patchwork text in the way that he regularly writes of 'unspeakable nature' (φύσις τις ἀπόρρητος, *vel sim.*) with the language of religious awe.[22]

Aelian's engagement with this contemporary philosophical debate should be understood as informing his criticism of artificial mnemonic aids in all areas of human life, whether that criticism is explicit or merely implied. In one narrative, Aelian describes the strange harvesting of the plant known as the *kunospastos* or *aglaophōtis*: at night, the plant 'shines out and is distinguished like a star, for it is of a fiery nature and is like fire' (νύκτωρ δὲ ἐκφαίνεται καὶ διαπρέπει, ὡς ἀστήρ· φλογώδης γάρ ἐστι καὶ ἔοικε πυρί, 14.27, p. 352, lines 24–5). When men find the plant glowing at night, they place a marker (σημεῖόν τι, line 25), since they would be unable to remember (μνημονεῦσαι, line 27) either the colour or shape of the plant when they return by day. The plant is also deadly to pluck, so when they do return to the marker by day, they bring a dog that will pluck the plant for them. After the dog has done his fatal duty, 'they bury it on that very spot, and having performed certain mysterious rites and honouring the dog's corpse in the belief that it died on their behalf, they then dare to touch the aforementioned plant' (θάπτουσι δὲ ἐν αὐτῷ τῷ χώρῳ αὐτόν, καί τινας δράσαντες ἀπορρήτους ἱερουργίας καὶ τιμήσαντες τοῦ κυνὸς τὸν νεκρὸν ὡς ὑπὲρ αὐτῶν τεθνεῶτος εἶτα μέντοι προσάψασθαι τολμῶσι τοῦ φυτοῦ τοῦ προειρημένου, p. 353, lines 16–19). Nature provides the plant with its own distinguishing features (the mysterious nocturnal glow), but humans must employ artificial signs and symbols to mark out the plant for their own acquisitive needs. Granted, the plant is used for medicinal purposes,

---

[21] See Wygoda's chapter (above, pp. 200–9) for an in-depth discussion.

[22] *NA* 1.17, 34; 2.22, 48; 4.11, 24, 42; 5.1, 33, 49; 6.60; 8.9, 27; 9.36; 10.48; 11.7; 13.22; 15.1, 5, 17, 19; 16.34, 38; 17.15, 46; *Ep.* 430, line 20. Cf. D.L. 7.85–9.

such as curing epilepsy and improving human eyesight, but Aelian clearly presents the humans' harvest of the plant as a corrupting intervention and manipulation of the natural order. It is telling that Aelian describes the death of the dog as occurring at the moment 'when Hēlios sees the roots' (ἐπὰν δὲ ὁ ἥλιος ἴδῃ τὰς ῥίζας, line 15): the sun god is depicted as being angered at the destruction of a plant that shares his own fiery nature.[23] Furthermore, the 'mysterious rites' that accompany the burial of the dog reveal the religious anxiety of the humans who have harvested the plant, as they surely feel the need to expiate the angry spirit of their canine instrument.

Even human law is criticized by Aelian as something artificial of which animals have no need. In another narrative Aelian compares the respect shown by elephants toward their elders to the Spartan law established by Lykurgos, according to which young men regularly gave up their seats or stepped out of the way of their elders in the street. Aelian asks, 'How would the noble son of Eunomos [Lykourgos] be able to compete with the laws of nature? At any rate, o you Lykourgoi and Solons and Zaleukoi and Charondai, the race of elephants obey laws that you yourselves do not even begin to ordain' (ποῦ δὲ ὁ γενναῖος ὁ τοῦ Εὐνόμου δύναιτο ἂν τοῖς τῆς φύσεως νόμοις ἁμιλλᾶσθαί τε καὶ ἀντικρίνεσθαι; ἐπαΐουσι γοῦν τὸ τῶν ἐλεφάντων γένος, ὦ Λυκοῦργοί τε καὶ Σόλωνες καὶ Ζάλευκοι καὶ Χαρῶνδαι, ὧνπερ οὖν ὑμεῖς νομοθετεῖτε οὐδὲ τὴν ἀρχήν, 6.61, p. 157, line 27–p. 158, line 1). Elephants, in other words, endowed as they are with a superlative natural memory, are forever mindful of the respect due to their elders and have no need of artificial laws to remind them how to act.

Though he participates in the contemporary division between natural and artificial memory, and though he privileges the natural memory that animals enjoy, Aelian is also aware that the commemoration of such natural phenomena is achieved through the medium of literature. It is the written word that conveys to humans, across generations, the morality of animals that live in harmony with nature. The *NA* is not a call for the unmediated experience of nature; on the contrary, Aelian's book documents the experience of nature insofar as it is mediated through other books. Furthermore, Aelian's collection is self-consciously aware of its own *constructed* nature. Proudly disdaining any kind of organizational structure and vaunting the random ordering of its varied entries, this text continually employs a repetitive prose formula (ἀνωτέρω μνήμην ἐποιησάμην, *vel sim.*) to draw attention to the mnemonics of its own literary composition. In other

---

[23] On the religious significance of Helios in Aelian's collection, see Smith 2014: 125–7.

words, the reader continually witnesses the narrative voice recalling its own act of narration.

The text can even be quite playful in this regard. The entry on the deadly plant known as the *kunospastos* or *aglaophōtis*, for example, was anticipated earlier in the text: at the conclusion of a discussion of poison harvested from seaweed, Aelian writes that 'this poison is second to that called *aglaophōtis* on land. And they also give it the name *kunospastos*. And what the reason is, if I remember to tell you, you will learn' (δεύτερον καὶ κακὸν τοῦτο τῆς καλουμένης χερσαίας ἀγλαοφώτιδος. ὄνομα δὲ αὐτῇ ἄρα ἔθεντο καὶ κυνόσπαστον· καὶ τίς ἡ αἰτία, ἐὰν ὑπομνησθῶ εἰπεῖν, εἴσεσθε αὐτήν, 14.24, p. 348, lines 1–4). Three entries later, Aelian makes good on his promise and explains the strange rite of harvesting the *kunospastos*, writing 'for I wish to fulfill my obligation, since I have remembered' (βούλομαι γὰρ ἐκτῖσαι χρέος ὑπομνησθείς, 14.27, p. 352, line 22). This textual marking of course corresponds with the content of the narrative itself, in which humans must employ markers to designate the location of the plant that glows at night but is indistinguishable by day. Aelian tells us that he has remembered his intention to describe the harvest of the *kunospastos*, but we are left to wonder whether he remembered to do so unprompted (like the elephant), or whether he remembered because he was reminded by the marker that he had placed in his own text. For as much as Aelian privileges the natural memory of animals, he does not hesitate to remind his readers that his own book was inextricably created within a human, artificial system of signification.

By way of conclusion, I would like to consider briefly Aelian's interest in memory not just within the context of contemporary philosophical or literary trends, but within the context of contemporary political events. I concede that this move is somewhat speculative, as there is hardly anything in Aelian's text that explicitly addresses the political landscape of Severan Rome. This silence in the *NA* should not, however, be taken as an indication that Aelian was not interested in or could not reflect upon the political climate of the day. In fact, in the *Lives of the Sophists*, Philostratos informs us that Aelian composed an outspoken invective against the recently assassinated emperor Elagabalus; Aelian therefore clearly felt comfortable voicing political sentiments – so long as the moment was right and so long as he felt safe doing so.[24] Moreover, the morally critical tone of much of the *NA* indicates a general dissatisfaction with the culture of

---

[24] On the political diatribe, see Smith 2014: 21–2, 274–9.

Rome under the Severans. Aelian's remarks in the epilogue of the *NA* are worth considering. He writes:

οὐκ ἀγνοῶ δὲ ἄρα ὅτι καὶ τῶν εἰς χρήματα ὁρώντων ὀξὺ καὶ τεθηγμένων ἐς τιμάς τε καὶ δυνάμεις τινὲς καὶ πᾶν τὸ φιλόδοξον δι᾽ αἰτίας ἕξουσιν, εἰ τὴν ἐμαυτοῦ σχολὴν κατεθέμην καὶ εἰς ταῦτα, ἐξὸν καὶ ὠφρυῶσθαι καὶ ἐν ταῖς αὐλαῖς ἐξετάζεσθαι καὶ ἐπὶ μέγα προήκειν πλούτου. (*NA* epilogue 430.8–12)

And I am not unaware indeed that even of those who have a sharp eye for money and who have been whetted for honours and influence and every ambition, some will find fault if I set aside my free time even for these things [the study of animals], when it is possible to raise my brow in arrogance and to appear in palaces and to come into great wealth.

These statements reveal a self-representation starkly at odds with the world around him, and we might therefore profit from considering the ways in which the *NA* was informed, at least in part, as a response to the turbulence and the violent political transformations of Rome in the first quarter of the third century.

Once we contextualize the *NA* within the sophistic culture of Severan Rome in this way, Aelian's valorization of the natural memory of animals and his criticism of human reliance on artificial mnemonic aids becomes newly relevant. I have in mind, of course, the practice known today as *damnatio memoriae*, rampant under the Severans, whereby the images and name of a deceased political rival were expunged from the visual record of the city and of the empire: statues were toppled, portrait busts radically reworked, names and faces chiselled away from public monuments. One thinks immediately of the systematic erasure of the visual depictions of Geta that was imposed by Caracalla after his brother's murder in 211 AD. Dio Cassius provides the literary evidence that complements the absence of Geta from monuments across the empire: Caracalla 'exhibited his hatred for his dead brother by abolishing the observance of his birthday, and he vented his anger upon the stones that had supported his statues, and melted down the coinage that displayed his features. And not content with even this, he now more than ever practised unholy rites, and would force others to share his pollution, by making a kind of annual offering to his brother's Manes'[25] (78.12.6). But Caracalla's attempt to negate the existence of his dead brother was only the most elaborate example of *damnatio memoriae* that Aelian witnessed in the 42-year reign of the Severi. Eric

---

[25] Loeb translation by Earnest Carey.

Varner reminds us that during these four decades, '*damnationes memoriae* were enacted against numerous members of the imperial family as well as rival emperors. Didius Julianus, Pescennius Niger, Clodius Albinus, Plautianus, Plautilla, Geta, Macrinus, Diadumenius, Elagabalus, and Julia Soaemias all suffered some form of official sanctions after their deaths'.[26]

Caracalla's *damnatio memoriae* of Geta nevertheless stands out, since this was brother against brother, a rupture within the imperial family that evoked the fratricidal mythology at the heart of Rome's legendary past. And indeed there are two important narratives of fraternal enmity and fratricide in Aelian's *NA*. In one very elaborate narrative about the remarkable relationship between the Macedonian boy Pindos and a giant snake, Pindos is brutally murdered by his hateful brothers, but his death is avenged by the sudden appearance of the friendly snake. Aelian concludes the story with an etiological notice that Pindos 'was given a lavish burial and the river adjacent to the murder was called Pindos from the dead man and his tomb' (ἐτάφη μεγαλοπρεπῶς καὶ ὁ γείτων τῷ φόνῳ ποταμὸς ἐκλήθη Πίνδος ἐκ τοῦ νεκροῦ καὶ τοῦ κατ' αὐτὸν τάφου, 10.48, p. 256, lines 8–10). Aelian thus combines the themes of fratricide and human commemoration, and contemporary readers might reasonably be motivated to think about the violence committed by Caracalla against the memory of Geta. Unlike Pindos, however, Geta would have no quasi-divine animal avenger, and his memory would live on in artistic monuments only by negation.

In another passage, Aelian tells a story from India about a boy who accompanied his parents into exile because of the hatred of his older brothers. When the parents die as a result of the arduous journey, the good son buries their bodies in his head; the god Helios witnesses the boy's surreal act of piety and transforms him into the hoopoe, placing a crest atop the bird's head, 'as if this was a commemoration of the things that had been done when he was in exile' (οἱονεὶ μνημεῖον τοῦτο τῶν πεπραγμένων ὅτε ἔφυγεν, 16.5, p. 381, line 16). Aelian's readers would doubtless recall the violent myth of Tereus, but this competing, alternative narrative introduces into the aetiology for the hoopoe themes newly relevant for a Severan audience. Not only does Aelian's story combine fraternal enmity with the theme of commemoration, but the involvement of the god Helios and the eastern setting suggest also the connection between Julia Domna's family and the solar cult of Elagabal at Emesa.[27] I do not suggest that we read

---

[26] Varner 2004: 156.
[27] Levick 2007: 15–17. On allusions to the solar cult in Severan literature, see Morgan 2009.

these narratives allegorically. I do suggest, however, that these narratives about hatred between brothers and about the memorialization of *pietas* would have resonated with Aelian's reading public in the years following Geta's murder and *damnatio memoriae*.

But though Caracalla attempted to wipe out the memory of his brother, we may find in the pages of the *NA* yet one more vague memory of Geta. If the evidence of Spartianus in the fourth century *Historia Augusta* is to be trusted,[28] we know that Geta was fond of asking the *grammatici* to describe the voices of different animals; thus, for example, 'the lamb bleats, the pig squeals, the dove coos, the hog grunts, the bear growls, the lion roars, the leopard snarls, the elephant trumpets, the frog croaks, the horse neighs, the ass brays, the bull bellows; and in proof he would cite the ancient writers'[29] (*agni balant, porcelli grunniunt, palumbes minurriunt, porci grunniunt, ursi saeuiunt, leones rugiunt, leopardi rictant, elephanti barriunt, ranae coaxant, equi hinniunt, asini rudunt, tauri mugiunt, easque de ueteribus adprobare, HA Geta 5.5*). This is exactly the kind of philological-zoological exercise that excited Aelian, who would have been just the sort of *grammaticus* to satisfy the inquisitive Geta. In the *NA*, Aelian writes: 'Nature made animals most varied in voice and sound, so you might say, just as humans ... for one roars, another moos, and whinnying belongs to another, and braying and bleating belong to another, and to some howling is dear, and to another snarling. And grunts, whistles, gnashing, singing, melody, lisping, and countless other gifts of nature are the distinct qualities of animals, some belonging to some, and others belonging to others' (Πολυφωνότατα δὲ τὰ ζῷα καὶ πολύφθογγα ὡς ἂν εἴποις ἡ φύσις ἀπέφηνεν, ὥσπερ οὖν καὶ τοὺς ἀνθρώπους ... τὸ μὲν γὰρ βρυχᾶται, μυκᾶται δὲ ἄλλο, καὶ χρεμέτισμα ἄλλου καὶ ὄγκησις ἄλλου βληχηθμός τε καὶ μηκασμός, καί τισι μὲν ὠρυγμός, τισὶ δὲ ὑλαγμὸς φίλον, καὶ ἄλλῳ ἀρράζειν· κλαγγαὶ δὲ καὶ ῥοῖζοι καὶ κριγμοὶ καὶ ᾠδαὶ καὶ μελῳδίαι καὶ τραυλισμοὶ καὶ μυρία ἕτερα δῶρα τῆς φύσεως ἴδια τῶν ζῴων ἄλλα ἄλλων, 5.51). Was Aelian acquainted with the young Geta? It is impossible to know for certain, but given Aelian's prominence among the community of sophists at Rome it is not out of the question. Alternatively, the author of the *Historia Augusta* has fabricated the story completely. But the fiction remains interesting because it invites learned readers to speculate about Geta's intellectual circle and even draws such readers back to Aelian's text, reminding them that a collection of apparently benign animal narratives may in fact suggest

[28] On the problem of the *Historia Augusta*, see Barnes 1978.
[29] Loeb translation by David Magie.

direct engagement with the imperial court. If Aelian's passage does preserve a memory of Geta's intellectual curiosity, it is eloquent testimony of literature's slippery ability to escape the violent reach of Caracalla. The tutors and personal attendants of the young emperors were not always safe: Dio Cassius tells of Caracalla's eagerness to murder his *tropheis* Euodos and Kilo.[30]

Even if the above interpretations are only speculative, they at least indicate that Aelian's narratives about animal memory may be read as part of broader trends within public and intellectual life at Rome in the early third century. Like others of his time, Aelian idealized the natural memory of animals, while seeing human reliance on artificial forms of memory as yet one more indication of our inability to live in harmony with nature. At the same time, however, Aelian's text is self-consciously aware that it is itself a product of human art and could not therefore be more distant from the idealized world of nature that it seeks to depict. And this, I think, partially explains the form of the text: a disjointed collection of randomly arranged short passages. There was of course a long tradition of literary *poikilia* that preceded Aelian and to which his own collection was responding in complex ways. This apparent randomness is an integral part of the collection's aesthetic, simultaneously delighting and challenging readers. Rejecting any overarching, grand narrative of the natural world, the *NA* offers a sober meditation on cultural memory as fragmented, partial, and vulnerable to manipulation. Through his own sophisticated Hellenism, Aelian responds to the fraught atmosphere of Severan Rome, when public intellectuals and the imperial court were both laying claim to memory itself or, more properly, to the power to control the past.

---

[30] D.C. 77.6, 78.1, 4.

CHAPTER 14

Plotinus on Memory, Recollection and Discursive Thought

Riccardo Chiaradonna

De natura Rationis est res sub quadam æternitatis specie percipere.
Spinoza, *Ethica*, Pars II, Prop. 44, Corollarium II

For the ancient Platonists memory has a crucial position in the account of knowledge. This of course depends on the association of memory with what Plato had called *anamnēsis*, i.e. the recollection of real beings.[1] For example Alcinous (ca. second century AD) holds that 'natural conceptions', i.e. inborn memories of the Ideas, are stored in our souls and these memories should be properly awakened in order to attain genuine knowledge (Alc., *Did.* 4.155.27–34; 156.19–23; 5.158.4).[2] In this chapter I aim to show that Plotinus develops these ideas in a highly distinctive way against the background of his account of the higher soul as something that involves direct acquaintance with intelligible Forms. As a matter of fact Plotinus has a lot to say on memory; but it is extremely difficult to outline his 'theory of memory'.[3] One reason for this is that his most extensive treatment of the topic, which takes up more than ten chapters in treatises 4.3 [27] and 4.4 [28] according to Ficino's *diuisio textus*, does not focus on memory as such; rather, Plotinus aims to enquire into 'what it is that remembers' (4.3.25.6: τί ποτε τὸ μνημονεῦόν ἐστι),[4] which is to say: in what kind of realities memory naturally exists (25.9–10). Plotinus' research, then,

---

[1] For an introduction to Platonic recollection, with further references, see the Introduction of this volume (especially section 6) and Capra's chapter.

[2] Helmig 2012: 147–54 and 282–6 provides an updated discussion of these and other parallel passages.

[3] On Plotinus' views on memory, see Warren 1965; Blumenthal 1971: 80–99; Guidelli 1988. A number of recent studies have been devoted to this topic: Brisson 2006; D'Ancona 2007; Remes 2007: 111–19; Chiaradonna 2009; Taormina 2011; Hutchinson 2011; Nikulin 2014. King 2009 provides certainly the most accurate discussion of Plotinus' theory of memory and recollection. On the key role of forgetting in Plotinus, see Clark's chapter in this volume.

[4] For the translations, see Armstrong 1984 (with slight alterations). The text is that of Henry and Schwyzer's *editio minor* in the OCT series. A translation with detailed commentary of these treatises is given by Dillon and Blumenthal 2015.

focuses on the soul, since he regards this as the subject of memory.[5] This view has crucial consequences for Plotinus' treatment of memory, which is intertwined with a set of further questions, both metaphysical (the relation between the soul's nature, its embodied existence and its vicissitudes after leaving the physical body) and epistemological (the distinction between the different cognitive powers of the soul, from sense-perception to non-discursive thought). Plotinus' numerous remarks on memory should in no way be isolated from this wider background. Plotinus' subsequent and briefer discussion in treatise 4.6 [41] is explicitly devoted to memory and yet, once again, it is the ontological and cognitive status of the soul as such that comes to the forefront (see 4.6.3.5–19).

Plotinus' inquiry into 'what it is that remembers' in 4.3 and 4.4 is part of his extensive discussion on the nature of the soul and the difficult questions this raises (Περὶ ψυχῆς ἀποριῶν: 4.3 [27]; 4.4 [28]; 4.5 [29]). More specifically, Plotinus aims to answer the question of whether and to what degree souls have the power to remember things after leaving 'these regions' (4.3.25.1–2), i.e. their embodied lives. In order to carry out this investigation, Plotinus addresses the question of 'what it is that has the natural capacity of remembering' (4.3.25.9–10). Plotinus claims that he has focused elsewhere on 'what memory is', so that this question can now be left aside (25.8–9). Actually, this is an obscure allusion to say the least, since no extensive treatment of memory as such can be found in Plotinus' previous treatises (arguably, in fact, no such discussion is featured in the *Enneads*). I will not go into this question, however, and I will limit myself to examining the structure of the first chapter of this section (4.3.25): here we find the basic distinctions Plotinus draws with regard to memory and its cognitive power.

When starting his discussion on 'what it is that remembers', Plotinus shows great care in dealing with what it is that does *not* remember, i.e. with those realities whose thought-activity is incompatible with memory. Why? I will propose a tentative answer at the end of this paper. Let me first paraphrase Plotinus' rather surprising argument; I will then provide a more systematic outline of it and, after a number of supplementary remarks, I will try to give an answer to the question I have just raised.

---

[5] As King 2009: 141 and 235 shows, this is Plotinus' major point of disagreement with Aristotle, who regards the concrete living being as the subject of memory. According to Plotinus, memory belongs to the soul alone, unlike perception. However, memory does not belong to each kind of soul: souls of the heavenly bodies and the world soul have no memory (see 4.4.12 with Brisson 2006: 25–6). Plotinus' discussion of memory is actually limited to human souls.

Memory is first presented as something whose object is acquired: it is either learnt or experienced (4.3.25.11: ἐπικτήτου τινὸς ἢ μαθήματος ἢ παθήματος). Accordingly, memory does not belong to those realities that are unaffected (τοῖς ἀπαθέσι) and outside time.[6] Consequently, Plotinus points out that God, Being and Intellect are not connected to memory (also, see 4.4.1.11–14; 4.4.2.1–8; 4.4.15.2). Basically what Plotinus offers here is a sketchy account of intelligible Being.[7] Nothing external comes to it (see 25.14: οὐδὲν γὰρ εἰς αὐτούς) and its structure does not admit any change. Accordingly, memory does not belong to the Intellect, since it was stated before that memory requires 'something acquired' and is intrinsically connected to time (see 5.9 [5] 8.15–18 and 5.3 [49] 5.31–9: the Intellect shares the same activity with the intelligible Forms; so Forms are not acquired thought-contents). As Plotinus remarks, it cannot even be said that the Intellect remembers its own thoughts, 'for they did not come in such a way that it has to hold them fast to prevent them from going away' (25.25–6). When moving on to the soul, Plotinus first argues that in the same sense (25.28: τὸν αὐτὸν τρόπον: he is referring to the above-specified notion of memory as something connected with an acquired object and with time) not even the soul remembers those things which it possesses as part of its nature, 'but when it is here below it possesses them and does not act by them' (25.29–30). Finally, Plotinus remarks that the 'ancients' seem to apply the terms 'memory' and 'recollection' to a certain activity of souls 'which brings into act what they possessed' (25.31–2). This, i.e. recollection, as Plotinus concludes, is a 'different kind of memory and therefore time is not involved in memory understood in this sense' (25.33–4). But from what is this kind of memory different? Arguably, from the kind of memory which was mentioned in the previous lines and entails both an acquired object and time.[8] Plotinus then stops and remarks 'but perhaps we are being too easy-going about this and not really examining it critically' (25.34–5). Although Ficino's *diuisio textus* does not mark this as a break, it would not be inappropriate to end chapter 25 at line 34, i.e. just before this remark (Ἀλλ' ἴσως), which announces the start of Plotinus' proper treatment of the issue of the subject of memory.[9] Indeed, after a

[6] At 4.3.25.12 οὔτε τοῖς ἐν χρόνῳ ἐγγίνοιτο (MSS) cannot make sense: H.-S. accept Kirchhoff's insertion of μὴ before ἐν χρόνῳ. See Dillon and Blumenthal 2015: 284–5. As Dillon and Blumenthal 2015: 284 rightly explain: 'The point is that, if memories are of something acquired from the outside, or something that has happened, they can only belong to things that exist in a temporal framework, since there must have been a time before the acquisition of the happening.'
[7] See Emilsson 2007.
[8] Nikulin 2014: 196 outlines a different interpretation.
[9] This transition is rightly emphasized in Dillon and Blumenthal 2015: 289.

series of aporetic remarks, Plotinus restates the topic of his inquiry ('So we must enquire what is of the things within us that possesses memory, which is just what we were enquiring at the beginning': 25.39–41). He then moves on to deal with this topic in the following chapter (26 in Ficino's *diuisio textus*).

Plotinus' argument is structured as follows:

A) Plotinus announces the topic he is going to focus on ('what it is that remembers').

B) He provides a summary outline of memory (M1) without defining it in any detail; he only specifies one of its characterizing aspects, namely that memory concerns an acquired object, an object either learnt or experienced. We would then expect Plotinus to immediately explain the nature of that reality whose cognitive power is connected with learning or experiencing and which, accordingly, can be regarded as the proper subject of memory. As previously noted, however, Plotinus adopts a different strategy, since he first explains what it is that does not remember, i.e. what it is that cannot be connected with M1. Memory does not in fact belong to what has no affection and is outside time. What follows, then, is a detour which includes the following points. Plotinus focuses on:

Ci) The non-discursive Intellect, which is not receptive of its objects of thought and does not admit any temporal change;

Cii) The soul, which does not remember (in the above specified sense of M1, which entails both an acquired object and time) those things which it possesses as part of its nature (συμφύτων). Plotinus, however, argues (i) that the soul in its physical existence (ἐνταῦθα) is not active according to those things, even if it possesses them latently; (ii) that the soul can recover conscious knowledge of those things.

D) Accordingly, Plotinus admits another type of memory (M2, i.e. a type of memory different from M1), which (a) does not require an acquired object (since M2 concerns those things which the soul already possesses as part of its nature) and (b) does not entail time. I will discuss later why M2 does not entail time. For the time being, it may provisionally be assumed that according to M2 the soul does not need to *first* acquire what it *then* remembers. Accordingly, this kind of memory does not entail time, or at least does not entail time in the way in which time is entailed by M1.

According to M2, souls 'bring into act what they possessed' (but never acquired). M2 guarantees that those things which the soul does not need to acquire, since they are part of its nature, emerge from a latent, uncon-scious condition (which depends on the soul having arrived ἐνταῦθα, i.e. in the bodily world), so that the soul can 'act by them' (ἐνεργεῖν κατ' αὐτά).[10] In Plotinus' view, M2 is identical with what the ancients called 'memory' or 'recollection'; arguably, then, M2 is identical with Plotinus' reading of Plato's recollection.

E) Until now, Plotinus has not spent a single word on 'what it is that remembers'. He makes a break here and starts afresh discussing this issue which he had announced in A).[11]

Chapter 26 provides a detailed treatment of the soul as 'that which remembers'. Plotinus explains that memory (M1) is connected to (but not identical with or strictly dependent on) perception. Now, according to Plotinus perception cannot be identified with a bodily affection. Rather, perception entails a spontaneous judgement (κρίσις) which the soul (an incorporeal and self-subsisting substance incapable of being affected by bodies) makes in correspondence to the affections received by the sense-organs of the living ensouled body (see 3.6.1.1–2; 4.4.23.36–42).[12] The details of Plotinus' theory of perception are complex to say the least, but they need not concern us here (in particular, it is difficult to get a clear idea of the status of Plotinus' perceptual judgements).[13] Suffice it to recall some general features of this theory. According to Plotinus, neither perception nor memory entail any physical or quasi-physical alteration of the soul which perceives and remembers: accordingly, there is no physical impres-sion of the perceived qualities in the soul and Plotinus consistently rejects the theory according to which sense-perceptions are impressions or seal-stamps on the soul. Memory, then, cannot be conceived of as the retention (κατοχή) of any such quasi-physical impressions (τυπώσεις: 4.6.1.1–4).[14] Each cognitive activity of the soul, starting from perception, is instead regarded by Plotinus as a spontaneous thought-activity, which is based on *a priori* capacities of the soul (and possibly *a priori* contents too, although this is never completely made clear in the texts about perception: but see

[10] On Plotinus' use of ἐνεργεῖν in this passage, see Chiaradonna 2015.
[11] King 2009: 139–46 outlines clearly the distinction between M1 and M2; also, see Nikulin 2014: 193.
[12] This issue is further developed in Clark's chapter in this volume (especially pp. 327–8).
[13] See the standard discussion by Emilsson 1988. Further developments and criticism of Emilsson in Lavaud 2006; Remes 2007: 145 and Magrin 2010. See also Chiaradonna 2012.
[14] Note, however, that in 4.3.29.24 Plotinus claims that memory *is* retention or κατοχή, and this seems to contradict what he says 4.6.1.3, i.e. that memories are not retentions. On this, see Taormina 2011 and Nikulin 2014: 191. On the role of impressions and imprints in Plato and Aristotle, see Castagnoli's chapter in this volume.

4.6.3.18–19). As for memory, in 4.6.3 Plotinus argues that it cannot merely consist of the passive capacity of storing past perceptions; rather, memory involves an active power of the soul, which 'makes the objects of sense, which are, so to speak, connected with it, shine out by its own power and brings them before its eyes' (4.6.3.16–18). Obviously these views entail the rejection of materialist analogies like that of the wax block (4.6.1.19–21; 4.3.26.29–32).

Plotinus' views can interestingly be compared to those of Aristotle, who claims that the objects of our knowledge are only incidentally remembered, since memory belongs to the same part of the soul as 'representation' (*phantasia*), so that all things which are representational are essentially objects of memory, while those (such as thought-objects) which necessarily involve representation (without being themselves representational) are objects of memory only incidentally (*Mem.* 450a22–5; 451a28–9). Like Aristotle, Plotinus connects memory with *phantasia* or *to phantastikon*, i.e. with the faculty of representation (4.3.29.31–2).[15] However, in 4.3.29 and 30 Plotinus raises a further question, which hardly fits Aristotle's conceptual framework: since we have memory of thoughts as well, what is it that remembers thoughts? Plotinus argues from the very beginning of his enquiry that memory can be 'of what has been learnt'. He also points out that it is not only what has been perceived that can be remembered: for example, the soul must have memory of its own movements, of what it desired, even if it did not enjoy these desired objects and these objects did not enter the body (4.3.26.34–6).

It is difficult to interpret Aristotle's view that we do not properly remember thought-contents. I would rely here on the reading proposed by Castagnoli, who draws the following distinction.[16] According to Aristotle, one can only *know* – for instance – what a triangle is or what the theorem of Pythagoras is and how to demonstrate it. Such things, however, cannot properly be *remembered*, unless we use 'remembering' in a secondary ('incidental') sense, according to which we can remember abstract thought-contents, only in that we remember events or objects of our past experiences which are related to them (e.g. we can remember

---

[15] See, along these lines, King 2009: 176 n. 749. King 2009: 4–13 and *passim* suggests that *phantasia* should be translated with 'representation' (rather than 'imagination'). A *phantasia* is 'what remains when perception is over and requires a preceding perception to exist' (King 2009: 5). As he argues, Aristotle and Plotinus regard *phantasia* as a propositional and, thus, conceptual capacity, which cannot (merely) be equated with the preservation of images or pictures in the soul (on Plotinus, see King, 2009: 183). As King himself recognizes, however, sometimes Plotinus comes very close to suggesting that representation is a kind of image of the thought: see 4.3.30.3–4.

[16] See Castagnoli 2006b. This proposal is expanded in Castagnoli's chapter in this volume, pp. 248–55.

episodes in which we thought of that theorem; or we may remember the diagrams drawn on those occasions). Unlike Aristotle, Plotinus is quite happy to apply both M1 and M2 to thought-contents: through M1 we can remember thought-contents we previously learnt (4.3.25.11); through M2 we can remember thought-contents that are latently connatural to our soul (25.29–33). The difference between Plotinus and Aristotle can be explained in several ways:

1) Plotinus is not aware of Aristotle's technicalities and simply uses the verb 'to remember' in its ordinary sense which corresponds to Aristotle's 'incidental' sense.

2) Plotinus is a Platonic philosopher and an exegete of Plato: accordingly, he cannot but assume as a starting point Plato's well-known thesis in the *Meno* (81d), according to which 'searching and learning are, as a whole, recollection'.[17]

3) There is a particular sense in which thought-contents can be remembered according to Plotinus and this fact marks his difference from Aristotle.

In my view, explanation 1) is simply false, because Plotinus alludes to Aristotle's view (in the free manner that is usual of him) at the beginning of 4.3.30. Explanation 2) is not implausible in itself, since Plotinus presents M2 as his own version of what the ancients (presumably Plato) had called ἀνάμνησις (4.3.25.33);[18] and besides, it is well known that Plotinus never claimed to be original, and presented his own philosophy as an exegesis of Plato (4.8 [6] 1.23–8; 5.1 [10] 8.10–14). Still, explanation 2) is not enough in itself, unless we get a clear idea of how Plotinus tries to make sense of Plato's view (indeed, Plotinus' way of making sense of Plato's authoritative views can be remarkably different from what we actually find in Plato: among several possible examples, I would refer here to Plotinus' highly original interpretation of the μέγιστα γένη of the *Sophist* in 6.2, or to his interpretation of the Demiurge described in the *Timaeus* in 6.7.1–2). To claim that Plotinus adopted a given view merely because he was a Platonist and that a similar view can be found in Plato is, in my opinion, unsatisfactory.[19] As I see it, explanation 3) is correct, and furthermore reveals some interesting features of Plotinus' theory of knowledge.

---

[17] Note that Plotinus' use of *anakinein* in passages such as 4.4.5.23 and 6.6 [34] 4.23 is reminiscent of Plato, *Meno* 85c, where the notions (*doxai*) of the slave boy are said to have been 'activated' (*anakekinēntai*) by the dialectic.

[18] See King, 2009: 117 n. 506; 145.

[19] On the difference between Plato's and Plotinus' views on recollection, see Chiaradonna 2009.

Let me quote the first lines of 4.3.30:

> But what is it that remembers thoughts? Does the power of representation remember these too [i.e.: does τὸ φανταστικόν, which is in charge of preserving perceptions in memory, also grant that thoughts be remembered?]. But if [εἰ μέν] a representation accompanies every intellectual act, perhaps if this image remains, being a kind of picture of the thought, in this way there would be memory of what was known; but if not [εἰ δὲ μή], we must look for some other explanation. (4.3.30.1–5)

As the sequence of εἰ μέν ... εἰ δέ ... makes clear, two alternative hypotheses are brought into discussion, in order to explain how representation can grant that thoughts be remembered. The first hypothesis is obviously reminiscent of Aristotle's view about the relation between thoughts and representation.[20] Indeed, Plotinus' words 'if a representation accompanies every intellectual act' can be seen as a loose paraphrase of Aristotle's well-known view that while thoughts are not φαντάσματα, they do not occur without (οὐκ ἄνευ) φαντάσματα (*An.* 3.8.432a14). Plotinus' hypothesis introduced by εἰ μέν is at least very closely related to Aristotle's view in the treatise *De memoria et reminiscentia*: if representation accompanies (παρακολουθεῖ) every thought-act (without being identical with it), then we may have memory of those representational contents which are connected with abstract thoughts and can be regarded as a sort of 'picture' (4.3.30.3–4: οἷον εἰκόνος οὔσης τῆς διανοήματος) of them. In other words, we may have memory of thoughts since we have memory of the representational contents that accompany thoughts. Plotinus does not reject this hypothesis. Possibly he regards the Aristotelian view as apt to explain how we can (at least incidentally) remember thought-contents we previously learnt in our embodied life (i.e. acquired thought-contents that cannot occur without representations).[21] However this account cannot explain

---

[20] See King 2009: 181 and Hutchinson 2011: 266.

[21] It is doubtful whether Plotinus would have claimed that we have thought-contents acquired from perception through an Aristotelianizing process of abstraction. He rather suggests that our soul has in itself everything (*ta panta*) as if written in it (see 5.3 [49] 4.21–2 and 4.6.3.1–8: the soul is *logos pantōn*). If this is the case, even the production of concepts derived from experience actually entails the activation of formal *a priori* contents. On this, see Chiaradonna 2012. Yet it can still be argued that the *a priori* contents involved in discursive and temporal thought (i.e. what Plotinus calls the imprints or traces of the intelligible Forms in us: 5.3.2.7–13) are different from the *a priori* contents involved in M2 (i.e. our direct and connatural thoughts of the Forms – not of their discursive *imprints* in us). From this perspective, the connection with *phantasia* can be seen as different too. In 4.3.30.3–4 Plotinus suggests that a representation actually accompanies lower discursive intellectual acts. This does not hold true of our higher and ordinarily unconscious thoughts. That said, a certain tension seems to subsist between Plotinus' account of acquired thoughts in 4.3.25 and 30 and his innatism about discursive thought-contents stated elsewhere (5.3.2–3).

all memories of thoughts, since, as the second hypothesis makes clear (εἰ δὲ μή), there are some thought-contents which representation does not accompany and which our souls are nonetheless able to remember. If this is true, 'we must look for some other explanation'.

Some supplementary remarks are necessary. It is somewhat misleading to distinguish between 'thought-activities' and 'thought-contents' in Plotinus' philosophy, because all proper thought-contents are conceived by Plotinus as essentially connected to a corresponding thought-activity. I did not say 'because all thought-contents *depend* on a corresponding thought-activity', since this would entail a psychologizing notion of thought-contents as the result of an independent thought-activity. Plotinus rejects this position with regard to the divine non-discursive Intellect at 5.9.7–8: his view is rather that of a necessary mutual entailment between thought-activity and thought-content. Plotinus famously conceives of archetypal Forms (i.e. the highest possible type of being and reality, since the One is situated beyond being) as the thought-contents of the divine Intellect and, at the same time, as the aspects that are constitutive of the essence of the divine Intellect. Thought-activity and thought-content coincide in the Intellect which, accordingly, does not acquire its thought-objects from something else: rather, its thought-objects and its thought-activities (i.e., its very essence) are one and the same thing (see 5.5 [32] 1–2). Plotinus' metaphysical hierarchy consists of several levels. The One is the principle of being and thought, without being itself being and thought. At the level of the divine Intellect, Forms are perfectly unified aspects through which the internal plurality of the Intellect is structured; this perfect unification of plurality is Plotinus' highest type of being and thought. As we proceed downwards in the metaphysical hierarchy, we encounter increasingly lower, less unified levels of Forms which correspond to lower, more 'unfolded' and less unified levels of thought; the lower levels are images or (obviously non-corporeal) imprints (see 5.3.2.9–11) deriving from the higher ones. The characteristic property of the soul lies in the fact that it displays a kind of thought which entails a succession of contents and a temporal structure (see 3.7 [45] .11). This kind of activity is a 'diminution' of the Intellect (4.3.18.4) and is what Plotinus calls διάνοια, discursive thought (see 5.1.7.42, where the soul is referred to as τὸ διανοούμενον). In Intellect, Forms are 'all together', whereas in soul they are 'unfolded and separated' (1.1 [53] 8.6–8).[22] Although the details of Plotinus' view remain very difficult to pin down (and differences subsist between the thought-activity of

---

[22] Further details in Emilsson 1988: 134 and Hutchinson 2011: 270–1.

the different levels of the soul),[23] it is safe to assume that the soul receives images of the archetypal Forms from the Intellect and that such images are the objects of the successive and temporal thought-activity of the soul. The soul, then, is intrinsically 'ectype', since it is receptive of thought-contents that derive from a higher hypostasis. This holds for all levels of the soul (the hypostasis soul, the world soul and our individual, embodied soul); in addition, our embodied soul is 'doubly ectype', since it is receptive both of the imprints of the Forms which stem from the Intellect and of the contents which derive from sense-perception (5.3.2.7–11; 3.36–40). What we find in our physical world are even lower, non-essential images of the soul's Forms in matter, which derive from the soul via the activity of the spermatic *logoi* (6.3.15.24–38). This sketchy general account not only applies to Plotinus' macrocosmos, but also to his view of human nature. According to Plotinus 'we' are structured according to the same pattern which can be found at the level of the macrocosmos.[24] A key aspect of this view is that 'a part' of us never leaves the level of the transcendent Intellect. Even if we are not ordinarily conscious of this fact, 'something in us' (i.e. the highest part of our soul or its noetic counterpart) always remains at the level of the Intellect and shares its non-discursive, archetypal thought-activity. Hence we are never really cut off from the *nous* (see 1.4.10; 5.1.11– 12; 5.3.4.1–5; 6.4.14.16–22). Our ordinary thought-activity is situated at the level of discursive thought, which entails a temporal succession and is directed towards external objects. Furthermore, we have a body and this shares the non-essential mode of existence that characterizes the physical world. Still, as Plotinus emphatically claims in 4.8.8.1–4, 'even our soul does not altogether come down, but there is always something of it in the intelligible'. Ordinarily we are not aware of the activity of this undescended part of us.[25] In everyday life, our thought proceeds discursively and is directed towards external objects (see 5.3.2–3). This, however, is not an unavoidable condition: we can in fact become aware of the highest thought-activity, which is connatural to our soul, even if this escapes our ordinary conscious reasoning. How is this possible? Plotinus' answer in 4.3 is: thanks to a peculiar kind of memory, namely M2. M2, i.e. Plotinus'

---

[23] In particular, Plotinus conceives of the world soul's discursive thought as successive and temporal, but not as an inferential reasoning. See on this Emilsson 2007: 183. On levels or 'parts' of the Soul in Plotinus, see Karfík 2014.

[24] Plotinus famously claims that the three highest principles are present 'in ourselves' (παρ' ἡμῖν: 5.1.10.5–6 and 12.1–5).

[25] Plotinus' theory of the undescended soul has been the focus of much research; it is sufficient here to mention the recent contribution by Tornau 2009 (with further references). An excellent overview is given by Emilsson 2017: 269–95.

version of Plato's recollection, brings into act those connatural activities
of the soul, which we are ordinarily not aware of. It is through M2 (i.e.
through the memory of our connatural and ordinarily latent thoughts)
that 'the recovery of the *noetic* self begins'.[26]

Possibly representation accompanies all those thought-contents which
have been discursively learnt by our embodied soul.[27] But thoughts which
are connatural to our soul since they belong to its higher, non-discursive
and ordinarily unconscious activity are in all likelihood not accompanied
by representational contents in themselves. Plotinus actually claims that
thought of the intelligibles is as such without images or representational
contents (see 1.4.10.17–22; 4.6.2.18–19).[28] In fact, such representational
contents proper to intelligibles should be different from those representational contents ultimately derived from perception, which accompany
discursive thought. Plotinus emphasizes that a hypothesis like this would
have very unwelcome consequences, as it would jeopardize the unity
of the living being (see 4.3.31.6–9).[29] Aristotle's account, then, cannot
hold for thoughts of this kind: if such thoughts (i.e. our connatural and
superior thoughts of the intelligible Forms) are the objects of memory,
this cannot be because we remember the representational contents which
accompany these thoughts as such. Plotinus' account of the role played
by *phantasia* when our soul remembers its higher thoughts is rather
complicated:

> Perhaps the reception into the power of representation would be of the
> *logos*, which accompanies the thought. The thought is without parts and has
> not, so to speak, come out into the open, but remains unobserved within,
> but the *logos* unfolds its content, and brings it out of the thought into the
> power of representation and so shows the thought as if in a mirror, and this
> is how there is apprehension and persistence and memory of it. Therefore,
> even though the soul is always moved to thinking, it is when it comes

---

[26] I borrow these words from Hutchinson 2011: 278. We might indeed wonder how this process really begins, i.e. what causes the recovery of our noetic self. This is too large a question to be dealt with here, and I only refer to Remes 2007: 148 for some interesting remarks about the intellectual char-acter of the process.

[27] For qualifications, see above n. 21.

[28] Cf. Plato *Resp.* 509d–511e and 532a–534b. See Hutchinson 2011: 267 and Linguiti 2004–2005.

[29] The interpretation of 4.3.31 is problematic. Plotinus raises the hypothesis that there are two *phantasiai*, i.e. that both the higher and the lower soul have representative faculties, each of which is responsible for its own memories. Yet Plotinus clearly says that if this were the case, the living being would have no unity at all (4.3.31.6–9: οὕτω γὰρ ἂν παντάπασι δύο ζῷα οὐδὲν ἔχοντα κοινὸν πρὸς ἄλληλα ἔσται). See Hutchinson 2011: 265. I agree with King 2009: 171 that Plotinus' reference to two *phantasiai* actually conveys the idea that there are two functions of the same faculty. For fur-ther details, see Gritti 2005; Chiaradonna 2009: 20 n. 32; and Clark's chapter in this volume.

to be in the power of representation that we apprehend it. (4.3.30.5–13; see also 1.4.10.6–16)

I will limit myself to an examination of a couple of general points.[30] Plotinus is here describing the same memory, M2, he outlined in 25.27–34. As Plotinus argues in that passage, the ancients applied the terms 'memory' and 'recollection' to the souls bringing into act what they possessed (ταῖς ἐνεργούσαις ἃ εἶχον). This process is further specified in 30.11–13 as that by which we (i.e. our discursive and ordinarily conscious self) apprehend (ἀντίληψις) the intelligent activity towards which our higher soul is always inclined.[31] This intelligent and latent activity is brought into consciousness when representation acts as a mirror (something clearly reminiscent of Plato's description of the function of the liver in Plato, *Tim.* 71b), a mirror that reflects our higher intellectual contents, i.e. our connatural non-discursive knowledge of the archetypal Forms.

Plotinus' argument in this chapter concerns three elements: (i) our higher, connatural and ordinarily latent thoughts, which in themselves are not accompanied by any representation; (ii) our faculty of representation, which brings such thoughts into consciousness, acting as a mirror which reflects them (this idea is obscure, but we may suppose that *phantasia* provides a content derived from perception for our higher unconscious thoughts and consequently makes it possible for the whole soul to apprehend them); (iii) *logos*, which acts as a middle term between our higher thoughts and their apprehension in *phantasia*. What exactly is this *logos*? Plotinus' words are far from clear and the opinions of interpreters greatly vary.[32] Armstrong translates *logos* as 'verbal expression'. Plotinus, however, seems to present *logos* as a thought-structure rather than a verbal expression. More specifically, he regards *logos* as a discursive or predicative unfolding of our higher thoughts: Blumenthal and Dillon aptly talk of a 'discursive sequel'.[33] This unfolding entails a discursive and propositional analysis of the same content that is non-discursively thought of without any parts in its highest and ordinarily unconscious mode. As a consequence of this

---

[30] The literature on 4.3.30 is extensive. Here I only refer to Hutchinson 2011, who provides a detailed and, in my view, persuasive exegesis of this chapter.

[31] On ἀντίληψις, see Hutchinson 2001: 264 and 277. It is crucial to note, with Hutchinson, that the subject of ἀντίληψις is our discursive and ordinarily conscious self: 'the subject of a thought is the *noetic* self, the subject of the apprehension of a thought is the *dianoetic* self' (Hutchinson 2001: 277).

[32] Further discussion in D'Ancona 2007: 87 n. 36; King 2009: 184. See the excellent accounts in Karfik 2014: 133–6; Hutchinson 2011: 268–70.

[33] See Dillon and Blumenthal 2015: 311.

discursive unfolding, higher thoughts (the non-discursive thoughts of the archetypal Forms) come to be 'mirrored' by *phantasia* so that our soul apprehends them (i.e. becomes conscious of them).[34] Plotinus' *phantasia* has aptly been characterized as 'a single faculty that is in itself Janus-faced'.[35] *Phantasia* can be directed both 'downwards' and 'upwards'; it receives both acts of thoughts and perceptions. Its highest power is described in 1.4.10 and 4.3.30 and resides in mirroring the non-discursive thoughts of our higher soul.

Let us now turn to Aristotle again. It may be said that an abstract thought is incidentally remembered when we have memory of a representational content associated with it; however, the thought-content is not remembered in itself, but only known as such. This entails that the known thought-content does not undergo any change through the memory of the representational contents associated with it. For example, we remember the particular diagrams by which we have first learnt the theorem of Pythagoras and we know the abstract content of that theorem. These two things remain, so to speak, independent of each other and our knowledge of the theorem does not change when we remember the representational contents associated with it. This, however, does not hold for M2, since apprehending our higher and latent thoughts in the *phantasia* entails a discursive unfolding of them. It is only when *logos* unfolds our higher thoughts that they come to acquire a discursive structure such that representation can mirror them. Or, rather, it is only the discursive counterpart of our higher thoughts that can be mirrored by representation and, therefore, remembered.[36] Insofar as our higher thoughts are only known in themselves, they are instead non-conscious, independent of perception, free from images and non-discursive.[37]

---

[34] As Hutchinson 2011: 268 says, 'it belongs to the very nature of a *logos* that having it in the imagination leads to the conscious apprehension of it and the object of thought it unfolds under the appropriate circumstances'.

[35] King 2009: 171. The 'Janus-faced' nature of representation is brought out in 4.3.27.1–6; 31.1–5, where Plotinus speaks of two different powers of representation (see above n. 29).

[36] On this, I fully agree with Hutchinson 2011: 274.

[37] It is debated whether according to Plotinus our soul has a direct cognitive access to the intelligible Forms, independently of sense-perception, even in its embodied condition. I tried to develop the interpretation set out here in Chiaradonna 2009 and 2012; for a different account, see Gerson 1994: 177–80. I suggest that M2 is a crucial but *preliminary* stage for attaining the highest goal of our cognitive activity, i.e. the condition in which our intellect functions without representation so that we fully recover our higher and noetic self. At that stage, memory and *phantasia* do not play a role any more (see Remes 2007: 123 and Chiaradonna 2009: 27–8) and we fully share the noetic non-discursive mode of knowledge (see Plotinus' famous first-person description of this experience in 4.8.1).

It is not easy to make sense of Plotinus' views; here I propose the following tentative explanation. Each of us has an intrinsically double nature: our soul has descended into a body and our ordinary cognitive activities have a discursive structure and are ultimately directed towards the mundane objects of our experience. This, however, does not exhaust our soul's cognitive powers, since a part of us (our undescended soul) never leaves the intelligible world and shares the Intellect's non-discursive knowledge of the archetypal Forms. M2, Plotinus' recollection, is the process whereby we may become conscious, even in our mundane existence, of this higher thought-activity which is connatural to us and ordinarily remains latent. By doing so, we start to recover our noetic self. This process does not entail that we suppress our discursive and representational knowledge. Those who attain M2 do not stop having ordinary discursive thoughts and perceptions; they do no stop living in the bodily world. According to Plotinus, however, their everyday experience is only superficially similar to that of other human beings. Actually, in those who attain M2, discursive thoughts and their perceptions acquire a different function, since they unfold and discursively mirror a higher non-discursive knowledge of the archetypal Forms. A Plotinian sage obviously perceives the same things as other people, but – at least in some cases – he can do so in a different way (he does so, so to speak, *sub specie aeternitatis*), since the cognitive activities of his soul are nothing but expressions of his higher knowledge of the intelligible world.[38] We may suppose, then, that a Plotinian sage is able to understand (at least some of) the aspects comprising his mundane experience as manifestations of the intelligible principles of our world.

This may help answer the question about the a-temporal character of M2. Indeed, M2 does not concern thoughts that have been acquired at a previous time; in this sense, M2 does not involve time. One may object, however, that M2 entails discursive *logos* and *phantasia*, which are, in turn, connected to time: so how can it be that time is not involved in M2 (25.33–4)? In my view the answer to this question lies in the fact that, through M2, representation and discursive thought attempt to transcend, so to speak, their constitutive boundaries and come to mirror temporally an eternal mode of knowledge. I would call this a 'qualified use' of our discursive thought (a use *sub specie aeternitatis*), which is only possible in virtue of our direct preliminary intellectual grasp of the Forms. What really matters is not only that our higher thoughts come to be mirrored in

---

[38] These conclusions come close to Wilberding's (2008) fine analysis of the way in which the Plotinian sage may perform some of his actions.

our temporal experience, but also that our ordinary and temporal experience acquires thus a different sense, i.e. one that is influenced by our
higher, non-discursive and non-temporal thoughts of the Forms. I suggest
that Plotinus refers to this favourable condition when he describes the
situation in which the higher soul exerts its influence over the lower soul
and the two souls are in tune, so that 'the *phantasma* becomes one, as if
a shadow followed the other and as if a little light slipped under a greater
one' (4.3.31.11–13).[39]

We can now get back to the original question raised in this article: why
does Plotinus start his enquiry on the subject of memory with a long
digression concerning that which does not remember? The answer is
simple, once we understand that Plotinus' argument (here as elsewhere
in the *Enneads*) is not linear but circular: the beginning of his research
points to its end.[40] Plotinus believes that right from the outset we must
have a preliminary grasp of the goal of his research, if we are to properly understand the development of his argument. Plotinus' discussion on
'what it is that remembers' is nothing but a complex discussion of the
soul's cognitive powers, from the lowest to the highest. Memory has the
crucial role of revealing the soul's internal structure, with its different and
hierarchically ordered metaphysical and cognitive levels. The highest kind
of memory lies in the conscious apprehension of our highest connatural
knowledge of the archetypal Forms. It is not surprising, then, that at the
very beginning Plotinus outlines what it is that does not remember and
lies outside time, since this, so to speak, is the very goal of his discussion,
which presents memory (M2) as the temporal and discursive expression of
our non-temporal and non-discursive grasp of the intelligible world: as the
discursive and temporal expression, that is, of a mode of knowledge which
is homogeneous to that of the divine Intellect.

---

[39] See Hutchinson 2011: 265.
[40] On this argumentative structure, see Chiaradonna 2002: 42; 156–7.

CHAPTER 15

Plotinus: Remembering and Forgetting

Stephen R. L. Clark

1 A Summary Introduction

Memory, for Plotinus, is not a passive affair, but an active use of imagination: the traditional notion that memories are, as it were, inscribed on mental tablets is an error (*Ennead* III.6 [26] .2, 39–45).[1] There is some evidence that Plotinus was familiar with 'topical' techniques of memory, which involve the imaginative creation of a house or landscape within which appropriate mnemonic images can be placed. Porphyry notes Plotinus' remarkable capacity to pick up conversations and writings after he had left off in order to attend to something else (*Life of Plotinus* 8.8–19). And Plotinus refers often enough to temples, statues, and inner shrines to represent the workings of the soul to suggest that he may have established some such order. But the use he made of those images was not, after all, straightforwardly mnemonic. The point was to scrub the statues clean, clear away impedimenta, and at last go naked into the shrine, where there would be no statues.[2]

We remember best what we are moved by: 'the more strongly [the soul] is moved, the more lasting the presence' (*Ennead* IV.6 [41].3, 21). Plotinus' innovation was to distinguish two sorts of imagination, two organs of imagination (*Ennead* IV.3 [27].31): one is that by which, as bodily beings, we recall whatever is personal to us, and the other that by which we recall the larger, eternal reality. Our 'fall' into bodily, personal life, as Plato suggested, involves our forgetting that larger world. Conversely, our reascent to reality means that we must shed the merely personal, accidental

---

[1] All quotations are taken from Armstrong 1966–88. On the language and imagery of the tablets of memory, see Agócs' chapter in this volume, and also Chiaradonna's chapter in this volume on memory as 'the temporal and discursive expression of our non-temporal and non-discursive grasp of the intelligible world' (as Chiaradonna well describes Plotinus' conception on p. 324).

[2] See Clark 2008, and in more developed form Clark 2016 (which employs some of the material in this chapter).

memories of our lives here.[3] 'Souls that descend, souls that change their
state – these, then, may be said to have memory, which deals with what
has come and gone; but what subjects of remembrance can there be for
souls whose lot is to remain unchanged?' (*Ennead* IV.4 [28].6). It is this
process of *forgetting* that is more significant for Plotinus than this-worldly
uses of the art of memory. Heracles' shadow might recall his earthly life,
but Heracles himself does not remember it.[4] These processes of descent
and ascent are determined by whatever it is that we most love: we are
pulled away from reality by a wish to have things all our own way (*Ennead*
V.2 [11].2), and return by attending first to images of beauty. This is to
forget ourselves, as an attentive reader or accomplished dancer also has no
attention to spare for herself (*Ennead* I.4 [46].10; IV.4 [28].33). Even beauty
may be forgotten: 'like a man who enters into the sanctuary and leaves
behind the statues in the outer shrine' (*Ennead* VI.9 [9].11).

The two movements, of remembering and forgetting, can also be linked
to Plotinus' use of astrological themes, especially that the soul acquires
various characters in its descent through the planetary spheres, and must
relinquish them as it returns to its first material home, in the fixed stars.[5]
Although the astrological details cannot easily now be taken seriously, it is
worth noting that we may still put aside our this-worldly memories and
concerns by attending to modern visions of astronomical immensity. The
difference between Plotinus' vision and that modern, more nihilistic vision
does not turn on the astrological details but on metaphysical and ethical
commitments: but that is another story.

2   The Art of Memory

That there were mnemonic 'mental exercises' in common use in Plotinus'
day is attested by his remarks on memory, designed to show that memory
is not a passive matter. Remembering is a power of the soul that can be
improved by exercise, 'just like physical training of our arms and legs to
make them do easily what does not lie in the arms or legs, but what they
are made ready for by continuous exercise' (*Ennead* IV.6 [41] .3, 29f). The
obvious reference is to the ordinary use of memory, though no Platonist
can entirely escape the association of 'memory' with what Plato called
anamnēsis, recollection of real things.[6] But even if these exercises do not

---

[3] For analysis of Plato's original idea, see Capra's chapter in this volume.
[4] *Ennead* IV.3 [27].27, after Homer *Odyssey* 11.601–4; see also IV.3 [27].32, 24f.
[5] Macrobius *Commentary on the Dream of Scipio* I 13.
[6] See Warren 1965.

empower us to do more than remember dates, data or persons' faces, it is worth considering what they were. Exercises for the arms and legs are not simply a matter of doing more of what one does in any case (as it might be, walking or lifting books). Rather those who exercise will train carefully with sticks or balls, or dance, or practise yoga. Just so, those who would improve their memory do not simply learn long lists, in the hope that this will somehow help them to remember dates, data or persons' faces. Learning long lists may help, but only if we thereby learn *how* to remember, how to do something more than what comes naturally. 'The Art of Memory' was well known in rhetorical and philosophical circles from the fifth century BC[7] till well into the Renaissance, and had more than merely 'utilitarian' significance.[8]

The first step in remembering anything is to have it to remember, by attending to its first appearance. Children, Plotinus says, are better at remembering because they are more attentive, or less easily distracted by other things to think about (*Ennead* IV.6 [41] 3.22).[9] We remember best what we are moved by: 'the more strongly [the soul] is moved, the more lasting the presence' (*Ennead* IV.6 [41] .3, 21). Remembering is primarily a function of the imagination, so that it will be easier to remember an image that excites us – which explains the violence and obscenity of myths intended to convey more abstract truths. But the images are not simply fading impressions.

> There is no stamp impressed on it internally but it has what it sees and in another way does not have it; it has it by knowing it, but does not have it in that something is not put away in it from the seeing, like a shape in wax. And we must remember that memories too do not exist because things are put away in our minds but the soul awakes the power in such a way as to have what it does not have. (*Ennead* III.6 [26] .2, 39–45)

Despite not being stored somewhere in the soul as 'imprints',[10] memories are there even when they are not recalled – and these 'unconscious' memories may have more effect than the conscious ones.[11] We might rely simply

---

[7] See Sassi's chapter in this volume.

[8] See Yates 1966. Carruthers (1998: 8) offers a more sympathetic account, criticizing Yates's assumption that the memorist aims to recall entire speeches verbatim: 'the art of memory was not an art of recitation and reiteration, but an art of invention'.

[9] Luca Castagnoli reminds me that Plotinus is here contradicting Aristotle's claim (*De Memoria* 453a32) that: 'Infants and very old persons have bad memories, owing to the amount of movement going on within them.' Memory is not so dependent on the merely physical, and so not necessarily affected by bodily change. See King 2009: 127–9.

[10] For analysis of this Plotinian doctrine, see Chiaradonna's chapter in this volume.

[11] Warren 1965: 255, after *Ennead* IV.4 [28].4, 7–14.

on chance associations to revive them, but it is better to put them in some accessible order so that we can remember where our forgotten images are – and know what to do with them. Modern manuals often suggest that they be ordered in a narrative or musical sequence, so that what needs to be recalled is set to music or incorporated in a – precisely – *memorable* story. As Hacking suggested,

> Memory is not like a video record. It does not need images, and images are never enough; moreover, our memories shade and patch and combine and delete. This thought leads to a second one: the best analogy to remembering is storytelling. The metaphor for memory is narrative.[12]

The disadvantage is that things must then be remembered *in that order*, and often the whole song or story must be recited to reach a later item. Though memory does not *need* images, they help. The method preferred in ancient manuals is the 'topical', first devised, according to the tradition, by the poet Simonides, who realized that he could recall where each member of his audience had been since he had a vivid visual memory of the couches where they lay.[13] The technique he pioneered (though he probably had many predecessors, from the beginnings of human consciousness) was first to memorize a familiar building, and then put mementos around its walls, windows, and niches. Everything could then be relocated merely by going, in imagination, to that part of the building, from any direction and starting point. The adept might use an actual building, which could be populated for his or for anyone's imagination with mementos – very much as members of oral cultures identify stories with particular features of a landscape.[14] Medieval cathedrals similarly contained sacred memories, embodied in pictures and carvings rather than mere words, very much as the Egyptian priests expressed *their* doctrines (*Ennead* IV.3 [27].11; v.8 [31].6). The further advantage of the system was that the architectural ordering itself might make new associations, and the images change to reveal new aspects of the things remembered.

This may give a credible sense to the odd stories of moving statues created by Egyptian priests.[15] It is possible that these were corporeal images, powered by whatever technical trick to deceive or amuse the faithful. But it is more helpful now to conceive them as *imagined* statues, which could

---

[12] Hacking 1995: 250.
[13] It was good that he could, since the roof had fallen in and killed all the members of his audience, and their bodies were otherwise unidentifiable.
[14] See Abram 1996: 173–4.
[15] See *Asclepius* 24; Copenhaver 1992: 81.

come to life in us. Such images could be drawn from public exhibition – Pheidias' Zeus, Praxiteles' Aphrodite, or allegorical depictions of *sōphrosunē* or justice: the soul sees 'them standing in itself like splendid statues all rusted with time which it has cleaned'.[16]

The Romans, and their many imitators, chose to depict Virtues on their public monuments as clothed female figures: the four statues ornamenting the Library of Celsus in Ephesus, for example, are of *aretē, ennoia, epistēmē*, and *sophia*. Roman coins carry similar figures to represent equity, good faith, modesty, and the like. Whether those who admired the statues or glanced at the coins ever *invoked* these personified virtues, constructing moving images of them, is unknown, though it is likely that even what seem to us to be lifeless abstractions had some real emotional significance.[17] Such public, 'civic', virtues are not all that Plotinus praised: indeed they can barely qualify as human, and their exemplars can expect to be born again as ants or bees, in happy service of society.[18] 'Real' virtues – of which those civic virtues are themselves no more than images – are not dependent on a fallen world to give them sense (as the exercise of courage requires that there be wars), and the virtuous themselves would wish *not* to have to exercise their civic virtue in that way, 'as if a physician were to wish that nobody needed his skill' (*Ennead* VI.8 [39] .5, 13–21). *Sōphrosunē*, as seen by those who gaze on the divine beauty, is 'not the kind which men have here below, when they do have it (for this is some sort of imitation of that other)' (*Ennead* V.8 [31] .10, 14–16). But we have to start somewhere: to be virtuous even in ordinary civil practice we must awaken a right spirit in us – one which was sleeping in us already. Imagining true virtue in ourselves we may, perhaps, become virtuous.

3 The Art of Oblivion

The chief point of Plotinus' art was to clean the statues, clear away impedimenta, and go naked into the shrine, beyond the statues: 'We must certainly not attribute memory to God, or [to] real being or Intellect' (*Ennead* VI.3 [27] .25, 13–14). Purification is a waking up from inappropriate images (*Ennead* III.6 [26] .5, 23–6), as dreams dissolve and are forgotten.[19] But in the heavens, he says, we may still remember enough to recognize our

---

[16] *Ennead* IV.7 [2] .10, 47, after Plato *Phaedrus* 247d.
[17] See, for example, Stafford 2000: 26–7 on Homonoia.
[18] See *Ennead* VI.3 [44] .16, 28–32; *Ennead* VI.8.5
[19] See Detienne 1996: 181, n. 107, citing IV.3 [27] .32, IV.4 [28] .1 after Schaerer 1964: 193–4.

friends, 'by their characters and the individuality of their behaviour' (*Ennead* IV.4 [28] .5, 20), even if they have spherical bodies (even, that is, if they are stars),[20] and even if neither they nor we have any memory of our lives below. Nor do they need to *speak*: 'For here below, too, we can know many things by the look in people's eyes when they are silent; but there all their body is clear and pure and each is like an eye, and nothing is hidden or feigned, but before one speaks to another that other has seen and understood' (*Ennead* IV.3 [27] .18, 19–24). But it is hard to see how this should matter: 'the man of quality (*asteios*) would have his memories of [friends and children and wife] without emotion' (*Ennead* IV.3 [27] .32). And in going further 'up', we forget even particular friends. The way down from the intelligible is when we acquire memory, that is, when we fell: 'When the soul comes out of the intelligible world and cannot endure unity but embraces its own individuality and wants to be different and so to speak puts its head outside, it thereupon acquires memory' (*Ennead* IV.4 [28] .3).

The opposition – and occasional conjunction – of Truth (*alētheia*) and Forgetfulness (*lēthē*) is a rhetorical trope dating back at least to Hesiod. One who sees and speaks the truth, *alēthēs*, is one who has not forgotten. Truth lies, for the most part, in memory, *mnēmosynē*, but 'when the Muses tell the truth, they simultaneously bring "a forgetting of ills and a rest from sorrows"'.[21] Plotinus remarks that 'the higher soul ought to be happy to forget what it has received from the worse soul' (*Ennead* IV.3 [27] .32, 10–11). So also Maximus the Confessor (580–662):

> We carry along with us the voluptuous images of the things we once experienced. Now the one who overcomes these voluptuous images completely disdains the realities of which they are images. In fact, the battle against memories is more difficult than the battle against deeds, as sinning in thought is easier than sinning in deed. (*Four Hundred Chapters on Love* 1.63, transl. Berthold 1985)

There is more to be said about those images, and the living statues that 'wise men of old' created. Here the point is only that there is another use for 'mental exercises' than that meant by their creators, a use that may explain one of the oddest of Plotinus' similes:

> It is as if someone went into a house richly decorated and so beautiful, and within it contemplated each and every one of the decorations and admired

---

[20] That the stars are *spherical* is not as obvious as we now might think: after all, to the astronomers of Plotinus' day they were only visible as *points* (see *Ennead* I.6 [1] .1, 34–5). They are *spherical*, perhaps, because they travel in circles: their bodies are their transit across the sky.

[21] Detienne 1996: 81, after Hesiod *Theogony* 55f.

them before seeing the master of the house, but when he sees the master with delight, who is not of the nature of the images, but worthy of genuine contemplation, he dismisses those other things and thereafter looks at him alone ... And perhaps the likeness would keep in conformity with the reality if it was not a mortal who encountered the one who was seeing the sights of the house but one of the gods, and who did not appear visibly but filled the soul of the beholder. (*Ennead* vi.7 [38] .35)

It is certainly not usual to find the master of a beautiful house more *beautiful* than the house and ornaments, unless one is in love.[22] But if the house intended is the memory house, we should attend to the *maker* of that house, the inspiring spirit, so turning aside from images to let them wither.

Let every soul first consider this, that it [that is, the soul] made all living things itself, breathing life into them, those that the earth feeds and those that are nourished by the sea, and the divine stars in the sky; it made the sun itself, and this great heaven, and adorned itself, and drives it round itself, in orderly movement; it is a nature other than the things which it adorns and moves and makes live; and it must necessarily be more honourable than they. (*Ennead* v.1 [10] .2)

This can be read in at least two ways. It may be a cosmological thesis, about the earth, sea, and stars and the creatures that inhabit them. It is after all literally and clearly true that the whole world has been made, and constantly remade – soil and air as well as our fuel and food – by living things, by the life in them. But the story is also about the world that each of us severally creates, the world as it is for us, the subjective world. We need to understand both that the world of our immediate experience is personal to us, constructed according to our own needs and fancies, and also that it is a *lesser* world than the one that guides and sustains us.[23] These revelations are not distinct: in realizing that I make my world I also realize that I do not make *myself*, that the power I display in attending to this or that, in populating my world with phantom memories and plans, lies deeper than I ordinarily conceive.

Much as your body is built from the foods you eat, your mind is built from the experiences you have. The flow of experience gradually sculpts your brain, thus shaping your mind. Some of the results can be explicitly

---

[22] Though see Clark 2016: 130: Roman society made more of the ceremonial role of a householder.

[23] Cf. Wilson 1969: 129: 'Man is the first *objective* animal. All others live in a subjective world of instinct, from which they can never escape; only man looks at the stars or rocks and says "How interesting ..." instantly leaping over the wall of his mere identity.' I am not so sure that we are the first or only such animals.

recalled: *This is what I did last summer; that is how I felt when I was in love*. But most of the shaping of your mind remains forever unconscious. This is called implicit memory, and it includes your expectations, models of relationships, emotional tendencies, and general outlook. Implicit memory establishes the interior landscape of your mind – what it feels like to be you – based on the slowly accumulating residues of lived experience.[24]

Hanson draws on modern neuroscience and Buddhist theory to suggest how this interior landscape can be reshaped once we recognize that memories are not fixed objects, but part of an ongoing story. Similarly, Plotinus' goal is not Remembrance, but Forgetfulness, not because he was 'ashamed to be in a body', as Porphyry supposed,[25] but because there were things better worth 'remembering' than childhood fears or fancies, even than grown-up fears and fancies. It may be necessary to bring those unconscious memories to light, but only to deconstruct them. By concentrating on what he wished to remember, on the very poetic genius that creates those images, 'the master of the house',[26] he could hope to cleanse the past – and also the future. Everyday life is conditioned by our hopes and memories: we must remember our mistakes in the hope of avoiding like mistakes, but the very memories remind us of the likeliest future, that we will make mistakes again.[27] If we are ever actually to change, we must change the way we see things. We must repopulate our inner landscape. And the first step in that process is forgetting. Similarly Wilson: 'to be possessed by a strong sense of purpose is to ignore ninety-nine per cent of your experience, and to forget all the unimportant things that have happened to you'.[28]

Medieval 'mnemotechnicians' imagined the items written on papyrus and then burnt up.[29] Eco (1988) has suggested that this could only be a way of recalling that there is something that we wanted to forget – though it is not clear that he had actually attempted the technique.[30] His own suggestion, not for forgetting what we do not want to remember but at

---

[24] Hanson-Mendius 2009: 69.

[25] *Life of Plotinus* 1: vol. 1 of Armstrong 1966–88: 3.

[26] See William Blake *The Marriage of Heaven and Hell* 12–13 in Keynes 1966: 153.

[27] See Ouspensky 1947: Osokin is magically permitted to go back to his schooldays and attempt to remake his life. He merely repeats the very same mistakes, even though he knows or half-knows what will happen. My thanks to Richard Lawrence for this reference.

[28] Wilson 2009: 56, commenting on Borges 1970.

[29] See Carruthers 1996. Luria (1968: 66–71) reports that his mnemonist, Shereshevski, found this technique unhelpful, but that he could simply will his images away.

[30] Eco argues that there can be no real 'art of oblivion' since all attempts to identify what is to be forgotten must inevitably bring it to mind. But this only really shows, at most, that the art requires a sort of indirection, not that we cannot learn or identify effective ways of forgetting.

least for obscuring it, or forgetting whether this or that is true, is rather to overlay the memory. If we wished to forget the rhyme recalling the valid figures of the syllogism ('Barbara Celarent Darii Ferioque prioris' and the rest) we should recite some spurious version till we cannot remember which is right, which wrong, so rendering them all ridiculous. Maimonides (1135–1204) proposed that the Law was also an overlay, a counter to 'Sabian idolatry', the worship, as he supposed, of stars.[31] A still easier technique for forgetting things like that is simply: not to recall them. Students who once achieved distinctions for their memory of 'Barbara', the formula for solving quadratic equations, or 'the Causes of the Peloponnesian War' will forget them when their exams are over. Unfortunately neither overlaying memories nor not-recalling them are foolproof ways of forgetting more emotive matters: showing oneself an idiot at the age of seven (seventeen, twenty-seven, forty, or a week ago) is something likely to recur however we attempt to overlay the memory, and even after months or years of not recalling it. And most of us nowadays are plagued by memories of telephone numbers and pin codes that we have not used for years. This indeed is one reason Plotinus had for rejecting the idea that memories are impressions: that would not explain why we need to search for them, how we lose them for a while, and then find they reappear (*Ennead* iv.6 [41] 3.27). 'It is rather difficult to forget unwanted memories at will.'[32] The only way of addressing this is somehow to live through the memories and 'throw them away' or (in another spiritual tradition) 'lay them on the Lord'. We must redirect our attention to the beauties we have encountered, the living presences covered in rust or lichen or barnacles, and let them shake free.

4 Circling About the One

The world as we ordinarily experience it is private and delusional in a way that we can only escape by intellectual awakening: 'the fool on the hill sees the sun going down, and the eyes in his head' – that is, the eye of reason – 'see the world spinning round'.[33] So far, so Stoical: is the advice just to abandon our *personal* perceptions, memories and attitudes, in favour of as *impersonal*, as *universal*, a stance as possible? Should we seek to see and feel things as 'just anyone' would see and feel them, or at least as just

---

[31] See Moses Maimonides *The Guide of the Perplexed* iii 29: 'the first purpose of the whole law is to remove idolatry and to wipe out its traces and all that belongs to it, even in memory'. See also Assman 1997: 58.

[32] Nørby-Lange-Larsen 2010.

[33] Paul McCartney, in *The Magical Mystery Tour* (Parlophone 1967).

anyone sane and sensible would, free of passion and unimportant detail? But Plotinus' notion of awakening is more passionate:

> Intellect has one power for thinking, by which it looks at the things in itself, and one by which it looks at what transcends it by a direct awareness and reception, by which also before it saw only, and by seeing acquired intellect and is one. And that first one is the contemplation of Intellect in its right mind, and the other is Intellect in love, when it goes out of its mind 'drunk with the nectar'; then it falls in love, simplified into happiness by having its fill, and it is better for it to be drunk with a drunkenness like this than to be more respectably sober. (*Ennead* VI.7 [38] .35)

The beauty that such drunken lovers see has 'penetrated through the whole of their soul', and they are not simply spectators – 'as if someone possessed by a god, taken over by Phoebus or one of the Muses, could bring about the vision of the god in himself, if he had the power to look at the god in himself'.[34] The lovers are so far involved in what is happening that they 'forget themselves', as dancers do when they dance well:[35]

> The dancer's intention looks elsewhere; his limbs are affected in accordance with the dance and serve the dance, and help to make it perfect and complete; and the connoisseur of ballet can say that to fit a particular figure one limb is raised, and other bent together, one is hidden, another degraded; the dancer does not choose to make these movements for no reason, but each part of him as he performs the dance has its necessary position in the dancing of the whole body. (*Ennead* IV.4 [28] .33)[36]

But we do not stay forgetful, unselfconscious, passionately involved, for long. However gripping those moments, we forget *them* in their turn, and imagine that the common world, the projection of our more parochial and personal fears, is real:

> It is as if people who slept through their life thought the things in their dreams were reliable and obvious, but, if someone woke them up, disbelieved in what they saw with their eyes open and went to sleep again. (*Ennead* V.5 [32] .11)

Conversely, factors in our ever-changeful bodies cause us to forget what once we knew – and we can hope that 'when they are removed and purged away the memory revives' (*Ennead* IV.3 [27]. 26, 52). Forgetting is of two sorts, just as there are two sets of memories, and two *phantastika*, the

---

[34] *Ennead* V.8 [31] .10, after Plato *Phaedrus* 246e.
[35] Barbara Montero 2010 has cast some doubt on this familiar trope.
[36] See also VI.9 [9] .38. I examined this sort of unconsciousness in more detail in Clark 2010: 21–44.

organs of imagination: one belongs to our real self, and one to the soul of the world as it moves and maintains us according to its own, quite proper, policies (*Ennead* iv.3 [27] .27). And the former is the more divine. So the straightforwardly *Stoical* version, despite appearances, is wrong. Our real selves are to be found in admiration of beauty, and we must forget the very things that first seduced us from the better beauty. The lover, as Socrates said, 'forgets mother, brothers, friends, all together, not caring about the loss of its wealth through neglect, and with contempt for all accepted standards of propriety and good taste'.[37]

So how shall we remember beauty, and forget or put aside the bodily entanglements and confusions that the worldly count as reason? And what would it be like to live like that? It is – or at least it approximates – the life of stars, who need not remember where they have been (*Ennead* iv.4 [28] .8, 41–2): 'What subjects of remembrance can there be for souls whose lot is to remain unchanged?' (*Ennead* iv.4 [28] .6). And this too is a way of guiding our minds and memories. Later mnemotechnicians sometimes used the constellations and the Houses of the Zodiac as their imagined building, to the scandal of the Church. Plotinus may have done something similar – but what does the method amount to? The heavens, or the sphere of the fixed stars, move in a circle 'because it imitates intellect' (*Ennead* ii.2 [14] .1), and the soul that animates them conveys a literally or spatially circular motion to them because she is herself 'in orbit' around God (*Ennead* ii.2 [14] .2, 13–14; 3, 20–1), as also are our 'real selves'. We are to look toward the example of the heavens to get some sense of our real lives. Plato suggested that we 'must correct the orbits in the head which were corrupted at our birth' (*Timaeus* 90d), and so bring ourselves into line with the heavens. Plotinus supposed rather that our real selves were already thus 'in orbit', and that only our lower selves needed the reminder – but what this means remains obscure. In what sense is the light from above divided 'among the houses' (*Ennead* iv.3 [27] .4, 21)? What does 'circular motion' *mean*, in this spiritual sense? Why should we regret that our bodies do not 'go round', or that 'our spherical parts', our heads, do not 'run easily, being earthy' (*Ennead* ii.2 [14] .2, 18f)? *How* are we to 'imitate the soul of the universe and of the stars' (*Ennead* ii.9 [33].18, 32)? And should we draw any morals from *planetary* motions, whether their visible shape or the nested spheres which are postulated to predict how they will seem to us?

---

[37] Plato *Phaedrus* 252a. Thanks to Andrea Capra for the reminder of this passage. On this theme in Plato, cf. Capra's chapter in this volume.

The intended motion, obviously, is not spatial: 'one must use "centre" analogically' (*Ennead* 11.2 [14] .2, 10). 'Circular motion' is – in principle – unending, and never nearer or further from its goal. It is therefore more 'perfect' than 'linear motion', since its end and its beginning are the same: it has nowhere *else* to go. 'Linear motion' is a process, culminating in arrival or completion (after which, it ceases). 'Circular motion' is always already There, and because it needs nothing else to complete it, can be forever. A similar distinction had been drawn by Aristotle, between 'motions' (*kinēseis*) and 'activities' (*energeiai*)[38] – a distinction which is not exactly mapped by the grammatical or semantic distinctions he offered, but which had important ethical implications. Nothing qualifies as the essential element of *eudaimonia*, the good life, if it must, of its nature, end, and cannot, of its nature, be complete until that end. *Eudaimonia* is an activity, not a motion, and its highest form is God's life, the life enjoyed by the celestials: 'On such a principle depend the heavens and the world of nature. And it is a life such as the best that we enjoy, and enjoy for but a short time ... So that life and *aiōn* continuous and eternal belong to the god, for this is what the god is' (Aristotle *Metaphysics* 12.1072b13ff). So also pseudo-Dionysius, writing in *The Divine Names*: 'the soul moves in a circle [like the divine intelligences], that is, it turns within itself and away from what is outside and there is an inner concentration of its intellectual powers ... From there the revolution brings the soul the Beautiful and the Good, which is beyond all things, is one and the same, and has neither beginning nor end.'[39] Even a more recent Neo-Platonist tells us that 'by contemplating the equivalence of the future and the past [in the circling heavens] we pierce through time right to eternity'.[40]

> One must think that there is a universe in our soul, not only an intelligible one but an arrangement like in form to that of the soul of the world: so, as that, too, is distributed according to its diverse powers into the sphere of the fixed stars and those of the moving stars, the powers in our soul also are of like form to these powers, and there is an activity proceeding from each power, and when the souls are set free they come there to the star which is in harmony with the character and power which lived and worked in them; and each will have a god of this kind as its guardian spirit, either the star itself or the god set above this power. (*Ennead* 111.4 [15] .6)

---

[38] Aristotle *Metaphysics* 9.1048b18–35, *Nicomachean Ethics* 10.1174a14–29; see Ackrill 1965.
[39] Ps-Dionysius 'The Divine Names' 705a: *Ps-Dionysius, the Complete Works*, transl. Colm Luibheid and Paul Rorem (SPCK: London 1987), p. 78. See also Berthold 1985: 219 n. 58 with Maximus' *Scholia on the Divine Names* 257CD (Migne *Patrologia Graeca* vol. 4).
[40] Weil 1957: 96.

Numenius (whom Plotinus was said by some to have copied) and Amelius (one of Plotinus' followers) both suggested that the soul was corrupted in its descent through the planetary spheres.[41] It was a familiar notion of the time. The planets, so-called because they did not keep the steady onward march of the 'fixed stars', could be thought perverse, and so responsible for unwelcome features of our terrestrial souls. According to the Hermetic text *Poimandres*, in its ascent:

> the human being rushes up through the cosmic framework, at the first zone surrendering the energy of increase and decrease; at the second evil machination, a device now inactive; at the third the illusion of longing; at the fourth the ruler's arrogance, now freed of excess; at the fifth unholy presumption and daring recklessness; at the sixth the evil impulses that come from wealth, now inactive; and at the seventh zone the deceit that lies in ambush. And then, stripped of the effects of the cosmic hierarchy, the human enters the region of the ogdoad. (*Poimandres* 1.25, transl. Copenhaver 1992)[42]

Plotinus himself gives a less detailed story – and one that he immediately qualifies:

> In the *Timaeus* the God who makes the world gives 'the first principle of soul', but the gods who are borne through the heavens 'the terrible and inevitable passions', 'angers', and desires and 'pleasures and pains', and the 'other kind of soul', from which comes passions of this kind. These statements bind us to the stars, from which we get our souls, and subject us to necessity when we come down here; from them we get our moral characters, our characteristic actions, and our emotions, coming from a disposition which is liable to emotion. So what is left which is 'we'? Surely, just that which we really are, we to whom nature gave power to master our passions. (*Ennead* II.3 [52] .9,7–16)[43]

Each of us is double, Plotinus goes on to say, and our liberty lies in rising to a higher world. That progress upwards can be conceived as a successive stripping away of the garments donned in the earlier descent from heaven through the planetary spheres or the four elements.[44] Plotinus insists that 'the sun and other heavenly bodies ... communicate no evil to the other pure soul' unless such evil comes from the mixed, double souls of those stars – or rather, of those planets. Plotinus' schema may accommodate

---

[41] See Scott 1991: 85–9. See also Couliano 1991.
[42] See Scott 1991: 89. Cf. Macrobius *Commentary on the Dream of Scipio* I.13, who had a more positive idea of the qualities we acquire in our descent. See also Moore 1989.
[43] Cf. Plato *Timaeus* 69c5–d4.
[44] Proclus *The Elements of Theology*, on Proposition 209; see Rist 1967: 190–1. See also Plotinus *Ennead* IV.3 [27].15.

both opinions, the more positive one recorded by Macrobius and the negative account from the Hermetic Corpus:

> What comes from the stars will not reach the recipients in the same state in which it left them ... If it is a loving disposition it becomes weak in the recipient and produces a rather unpleasant kind of loving (*ou mala kalēn tēn philēsin*);[45] and manly spirit ... produces violent temper or spiritlessness; and that which belongs to honour in love and is concerned with beauty produces desire of what only seems to be beautiful, and the efflux of intellect produces knavery (*panourgia*); for knavery wants to be intellect, only it is unable to attain what it aims at. So all these things become evil in us, though they are not so up in heaven. (*Ennead* II.3 [52] .11)[46]

Plotinus' objection to the astrology of his day was not founded on the empirical observation that 'it did not work', but on his refusal to agree that even the planetary stars could intend evil, or that we were ourselves bound by astral necessity to do or to be evil. The stars could serve as *signs* of terrestrial events or characters, but they were not to be conceived as squabbling superpowers, intent on doing us harm, and our 'ascent' should not be conceived as shaking off all their influence, even if we should eventually pass beyond them (*Ennead* III. 4 [15] .6, 31–3). But it does involve a stripping and forgetting not far removed from Maimonides' rejection of Sabian idolatry, a movement beyond the images in the outer sanctuary (see *Ennead* VI.9 [9] .11). So also Damascius, writing on *Phaedo* 66d: 'The last garment and the one most difficult to cast off is, on the appetitive level, ambition, and on the cognitive level, *phantasia*. Hence even the majority of philosophers are hampered by these, and especially by *phantasia*. Therefore Plato here bids the philosopher to strip himself even of this last garment.'[47]

But how seriously can we take all this? We may take the goal seriously: to recall and seek to live by the vision of beauty rather than by personal or parochial concerns. The arts of memory and oblivion may help. But the

---

[45] Armstrong's translation of *ou mala kalēn* as 'rather unpleasant' seems uncharacteristically weak. Better: 'not very beautiful (fine, noble)'.

[46] Similarly Hildegard of Bingen tells us that before Adam fell 'what is now gall in him sparkled like crystal, and bore the taste of good works, and what is now melancholy in man shone in him like the dawn and contained in itself the wisdom and perfection of good works' (Klibansky-Panofsky-Saxl 1964: 80). And Pseudo-Dionysius: 'their fury of anger represents an intellectual power of resistance of which anger is the last and faintest echo; their desire symbolizes the Divine Love; and in short we might find in all the irrational tendencies and many parts of irrational creatures, figures of the immaterial conceptions and single powers of the Celestial Beings' (*The Celestial Hierarchy* 337B; see Louth 1989: 47).

[47] Watson 1988: 125.

specifically astrological aspects of the story are likely to be unconvincing. In Plotinus' day, and for many centuries thereafter, we might meditate on the heavens and expect to get some measure of calm from their example. The planetary spheres might offer a sort of checklist for the things that we should take care to forget, abandon or correct. But nowadays we know that it is the earth that is revolving (and also orbiting a minor star). And we also know that the superlunary realm does change: stars too have their predictable life-spans, even if they are not – quite – alive. This is not to repeat the familiar story that our predecessors thought that the earth was significantly central in the scheme of things. Their problem was that they thought that the earth was at the bottom, and insignificant.[48] Ours is that the visible heavens are no more than backdrop: we mind far more than our ancestors about *this* life and world, and hardly anyone seeks to remember what we say we believe about the *wider* world. But it does seem that we can still – occasionally – be moved by thinking of what we still call the heavens.

> Whenever life get you down, Mrs. Brown,
> And things seem hard or tough
> And people are stupid, obnoxious or daft
> And you feel that you've had quite enu-hu-hu-huuuuff.
> Just remember that you're standing on a planet that's evolving
> And revolving at 900 miles an hour,
> That's orbiting at 19 miles a second, so it's reckoned,
> A sun that is the source of all our power.
> The sun and you and me, and all the stars that we can see
> Are moving at a million miles a day
> In an outer spiral arm, at 40,000 miles an hour,
> Of the galaxy we call the Milky Way.[49]

This is a more nihilistic and defeatist vision than the Plotinian instruction to 'imitate the soul of the universe and the stars',[50] but it does at least provide a suitable closure, before we all fall asleep again. The larger world is the one from which we should take life and light, and learn to forget our troubles.

---

[48] Scipio, on his ascent through the planetary spheres, saw 'stars which we never see from here below, and all the stars were vast far beyond what we have ever imagined. The least of them was that which, farthest from heaven, nearest to the earth, shone with a borrowed light. But the starry globes very far surpassed the earth in magnitude. The earth itself indeed looked to me so small as to make me ashamed of our empire, which was a mere point on its surface': Cicero *Republic* VI 16, transl. Peabody.

[49] 'The Galaxy Song', from Monty Python's *The Meaning of Life* (Universal Pictures 1983).

[50] *Ennead* II.9 [33] .18, 31.

PART V

Envoi

CHAPTER 16

The Greek Philosophers on How to Memorise – and Learn

*Maria Michela Sassi**

Half a century ago, at the beginning of his memorable essay on the mythic aspects of memory in ancient Greece, Jean-Pierre Vernant noted that there are close links in different times and cultures between the ways in which memory is practised and the ideas men have on the organisation of this mental function and its place in the 'system of the ego'.[1] Taking this remark as a starting point, I will focus in this chapter on the reflections of Greek philosophers on the good reasons for memorising, and for memorising what, and how. In particular, by surveying a number of texts from the Pre-Socratic age to late antiquity, I will try to trace, and stress the theoretical interest of, a trend of thought that insisted on memorisation as a *natural* process, more or less explicitly refusing the *artificial* devices adopted by the practitioners of various kinds of mnemotechnics.

A number of scholars, in the wake of the seminal studies of Frances Yates, have cast light upon the technique of placing mnemonic images in a predetermined set of *topoi*. I am far from underrating the documentary evidence of the Greek beginnings of this technique, however scattered it is, and thus the role this *technē* may have played in the cultural arena between the late fifth century and the fourth century BC. However, I am interested in that 'antagonism between two varieties of *mnēmē*' (that is, natural vs. artificial), which Friedrich Solmsen claimed some time ago to be worthy of thorough investigation.[2] The distinction between two different ways of improving the natural talent of memory, namely, mere practice or adoption of a system of rules, is clearly made both in ancient and in medieval writers (cfr. *Rhet. Her.* III, 29–39; Albertus Magnus, *De bono*, Tractatus IV, Quaestio 2). Nevertheless, this topic has been neglected

* For invaluable written comments and suggestions I would like to thank Luca Castagnoli (who also generously helped to improve my English) and Andrea Capra. Any remaining faults in the paper are, of course, solely mine.

1 Vernant 1959.
2 On at least two occasions, both of them earlier than Vernant's essay: Solmsen 1929: 172 n. 3; 1944: 29.

in the last decades, while the scholarship was falling, with few exceptions,[3] under the spell of the 'places and images' art of memory. The time may be ripe to remind ourselves that a number of ancient philosophers, and rhetoricians too, preferred to stick to the natural side of memory. This may lead to a clash with some consolidated views, for instance, the common opinion that Aristotle was sort of adept of artificial memory. I will argue instead that his references to mnemotechnic terminology and patterns do not commit him to seeing the *manipulation* of mental images as central to the workings of memory.[4]

1   Pleading for 'Natural' Memory

Let us start from the well-known passage in the *Phaedrus* (274c–275b) in which the Pharaoh acutely objects to the *technikōtatos* Theuth that writing looks like a remedy not so much for 'memory and wisdom' (*mnēmēs te gar kai sophias*) as for 'reminding' (*hupomnēseōs*). If we leave aside for the moment the theoretical problem of the opposite rating Plato assigns to 'dialogue' and 'writing' in relation to the search for and the communication of truth, that is to say, the problem of philosophical recollection,[5] we may note that Plato seems to be interested in a 'mundane' sense of memory as well. He seems actually to be worried not about the act of writing itself, but about its product, books, that he judges to be a tremendous threat to the human capacity for memorising. In fact, he claims that the possibility of written records seduces the souls into relying on external signs rather than reminding inwardly by themselves (*exōthen hyp'allotriōn tupōn, ouk endothen autous huph'hautōn anamimnēiskomenous*), so that men give up the habit of practising memory (*mnēmēs ameletēsiai*) and fall prey to oblivion. As William Harris has noted, Plato was justified in his concern with the fortunes of memory in a world of increasing literacy.[6] While contemporary psychological research has proven that the mnemonic capacity does not grow weaker as soon as one becomes able to write and read, there are reasons to believe that individual memory skills tend to be less

---

[3] Among them, Simondon 1982: 320–1; Carruthers 1990: 70, 78, 269–71.

[4] One could say something analogous for Augustine, as I have been convinced of by Tell 2006 and Castagnoli 2006a.

[5] For some notes on Plato's theory of recollection, with references, cf. the Introduction to this volume, pp. 26–8; cf. also Capra's chapter in this volume.

[6] Cf. Harris 1989: 29–33. Small 1997: 9–10, mentions a number of Roman writers making similar complaints. Carruthers 1990: 16, 30–1, makes useful comments on the relationship between writing and memory in the *Phaedrus*. For the relation between memory and literacy, cf. also Agócs' chapter in this volume.

cultivated as literacy increases – or as other kinds of 'prosthetic memories' do:[7] just think of how fast we have got out of the habit of memorising, and thus have become slower, or even unable, to recall telephone numbers, even of relatives and close friends, since we have them ready-to-dial in our cell phone lists. Nor was Plato alone in worrying. In fact, we are told that Antisthenes – significantly, another pupil of Socrates – blamed an acquaintance who was complaining of having lost his written records for not having written those things 'in the soul' instead (Diogenes Laertius, VI 5 = fr. 188 Decleva Caizzi).[8]

Alcidamas, an orator, was part of this company. In his work *On those who write written speeches* (or *On the Sophists*), which is probably to be dated around 390 BC – so before the *Phaedrus*, variously dated after 380 BC – he attacks the *logographoi*, namely, the rhetoricians who write speeches for their clients to deliver by heart in the court, claiming that this practice is inadequate to the demands of the rhetorical context. Memorising entire ready-made speeches is a vain effort and is detrimental to the performance, because the speaker is a prisoner of the *akribeia* of the written speech that he aims to reproduce,[9] and is unable to adjust his words to the circumstances (the key term *kairos* occurs several times in this text) and to the changeable expectations of the audience (18–20, 25). Therefore, what the orator should learn is, rather, the capacity to improvise. By doing so, provided he keeps in mind a few basic points, he would be able to modulate them in the best way while speaking, as well as to react promptly to the arguments of his opponents and/or to insert fresh reflections of his own (*dia tēn suntonian tēs dianoias*, 24), with no trouble at all for the whole structure of the speech. Alcidamas argues that the spoken word is superior to the written one because passive repetition of what someone else wrote inhibits active thinking, in terms which are strikingly similar to Plato's in another famous passage of the final section of the *Phaedrus* – he also says that written *logoi* are like motionless images (*eidōla*), patterns (*schēmata*), and imitations (*mimēmata*) of speeches, just as art works are imitations of real bodies, whereas the spoken speech drawn on the spot from one's *dianoia* is like a real body, i.e. has got soul and living power (*empsuchos*

---

[7] See Draaisma 2000, for the notion of 'prosthetic memory' – a notion that is effectively conveyed by the Greek word *hupomnēma*.

[8] See also Antisthenes' fr. 174 Decleva Caizzi, to be interpreted perhaps as a praise of learning by heart.

[9] Arist. *Rhet.* III 12, 1413 b5–10 makes a clear distinction between the written and the 'agonistic' style, the former being 'most exact' (*akribestatē*), the latter more flexible. On the discussion of written and oral rhetoric going on throughout Greek and Roman antiquity, see Small 1997: 206–9.

esti kai zei, 27–8, to be compared to *Phdr.* 275d4–276a9).[10] It is important
to note that an insider of rhetoric such as Alcidamas is as worried as
Plato about the effects of books, if they are used as tools for mechanical
learning. Of course there are differences; the main one is that, according
to Alcidamas, the strain in memorising and repeating written speeches
word by word will inhibit us from intelligently interacting with others in
a dynamic social frame, and so he stays within the limits of a rhetorical
discourse indifferent to the truth and therefore opposed by Plato. Plato
thinks instead that *mnēmē* is a property essential for the soul approaching
the vision of the absolutely good, i.e., the Forms (see Section 2 below),
and in thinking so he proves to be the most genuine heir and champion of
the old Greek habit of establishing a fundamental link between memory
and *sophia* – suffice it to remind here that learning by heart the traditional
poems, where moral models to internalize are stored, was an integral part
of Greek *paideia*.[11] That link was not in jeopardy in itself, but there had
been in the late fifth century a dramatic change in the very notions of
memory and wisdom, and this prompted Plato to engage in battle.

Let's go back a little. It is well known that some of the Sophists, while
identifying *aretē* with oratorical excellence and professing to be able to teach
skills in this field, promoted a provocatively new concept of *sophia* as well.
That the notion of memory tended to change correspondingly is clearly
testified by the *exploits* of Hippias of Elis, who, moreover, rehabilitated the
polymathia that earlier sages such as Xenophanes or Heraclitus had rejected
while advocating a deeper understanding of reality. Hippias favoured the
possession of a heap of notions to be displayed before astonished audiences,
and must have had a natural talent for storing and pouring out in fixed
order an extraordinary quantity of data, such as fifty names after hearing
them just once, besides a number of genealogies of heroes and men and
foundations of towns (Pl. *Hipp. Mai.* 285d–286a, 86 A 11 DK, on which
Philostr. *V. Soph.* 1 11, 1, 86 A 2 DK, clearly depends). Yet it is likely that he
had to resort to some sort of artificial memory, the *mnēmonikon technēma*
for which he was famous according to *Hipp. Min.* 368d (86 A 12 DK).

One can guess that Hippias organised his material by manipulating
letters and bits of texts and/or by associating the various items to be
memorised to a precise set of images. In any case, a passage in the *Dissoi*

---

[10] Cf. Berzins Mc Coy 2009 for a careful comparison of Alcidamas' and Plato's (as well as Isocrates')
reflections on speech, writing, and philosophy.

[11] This practice is mentioned by Plato himself at *Prot.* 325e–326a. No wonder that memorising
both poems and written laws in order to 'inwardize' moral precepts is highly recommended in
Magnesia: cf. *Leg.* 732b8ff., 810e, 811d.

logoi (90 DK, 9) confirms that such heuristic schemes were part of the Sophistic equipment.[12] After celebrating memory as a supreme invention (*exeurēma*) helpful both to wisdom and to life, the author mentions four ways of improving memory, which are apparently listed according to a scale of increasing technicality: (1) concentrating on things (*ean prosecheis ton noun*) while perceiving; (2) exercising (*meletan*) through repeating the same things again and again; (3) 'placing' (*katathesthai*) the proper names 'on' things one already knows (e.g. the name *Chrusippos* on *chrusos* and *hippos*, *Purilampē* on *pur* and *lampein*); (4) placing things, again, on what they are commonly associated with (e.g. courage with Ares and Achilles, the blacksmith art with Hephaestus).[13]

Actually, mental concentration and *meletē* through repetition were not a 'discovery' of the day: Pythagoras was probably the wise man famous for remembering his former lives by stretching his *prapides* (as Empedocles put it in B 129; cf. D. L. VIII 4), and the practice of thinking back over the events of the day every night was one of the rules of the *Puthagorikos bios*, perhaps since the earliest times of the school (Iambl. *VP* 94, 97, 164–6, 256). This was an entirely inward practice, which did not require anything but intensifying the subject's mental energy, and was directed to disclosing unseen realities of the past or the underworld – the 'Orphic' notion of memory, as it emerges from the gold leaves, had similar features.[14] However, the Sophists did not discard mental concentration as a path to wisdom, although the latter's scope was quite different for some of them. Gorgias' Palamedes, at the end of *Palamedes' Apology* (82 B 11a.37 DK), claims that a final recapitulation (*hupomnēsai*) of his long speech would be reasonable but is not necessary, since his judges are the best among the Greeks, and they certainly remember all that has been said just in virtue of having paid attention (*prosechein ton noun*) during the delivery.[15]

It remains true that some Sophists, by playing on a different concept of *sophia* and her sibling *mnēmē*, searched new aids to be added to the old ones. Next to Hippias we should mention Euenus of Paros, the rhetorician

---

[12] While the suggestion that this writing could be dated much later (see e.g. Burnyeat 1998) is worth taking into account, the Sophistic origin of most of its contents cannot be denied.

[13] The verb *katathesthai* may be our earliest evidence for the method based on 'placing' the mnemonic images in proper *topoi*. Blum 1969 offers a fundamental reconstruction of the Greek and Roman mnemotechnics, on the basis of admittedly meagre evidence.

[14] On the role of Mnemosyne/*mnēmosunē* in the gold 'Orphic' leaves, cf. Bernabé – Jiménez San Cristóbal 2011: 15–18, with further references, as well as the Introduction to this volume (pp. 18–20), and Agócs's chapter (pp. 82–3).

[15] The final recapitulation of the main points of a speech, mentioned also in Plato, *Phdr.* 267d (*epanodos*), must have been a common practice at the time.

and poet who is deemed *sophos* in the *Phaedrus* (267a) for having not only invented 'covert allusion' and 'indirect praise' as technical parts of the rhetoric, but also composed in verse, 'as an aid to memory' (*en metrōi ... mnēmēs charin*), the 'indirect censures'. Such development from a natural to a technical concept of memory is sharply reflected in the sequence from point (1) to (4) described in the *Dissoi logoi*. Nevertheless, we need not assume that the more 'modern' mnemonic aids were commonly approved and used in the Sophistic *milieu*. Antiphon of Rhamnus, for instance, seems to have considered the very retention of a sharp imprint of one's perceptions as 'unnatural' (*para phusin*), if compared to the 'natural' (*kata phusin*) perception of present things – in a fragment attributed to the *Rhētorikai Technai* (Longinus, *Ars Rhet.* 174–9 Patillon-Brisson = Antiphon, fr. 71 Thalheim).[16] One may wonder if Plato, while erasing from his agenda points (3) and (4) as incompatible with his 'Pythagorean' conception of the virtue of memory, was more interested than we would expect in the work which some Sophists and the orators were doing on points (1) and (2), namely, on the worth of memorising and the best (i.e. natural) ways for doing it.

2 The Gist and the Words

Significantly, indications of memory's growing importance as a specific philosophical issue start to emerge at the end of the fifth century in a number of writers who were connected to Socrates one way or another. For instance, in Aristophanes' *Clouds* both Socrates and the chorus make frequent jokes about Strepsiades' equal lack of memory and cleverness (*Nub.* 129, 414, 483, 785, 854).[17] Xenophon's emphasis in the *Oeconomicus* on the practical advantages of having a good memory is also notable (*Oec.* I 7.26, I 8, I 9.11, I 12.11, etc.), yet especially valuable is his mention that Socrates himself used to judge a man's nature by his memory *and* facility in learning (*eumatheia*: *Mem.* IV 1, 2). It is the same connection that often emerges in Plato, who considers *mnēmē* as an essential quality (and a natural one: *phusei*) of the philosopher's soul, whose power of retention is crucial to true learning (*eumatheia*: *Resp.* 486c–d, 487a; *Tht.* 194d).[18]

---

[16] I am inclined to think that the orator Antiphon is the same person as Antiphon the sophist. At any rate, the concern for the distinction between perception and memory is appropriate for an author imbued with sophistic culture.

[17] Cf. Milanezi's chapter, pp. 120–3, and Wygoda's chapter, 209–11 in this volume.

[18] I think there is no contradiction with *Epist.* VII 344a 2ff. and *Epin.* 976b–c, where emphasis is put on the fact that being endowed with a good *mnēmē* and *eumatheia* is not enough for attaining anything but superficial *sophia*.

Plato in the *Philebus* states very clearly that memory has the function of saving not merely perceptual data, but also the knowledge one obtains through them – memory quickly goes from being *sōtēria aisthēseōs*, at 34a, to being *eit' aisthēseōs eit' au mathēmatos*, at 34b.[19] This passage is an important precedent, along with *Phaedo* 96a–b, for the role which *mnēmē* would play in the sequence from *aisthēsis* to *epistēmē* in Aristotle's *Metaphysics* I 1 and *Posterior Analytics* II 19 (and *aisthēsis* and *mathēma* are regularly associated as objects both of *mnēmē* and *anamnēsis* in the *De memoria et reminiscentia*: 449b20–3, 450a20–1; 451b2–10). Of course, we must not forget that Plato's memory is, unlike Aristotle's, two-faced, its other face being directed toward the pre-natal life, in which the highest realities have been disclosed to the soul before being forgotten, apparently as the result of its union to the body. However, the anamnestic retrieval of what is latently stored in the soul, as it is described in the *Meno*, *Phaedo*, and *Phaedrus*, always starts from some entities in this world – be they geo-metrical drawings, equal sticks and stones, or beautiful bodies – whose perception sets a chain of associations going from the sensible world to the intelligible. Therefore, even though reaching true knowledge is a work the soul must do alone, it cannot be done but by processing the data that are stored in the body-soul complex thanks to the work of *mnēmē* as related to perception. I think this can explain why in the *Theaetetus*, where we find the strongest statement of the idea that the soul reaches *epistēmē* by 'comparing *in herself* [i.e. apart from the body] the past and present things to the future ones' (186a10), Plato makes room for the physiological model of memory as a tablet made of more or less pure wax, on which images are impressed, like stamps of seal rings, with different degrees of depth, clearness, and stability which cause the differences in the individual capacities for storing not only perceptions but objects of thought as well (*hoti an boulēthōmen mnēmoneusai hōn an idōmen ē akousōmen ē an autoi ennoēsōmen*, 191d4–5). While it is admittedly difficult to determine to what extent Plato may have endorsed this particular view,[20] it is beyond doubt that in another passage of this dialogue Plato does suggest, indirectly but significantly, that con-stant exercise of the mind on sensible data – with, *inter alia*, repetition – is crucial to storing and preserving knowledge. This is the case of learning letters, mentioned later in the dialogue in the discussion on the nature

---

[19] On Plato's treatment of memory in the *Philebus*, cf. also King's chapter in this volume.

[20] It is my opinion that the wax tablet model, while being apparently rejected at *Tht.* 196c4–5, is not quite superseded by the aviary model, inasmuch as it remains a 'satisfactory account of empirical judgments' (Sedley 2004: 139).

of true *doxa* with *logos*. Learning letters requires, we are told at 206a5–9, distinguishing carefully (*diagignōskein*) every single element, by itself, both by sight and by hearing, and in addition doing this *continuously* (*diatelesas*) in order not to be confused when we identify the position of the letter in the word, whether spoken or written. The prefix *dia-* in *diatelesas*, by reminding us of the soul's *diexerchesthai* and *dialeghesthai* in reasoning (189e6–8), shows how the temporal, and thus mnemonic, dimension is central to the workings of thought.

To sum up, for Plato true learning requires the hard work of one's individual endowment of memory, and this is based on what one retains in one's soul. We can thus return to the *Phaedrus*, where writing is seen as an external device that, like any other technical aid, aims to improve the performances of memory, but actually ends up weakening its cognitive power. However, *this* power is worth enhancing. The 'mathematical experiment' with the slave in the *Meno* is sufficient proof of how Socratic dialectic offered Plato a model which was opposed to that of the Sophists: it assumes that to learn is not to be mechanically imbued with the master's notions, but to be reminded, through a common search for truth, of something known in previous lives and now buried in one's soul – how this model would be crucial to Augustine, especially in the *De magistro*, can only be mentioned here.[21] Socrates' frequent claims that he is unable to memorise long speeches (*Menex.* 236b 8–c 1, *Prot.* 334c–d) or has forgotten an opinion he has heard from someone else (like Gorgias on the possibility of teaching virtue in the *Meno*, 71c8–d1) also imply that live and responsible discussion is to be preferred to passively drawing on other people's opinions.[22]

However, Plato does not deny that thoughts may be awakened by examining others' philosophical positions, even if the author is not there;[23] nor does he deny that it is important to memorise them, if they are to be preserved in oral or written texts.[24] In fact, since large part of Plato's corpus pretends to record Socrates' 'teaching', however resistant he was to such an operation, the 'narrated' dialogues are scattered with countless references to the careful ways in which Socrates' own conversations were memorised, and even fixed in writing if necessary, by his friends and disciples (cf. e.g. *Phaed.* 58d and *Tht.* 142c–143b). This concern, as feigned as it might be,

---

[21] See Castagnoli 2006a: 120–9.

[22] On the *Meno* in particular, see Wygoda's chapter in this volume, pp. 202–8, which shows how forgetting what one has 'learnt' in order to achieve a deeper recollection is crucial to real learning.

[23] Cf. Cambiano 2007a for deep analysis of this issue.

[24] I am using here a broad notion of 'text' as defined by Carruthers 1990: 12–13.

seems to pervade the whole Socratic literature,[25] and this is not by chance, since reflecting on the relationship between memory and knowledge must have been greatly fostered by Socrates' peculiar method of inquiring, and at the same time by his choice not to write.

Plato seems to appreciate the advantages of memorising long texts of various kinds. The way in which Critias the Younger explains in the *Timaeus* his elaborate recall of the Atlantis story that Critias the Older had heard from Solon and told him a long time ago, impressing him from the start with his smiling attitude (*sphodra gar oun memnēmai*, 21c), is significant. The passionate speaking of the old man and the many questions the tale provoked in his grandchild contributed to leaving in the latter's mind an indelible memory, as often happens to one learning something as a child – notably, the durability of the original impression is highlighted through a metaphor drawn from the technique of encaustic painting: *hoion enkaumata anekplutou graphēs emmona moi gegonen* (26c).[26] It was the conversation of the previous day, which is supposed to be reported in the *Republic*, that reminded Critias (*ethaumazon anamimnēiskomenos*, 25e) of that ancient *muthos*, because of the striking similarity between Atlantis and the ideal city Socrates was describing. We find applied here that principle of similarity that is mentioned at *Phaed.* 73d–74a, along with those of dissimilarity and contiguousness, as a trigger for the recollection process; this offers an opportunity to note how the theory of *anamnēsis*, being based on a deep understanding of the mechanisms of memory, is primarily a matter of psychological interest to Plato, over and above its metaphysical and epistemological significance.[27] Critias immediately tried to recall the outline of his grandfather's tale with his friends, and then thought over it all the night. Having repeated the tale again to his friends in the morning, he is finally ready to narrate the story not just summarily (*en kephalaiois*), but in detail and faithfully (*hōsper ēkousa kath' hekaston*, 26c).

Therefore, paying attention to a speech while it is uttered and repeating it afterwards several times, both alone – silently or murmuring – and aloud, addressing the occasional listeners, are presented by Plato as good ways of memorising a speech. That this was a common practice among the orators is confirmed by Plato himself in the introductory section of the *Phaedrus*. Phaedrus, having been struck by the 'sophisticated' statement of

---

[25] This point was made by Rossetti 1991.

[26] Roselli 2013, while tracing the interesting history of this metaphor, has suggested an alternative reading of it, as alluding to firebranding rather than to encaustic painting.

[27] The principles of association mentioned in the *Phaedo* were interesting enough for Aristotle to integrate them into his treatment of *anamnēsis* (*Mem.* 451b20–2).

Lysias on love (227c), asked the orator to repeat his speech at once in order to fix it in his mind, then repeatedly read the most impressive passages (*ha malista epethumei*, 228b 2) in the book, and finally went walking through the countryside to practise (*ina meletōiē*, 228b 6); only at this point did he feel ready to summarise for Socrates the gist of each of Lysias' arguments in the right order (*tēn mentoi dianoian schedon hapantōn ... en kephalaiois hekaston ephexēs dieimi, arxamenos apo tou prōtou*).

Notably, Socrates prefers Phaedrus to read directly Lysias' writing, thus showing to like the original written text, if available, better than an oral report as a substitute for the absent author (228d–e).[28] However, it is more important here to note that Phaedrus, in saying that he is inclined to exposing the text memorised *summatim* rather than *verbatim*, assumes the distinction that Latin orators would label as the distinction between *memoria rerum* and *memoria uerborum* (*Rhet. Her.* 1, 2, 3; Cic. *Inv.* 1, 7, 9), thus showing that the distinction was drawn in rhetorical practice as early as the late fifth century.[29] This is remarkable, because we tend to think that 'the' teaching method in the rhetorical schools was giving students long speeches to memorise word by word. Such method is attributed to the Sophists, and is censured as the worst example of passive learning, both in the *Theages* attributed to Plato (121c–d) and by Aristotle, who at the end of the *Sophistical Refutations* (183b34–184a8) famously attacked Gorgias and the teachers of eristic for giving their students ready-made *logoi* to be learned by heart, thus transmitting to them not the rules of the dialectical art, but its mere products. However, we must not think that rote repetition was the standard training in the Athenian schools of rhetoric.[30] Alcidamas, for instance, in his pleading for improvisation, emphasises that learning written speeches word by word is extremely difficult and liable to probable and shameful failure, while remembering the most important arguments (*enthumēmata*) to be developed with the words occurring at the right moment is much easier (*Soph.* 18ff.). Thus he disparages the *memoria uerborum* which was central both to the practice of the *logographoi* and

---

28 The commonsense explanation of Socrates' choice is that the written text is separated from the author by just one degree.

29 This has been acutely pointed out by Velardi 2007. See also Rispoli 2004: 119–20. Small 1997: 202–6 makes the excellent point that the need of *verbatim* accuracy is a scholarly projection onto non-literate cultures, where reporting the gist of conversations is usually held in higher regard than parroting reproduction. Memory 'of things' would actually tend to be preferred both in Greek and in Roman rhetoric, while memory 'of words', from Hippias onwards, seems to have been exhibited mostly by individuals fond of public displays.

30 Aristotle, if we interpret the word *logoi* in *SE* as Natali 1986 suggested, might be arguing against giving entire 'arguments', not 'speeches', to learn.

to mnemonic performances like those of Hippias, and states the *memoria rerum* to be superior; in this way, he comes close to Aristotle's recommendation to his students in the *Topics* (163b 18–33) to learn by heart just a limited set of basic propositions, so as to keep them ready to be promptly articulated in the debate.[31]

The positive overtones in the descriptions of Critias' and Phaedrus' efforts prove that Plato was also ready to appreciate those memory practices aimed at retaining the gist of a speech that is worth preserving. Moreover, the physiological model of memory he introduces in the *Theaetetus* seems to offer a theoretical basis for the procedures of the *memoria rerum*, since it makes different capabilities of learning *cum* remembering correspond to differences in the depth and quality of the mnemonic imprints, these depending in turn on the qualities of the psychic matter (*Tht.* 194e). It is interesting to see how this model resurfaced in fuller form in the brief treatise *Peri mnēmēs*, whose author is a Platonist, writing probably in the second half of the second century AD. This text was certainly added to the manuscripts of Longinus' *Ars rhetorica* because Longinus had made no room in his work for memory, which had become since the start of the Hellenistic period one of the formal divisions of rhetoric. What is striking is how little importance the text attaches, despite its scholastic purpose, to the 'places and images' mnemotechnics, which had gained a major role in Latin rhetoric, but is just briefly mentioned here, with its *primus inuentor*, Simonides (Long. *Ars Rhet.* 201 Speng.-Hamm. = 105–10 Patillon-Brisson).[32] After initially stating the parallel links of *mnēmē* and *sophia* (16–17 Patillon-Brisson) and *anamnēsis* and *mathēsis* (41–2 Patillon-Brisson), the author of the *Peri mnēmēs* attributed to Longinus prefers to indulge in a whirl of variations on the theme of how to improve the performance of memory. The basic notion is that human beings retain the contents of the perceptions by having them imprinted in their soul, and this behaves as a dirty parchment in dull and oblivious people, while it looks like a bronze tablet in people who are good-natured and blessed with good memory (105–10 Patillon-Brisson). Since what someone has learnt is stored in his mind like an imprint (*tupos*) or a track (*ichnos*), the practice of memory has to be directed toward keeping these marks deep, so as to

---

[31] The first principles are called, notably, *topoi* – where the title of the work comes from – and it is quite possible that this term derived from the place system used by some mnemonists.

[32] Post 1932: 108 thinks this is 'wretched stuff', yet the opposite evaluation in Patillon-Brisson 2002: 126 is to be preferred: 'notre exposé est supérieur à tout ce qu'on peut lire sur le sujet dans les anciens traités de rhétorique'. The notes in the Patillon-Brisson edition are useful in indicating the number of Plato's passages (mainly from the *Meno*, the *Phaedrus*, the *Theaetetus*, and the *Philebus*) the author draws on.

prevent them from diminishing or disappearing. And for this purpose both mental concentration (*prosesche ton noun*, 84 Patillon-Brisson) and reiteration are essential. An original metaphor is coined to stress the advantages of reiteration. If one listens to or utters many times what one has previously heard or learnt through whatever sensible channel, it happens in one's soul what happens to the tracks in the ground, which are increasingly deepened by the carts passing over them again and again (93–102 Patillon-Brisson). Pseudo-Longinus' work is still waiting for thorough study; nevertheless, it is clear how intelligently he developed and organised the various elements of the Platonic account of memory, to make it not only palatable but also useful to the teachers of rhetoric.

The role that *memoria rerum* played in Greek philosophy may also be detected in the care which some philosophers took to epitomise their own doctrines. Iamblichus is probably anachronistic when he says that Pythagoras inaugurated this practice expressly for Abaris, whose capacity of learning had been impaired by ageing (*VP* 90 and 93, and 34, on Pythagoras' use of an *apopthegma* as a sort of *epitomē* and *anakephalaiōsis*).[33] It is more likely that Diogenes from Sinope was the first to realise the potential of summaries for memorising and learning, and taught that to his disciples (*pasan t'ephodon suntomon pros to eumnēmoneuton epēskei*: D. L. VI 31). In any case, it was Epicurus who fully exploited the advantages of summarising. Not only are we told that he used to train his friends in committing his own writings to memory (*egumnaze … tous gnōrimous kai dia mnēmēs echein ta heautou sungrammata*, D. L. X 12), but he himself states that the letter to Herodotus had been conceived as an *epitomē* of his physics in order to help (*boēthein*) both those who were unable to study his works *in extenso*, and those who had already progressed in philosophy, by making easier to remember (*kataschein … tēn mnēmēn*) the most significant points – one may recognise Platonic resonances in the claim that recalling the outline (*tupon*) rather than the details is needed to do philosophy (D. L. X 35–6, 83). The letter to Pythocles is part of the same project. In fact, it is introduced as a memory aid on the celestial phenomena,

---

[33] The Neoplatonists were well acquainted with the practice. Porph. *Vit. Plot.* 17 mentions a compendium Amelius made *On the difference between Plotinus' and Numenius' doctrines*, in order not only to defend the former from the charge of plagiarism, but also to have his doctrines ready for recollection (*procheirotera eis anamnēsin*). Moreover, Porphyry is clear in saying that the work was not a collection of passages but a recalling of the old conversations with his master. The model of the Socratic literature may have worked here. Plotinus was actually unwilling to put down his ideas in writing, and Porphyry took pains to convince him to do so (*Vit. Plot.* 18). For Plotinus' own reflections on memory and recollection, cf. Chiaradonna's and Clark's chapters in this volume.

thanks to its conciseness (*suntomon kai euperigraphon*: D. L. x 84–5, and see the final *mnēmoneuson* at 116).

While Michael Frede has shown how memory is central to Epicurean epistemology,[34] I am interested here in emphasising that Epicurus took a crucial step in letting the practice of memory merge into a 'spiritual exercise'[35] – notably, the same Greek word, *meletē*, is used for both the practice and the exercise. The beginning of the letter to Menoeceus is revealing. While not mentioning memory, Epicurus is clear in his purpose to provide his disciple with the main elements (*stoicheia*) of 'living well', as a ground for 'exercising' or 'meditating' (*meletan*: D. L. x 123, cf. 135). The famous *tetrapharmakos* was also seen as meeting the need for keeping a simple prescription for life always 'handy' (*parepomenon*, cf. Philod. *Adu. soph.* col. 4, 10–14, p. 87 Sbordone), and so did both the *Key doctrines* and the collections of sentences the Epicureans were particularly fond of – think of the *Capital Sentences* or the *Gnomologium Vaticanum*. All in all, the Epicurean discourse seems to be a mature outcome of the long trend of thought on the connection between memory and wisdom we have traced so far. On the other hand, it also sounds surprisingly close to the Christian notion of meditation as an essential *memorial* activity with which we are well acquainted thanks to Mary Carruthers' books.[36] There are further traces of continuity, worth investigating, from the ancient to the medieval conception of memory; I will focus on them in the next section.

3 The Dialogue Within the Soul

In his seminal reading of the *De memoria et reminiscentia*, Richard Sorabji made much of Aristotle's references in his psychological writings to the mnemonists' work on places and images (*An.* 427b18, *De ins.* 458b20, and the above-mentioned *Top.* 163b28), in support of his claim that *pictorial* mental images are central to the Aristotelian account of *phantasia* – *aisthēmata* become *phantasmata* by being imprinted upon memory as if with signet rings (*Mem.* 450a25–b17).[37] In particular, Sorabji managed to make intelligible, through a few emendations, a difficult passage in the second chapter of the treatise on memory and recollection where Aristotle

---

[34] Cf. Frede 1990.
[35] This is of course Hadot's formula: see in particular Hadot 1995 (1981): 81–125. See also Spinelli's focus in this volume on the ethical significance of memorisation for Epicurus.
[36] Carruthers 1990; 1998.
[37] I discussed elsewhere (Sassi 2007) this and other details of Aristotle's account of memory. For a discussion of Aristotle's theory of memory and its objects, cf. also Castagnoli's chapter in this volume.

seems to describe the best method for recalling a given set of items, by
moving through an ordered sequence of 'places' – the so-called 'technique
of mid-points':

> But one should get a starting-point: And this is why people are thought
> sometimes to recollect starting from places. The reason is that people go
> quickly from the one thing to another, e. g. from milk to white, from white
> to air, and from this to fluid, from which one remembers autumn, the
> season one is seeking. In general in every case the middle also looks like a
> starting-point. For if no sooner, a person will remember when he comes to
> this, or else he will no longer remember from any position, as for example
> if someone were to think of the things denoted by A B Γ Δ E Z H Θ. For
> if he has not remembered at Θ, he will remember at Z for from here he can
> move in either direction to H or to E. But if he was not seeking one of these,
> after going to Γ he will remember, if he is searching for Δ or B, or if he is
> not, he will remember after going to A. And so in all cases. (Arist. *Mem.*
> 452a12–24)[38]

There is no doubt that Aristotle is mentioning here a system of memory
places, and Sorabji is certainly right in emphasising his interest in artificial
memory systems. I am also inclined to think that Aristotle, as Sorabji put
it, 'seems very much alive to the idea that artifice, rather than nature, may
influence the order in which images occur'.[39] However, it is my impression that this statement needs to be qualified on at least one point, that
is the prescriptive programme which Sorabji attributes to Aristotle when
he claims that 'here Aristotle is giving *advice* on recollecting'.[40] In fact,
this attribution gave birth to a *vulgata* that may be summarised in the
misleading judgement of an otherwise perceptive scholar: 'Aristotle wrote a
separate treatise on memory that is the earliest surviving how-to manual on
the subject.'[41] On the contrary, I do not think that Aristotle's purpose was
to give any 'recommendations'. His references to mnemonic techniques
in the *De memoria* and elsewhere must have the function which technical
analogies usually have in his work, i.e. explaining how *phusis* works at a
deeper level by identifying in the *technai*, since they imitate the natural
processes, some similar features that are just more visible therein.

One may add that, while Aristotle's dialectical use of the word *topos*
may be derived from mnemonic techniques, as Sorabji suggested,[42] this has

---

[38] Henceforth I adopt Sorabji's translation of Aristotle's text (my italics).
[39] Sorabji 1972: 44.
[40] Cf. Sorabji 1972: 31 (my italics).
[41] Small 1997: 87; cf. also p. 126: 'Aristotle bases his recommendations …'.
[42] Cf. Sorabji 1972: 26–31.

nothing to do with the construction of *loci* as *spatial* places pre-fabricated for being filled with visual images, which is typical of the mnemotechnic practice from Roman rhetoric onwards. Catherine Baroin has argued, remarkably, that the 'architectural' art of memory based on elaborate setting of images in buildings may be a Roman invention, as well as the tradition that it was 'discovered' by Simonides when he identified the disfigured victims of a collapsed building by remembering the places they had taken in the banquet they were attending.[43] Moreover, at Aristotle's time memory was not a formal division of rhetoric yet, and thus no 'handbook' of codified rules was needed, unlike what would later happen in the Roman world.[44] In fact, Aristotle does not even make room for the question in the *Rhetoric*, where he hardly touches upon it when he says that a style based on *periodoi* of moderate length must be preferred, because a phrase that one can 'embrace in a glance' (*eusunopton*) is more understandable *since* more easily memorable (*eumathes hoti eumnēmoneuton*),[45] and that poetry is more easily remembered than prose[46] because of the *metron*, just like any thing ordered by number (1409b). In the *Poetics* the similar remark is made that, just as animal bodies must be well-proportioned so as to be embraced in a single glance (*eusunopton*), so *muthoi* have to be not too long in order to be easily memorised (*eumnēmoneuton*, 1451a1–6; cf. 1459b18–20 on epic composition).[47] It is significant that in such passages belonging to a prescriptive context Aristotle does not mention any rules based on images, focusing rather on the length and the ordering of the sentences. Reflecting on the principles of epic composition may have inspired his attention to these features. As for the role which order plays in memorisation, a further model must have been provided by the structured construction of the scientific disciplines, in particular, mathematics. This was the case for

---

[43] Baroin 2007.

[44] According to D. L. v 26, Aristotle wrote a *Mnēmonikon*, but this may be another title for *Peri mnēmēs kai anamnēseōs*. See Simondon 1982: 319.

[45] Size matters also in the remark that 'connecting particles should be made to correspond while the hearer still recollects (*heōs memnētai*)' (*Rhet.* 1407a24–6, transl. Freese).

[46] While the practical point had been previously exploited by Euenus, as we have seen above (pp. 347–8), the notion that 'measure' fosters memory would resurface in Plutarch observing that things 'bound' (*dethenta*) and 'interwoven' (*sumplakenta*) in metres are better remembered and firmly kept in mind. That is why men in ancient times had to be endowed with excellent memories, due to the huge number of indications they had to draw from the responses of the oracles, which were put into verse (*Pyth. orac.* 407F).

[47] In other words, Aristotle recommends here conciseness (*suntomia*) as a feature that improves the memorability of a text. The neglected history of the Greeks writers' concern for the stylistic and structural features that make a text easier to memorise *for the audience* has been recently traced by Vatri 2015, in an insightful article that appeared after the present chapter was submitted.

Plato when he chose a mathematical problem for the anamnestic 'experiment' of the slave in the *Meno*, and so it is for Aristotle when he states that 'whatever has some order, like things in mathematics (*hōsper mathēmata*), is easily remembered. Other things are remembered badly and with difficulty' (*Mem.* 452a2–4).[48] Yet, again, mathematics seems to be here an analogical *inlustrans* of the order that is to be found in the things themselves, and which the mind has to draw out from them.

Therefore, we need not think of the exercises (*meletai*) preserving memory through repetition mentioned at *Mem.* 451a12–15 as part of any *artificial* method.[49] Aristotle clearly says that one is quicker in recollecting things when thinking of them frequently, 'for just as by nature (*phusei*) one thing is after another, so also in the activity (*energeiai*) [of recollecting the same things]. And frequency creates nature' (452a28–30). This comment – which is framed, notably, in the description of the 'technique of midpoints' – is built on the assumption that there is a direct correspondence between things in the world and cognitive items, so that memory can be improved by merely focusing again and again on the internal images. Frequent exercise creates a habit of recollecting that is a second nature, nonetheless individual abilities come first. As a matter of fact, the soul has the natural tendency to associate mental images according to mechanisms of similarity, contrariety, and contiguousness that Plato was probably the first to identify – as we noted above – and provided the mnemonists an empirical basis for building their systems. As Aristotle put it, 'acts of recollection happen because one change is *of a nature* to occur after another' (451b11–12). Recollection mostly occurs deliberately, of course, and this is why Aristotle likens the anamnestic process to a search and even to a hunt (451b 15–25).[50] Yet it is, in any case, a primarily natural process, so that '*also when* [people] *do not search* in this way they recollect, whenever the change in question occurs after another one' (451b22–3). One must not forget that memory is 'common' to body and soul for Aristotle, and the bodily substratum, varying according to physical constitution and age, directly causes the individual power to move from change to change in a certain sequence of associations (450a32–b11, 453a14–b7).

---

[48] I suspect that Pseudo-Longinus drew on Aristotle for his remarks on memorability, *metra*, and *mathēmata* (105–25 Patillon-Brisson).

[49] As Sorabji 1972: 43–4 does. Coleman 1992: 24–6 is more willing to point out the physiological dimension of the recollection process.

[50] That both habit and deliberation are central to Aristotle' ethics is revealing of a moral subtext in his discourse on memory. A number of interesting remarks on this point are made by Riccardo 1999, Morel 2006.

Last but not at all least, while sharing Sorabji's view that *visual* images are paradigmatic for Aristotle's theory of *phantasmata* (which is not surprising, given the place of honour the Greeks bestowed on the sense of sight), I think that this did not prevent him from conceiving of the possibility that non-visual *percepta*, say, a melody or a flavour, be encoded as merely 'iconic' *phantasmata*, i.e. *representations* of the essential features of the remembered thing that are not to be literally 'seen' by the soul.[51] One should note that connecting the internal image to the thing once perceived or learnt, which is central to remembering, is a *verbal* rather than a visual operation:

> For whenever someone is actively engaged in remembering, he always *says in his soul* in this way that he heard, or perceived, or thought this before. Therefore memory is not perception or conception, but a state or affection connected with one of these, when time has elapsed. (Arist. *Mem.* 449b22–5; cf. 450a20–2)

What is more, recollection is an essentially linguistic act, more intellectual than memory, and thus specifically human, in that it is activated by consciously searching for the *phantasmata* in the soul:

> Recollecting differs from remembering not only in respect of the time, but in that many other animals share in remembering, while of the known animals one may say that none other than man shares in recollecting. The explanation is that recollecting is, as it were, a sort of reasoning (*sullogismos tis*). For in recollecting, a man reasons (*sullogizetai ho anamimnēskomenos*) that he formerly saw, or heard, or had some such experience, and recollecting is, as it were, a sort of search. And this kind of search is a *natural*[52] attribute (*phusei ... sumbebēke*) only of those animals which also have the deliberating part. For indeed deliberation is a sort of reasoning (*sullogismos tis*). (Arist. *Mem.* 453a6–14)

What is described here is an intra-psychic *logos*, strongly reminiscent of the Platonic image of reasoning as a silent dialogue occurring within the soul (*Tht.* 189e–190a, *Soph.* 263e–264a, *Phlb.* 38c–e). Moreover, what Plato and Aristotle share in their thinking on the practice of memorisation and retrieval is the notion that 'true' recall occurs by internalising and pondering what one had perceived or learnt by reading or listening, and then forgotten. Aristotle is clear indeed in stating that 'people recollect when a principle is within them over and above the principle by which

---

[51] On the representational nature of *phantasmata*, cf. King 2009: 40–62.

[52] 'Natural' is my addition (the reference to the natural quality to the process is lost in Sorabji's translation).

they learn' (451b5–6), i.e. they recollect when ransacking no storages of knowledge but *themselves*.

The difference is of course that while for Plato the soul is apparently alone in doing the final work, for Aristotle the body is involved not only in the initial stage of storing images, but also in retrieving and reasoning on them, and this has an intriguing by-product, namely, emotions:

> The following is a sign that the affection is something to do with the body, and that recollection is a search in something bodily for an image. It upsets some people when they are unable to recollect in spite of applying their thought hard, and when they are no longer trying, they recollect none the less. This happens most to melancholic people. For images move them most ... The people who get upset most are those who happen to have fluid around the perceptive region. For once moved, the fluid is not easily stopped until what is sought returns and the movement takes a straight course. And this is also why, when cases of anger and of fear set something moving, they are not halted, even though the people set up counter-movements in turn, but rather the anger and fear make counter-movements in the original direction. (Arist. *Mem.* 453a14–28)

The notion that recollection or the failure of it, being physiological facts, are linked to emotions is not new to Greek philosophy. Diogenes of Apollonia had noted that the fact that we feel our chest heavy while straining to remember, and then we feel relieved after recalling, is a proof that memory is a physical process, determined by air movements through the body (Theophr. *De sens.* 45, in 64 A 19 Diels-Kranz) – think also of the wise man stretching his *prapides* in Empedocles' fragment 129 mentioned above.[53] On the other hand, Plato was keen on noting that emotions can, in turn, influence recollection. He actually stressed the role of *eros* in triggering the work of memory, in saving and/or retrieving knowledge, in the *Symposium* (207c–208b),[54] in the *Phaedrus* (249d–253c), and even in the *Phaedo*, where we read that lovers are reminded of their beloved by seeing a lyre or whatever else they may associate with him (73d). Our Platonist most interested in memory, the Pseudo-Longinus author of *Peri mnēmēs*, would later remark that *fear* of forgetting is the greatest spur to remember (127–8 Patillon-Brisson), and, on the other hand, the names of the beloved are unlikely to be forgotten, thanks to the concern (*phrontis*) and the practice (*meletē*) one has with her or him (146–50)[55] – the same

---

[53] P. 347. See also Simondon 1982: 174–5, who finds a similar conception of emotional memory in Heraclitus and Critias.

[54] It is noteworthy that *meletan* and *meletē* occur at *Symp.* 208a, meaning, at the same time, 'exercising' to preserve one's knowledge from oblivion, and 'meditation'.

[55] A passage echoing *Phdr.* 249c–d follows at 152–9.

happens to the money lovers, not forgetting at all where they hid their treasures, so much care (*phrontis*) they took in accumulating riches. These observations, striking for their acuteness, show Pseudo-Longinus to be the heir of an attitude towards memory practice that was deeply rooted in Greek culture. The truth is that the emotional character of memory is clearly implied in the standard word *meletē*, whose root connotes 'care'.[56]

To internalise in order to memorise, and to intensify a mix of intellectual and emotional energies: these seem to me the most important recipes which Greek philosophers prescribed for having a good memory. And, since they were to be found in human nature, they never sunk into oblivion.[57]

---

[56] At Pl. *Prot.* 339b Socrates claims to be perfectly acquainted with Simonides' poem (*epistamai*) for 'having taken much care' (*panu ... memelēkos*) of it, perhaps because of its difficulty (cf. 347a).

[57] Much work should be done to fill the gaps remaining in the journey of natural memory which I have just sketched. Mary Carruthers' books of course show the way, especially the later one. Concerning the early Christian times, see also Tell 2006 and Castagnoli 2006a, on Augustine, and Roselli 2007 and 2008 on the Pseudo-Clementine *Recognitiones* (where meditation feeds on memorising conversations *without* artificial aids).

References

Abram, D. (1996). *The Spell of the Sensuous: Perception and Language in a More-than-Human World*. New York.

Ackrill, J. D. (1965). 'Aristotle's Distinction Between *Energeia* and *Kinesis*', in R. Bambrough (ed.) *New Essays on Plato and Aristotle*. London: 121–41.

Acosta-Hughes, B. (2010). *Arion's Lyre. Archaic Lyric into Hellenistic Poetry*. Princeton and Oxford.

Acosta-Hughes, B. and Stephens, S. A. (2012). *Callimachus in Context: From Plato to the Augustan Poets*. Cambridge and New York.

Adalier, G. (2001). 'The Case of *Theaetetus*', *Phronesis* 48: 1–37.

Ademollo, F. (2011). *The Cratylus of Plato: A Commentary*. Cambridge and New York.

Agócs, P. (2009). 'Memory and Forgetting in Pindar's Seventh *Isthmian*', in L. Doležalová (ed.) *Strategies of Remembrance: From Pindar to Hölderlin*. Newcastle upon Tyne: 33–92.

Agócs, P., Carey, C., and Rawles, R. (eds.) (2012). *Reading the Victory Ode*. Cambridge.

Ahearne-Kroll, S. P. (2014). 'Mnemosyne at the Asklepieia', *Classical Philology* 109: 99–118.

Alcock, S. E. (1996). 'Landscapes of Memory and the Authority of Pausanias', in J. Bingen (ed.) *Pausanias Historien*. Geneva: 241–67.

(2002). *Archaeologies of the Greek Past. Landscape, Monuments, and Memories*. Cambridge.

Alcock, S. E., Cherry, J., and Elsner, J. (eds.) (2001). *Pausanias. Travel and Memory in Roman Greece*. Oxford.

Alexiou, M. (2002 – first published in 1974). *The Ritual Lament in Greek Tradition*. 2nd edn. Lanham.

Allen, R. E. (1996). *The Dialogues of Plato*, III: *Ion, Hippias Minor, Laches, Protagoras*, with transl. and comm. New Haven and London.

Aloni, A. (1997). *Saffo. Frammenti*. Firenze.

Andriopoulos, D. Z. (2015). 'Can We Identify an Empiricist Theory of Memory in Plato's Dialogues?', *Philosophical Inquiry* 39: 124–38.

Angeli, A. (1985). 'L'esattezza scientifica in Epicuro e Filodemo', *Cronache Ercolanesi* 15: 63–84.

(1986). 'Compendi, *eklogai, tetrapharmakos*: due capitoli di dissenso nell'epicureismo', *Cronache Ercolanesi* 16: 53–66.

(ed.) (1988). *Filodemo. Agli amici di scuola (PHerc. 1005)*. Naples.

Annas, J. (1982). 'Plato's Myths of Judgement', *Phronesis* 27: 119–43.

(1992). 'Aristotle on Memory and the Self', in M. Nussbaum and A. Oksenberg Rorty (eds.) *Essays on Aristotle's* De Anima. Oxford: 297–311.

(1993). *The Morality of Happiness*. Oxford.

Appadurai, A. (1981). 'The Past as a Scarce Resource', *Man* 16: 201–19.

Armstrong, A. H. (1966–1988). *Plotinus: Enneads*, vols. 1–7. London.

(1984). *Plotinus. Ennead IV*. Cambridge (Mass.).

Arrighetti, G. (ed.) (1973). *Epicuro. Opere*. 2nd edn. Turin.

(2006). *Poesia, poetiche e storia nella riflessione dei Greci. Studi*. Pisa.

(2010). 'Epicuro, la κυρία λέξις e i πράγματα', *Cronache Ercolanesi* 40: 17–22.

(2013). 'Forme della comunicazione in Epicuro', in M. Erler and J. H. Heßler (eds.) *Argument und literarische Form in antiker Philosophie*. Berlin and Boston: 315–37.

Arrington, N. T. (2015). *Ashes, Images, and Memories: The Presence of the War Dead in Fifth-Century Athens*. Oxford.

Arthur Katz, M. (1981). 'The Divided World of *Iliad* VI', in H. P. Foley (ed.) *Reflections of Women in Antiquity*. New York: 19–44.

Asheri, D., Lloyd, A. B., and Corcella, A. (2007). *A Commentary on Herodotus I-IV*. Oxford.

Asmis, E. (1984). *Epicurus' Scientific Method*. Ithaca and London.

(2009). 'Epicurean Empiricism', in J. Warren (ed.) *The Cambridge Companion to Epicureanism*. Cambridge: 84–104.

(2016). 'Lucretius' Reception of Epicurus: *De Rerum natura* as a Conversion Narrative', *Hermes* 144: 439–61.

Asper, M. (2007). *Griechische Wissenschaftstexte: Formen, Funktionen, Differenzierungs-geschichten*. Stuttgart.

Assaël, J. (2006). *Pour une poétique de l'inspiration d'Homère à Euripide*. Namur.

Assmann, J. (1992). *Das kulturelle Gedächtnis. Schrift, Erinnerung und politische Identität in frühen Hochkulturen*. Munich. (Engl. transl.: Assmann 2011.)

(1997). *Moses the Egyptian*. Cambridge (Mass.).

(2000). *Religion und Kulturelles Gedächtnis. Zehn Studien*. Munich. (Engl. transl.: Assman, J. (2006). *Religion and Cultural Memory: Ten Studies*. Stanford.)

(2008). 'Communicative and Cultural Memory', in A. Erll and A. Nünning (eds.) *Cultural Memory Studies. An International and Interdisciplinary Handbook*. Berlin and New York: 109–18.

(2011). *Cultural Memory and Early Civilization. Writing, Remembrance, and Political Imagination*. Cambridge.

Athanassaki, L. (2012). 'Performance and Reperformance: The Siphnian Treasury Evoked (Pindar's *Pythian* 6, *Olympian* 2 and *Isthmian* 2)', in P. Agócs, C. Carey, and R. Rawles (eds.) *Reading the Victory Ode*. Cambridge: 134–57.

Atherton, C. (2009). 'Epicurean Philosophy of Language', in J. Warren (ed.) *The Cambridge Companion to Epicureanism*. Cambridge: 197–215.

Austin, C. and Olson, S. D. (2003–2004). 'On the Date and Plot of Aristophanes' Lost *Thesmophoriazusae* II', *Leeds International Classical Studies* 3: 1–11.

(eds.) (2004). *Aristophanes' Thesmophoriazusae*. Oxford.

Austin, N. (1967). 'Idyll 16: Theocritus and Simonides', *Transactions of the American Philological Association* 98: 1–21.

Azoulay, V. (2004). *Xénophon et les Grâces du pouvoir. De la* charis *au charisma*. Paris.

Badian, E. (2000). 'The Road to Prominence', in I. Worthington (ed.) *Demosthenes: Statesman and Orator*. London: 9–44.

Bagnall, R. (2000). 'Jesus Reads a Book', *Journal of Theological Studies* n.s. 51: 577–88.

Bakker, E. J. (ed.) (1997). *Grammar as Interpretation. Greek Literature in its Linguistic Contexts*. Leiden.

(2002a). 'Remembering the God's Arrival', *Arethusa* 35: 63–81.

(2002b). 'Khronos, Kleos, and Ideology from Herodotus to Homer', in M. Reichel and A. Rengakos (eds.) *Epea Pteroenta: Beitrage zur Homerforschung*. Stuttgart: 11–30.

(2005). *Pointing at the Past: From Formula to Performance in Homeric Poetics*. Cambridge (Mass.).

(2008). 'Epic Remembering', E. A. Mackay (ed.) *Orality, Literacy, Memory in the Greek and Roman World*. Leiden: 65–77.

Bakker, F. A. (2016). *Epicurean Meterology: Sources, Method, Scope and Organization*. Leiden and Boston.

Bakola, E. (2010). *Cratinus and the Art of Comedy*. Oxford.

Baracchi, C. (2001). 'Beyond the Comedy and Tragedy of Authority: The Invisible Father in Plato's *Republic*', *Philosophy and Rhetoric* 34: 151–76.

Baragwanath, E. (2008). *Motivation and Narrative in Herodotus*. Oxford and New York.

Barbantani, S. (2005). 'Goddess of Love and Mistress of the Sea. Notes on an Hellenistic Hymn to Arsinoe-Aphrodite (*P. Lit. Goodsp.* 2, I-IV)', *Ancient Society* 35: 135–65.

Barker, E. T. E. (2009). *Entering the Agon: Dissent and Authority in Homer, Historiography and Tragedy*. Oxford.

Barnes, T. D. (1978). *The Sources of the Historia Augusta*. Brussels.

Baroin, C. (2007). 'Techniques, arts et pratiques de la mémoire en Grèce et à Rome', *Métis* N. S. 5: 135–60.

Barrett, J. (2002). *Staged Narrative: Poetics and the Messenger in Greek Tragedy*. Berkeley.

Barrett, W. S. (1964). *Euripides. Hippolytos*. Oxford.

Bassi, K. (2005). 'Things of the Past: Objects and Time in Greek Narrative', *Arethusa* 38: 1–32.

Baumbach, M., Petrovic, A., and Petrovic, I. (eds.) (2010). *Archaic and Classical Greek Epigram*. Cambridge.

Baxter, E. (2007). 'The "New Sappho" and the *Phaedo*: Reflections on Immortality', *Dionysius* 25: 7–19.

Beazley, J. D. (1948). 'Hymn to Hermes', *American Journal of Archaeology* 52: 336–40.

Beck, F. A. G. (1975). *Album of Greek Education*. Sydney.

Becker, A. and Scholz, P. (2004). *Dissoi Logoi. Zweierlei Ansichten: Ein sophistischer Traktat*. Berlin.

Beecroft, A. J. (2006). ' "This Is Not a True Story": Stesichorus's "Palinode" and the Revenge of the Epichoric', *Transactions of the American Philological Association* 136: 47–69.

Beekes, R. (2010). *Etymological Dictionary of Greek*. 2 vols. Leiden and Boston.

Beer, B. (2009). *Lukrez und Philodem: poetische Argumentation und poetologischer Diskurs*. Basel.

Bénatouïl, T. (2003). 'La méthode épicurienne des explications multiples', in T. Bénatouil, V. Laurand and A. Macé (eds.) *L'Épicurisme antique*. Paris: 15–47.

Benveniste, E. (1954). 'Formes et sens de μνάομαι', in *Sprachgeschichte und Wortbedeutung*. Bern: 13–18.

Bernabé, A. (1987–2007). *Poetae Epici Graeci*. 4 vols. Leipzig, Stuttgart, Berlin and New York.

(2011). *Platón y el orfismo: diálogos entre religión y filosofía. Referencias de religión*. Madrid.

(2013). 'Ὁ Πλάτων παρωιδεῖ τὰ Ὀρφέως: Plato's Transposition of Orphic Netherworld Imagery', in V. Adluri (ed.) *Philosophy and Salvation in Greek Religion*. Berlin: 117–150.

Bernabé, A. and Jiménez San Cristóbal, A. I. (2008). *Instructions for the Netherworld. The Orphic Gold Tablets*. Leiden and Boston.

(2011). 'Are the "Orphic" Gold Leaves Orphic?', in R. G. Edmonds III (ed.) *The "Orphic" Gold Tablets and Greek Religion: Further Along the Path*. Cambridge: 68–101.

Berthold, C. (1985). *Maximus Confessor: Selected Writings*. London.

Berzins Mc Coy, M. (2009). 'Alcidamas, Isocrates, and Plato on Speech, Writing, and Philosophical Rhetoric', *Ancient Philosophy* 29: 45–66.

Beta, S. (2004). *Il linguaggio nelle commedie di Aristofane*. Rome.

Betegh, G. (2004). *The Derveni Papyrus: Cosmology, Theology and Interpretation*. Cambridge.

Bettini, M. and Brillante, C. (2002). *Il mito di Elena. Immagini e racconti dalla Grecia a oggi*. Turin.

Beversluis, J. (2000). *Cross Examining Socrates: A Defense of the Interlocutors in Plato's Early Dialogues*. Cambridge.

Bierl, A. (2003). ' "Ich aber (sage), das Schönste ist, was einer liebt!": eine pragmatische Deutung von Sappho Fr. 16 LP/V', *Quaderni Urbinati di Cultura Classica* 74: 91–124.

Biles, Z. (2002). 'Intertextual Biography in the Rivalry of Cratinus and Aristophanes', *American Journal of Philology* 123: 169–204.

(2011). *Aristophanes and the Poetics of Competition*. Cambridge.

Bing, P. (1988). *The Well-Read Muse.* Göttingen.

(2009). *The Scroll and the Marble: Studies in Reading and Reception in Hellenistic Poetry.* Ann Arbor.

Blake, W. (1966). *The Marriage of Heaven and Hell,* in G. Keynes (ed.) *Blake. Complete Writings.* Oxford: 12–13.

Bloch, D. (2007). *Aristotle on Memory and Recollection.* Leiden.

Bluck, R. S. (1978). *Plato's Meno.* Cambridge.

Blum, H. (1969). *Die antike Mnemotechnik.* Hildesheim and New York.

Blumenthal, H. J. (1971). *Plotinus' Psychology: His Doctrines of the Embodied Soul.* The Hague.

Blundell, M. W. (1989). *Helping Friends and Harming Enemies: A Study in Sophocles and Greek Ethics.* Cambridge.

Boedeker, D. (1995). 'Simonides on Platea: Narrative Elegy, Mythodic History', *Zeitschrift für Papyrologie und Epigraphik* 107: 217–29.

(1998). 'Presenting the Past in Fifth-Century Athens', in D. Boedeker and K. A. Raaflaub (eds.) *Democracy, Empire, and the Arts in Fifth-Century Athens.* Cambridge (Mass.): 185–202.

(2001). 'Heroic Historiography: Simonides and Herodotus on Platea', in D. Boedeker and D. Sider (eds.) *The New Simonides, Contexts of Praise and Desire.* Oxford and New York: 120–34.

Boedeker, D. and Sider, D. (eds.) (2001). *The New Simonides, Contexts of Praise and Desire.* Oxford and New York.

Bolmarcich, S. (2007). 'The Afterlife of a Treaty', *Classical Quarterly* n.s. 57: 477–89.

Borges, J. L. (1970). 'Funes the Memorious', in D. A. Yates and J. E. Irby (eds.) *Jorge Luis Borges. Labyrinths.* Harmondsworth.

Borges, J. L. (1985). *Conférences.* Paris.

Bouchet, C. (2008). 'Les lois dans le *Contre Timarque* d'Eschine', *Rivista di Cultura Classica e Medioevale* 50: 267–88.

Bouvier, D. (2011). 'Chanter les morts dans l'*Iliade*: entre mémoire feminine et mémoire masculine', *Gaia* 14: 11–34.

Bouvrie Thorsen, S. des (1978). 'The Interpretations of Sappho's Fragment 16 L.P.', *Symbolae Osloenses* 53: 5–23.

Bowie, A. M. (1993). *Aristophanes: Myth, Ritual and Comedy.* Cambridge.

(1997). 'Tragic Filters for History: Euripides' *Supplices* and Sophocles' *Philoctetes*', in C. B. R. Pelling (ed.) *Greek Tragedy and the Historian.* Oxford: 39–62.

Bowie, E. (1986). 'Early Greek Elegy, Symposium and Public Festival', *Journal of Hellenic Studies* 106: 13–35.

(2001). 'Ancestors of Historiography in Early Greek Elegiac and Iambic Poetry?', in N. Luraghi (ed.) *The Historian's Craft in the Age of Herodotus.* Oxford: 44–66.

Boys-Stones, G., El Murr, D., and Gill, C. (eds.) (2013). *The Platonic Art of Philosophy.* Cambridge.

Bredlow Wenda, L. A. (2008). 'Epicurus's Letter to Herodotus: Some Textual Notes', *Harvard Studies in Classical Philology* 104: 171–7.

Brescia, C. (1955). *Ricerche sulla lingua e sullo stile di Epicuro*. Naples.

Brillante, C. (2015). 'La memoria e il tempo nella testimonianza di Simonide', *Gaia* 18: 211–23.

Brisson, L. (2006). 'La place de la mémoire dans la psychologie plotinienne', *Etudes platoniciennes* 3: 13–27.

Brown, C. (1989). 'Ἀnactoria and the Χαρίτων ἀμαρύγματα. Sappho fr. 16,18 Voigt', *Quaderni Urbinati di Cultura Classica* 61: 7–15.

Buck, C. D. (1920). 'A Semantic Note', *Classical Philology* 15: 39–46.

Buckler, J. (2000). 'Demosthenes and Aeschines', in I. Worthington (ed.) *Demosthenes: Statesman and Orator*. London: 114–58.

Budelmann, F. (ed.) (2009). *The Cambridge Companion to Greek Lyric*. Cambridge.

(2017). 'Performance, Reperformance, Preperformance: The Paradox of Repeating the Unique in Pindaric Epinician and Beyond', in A. Uhlig and R. Hunter (eds.) *Imagining Reperformance in Classical Culture: Studies in the Traditions of Drama and Lyric*. Cambridge: 42–62.

Bundy, E. L. (1986). *Studia Pindarica*. Berkeley and Los Angeles. [Reprint of (1962) *California Publications in Classical Philology* 18.]

Burgess, D. L. (1990). 'Pindar's *Olympian* 10: Praise for the Poet, Praise for the Victor', *Hermes* 118: 273–81.

Burian, P. (1997). 'Myth into Muthos: The Shaping of the Tragic Plot', in P. E. Easterling (ed.) *The Cambridge Companion to Greek Tragedy*. Cambridge: 178–208.

Burnet, J. (ed.) (1901–1907). *Platonis Opera*. 5 vols. Oxford.

Burnett, A. (1979). 'Desire and Memory (Sappho frag. 94)', *Classical Philology* 74: 16–27.

Burnyeat, M. F. (1976). 'Plato on the Grammar of Perceiving', *Classical Quarterly* n.s. 26: 29–51.

(1987). 'Wittgenstein and Augustine *De magistro*', *Proceedings of the Aristotelian Society*, s.v. 61: 1–24.

(1998). 'Dissoi logoi', in E. Craig (ed.) *Routledge Encyclopaedia of Philosophy*. London.

Butrica, J. J. (2001). 'The Lost *Thesmophoriazusae* of Aristophanes', *Phoenix* 55: 44–76.

(2004). 'The Date of Aristophanes' Lost *Thesmophoriazusae*: A Response to Austin and Olson', *Leeds International Classical Studies* 3: 1–5.

Buxton, R. (1994). *Imaginary Greece. The Contexts of Mythology*. Cambridge.

(ed.) (1999). *From Myth to Reason? Studies in the Development of Greek Thought*. Oxford.

Cairns, D. (2013). 'The Imagery of *Eros* in Plato's *Phaedrus*', in E. Sanders, C. Thumiger, C. Carey and N. Lowe (eds.) *Eros in Ancient Greece*. Oxford: 233–50.

Calame, C. (1983). *Alcman. Introduction, texte critique, témoignages, traduction et commentaire*. Rome.

(1988). 'Spartan Genealogies: The Mythological Representation of a Spatial Organisation', in J. Bremmer (ed.) *Interpretations of Greek Mythology*. London: 153–86.

(1990). 'Mythe, récit épique et histoire. Le récit hérodotéen de la fondation de Cyrène', in C. Calame (ed.) *Métamorphoses du mythe en Grèce antique*. Geneva: 105–25.

(1992). 'Espaces liminaux et voix discursives dans l'*Idylle* I de Théocrite: une civilisation de poètes', *Etudes de Lettres* 2: 59–85.

(1995). *The Craft of Poetic Speech in Ancient Greece*. Ithaca (NY). [Transl. of: (1986) *Le récit en Grèce ancienne*, Paris.]

(1996). 'Sappho's Group: An Initiation into Womanhood', in E. Greene (ed.) *Reading Sappho. Contemporary Approaches*. Berkeley, Los Angeles and London: 113–24.

(1998). 'La poésie lyrique grecque, un genre inexistant?', *Littérature* III: 87–110.

(2001). *Choruses of Young Women in Ancient Greece: Their Morphology, Religious Role, and Social Functions*. 2nd edn. Lanham, Boulder, New York and Oxford.

(2002). *L'Éros dans la Grèce antique*. 2nd edn. Paris.

(2004). 'Choral Forms in Aristophanic Comedy: Musical Mimesis and Dramatic Performance in Classical Athens', in P. Murray and P. Wilson (eds.) *Music and the Muses: The Culture of Mousike in the Classical Athenian City*. Oxford: 157–84.

(2005). *Masques d'autorité. Fiction et pragmatique dans la poétique grecque antique*. Paris.

(2006a). 'Récit héroïque et pratique religieuse: le passé poétique des cités grecques classiques', *Annales. Histoire, Sciences Sociales* 61: 527–51.

(2006b). *Pratiques poétiques de la mémoire. Représentations de l'espace-temps en Grèce ancienne*. Paris 2006. [Engl. transl: (2009) *Poetic and performative memory in ancient Greece*. Cambridge (Mass.).]

(2008). *Sentiers transversaux. Entre poétiques grecques et politiques contemporaines*, Grenoble.

(2009a). 'Age, Peers Groups, Rites of Passage', in G. Boys-Stones, B. Graziosi, and P. Vasunia (eds.) *The Oxford Handbook of Hellenic Studies*. Oxford: 281–93.

(2009b). 'L'enlèvement de la belle Hélène et la tradition politique de la poétique grecque: réinterprétations et controverses', in J.-P. Aygon, C. Bonnet and C. Noacco (eds.) *La Mythologie de l'Antiquité à la Modernité. Appropriation – Adaptation – Détournement*. Rennes: 19–33.

(2010). 'La pragmatique poétique des mythes grecs: fiction référentielle et performance rituelle', in F. Lavocat and A. Duprat (eds.) *Fiction et cultures*. Paris: 33–56.

(2015). *Qu'est-ce que la mythologie grecque?* Paris.

(2016). 'The Amorous Gaze: A Poetic and Pragmatic *Koinê* for Erotic *Melos*?', in V. Cazzato and A. Lardinois (eds.) *The Look of Lyric: Greek Song and the Visual*. Leiden and Boston: 288–306.

Calder, W. M. (1984). 'An Echo of Sappho Fragment 16 L.P. at Aeschylus, *Agamemnon* 403–419?', *Estudios Clásicos* 87: 215–18.

Cambiano, G. (2007a). 'Come confutare un libro? Dal *Fedro* al *Teeteto* di Platone', *Antiquorum Philosophia* 1: 99–122.

(2007b). 'Problemi della memoria in Platone', in M. M. Sassi (ed.) *Tracce nella mente. Teorie della memoria da Platone ai moderni*. Pisa: 1–23.

Campanile, D. (2006). 'Eliano e la sua *Varia Historia*', in E. Amato (ed.) *Approches de la Troisième Sophistique. Homages à Jacques Schamp*. Brussels: 420–30.

Campos Daroca, F. J. and López Martínez, M. P. (2010). 'Communauté épicurienne et communication épistolaire. Lettres de femmes selon le *PHerc*. 176: la correspondance de Batis', in A. Antoni, G. Arrighetti, M. I. Bertagna and D. Delattre (eds.) *Miscellanea Papyrologica Herculanensia*. Pisa and Rome: 21–36.

Caneva, S. G. (2014). 'Courtly Love, Stars and Power. The Queen in 3rd Century Royal Couples, Through Poetry and Epigraphic Texts', in M. A. Harder, R. F. Regtuit and G. C. Wakker (eds.) *Hellenistic Poetry in Context*. Leuven: 25–58.

Canevaro, L. G. (2014). 'The Homeric Ladies of Shalott', *Classical Receptions Journal* 6: 198–220.

(forthcoming). 'Commemoration Through Objects? Homer on the Limitations of Material Memory', in M. Giangiulio, E. Franchi and G. Proietti (eds.) *Commemorating War and War Dead. Ancient and Modern*. Stuttgart.

Canevaro, M. (2013). *The Documents in the Attic Orators. Laws and Decrees in the Public Speeches of the Demosthenic Corpus*. Oxford.

Capasso, M. (1984). 'Prassifane, Epicuro e Filodemo. A proposito di Diog. Laert. X 13 e Philod. *Poem*. V IX 10-X 1', *Elenchos* 5: 391–415.

(1987). *Comunità senza rivolta. Quattro saggi sull'epicureismo*. Naples.

(1988). 'Gli Epicurei e il potere della memoria (*PHerc*. 1041 e 1040)', in G. Mandilaras (ed.) *Proceedings of the XVIII International Congress of Papyrology*. Athens, I: 257–70.

Capra, A. (2001). Ἀγὼν λόγων: *Il 'Protagora' di Platone tra eristica e commedia*. Milan.

(2014a). *Plato's Four Muses: The* Phaedrus *and the Poetics of Philosophy*. Cambridge (Mass.) and Washington.

(2014b). 'Lyric Poetry and Its Platonic Pedigree', in C. Werner and B. B. Sebastian (eds.) *Gêneros poéticos na Grécia antiga: confluências e fronteiras*. São Paulo: 125–48.

Carawan, E. (2008). 'What the *MNEMONES* know', in E. A. Mackay (ed.) *Orality, Literacy, Memory in the Greek and Roman World*. Leiden: 163–84.

Carey, C. (2005). 'Propaganda and Competition in Athenian Oratory', in K. Enenkel and I. L. Pfeijffer (eds.) *The Manipulative Mode. Political Propaganda in Antiquity: A Collection of Case Studies*. Leiden: 65–100.

Carpenter, A. D. (2010). 'What is Peculiar in Aristotle's and Plato's Psychologies? What is Common to Them Both?', in V. Harte, M. M. McCabe, R. W. Sharples and A. Sheppard (eds.) *Aristotle and the Stoics Reading Plato*. London: 21–44.

Carruthers, M. (1990). *The Book of Memory. A Study of Memory in Medieval Culture*. Cambridge. [2nd edn published in 2008.]

(1996). 'Review of Lina Bolzoni's *La Stanza della Memoria: modelli letterari e iconografici nell'età della stampa*', *Speculum* 71: 689–92.

(1998). *The Craft of Thought: Meditation, Rhetoric, and the Making of Images, 400–1200*. Cambridge.

Carson, A. (1992). 'Simonides Painter', in R. Hexter and D. Selden (eds.) *Innovations of Antiquity*. New York and London: 51–64.

Carter, R. E. (1967). 'Plato and Inspiration', *Journal of the History of Philosophy* 5: 111–21.

Casali, C. (1989). 'Le *Baccanti* e l'esempio di Elena', *Lexis* 3: 37–41.

Cashdollar, S. (1973). 'Aristotle's Account of Incidental Perception', *Phronesis* 18: 156–75.

Castagnoli, L. (2006a). 'Liberal Arts and Recollection in Augustine's *Confessions*', *Philosophie Antique* 6: 107–35.

(2006b). 'Memoria aristotelica, memoria agostiniana', in U. La Palombara and G. Lucchetta (eds.) *Mente, anima e corpo nel mondo antico: immagini e funzioni*. Pescara: 141–60.

Caston, V. (1996). 'Why Aristotle Needs Imagination', *Phronesis* 41: 20–55.

(2005). 'The Spirit and the Letter: Aristotle on Perception', in R. Salles (ed.) *Metaphysics, Soul, and Ethics: Themes from the work of Richard Sorabji*. Oxford: 245–320.

Catenacci, C. (1999). 'Ἀπονέμειν/«leggere»: Pind. *Isthm.* 2, 47; Soph. fr. 144; Aristoph. *Av.* 1289', *Quaderni Urbinati di Cultura Classica* n.s. 62: 49–61.

(2013). 'Saffo, un'immagine vascolare e la poesia del distacco', *Quaderni Urbinati di Cultura Classica* 133: 69–74.

Ceccarelli, P. (2010). 'Changing Contexts: Tragedy in the Civic and Cultural Life of Hellenistic City-States', in I. Gildenhard and M. Revermann (eds.) *Beyond the Fifth Century: Interactions with Greek Tragedy from the Fourth Century BCE to the Middle Ages*. Berlin: 99–150.

(2013). *Ancient Greek Letter Writing: A Cultural History (600–150 BC)*. Oxford.

Cerri, G. (2012). 'Le *Nuvole* di Aristofane e la realtà storica di Socrate', in F. Perusino and M. Colantonio (eds.) *La commedia greca e la storia*. Pisa: 151–94.

Chaniotis, A. (2009). 'Travelling Memories in the Hellenistic world', in R. Hunter and I. Rutherford (eds.) *Wandering Poets in Ancient Greek Culture: Travel, Locality, and Panhellenism*. Cambridge: 249–69.

Chantraine, P. (1950). 'Les verbes grecs signifiant "lire"', in *Mélanges H. Grégoire II*. Brussels: 115–26.

(1968–1980). *Dictionnaire étymologique de la langue grecque. Histoire des mots*. Paris.

Chiaradonna, R. (2002). *Sostanza movimento analogia. Plotino critico di Aristotele*. Naples.

(2009). 'Plotin, la mémoire et la connaissance des intelligibles', *Philosophie antique* 9: 5–33.

(2012). 'Plotinus' Account of the Cognitive Powers of the Soul: Sense-Perception and Discursive Thought', *Topoi* 31: 191–207.

(2015). 'Dualismo metafisico e teoria dell'azione in Plotino', in E. Canone (ed.) *La riflessione morale di fronte al problema anima-corpo: Antichi e Moderni*. Florence: 117–31.

Cingano, E. (2005). 'A Catalogue Within a Catalogue: Helen's Suitors in the Hesiodic *Catalogue of Women* (frr. 196–204)', in R. Hunter (ed.) *The Hesiodic Catalogue of Women. Constructions and reconstructions.* Cambridge: 118–52.

Clark, G. (2004). *Augustine. The Confessions.* Bristol.

Clark, S. R. L. (2008). 'Going Naked into the Shrine: Herbert, Plotinus and the Constructive Metaphor', in D. Hedley and S. Hutton (eds.) *Platonism at the Origins of Modernity.* Dordrecht: 45–61.

(2010). 'How to Become Unconscious', in P. Basile, J. Kiverstein and P. Phemister (eds.) *The Metaphysics of Consciousness.* Cambridge: 21–44.

(2016). *Plotinus: Myth, Metaphor and Philosophical Practice.* Chicago.

Clarke, K. (2008). *Making Time for the Past: Local History and the Polis.* Oxford.

Clarke, M. (1999). *Flesh and Spirit in the Songs of Homer: A Study of Words and Myths.* Oxford.

Clay, D. (1973). 'Epicurus' Last Will and Testament', *Archiv für Geschichte der Philosophie* 55: 252–80.

(1982). 'Epicurus in the Archives of Athens', *Hesperia* 19: 17–26.

(1986). 'The Cults of Epicurus', *Cronache Ercolanesi* 16: 11–28.

Clay, J. S. (2011). *Homer's Trojan Theater: Space, Vision, and Memory in the* Iliad. Cambridge.

(2016). 'Homer's Epigraph: *Iliad* 7.87–91', *Philologus* 160: 185–96.

Clayton, B. (2004). *A Penelopean Poetics: Reweaving the Feminine in Homer's Odyssey.* Lanham.

Clements, A. (2014). *Aristophanes'* Thesmophoriazusae: *Philosophizing Theatre and the Politics of Perception in Late Fifth-Century Athens.* Cambridge.

Cohoe, C. (2016). 'When and Why Understanding Needs *Phantasmata*: A Moderate Interpretation of Aristotle's De Memoria and De Anima on the Role of Images in Intellectual Activities', *Phronesis* 61: 337–72.

Cole, S. G. (2004). *Landscapes, Gender, and Ritual Space: the Ancient Greek Experience.* Berkeley.

Cole, T. (1983). 'Archaic Truth', *Quaderni Urbinati di Cultura Classica* 13: 7–28.

Coleman, J. (1992). *Ancient and Medieval Memories: Studies in the Reconstruction of the Past.* Cambridge.

Collard, C. (1975). *Euripides Supplices.* Groningen.

(2007). 'The Date of Euripides' *Suppliants* and the Date of Tim Rice's *Chess*', in C. Collard, *Tragedy, Euripides and Euripideans.* Liverpool: 138–40. [Revised version of an article first printed in *Liverpool Classical Monthly* 15 (1990): 48.]

Collard, C. and Cropp, M. J. (2008). *Euripides. Fragments.* 2 vols. (vol. VII: *Aegeus-Meleager*; vol. VIII: *Oedipus-Chrysippus, Other Fragments).* Cambridge (Mass.) and London.

Collard, C., Cropp, M. J., and Lee, K. H. (1995). *Euripides. Selected Fragmentary Plays*, vol. 1. Warminster.

Collard, C., Cropp, M. J., and Gilbert, J. (2004). *Euripides. Selected Fragmentary Plays*, vol. 2. Warminster.

Collins, D. (1999). 'Hesiod and the Divine Voice of the Muses', *Arethusa* 32: 241–61.

Conche, M. (1987). *Épicure. Lettres et maximes.* Paris.

Connerton, P. (1989). *How Societies Remember*. Cambridge.

Connor, W. R. (1985). 'The Razing of the House in Greek Society', *Transactions of the American Philological Association* 115: 79–102.

Contiades-Tsitsoni, E. (1990). *Hymenaios und Epithalamion. Das Hochzeitslied in der frühgriechischen Lyrik*. Stuttgart.

Coope, U. (2005). *Time for Aristotle*: Physics *IV.10–14*. Oxford.

Cooper J. M. (1970). 'Plato on Sense-Perception and Knowledge (*Theaetetus* 184–186)', *Phronesis* 15: 123–46.

Copenhaver, B. P. (1992). *Hermetica*. Cambridge.

Cornea, A. (2011–2012). 'La prénotion d'Épicure est-elle d'inspiration platonicienne?', *Chora* 9–10: 203–16.

Couliano, I. P. (1991). *Out of this World: Otherworldly Journeys from Gilgamesh to Albert Einstein*. Boston and London.

Crielaard, J. P. (2003). 'The Cultural Biography of Material Goods in Homer's Epics', *Gaia* 7: 49–62.

Csapo, E. (2004). 'Some Social and Economic Conditions Behind the Rise of the Acting Profession in the Fifth and Fourth Centuries BC', in C. Hugoniot, F. Hurlet and S. Milanezi (eds.) *Le Statut de l'acteur dans l'Antiquité grecque et romaine*. Tours: 53–76.

Csapo, E. and Miller, M. (1998). 'Democracy, Empire, and Art: Toward a Politics of Time and Narrative', in D. Boedeker and K. A. Raaflaub (eds.) *Democracy, Empire, and the Arts in Fifth-Century Athens*. Cambridge (Mass.) and London: 87–125.

Csapo, E. and Slater, W. (1995). *The Context of Ancient Drama*. Ann Arbor.

D'Alessio, G. B. (2004). 'Past Future and Present Past: Temporal Deixis in Greek Archaic Lyric', *Arethusa* 37: 267–94.

D'Ancona, C. (2007). 'Plotino: memoria di eventi e anamnesi di intelligibili', in M. M. Sassi (ed.), *Tracce nella mente. Teorie della memoria da Platone ai Moderni*. Pisa: 67–98.

Dagnini, I. (1986). 'Elementi saffici e motivi tradizionali in Teocrito, *Idillio* XVIII', *Quaderni Urbinati di Cultura Classica* 53: 38–46.

Damiani, V. (2015). 'Die kommunikativen Merkmale von Epikurs Kompendien und ihr Verhältnis zum Traktat Περὶ φύσεως', *Würzburger Jahrbücher für die Altertumswissenschaft* 39: 197–236.

(2016). 'Le epitomi di Epicuro: un modello di strategie comunicative per il *De rerum natura*', in M. Tulli (ed.) *Testo e forme del testo: Ricerche di filologia filosofica*. Pisa and Rome: 257–79.

Dancy, R. (2004). *Plato's Introduction of Forms*. Cambridge.

Dane, J. A. (1981). 'Sappho fr. 16: An analysis', *Eos* 79: 185–92.

Darbo-Peschanski, C. (1987). *Le discours du particulier. Essai sur l'enquête hérodotéenne*. Paris.

(ed.) (2000). *Constructions du temps dans le monde grec ancien*. Paris.

(2007). *L'historia. Commencements grecs*. Paris.

Darcus Sullivan, S. (1989). 'A study of φρένες in Pindar and Bacchylides', *Glotta* 67: 148–89.

(1990). 'An Analysis of the Psychic term νόος in Pindar and Bacchylides', *Glotta* 68: 179–202.

(1994). *Psychological and Ethical Ideas: What Early Greeks Say*. Leiden, New York and Cologne.

Davies, J. K. (1971). *Athenian Propertied Families 600–300 B.C.* Oxford.

Davies, M. and Finglass, P. J. (2014). *Stesichorus. The Poems*. Cambridge.

Day, J. W. (2010). *Archaic Greek Epigram and Dedication. Representation and Reperformance*. Cambridge.

De Jong, I. (2012). *Homer: Iliad. Book XXII*. Cambridge.

De Sanctis, D. (2012). 'Utile al singolo, utile a molti: il proemio dell'*Epistola a Pitocle*', *Cronache Ercolanesi* 42: 95–109.

(2015). 'Questioni di stile: osservazioni sul linguaggio e sulla comunicazione del sapere nelle lettere maggiori di Epicuro', in D. De Sanctis, E. Spinelli, M. Tulli and F. Verde (eds.) *Questioni epicuree*. Sankt Augustin: 55–73.

(2016). 'La biografia del Κῆπος e il profilo esemplare del saggio epicureo', in M. Bonazzi and S. Schorn (eds.) *Bios Philosophos: Philosophy in Ancient Greek Biography*. Turnhout: 71–99.

Del Mastro, G. (2014). *Titoli e annotazioni bibliologiche nei papiri greci di Ercolano*. Naples.

Delattre, C. (2009). 'AITIOLOGIA: mythe et procédure étiologique', *Métis* n.s. 7: 285–310.

Delcomminette, S. (2006). *Le Philèbe de Platon*. Leiden.

Derderian, K. (2001). *Leaving Words to Remember: Greek Mourning and the Advent of Literacy*. Leiden and Boston.

Detienne, M. (1967). *Les Maîtres de vérité dans la Grèce archaïque*. Paris. (Engl. transl.: Detienne 1996.)

(1996). *The Masters of Truth*. New York.

Deubner, L. (1932). *Attische Feste*. Berlin.

Dewald, C. (2002). ' "I Didn't Give My Own Genealogy": Herodotus and the Authorial Persona', in E. J. Bakker, I. J. F. de Jong and H. van Wees (eds.) *Brill's Companion to Herodotus*. Leiden: 267–89.

Di Benedetto, V. (1971). *Euripide: teatro e società*. Turin.

Di Marco, M. (1980). 'Una parodia di Saffo in Euripide (*Cycl.* 182–186)', *Quaderni Urbinati di Cultura Classica* 34: 39–45

Diano, C. (1974). *Scritti epicurei*. Florence.

Dillon, J. M. and Blumenthal, H. J. (2015). *Plotinus: Ennead IV.3–4.29. Problems Concerning the Soul*. Las Vegas.

Dimock, G. E. (1989). *The Unity of the Odyssey*. Amherst, Mass.

Dodson-Robinson, E. (2010). 'Helen's "Judgment of Paris" and Greek Marriage Ritual in Sappho 16', *Arethusa* 43: 1–20.

Dorandi, T. (2007). 'Le *corpus* épicurien', in A. Gigandet and P.-M. Morel (eds.) *Lire Épicure et les épicuriens*. Paris: 29–48.

Dover, K. J. (1968). *Aristophanes Clouds*. Oxford.

(1974). *Greek Popular Morality in the Time of Plato and Aristotle*. Oxford.

(1976). 'The Freedom of the Intellectual in Greek Society', *Talanta* 7: 24–54 (reprinted in Dover (1988), 135–58).

(1988). *The Greeks and their Legacy: Prose Literature, History, Society, Transmission, Influence.* Oxford.

Draaisma, D. (2000). *Metaphors of Memory. A History of Ideas About the Mind.* Cambridge.

Drachmann, A. B. (1903–1927). *Scholia Vetera in Pindari Carmina.* 3 vols. Leipzig.

Dubischar, M. (2016). 'Preserved Knowledge. Summaries and Compilations', in M. Hose and D. Schenker (eds.) *A Companion to Greek Literature.* Malden (Mass.): 427–40.

Dubois, P. (1985). 'Phallocentrism and Its Subversion in Plato's *Phaedrus*', *Arethusa* 18: 91–103.

(1995). *Sappho is Burning*, Chicago and London.

(2010). *Out of Athens: The New Ancient Greeks.* Cambridge (Mass.) and London.

Dumortier, J. (1975). *Les images dans la poésie d'Eschyle.* Paris.

Dunn, F. M. (2000). 'Euripidean Aetiologies', *Classical Bulletin* 76: 3–27.

(2007). *Present Shock in Late Fifth-Century Greece.* Ann Arbor.

Dunsloky, J. and Tauber, S. (eds.) (2016) *The Oxford Handbook of Metamemory.* Oxford.

Easterling, P. E. (1985). 'Anachronism in Greek Tragedy', *Journal of Hellenic Studies* 105: 1–10.

(1988). 'Tragedy and Ritual', *Métis* 3: 87–109.

(1991). 'Men's κλέος and Women's γόος: Female Voices in the *Iliad*', *Journal of Modern Greek Studies* 9: 145–51.

Eckerman, C. (2008). 'Pindar's κοινὸς λόγος and Panhellenism in Olympian 10', *Rheinisches Museum für Philologie* 151: 37–48.

Eco, U. (1988). 'An *Ars Oblivionalis*? Forget It!', *Proceedings of the Modern Language Association* 103: 254–61.

Eijk, P. J. van der (1997). 'Towards a Rhetoric of Ancient Scientific Discourse: Some Formal Characteristics of Greek Medical and Philosophical Texts (Hippocratic Corpus, Aristotle)', in E. J. Bakker (ed.) *Grammar as Interpretation. Greek Literature in its Linguistic Context.* Leiden: 77–129.

Eliade, M. (1963). 'Mythologies of Memory and Forgetting', *History of Religions* 2: 329–44.

Ellis, W. M. (1989). *Alcibiades.* London and New York.

Elmer, D. F. (2005). 'Helen *Epigrammatopoios*', *Classical Antiquity* 24: 1–39.

Elsner, J. and Squire, M. (2016). 'Sight and Memory: The Visual Arts of Roman Mnemonics', in M. Squire (ed.) *Sight and the Ancient Senses.* London and New York: 180–204.

Emilsson, E. K. (1988). *Plotinus on Sense-Perception. A Philosophical Study.* Cambridge.

(2007). *Plotinus on Intellect.* Oxford.

(2017). *Plotinus.* London and New York.

Erbì, M. (2013). 'Il βίος di Dionisio di Eraclea nella *Stoicorum Historia* di Filodemo (*PHerc.* 1018, coll. XXIX 5–XXXIII 4)', *Cronache Ercolanesi* 43: 27–34.

Erbse, H. (ed.) (1969). *Scholia Graeca in Homeri Iliadem*. Berlin.

Erler, M. (1991). '*Epitedeuein asapheian*', *Cronache Ercolanesi* 21: 83–8.

(1994). 'Epikur-Die Schule Epikurs-Lukrez', in H. Flashar (ed.) *Grundriss der Geschichte der Philosophie. Die Philosophie der Antike*, 4. *Die hellenistische Philosophie*. Basel: 29–490.

(2002). 'Epicurus as *deus mortalis*. Homoiosis theoi and Epicurean Self', in D. Frede and A. Laks (eds.) *Traditions of Theology. Studies in Hellenistic Theology, Its Background and Aftermath*. Leiden, Boston and Cologne: 159–81.

(2003). '*Philologia medicans*. Comment les Épicuriens lisaient les textes de leur maître?', in T. Bénatouil, V. Laurand and A. Macé (eds.) *L'Épicurisme antique*. Paris: 217–53.

(2009). 'La felicità del *proficiens* in Platone e negli Epicurei', in P. Donatelli and E. Spinelli (eds.) *Il senso della virtù*. Rome: 49–60.

(2014). 'La sacralizzazione di Socrate e di Epicuro', in M. Beretta, F. Citti and A. Iannucci (eds.) *Il culto di Epicuro: Testi, iconografia e paesaggio*. Florence: 1–13.

Erll, A. and Nünning, A. (eds.) (2008). *Cultural Memory Studies. An International and Interdisciplinary Handbook*. Berlin and New York.

Essler, H. (2011). *Glückselig und unsterblich. Epikureische Theologie bei Cicero und Philodem. Mit einer Edition von* PHerc. *152/157*, Kol. 8–10. Basel.

Evans, J. A. S. (1991). *Herodotus, Explorer of the Past: Three Essays*. Princeton.

Everson, S. (1994). 'Epicurus on mind and language', in S. Everson (ed.) *Language*. Cambridge: 74–108.

(1997). *Aristotle on Perception*. Oxford.

Faraguna, M. (1992). *Atene nell'età di Alessandro. Problemi politici, economici e finanziari*. Florence.

(2006). 'Tra oralità e scrittura: diritto e forme della comunicazione dai poemi omerici a Teofrasto', *Dike* 9: 63–91.

Farnell, L. R. (1930–1932). *The Works of Pindar*. 3 vols. London.

Fearn, D. (2013). '*Kleos* versus Stone? Lyric Poetry and Contexts for Memorialization', in P. Low and P. Liddel (eds.) *Inscriptions and their Uses in Greek and Latin Literature*. Oxford: 231–53.

Fentress, J. and Wickham, C. (1992). *Social Memory*. Oxford and Cambridge (Mass.).

Ferrari, F. (2010). *Sappho's Gift: The Poet and Her Community*. Ann Arbor.

Ferrari, G. R. F. (1987). *Listening to the Cicadas: A Study of Plato's Phaedrus*. Cambridge.

Ferrario, S. (2006). 'Replaying Antigone: Changing Patterns of Public and Private Commemoration at Athens c. 440–350', in C. Patterson (ed.) *Antigone's Answer: Essays on Death and Burial, Family and State in Classical Athens. Helios Suppl.* 33: 79–117.

Festugière, A. J. (1968). *Épicure et ses dieux*, 2nd edn. Paris.

Fine, G. (2004). 'Knowledge and True Belief in the *Meno*', *Oxford Studies in Ancient Philosophy* 27: 41–81.

(2014). *The Possibility of Inquiry. Meno's Paradox from Socrates to Sextus*. Oxford.

Finglass, P. J. (2011). *Sophocles. Ajax*. Cambridge and New York.

Finkelberg, M. (1998). *The Birth of Literary Fiction in Ancient Greece*. Oxford.

(2007). 'More on ΚΛΕΟΣ ΑΦΘΙΤΟΝ', *Classical Quarterly* 57: 341–50.

Finley, M. I. (1973). *Democracy Ancient and Modern*. New Brunswick, New Jersey.

(1975). *The Use and Abuse of History*. London.

(1983). *Politics in the Ancient World*. Cambridge.

Fisher, N. (2010). '*Kharis, Kharites*, Festivals, and Social Peace in the Classical Greek City', in R. M. Rosen and I. Sluiter (eds.) *Valuing Others in Classical Antiquity*. Leiden: 71–112.

Fisher, R. K. (1984). *Aristophanes' Clouds: Purpose and Technique*. Amsterdam.

Fletcher, J. (2012). *Performing Oaths in Classical Greek Drama*, Cambridge.

Flower, H. I. (2006). *The Art of Forgetting: Disgrace and Oblivion in Roman Political Culture*. Chapel Hill.

Flower, M. A. (2008). *The Seer in Ancient Greece*. Berkeley.

Foley, H. P. (1998). '"The Mother of the Argument": Eros and the Body in Sappho and Plato's *Phaedrus*', in M. Wyke (ed.) *Parchments of Gender: Deciphering the Bodies of Antiquity*. Oxford: 39–70.

Foley, J. M. (1996). 'Guslar and Aoidos: Traditional Register in South Slavic and Homeric Epic', *Transactions of the American Philological Association* 126: 11–41.

Ford, A. (1985). 'The Seal of Theognis: The Politics of Authorship in Archaic Greece', in T. J. Figueira and G. Nagy (eds.), *Theognis of Megara: Poetry and the Polis*. Baltimore: 82–95.

(1992). *Homer: the Poetry of the Past*. Ithaca (NY).

(1999). 'Reading Homer From the Rostrum: Poems and Laws in Aeschines' *Against Timarchus*', in S. Goldhill and R. Osborne (ed.) *Performance Culture and Athenian Democracy*. Cambridge: 231–56.

(2002). *The Origins of Criticism. Literary Culture and Poetic Theory in Classical Greece*. Princeton and Oxford.

(2003). 'From Letters to Literature: Reading the "Song Culture" of Classical Greece', in H. Yunis (ed.) *Written Texts and the Rise of Literate Culture in Ancient Greece*. Cambridge: 15–37.

Fortenbaugh, W. W. (1966). 'Plato's *Phaedrus* 235c3', *Classical Philology* 61: 108–9.

Fowler, R. L. (1996). 'Herodotos and His Contemporaries', *Journal of Hellenic Studies* 116: 62–87.

(2001). 'Early *Historie* and Literacy', in N. Luraghi (ed.) *The Historian's Craft in the Age of Herodotus*. Oxford: 95–115.

Foxhall, L., Gehrke, H.-J. and Luraghi, N. (eds.) (2010). *Intentional History: Spinning Time in Ancient Greece*. Stuttgart.

Fraenkel, E. (1950). *Aeschylus: Agamemnon*. 3 vols. Oxford.

Fränkel, H. (1955). *Wege und Formen frühgriechischen Denkens*. Munich.

(1975). *Early Greek Poetry and Philosophy: A History of Greek Epic, Lyric, and Prose to the Middle of the Fifth Century*. Oxford.

Fraser, P. M. (1972). *Ptolemaic Alexandria* I. Oxford.

Frede, D. (1992). 'The Cognitive Role of *Phantasia* in Aristotle', in M. C. Nussbaum and A. O. Rorty (eds.) *Essays on Aristotle's De Anima*. Oxford: 279–95.

(1997). *Platon. Philebos*. Göttingen.

Frede, M. (1987). 'Observations on Perception in Plato's later Dialogues', in M. Frede, *Essays in Ancient Philosophy*. Minneapolis: 3–10.

(1990). 'An Empiricist View of Knowledge: Memorism', in S. Everson (ed.) *Epistemology*. Cambridge: 225–50.

French, R. (1994). *Ancient Natural History: Histories of Nature*. London and New York.

Friedländer, P. (1958). *Plato*, I. New York.

Friis Johansen, H. and Whittle, E. W. (1980). *Aeschylus: The Suppliants*. 3 vols. Copenhagen.

Fronterotta, F. (2001). ΜΕΘΕΞΙΣ. *La teoria platonica delle idee e la partecipazione delle cose empiriche. Dai dialoghi giovanili al Parmenide*. Pisa.

Frontisi-Ducroux, F. and Vernant, J.-P. (1997). *Dans l'oeil du miroir*. Paris.

Furley, W. D. (2011). 'Life in a Line: A Reading of Dedicatory Epigrams From the Archaic to the Classical Period', in M. Baumbach, A. Petrovic and I. Petrovic (eds.) *Archaic and Classical Greek Epigram*. Cambridge: 151–66.

Gadamer, H.-G. (1980). *Dialogue and Dialectic: Eight Hermeneutical Studies on Plato*. New Haven.

(2000). *Platons Dialektische Ethik*. Hamburg (first published in 1931).

Gagarin, M. (2008). *Writing Greek Law*. Cambridge.

Gagliardi, P. (2007). *I due volti della gloria*. Bari.

Galli, M. (2005). 'Pilgrimage as Elite *Habitus*: Educated Pilgrims in Sacred Landscape During the Second Sophistic', in J. Elsner and I. Rutherford (eds.) *Pilgrimage in Greco-Roman and Early Christian Antiquity. Seeing the Gods*. Oxford: 253–90.

Garcia, L. F., Jr. (2013). *Homeric Durability: Telling Time in the Iliad*. Washington, DC. [URL = http://nrs.harvard.edu/urn-3:hul.ebook:CHS_GarciaL.Homeric_Durability_Telling_Time_in_the_Iliad.2013.]

García Valdes, M., Llera Fueyo, L. A., and Rodríguez-Noriega Guillén, L. (2009). *Claudius Aelianus. De Natura Animalium*. Berlin.

Garvie, A. F. (1986). *Aeschylus* Choephori. Oxford.

(2009). *Aeschylus* Persae. Oxford.

Gauthier, P. (1985). *Les cités grecques et leurs bienfaiteurs (IVᵉ–Iᵉʳ siècle av. J.-C.): contribution à l'histoire des institutions*. Paris.

Gavran Miloš, A. (2012). 'Epicurus on the Origin and Formation of Preconceptions', *Croatian Journal of Philosophy* 12: 239–56.

Gavrilov, A. K. (1997). 'Techniques of Reading in Classical Antiquity', *Classical Quarterly* 47: 56–73.

Gehrke, H.-J. (2001). 'Myth, History and Collective Identity: Uses of the Past in Ancient Greece and Beyond', in N. Luraghi (ed.) *The Historian's Craft in the Age of Herodotus*. Oxford: 286–313.

Genette, G. (1979). *Introduction à l'architexte*. Paris.

Gentili, B. (2011). *Poesia e pubblico nella Grecia antica. Da Omero al V secolo*. 2nd edn. Milan.

Gentili, B., Catenacci, C., Giannini, P., and Lomiento, L. (2013). *Pindaro: Le Olimpiche*. Milan.

Gerson, L. P. (1994). *Plotinus*. London.

Gesner, C. (ed.) (1556). *Claudii Aeliani praenestini pontificis et sophistae ... opera, quae extant, omnia, graece latineque*. Zurich.

Ghiron-Bistagne, P. (1976). *Recherches sur les acteurs dans la Grèce antique*. Paris.

Giangiulio, M. (2001). 'Constructing the Past: Colonial Traditions and the Writing of History. The Case of Cyrene', in N. Luraghi (ed.) *The Historian's Craft in the Age of Herodotus*. Oxford: 116–37.

(2010). 'Le società ricordano? Paradigmi e problemi della "memoria collettiva" (a partire da Maurice Halbwachs)', in M. Giangiulio (ed.) *Memorie coloniali*. Rome: 29–43.

Giangiulio, M., Franchi, E., and Proietti, G. (eds.) (forthcoming). *Commemorating War and War Dead. Ancient and Modern*. Stuttgart.

Gigante, M. (1975). '*Philosophia medicans* in Filodemo', *Cronache Ercolanesi* 5: 53–61.

(1990). 'I frammenti di Sirone', *Paideia* 45: 175–98.

Gildersleeve, B. L. (1885). *Pindar: The Olympian and Pythian Odes*. New York.

Gill, C., Postlethwaite, N., and Seaford, R. (eds.) (1998). *Reciprocity in Ancient Greece*. Oxford.

Glidden, D. K. (1983). 'Epicurean Semantics', in *Syzetesis: Studi sull'epicureismo greco e romano offerti a Marcello Gigante*. Naples: vol. II, 185–226.

Goldhill, S. (1987). 'The Great Dionysia and Civic Ideology', *Journal of Hellenic Studies* 107: 58–76.

(1991). *The Poet's Voice. Essays on Poetics and Greek Literature*. Cambridge.

(2000). 'Civic Ideology and the Problem of Difference: The Politics of Aeschylean Tragedy, Once Again', *Journal of Hellenic Studies* 120: 34–56.

(2002). *The Invention of Prose*. Oxford.

(2004). *Aeschylus. The Oresteia*. Cambridge.

(2009). 'The Anecdote: Exploring the Boundaries Between Oral and Literate Performance in the Second Sophistic', in W. A. Johnson and H. N. Parker (eds.) *Ancient Literacies: the Culture of Reading in Greece and Rome*. Oxford and New York: 96–113.

Goldschmidt, V. (1979). *Le système stoïcien et l'idée de temps*. Paris.

Gonzalez, F. J. (2007). 'How is the Truth of Beings in the Soul? Interpreting *Anamnesis* in Plato', *Elenchos* 28: 275–301.

Goody, J. (1977). *The Domestication of the Savage Mind*. Cambridge.

Gordon, P. (2013). 'Epistolary Epicureans', in O. Hodkinson, P. A. Rosenmeyer and E. Bracke (eds.) *Epistolary Narratives in Ancient Greek Literature*. Leiden and Boston: 133–51.

Gosling, J. C. B. (1975). *Plato. Philebus*. Oxford.

Gow, A. S. F. (ed.) (1950). *Theocritus*. 2 vols. Cambridge.

Graf, F. (2009). 'Serious Singing: The Orphic Hymns as Religious Texts', *Kernos* 22: 169–82.

Graf, F. and Johnston, S. I. (2007). *Ritual Texts for the Afterlife. Orpheus and the Bacchic Gold Tablets.* London.

Gray, B. (2015). *Stasis and Stability. Exile, the Polis, and Political Thought, ca. 404–146 BC.* Oxford.

Graziosi, B. (2002). *Inventing Homer: The Early Reception of Epic.* Cambridge.

Graziosi, B. and Haubold, J. (2005). *Homer: The Resonance of Epic.* London.

(2009). 'Greek Lyric and Early Greek Literary History', in F. Budelmann (ed.) *The Cambridge Companion to Greek Lyric.* Cambridge: 95–113.

(2010). *Iliad 6: A Commentary.* Cambridge.

Greene, E. and Skinner, M. B. (eds.) (2009). *The New Sappho on Old Age: Textual and Philosophical Issues.* Cambridge (Mass.) and Washington.

Gregoric, P. (2007). *Aristotle on the Common Sense.* Oxford.

Grethlein, J. (2003). *Asyl und Athen. Die Konstruktion kollektiver Identität in der griechischen Tragödie.* Stuttgart and Weimar.

(2007). 'The Poetics of the Bath in the *Iliad*', *Harvard Studies in Classical Philology* 103: 25–49.

(2008). 'Memory and Material Objects in the *Iliad* and the *Odyssey*', *Journal of Hellenic Studies* 128: 27–51.

(2010). *The Greeks and Their Past: Poetry, Oratory and History in the Fifth Century BCE.* Cambridge.

Griffith, M. (1977). *The Authenticity of* Prometheus Bound. Cambridge.

(1983). *Aeschylus.* Prometheus Bound. Cambridge.

Griffiths, F. T. (1979). *Theocritus at Court.* Leiden.

Grilli, A. (1983). 'ΔΙΑΘΕΣΙΣ in Epicuro', in *Syzetesis: Studi sull'epicureismo greco e romano offerti a Marcello Gigante.* Naples: 93–109.

Gritti, E. (2005). 'La φαντασία plotiniana tra illuminazione intellettiva e impassibilità dell'anima', in R. Chiaradonna (ed.) *Studi sull'anima in Plotino.* Naples: 251–74.

Grondin, J. (1982). 'L'ἀλήθεια entre Platon et Heidegger', *Revue de Métaphysique et de Morale* 87: 551–6.

Grote, G. (1888). *Plato and the Other Companions of Plato*, vol. II. London.

Guidelli, C. (1988). 'Note sul tema della memoria nelle *Enneadi* di Plotino', *Elenchos* 9: 75–94.

Guthrie, W. K. C. (1952). *Orpheus and Greek Religion: A Study of the Orphic Movement.* Princeton.

(1987). *A History of Greek Philosophy*, vol. III. Cambridge.

Gutzwiller, K. (1992). 'Callimachus' Lock of Berenice: Fantasy, Romance, and Propaganda', *American Journal of Philology* 113: 359–85.

(1996). 'The Evidence for Theocritean Poetry Books', in M. A. Harder, R. F. Regtuit, and G. C. Wakker (eds.) *Theocritus (Hellenistica Groningana II).* Groningen: 119–48.

Habicht, C. (1998). '«Zur ewig währenden Erinnerung». Ein auf das Nachleben zielender Topos', *Chiron*: 35–41.

Hackforth, R. (1945). *Plato's Examination of Pleasure.* Cambridge.

Hacking, I. (1995). *Rewriting the Soul: Multiple Personality and the Sciences of Memory*. Princeton.

Hadot, I. (1969). 'Épicure et l'enseignement philosophique hellénistique et romain', in *Association Guillaume Budé. Actes VIIIᵉ Congrès*, Paris 5–10 avril 1968. Paris: 347–54.

Hadot, P. (1981). *Exercices spirituels et philosophie antique*. Paris. [Engl. transl: (1995) *Philosophy As a Way of Life: Spiritual Exercises from Socrates to Foucault*. Malden.]

Halbwachs, M. (1925). *Les cadres sociaux de la mémoire*. Paris (2nd edn. 1952). [Engl. transl.: (1992) *On Collective Memory*. Chicago.]

Hall, E. M. (1989). 'The Archer Scene in Aristophanes' Thesmophoriazusae', *Philologus* 133: 38–54.

(1996). *Aeschylus Persians, edited with an Introduction, Translation and Commentary*. Warminster.

Halliwell, S. (2007). 'The Life-and-Death Journey of the Soul: Interpreting the Myth of Er', in G. R. F. Ferrari (ed.) *The Cambridge Companion to Plato's Republic*. Cambridge: 445–73.

Hammerstaedt, J. (1996). 'Il ruolo della *prolepsis* epicurea', in G. Giannantoni and M. Gigante (eds.) *Epicureismo greco e romano*. Naples: vol. I, 221–37.

Hanink, J. (2010). 'The Life of the Author in the Letters of "Euripides"', *Greek, Roman, and Byzantine Studies* 50: 537–64.

(2013). 'Epitaphioi Mythoi and Tragedy as Encomium of Athens', *Trends in Classics* 5: 289–317.

(2014). *Lycurgan Athens and the Making of Classical Tragedy*. Cambridge.

(2017). 'Archives, Repertoires, Bodies, and Bones: Thoughts on Reperformance for Classicists', in R. Hunter and A. Uhlig (eds.) *Imagining Reperformance in Ancient Culture*. Cambridge: 21–41

Hanson, R. and Mendius, R. (2009). *Buddha's Brain: The Practical Neuroscience of Happiness, Love and Wisdom*. Oakland (Cal.)

Harder, A. (2012). *Callimachus AETIA. Introduction, Text, Translation and Commentary*. Oxford.

Hardie, A. (2013). 'Empedocles and the Muse of the *Agathos Logos*', *American Journal of Philology* 134: 209–46.

Harriot, R. (1962). 'Aristophanes' Audience and the Plays of Euripides', *Bulletin of the Institute of Classical Studies* 9: 1–9.

Harris, E. M. (1995). *Aeschines and Athenian Politics*. Oxford.

(2000). 'Open Texture in Athenian law', *Dike* 3: 29–79.

(2006). *Democracy and the Rule of Law in Classical Athens: Essays on Law, Society, and Politics*. Cambridge.

Harris, E. M., Leão, D. F., and Rhodes, P. J. (eds.) (2010). *Law and Drama in Ancient Greece*. London.

Harris, W. V. (1989). *Ancient Literacy*. Cambridge (Mass.).

Harte, V. (2014). 'Desire, Memory and the Authority of Soul: Plato *Philebus* 35C-D', *Oxford Studies in Ancient Philosophy* 46: 33–72.

Hartmann, A. (2010). *Zwischen Relikt und Reliquie. Objektbezogene Erinnerungspraktiken in Antiken Gesellschaften*. Berlin.

Hartwig, A. (2014). 'The Evolution of Comedy in the Fourth Century', in E. Csapo, H. R. Goette, J. R. Green and P. Wilson (eds.) *Greek Theatre in the Fourth Century BC*. Berlin: 207–27.

Harvey, F. D. (1966). 'Literacy in the Athenian Democracy', *Revue des Études Grecques* 79: 585–635.

Harvey, D. (2000). 'Phrynichos and his Muses', in D. Harvey and J. Wilkins (eds.) *The Rivals of Aristophanes. Studies in Athenian Old Comedy*. Swansea: 91–134.

Havelock, E. A. (1963). *Preface to Plato*. Cambridge, Mass.

(1982). *The Literate Revolution in Greece and its Cultural Consequences*. Princeton.

Hawes, G. (ed.) (2017). *Myths on the Map: The Storied Landscapes of Ancient Greece*. Oxford.

Hawke, J. (2011). *Writing Authority: Elite Competition and Written Law in Early Greece*. DeKalb (Ill.).

Heath, M. (1990). 'Aristophanes and His Rivals', *Greece and Rome* 37: 143–58.

Hedrick, Ch. W., Jr. (1999). 'Democracy and the Athenian Epigraphical Habit', *Hesperia* 68: 387–439.

Heerink, M. A. J. (2010). 'Merging Paradigms: Translating Pharaonic Ideology in Theocritus' Idyll 17', in R. Rollinger, M. Lang, B. Gufler, I. Madreiter (eds.) *Interkulturalität in der Alten Welt: Vorderasien, Hellas, Ägypten und die vielfältigen Ebenen des Kontakts*. Wiesbaden: 383–408.

Heidegger, M. (1998). 'Plato's Doctrine of Truth', in W. McNeill (ed.) *Pathmarks*. Cambridge: 155–82.

Heitsch, E. (1962). 'Die Nicht-Philosophische ΑΛΗΘΕΙΑ', *Hermes* 90: 24–33.

(1963). 'Wahrheit als Erinnerung', *Hermes* 91: 36–52.

(2011). *Aletheia: eine Episode aus der Geschichte des Wahrheitsbegriffs*. Meinz and Stuttgart.

Held, K. (2007). *Hedone und Ataraxia bei Epikur*. Paderborn.

Helmig, C. (2012). *Forms and Concepts: Concept Formation in the Platonic Tradition*. Berlin and Boston.

Henrichs, A. (1993). 'The Tomb of Aias and the Prospect of Hero Cult in Sophokles', *Classical Antiquity* 12: 165–80.

Henry, O. and Kelp, U. (eds.) (2016). *Tumulus as Sema: Space, Politics, Culture and Religion in the First Millennium BC*. Berlin.

Hercher, R. (1864). *De natura animalium libri XVII, Varia historia, Epistolae, Fragmenta*, vol. 1. Leipzig.

Herrmann, P. (1981). 'Teos und Abdera im 5. Jahrhundert v. Chr.', *Chiron* 11: 1–30.

Hesk, J. (1999). 'The Rhetoric of Anti-rhetoric in Athenian Oratory', in S. Goldhill and R. Osborne (eds.) *Performance Culture and Athenian Democracy*. Cambridge: 201–30.

(2000). *Deception and Democracy in Classical Athens*. Cambridge.

Heßler J. E. (2012). 'Epikur/Epikureismus: Sklaverei im Kepos', in H. Heinen (ed.) *Handwörterbuch der antiken Sklaverei*. Stuttgart.

Heubeck, A. (1979). *Schrift. Archaeologia Homerica*, vol. III. Göttingen.

Hicks, R. D. (1907). *Aristotle. De Anima*. Cambridge.

(1972). *Diogenes Laertius. Lives of Eminent Philosophers*. 2 vols. 2nd edn. Cambridge (Mass.) (1st edn: 1925).

Higbie, C. (2003). *The Lindian Chronicle and the Greek Creation of their Past*. Oxford.

Hinds, S. (1998). *Allusion and Intertext: Dynamics of Appropriation in Roman Poetry*. Cambridge.

Hochschild, P. E. (2012). *Memory in Augustine's Theological Anthropology*. Oxford.

Hoerber, R. G. (1960). 'Plato's Meno', *Phronesis* 5: 78–102.

Hoffmann, P. and Rashed, M. (2008). 'Platon: *Phèdre* 249b8-c1: les enjeux d'une faute d'onciales', *Revue des Études Grecques* 121: 43–64.

Hornblower, S. (2001). 'Epic and Epiphanies: Herodotus and the New Simonides', in D. Boedeker and D. Sider (eds.) *The New Simonides, Contexts of Praise and Desire*. Oxford and New York: 135–47.

(2008). *A Commentary on Thucydides, vol. III: Books 5.25–8.109*. Oxford.

Hubbard, B. A. F. and Karnofsky, E. S. (1982). *Plato: Plato's Protagoras*. London.

Hubbard, T. K. (1985). *The Pindaric Mind: A Study of Logical Structure in Early Greek Poetry*. Leiden.

(1991). *The Mask of Comedy: Aristophanes and the Intertextual Parabasis*. Ithaca and London.

Humbert, J. (1972). *Syntaxe grecque*. 3rd edn. Paris.

Hunter, R. (1989). *Apollonius of Rhodes. Argonautica book III*. Cambridge.

(1996). *Theocritus and the Archaeology of Greek Poetry*. Cambridge.

(2003a). *Theocritus. Encomium of Ptolemy Philadelphus*. Berkeley, Los Angeles and London.

(2003b). 'Reflecting on Writing and Culture: Theocritus and the Style of Cultural Change', in H. Yunis (ed.) *Written Texts and the Rise of Literate Culture in Ancient Greece*. Cambridge: 213–34.

(2012). *Plato and the Traditions of Ancient Literature: The Silent Stream*. Cambridge.

Hunter, R. and Uhlig, A. (2017). *Imagining Reperformance in Ancient Culture*. Cambridge.

Hutchinson, D. M. (2011). 'Apprehension of Thought in *Ennead* 4.3.30', *The International Journal of the Platonic Tradition* 5: 262–82.

Ierodiakonou, K. (2007). 'The Stoics and the Skeptics on Memory', in M. M. Sassi (ed.) *Tracce nella mente: teorie della memoria da Platone ai moderni*. Pisa: 47–65.

Immerwahr, H. (1964). 'Book Rolls on Attic Vases', in C. Henderson Jr. (ed.) *Classical and Renaissance Studies in Honor of Berthold Louis Ullman*, vol. I. Rome: 17–48.

(1973). 'More Book Rolls on Attic Vases', *Antike Kunst* 16 (1973): 143–7.

Imperio, O. (2004). *Parabasi di Aristofane. Acarnesi Cavalieri Vespe Uccelli*. Bari.

Ireland, S. and Steel, F. L. (1975). 'Phrenes as an Anatomical Organ in the Works of Homer', *Glotta* 53: 183–94.

Jacobs, F. (1832). *Aeliani de natura animalium libri XVII*, 2 vols. Jena.

Jahn, T. (1987). *Zum Wortfeld 'Seele-Geist' in der Sprache Homers*. Munich.

Jankélévitch, V. (1964). *L'ironie*. Paris.

Jarrett, S. C. (2002). 'Sappho's Memory', *Rhetoric Society Quarterly* 32: 11–43.

Jebb, R. C. (2004). *Sophocles Plays: Trachiniae*. London. [1st edn, 1892.]

Jeffery, L. and Morpurgo-Davies, A. (1970). 'ΠΟΙΝΙΚΑΣΤΑΣ and ΠΟΙΝΙΚΑΖΕΝ: A New Archaic Inscription from Crete', *Kadmos* 9: 118–54.

Jiménez San Cristóbal, A. I. (2011). 'Do not Drink the Water of Forgetfulness (*OF* 474–477)', in M. Herrero de Jáuregui, A. I. Jiménez San Cristóbal, M. A. Santamaria et al. (eds.) *Tracing Orpheus. Studies of Orphic Fragments in honour of Alberto Bernabé*. Berlin: 165–70.

Johnson, M. (2012). 'The Role of *Eros* in Improving the Pupil, or What Socrates Learned from Sappho', in M. Johnson and H. Tarrant (eds.) *Alcibiades and the Socratic Lover-Educator*. London: 7–29.

Johnson, W. A. (2000). 'Toward a Sociology of Reading in Classical Antiquity', *American Journal of Philology* 121: 593–627.

(2010). *Readers and Reading Culture in the High Roman Empire: A Study of Elite Reading Communities*. Oxford.

Jost, K. (1935). *Das Beispiel und Vorbild der Vorfahren bei den attischen Rednern und Geschichtschreibern bis Demosthenes*. Basel.

Jouan, F. and Van Looy, H. (eds.) (1998). *Euripide, vol. 8. Fragments 1: Aigeus– Autolykos*. Paris.

Julião, R., Lo Presti, R., Perler, D., and van der Eijk, P. (2016). 'Mapping Memory: Theories in Ancient, Medieval and Early Modern Philosophy and Medicine', *eTopoi* 6: 678–702.

Jung, M. (2006). *Marathon und Plataiai: Zwei Perserschlachten als "lieux de mémoire" im antiken Griechenland*. Göttingen.

Kahn, C. (2006). 'Plato on Recollection', in H. H. Benson (ed.) *A Companion to Plato*. Oxford: 119–32.

Kakrides, J. T. (1949). *Homeric Researches*. Lund.

Kany-Turpin, J. (2007). 'Les dieux. Représentation mentale des dieux, piété et discours théologique', in A. Gigandet and P.-M. Morel (eds.) *Lire Épicure et les épicuriens*. Paris: 145–65.

Kapparis, K. (1999). *Apollodoros. Against Neaira [D 59]*. Berlin.

Karfik, F. (2014). 'Parts of the Soul in Plotinus', in K. Corcilius, D. Perler, and C. Helmig (eds.) *Partitioning the Soul: Debates from Plato to Leibniz*. Berlin and New York: 107–48.

Kavoulaki, A. (2008). 'The Last Word: Ritual, Power, and Performance in Euripides' *Hiketides*', in M. Revermann and P. Wilson (eds.) *Performance, Iconography, Reception: Studies in Honour of Oliver Taplin*. Oxford: 291–317.

Keesling, C. M. (2009). 'Exemplary Animals: Greek Animal Statues and Human Portraiture', in T. Fögen and M. Lee (eds.) *Bodies and Boundaries in Graeco-Roman Antiquity*. Berlin and New York: 283–310.

Kelly, A. (2007). 'Stesikhoros and Helen', *Museum Helveticum* 64: 1–21.

Keynes, G. (1966). *The Complete Writings of William Blake: With Variant Readings.* Oxford.

Kindstrand, J. F. (1998). 'Claudius Aelianus und sein Werk', *Aufstieg und Niedergand der Römischen Welt* II.34.4: 2954–96.

King, R. A. H. (2004). *Aristoteles: De Memoria et Reminiscentia.* Berlin.

(2009). *Aristotle and Plotinus on Memory.* Berlin and New York.

(2016). 'Sensation in the *Philebus*: Common to Body and Soul', in J. Jirsa and Š. Špinka (eds.) *Plato's* Philebus: *Proceedings of the 9th Plato Symposium Platonicum Pragense.* Prague: 93–109.

Kirk, G. S. (1990–1993). (ed.) *The Iliad: A Commentary.* 3 vols. Cambridge.

Kirk, G. S. and Raven, J. E. (1957). *The Presocratic Philosophers.* Cambridge.

Klein, J. (1989 – first published Chapel Hill, 1965). *A Commentary on Plato's Meno.* Chicago.

Kleve, K. (1963). 'Zur epikureischen Terminologie', *Symbolae Osloenses* 38: 25–31.

Klibansky, R., Panofsky, E., and Saxl, F. (1964). *Saturn and Melancholy.* Edinburgh.

Klosko, G. (1979). 'Toward a Consistent Interpretation of the *Protagoras*', *Archiv für Geschichte der Philosophie* 61: 125–42.

Kloss, G. (2001). *Erscheinungsformen komischen Sprechens bei Aristophanes.* Berlin and New York.

Knox, B. M. W. (1961). 'The *Ajax* of Sophocles', *Harvard Studies in Classical Philology* 65: 3–24.

(1968). 'Silent Reading in Antiquity', *Greek, Roman, and Byzantine Studies* 9: 421–35.

Koljević, S. (1980). *The Epic in the Making.* Oxford.

Koniaris, G. L. (1967). 'On Sappho, fr. 16 LP.', *Hermes* 95: 257–68.

Konstan, D. (2007). 'Commentary on Morel', in *Proceedings of the Boston Area Colloquium in Ancient Philosophy* 23: 49–55.

(2011). 'Epicurus on the Gods', in J. Fish and K. R. Sanders (eds.) *Epicurus and the Epicurean Tradition.* Cambridge: 53–71.

(2015). 'Sappho 16 and the Sense of Beauty', *EuGeStA* 5: 14–26.

Kottman, P. A. (2003). 'Memory, "Mimesis," Tragedy: The Scene before Philosophy', *Theatre Journal* 55: 81–97.

Kromer, G. (1976). 'The Value of Time in Pindar's *Olympian* 10', *Hermes* 104: 420–36.

Labarrière, J. L. (2000). 'Sentir le temps, regarder un tableau: Aristotle et les images de la mémoire', in C. Darbo-Péschanski (ed.) *Constructions du temps dans le monde grec ancien.* Paris: 269–83.

Lai, A. (1997). 'La circolazione delle tragedie eschilee in ambito simposiale', *Lexis* 15: 143–8.

Lambert, S. (2010). 'Connecting with the Past in Lykourgan Athens: an Epigraphic Perspective', in L. Foxhall, N. Luraghi and H.-J. Gehrke (eds.) *Intentional History: Spinning Time in Ancient Greece.* Stuttgart: 225–38.

Lambrinoudakis, V. and Wörrle, M. (1983). 'Ein hellenistischen Reformgesetz über das öffentliche Urkundenwesen von Paros', *Chiron* 13: 283–368.

Lammermann, K. (1936). 'Von der attischen Urbanität und ihrer Auswirkung in der Sprache'. Dissertation, Göttingen.

Lane Fox, R. (1997). 'Demosthenes, Dionysius and the dating of six early speeches', *Classica et Mediaevalia* 48: 167–203.

Lang, H. S. (1980). 'On Memory: Aristotle's Corrections to Plato', *Journal of the History of Philosophy* 18: 379–93.

Lardinois, A. (2008). ' "Someone, I Say, Will Remember Us": Oral Memory in Sappho's Poetry', in E. A. MacKckay (ed.) *Orality, Literacy, Memory in the Ancient Greek and Roman World*. Leiden and Boston: 79–96.

(2009). 'The New Sappho Poem (P. Koln 21351 and 21376): Key to the Old Fragments', in E. Greene and M. B. Skinner (eds.) *The New Sappho on Old Age: Textual and Philosophical Issues*. Cambridge (Mass.) and Washington: 41–57.

Lateiner, D. (1989). *The Historical Method of Herodotus*. Toronto.

Lattimore, R. (1951). *The Iliad of Homer*. Chicago and London.

Laurand, V. (2003). 'Le traitement épicurien de la douleur', in T. Bénatouil, V. Laurand and A. Macé (eds.) *L'Épicurisme antique*. Paris: 91–117.

Lavaud, L. (2006). 'La dianoia médiatrice entre le sensible et l'intelligible', *Etudes Platoniciennes* 3: 29–55.

Ledesma, F. (2016). 'Amor, lenguaje y olvido. Sobre memoria y desmemoria en los diálogos de Platón', *Logos: Anales del Seminario de Metafísica* 49: 91–109.

Lee, M.-K. (2008). 'The *Theaetetus*', in G. Fine (ed.) *The Oxford Handbook of Plato*. Oxford: 411–36.

Lembo, D. (1981–1982). '*Typos* e *sympatheia* in Epicuro', *Annali della Facoltà di Lettere e Filosofia della Università di Napoli* 24: 17–67.

Levick, B. (2007). *Julia Domna: Syrian Empress*. London and New York.

Linguiti, A. (2004–2005). 'Immagine e concetto in Aristotele e Plotino', *Incontri triestini di filologia classica* 4: 69–80.

Lissarrague, F. (1987). *Un Flot d'Images, Une esthétique du banquet grec*. Paris.

Lloyd, G. E. R. (1966). *Polarity and Analogy: Two Types of Argumentation in Early Greek Thought*. Cambridge.

(1987). *The Revolutions of Wisdom: Studies in the Claims and Practice of Ancient Greek Science*. Berkeley.

(1990). *Demystifying Mentalities*. Cambridge.

(1999). 'Mythology: Reflections from a Chinese Perspective', in R. Buxton (ed.) *From Myth to Reason? Studies in the Development of Greek Thought*. Oxford: 145–65.

Lloyd, G. E. R. and Owen, G. E. (eds.) (1978). *Aristotle on Mind and the Senses*. Cambridge.

Long, A. A. (1971). 'Aisthesis, Prolepsis and Linguistic Theory in Epicurus', *Bulletin of the Institute of Classical Studies* 18: 114–33.

Long, A. A. and Sedley, D. N. (eds.) (1987). *The Hellenistic Philosophers*. 2 vols. Cambridge.

Loraux, N. (1986). *The Invention of Athens: The Funeral Oration in the Classical City*. Cambridge. [First published as *L'Invention d'Athènes. Histoire de l'oraison funèbre dans la 'cité classique'*. Paris 1981.]

(1988). 'De l'amnistie et de son contraire', in *Usages de l'Oubli*. Paris: 23–48. [Engl. transl.: Loraux 1998.]

(1990). *Les mères en deuil*. Paris. [Engl. transl.: Loraux 1998.]

(1997). *La cité divisée. L'oubli dans la mémoire d'Athènes*. Paris. [Engl. transl.: Loraux 2002.]

(1998). *Mothers in Mourning. With the Essay on Amnesty and its Opposite*. Ithaca and London.

(2002). *The Divided City: On Memory and Forgetting in Ancient Athens*. New York.

Lord, A. (ed.) (1954). *Serbocroatian Heroic Songs – Collected by Milman Parry*. Cambridge.

Louth, A. (1989). *Denys the Areopagite*. London.

Low, P., Oliver, G., and Rhodes, P. J. (eds.) (2012). *Cultures of Commemoration. War Memorials, Ancient and Modern*. Oxford.

Luginbill, R. D. (2009). 'The Occasion and Purpose of Alcman's *Partheneion* (1 *PMGF*)', *Quaderni Urbinati di Cultura Classica* 121: 27–54.

Luraghi, N. (2010). 'The Demos as Narrator: Public Honors and the Construction of Future and Past', in L. Foxhall, N. Luraghi and H.-J. Gehrke (eds.) *Intentional History: Spinning Time in Ancient Greece*. Stuttgart: 247–64.

Luria A. R. (1968). *The Mind of a Mnemonist*. New York.

Luther, W. (1935). *'Wahrheit' und 'Lüge' im ältesten Griechentum*. Borna and Leipzig.

Ma, J. (1999). *Antiochos III and the Cities of Western Asia Minor*. Oxford.

(2009). 'City as Memory', in B. Graziosi, P. Vasunia and G. Boys-Stones (eds.) *The Oxford Handbook of Hellenic Studies*. Oxford: 248–59.

MacDowell, D. M. (2009). *Demosthenes the Orator*. Oxford.

MacLachlan, B. (1993). *The Age of Grace: Charis in Early Greek Poetry*. Princeton and Oxford.

Maffi, A. (1988). *L'iscrizione di Lygdamis*. Trieste.

Magrin, S. (2010). 'Sensation and Scepticism in Plotinus', *Oxford Studies in Ancient Philosophy* 39: 249–97.

Makin, S. (2006). *Aristotle*. Metaphysics *Book Theta*. Oxford.

Manolidis, G. (1987). *Die Rolle der Physiologie in der Philosophie Epikurs*. Frankfurt am Main.

Mansfeld, J. (2002). 'Zeno on the unity of philosophy', in T. Scaltsas and A. S. Mason (eds.). *The Philosophy of Zeno*. Larnaca: 59–79.

Manuwald, A. (1972). *Die Prolepsislehre Epikurs*. Bonn.

Marincola, J. (1997). *Authority and Tradition in Ancient Historiography*, Cambridge.

(2001). *Greek Historians*. Cambridge.

Marmodoro, A. (2014). *Aristotle on Perceiving Objects*. Oxford.

Martin, C. B. and Deutscher, M. (1966). 'Remembering', *Philosophical Review* 75: 161–96.

Martinelli Tempesta, S. (1999). 'Nota a Saffo, fr. 16, 12–13 V. (P.Oxy. 1231)', *Maia* 69: 7–14.

Masi, F. (2014a). 'Gli atomi ricordano? Fisicalismo e memoria nella psicologia di Epicuro', *Antiquorum Philosophia* 8: 121–41.

(2014b). 'The Method of Multiple Explanations: Epicurus and the Notion of Causal Possibility', in C. Natali and C. Viano (eds.) *AITIA II, Avec ou sans Aristote: Le débat sur les causes à l'âge hellénistique et impérial.* Leuven: 37–63.

Massimilla, G. (1996). *Aitia. Libri primo e secondo. Callimaco.* Pisa.

Masson, E. (1967). *Recherches sur les plus anciens emprunts sémitiques en grec.* Paris.

Mastromarco, G. (1987). 'Trame allusive e memoria del pubblico (*Acarn.* 300–301, *Caval.* 314)', in S. Boldrini et al. (eds.) *Filologia e forme letterarie. Studi offerti a F. Della Corte, vol. 1, Letteratura greca.* Urbino: 239–43.

(1997). 'Pubblico e memoria teatrale nell'Atene di Aristofane', in P. Thiercy and M. Menu (eds.) *Aristophane: La langue, la scène, la cité. Actes du colloque de Toulouse. 17–19 mars 1994.* Bari: 530–48.

(2006a). 'La paratragodia, il libro, la memoria', in E. Medda, M. S. Mirto, and M. P. Pattoni (eds.) *ΚΩΜΩΙΔΟΤΡΑΓΩΙΔΙΑ. Intersezioni del tragico e del comico nel teatro del V secolo a.C.* Pisa: 137–91.

(2006b). 'Aristofane a simposio', in M. Vetta and C. Catenacci (eds.) *I luoghi della poesia nella Grecia antica.* Alessandria: 265–78.

Mastronarde, D. J. (2002). *Euripides. Medea.* Cambridge.

Matelli, E. (2012). 'Praxiphanes of Mytilene (called "of Rhodes"): The Sources, Text and Translation', in A. Martano, E. Matelli and D. Mirhady (eds.) *Praxiphanes of Mytilene and Chamaeleon of Heraclea: Text, Translation, and Discussion.* New Brunswick (New Jersey): 1–156.

Mathieu, G. (1914). 'Survivances des luttes politiques du Ve siècle chez les orateurs attiques du IVe siècle', *Revue de Philologie* n.s. 38: 182–205.

Meiggs, R. and Lewis, D. M. (1988). *A Selection of Greek Historical Inscriptions to the End of the Fifth Century.* 2nd edn. Oxford.

Mette, H. J. (1977). *Urkunden dramatischer Aufführungen in Griechenland.* Berlin and New York.

Meyer, D. (2005). *Inszeniertes Lesevergnügen. Das inschriftliche Epigramm und seine Rezeption bei Kallimachos.* Stuttgart.

Meyer, E. (2013). 'Inscriptions as Honors and the Athenian Epigraphic Habit', *Historia* 62: 453–505.

Michaelian, K. and Sutton, J. (2017). 'Memory', *The Stanford Encyclopedia of Philosophy* (Summer 2017 edition), E. N. Zalta (ed.). [URL = https://plato .stanford.edu/archives/sum2017/entries/memory/.]

Milanese, G. (1989). *Lucida carmina. Comunicazione e scrittura da Epicuro a Lucrezio.* Milan.

(1996). 'Aspetti del rapporto fra tra denominazione e referenzialità in Epicuro e nella tradizione epicurea', in G. Giannantoni and M. Gigante (eds.) *Epicureismo greco e romano.* Naples: vol. I, 269–86.

Milanezi, S. (2000). 'Le suffrage du rire, ou le spectacle du politique en Grèce', in M.-L. Desclos (ed.) *Le Rire des Grecs. Anthropologie du rire en Grèce ancienne.* Grenoble: 369–96.

(2011). 'Spectacles de l'amitié et de la haine dans les concours en l'honneur de Dionysos', in J. Peigney (ed.) *Amis et Ennemis en Grèce ancienne.* Bordeaux: 141–59.

Millis, B. W. and Olson, D. S. (2012). *Inscriptional Records for the Dramatic Festivals in Athens: IG II² 2318–2325 and Related Texts*. Leiden and Boston.

Minchin, E. (2001). *Homer and the Resources of Memory: Some Applications of Cognitive Theory to the* Iliad *and the* Odyssey. Oxford.

(2016). 'Heritage in the Landscape: The "Heroic Tumuli" in the Troad Region', in J. McInerney and I. Sluiter (eds.) *Valuing Landscape in Classical Antiquity: Natural Environment and Cultural Imagination*. Leiden: 255–75.

Mitsis, P. (1988). *Epicurus' Ethical Theory: The Pleasures of Invulnerability*. Ithaca.

Moggi, M. (2009). 'Strategie e forme della riconciliazione: μὴ μνησικακεῖν', *I quaderni del ramo d'oro* 2: 167–91.

Moles, J. (1999). '*Anathēma kai Ktēma*: the Inscriptional Inheritance of Ancient Historiography', *Histos* 3: 27–69.

Montero, B. (2010). 'Does Bodily Awareness Interfere with Highly Skilled Movement?', *Inquiry* 5: 105–22.

Moore, C. (2015). 'Socrates and Self-knowledge in Aristophanes' Clouds', *Classical Quarterly* 65: 534–51.

Moore, T. (1989). *The Planets Within: the Astrological Psychology of Marsilio Ficino*. 2nd edn. Great Barrington (Mass.).

Morand, A.-F. (2001). *Études sur les Hymnes Orphiques*. Leiden and Boston.

Morel, J.-P. (2006). 'Mémoire et caractère – Aristote et l'histoire personnelle', in A. Brancacci and G. Gigliotti (eds.) *Mémoire et souvenir. Six études sur Platon, Aristote, Hegel et Husserl*. Rome: 49–87.

Morel, P.-M. (2003). 'Épicure et la "fin de la nature"', in T. Bénatouïl, V. Laurand and A. Macé (eds.) *L'Épicurisme antique*. Paris: 167–96.

(2007). 'Method and Evidence: on the Epicurean Preconception', *Proceedings of the Boston Area Colloquium in Ancient Philosophy* 23: 25–48.

(2009). *Épicure. La nature et la raison*. Paris.

(2011). *Épicure: Lettres, maxims et autres texts*. Paris.

Morgan, J. R. (2009). 'The Emesan Connection: Philostratus and Heliodorus', in K. Demoen and D. Praet (eds.) *Theios Sophistes: Essays on Flavius Philostratus' Vita Apollonii*. Leiden and Boston: 263–81.

Morgan, K. A. (2000). *Myth and Philosophy from the Presocratics to Plato*. Cambridge.

Morrison, A. D. (2007). *The Narrator in Archaic Greek and Hellenistic Poetry*. Cambridge.

(2011). 'Callimachus' Muses', in B. Acosta-Hughes, L. Lehnus and S. Stephens (eds.) *Brill's Companion to Callimachus*. Leiden and Boston: 329–48.

(2013). 'Speaking from the Tomb? The Disappearing Epitaph of Simonides in Calimachus, *Aetia* fr. 64 Pf.', in P. Low and P. Liddel (eds.) *Inscriptions and their Uses in Greek and Latin Literature*. Oxford: 289–301.

Morstein-Marx, R. (2004). *Oratory and Political Power in the Late Roman Republic*. Cambridge.

Morwood, J. (2007). *Euripides. Suppliant Women*. Oxford.

Most, G. W. (1981). 'Sappho fr. 16.6–7 L-P', *Classical Quarterly* 31: 11–17.

(1996). 'Reflecting Sappho', in E. Greene (ed.) *Re-Reading Sappho: Reception and Transmission*. Berkeley, Los Angeles and London: 11–35.

Mueller, M. (2007). 'Penelope and the Poetics of Remembering', *Arethusa* 40: 337–62.

(2010). 'Helen's Hands: Weaving for *Kleos* in the *Odyssey*', *Helios* 37: 1–21.

(2016). *Objects as Actors: Props and the Poetics of Performance in Greek Tragedy*. Chicago.

Muellner, L. (1996). *The Anger of Achilles: Mênis in Greek Epic*. Ithaca and London.

Muir, J. V. (2001). *Alcidamas. The Works and Fragments*. London.

Mullen, W. C. (1982). *Choreia: Pindar and Dance*. Princeton.

Munn, M. (2000). *The School of History: Athens in the Age of Socrates*, Berkeley.

Murray, P. (1981). 'Poetic Inspiration in Early Greece', *The Journal of Hellenic Studies* 101: 87–100.

(2004). 'The Muses and their arts', in P. Murray and P. J. Wilson (eds.) *Music and the Muses: The Culture of 'Mousike' in the Classical Athenian City*. Oxford: 365–89.

Murray, P. and Wilson, P. J. (eds.) (2004). *Music and the Muses: The Culture of 'Mousike' in the Classical Athenian City*. Oxford.

Muth, R. (1954). ' "Hymenaios" und "Epithalamion" ', *Wiener Studien* 67: 5–45.

Nagy, G. (1979). *The Best of the Achaeans: Concepts of the Hero in Archaic Greek Poetry*. Baltimore.

(1983). '*Sema* and *Noesis*: Some Illustrations', *Arethusa* 16: 35–55.

(1990). *Greek Mythology and Poetics*. Ithaca.

(2009). 'The "New Sappho" Reconsidered in the Light of the Athenian Reception of Sappho', in E. Greene and M. B. Skinner (eds.) *The New Sappho on Old Age: Textual and Philosophical Issues*. Cambridge (Mass.) and Washington: 176–99.

Nassen, P. J. (1975). 'A Literary Study of Pindar's *Olympian* 10', *Transactions of the American Philological Association* 105: 219–40.

Natali, C. (1986). 'Aristote et les méthodes d'enseignement de Gorgias', in B. Cassin (ed.) *Positions de la sophistique*. Paris: 105–16.

Nehamas, A. (1999). *Virtues of Authenticity: Essays on Socrates and Plato*. Princeton.

Nervegna, S. (2014). 'Performing Classics: The Tragic Canon in the Fourth Century and Beyond', in E. Csapo, H. R. Goette, J. R. Green and P. Wilson (eds.) *Greek Theatre in the Fourth Century B.C.* Berlin: 157–86.

Nesselrath, H. G. (1990). *Die attische Mittlere Komödie: ihre Stellung in der antiken Literaturkritik und Literaturgeschichte*. Berlin.

Nieddu, G. F. (1984). 'La metafora della memoria come scrittura e l'immagine dell'animo come *deltos*', *Quaderni di Storia* 19: 213–9.

Nietzsche, F. (1980). *Zur Genealogie der Moral*, in G. Colli and M. Montinari (eds.) *Sämtliche Werke, Kritische Studienausgabe*, vol. 5. Munich and New York.

Nightingale, A. (1995). *Genres in Dialogue: Plato and the Construct of Philosophy*. Cambridge.

Nikkanen, A. (2012). 'A Note on Memory and Reciprocity in Homer's Odyssey', in V. Bers et al. (eds.) *Donum natalicium digitaliter confectum Gregorio*

Nagy septuagenario a discipulis collegis familiaribus oblatum. Washington. (URL = http://chs.harvard.edu/wa/pageR?tn=ArticleWrapper&bdc=12 &mn=4616 - n.7).

Nikulin, D. (2014). 'Memory and Recollection in Plotinus', *Archiv für Geschichte der Philosophie* 96: 183–201.

———— (ed.) (2015). *Memory: A History.* Oxford: 3–34.

Nora, P. (ed.) (1984–1992). *Les Lieux de mémoire.* 3 vols. Paris.

———— (1989). 'Between Memory and History: Les Lieux de Mémoire', *Representations* 26: 7–24.

Nørby, S., Lange, M., and Larsen, A. (2010). 'Forgetting to Forget: On the Duration of Voluntary Suppression of Neutral and Emotional Memories', *Acta Psychologica* 133: 73–80.

Norden, E. (1916). *P. Vergilius Maro Aeneis Buch VI.* Leipzig.

North, H. (1952). 'The Use of Poetry in the Training of the Ancient Orator', *Traditio* 8: 1–33.

Notopoulos, J. A. (1938). 'Mnemosyne in Oral Literature', *Transactions and Proceedings of the American Philological Association* 69: 465–93.

Nouhaud, M. (1982). *L'utilisation de l'histoire par les orateurs attiques.* Paris.

———— (1986). 'Sur une allusion d'Eschine (*Ambassade, 75*) au stratège athénien Tolmidès', *Revue des Études Grecques* 99: 342–6.

Nünlist, R. (1998). *Poetologische Bildersprache in der frühgriechischen Dichtung.* Stuttgart.

Nussbaum, M. (1978). *Aristotle's De Motu Animalium.* Princeton.

———— (1980). 'Aristophanes and Socrates on Learning Practical Wisdom', *Yale Classical Studies* 26: 43–97.

Nussbaum, M. and Oksenberg Rorty, A. (eds.) (1992). *Essays on Aristotle's De Anima.* Oxford.

O'Keefe, T. (2010). *Epicureanism.* Durham.

Obbink, D. (2016). 'The Newest Sappho: Text, Apparatus Criticus, and Translation', in A. Bierl and A. Lardinois (eds.) *The Newest Sappho: P. Sapph. Obbink and P.GC inv. 105, frs. 1–4.* Leiden and Boston: 13–33.

Ober, J. (1989). *Mass and Elite in Democratic Athens. Rhetoric, Ideology, and the Power of the People.* Princeton.

Ober, J. and Strauss, B. (1990). 'Drama, Political Rhetoric and the Discourse of Athenian Democracy', in J. Winkler and F. Zeitlin (eds.) *Nothing to do with Dionysos?* Princeton: 237–70.

Ogden, D. (2001). *Greek and Roman Necromancy.* Princeton.

Olding, G. (2007). 'Myth and Writing in Aeschines' *Against Timarchus*', in C. Cooper (ed.) *Politics of Orality.* Leiden: 155–70.

Olson, S. D. (2002). *Aristophanes Acharnians.* Oxford.

———— (2007). *Broken Laughter: Select Fragments of Greek Comedy.* Oxford.

Onians, R. B. (1951). *The Origins of European Thought About the Body, the Mind, the Soul, the World, Time, and Fate.* Oxford.

Osborne, C. (2007). *Dumb Beasts and Dead Philosophers: Humanity and the Humane in Ancient Philosophy and Literature.* Oxford and New York.

Osborne, R. (1985). *Demos: the Discovery of Classical Attika*. Cambridge.

(2011). 'Local Environment, Memory, and the Formation of the Citizen in Classical Attica', in S. D. Lambert (ed.) *Sociable Man: Essays on Ancient Greek Social Behaviour in Honour of Nick Fisher*. Swansea: 25–43.

Osborne, R. and Rhodes, P. J. (2017). *Greek Historical Inscriptions 479–404 BC*. Oxford.

Ostwald, M. (1986). *From Popular Sovereignty to the Sovereignty of Law: Law, Society, and Politics in Fifth-century Athens*. Berkeley.

Otto, W. F. (1956). *Die Musen und der göttliche Ursprung des Singens und Sagens*. Düsseldorf.

Ouspensky, P. D. (1947). *Strange Life of Ivan Osokin*. London.

Padel, R. (1992). *In and Out of the Mind: Greek Images of the Tragic Self*. Princeton.

Page, D. (1955). *Sappho and Alcaeus*. Oxford.

Panofsky, E. (1939). *Studies in Iconology: Humanistic Themes in the Art of the Renaissance*. Oxford.

Pantelia, M. C. (1993). 'Spinning and Weaving: Ideas of Domestic Order in Homer', *American Journal of Philology* 114: 493–501.

(2002). 'Helen and the Last Song for Hector', *Transactions of the American Philological Association* 132: 21–7.

Parke, H. W. (1977). *Festivals of the Athenians*. London.

Parker, G. (2008). *The Making of Roman India*. Cambridge and New York.

Parker, H. N. (1996). 'Sappho Schoolmistress', in E. Greene (ed.) *Re-Reading Sappho: Reception and Transmission*. Berkeley, Los Angeles and London: 146–86.

Parker, R. (1997). *Athenian Religion. A History*. Oxford.

(1998). 'Pleasing Thighs: Reciprocity in Greek Religion', in C. Gill, N. Postlethwaite and R. Seaford (eds.) *Reciprocity in Ancient Greece*. Oxford: 105–25.

(2005). *Polytheism and Society in Athens*, Oxford.

Parry, M. and Parry, A. (eds.) (1971). *The Making of Homeric Verse: The Collected Papers of Milman Parry*. Oxford.

Parsons, P. J. (1992). '3965: Simonides, Elegies', *The Oxyrhynchus Papyri* 59: 4–50.

Parsons, R. G. (2016). 'Aristotle on Remembering and Recollecting'. Dissertation, Princeton.

Pataki, E. (2015) 'Variations sur l'immortalité: Tithon et la cigale chez Sappho (fragment 58) et dans la tradition homérique', *Gaia* 18: 535–47.

Patillon, M. and Brisson, L. (2002). *Longin. Fragments – Art rhétorique*. Paris.

Payne, M. (2007). *Theocritus and the Invention of Fiction*. Cambridge.

Pearson, L. (1941). 'Historical Allusions in the Attic Orators', *Classical Philology* 36: 209–29.

Pellegrin, P. (1986). *Aristotle's Classification of Animals: Biology and the Conceptual Unity of the Aristotelian Corpus*. Berkeley.

Pelliccia, H. (1992). 'Sappho 16, Gorgias' *Helen*, and the Preface to Herodotus' *Histories*', *Yale Classical Studies* 29: 63–84.

Pelling, C. (2000). *Literary Texts and the Greek Historian*. London.

Pender, E. E. (2007). 'Sappho and Anacreon in Plato's *Phaedrus*', *Leeds International Classical Studies* 6: 1–57.

(2011). 'A Transfer of Energy: Lyric Eros in *Phaedrus*', in P. Destrée and F.-G. Hermann (eds.) *Plato and the Poets*. Leiden and Boston: 327–48.

Penner, T. (2013). 'The Wax Tablet, Logic and Protagoreanism', in G. Boys-Stones, D. El Murr and C. Gill (eds.) *The Platonic Art of Philosophy*. Cambridge: 186–220.

Perlman, S. (1961). 'The Historical Example, Its Use and Importance in the Attic Orators', *Scripta Hierosolymitana* 7: 150–66.

(1964). 'Quotations from Poetry in Attic Orators of the Fourth Century BC', *American Journal of Philology* 85: 155–72.

Petrovic, A. (2013). 'Inscribed Epigrams in Orators and Epigrammatic Collections', in P. Liddel and P. Low (eds.) *Inscriptions and Their Uses in Greek and Latin Literature*. Oxford: 197–213.

(2016). 'Archaic Funerary Epigram and Hector's Imagined *Epitymbia*', in A. Efstathiou and I. Karamanou (eds.) *Homeric Receptions Across Generic and Cultural Contexts*. Berlin: 45–58.

Petrovic, I. (2016). 'On Finding Homer: The Impact of Homeric Scholarship on the Perception of South Slavic oral traditional poetry', in A. Efstathiou and I. Karamanou (eds.) *Homeric Receptions Across Generic and Cultural Contexts*. Berlin: 315–28.

Pfeiffer, R. (1968). *History of Classical Scholarship: from the Beginnings to the End of the Hellenistic Age*. Oxford.

Pickard-Cambridge, A. W. (1988). *The Dramatic Festivals of Athens*. Second edition (1968) revised with a new supplement (1988) by J. Gould and D. M. Lewis. Cambridge.

Piergiacomi, E. (2017). *Storia delle antiche teologie atomiste*. Rome.

Platter, C. (2007). *Aristophanes and the Carnival of Genres*. Baltimore.

Podolak, P. (2010). 'Questioni Pitoclee', *Würzburger Jahrbücher für die Altertumswissenschaft. Neue Folge* 34: 39–80.

Polansky, R. M. (1992). *Philosophy and Knowledge: A Commentary on Plato's Theaetetus*. Lewisburg and London.

(2007). *Aristotle's De Anima*. Cambridge.

Poltera, O. (2008). *Simonides Lyricus. Testimonia und Fragmente*. Basel.

Pomeroy, S. (1984). *Women in Hellenistic Egypt: From Alexander to Cleopatra*. New York.

Popescu, C. (2014). 'Memory and Forgetfulness', in H. M. Roisman (ed.) *The Encyclopedia of Greek Tragedy*. 3 vols. Malden: vol. II, 809–12.

Porter, J. I. (2010). *The Origins of Aesthetic Thought in Ancient Greece: Matter, Sensation, and Experience*. Cambridge.

Post, L. A. (1932). 'Ancient Memory Systems', *Classical Weekly* 25: 105–10.

Prandi, L. (2005). *Memorie storiche dei greci in Claudio Eliano*. Rome.

Pretagostini, R. (2009). 'Occasioni di *performances* musicali in Callimaco e in Teocrito', in M. C. Martinelli (ed.) *La Musa dimenticata. Aspetti dell'esperienza musicale greca in età ellenistica*. Pisa: 3–30.

Price, S. (2012). 'Memory and Ancient Greece', in B. Dignas and R. R. R. Smith (eds.) *Historical and Religious Memory in the Ancient World*. Oxford: 15–36.

Privitera, G. A. (1967). 'Su una nuova interpretazione di Saffo fr. 16 LP', *Quaderni Urbinati di Cultura Classica* 4: 182–7.

Proietti, G. (2012). 'Memoria collettiva e identità etnica: nuovi paradigmi teorico-metodologici nella ricerca storica', in E. Franchi and G. Proietti (eds.) *Forme della memoria e dinamiche identitarie dell'antichità greco-romana*. Trento: 13–41.

Pucci, P. (1977). 'Euripides: The Monument and the Sacrifice', *Arethusa* 10: 165–95.

(1979). 'The Song of the Sirens', *Arethusa* 12: 121–32.

(2007). *Inno alle Muse (Esiodo, Theogonia 1–115)*. Pisa and Rome.

Purves, A. C. (2010). *Space and Time in Ancient Greek Narrative*. Cambridge and New York.

Race, W. H. (1989–1990). 'Sappho, fr. 16 L-P and Alkaios, fr. 42 L-P. Romantic and Classical Strains in Lesbian Lyric', *Classical Journal* 85: 16–33.

(1997). *Pindar*. Cambridge (Mass.) and London.

Rankin, H. D. (1963). 'ΑΛΗΘΕΙΑ in Plato', *Glotta* 41: 51–4.

Rawles, R. (2006). 'Notes on the Interpretation of the "New Sappho"', *Zeitschrift für Papyrologie und Epigraphik* 157: 1–7.

Rayor, D. J. (2005). 'The Power of Memory in Erinna and Sappho', in E. Greene (ed.) *Women Poets in Ancient Greece and Rome*. Norman (Okl.): 59–71.

Remes, P. (2007). *Plotinus on Self: The Philosophy of the 'We'*. Cambridge.

Revermann, M. (2006a). *Comic Business: Theatricality, Dramatic Technique, and Performance Contexts of Aristophanic Comedy*. Oxford.

(2006b). 'The Competence of Theatre Audiences in Fifth- and Fourth-Century Athens', *Journal of Hellenic Studies* 126: 99–124.

Rhodes, P. J. (2003). 'Nothing to Do With Democracy: Athenian Drama and the Polis', *Journal of Hellenic Studies* 123: 104–19.

Riccardo, A. (1999). 'Immaginazione e reminiscenza. (Qualche considerazione sul *De memoria et reminiscentia* di Aristotele)', in L. Formigari, G. Casertano and I. Cubeddu (eds.) *Imago in phantasia depicta. Studi sulla teoria dell'immaginazione*. Rome: 123–37.

Richardson, N. (1993). *The Iliad: A Commentary. Volume iv: books 21–24*. Cambridge.

Riddell, J. (1877). *Apology: With a rev. text and English notes, and a digest of Platonic idioms*. Oxford.

Rink, A. (1997). *Mensch und Vogel bei römischen Naturschriftstellern und Dichtern: untersucht insbesondere bei Plinius, Älian und Ovid*. Frankfurt am Main and New York.

Rispoli, G. M. (2004). 'Tra oralità e scrittura. L'ingresso della memoria nella trattatistica retorica', in S. Cerasuolo (ed.) *Mathesis e Mneme. Studi in memoria di Marcello Gigante*. Naples: vol. I, 105–30.

Rist, J. M. (1967). *Plotinus: The Road to Reality*. Cambridge.

Roark, T. (2011). *Aristotle on Time: A Study of the Physics*. Cambridge.

Rodighiero, A. (2016). ' "Sail with your Fortune": Wisdom and Defeat in Euripides' *Trojan Women*', in P. Kyriakou and A. Rengakos (eds.) *Wisdom and Folly in Euripides*. Berlin: 177–93.

Roediger, H. L and Wertsch, J. V. (2008). 'Creating a New Discipline of Memory Studies', *Memory Studies* 1: 9–22.

Rootham, H. (1920). *Kossovo: Heroic Songs of the Serbs*. New York.

Roselli, A. (2007). Ἀναπεμπάζεσθαι: termine tecnico del lessico della memoria', *AION* 29: 111–26.

(2008). '*Solita noctis hora consurgens*. Insegnamento e apprendimento nelle *Recognitiones* pseudoclementine: il ruolo della memoria', in *Filologia, papirologia, storia dei testi. Giornate di studio in onore di Antonio Carlini*. Pisa and Rome: 289–315.

(2013). 'οἶον ἐγκαύματα: una metafora platonica nel *Timeo* di Platone', in L. M. Pino Campos and G. Santana Henríquez (eds.) *Homenaje al Profesor Juan Antonio López Férez. Καλὸς καὶ ἀγαθὸς ἀνήρ. διδασκάλου παράδειγμα*. Madrid: 741–7.

Rosen, R. (2000). 'Cratinus' *Pytine* and the Construction of the Comic Self', in D. Harvey and J. Wilkins (eds.) *The Rivals of Aristophanes: Studies in Athenian Old Comedy*. Swansea: 23–39.

Rosen, S. (2005). *Plato's Republic: A Study*. New Haven and London.

Rosenbloom, D. (1993). 'Shouting "Fire" in a Crowded Theater: Phrynichos' *Capture of Miletos* and the Politics of Fear in Early Attic Tragedy', *Philologus* 137: 159–96.

Rösler, W. (1975). 'Ein Gedicht und sein Publikum. Überlegegungen zu Sappho Fr. 44 Lobel-Page', *Hermes* 103: 275–85.

Ross, G. R. T. (1906). *Aristotle. De Sensu and De Memoria*. Cambridge.

Ross, W. D. (1955). *Aristotle. Parva Naturalia*. Oxford.

Rossetti, L. (1991). '*Logoi sokratikoi* anteriori al 399 a. C.', in L. Rossetti and O. Bellini (eds.) *Logos e logoi*. Naples: 21–40.

Rousseau, P. (2003). 'La toile d'Hélène (*Iliade* III, 125–128)', in M. Broze, L. Couloubaritsis et al. (eds.) *Le mythe d'Hélène*. Brussels and Paris: 9–43

Rubinstein, L. (2013). 'Forgive and Forget? Amnesty in the Hellenistic Period', in K. Harter-Uibopuu and F. Mitthof (eds.) *Vergeben und Vergessen? Amnestie in der Antike*. Vienna: 127–61.

Russell, B. (1921). *The Analysis of Mind*. London.

Rusten, J. (ed.) (2011). *The Birth of Comedy: Texts, Documents, and Art from Athenian Comic Competitions, 486–280*. Baltimore.

Rutherford, I. (2001). *Pindar's Paeans: A Reading of the Fragments with a Survey of the Genre*. Oxford.

(2013). 'Strictly Ballroom: Egyptian Mousike and Plato's Comparative Poetics', in A. E. Peponi (ed.) *Performance and Culture in Plato's Laws*. Cambridge: 67–84.

Ruzé, F. (1988). 'Aux débuts de l'écriture politique: le pouvoir de l'écrit dans la cité', in M. Detienne (ed.) *Les savoirs de l'écriture en Grèce antique*. Lille: 82–94.

Saetta-Cottone, R. (2003). 'Agathon, Euripide et le thème de la μίμησις dramatique dans les *Thesmophories* d'Aristophane', *Revue des Études Grecques* 116: 445–69.

Sandbach, F. H. (ed.) (1967). *Plutarchi Moralia*, vol. VII. Leipzig.

Sansone, D. (1975). *Aeschylean Metaphors for Intellectual Activity*. Wiesbaden.

Santoro, M. (ed.) (2000). *[Demetrio Lacone] [La forma del dio] (PHerc. 1055)*. Naples.

Sassi, M. M. (2007). 'Aristotele fenomenologo della memoria', in M. M. Sassi (ed.) *Tracce nella mente. Teorie della memoria da Platone ai moderni*. Pisa: 25–46.

Schaerer, R. (1964). *Le Héros, le sage et l'événement*. Paris.

Scheer, T. S. (1996). 'Ein Museum griechischer „Frühgeschichte" im Apollontempel von Sikyon', *Klio* 78: 353–73.

Scheid, J. and Svenbro, J. (1996). *The Craft of Zeus: Myths of Weaving and Fabric*. Cambridge (Mass.).

Scheiter, K. M. (2012). 'Images, Appearances and *Phantasia* in Aristotle', *Phronesis* 57: 251–78.

Schenkeveld, D. M. (1992). 'Prose Usages of AKOYEIN, "To Read"', *Classical Quarterly* 42: 129–41.

Schettino, M. T. (2005). 'Il passato e il presente di Roma nell'opera di Eliano', in L. Troiani and G. Zecchini (eds.) *La cultura storica nei primi due secoli dell'impero romano*. Rome: 283–307.

Schibli, H. S. (1990). *Pherekydes of Syros*. Oxford.

Schiesaro, A. (1989). '*Pedetemptin progredientis* (Lucr. 5, 533)', *Rivista di Filologia e di Istruzione Classica* 117: 286–96.

Schleiermacher, F. (1991). 'Platon, Philebos, Timaios, Kritias, Griechisch und Deutsch', in *Platon. Sämtliche Werke VIII*. Frankfurt.

Schlesier, R. (2010). 'Tragic Memories of Dionysos', in L. Foxhall, H.-J. Gehrke and N. Luraghi (eds.) *Intentional History. Spinning Time in Ancient Greece*. Stuttgart: 245–63.

Schmid, W. (1961). 'Epikur', in T. Klauser (ed.) *Reallexikon für Antike und Christentum*, vol. V, 681–819.

Schmitz, T. A. (2010). 'Speaker and Addressee in Early Greek Epigram and Lyric', in M. Baumbach, A. Petrovic and I. Petrovic (eds.) *Archaic and Classical Greek Epigram*. Cambridge: 25–41.

Schofield, M. (1978). 'Aristotle on the Imagination', in G. E. R. Lloyd and G. E. Owen (eds.) *Aristotle on Mind and the Senses*. Cambridge: 99–140.

Schur, D. (2014). 'The Silence of Homer's Sirens', *Arethusa* 47: 1–17.

Scodel, R. (1992). 'Inscriptions, Absence and Memory: Epic and Early Epitaph', *Studi Italiani di Filologia Classica* 3: 57–76.

(1997). 'Teichoscopia, Catalogue, and the Female Spectator in Euripides', *Colby Quarterly* 33: 76–93.

(2002). 'Homeric Signs and Flashbulb Memory', in I. Worthington and J. M. Foley (eds.) *Epea and Grammata: Oral and Written Communication in Ancient Greece*. Leiden: 99–116.

(2008). 'Social Memory in Aeschylus' *Oresteia*', in E. A. Mackay (ed.) *Orality, Literacy, Memory in the Ancient Greek and Roman World*. Leiden: 115–41.

Scolnicov, S. (1988). *Plato's Metaphysics of Education*. London and New York.

Scott, A. (1991). *Origen and the Life of the Stars*. Oxford.

Scott, D. (1995). *Recollection and Experience: Plato's Theory of Learning and Its Successors*. Cambridge.

  (2006). *Plato's Meno*. Cambridge.

Scullion, S. (1999–2000). 'Tradition and Invention in Euripidean Aetiology', *Illinois Classical Studies* 24–25: 217–33.

Scully, S. (1990). *Homer and the Sacred City*. Ithaca and London.

Seaford, R. (2009). 'Aitiologies of Cult in Euripides: A Response to Scott Scullion', in J. R. C. Cousland and J. R. Hume (eds.) *The Play of Texts and Fragments: Essays in Honour of Martin Cropp*. Leiden: 221–34.

Sealey, R. (1967). 'Pseudo-Demosthenes XIII and XXV', *Revue des Études Grecques* 80: 250–5.

  (1993). *Demosthenes and his Time: A Study in Defeat*. New York.

Sedley, D. N. (1973). 'Epicurus, *On nature*, Book XXVIII', *Cronache Ercolanesi* 3: 5–83.

  (2004). *The Midwife of Platonism: Text and Subtext in Plato's Theaetetus*. Oxford.

  (2011). 'Epicurus' Theological Innatism', in J. Fish and K. R. Sanders (eds.) *Epicurus and the Epicurean Tradition*. Cambridge: 29–52.

  (2017). 'Epicurean Versus Cyrenaic Happiness', in R. Seaford, J. Wilkins and M. Wright (eds.) *Selfhood and the Soul: Essays on Ancient Thought and Literature in Honour of Christopher Gill*. Oxford: 89–106.

Segal, C. (1971). 'Andromache's *Anagnorisis*: Formulaic Artistry in *Iliad* 22: 437–76', *Harvard Studies in Classical Philology* 75: 33–57.

  (1989). 'Song, Ritual and Commemoration in Early Greek Poetry and Tragedy', *Oral Tradition* 4: 330–59.

  (1993). *Euripides and the Poetics of Sorrow*. Durham and London.

  (1995). *Sophocles' Tragic World: Divinity, Nature, Society*, Cambridge (Mass.).

Segvic, H. (2006). 'Homer in Plato's *Protagoras*', *Classical Philology* 101: 247–62.

Senor, T. D. (2009). 'Epistemological Problems of Memory', in E. N. Zalta (ed.) *The Stanford Encyclopedia of Philosophy* (Autumn 2009 edition). [URL = http://plato.stanford.edu/archives/fall2009/entries/memory-episprob/.]

Seremetakis, C. N. (1991). *The Last Word: Women, Death and Divination in Inner Mani*. Chicago.

Sharples, R. W. (1985). *Plato:* Meno. Warminster.

Shear, J. L. (2011). *Polis and Revolution: Responding to Oligarchy in Classical Athens*. Cambridge and New York.

  (2012). 'The Politics of the Past: Remembering Revolution at Athens', in J. Marincola, L. Llewellyn-Jones and C. A. Maciver (eds.) *Greek Notions of the Past in the Archaic and Classical Eras: History without Historians*. Edinburgh: 276–300.

  (2013). ' "Their Memories Will Never Grow Old": The Politics of Remembrance in the Athenian Funeral Orations', *Classical Quarterly* 63: 511–36.

Shoemaker, S. (1967). 'Memory', in P. Edwards (ed.) *The Encyclopedia of Philosophy*, vol. 5. New York and London: 265–74.

Shrimpton, G. S. (1997). *History and Memory in Ancient Greece*. Montreal.

(2014). 'Memory and History in the Ancient World', in S. Berger and B. Niven (eds.) *Writing the History of Memory*. London: 25–45.

Sickinger, J. P. (1999). *Public Records and Archives in Classical Athens*. Chapel Hill.

(2009). 'Nothing to Do with Democracy: Formulae of Disclosure and the Athenian Epigraphic Habit', in L. Mitchell and L. Rubinstein (eds.) *Greek Epigraphy and History: Essays in honour of P. J. Rhodes*. Swansea: 87–102.

Sider, D. (2001). 'Fragments 1–22 W². Text, Apparatus Criticus and Translation', in D. Boedeker and D. Sider (eds.) *The New Simonides, Contexts of Praise and Desire*. Oxford and New York: 13–29.

(2010). 'Greek Verse on a Vase by Douris', *Hesperia* 79: 541–54.

Silk, M. (1974). *Interaction in Poetic Imagery, with Special Reference to Early Greek Poetry*. Cambridge.

Simon, E. (2002). *Festivals of Attica: An Archaeological Commentary*. Chicago.

Simondon, M. (1982). *La mémoire et l'oubli dans la pensée grecque jusqu'à la fin de Vᵉ siècle av. J-C. Psychologie archaïque, mythes et doctrines*. Paris.

Skarsouli, P. (2006). 'Calliope, a Muse Apart: Some Remarks on the Tradition of Memory as a Vehicle of Oral Justice', *Oral Tradition* 21: 210–28.

Slater, N. W. (1988). 'Making the Aristophanic Audience', *American Journal of Philology* 120: 351–68.

(2002). *Spectator Politics: Metatheatre and Performance in Aristophanes*. Philadelphia.

Small, J. P. (1997). *Wax Tablets of the Mind: Cognitive Studies of Memory and Literacy in Classical Antiquity*. London and New York.

Smith, C. (2012). 'Foreword: Memory History, Forgetting', in M. Bommas, J. Harrisson and P. Roy (eds.) *Memory and Urban Religion in the Ancient World*. London and New York: xiv–xxv.

Smith, S. D. (2014). *Man and Animal in Severan Rome: The Literary Imagination of Claudius Aelianus*. Cambridge and New York.

Snell, B. (1924). *Die Ausdrücke für den Begriff des Wissens in der vorplatonische Philosophie*. Berlin.

(1953). *The Discovery of the Mind: The Greek Origins of European Thought*. Oxford.

(1977). 'φρένες – φρόνησις', *Glotta* 55: 34–64.

Snyder, J. M. (1981). 'The Web of Song: Weaving Imagery in Homer and the Lyric Poets', *Classical Journal* 76: 193–6.

Solmsen, F. (1929). *Die Entwicklung der aristotelischen Logik und Rhetorik*. Berlin.

(1944). 'The Tablets of Zeus', *Classical Quarterly* 38: 27–30.

Sommerstein, A. H. (1989). *Aeschylus, Eumenides. Edited with an Introduction, Translation and Commentary*. Warminster.

(1994). *The Comedies of Aristophanes. Vol. 8. Thesmophoriazusae*. Warminster.

(2008). *Aeschylus*. 3 vols. Cambridge (Mass.) and London.

Sommerstein, A. H. and Bayliss, A. J. (2013). *Oath and State in Ancient Greece*. Berlin.

Sorabji, R. (1972). *Aristotle on Memory*. London. [2nd edn. 2004.]

(2006). *Self: Ancient and Modern Insights About Individuality, Life, and Death*. Chicago.

Sourvinou-Inwood, C. (1995). *'Reading' Greek Death: To the End of the Classical Period*. Oxford.

Spentzou, E. (2002). 'Secularizing the Muse', in E. Spentzou and D. Fowler (eds.) *Cultivating the Muses: Struggles for Power and Inspiration in Classical Literature*. Oxford: 1–28.

Spinelli, E. (2007). 'Ancient Stoicism, "Robust Epistemology", and Moral Philosophy', in P. Machamer and G. Wolters (eds.) *Thinking About Causes: From Greek Philosophy to Modern Physics*. Pittsburgh: 37–46.

(2012). 'Physics as Philosophy of Happiness: The Transmission of Scientific Tenets in Epicurus', in M. Sgarbi (ed.) *Translatio studiorum: Ancient, Medieval, and Modern Bearers of Intellectual History*. Leiden: 25–36.

Spinelli, E. and Verde, F. (2010). *Epicuro. Epistola a Erodoto*. Rome.

Sprague, R. K. (ed.) (1972). *The Older Sophists*. Columbia (South Carolina).

Stafford, E. (2000). *Worshipping Virtues: Personification and the Divine in Ancient Greece*. London.

Stamm, C. (2003). *Vergangenheitsbezug in der Zweiten Sophistik: die Varia Historia des Claudius Aelianus*. Frankfurt am Main and New York.

Starr, R. (1990–1991). 'Lectores and Book Reading', *Classical Journal* 86: 337–43.

Stehle, E. (2001). 'A Bard of the Iron Age and his Auxiliary Muse', in D. Boedeker and D. Sider (eds.) *The New Simonides, Contexts of Praise and Desire*. Oxford and New York: 106–19.

Steinbock, B. K. (2013a). 'Contesting the Lessons of the Past: Aeschines' Use of Social Memory', *Transactions of the American Philological Association* 142: 65–103.

(2013b). *Social Memory in Athenian Public Discourse: Uses and Meanings of the Past*. Ann Arbor.

Steiner, D. T. (1993). 'Pindar's "Oggetti Parlanti"', *Harvard Studies in Classical Philology* 95: 159–80.

(1994). *The Tyrant's Writ: Myths and Images of Writing in Ancient Greece*. Princeton.

(1999). 'To Praise, not to Bury: Simonides fr. 531P', *Classical Quarterly* 49: 383–95.

(2001). *Images in Mind: Statues in Archaic and Classical Greek Literature and Thought*. Princeton.

Stein-Hölkeskamp, E. and Hölkeskamp, K.-J. (eds.) (2010). *Die griechische Welt. Erinnerungsorte der Antike*. Munich.

Stephens, S. A. (2003). *Seeing Double: Intercultural Poetics in Ptolemaic Alexandria*. Berkeley and Los Angeles.

(2015). *Callimachus: Aetia*. Carlisle (Penn.).

Stone, L. M. (1977). *Costume in Aristophanic Poetry*. Chapel Hill.

Storey, I. (2008). *Euripides. Suppliant Women*, London.

Striker, G. (1970). *Peras und Apeiron: das Problem der Formen in Platons Philebos*. Göttingen.

(1990). 'The Problem of the Criterion', in S. Everson (ed.) *Epistemology*. Cambridge: 143–60.

Sutton, J. (2010). 'Memory', in E. N. Zalta (ed.) *The Stanford Encyclopedia of Philosophy* (Summer). [URL = http://plato.stanford.edu/archives/sum2010/entries/memory/.]

Svenbro, J. (1984). 'La stratégie de l'amour. Modèle de la guerre et théorie de l'amour dans la poésie de Sappho', *Quaderni di storia* 19: 57–79.

(1993). *Phrasikleia: An Anthropology of Reading in Ancient Greece*. Ithaca (NY). (First published as (1988) *Phrasikleia. Anthropologie de la lecture en Grèce ancienne*. Paris.)

Taillardat, J. (1965). *Les Images d'Aristophane. Etudes de langue et de style*. Paris.

Taormina, D. P. (2011). 'Dalla potenzialità all'attualità: Un'introduzione al problema della memoria in Plotino', in T. Bénatouïl, E. Maffi and F. Trabattoni (eds.) *Plato, Aristotle, or Both? Dialogues between Platonism and Aristotelianism in Antiquity*. Hildesheim: 139–59.

Taplin, O. (2010). 'Antifane, Antigone e la malleabilità del teatro tragico', in A. M. Belardinelli and G. Greco (eds.) *Antigone e le Antigoni. Storia, forme, fortuna di un mito*. Florence: 27–36.

Tarrant, H. (1988). 'Midwifery and the *Clouds*', *Classical Quarterly*, n.s. 38: 116–22. (2005). *Recollecting Plato's* Meno. London.

Taub, L. (2009). 'Cosmology and Meteorology', in J. Warren (ed.) *The Cambridge Companion to Epicureanism*. Cambridge: 105–24.

Taylor, A. E. (1956). *Plato. Philebus and Epinomis*. London.

Taylor, C. C. W. (1991). *Plato. Protagoras*. Oxford.

Tedeschi, A. (1985). 'L'invio del carme nella poesia lirica arcaica: Pindaro e Bacchilide', *Studi italiani di filologia classica* 78: 29–54.

Tell, D. (2006). 'Beyond Mnemotechnics: Confession and Memory in Augustine', *Philosophy and Rhetoric* 39: 233–53.

Tepedino Guerra, A. (1990). 'Il contributo di Metrodoro di Lampsaco alla formazione della teoria epicurea del linguaggio', *Cronache Ercolanesi* 20: 17–25.

(2010). 'Le lettere private del *Kepos*: Metrodoro, i maestri e gli amici epicurei (*PHerc*. 176 e *PHerc*. 1418)', in A. Antoni, G. Arrighetti, M. I. Bertagna and D. Delattre (eds.) *Miscellanea Papyrologica Herculanensia*. Pisa and Rome: 37–59.

Teske, R. (2001). 'Augustine's Philosophy of Memory', in E. Stump and N. Kretzmann (eds.) *The Cambridge Companion to Augustine*. Cambridge: 148–58.

Thein, K. (2012). 'Imagination, Self-awareness and Thought in the *Philebus*', *Oxford Studies in Ancient Philosophy* 42: 109–49.

Thévenaz, O. (2015). 'Sappho's Soft Heart and Kypris' Light Wounds: The Restoration of the Helen Poem (esp. Sa. 16.13–14) and Ovid's Sappho Epistle', *Zeitschrift für Papyrologie und Epigraphik* 196: 31–43.

Thomas, R. (1989). *Oral Tradition and Written Record in Classical Athens*. Cambridge.

(1992). *Literacy and Orality in Ancient Greece*. Cambridge.

(2000). *Herodotus in Context: Ethnography, Science, and the Art of Persuasion.* Cambridge.

(2001). 'Herodotus' *Histories* and the Floating Gap', in N. Luraghi (ed.) *The Historian's Craft in the Age of Herodotus.* Oxford: 198–210.

(2009). 'Writing, Reading, Public and Private "Literacies": Functional Literacy and Democratic Literacy in Greece', in W. A. Johnson and H. R. Parker (eds.) *Ancient Literacies.* Oxford: 13–46.

Thyresson, I. L. (1977). *The Particles in Epicurus.* Malmö.

Todd, S. C. (2007). *A Commentary on Lysias, Speeches 1–11.* Oxford.

Too, Y. L. (2010). *The Idea of the Library in the Ancient World.* Oxford.

Tornau, C. (2009). 'Qu'est-ce qu'un individu? Unité, individualité et conscience de soi dans la métaphysique plotinienne de l'âme', *Les études philosophiques* 90: 333–60.

Torrance, I. C. (2013). *Metapoetry in Euripides.* Oxford.

(2014). '6 Ways to Give Oaths Extra-sanctity', in A. H. Sommerstein and I. C. Torrance (eds.) *Oaths and Swearing in Ancient Greece.* Berlin: 132–55.

Trabattoni, F. (2012). 'Myth and Truth in Plato's *Phaedrus*', in C. Collobert, P. Destrée and F. Gonzalez (eds.) *Plato and Myth: Studies on the Use and Status of Platonic Myths.* Leiden and Boston: 305–21.

Treu, M. (1999). *Undici cori comici. Aggressività, derisione e tecniche drammatiche in Aristofane.* Genoa.

Trevett, J. (1990). 'History in [Demosthenes] 59', *Classical Quarterly* 40: 407–20.

(1994). 'Demosthenes' Speech *On Organization* (Dem. 13)', *Greek, Roman, and Byzantine Studies* 35: 179–93.

Tsouna, V. (2006). 'Rationality and the Fear of Death in Epicurean Philosophy', *Rhizai* 3: 79–117.

(2016). 'Epicurean Preconceptions', *Phronesis* 61: 160–221.

Tueller, M. A. (2010). 'The Passer-By in Archaic and Classical Epigram', in M. Baumbach, A. Petrovic and I. Petrovic (eds.) *Archaic and Classical Greek Epigram.* Cambridge: 42–60.

Tulli, M. (2000). 'L'epitome di Epicuro e la trasmissione del sapere nel Medioplatonismo', in M. Erler and R. Bees (eds.) *Epikureismus in der späten Republik und der Kaiserzeit.* Stuttgart: 109–21.

(2008). 'Isocrate storico del pensiero: Antistene, Platone, gli eristi nell'*Encomio di Elena*', in L. Rossetti and A. Stravru (eds.) *Socratica 2005. Studi sulla letteratura socratica antica presentati alle Giornate di studio di Senigallia.* Bari: 91–105.

(2014). 'Epicuro a Pitocle: La forma didattica del testo', in M. Tulli (ed.) Φιλία: *Dieci contributi per Gabriele Burzacchini.* Bologna: 67–78.

Tulving, E. (2007). 'Are There 256 Different Kinds of Memory?', in J. S. Nairne (ed.) *The Foundations of Remembering: Essays in Honor of Henry L. Roediger, III.* New York: 39–52.

Tulving, E. and Craik, F. (eds.) (2000). *The Oxford Handbook of Memory.* Oxford.

Uhlig, A. and Hunter, R. (eds.) (2017). *Imagining Reperformance in Classical Culture: Studies in the Traditions of Drama and Lyric.* Cambridge.

Untersteiner, M. (1980). *Problemi di filologia filosofica*. Milan.

(2002). *Eschilo, Le Coefore*. Amsterdam.

Usener, H. (1977). *Glossarium Epicureum edendum curaverunt M. Gigante et W. Schmid*. Rome.

Ustinova, Y. (2012). 'Madness into Memory: *Mania* and *Mneme* in Greek Culture', *Scripta Classica Israelica* 31: 109–31.

Van der Eijk, P. (1997). 'Towards a Rhetoric of Ancient Scientific Discourse: Some Formal Characteristics of Greek Medical and Philosophical Texts (Hippocratic Corpus, Aristotle)', in E. J. Bakker (ed.) *Grammar as Interpretation*. Leiden: 77–129.

van Effenterre, H. (1973). 'Le contrat de travail du scribe Spensithios', *Bulletin de correspondance hellénique* 97: 31–46.

van Looy, H. (1964). *Zes verloren Tragedie van Euripides: Studie met kritische uitgave en vertaling der fragmenten*. Brussels.

van Minnen, P. (2001). 'Luke 4. 17–20 and the Handling of Ancient Books', *Journal of Theological Studies* n.s. 52: 689–90.

Vansina, J. (1985). *Oral Tradition as History*. Madison.

Varner, E. R. (2004). *Mutilation and Transformation:* Damnatio Memoriae *and Roman Imperial Portraiture*. Leiden and Boston.

Vasunia, P. (2001). *The Gift of the Nile: Hellenizing Egypt from Aeschylus to Alexander*. Berkeley.

Vatri, A. (2015). 'Ancient Greek Writing for Memory: Textual Features as Mnemonic Facilitators', *Mnemosyne* 68: 750–73.

Velardi, R. (1991). 'Le origini dell'inno in prosa tra V e IV secolo a.C.: Menandro Retore e Platone', in A. C. Cassio and G. Cerri (eds.) *L'inno tra rituale e letteratura nel mondo antico*. Rome: 205–31.

(2001). *Retorica filosofia letteratura: saggi di storia della retorica greca su Gorgia, Platone e Anassimene di Lampsaco*. Naples.

(2007). '*Memoria rerum* e *memoria verborum* nel *Fedro* di Platone (228d1-4)', *AION* 29: 39–49.

Verde, F. (2011). 'Minimi in movimento? Note sulle coll. XLVIII-L Puglia del *PHerc.* 1012 (*Demetrii Laconis Opus incertum*)', *Cronache Ercolanesi* 41: 49–61.

(2013a). *Epicuro*. Rome.

(2013b). 'Cause epicuree', *Antiquorum Philosophia* 7: 127–42.

(2016). 'Epicuro nella testimonianza di Cicerone: la dottrina del criterio', in M. Tulli (ed.) *Testo e forme del testo: Ricerche di filologia filosofica*. Pisa and Rome: 335–68.

(forthcoming). 'L'empirismo di Teofrasto e la meteorologia epicurea', *Rivista di Filosofia Neo-Scolastica*.

Verdenius, W. J. (1988). *Commentaries on Pindar: Olympian Odes 1, 10, 11; Nemean 11; Isthmian 2*. Leiden.

Verlinsky, A. (2005). 'Epicurus and His Predecessors on the Origin of Language', in D. Frede and B. Inwood (eds.) *Language and Learning: Philosophy of Language in the Hellenistic Age*. Cambridge: 56–100.

Vernant, J.-P. (1959). 'Aspects mythiques de la Mémoire et du temps', *Journal de Psychologie* 56: 1–29. [Repr. in Vernant 1965: 51–78; Engl. transl. in Vernant 1983: 75–105; and in Vernant 2006: 115–38.]

    (1960). 'Le fleuve "Amélès" et la "Mélétè Thanatou"', *Revue philosophique* 150: 163–79. [Repr. in Vernant 1965: 79–94; Engl. transl. in Vernant 1983.]

    (1965). *Mythe et pensée chez les Grecs. Études de psychologie historique.* Paris. [Translated into English as Vernant 1983.]

    (1983). *Myth and Thought Among the Greeks.* London.

    (2006). *Myth and Thought Among the Greeks.* New York (translation of the new, enlarged French edition 1996).

Vestrheim, G. (2010). 'Voice in Sepulchral Epigrams: Some Remarks on the Use of First and Second Person in Sepulchral Epigrams, and a Comparison with Lyric Poetry', in M. Baumbach, A. Petrovic and I. Petrovic (eds.) *Archaic and Classical Greek Epigram.* Cambridge: 61–78.

Vivian, B. (2010). *Public Forgetting: The Rhetoric and Politics of Beginning Again.* University Park.

Vlastos, G. (1991). *Socrates: Ironist and Moral Philosopher.* Ithaca.

    (1994). 'Anamnesis in the *Meno*', in J. Day (ed.) *Plato's Meno in Focus.* London and New York: 88–111.

Voelke, P. (2004). 'Euripide, héros et poète comique: à propos des *Acharniens* et des *Thesmophories* d'Aristophane', in C. Calame (ed.) *Poétique d'Aristophane et langue d'Euripide en dialogue.* Paris: 117–38.

Wagner-Hasel, B. (2011). 'Mnemosyne – die Göttin der Erinnerung: Zum Verhältnis von Traditionsbildung und Geschlecht in der Antike', in H. Brandt, A. M. Auer, J. Brehm, D. de Brasi and L. K. Hörl (eds.) *Genus und Generatio. Rollenerwartungen und Rollenerfüllungen im Spannungsfeld der Geschlechter und Generationen in Antike und Mittelalter.* Bamberg: 23–48.

Walters, K. R. (1981). ' "We Fought Alone at Marathon": Historical Falsification in the Attic Funeral Oration', *Rheinisches Museum für Philologie* 124: 204–11.

Warren, E. W. (1965). 'Memory in Plotinus', *Classical Quarterly* 15: 252–60.

Warren, J. (2001). 'Lucretian *Palingenesis* Recycled', *Classical Quarterly* 51: 499–508.

    (2004). *Facing Death: Epicurus and his Critics.* Oxford.

    (2009). 'Removing Fear', in J. Warren (ed.) *The Cambridge Companion to Epicureanism.* Cambridge: 234–48.

    (2014). *The Pleasures of Reason in Plato, Aristotle, and the Hellenistic Hedonists.* Cambridge.

Watson, G. (1988). *Phantasia in Classical Thought.* Galway.

Weber, G. (1993). *Dichtung und höfische Gesellschaft. Die Rezeption von Zeitgeschichte am Hof der ersten drei Ptolemäer.* Stuttgart.

Wedin, M. V. (1988). *Mind and Imagination in Aristotle.* New Haven (Conn.).

Weil, S. (1957). *Intimations of Christianity.* London.

Werner, D. S. (2012). *Myth and Philosophy in Plato's Phaedrus.* Cambridge and New York.

West, M. L. (1966). *Hesiod. Theogony*. Oxford.

(1992). *Iambi et Elegi Graeci. Vol. II*. Oxford.

(1997). *The East Face of Helikon*. Oxford.

(1998). *Homeri Ilias I-XII*. Stuttgart.

(2000). *Homeri Ilias XIII-XXIV*. Munich and Leipzig.

West, T. G. and West, G. S. (1984.) *Aristophanes: Clouds*, in *Plato and Aristophanes: Four Texts on Socrates*. Ithaca and London.

Whitmarsh, T. (2007). 'Prose Literature and the Severan Dynasty', in S. Swain, S. Harrison and J. Elsner (eds.) *Severan Culture*. Cambridge and New York: 29–51.

Wifstrand Schiebe, M. (2003). 'Sind die epikureischen Götter "thought-constructs"?', *Mnemosyne* 56: 703–27.

Wilberding, J. (2008). 'Automatic Action in Plotinus', *Oxford Studies in Ancient Philosophy* 34: 443–77.

Willetts, R. F. (1967). *The Law Code of Gortyn*. Berlin.

Wills, G. (1967). 'The Sapphic "Umwertung aller Werte"', *American Journal of Philology* 88: 434–42.

Wilson, C. (1969). *The Philosopher's Stone*. London.

(2009). *Existential Criticism: Selected Book Reviews*. Nottingham.

Wilson, P. (2000). *The Athenian Institution of Khoregia. The Chorus, the City and the Stage*. Cambridge.

(2009). 'Tragic Honours and Democracy: Neglected Evidence for the Politics of the Athenian Dionysia', *Classical Quarterly* 59, 8–29.

Winnington-Ingram, R. (1980). *Sophocles: An Interpretation*. Cambridge.

Wohl, V. (2015). *Euripides and the Politics of Form*. Princeton.

Wolff, F. (2000). *L'être, l'homme, le disciple. Figures philosophiques empruntées à des Anciens*. Paris.

Wolpert, A. (2002). *Remembering Defeat: Civil War and Civic Memory in Ancient Athens*. Baltimore and London.

(2003). 'Addresses to the Jury in the Attic Orators', *American Journal of Philology* 124: 537–55.

Woolf, R. (2009). 'Pleasure and Desire', in J. Warren (ed.) *The Cambridge Companion to Epicureanism*. Cambridge: 158–78.

Worthington, I. (1994). 'History and Oratorical Exploitation', in I. Worthington (ed.) *Persuasion: Greek Rhetoric In Action*. London and New York: 109–29.

Worthington, I. and Foley, J. M. (eds.) (2002). *Epea and Grammata: Oral and Written. Communication in Ancient Greece*. Leiden and Boston.

Yamagata, N. (2005). 'Plato, Memory and Performance', *Oral Tradition* 20: 111–29.

Yates, F. A. (1966). *The Art of Memory*. London.

Yunis, H. (2000). 'Politics as Literature: Demosthenes and the Burden of the Athenian Past', *Arion* 8: 97–118.

(2011). *Plato. Phaedrus*. Cambridge.

Zadorojny, A. V. (1999). 'Sappho and Plato in Plutarch, Demetrius 38', in A. Pérez Jiménez, J. García López and R. M. Aguilar (eds.) *Plutarco, Platón y Aristóteles*. Madrid: 515–32.

Zeitlin, F. (1995). 'Art, Memory and kleos in Euripides' Iphigenia in Aulis', in B. Goff (ed.) *History, Tragedy, Theory: Dialogues on Athenian Drama.* Austin: 174–201.

(2001). 'Visions and Revisions of Homer', in S. Goldhill (ed.) *Being Greek under Rome: Cultural Identity, the Second Sophistic and the Development of Empire.* Cambridge: 195–266.

Zellner, H. M. (2007). 'Sappho's Alleged Proof of Aesthetic Relativity', *Greek, Roman, and Byzantine Studies* 47: 257–70.

Zimmermann, B. (2006). 'Aischylos-Rezeption im 5. Jahrhundert v. Chr.', *Lexis* 24: 53–62.

Zuckerman, V. G. (2015). 'The Wax Tablet in the Soul: From Metaphor to Model. Plato's *Theaetetus* 191a5–196c9 in Light of 5th Century Metaphors of Memory'. MA thesis, Copenhagen.

Zuntz, G. (1955). *The Political Plays of Euripides.* Manchester.

Index Locorum

Plutarch (Plut.)

Subject Index